# INTERNATIONAL
# FILM NECROLOGY

GARLAND REFERENCE LIBRARY
OF THE HUMANITIES
(VOL. 215)

# INTERNATIONAL FILM NECROLOGY

William T. Stewart
Arthur F. McClure
Ken D. Jones

GARLAND PUBLISHING, INC. • NEW YORK & LONDON
1981

**Library of Congress Cataloging in Publication Data**

Stewart, William T
    International film necrology.

    (Garland reference library of the humanities ; v. 215)
    1. Moving-picture actors and actresses—Biography.
2. Obituaries.    I. McClure, Arthur F., joint author.
II. Jones, Ken D., joint author.    III. Title.
PN1998.A2S673      791.43'028'0922 [B]      80-17636
ISBN 0-8240-9552-9

Printed on acid-free, 250-year-life paper
Manufactured in the United States of America

To my mother and father,
Bess and Brooks Stewart

# CONTENTS

# ACKNOWLEDGMENTS

I would like to acknowledge the kind assistance of the following over 22 years of research: Dolores Kleinke and her staff at the California Department of Public Health, Bureau of Vital Statistics; Roi A. Uselton; Bill H. Doyle; Bill McDowell; various contributors to *Films in Review*; a host of periodicals and yearbooks, foreign and domestic, such as *Variety*, *The Stage*, *Who's Who in the Theatre*, *Billboard*, *The New York Times*, and *The Los Angeles Times*; Walter Rigdon and his *Biographical Encyclopaedia & Who's Who of the American Theatre*; and the following institutions: The Academy of Motion Picture Arts & Sciences, Stanford University, the Library of Congress, the University of Texas, and the California State Library. I am also grateful for the support of Mary and Lola McGee and of my wife, Vita.

And finally, I thank my co-authors: Arthur F. McClure, for his unwavering faith in and support of the project; and Ken D. Jones—whose positive attitude matches his superlative collection of stills.

William T. Stewart
*Fair Oaks, Calif.*

# INTRODUCTION

Interest in the history and criticism of the motion picture has increased tremendously in recent years. The number of reference books—including indexes, dictionaries, encyclopedias, and other types of guide books—in this area has increased rapidly. As is the case in any new field, however, the quality and accuracy of these works is uneven. In screen obituaries, errors of all kinds abound, such as incorrect dates, misspelled names, incorrect titles, and mixed-up identifications. The task of checking the accuracy of obituaries is one that is influenced by many factors, including name changes, family reluctances about cause of death (especially where suicide is involved), and the erasure of all traces of early marriages. Families also sometimes misrepresent screen credits, either intentionally or unintentionally.

The primary sources for obituary information include, among other publications, *Variety*, the old *Hollywood Citizen-News*, *The New York Times*, and *Films in Review*. Often these journals duplicate existing inaccuracies and thus further complicate matters. Most previous reports and compilations in yearbooks, magazines, and trade papers have relied on sometimes inaccurate firsthand and secondhand reports. Such incomplete or inaccurate information is often repeated in subsequent publications. Unfortunately, the compilers of these reference works have rarely consulted the most important primary source: the death certificates. Therefore, false birth dates, guessed-at death dates, and incorrectly reported birthplaces proliferate in books that claim to be accurate and complete.

Much of the statistical research for this necrology was done in the vital statistics files at the California Department of Public Health in Sacramento. These files contain death certificates for people who have died in California since 1905. Birth date, place of birth, date of death, cause of death, and last spouse are given on each certificate. Research for this necrology was restricted to the first three items.

However, this volume cannot claim complete accuracy. The only death certificates available to the compilers were those of the State of California. We were dependent on secondhand sources for out-of-state and foreign dates; all available English and foreign-language reference material has been consulted. Where there were two conflicting dates, the one from the more reliable source was chosen.

Similarly, not all death certificates in California could be checked, because of limitations of time and expense. In addition, lack of marital information has hindered research on women in film. In time, more and more certificates will be consulted, and any update of this volume will include more accurate information. Many names from the 1978 and 1979 Screen Actors Guild obituary lists have been excluded because the microfiche for these years was not available at the Department of Public Health, and the listings could not be verified. Most Eastern European players (Poland and Czechoslovakia) have been excluded for lack of time.

Some film buffs will have dates at variance with those in this volume. This is because the dates, particularly birth dates, on a vast majority of the death certificates were different from those cited elsewhere, since many players were reluctant to give their real age during their lifetime.

Again, *much*, but not all, of the research for this volume was done at the California Department of Public Health. There are included here hundreds of players whose death dates have never before been reported in a publication. These, and the accurate dates for those that have been cited incorrectly elsewhere, make this a unique compilation. Therefore, in spite of any shortcomings, the authors consider it the most complete and accurate work of its kind ever produced.

# EXPLANATION OF ENTRY FORMAT

Entries take the following form: the individual's name, followed by his or her occupation; date and place of birth, if known; date of death, with age at death in parentheses. An individual's real name (indicated by "r.n.") is given in parentheses following the professional name, as is any additional name by which the individual was known. For example, the entry:

Bailey, William Norton (Rusty Wescoatt; Norman (Rusty) Wescoatt) (r.n. Gordon Reineck), actor & director; b. Sept. 26, 1886, Nebraska; d. Nov. 8, 1962 (76).

translates thus: Actor-director William Norton Bailey, also known as Rusty Wescoatt and Norman (Rusty) Wescoatt, whose real name was Gordon Reineck, was born Sept. 26, 1886, in Nebraska, and died Nov. 8, 1962, at the age of 76.

# INTERNATIONAL
# FILM NECROLOGY

Aasen, John, actor; d. Aug. 1, 1938 (51).
Abbas, Hector, actor; d. Nov. 11, 1942 (58).
Abbe, Charles S., actor; b. Windham, Conn.; d. June 16, 1932 (72).
Abbe, Jack Yutaka, actor; d. Jan. 3, 1977 (81).
Abbey, May, actress; b. Hartford, Conn.; d. Aug. 20, 1952 (80).
Abbot, Frank, actor; b. July 16, 1878, California; d. Feb. 2,
    1957 (78).
Abbot, Franklin J. (see Abbot, Frank)
Abbott, Al, actor; b. Mar. 28, 1884, Iowa; d. Sept. 4, 1962 (78).
Abbott, Bud (r.n. William Alexander Abbott), actor; b. Oct. 2,
    1895 or 1898 (cert.), Atlantic City, N.J.; d. Apr. 24, 1974 (78).
Abbott, Dorothy, actress; b. Dec. 16, 1920, Missouri; d. Dec. 5,
    1968 (47).
Abbott, Gypsy, actress; b. Jan. 31, 1897, Georgia; d. July 25,
    1952 (55).
Abbott, James Francis, actor; d. Jan. 19, 1954 (81).
Abbott, Marian, actress; b. Danville, Ky.; d. Jan. 15, 1937 (71).
Abbott, Nancy Ann, actress; b. Feb. 22, 1901, California; d. Aug.
    10, 1964 (63).
Abdulov, Osip N., actor; b. Nov. 16, 1900; d. June 14, 1953 (52).
Abel, Alfred, actor; d. Dec. 12, 1937 (72).
Abel, Ilse, actress; d. Apr., 1959.
Abeles, Edward S., actor & director; b. Nov. 4, 1869, St. Louis,
    Mo.; d. July 10, 1919 (49).
Abington, W.L., actor; d. May 19, 1918 (59).
Abramson, Ivan, director & writer; d. Sept. 15, 1934 (65).
Abramson, Mrs. Ivan, actress; d. Jan. 14, 1945 (87).
Abril, Dorothy, actress; b. June 10, 1897, Paterson, N.J.; d. Apr.
    28, 1977 (79).
Aburto, Armando, actor; d. July 16, 1955 (45).
Achterberg, Fritz, actor; b. Nov. 2, 1888, Berlin, Germany; d. Oct.,
    1971 (82).
Acker, Jean, actress; d. Aug. 16, 1978 (85).
Ackerman, Rick, actor; b. Apr. 8, 1948, Maine; d. Mar. 13, 1974 (25).
Ackerman, Walter, actor; b. June 28, 1881, New York City; d. Dec.
    12, 1938 (57).
Acord, Art, actor; b. Apr. 17, 1890, Glenwood, Sevier, Utah; d. Jan.
    4, 1931 (40).
Acosta, Enrique, actor; b. Feb. 26, 1870, Mexico; d. May 22, 1949 (79).
Acosta, Rodolfo, actor; b. July 29, 1920, Chihuahua, Mexico; d. Nov.
    7, 1974 (54).
Acuff, Eddie, actor; b. June 3, 1908, Caruthersville, Mo.; d. Dec. 17,
    1956 (48).
Adair, Jack, actor; b. Nov. 29, 1895, Franklin, Ind.; d. Sept. 22,
    1940 (44).
Adair, Jean, actress; b. Hamilton, Ont., Canada; d. May 11, 1953
    (80).
Adair, John, actor; d. Jan. 22, 1952 (67).
A'Dair, Robert, actor; b. Jan. 3, 1900, San Francisco, Calif.; d.
    Aug. 10, 1954 (54).

3

Adalbert, Max, actor; b. Dec. 19, 1874, Danzig; d. Sept. 7, 1933 (58).
Adam, Ronald, actor; b. Dec. 31, 1896, Herefordshire, England; d.
    Mar. 27, 1979 (82).
Adams, Abigail (Tommye Adams), actress; b. Jan. 11, 1922, South
    Carolina; d. Feb. 13, 1955 (33).
Adams, Blake, actor; d. Aug. 17, 1913.
Adams, Claire, actress; b. 1898, Winnipeg, Canada; d. Sept. 25,
    1978 (80).
Adams, Edith, actress; d. Jan. 10, 1957 (78).
Adams, Ernie, actor; b. June 18, 1885, San Francisco, Calif.; d. Nov.
    26, 1947 (62).
Adams, Jimmie, actor; b. Oct. 4, 1888, Paterson, N.J.; d. Dec. 19,
    1933 (45).
Adams, Kathryn, actress; b. St. Louis, Mo.; d. Feb. 17, 1959 (65).
Adams, Leslie, actor; b. Stark, Fla.; d. Mar. 26, 1936 (49).
Adams, Lionel, actor; b. New Orleans, La.; d. Aug. 10, 1952 (86).
Adams, Nick, actor; b. July 10, 1931, Nanticoke, Pa.; d. Feb. 7,
    1968 (36).
Adams, Sam, actor; b. Dec. 16, 1870, Canada; d. Mar. 24, 1958 (87).
Adams, Stanley, actor; d. Apr. 27, 1977 (62).
Adams, Stella, actress; b. Apr. 24, 1883, Texas; d. Sept. 17, 1961
    (78).
Adams, Ted (r.n. Richard Ted Adams), actor; b. Mar. 17, 1890, New
    York; d. Sept. 24, 1973 (83).
Adams, Victoria, actress; b. June 17, 1897, Missouri; d. May 13,
    1961 (63).
Adams, William Perry, actor; d. Sept. 30, 1972 (85).
Adamson, Evelyn, actress; d. Oct. 29, 1958 (57).
Adamson, Ewart, writer; b. Oct. 23, 1882, Dundee, Scotland; d. Nov. 28,
    1945 (63).
Adderley, Frederick, actor; b. Oct. 18, 1887, England; d. Nov. 13,
    1967 (80).
Addinsell, Richard, composer; d. Nov. 14, 1977 (73).
Ade, George, writer; d. May 16, 1944 (78).
Adeson, Martin, actor; d. Jan. 18, 1936 (68).
Adin, Oris Lyle, actor; d. Apr. 28, 1972 (51).
Adler, Buddy, producer; b. June 22, 1909, New York City; d. July
    12, 1960 (51).
Adler, Celia, actress; d. Jan. 31, 1979 (89).
Adler, Harry, actor; d. May 5, 1944 (61).
Adler, Jacob, actor; b. Odessa, Russia; d. Apr. 1, 1926 (71).
Adler, Jay, actor; d. Sept. 23, 1978 (82).
Adlon, Duke (see Adlon, Louis)
Adlon, Louis (Michael Duke; Duke Adlon), actor; b. Oct. 7, 1907,
    Berlin, Germany; d. Mar. 31, 1947 (39).
Adolfi, John G., director; d. May 11, 1933 (44).
Adoree, Renee, actress; b. Sept. 30, 1898, Lille, France; d. Oct. 5,
    1933 (35).
Adrian, Max, actor; b. Nov. 1, 1903, Enniskillen, Northern Ireland;
    d. Jan. 19, 1973 (69).
Afrique, actor, vocalist, & impressionist; b. Johannesburg, South
    Africa; d. Dec. 17, 1961 (54).
Agar, Jane, actress; d. June 10, 1948 (59).
Agay, Irene, actress; b. Feb. 23, 1913, Budapest, Hungary; d. Sept.
    2, 1950 (37).
Agee, James, writer; d. May 16, 1955 (45).

Agresti, Edward, actor; b. Oct. 4, 1900, Italy; d. Jan. 1, 1971 (70).
Aguglia, Mimi, actress; b. Dec. 21, 1884, Italy; d. July 30, 1970
    (85).
Aguilar, Marcus R., actor; b. Sept. 5, 1894, Texas; d. May 3, 1960
    (65).
Aguirre, Manuel B., actor; d. Dec. 3, 1957 (50).
Ahearne, Tom, actor; d. Jan. 5, 1969 (63).
Aherne, Patrick, actor; b. Jan. 6, 1901, England; d. Sept. 30,
    1970 (69).
Ahlers, Anny, actress; d. Mar. 14, 1933 (26).
Ahlm, Philip E., actor; b. July 15, 1905, Sweden; d. July 5, 1954
    (48).
Ahn, Philip, actor; b. Mar. 29, 1905, Los Angeles, Calif.; d. Feb.
    28, 1978 (72).
Ahrensborg, Henning, actor; d. Oct. 25, 1951 (26).
Aimos, Raymond, actor; b. 1889; d. Aug. 22, 1944 (55).
Ainley, Henry, actor; b. Aug. 21, 1879, Leeds, England; d. Oct. 31,
    1945 (66).
Ainley, Richard, actor; b. Dec. 22, 1910, Stanmore, Middlesex,
    England; d. May 18, 1967 (56).
Ainsley, Norman (r.n. Norman A. Blume), actor; b. May 4, 1881,
    Edinburgh, Scotland; d. Jan. 23, 1948 (66).
Ainsworth, Cupid (r.n. Helen Ainsworth), actress; b. Oct. 10, 1901,
    San Jose, Calif.; d. Aug. 18, 1961 (59).
Ainsworth, Sidney, actor; b. Manchester, England; d. May 21, 1922
    (50).
Aitken, Spottiswoode (r.n. Frank Spottiswoode Aitken), actor;
    b. Apr. 16, 1868, Edinburgh, Scotland; d. Feb. 24, 1933 (64).
Aked, Muriel, actress; b. Nov. 9, 1887, Bingley, England; d. Mar.
    21, 1955 (67).
Akers, Henry Carl (Hank), stand-in for J. Weissmuller; d. Aug. 22,
    1967 (53).
Akst, Harry, composer & actor; d. Mar. 31, 1963 (68).
Aladdin (Pallante), actor & musician; d. June 9, 1970 (57).
Alanova, Kyra, actress; d. Sept. 1, 1965 (63).
Albach-Retty, Wolf, actor; b. May 28, 1908, Vienna, Austria; d. Feb.
    21, 1967 (58).
Albanesi, Meggie, actress; d. Dec. 9, 1923 (24).
Albani, Olga, singer; d. June 3, 1940 (36).
Alberg, Somer, actor; d. May 31, 1977 (69).
Alberni, Louis, actor; b. Oct. 4, 1886, Spain; d. Dec. 23, 1962 (76).
Albers, Hans, actor; b. Sept. 22, 1892, Hamburg, Germany; d. July
    24, 1960 (67).
Albert, Dan, actor; d. Aug., 1919 (29).
Alberti, Fritz, actor; b. Oct. 22, 1877, Hanau, Germany; d. Sept.,
    1954 (76).
Albertson, Frank, actor; b. Feb. 2, 1909, Fergus Falls, Minn.;
    d. Feb. 29, 1964 (55).
Albright, Hardie, actor; b. Dec. 16, 1903, Pittsburgh, Pa.; d. Dec.
    7, 1975 (71).
Alcalde, Mario, actor; b. Sept. 6, 1926, Florida; d. Apr. 22,
    1971 (44).
Alcock, Douglas, actor; d. Oct. 14, 1970 (62).
Alcovar, Pierre, actor; b. Mar 14, 1893; d. 1954 (61).
Aldea, Mercedes, actress; d. Oct. 28, 1954.

Alden, Betty (r.n. Elsa Maxwell), actress; b. Aug. 21, 1891, India-
    napolis, Ind.; d. Apr. 7, 1948 (56).
Alden, Lester, actor; d. July 28, 1956 (84).
Alden, Mary, actress; b. June 18, 1883, New York City; d. July 2,
    1946 (63).
Alden, Newton C., actor; d. Apr. 1, 1953 (88).
Alderson, Erville, actor; b. Sept. 11, 1882, Missouri; d. Aug. 4,
    1957 (74).
Aldrich, Fred, actor; b. Dec. 23, 1904, New York; d. Jan. 25, 1979 (74).
Aldrich, Mariska, actress; b. Mar. 27, 1881, Massachusetts; d. Sept.
    28, 1965 (84).
Aldridge, Alfred, actor; d. May 4, 1934 (58).
Alekin, Boris, actor; d. Mar., 1942 (38).
Alerme, Andre, actor; b. Sept. 9, 1877, Dieppe, France; d. 1960 (83).
Alexander, Alex, actor; d. Apr. 24, 1977 (66).
Alexander, Ben (r.n. Nicholas Benton Alexander), actor; b. May 26,
    1911, Goldfield, Nev.; d. July 5, 1969 (58).
Alexander, Edward, actor; d. Aug. 15, 1964 (76).
Alexander, Frank, actor; d. Sept. 8, 1937 (58).
Alexander, Georg, actor; b. Apr. 3, 1889, Hannover, Germany; d.
    1946 (57).
Alexander, Sir George, actor; b. June 19, 1858, Reading, England;
    d. Mar. 16, 1918 (59).
Alexander, Gerard (Mrs. Bertram Grassby), actress; d. Apr. 6, 1962
    (85).
Alexander, James, actor; b. May 20, 1914, Indiana; d. Feb. 1, 1961
    (46).
Alexander, John, actor; d. Apr. 5, 1951 (86).
Alexander, Lilla, actress; d. July 15, 1968 (56).
Alexander, Ross, actor; b. July 27, 1907, Brooklyn, N.Y.; d. Jan. 2,
    1937 (29).
Alexandre, Rene, actor; d. Aug. 19, 1946 (61).
Alexandre, Roland, actor; b. 1937; d. 1956 (19).
Alexis, Demetrius, actor; b. Dec. 1, 1905, Greece; d. Mar. 12, 1973
    (67).
Algaro, Gabriel, actor; d. Oct., 1951 (63).
Algier, Sidney, actor, production manager, & director; b. Dec. 5,
    1885, Examokin, Pa.; d. Apr. 25, 1945 (59).
Ali, George, actor; d. Apr. 26, 1947 (81).
Alippi, Elias, actor; b. Feb. 20, 1883, Buenos Aires, Argentina;
    d. May 3, 1942 (59).
Allan, Maud, actress; b. Aug. 27, 1880, Canada; d. Oct. 7, 1956 (76).
Allbeury, Daisy, extra; d. Oct. 20, 1961 (76).
Allbritton, Louise, actress; b. July 3, 1920, Oklahoma City, Okla.;
    d. Feb. 16, 1979 (58).
Alleborn, Al, stuntman & asst. director; d. June 14, 1968 (76).
Allegret, Marc, director; b. Dec. 22, 1900, Bale, Switzerland;
    d. Nov. 3, 1973 (72).
Allen, A. Hylton, actor; b. Oct. 25, 1879, Pulborough, Sussex,
    England; d. Feb. 6, 1975 (95).
Allen, Alfred, actor; b. Apr. 8, 1866, New York; d. June 18, 1947
    (81).
Allen, Arthur B., actor; d. Aug. 25, 1947 (66).
Allen, Barbara Jo (see Vague, Vera)
Allen, Christopher C., actor; d. Nov. 7, 1955 (86).
Allen, Dave, actor & director; b. Aug. 15, 1885, Albany, N.Y.;
    d. Jan. 3, 1955 (69).

Allen, Dorothy, actress; d. Sept. 30, 1970 (74).
Allen, Edwin Hampton (Richard Allen), actor; b. Nov. 15, 1885,
   Canton Lewis Co., Mo.; d. Aug. 13, 1942 (56).
Allen, Estelle, actress; b. Jan. 5, 1892, Portland, Ore.; d. July
   14, 1970 (78).
Allen, Ethan, actor; b. May 11, 1882, Missouri; d. Aug. 21, 1940 (58).
Allen, Fred, actor; b. May 31, 1894, Boston, Mass.; d. Mar. 17,
   1956 (61).
Allen, Gracie, actress; b. July 26, 1902, San Francisco, Calif.;
   d. Aug. 27, 1964 (62).
Allen, Harry, actor; b. July 10, 1883, Australia; d. Dec. 4, 1951
   (68).
Allen, Jack, actor; d. July 5, 1961 (32).
Allen, Jane Marie, dancer; d. Feb. 16, 1970 (54).
Allen, Joe, actor; d. Jan. 31, 1955 (67).
Allen, Joseph, actor; b. Jan. 2, 1840, Bristol, England; d. Jan. 12,
   1917 (77).
Allen, Joseph, actor; b. Boston, Mass.; d. Sept. 9, 1952 (80).
Allen, Joseph, Jr., actor; b. Mar. 30, 1918, Boston, Mass.; d. Nov.
   9, 1962 (44).
Allen, Kenneth, stuntman; d. Jan. 15, 1976 (72).
Allen, Lester, actor; b. Nov. 17, 1891, Utica, N.Y.; d. Nov. 6, 1949
   (57).
Allen, Maude, actress; d. Nov. 7, 1956.
Allen, Maude Pierce, actress; b. Nov. 30, 1887, Massachusetts;
   d. Apr. 24, 1960 (72).
Allen, Phyllis, actress; b. Nov. 25, 1861, Staten Island, N.Y.;
   d. Mar. 26, 1938 (76).
Allen, Ricca, actress; b. June 9, 1863, Victoria, B.C., Canada;
   d. Sept. 13, 1949 (86).
Allen, Rose, actress; d. May 3, 1977 (92).
Allen, Sam, actor; b. Dec. 25, 1861, Maryland; d. Sept. 13, 1934 (72).
Allen, Viola, actress; b. Oct. 27, 1869, Huntsville, Ala.; d. May
   9, 1948 (78).
Allenby, Frank, actor; b. Dec. 22, 1898, Hobart, Tasmania; d. May
   29, 1953 (54).
Allenby, Thomas, actor; d. Dec. 19, 1933 (72).
Allerton, Helen, actress; d. Nov. 4, 1959 (71).
Allerton, Marie, actress; d. Mar. 17, 1951.
Allgood, Sara, actress; b. Oct. 15, 1879, Dublin, Ireland; d. Sept.
   13, 1950 (70).
Allister, Claud (r.n. Claud Palmer), actor; b. Oct. 3, 1888, London,
   England; d. July 26, 1970 (81).
Allworth, Frank, actor; b. 1900; d. Sept. 2, 1935 (35).
Allwyn, Astrid, actress; b. Nov. 27, 1909, Manchester, Conn.;
   d. Mar. 31, 1978 (68).
Allyn, Alyce, actress; d. Feb. 11, 1976.
Allyn, Lilly, actress; d. May 5, 1944 (78).
Almirante, Luigi, actor; b. Sept. 30, 1886, Tunisia; d. May 6,
   1963 (76).
Alonso, Julio, actor; d. Feb. 9, 1955 (49).
Alonzo, Alberto, actor; b. Philippines; d. Oct. 6, 1967 (23).
Alsace, Gene (see Camron, Rocky)
Alsen, Elsa, singer; b. Apr. 7, 1880, Obra, Poland; d. Jan. 31,
   1975 (94).

Alstrup, Carl, actor; b. Apr. 11, 1877, Copenhagen, Denmark; d. Oct.
    2, 1942 (65).
Althoff, Charles R., actor; d. Oct. 14, 1962 (72).
Althouse, Earl F., actor; d. Feb. 6, 1971 (78).
Alton, Robert, director; d. June 14, 1957 (55).
Alvarado, Don, actor; b. Nov. 4, 1904, Albuquerque, N.M.; d. Mar. 31,
    1967 (62).
Amarante, Estevao, actor; d. Jan., 1952 (62).
Amato, Giuseppe, producer, actor, director, & author; b. Naples,
    Italy; d. Feb. 3, 1964 (64).
Amato, Pasquale, actor & opera singer; d. Aug. 12, 1942 (63).
Amaya, Carmen, flamenco dancer; b. Nov. 2, 1913, Barcelona, Spain;
    d. Nov. 19, 1963 (50).
Ames, Adrienne, actress; b. Aug. 3, 1907, Fort Worth, Tex.; d. May
    31, 1947 (39).
Ames, Gerald, actor; b. Sept. 12, 1881, Blackheath, England; d. July
    2, 1933 (51).
Ames, Jimmy, actor; b. July 11, 1909, Illinois; d. Aug. 14, 1965 (56).
Ames, Michael (see Andrews, Tod)
Ames, Robert, actor; b. Mar. 23, 1889, Hartford, Conn.; d. Nov. 27,
    1931 (42).
Amunarriz, Raul Cancio, actor; d. Oct. 23, 1961 (50).
Analla, Isabel, actress; d. Jan. 17, 1958 (38).
Anderson, Audley, actor; b. Mar. 5, 1885, Louisiana; d. Dec. 19,
    1966 (81).
Anderson, Bruce, actor; d. Sept. 14, 1979 (73).
Anderson, Cap (see Anderson, C.E.)
Anderson, C.E. (Cap), actor; b. Oct. 27, 1882, Sweden; d. Mar. 24,
    1956 (73).
Anderson, Claire Mathes, actress; b. May 8, 1895, Michigan; d. Mar.
    23, 1964 (68).
Anderson, Dallas, actor; b. Scotland; d. Nov. 16, 1934 (60).
Anderson, Eddie "Rochester," actor; b. Sept. 18, 1905, Oakland, Calif.;
    d. Feb. 28, 1977 (71).
Anderson, Edward, actor; d. May 7, 1943 (81).
Anderson, G.M. "Bronco Billy," actor; b. Mar. 21, 1884, Little Rock,
    Ark.; d. Jan. 20, 1971 (86).
Anderson, Gene, actress; b. London, England; d. May 5, 1965 (34).
Anderson, George, actor; b. Mar. 6, 1886, New York City; d. Aug. 26,
    1948 (62).
Anderson, Ivie, singer; b. July 10, 1905, Gilroy, Calif.; d. Dec.
    28, 1949 (44).
Anderson, James, actor; d. Mar. 22, 1953 (81).
Anderson, James, actor; d. Sept. 14, 1969 (48).
Anderson, John Murray, director; b. Sept. 20, 1886, St. John's,
    Newfoundland, Canada; d. Jan. 30, 1954 (67).
Anderson, Lawrence, actor; b. 1893, London, England; d. Mar. 28,
    1939 (46).
Anderson, Margaret, actress; d. Apr. 22, 1922.
Anderson, Mary, actress; b. July 28, 1859, Sacramento, Calif.; d. May
    29, 1940 (80).
Anderson, Maxwell, writer & playwright; b. Dec. 15, 1888, Atlantic
    City, N.J.; d. Feb. 23, 1959 (70).
Anderson, Warner, actor; b. Mar. 10, 1911, Brooklyn, N.Y.; d. Aug.
    26, 1976 (65).

Andra, Fern, actress; b. Nov. 24, 1893, Watseka, Ill.; d. Feb. 8, 1974 (80).

Andre, Carl Pierre, actor; b. Feb. 11, 1905, Pennsylvania; d. Mar. 20, 1972 (67).

Andre, Gaby, actress; d. Aug. 9, 1972.

Andre, Gwili, actress; b. Copenhagen, Denmark; d. Feb. 5, 1959 (51).

Andrews, Del, director; d. Oct. 27, 1942 (48).

Andrews, Laverne, recording artist & singer; b. July 6, 1915, Minneapolis, Minn.; d. May 8, 1967 (51).

Andrews, Lois, actress; b. Mar. 24, 1924, Los Angeles, Calif.; d. Apr. 5, 1968 (44).

Andrews, Orville, singer; d. Mar. 29, 1968.

Andrews, Stanley (r.n. Stanley Andrzejewski), actor; b. Aug. 28, 1891, Chicago, Ill.; d. June 23, 1969 (77).

Andrews, Tod (Michael Ames), actor; b. Nov. 10, 1914 or 1920 (cert.), New York City; d. Nov. 7, 1972 (57).

Andreyor, Yvette, actress; b. 1892; d. 1962 (70).

Androvskaya, Olga, actress; b. July 21, 1898, Moscow, Russia; d. Apr. 6, 1975 (76).

Angeles, Bert, director; d. May 30, 1950 (75).

Angeli, Pier, actress; b. June 19, 1932, Sardinia; d. Sept. 10, 1971 (39).

Angelica, Norma, actress; d. Dec. 24, 1962 (24).

Angelo, Jean, actor; b. May 17, 1875, Paris, France; d. Nov. 26, 1933 (58).

Angold, Edit, actress; b. Sept. 1, 1895, Germany; d. Oct. 4, 1971 (76).

Ankrum, Morris (Stephen Morris), actor; b. Aug. 28, 1897, Illinois; d. Sept. 2, 1964 (67).

Anry, Barat, actor; d. Jan. 4, 1929 (58).

Anselmi, Rosina, actress; b. July 26, 1880, Catania; d. May 23, 1965 (84).

Anson, Albert Edward, actor; b. Sept. 14, 1879, England; d. June 25, 1936 (56).

Anson, James (Yakima Jim), actor; d. 1925.

Anson, Lura, actress; b. Jan. 2, 1892, Nebraska; d. July 15, 1968 (76).

Anthony, Jack, actor; b. Pennistown, Glasgow, Scotland; d. Feb. 28, 1962 (61).

Anthony, Stuart, writer; d. Apr. 28, 1942 (56).

Antine, Gertrude, actress; b. Apr. 3, 1907, Washington; d. Apr. 10, 1974 (67).

Antonov, Aleksandr P., actor; b. Feb. 13, 1898; d. Nov. 26, 1962 (64).

Antony, P.J., actor; d. Apr., 1979 (55).

Antrim, Harry, actor; b. Aug. 27, 1884, Chicago, Ill.; d. Jan. 18, 1967 (82).

Antwerp, Van (see Van Antwerp, Albert)

Aoki, Tsuru, actress; d. Oct. 18, 1961 (69).

Apfel, Oscar, actor, director, & producer; b. Jan. 17, 1879, Cleveland, Ohio; d. Mar. 21, 1938 (59).

Appel, Anna, actress; b. Bucharest, Rumania; d. Nov. 19, 1963 (75).

Appel, Sam, actor; b. Aug. 8, 1871, Magdalina, Mexico; d. June 18, 1947 (75).

Applegarth, Jonas, actor; d. July 23, 1965 (45).

Applegate, Hazel, actress; d. Oct. 30, 1959 (73).
Appler, Walter F., actor; d. Sept. 13, 1956 (47).
Applewhite, Eric Leon, actor; b. Wilson, N.C.; d. May 29, 1973 (76).
Aquistapace, Jean, actor; b. Aug. 12, 1882, Nice, France; d. Oct.
    20, 1952 (70).
Arbenina, Stella, actress; d. Apr. 26, 1976 (91).
Arbenz, Arabella, actress; d. Oct. 5, 1965 (25).
Arbuckle, Andrew, actor; b. Sept. 5, 1887, Galveston, Tex.; d. Sept.
    21, 1939 (52).
Arbuckle, Macklyn, actor; b. July 9, 1866, San Antonio, Tex.; d. Mar.
    31, 1931 (64).
Arbuckle, Roscoe "Fatty," actor; b. Mar. 24, 1887, San Jose, Calif.;
    d. June 29, 1933 (46).
Arbury, Guy, actor; d. Dec. 26, 1972 (65).
Arcaro, Flavia, actress; b. June 22, 1876, Mejico, Tex.; d. Apr. 8,
    1937 (61).
Archainbaud, George, director; b. Paris, France; d. Feb. 20, 1959 (69).
Archer, Eugene (r.n. Samuel Eugene Archer), actor & critic; d. Jan.
    30, 1973 (42).
Archer, Louis A., actor; d. Aug., 1922 (48).
Ardavin, Eusebio Fernandez, director; b. July 31, 1898, Madrid,
    Spain; d. Jan. 9, 1965 (66).
Ardell, Franklyn (r.n. Franklyn Dziuba), actor; b. May 1, 1885,
    New Jersey; d. Apr. 17, 1960 (74).
Ardell, John E., actor; d. Apr. 26, 1949 (68).
Ardell, Lillian, actress; d. Mar. 15, 1950.
Arden, Eddie, actor; d. June 23, 1952 (44).
Arden, Edwin, actor; b. Feb. 13, 1864, St. Louis, Mo.; d. Oct. 2, 1918
    (54).
Ardrey, Robert, writer; d. Jan. 14, 1980 (71).
Arena, Maurizio, actor; d. Nov. 22, 1979 (46).
Arenas, Miguel, actor; b. Alicante, Spain; d. Nov. 3, 1965 (63).
Areola, Armando, actor; d. Nov., 1978 (73).
Arey, Wayne, actor; d. July 2, 1937 (57).
Argyle, Pearl, actress & dancer; b. Nov. 7, 1910, Johannesburg,
    South Africa; d. Jan. 29, 1947 (36).
Arledge, John, actor; b. Mar. 12, 1907, Crockett, Tex.; d. May 15,
    1947 (40).
Arlen, Judith, actress; b. Mar. 18, 1914, Los Angeles, Calif.;
    d. June 5, 1968 (54).
Arlen, Richard, actor; b. Sept. 1, 1900, Charlottesville, Va.;
    d. Mar. 28, 1976 (75).
Arliss, Florence, actress; d. Mar. 11, 1950 (77).
Arliss, George, actor; b. Apr. 10, 1868, London, England; d. Feb. 5,
    1946 (77).
Armand, Teddy V., actor; d. July 12, 1947 (73).
Armbrister, Cyril, actor; d. Sept. 18, 1966 (70).
Armendariz, Pedro, actor; b. May 9, 1912, Mexico; d. June 18, 1963
    (51).
Armengod, Ramon, actor; d. Oct. 31, 1976 (66).
Armetta, Henry, actor; b. July 4, 1888, Palermo, Italy; d. Oct. 21,
    1945 (57).
Armitage, Buford, actor; b. Aug. 27, 1898, Greeneville, Tenn.;
    d. Nov. 3, 1978 (80).
Armitage, Walter W., actor; b. Johannesburg, South Africa; d. Feb.
    22, 1953 (46).

Armstrong, Billy, actor; b. Jan. 14, 1891, Bristol, England; d. Mar. 1, 1924 (33).

Armstrong, Clyde, actor; d. Sept. 30, 1937 (58).

Armstrong, James, actor; b. July 23, 1891, Wyoming; d. June 20, 1973 (81).

Armstrong, Louis, actor & jazz artist; b. July 4, 1900, New Orleans, La.; d. July 6, 1971 (71).

Armstrong, R.L. (Tex), actor; d. Mar. 10, 1978.

Armstrong, Robert, actor; b. Nov. 20, 1890, Saginaw, Mich.; d. Apr. 20, 1973 (82).

Armstrong, Will, actor; b. Dec. 18, 1868, Peoria, Ill.; d. July 29, 1943 (74).

Arna, Lissi, actress; d. Jan. 22, 1964 (64).

Arnaud, Yvonne, actress; b. Dec. 20, 1892, Bordeaux, France; d. Sept. 20, 1958 (65).

Arnheim, Valy, actor; b. June 8, 1883, Waldau, Germany; d. Nov., 1950 (67).

Arno, Sig, actor; b. Dec. 27, 1895, Hamburg, Germany; d. Aug. 17, 1975 (79).

Arnold, Cecile, actress; d. 1931.

Arnold, Edward, actor; b. Feb. 18, 1890, New York City; d. Apr. 26, 1956 (66).

Arnold, Gertrud, actress; b. Mar. 3, 1873, Stolp, Poland; d. Jan. 11, 1931 (57).

Arnold, Grace, actress; b. Sept. 19, 1894, London, England; d. Feb. 26, 1979 (84).

Arnold, Jack (see also Hayworth, Vinton)

Arnold, Jack, actor; d. June 15, 1962 (59).

Arnold, Jessie, actress; b. Dec. 3, 1884, Lyons, Mich.; d. May 5, 1955 (70).

Arnold, Lois, actress; d. Jan. 26, 1947 (84).

Arnold, Mabel, actress; b. Apr. 25, 1888, Texas; d. Jan. 6, 1964 (75).

Arnold, Marcella, actress; d. Mar. 3, 1937 (26).

Arnold, Phil, actor; b. Sept. 15, 1909, New Jersey; d. May 9, 1968 (58).

Arnold, Seth, actor; b. London, England; d. Jan. 3, 1955 (70).

Arnold, William R., actor; b. Jan. 6, 1884, Brockton, Mass.; d. July 20, 1940 (56).

Arnoux, Robert, actor; b. Oct. 23, 1899, Lille, France; d. Mar. 15, 1964 (64).

Arnstaedt, Hansi, actress; d. May, 1945.

Arozamena, Eduardo, actor; d. 1951.

Arquette, Cliff, actor; b. Dec. 28, 1905, Toledo, Ohio; d. Sept. 23, 1974 (68).

Arras, Harry, actor; b. May 31, 1881, Buffalo, N.Y.; d. Jan. 29, 1942 (60).

Arroyo, Luis, actor; b. Nov. 19, 1915, Madrid, Spain; d. Nov. 4, 1956 (40).

Arruza, Carlos, actor & matador; d. May 20, 1966 (42).

Arshansky, Michael, actor & dancer; d. June 30, 1978 (82).

Artaud, Antonin, actor; b. Sept. 4, 1896, Marseille, France; d. Mar. 4, 1948 (51).

Arthur, Johnny, actor; b. May 20, 1883, Scottsdale, Pa.; d. Dec. 31, 1951 (68).

Arthur, Julia, actress; b. May 3, 1869, Hamilton, Ont., Canada; d. Mar. 28, 1950 (80).

Arthur, Louise, actress; d. June 9, 1925 (25).

Arundale, Sybil, actress; d. Sept. 5, 1965 (83).
Arvan, Jan, actor; d. May 24, 1979 (66).
Arvidson, Linda, actress; d. July 26, 1949 (65).
Arzner, Dorothy, director; b. Jan. 3, 1897, San Francisco, Calif.;
    d. Oct. 1, 1979 (82).
Asche, Oscar, actor & author; b. Jan. 26, 1871, Geelong, Australia;
    d. Mar. 23, 1936 (65).
Ascher, Anton, actor; d. Sept. 30, 1928 (60).
Ash, Arty, actor; d. Feb. 6, 1954 (61).
Ash, Jerome H. "Jerry," cinematographer & actor; d. Jan. 5, 1953
    (60).
Ash, Russell, actor; b. Dec. 12, 1910, Ohio; d. June 4, 1974 (63).
Ash, Sam, actor; b. Aug. 28, 1884, Kentucky; d. Oct. 20, 1951 (67).
Ashe, Warren, actor; b. New York City; d. Sept. 19, 1947 (44).
Asher, Max, actor; b. May 5, 1885, California; d. Apr. 15, 1957 (71).
Asher, Rollie, director; d. Apr. 18, 1953 (58).
Ashley, Arthur, actor; d. Dec. 28, 1970 (85).
Ashley, Beulah, actress; b. Jan. 24, 1899, Mississippi; d. July 6,
    1965 (66).
Ashley, Herbert, actor; b. Apr. 18, 1874, New York; d. July 23,
    1958 (84).
Ashton, Barry, actor; d. May, 1978 (43).
Ashton, Dorrit, actor; d. July 25, 1936 (63).
Ashton, Herbert, Jr., actor & writer; b. Sept. 25, 1902, San Francis-
    co, Calif.; d. Aug. 13, 1960 (57).
Ashton, Sylvia, actress; b. Jan. 26, 1880, Denver, Colo.; d. Nov.
    18, 1940 (60).
Ashton, Vera, actress; b. Feb. 28, 1900, Missouri; d. Apr. 27, 1965
    (65).
Askam, Earl, actor; b. May 10, 1898, Seattle, Wash.; d. Apr. 1,
    1940 (41).
Askam, Perry, actor & singer; b. Aug. 31, 1895, Seattle, Wash.;
    d. Oct. 22, 1961 (66).
Askan, Harry, actor; d. Sept. 30, 1934 (67).
Aslan, Raoul, actor; b. Oct. 16, 1890, Salonica, Greece; d. June 18,
    1958 (67).
Aslanov, Nikolay P., actor; b. 1877; d. 1944 (67).
Asquith, Anthony, director; b. London, England; d. Feb. 20, 1968
    (65).
Astangov, Mikhail, actor; b. Nov. 3, 1900, Warsaw, Poland; d. Apr. 20,
    1965 (64).
Astol, Paco, actor; d. Dec. 23, 1962.
Astor, Gertrude, actress; b. Nov. 9, 1887, Lakewood, Ohio; d. Nov.
    9, 1977 (90).
Astor, Junie, actress; d. Aug. 22, 1967 (49).
Atchley, Hooper, actor; b. Apr. 30, 1887, Ebenezer, Tenn.; d. Nov.
    16, 1943 (56).
Ates, Roscoe, actor; b. Jan. 20, 1895, Grange, Miss.; d. Mar. 1, 1962
    (67).
Atkins, Robert, actor; b. Aug. 10, 1886, Dulwich, England; d. Feb. 9,
    1972 (85).
Atkinson, Evelyn, actress; d. Dec. 16, 1954 (54).
Atkinson, Frank, actor & author; b. Mar. 19, 1890, Oldham, Lan-
    cashire, England; d. Feb. 23, 1963 (72).
Atkinson, Frank White, film editor; b. May 10, 1896, Canada; d.
    Nov. 23, 1951 (55).

Atkinson, George, actor; b. Dec. 15, 1877, England; d. May 1, 1968
(90).

Atkinson, Maude, actress; d. Mar. 7, 1944 (59).

Atkinson, Rosalind, actress; b. Apr. 11, 1900, New Zealand; d. Feb.
21, 1977 (76).

Atlas, Leopold, writer; b. Oct. 19, 1907, Brooklyn, N.Y.; d. Sept.
30, 1954 (46).

Atwater, Barry, actor; b. May 16, 1918, Colorado; d. May 24, 1978 (60).

Atwell, Grace, actress; b. July 13, 1872, Massachusetts; d. Nov. 2,
1952 (80).

Atwell, Roy, actor; d. Feb. 6, 1962 (83).

Atwill, Lionel (Lionel Alfred Wm. Atwill), actor; b. Mar. 1, 1885,
Kent, Croydon, England; d. Apr. 22, 1946 (61).

Aubert, Louis, actor; d. 1943.

Aubrey, Georges, actor; d. Nov. 1, 1975 (47).

Aubrey, Will, actor; d. Jan. 3, 1958 (64).

Audran, Edmond, actor; d. July, 1951 (32).

Auer, Florence, actress; b. May 14, 1962 (82).

Auer, John H., director, producer, & actor; b. Aug. 3, 1906, Budapest,
Hungary; d. Mar. 15, 1975 (68).

Auer, Mischa, actor; b. Nov. 17, 1905, St. Petersburg, Russia;
d. Mar. 5, 1967 (61).

Auerbach, Artie, actor; d. Oct. 3, 1957 (54).

Aug, Edna, actress; b. Cincinnati, Ohio; d. Nov. 30, 1938 (60).

August, Edwin, actor & director; b. Nov. 10, 1883, Missouri; d. Mar.
4, 1964 (80).

August, Hal, actor; d. Sept. 21, 1918 (28).

August, Joseph, cinematographer; d. Sept. 25, 1947 (57).

Augustin, William, actor; d. July, 1934.

Ault, Marie, actress; b. Sept. 2, 1870, Wigan, England; d. May 9,
1951 (80).

Aurthur, Robert Alan, writer; d. Nov. 20, 1978 (56).

Austen, Leslie, actor; d. Sept. 16, 1924 (36).

Austin, Albert, actor; d. Aug. 17, 1953 (71).

Austin, Charles, actor; d. Jan. 14, 1944 (63).

Austin, Edwin A., actor; b. Aug. 27, 1866, Paris, Idaho; d. Feb. 2,
1937 (70).

Austin, Frank (r.n. George Francis Austin), actor; b. Oct. 9, 1877,
Mound City, Mo.; d. May 13, 1954 (76).

Austin, Gene (r.n. Eugene Lucas), recording artist, actor, & singer;
b. June 24, 1900, Gainesville, Tex.; d. Jan. 24, 1972 (71).

Austin, Jere, actor; d. Nov. 12, 1927 (51).

Austin, Jerry, actor; b. July 20, 1892, Russia; d. Oct. 15, 1976 (84).

Austin, Johanna (Anna) R., actress; d. June 1, 1944 (91).

Austin, Stephen E., actor; d. May 12, 1955 (64).

Austin, William C.P. (r.n. William Crosby Piercy Austin), actor;
b. June 12, 1884, Georgetown, British Guiana; d. June 15, 1975
(91).

Avalier, Don, actor; b. Sept. 19, 1912, California; d. May 29,
1973 (60).

Avery, Charles, actor & director; b. May 28, 1873, Chicago, Ill.;
d. July 23, 1926 (53).

Avery, Eugene V. (r.n. Eugene Valentine Avery), actor; b. Aug. 11,
1907, Colorado; d. Nov. 17, 1975 (68).

Avery, Stephen Morehouse, writer; b. Dec. 20, 1893, Webster Grove,
Mo.; d. Feb. 10, 1948 (54).

Avery, Tol, actor; b. Aug. 28, 1915, Texas; d. Aug. 27, 1973 (57).
Axe, Harry D., actor; d. Aug. 29, 1955 (80).
Aye, Maryon, actress; b. Apr. 5, 1903, Illinois; d. July 20, 1951
    (48).
Ayerton, Robert, actor; d. May 18, 1924.
Aylesworth, Arthur, actor; b. Aug. 12, 1883, Apponaugh, R.I.; d. June
    26, 1946 (62).
Ayling, Robert, actor; d. Aug. 28, 1919.
Aylmer, David, actor; d. July 20, 1964 (31).
Aylmer, Felix, actor; b. Feb. 21, 1889, Corsham, Wilts, England;
    d. Sept. 2, 1979 (90).
Aynesworth, Allan, actor; b. Apr. 14, 1864, Sandhurst, England;
    d. Aug. 22, 1959 (95).
Ayres, Agnes, actress; b. Apr. 4, 1898, Carbondale, Ill.; d. Dec. 25,
    1940 (42).
Ayres, Robert, actor; d. Nov. 5, 1968 (54).
Ayres, Sidney, actor, d. Sept., 1916.
Ayrton, Randle, actor; b. Aug. 9, 1869, Chester, England; d. May 28,
    1940 (70).


Babbitt, Orrin, actor; d. July 5, 1941 (58).
Babcock, Theodore, actor; d. Sept. 7, 1930.
Baccaloni, Salvatore, actor & opera singer; b. Apr. 14, 1900, Rome,
    Italy; d. Dec. 31, 1969 (69).
Bach (Charles Pasquier), actor; b. 1882; d. Nov. 19, 1953 (71).
Bach, Reginald, director & actor; b. Sept. 3, 1886, Shepperton,
    England; d. Jan. 6, 1941 (54).
Bacigalupi, Louis, actor; d. Aug. 6, 1966 (56).
Backus, George, actor; b. Columbus, Ohio; d. May 21, 1939 (81).
Baclanova, Olga, actress; b. Aug. 19, 1899, Moscow, Russia; d. Sept.
    6, 1974 (75).
Bacon, David, actor; b. Mar. 24, 1914, Jamaica Plain, Mass.; d.
    Sept. 12, 1943 (29).
Bacon, Faith, actress; d. Sept. 26, 1956 (46).
Bacon, Frank, actor; b. Jan. 16, 1864, Marysville, Calif.; d. Nov.
    19, 1922 (58).
Bacon, Irving, actor; b. Sept. 6, 1893, St. Joseph, Mo.; d. Feb. 5,
    1965 (71).
Bacon, Lloyd, director & actor; b. Jan. 16, 1890, San Jose, Calif.;
    d. Nov. 15, 1955 (65).
Bacon, Rod, actor; b. June 6, 1914, Denver, Colo.; d. Feb. 28,
    1948 (33).
Bacon, Walter Scott, actor; d. Nov. 7, 1973 (82).
Baddeley, Angela, actress; b. July 4, 1904, London, England; d. Feb.
    22, 1976 (71).
Badger, Clarence, director; b. June 8, 1880; d. June 17, 1964 (84).
Badgley, Frank C., actor; d. Sept. 9, 1955 (62).
Badgley, Helen, actress; d. Oct. 25, 1977 (67).
Badolati, Louis, actor; d. 1968.
Baer, Max, actor & boxer; b. Feb. 11, 1909, Omaha, Neb.; d. Nov. 21,
    1959 (50).
Bagdad, William, actor; b. Mar. 12, 1921, Maryland; d. Nov. 20,
    1975 (54).

Bagdasarian, Ross (David Seville), actor, composer, & recording artist;
    d. Jan. 16, 1972 (52).
Bagget, Dave, actor; d. Oct., 1959.
Baggett, Lynne, actress; d. Mar. 22, 1960 (32).
Baggot, King, actor & director; b. Nov. 7, 1879, St. Louis, Mo.;
    d. July 11, 1948 (68).
Bagley, Sam, actor; d. July 3, 1968 (65).
Bagni, John, actor & author; b. Dec. 24, 1910, New York; d. Feb. 13,
    1954 (43).
Bahn, Roma, actress; b. Berlin, Germany; d. Jan. 11, 1975 (78).
Bailey, Albert, actor; d. July 31, 1952 (61).
Bailey, Bert (r.n. Albert Edward Bailey), actor; b. June 11, 1872,
    Auckland, New Zealand; d. Mar. 30, 1953 (80).
Bailey, Bill, dancer; d. Dec. 12, 1978 (66).
Bailey, Claude, actor; d. June, 1950.
Bailey, Edward Lorenz, actor; d. Oct. 16, 1951 (68).
Bailey, Edwin B., actor; d. July 22, 1950 (77).
Bailey, Harry A., actor; d. Aug. 9, 1954 (74).
Bailey, Jack, actor; b. Hampton, Iowa; d. Feb. 1, 1980 (72).
Bailey, Polly Vann, actress; b. July 29, 1882, Pennsylvania; d. Aug.
    25, 1952 (70).
Bailey, William Norton (Rusty Wescoatt; Norman (Rusty) Wescoatt)
    (r.n. Gordon Reineck), actor & director; b. Sept. 26, 1886,
    Nebraska; d. Nov. 8, 1962 (76).
Bainbridge, William, actor; b. Mar. 21, 1853, England; d. Oct. 24,
    1931 (78).
Baines, Beulah, actress; d. Aug. 16, 1930.
Bainter, Fay, actress; b. Dec. 7, 1893, Los Angeles, Calif.; d. Apr.
    16, 1968 (74).
Baird, Bobbie, dancer; d. Oct. 27, 1937.
Baird, Dorothea, actress; b. May 20, 1875, Teddington, England;
    d. Sept. 24, 1933 (58).
Baird, Leah, actress; b. June 20, 1883, Chicago, Ill.; d. Oct. 3,
    1971 (88).
Baird, Stewart, actor & singer; b. Boston, Mass.; d. Oct. 28, 1947
    (66).
Bajor, Gisi, actress; d. Feb. 12, 1951 (55).
Bakaleinikoff, Constantin, musical director at R.K.O.; b. Apr. 26,
    1896, Moscow, Russia; d. Sept. 3, 1966 (70).
Baker, Anna Auer, actress; d. Apr. 2, 1944 (84).
Baker, Art (Arthur Shank), actor; b. Jan. 7, 1898, New York; d. Aug.
    26, 1966 (68).
Baker, Belle, actress; b. New York City; d. Apr. 29, 1957 (60).
Baker, Bob, actor; b. Nov. 8, 1910, Forest City, Iowa; d. Aug. 29,
    1975 (64).
Baker, C. Graham, writer & producer; b. Evansville, Ind.; d. May 15,
    1950 (62).
Baker, Eddie, actor; b. Nov. 17, 1897, Davis, W. Va.; d. Feb. 4,
    1968 (70).
Baker, Elsie, actress; d. Aug. 16, 1971 (78).
Baker, Fay, actress; d. Nov. 13, 1954 (60).
Baker, Floyd (Silvertip), actor; d. Mar. 15, 1943 (56).
Baker, George, actor & singer; b. Feb. 10, 1885, Birkenhead, England;
    d. Jan. 8, 1976 (90).
Baker, Josephine, actress & dancer; b. June 3, 1901, St. Louis, Mo.;
    d. Apr. 12, 1975 (73).

Baker, Lee, actor; b. Ovid, Mich.; d. Feb. 24, 1948 (72).
Baker, Mark (r.n. Mark George Bakarian), actor; b. Jan. 28, 1910,
    Massachusetts; d. June 20, 1972 (62).
Baker, Phil, actor; b. Aug. 24, 1896, Philadelphia, Pa.; d. Dec. 1,
    1963 (67).
Baker, Snowy (r.n. Reginald Leslie Baker), actor; b. Feb. 8, 1884,
    Sydney, Australia; d. Dec. 2, 1953 (69).
Baker, Stanley, actor; b. Feb. 28, 1928, Glamorgan, Wales; d. June
    28, 1976 (48).
Baker, William, actor; d. Dec. 21, 1916.
Bakunas, A.J., stuntman; d. Sept. 22, 1978 (27).
Balaban, Barney, executive; b. June 8, 1887, Chicago, Ill.; d. Mar. 7,
    1971 (83).
Balachova, Tania, actress; d. Aug. 4, 1973 (71).
Balch, Joseph "Slim," actor; b. Dec. 31, 1898, Kansas; d. Jan. 30,
    1967 (68).
Balcon, Sir Michael, producer; b. May 19, 1896, England; d. Oct. 17,
    1977 (81).
Baldanello, Emilio, actor; b. Mar. 3, 1902, Padova, Italy; d. July
    21, 1952 (50).
Balderston, John, writer; b. Oct. 22, 1889, Philadelphia, Pa.;
    d. Mar. 8, 1954 (64).
Baldra, Charles M. (Chuck), actor; b. Aug. 18, 1899, New York;
    d. May 14, 1949 (49).
Baldwin, Earl W., writer; b. Newark, N.J.; d. Oct. 9, 1970 (69).
Baldwin, John, actor; d. Aug., 1969 (84).
Baldwin, Kitty, actress; d. July 27, 1934 (81).
Baldwin, Walter, actor; b. Jan. 2, 1889, Ohio; d. Jan. 27, 1977 (88).
Balfour, Lorna, actress; d. Mar. 2, 1932 (19).
Balhaus, Carl, actor; d. July, 1968.
Balieff, Nikita, actor; b. Russia; d. Sept. 3, 1936 (59).
Balin, Mireille, actress; b. France; d. Nov. 8, 1968 (57).
Ball, Suzan, actress; b. Feb. 3, 1933, Buffalo, N.Y.; d. Aug. 5,
    1955 (22).
Ballantine, E.J., actor; b. Edinburgh, Scotland; d. Oct. 20, 1968
    (80).
Ballantyne, Nell, actress; d. Feb. 19, 1959.
Ballard, Elmer, actor; b. May 7, 1879, South Dakota; d. June 5,
    1947 (68).
Ballin, Hugo, director & producer; b. New York City; d. Nov. 27,
    1956 (76).
Ballin, Mabel, actress; b. 1887, Philadelphia, Pa.; d. July 24,
    1958 (71).
Ballou, Marion, actress; d. Mar. 25, 1939 (68).
Balpetre, Antoine, actor; b. 1898; d. Mar. 30, 1963 (65).
Balser, Ewald, actor; b. Oct. 5, 1898, Elberfeld, Germany; d. Apr.
    17, 1978 (79).
Bamattre, Martha, actress; d. July 12, 1970 (78).
Bambury, John T. (r.n. John Thomas Bambury), actor; b. July 10,
    1891, Pennsylvania; d. Nov. 4, 1960 (69).
Bancroft, Charles (r.n. Fred Bently), actor; d. May 17, 1969 (58).
Bancroft, George, actor; b. Sept. 30, 1882, Philadelphia, Pa.;
    d. Oct. 2, 1956 (74).
Bando, Tsumasaburo, actor; b. Japan; d. July 7, 1953 (55).
Bankhead, Tallulah, actress; b. Jan. 31, 1903, Huntsville, Ala.;
    d. Dec. 12, 1968 (65).

Banks, Leslie, actor; b. June 9, 1890, West Derby, England; d. Apr.
    21, 1952 (61).
Banks, Monty, actor; b. 1897, Nice, France; d. Jan. 7, 1950 (52).
Banks, Perry, actor; b. Apr. 24, 1877, Victoria, B.C., Canada;
    d. Oct. 10, 1934 (57).
Banner, John, actor; b. Jan. 28, 1910, Vienna, Austria; d. Jan. 28,
    1973 (63).
Bannerman, Margaret, actress; b. Dec. 15, 1896, Toronto, Canada;
    d. Apr. 25, 1976 (79).
Bannister, Harry, actor; b. Sept. 29, 1888, Holland, Mich.; d. Feb.
    26, 1961 (72).
Banvard, Fifi, actress; d. June 24, 1962 (61).
Baptista, Carlos, actor; d. Jan. 7, 1950 (50).
Bara, Theda, actress; b. July 22, 1892, Cincinnati, Ohio; d. Apr. 7,
    1955 (62).
Baragrey, John, actor; b. Apr. 15, 1918, Haleyville, Ala.; d. Aug.
    4, 1975 (57).
Barasch, Max, actor; b. Dec. 30, 1891, Austria; d. Sept. 16, 1966
    (74).
Barbanell, Fred, actor; d. Sept. 11, 1959 (28).
Barbat, Percy, actor; d. June 20, 1965 (82).
Barbette, Vander, actor; b. Dec. 19, 1904, Round Rock, Tex.; d. Aug.
    5, 1973 (68).
Barbier, George, actor; b. Nov. 19, 1864, Philadelphia, Pa.; d. July
    19, 1945 (80).
Barbour, Dave, actor; b. May 28, 1912, New York; d. Dec. 11, 1965
    (53).
Barbour, Edwin, actor; d. 1914.
Barbour, Joyce, actress; b. Mar. 27, 1901, Birmingham, England;
    d. Mar. 14, 1977 (75).
Barclay, David (see O'Brien, Dave)
Barclay, Don, actor; b. Dec. 26, 1892, Astoria, Ore.; d. Oct. 16,
    1975 (82).
Barclay, John, actor; b. May 12, 1892, England; d. Nov. 21, 1978 (86).
Barcroft, Roy (r.n. Howard Ravenscroft), actor; b. Sept. 7, 1902,
    Crab Orchard, Neb.; d. Nov. 28, 1969 (67).
Bard, Ben, actor; b. Jan. 26, 1893, Milwaukee, Wisc.; d. May 17,
    1974 (81).
Bard, Maria, actress; d. Apr. 6, 1944 (43).
Bardette, Trevor, actor; b. Nov. 19, 1902, Nashville, Ark.; d. Nov.
    28, 1977 (75).
Barker, Adella, actress; d. Sept. 29, 1930 (73).
Barker, Bradley, actor & director; d. Sept. 29, 1951 (68).
Barker, Corinne, actress; d. Aug. 6, 1928 (35).
Barker, Florence, actress; b. Nov. 22, 1891, California; d. Feb. 15,
    1913 (21).
Barker, Lex, actor; b. May 8, 1919, Rye, N.Y.; d. May 11, 1973 (54).
Barker, Reginald, director & actor; b. Bothwell, Scotland; d. Feb.
    23, 1945 (59).
Barlow, Reginald, actor; b. June 17, 1866, Cambridge, Mass.; d. July
    6, 1943 (77).
Barnabo, Guglielmo, actor; b. May 11, 1888, Ancona, Italy; d. May
    31, 1954 (66).
Barnard, Ivor, actor; b. June 13, 1887, London, England; d. June 30,
    1953 (66).
Barnell, Nora Ely, actress; d. July 10, 1933 (51).

Barnes, Barry K., actor; b. Dec. 27, 1906, London, England; d. Jan. 12, 1965 (58).

Barnes, Edna Reming, actress; d. Mar. 7, 1935 (52).

Barnes, Frank, actor; d. Nov. 1, 1940 (65).

Barnes, Florence Lowe "Pancho," stunt pilot; d. Mar. 29, 1975 (73).

Barnes, George S., cinematographer; d. May 30, 1953 (60).

Barnes, Justus D., actor; d. Feb. 6, 1946 (84).

Barnes, Mable, actress; d. May 2, 1935 (54).

Barnes, T. Roy, actor; b. Aug. 11, 1880, Lincolnshire, England; d. Mar. 30, 1937 (56).

Barnes, V.L., actor; d. Aug. 9, 1949 (79).

Barnet, Boris V., director & actor; b. June 16, 1902, Moscow, Russia; d. Jan. 8, 1965 (62).

Barnett, Chester, actor; b. Piedmont, Mo.; d. Sept. 22, 1947 (62).

Barnett, Griff, actor; b. Nov. 12, 1884, Texas; d. Jan. 12, 1958 (73).

Barnett, Vince, actor; b. July 4, 1902, Pittsburgh, Pa.; d. Aug. 10, 1977 (75).

Baroncelli, Jacques, actor & director; b. June 25, 1881, Bouillargues, France; d. Jan. 12, 1951 (69).

Baroux, Lucien, actor; b. Sept. 21, 1888, Toulouse, France; d. May 21, 1968 (79).

Barr, Byron, actor; b. Aug. 18, 1917, Iowa; d. Nov. 3, 1966 (49).

Barr, Jeanne, actress; d. Aug. 10, 1967 (35).

Barrat, Robert H. (r.n. Robert Harriot Barrat), actor; b. July 10, 1889, New York City; d. Jan. 7, 1970 (80).

Barreiro, Luis G., actor; b. 1886, Mexico City, Mexico; d. May 24, 1947 (61).

Barreto, Pedro, actor; d. Dec., 1943 (59).

Barrett, Edith, actress; d. Feb. 22, 1977 (64).

Barrett, Gentry W., actress; d. Oct. 10, 1956 (64).

Barrett, Jane, actress; b. May 7, 1923, Highgate, London, England; d. July 20, 1969 (46).

Barrett, Maurice, director & author; d. June 9, 1963 (89).

Barrett, Minnette, actress; d. June 20, 1964 (80).

Barrett, Pat, actor; d. Mar. 25, 1959 (70).

Barrett, Tony, actor & author; d. Nov. 16, 1974 (58).

Barri, Mario, actor & director; d. Nov. 21, 1963.

Barrie, Wendy, actress; b. Apr. 18, 1912, Hong Kong; d. Feb. 2, 1978 (65).

Barrier, Edgar, actor; b. Mar. 4, 1907, New York; d. June 20, 1964 (57).

Barringer, Barry, author & actor; d. May 21, 1938 (49).

Barringer, Spencer Edward (Ned), actor & author; d. Feb. 13, 1976 (87).

Barrington, Herbert, actor; d. Oct. 26, 1933 (61).

Barris, Harry, actor & composer; b. Nov. 24, 1905, New York; d. Dec. 13, 1962 (57).

Barriscale, Bessie, actress; d. June 30, 1965 (81).

Barron, Frederick C., actor; b. Melbourne, Australia; d. Oct. 9, 1955 (67).

Barron, Marcus, actor; d. Mar. 15, 1944 (75).

Barrows, Henry A., actor; b. Apr. 29, 1875, Saco, Me.; d. Mar. 25, 1945 (69).

Barrows, James O., actor; b. Mar. 29, 1855, California; d. Dec. 7, 1925 (70).

Barry, Joe, actor; b. Feb. 18, 1924, California; d. July 9, 1974 (50).
Barry, John, production designer; d. June 1, 1979 (43).
Barry, Robert, actor; d. Mar. 21, 1931 (30).
Barry, Tom, author & actor; b. Kansas City, Mo.; d. Nov. 7, 1931 (47).
Barry, Viola, actress; d. Apr. 2, 1964 (70).
Barrye, Emily, actress; d. Dec. 15, 1957 (61).
Barrymore, Diana, actress; b. Mar. 3, 1921, New York City; d. Jan.
    25, 1960 (38).
Barrymore, Ethel, actress; b. Aug. 15, 1879, Philadelphia, Pa.;
    d. June 18, 1959 (79).
Barrymore, John, actor; b. Feb. 15, 1882, Philadelphia, Pa.; d. May
    29, 1942 (60).
Barrymore, Lionel, actor & director; b. Apr. 28, 1878, Philadelphia,
    Pa.; d. Nov. 15, 1954 (76).
Barrymore, William (Kit Carson; Boris Bullock), actor; b. Russia;
    d. Apr. 23, 1979 (79).
Barsam, Rene, actor; d. May 1, 1956 (52).
Barskiy, Vladimir G., actor; b. 1889; d. Jan. 24, 1936 (46).
Bartell, Richard, actor; b. Aug. 24, 1897, Pennsylvania; d. July 22,
    1967 (69).
Bartels, Louis John, actor; b. Oct. 19, 1895, Bunker Hill, Ill.;
    d. Mar. 4, 1932 (36).
Barter, Teddy, actor; d. Oct. 10, 1939 (50).
Barthelmess, Carolina Harris, actress; d. Apr. 23, 1937 (70).
Barthelmess, Richard, actor; b. May 9, 1895, New York City; d. Aug.
    17, 1963 (68).
Bartlett, Clifford, actor; b. June 14, 1903, Cardiff, Wales; d. Dec.
    25, 1936 (33).
Bartlett, Elise, actress; d. 1944.
Bartlett, Sy, writer; b. Russia; d. May 29, 1978 (78).
Barton, George C., actor; b. Jan. 8, 1897, California; d. Sept. 21,
    1955 (58).
Barton, Homer, actor; d. Oct. 29, 1935.
Barton, James, actor; b. Nov. 1, 1890, Gloucester, N.J.; d. Feb.
    19, 1962 (71).
Barton, Joan, actress; d. May, 1977 (52).
Barton, Joe, actor; d. July 5, 1937 (54).
Bartosch, Chester, actor; b. Feb. 10, 1911, California; d. Oct. 27,
    1967 (56).
Bartram, Gus M., actor; d. Oct. 7, 1951.
Barty, Jack, actor; b. Dec. 31, 1888, London, England; d. Nov. 25,
    1942 (54).
Bary, Leon, actor; b. 1880; d. 1954 (74).
Barzell, Wolfe, actor; b. Poland; d. Feb. 14, 1969 (72).
Basch, Felix, actor; b. Sept. 16, 1882, Vienna, Austria; d. May 17,
    1944 (61).
Baskcomb, A.W., actor; b. July 5, 1880, London, England; d. Dec. 10,
    1939 (59).
Baskcomb, Lawrence, actor; b. Oct. 13, 1883, London, England; d.
    Feb. 12, 1962 (78).
Baskett, James, actor; b. Feb. 16, 1904, Indianapolis, Ind.; d. July
    9, 1948 (44).
Basserman, Albert, actor; b. Sept. 7, 1867, Mannheim, Germany;
    d. May 15, 1952 (84).
Basserman, Elsa (r.n. Else Schiff), actress; b. Jan. 14, 1878,
    Leipzig, Germany; d. May 30, 1961 (83).

Bassett, H. Ellsworth, actor; d. May 22, 1943 (68).
Bassett, Russell, actor; b. Milwaukee, Wisc.; d. May 7, 1918 (72).
Bassett, Tony, actor; d. Aug. 4, 1955 (70).
Bastian, Bertha, actress; d. July 13, 1949 (81).
Baston, J. (Jack) Thornton, actor; b. Aug. 6, 1892, California;
    d. May 3, 1970 (77).
Batalov, Nikolay P., actor; b. Dec. 6, 1899, Moscow; d. Nov. 10,
    1937 (37).
Batcheff, Pierre, actor; b. 1901; d. Apr. 13, 1932 (31).
Bateman, Jessie, actress; b. Aug. 2, 1877; d. Nov. 14, 1940 (63).
Bateman, Victory, actress; b. Apr. 6, 1865, New York; d. Mar. 3,
    1926 (60).
Bates, Barbara, actress; b. Aug. 6, 1925, Denver, Colo.; d. Mar.
    18, 1969 (43).
Bates, Blanche, actress; b. Aug. 25, 1873, Portland, Ore.; d. Dec.
    25, 1941 (68).
Bates, Florence, actress; b. Feb. 21, 1888, Texas; d. Jan. 31,
    1954 (65).
Bates, Granville, actor; b. Jan. 7, 1882, Harvard, Ill.; d. July 8,
    1940 (58).
Bates, Kathryn, actress; b. Sept. 23, 1877, Rhode Island; d. Jan. 1,
    1964 (86).
Bates, Les, actor; b. June, 1877, Illinois; d. Aug. 8, 1930 (53).
Bates, Louise Emerald (see Mortimer, Louise Bates)
Bates, Michael, actor; b. Dec. 4, 1920, Jhansi, India; d. Jan. 11,
    1978 (57).
Bates, Tom, actor; d. Apr. 11, 1930 (66).
Batie, Franklin A., actor; b. Norwich, N.Y.; d. Dec. 31, 1949 (69).
Batterson, Earl, actor; b. Oct. 29, 1909, Connecticut; d. Mar. 20,
    1972 (62)
Battier, Robert, actor; b. Mar. 22, 1887, Tennessee; d. Dec. 16,
    1946 (59).
Battisti, Carlo, actor; b. Oct. 11, 1882, Trento, Italy; d. Mar. 6,
    1977 (94).
Batty, Archibald, actor & author; b. Nov. 6, 1887, North Mymms
    Vicarage, Herts., England; d. Nov. 24, 1961 (74).
Bauchens, Anne, film editor; d. May 7, 1967 (85).
Baucin, Escolastico, actor; b. Feb. 13, 1892, Philippine Islands;
    d. June 24, 1965 (73).
Baudin, Ginette, actress; d. Mar., 1971 (50).
Bauer, David, actor; d. Feb. 13, 1973 (55).
Bauler, William C. "Bill," actor; b. Feb. 7, 1919, Illinois;
    d. Feb. 21, 1962 (43).
Baum, Harry, actor; d. Jan. 31, 1974 (58).
Baumann-Tobien, Emmy, actress; b. Sept. 22, 1882, Braunschweig,
    Germany; d. Aug., 1961 (78).
Baumer, Jacques, actor; b. 1885; d. 1951 (66).
Baur, Esperanza, actress; d. Mar. 10, 1961 (35).
Baur, Harry, actor; b. Apr. 12, 1880, Montrouge, France; d. Apr. 8,
    1943 (62).
Baxley, Jack, actor; b. July 4, 1884, Texas; d. Dec. 10, 1950 (66).
Baxter, Alan, actor; b. Nov. 19, 1908, E. Cleveland, Ohio; d. May 8,
    1976 (67).
Baxter, Billy, actor; d. June 7, 1936.
Baxter, George, cinematographer; d. Dec. 27, 1975 (94).

Baxter, George, actor; b. Apr. 8, 1905, Paris, France; d. Sept. 10, 1976 (71).
Baxter, Jimmy, actor; d. Apr. 20, 1969 (46).
Baxter, Lora, actress; d. June 16, 1955 (47).
Baxter, Warner, actor; b. Mar. 29, 1889, Columbus, Ohio; d. May 7, 1951 (62).
Bay, Tom (r.n. William T. Bay), actor; b. Feb. 22, 1901, San Antonio, Tex.; d. Oct. 11, 1933 (32).
Bayley, Eleanor, actress & dancer; d. June 29, 1976 (60).
Bayley, Hilda, actress; d. May 25, 1971.
Bayliff, W. Lane, actor; d. Feb., 1938.
Beach, Brandon (r.n. Arthur W. Bache), actor; b. Oct. 18, 1879, Washington, D.C.; d. Nov. 22, 1974 (95).
Beach, Corra, actress; d. Oct. 5, 1963.
Beach, Guy, actor; b. Dec. 16, 1887, Keithburg, Ill.; d. Oct. 31, 1952 (64).
Beal, Frank, actor; b. Sept. 11, 1862, Cleveland, Ohio; d. Dec. 20, 1934 (72).
Beal, Royal, actor; b. June 2, 1899, Brookline, Mass.; d. May 20, 1969 (69).
Beal, Scott Rathbone, assistant director; b. 1890, Quinsick, Mich.; d. July 10, 1973 (83).
Beale, Ken, actor; d. June 20, 1979 (47).
Beamish, Frank, actor; b. 1881, Memphis, Tenn.; d. Oct. 3, 1921 (40).
Bear, Mary, actress; b. Mar. 10, 1910, California; d. Dec. 9, 1972 (62).
Beason, Nina, actress; d. Jan. 12, 1929.
Beaton, Mary, actress; d. Jan. 25, 1961.
Beatty, Clyde, actor & animal trainer; b. June 10, 1903, Chillicothe, Ohio; d. July 19, 1965 (62).
Beatty, George, actor; b. Sept. 5, 1895, Steubenville, Ohio; d. Aug. 6, 1971 (75).
Beatty, May, actress; b. Christchurch, New Zealand; d. Apr. 1, 1945 (64).
Beaubien, Julien, actress; d. Oct. 18, 1947 (51).
Beauchamp, D.D., writer; d. Mar. 20, 1969 (60).
Beaudet, Louise, actress; b. St. Emilie, Quebec, Canada; d. Dec. 31, 1947 (86).
Beaudine, William, director; b. Jan. 15, 1892, New York City; d. Mar. 18, 1970 (78).
Beaumont, Charles, writer; d. Feb. 21, 1967 (38).
Beaumont, Diana, actress; b. May 8, 1909, London, England; d. June 21, 1964 (55).
Beaumont, Harry, director; b. Feb. 10, 1888, Abilene, Kans.; d. Dec. 22, 1966 (78).
Beaumont, Lucy, actress; b. Bristol, England; d. Apr. 24, 1937 (73).
Beaumont, Vertee, actress; d. June 27, 1934 (45).
Beavers, Louise, actress; b. Mar. 8, 1902, Cincinnati, Ohio; d. Oct. 26, 1962 (60).
Beban, George, actor; b. San Francisco, Calif.; d. Oct. 5, 1928 (55).
Bech, Lily, actress; b. Dec. 29, 1885; d. 1939 (53).
Bechtel, William, actor; b. June 12, 1867, Berlin, Germany; d. Oct. 27, 1930 (63).
Beck, Danny, actor; d. Nov. 8, 1959 (55).
Beck, Nelson C., actor; d. Mar. 3, 1952 (65).

Becker, Jacques, director & actor; b. Sept. 15, 1906, Paris, France;
    d. Feb. 21, 1960 (53).
Becker, Philip, actor; d. Jan., 1975 (85).
Becker, Theodor, actor; d. June, 1952 (72).
Beckett, Guy (r.n. Guy Lauderdale Beckett), actor; d. Aug. 5, 1973
    (78).
Beckett, Scotty, actor; b. Oct. 4, 1929, Oakland, Calif.; d. May 10,
    1968 (38).
Beck-Gaden, Hanns, actor & director; d. June 20, 1956 (66).
Beckinsale, Richard, actor; d. Mar. 19, 1979 (31).
Beckwith, Reginald, actor; b. Nov. 2, 1908, York, England; d. June
    26, 1965 (56).
Becwar, George, actor; b. Sept. 16, 1917, Illinois; d. July 9, 1970
    (52).
Beday, Eugene, actor; b. Jan. 25, 1880, Switzerland; d. Aug. 1,
    1975 (95).
Bedoya, Alfonso, actor; b. Sonora, Mexico; d. Dec. 15, 1957 (53).
Beecher, Ada, actress; d. Mar. 30, 1935 (73).
Beecher, Janet, actress; b. Oct. 21, 1884, Jefferson City, Mo.;
    d. Aug. 6, 1955 (70).
Beecroft, Victor R., actor; b. London, England; d. Mar. 25, 1958
    (71).
Beers, Fannie, actress; d. Aug. 26, 1951 (81).
Beers, Fred C., actor; b. Oct. 8, 1895, Wilkes-Barre, Pa.; d. Nov.
    16, 1946 (51).
Beery, Noah, Sr., actor; b. Feb. 17, 1882, Smithville, Mo.; d. Apr.
    1, 1946 (64).
Beery, Wallace, actor; b. Apr. 1, 1885, Kansas City, Mo.; d. Apr. 15,
    1949 (64).
Beery, William, producer; d. Dec. 25, 1949 (70).
Begg, Gordon (r.n. Alexander Gordon Begg), actor; b. Jan. 14, 1868,
    Aberdeen, Scotland; d. Feb., 1954 (86).
Beggs, Lee, actor & director; d. Nov. 18, 1943 (72).
Beggs, Malcolm Lee, actor; d. Dec. 10, 1956 (49).
Begley, Ed, actor; b. Mar. 25, 1901, Hartford, Conn.; d. Apr. 28,
    1970 (69).
Behrens, Frederick, actor; d. Jan. 5, 1938 (84).
Behrle, Fred F., actor; d. May 20, 1941 (50).
Behrman, S.N., writer & playwright; b. June 9, 1893, Worcester, Mass.;
    d. Sept. 9, 1973 (80).
Beilby, Vangie (r.n. Thomasina Elizabeth Beilby), actress; b. Jan. 8,
    1872, England; d. Oct. 14, 1958 (86).
Bela, Nicholas, actor; b. July 18, 1900, Budapest, Hungary; d. Nov.
    19, 1963 (63).
Belasco, Arthur, actor; d. Nov. 8, 1979 (91).
Belasco, David, producer; b. San Francisco, Calif.; d. May 14, 1931
    (77).
Belasco, Genevieve, actress; b. London, England; d. Nov. 17, 1956
    (85).
Belasco, Walter, actor; d. June 21, 1939 (75).
Belcher, Alice, actress; d. May 9, 1939 (59).
Belcher, Charles, actor; b. July 27, 1872, San Francisco, Calif.;
    d. Dec. 10, 1943 (71).
Belden, Charles S., writer; b. Apr. 21, 1904, Montclair, N.J.;
    d. Nov. 3, 1954 (50).

Belfield, Richard, actor; b. July 23, 1873, Philadelphia, Pa.; d. Jan.
2, 1940 (66).
Belfrage, Bruce, actor; d. Aug., 1974 (73).
Belgard, Arnold, writer; b. July 31, 1907, Los Angeles, Calif.;
d. July 1, 1967 (59).
Bell, Diana, actress; d. Oct. 30, 1964.
Bell,-Digby, actor; b. Milwaukee, Wisc.; d. June 20, 1917 (66).
Bell, Gaston, actor; b. Sept. 27, 1877, Boston, Mass.; d. Dec. 11,
1963 (86).
Bell, Genevieve, actress; d. Oct. 3, 1951 (56).
Bell, George O. (r.n. Oren C. Bell), actor; b. Oct. 9, 1898, Texas;
d. Oct. 1, 1969 (70).
Bell, Hank, actor; b. Jan. 21, 1892, California; d. Feb. 4, 1950 (58).
Bell, James, actor; b. Dec. 1, 1891, Suffolk, Va.; d. Oct. 26, 1973
(81).
Bell, Leslie R., choral director & actor; d. Jan. 19, 1962 (55).
Bell, Monta, director, author, & producer; b. Feb. 5, 1891, Washing-
ton, D.C.; d. Feb. 4, 1958 (66).
Bell, Ralph W., actor; d. July 14, 1936 (53).
Bell, Rex (r.n. George Francis Beldam), actor & politician; b. Oct.
16, 1903, Chicago, Ill.; d. July 4, 1962 (58).
Bell, Rodney, actor; b. Oct. 21, 1915, Maryland; d. Aug. 3, 1968
(52).
Bell, Ruth, actress; d. June 17, 1933 (26).
Bell, Spencer, actor; b. Sept. 25, 1887, Lexington, Ky.; d. Aug. 18,
1935 (47).
Bellah, James Warner, writer; d. Sept. 22, 1976 (77).
Bellak, Adolf, actor & director; d. June 24, 1955 (69).
Bellamy, George, actor; d. Dec. 26, 1944 (78).
Bellew, Cosmo Kyrle, actor; b. Nov. 23, 1885, London, England;
d. Jan. 25, 1948 (62).
Bellew, Kyrle, actor; b. Mar. 28, 1855, Prescot, England; d. Nov. 2,
1911 (56).
Belmar, Henry, actor; b. 1849, at sea; d. Jan. 12, 1931 (81).
Belmont, Joseph (Baldy), actor; b. Aug. 18, 1875, Port Huron, Mich.;
d. May 16, 1939 (63).
Belmont, Michael, actor; b. July 6, 1919; d. Nov. 9, 1941 (22).
Belmont, Ralf, actor & writer; b. Apr. 9, 1882, Italy; d. Sept. 21,
1964 (82).
Belmonte, Herman, actor; d. Sept. 15, 1975 (84).
Belmore, Alice, actress; b. London, England; d. July 31, 1943 (73).
Belmore, Bertha, actress; b. Dec. 20, 1882, Manchester, England;
d. Dec. 14, 1953 (70).
Belmore, Daisy, actress; b. London, England; d. Dec. 12, 1954 (80).
Belmore, Lionel, actor; b. May 12, 1868, England; d. Jan. 30, 1953
(84).
Belmour, Harry, actor; b. Feb. 9, 1882, San Francisco, Calif.;
d. Sept. 8, 1936 (54).
Belokurov, Vladimir V., actor; d. Jan. 30, 1973 (69).
Belov, Grigoriy A., actor; b. Dec. 18, 1895; d. Jan. 8, 1965 (69).
Belson, Edward, extra; d. Dec. 1, 1975 (77).
Beltran, Ray, actor; b. 1892, Mexico; d. Oct. 17, 1967 (75).
Beltri, Ricardo, actor; d. May, 1962 (63).
Belwin, Alma, actress; d. May 8, 1924 (29).
Benaderet, Bea, actress; b. Apr. 4, 1906, New York City; d. Oct. 13,
1968 (62).

Ben-Ami, Jacob, actor & director; b. Nov. 23, 1890, Minsk, Russia;
    d. July 22, 1977 (86).
Benard, Raymond (see Corrigan, Ray (Crash))
Ben-Ari, Raikin, actor; b. Russia; d. Jan. 2, 1968 (64).
Benassi, Memo, actor; b. June 21, 1886, Parma, Italy; d. Feb. 24, 1957
    (70).
Benchley, Robert, actor & author; b. Sept. 15, 1889, Worcester,
    Mass.; d. Nov. 21, 1945 (56).
Bender, Russ, actor & author; b. Jan. 1, 1910, New York; d. Aug. 16,
    1969 (59).
Bendix, Doreen, actress; d. Aug. 7, 1931 (25).
Bendix, William, actor; b. Jan. 14, 1906, New York City; d. Dec.
    14, 1964 (58).
Bendow, Wilhelm (Emil Boden), actor; b. Sept. 29, 1884, Einbeck,
    Germany; d. May 29, 1950 (65).
Benedict, Brooks, actor; d. Jan., 1968.
Benedict, Kingsley, actor; b. Nov. 14, 1878, Buffalo, N.Y.; d. Nov.
    27, 1951 (73).
Benell, John Thomas, actor; d. Aug. 12, 1940 (23).
Benge, Sarah L., actress; d. Jan. 27, 1954 (71).
Benge, Wilson (r.n. George F. Benge), actor; b. Mar. 1, 1875,
    Greenwich, England; d. July 1, 1955 (80).
Benglia, Habib, actor; b. 1895; d. 1961 (66).
Benham, Dorothy, actress; b. Sept. 6, 1910; d. Sept. 19, 1956 (46).
Benham, Ethyle, actress; d. Apr. 20, 1949 (63).
Benham, Harry, actor; b. Feb. 26, 1886, Valparaiso, Ind.; d. July
    17, 1969 (83).
Benjamin, Jim, actor; d. June 21, 1978 (31).
Benkhoff, Fita, actress; b. Nov. 1, 1901, Dortmund, Germany; d.
    Oct., 1967 (65).
Benner, Yale Delespine, actor; b. Nov. 17, 1875, New York; d. Sept.
    29, 1952 (76).
Bennett, Alma, actress; b. Apr. 9, 1904, Seattle, Wash.; d. Sept. 16,
    1958 (54).
Bennett, Barbara, actress; b. Aug. 13, 1906, Palisades, N.J.; d. Aug.
    8, 1958 (51).
Bennett, Belle, actress; b. Apr. 22, 1891, Milcoon Rapids, Iowa;
    d. Nov. 4, 1932 (41).
Bennett, Billie (r.n. Emily B. Mulhausen), actress; b. Oct. 23,
    1874, Evansville, Ind.; d. May 19, 1951 (76).
Bennett, Billy, actor; d. June 30, 1942.
Bennett, Charles, actor; d. June, 1925.
Bennett, Charles J., actor; b. Mar. 11, 1889, Dunedin, New Zealand;
    d. Feb. 15, 1943 (53).
Bennett, Compton, director; b. Jan. 15, 1900, Tunbridge Wells,
    England; d. Aug. 13, 1974 (74).
Bennett, Constance, actress; b. Oct. 22, 1905, New York City;
    d. July 24, 1965 (59).
Bennett, Enid, actress; b. July 15, 1893, Western Australia; d. May
    14, 1969 (75).
Bennett, Frank, actor; d. Apr. 29, 1957 (66).
Bennett, Imogene, actress; d. Aug. 30, 1961 (67).
Bennett, Joe, actor; d. Aug. 31, 1967 (78).
Bennett, Joseph, actor; b. Aug. 28, 1894, Los Angeles, Calif.;
    d. Dec. 3, 1931 (37).
Bennett, Lee Hunt, actor-announcer; b. 1911; d. Oct. 10, 1954 (43).

Bennett, Mickey, actor; b. Victoria, B.C., Canada; d. Sept. 6, 1950
(35).
Bennett, Ralph Culver, actor; b. Mar. 14, 1878, Illinois; d. Mar. 29,
1959 (81).
Bennett, Raphael (see Bennett, Ray)
Bennett, Ray (Raphael Bennett), actor; b. Mar. 21, 1895, Portland,
Ore.; d. Dec. 18, 1957 (62).
Bennett, Richard, actor; b. May 21, 1873, Indiana; d. Oct. 21, 1944
(71).
Bennett, Sam, actor; d. Aug. 25, 1937 (50).
Bennett, Ted (r.n. William Oscar Houghton), actor; b. Nov. 5, 1872,
Glens Falls, N.Y.; d. May 10, 1941 (68).
Bennett, Wilda, actress; b. Dec. 19, 1894, Asbury Park, N.J.;
d. Dec. 20, 1967 (73).
Bennison, Andrew, actor, director, & author; d. Jan. 7, 1942 (55).
Bennison, Louis, actor & author; b. San Francisco, Calif.; d. June
9, 1929 (45).
Bennoit, Joseph, actor; d. June 23, 1925 (50).
Benny, Jack, actor; b. Feb. 14, 1894, Waukegan, Ill.; d. Dec. 26,
1974 (80).
Benoit, Victor, actor; d. Jan. 16, 1943 (66).
Benoit-Levy, Jean, director; b. Apr. 25, 1888, Paris, France; d. Aug.
3, 1959 (71).
Benson, Sir Frank, actor; b. Nov. 4, 1858, Alresford, England;
d. Dec. 31, 1939 (81).
Benson, Frank (r.n. Frank Waterhouse), actor; b. Jan. 6, 1876,
Australia; d. Apr. 7, 1950 (74).
Benson, John William, actor; d. July 12, 1926 (64).
Benson, Juliette V.P., actress; b. Aug. 15, 1875, Massachusetts;
d. Dec. 22, 1962 (87).
Benson, May "Mother," actress; d. Sept. 29, 1916.
Benson, Sanford, actor; d. Feb. 4, 1935 (21).
Bentley, Alice, actress; d. Sept. 3, 1956 (64).
Bentley, Irene, actress; b. Baltimore, Md.; d. June 3, 1940 (70).
Bentley, Irene, actress; b. Nov. 12, 1904, New York; d. Nov. 23,
1965 (61).
Bentley, Robert (Bob) (Bob Butt), actor; d. Apr. 19, 1958 (63).
Benton, Bessie, actress; d, Jan., 1917.
Benton, Curtis, actor; d. Sept. 14, 1938 (53).
Benton, Steve, actor; d. Aug. 4, 1976 (79).
Beranger, Andre (see Beranger, George Andre)
Beranger, Clara, writer; b. Jan. 14, 1886, Baltimore, Md.; d. Sept.
10, 1956 (70).
Beranger, George Andre, actor; b. Mar. 27, 1893, Sydney, Australia;
d. Mar. 8, 1973 (79).
Berangere, Mme., actress; d. Nov., 1928.
Beregi, Oscar, Sr., actor; b. Jan. 24, 1876, Hungary; d. Oct. 18,
1965 (89).
Beregi, Oscar, actor; b. May 12, 1918, Hungary; d. Nov. 1, 1976 (58).
Berenson, Abe, actor; d. Dec. 7, 1977 (68).
Beresford, Evelyn, actress; b. Feb. 22, 1881, England; d. Jan. 21,
1959 (77).
Beresford, Harry, actor; b. Nov. 4, 1863, London, England; d. Oct. 4,
1944 (80).
Berg, Gertrude, actress; b. Oct. 3, 1900, New York; d. Sept. 14, 1966
(65).

Bergen, Edgar, actor & ventriloquist; b. Feb. 16, 1903, Chicago, Ill.; d. Sept. 30, 1978 (75).
Berger, Gustav, actor; d. Oct. 18, 1958.
Berger, Ludwig, director; b. Jan. 6, 1892, Mainz, Germany; d. May 17, 1969 (77).
Berger, Nicole, actress; b. France; d. Apr. 19, 1967 (32).
Bergere, Ouida, actress & author; d. Nov. 29, 1974 (88).
Bergere, Valerie, actress; b. Feb. 2, 1867, Metz, Alsace-Lorraine, France; d. Sept. 16, 1938 (71).
Berghoefer, Beulah B., actress; b. Nov. 26, 1887, Kansas; d. Sept. 28, 1973 (85).
Bergman, Henri, actor; d. Jan. 9, 1917 (57).
Bergman, Henry, actor; d. Oct. 22, 1946 (76).
Berguland, William C., actor; d. Feb. 23, 1958.
Beristain, Leopoldo, actor; d. Jan. 5, 1948 (65).
Beristain, Luis, actor; d. Apr. 1, 1962 (45).
Berk, Sara, actress; d. Apr. 22, 1975 (77).
Berke, William (Lester Williams), director; b. Oct. 3, 1903, Milwaukee, Wisc.; d. Feb. 15, 1958 (54).
Berkeley, Arthur, actor; b. May 26, 1896, New York; d. July 29, 1962 (66).
Berkeley, Busby (r.n. William Berkeley Enos), director & choreographer; b. Nov. 29, 1895, Los Angeles, Calif.; d. Mar. 14, 1976 (80).
Berkeley, Gertrude, actress; b. Plattsburg, N.Y.; d. June 15, 1946 (81).
Berkeley, Reginald, writer; d. Mar. 30, 1935 (54).
Berkes, John (r.n. John Patrick Berkes), actor; b. June 13, 1895, Trenton, N.J.; d. July 5, 1951 (56).
Berlin, Abby, director; b. Aug. 7, 1907, New York City; d. Aug. 19, 1965 (58).
Berly, Andre, actor; d. Nov. 27, 1936.
Bern, Paul, producer; d. Sept. 4, 1932 (42).
Bernal, Robert, actor; d. May, 1973 (49).
Bernard, Barney, actor; b. Aug. 17, 1877, Rochester, N.Y.; d. Mar. 21, 1924 (46).
Bernard, Barry, actor; b. Oct. 4, 1899, England; d. June 24, 1978 (78).
Bernard, Carl, actor; d. May 4, 1972 (66).
Bernard, Dorothy, actress; b. July 25, 1890; d. Dec. 14, 1955 (65).
Bernard, Harry, actor; b. Jan. 13, 1878, San Francisco, Calif.; d. Nov. 4, 1940 (62).
Bernard, Joseph E., actor; b. June 1, 1880, Louisiana; d. Oct. 18, 1958 (78).
Bernard, Paul, actor; d. May 4, 1958.
Bernard, Peter, actor; d. Dec. 22, 1960 (72).
Bernard, Raymond, director; d. Jan., 1978 (86).
Bernard, Sam, actor; b. June 3, 1863, Birmingham, England; d. May 18, 1927 (63).
Bernard, Sam, actor; b. Apr. 23, 1889, New York City; d. July 5, 1950 (61).
Bernardi, Nerio, actor; b. July 23, 1899, Bologna, Italy; d. Jan. 12, 1971 (71).
Berne, Josef, director; d. Dec. 19, 1964 (60).
Bernes, Mark, actor & singer; d. Aug. 16, 1969 (57).
Bernhardt, Russ, actor; d. Oct. 9, 1978 (53).
Bernhardt, Sarah, actress; b. Oct. 23, 1844, Paris, France; d. Mar. 26, 1923 (78).

Bernivici, Count, actor; d. July 12, 1966 (82).
Bernoudy, Jane, actress; b. Aug. 19, 1893, New Castle, Colo.;
   d. Oct. 28, 1972 (79).
Berr, Georges, actor; d. July 21, 1942 (76).
Berrell, George, actor; b. Dec. 16, 1849, Philadelphia, Pa.; d. Apr.
   20, 1933 (83).
Berry, Aline, actress; d. Apr. 3, 1967 (62).
Berry, Arthur Frank, actor; b. Aug. 25, 1881, Jacksonville, Ill.;
   d. June 12, 1945 (63).
Berry, James J., actor; d. Jan. 28, 1969 (54).
Berry, Jules, actor; b. France; d. Apr. 25, 1951 (68).
Berry, Mady, actress; b. 1887; d. 1965 (78).
Berry, Nyas, dancer; d. Oct. 6, 1951 (36).
Berry, Patricia, actress; d. July 11, 1928 (23).
Berry, W.H., actor; b. Mar. 23, 1870, London, England; d. May 2,
   1951 (81).
Bersenev, Ivan N., actor & director; b. Apr. 23, 1889, Moscow, Russia;
   d. Dec. 25, 1951 (62).
Berthelet, Arthur, actor & director; b. Oct. 12, 1879, Wisconsin;
   d. Sept. 16, 1949 (69).
Bertone, Alfredo, actor; d. Mar., 1927.
Bertram, Vedah, actress; d. Aug. 27, 1912 (20).
Bertram, William, director & actor; b. Jan. 19, 1880, Canada;
   d. May 1, 1933 (53).
Bertrand, Mary, actress; d. May 12, 1955 (74).
Berubet, Magdeleine, actress; d. Oct., 1970.
Besozzi, Nino, actor; b. Feb. 6, 1901, Milan, Italy; d. Feb. 2,
   1971 (70).
Bessent, Marie, actress; d. Oct. 10, 1947 (49).
Besserer, Eugenie, actress; b. Dec. 25, 1868, Watertown, N.Y.;
   d. May 28, 1934 (65).
Best, Edna, actress; b. Mar. 3, 1900, Hove, England; d. Sept. 18,
   1974 (74).
Best, Willie (Sleep 'n' Eat), actor; b. May 27, 1916, Mississippi;
   d. Feb. 27, 1962 (45).
Bethke, Luise, actress; b. Dec. 17, 1889; d. Dec., 1952 (63).
Betrone, Annibale, actor; b. Dec. 9, 1883, Torino, Italy; d. Dec. 11,
   1950 (67).
Betton, George, actor; d. June 4, 1969 (73).
Betts, William E., actor; d. Apr. 5, 1929 (73).
Betz, Carl, actor; b. Mar. 9, 1921, Pittsburgh, Pa.; d. Jan. 18,
   1978 (56).
Betz, Mathew, actor; b. Sept. 13, 1881, St. Louis, Mo.; d. Jan. 26,
   1938 (56).
Bevan, Billy, actor; b. Sept. 29, 1887, Orange, Australia; d. Nov.
   26, 1957 (70).
Bevani, Alexander, actor & opera singer; d. Feb. 24, 1938 (67).
Bevans, Clem, actor; b. Oct. 16, 1879, Ohio; d. Aug. 11, 1963 (83).
Bevans, Philippa, actress; b. Feb. 10, 1913, London, England;
   d. May 10, 1968 (55).
Bevins, Mabel, actress; d. Dec. 23, 1916.
Beyer, Charles, actor; b. Feb. 28, 1893, Newark, N.J.; d. Nov. 28,
   1953 (60).
Bianchetti, Suzanne, actress; b. 1894, Paris, France; d. Oct. 17,
   1936 (42).
Bianchi, Giorgio, actor & director; d. Feb. 9, 1968 (63).

Biancini, Ferrucio, actor; b. Aug. 18, 1890, Pomponesco, Italy;
  d. Mar., 1955 (64).
Bianco, Ernesto, actor; d. Oct. 2, 1977 (54).
Bias, Chester, actor; d. Mar. 1, 1954 (37).
Biberman, Abner, actor; b. Apr. 1, 1909, Milwaukee, Wisc.; d. June
  20, 1977 (68).
Biberman, Herbert J., director; b. Mar. 4, 1900, Philadelphia, Pa.;
  d. June 30, 1971 (71).
Biberti, Leopold, actor; b. Sept. 18, 1894; d. Nov. 24, 1969 (75).
Biby, Edward, actor; b. Aug. 8, 1886, Illinois; d. Oct. 3, 1952 (66).
Bice, Robert, actor; b. Mar. 4, 1913, Dallas, Tex.; d. Jan. 8, 1968
  (54).
Bickel, George L., actor & director; b. Saginaw, Mich.; d. June 5,
  1941 (78).
Bickford, Charles, actor; b. Jan. 1, 1891, Cambridge, Mass.; d. Nov.
  9, 1967 (76).
Biebrach, Rudolf, actor; b. 1866; d. 1938 (72).
Biegel, Erwin, actor; d. May 24, 1954 (58).
Biensfeldt, Paul, actor; b. Mar. 4, 1869, Berlin, Germany; d. Apr. 2,
  1933 (64).
Big Bear, Chief, actor; d. Jan. 21, 1960 (78).
Bigelow, Frank, actor; d. Dec. 10, 1916 (46).
Biggar, Laura, actress; d. Jan. 3, 1935 (69).
Big Tree, Chief John, actor; d. July 6, 1967 (92).
Bilancia, Oreste, actor; b. Sept. 24, 1881, Catania, Italy; d. Oct.
  31, 1945 (64).
Bildt, Paul, actor; b. May 19, 1885, Berlin, Germany; d. Mar. 16,
  1957 (71).
Bill, Raffles (Andreas Aglassinger), actor; d. Feb. 21, 1940 (45).
Billings, Benjamin, actor; d. May 3, 1923 (20).
Billings, Elmo G., actor & film editor; b. June 24, 1912, California;
  d. Feb. 6, 1964 (51).
Billings, George, actor; b. Nov. 22, 1870, Preston, Minn.; d. Apr. 15,
  1934 (63).
Billings, Harry E. (Dad), actor; d. June, 1944 (73).
Billings, Ted, actor; d. July 5, 1947 (67).
Binder, Sybille, actress; b. Vienna, Austria; d. June 30, 1962 (62).
Bing, Herman, actor; b. Mar. 30, 1889, Frankfurt, Germany; d. Jan.
  9, 1947 (57).
Bingham, Leslie, actress; b. Boston, Mass.; d. Feb. 8, 1945 (61).
Bingham, S.J. (see Bingham, Stanley J.)
Bingham, Stanley J., actor; b. Apr. 28, 1880, Cleveland, Ohio;
  d. Jan. 9, 1962 (81).
Binney, Faire, actress; b. Aug. 24, 1900, Pennsylvania; d. Aug. 28,
  1957 (57).
Binney, Harold J. (Josh), director & producer; b. June 3, 1889,
  Kansas City, Mo.; d. Nov. 8, 1956 (67).
Binns, George H., actor; d. Oct. 27, 1918.
Binyon, Claude, writer; b. Oct. 17, 1905, Chicago, Ill.; d. Feb. 14,
  1978 (72).
Birch, Frank, actor; b. Dec. 5, 1889, London, England; d. Feb. 14,
  1956 (66).
Birch, Paul, actor; b. Jan. 13, 1912, Atmore, Ala.; d. May 24, 1969
  (57).
Birch, Wyrley (r.n. Ernest Wyrley Birch), actor; b. May 7, 1883,
  Montreal, Canada; d. Feb. 7, 1959 (75).

Birgel, Willy, actor; b. Sept. 19, 1891, Cologne, Germany; d. Dec. 29, 1973 (82).
Birkett, Viva, actress; b. Feb. 14, 1887, Exeter, England; d. June 26, 1934 (47).
Biro, Lajos, writer; d. Sept. 9, 1948 (68).
Birt, Dan, director; d. May 15, 1955 (48).
Bischoff, Samuel, producer; b. Aug. 11, 1890, Hartford, Conn.; d. May 21, 1975 (84).
Biscot, Georges, actor; b. Sept. 15, 1889, Paris, France; d. Dec. 18, 1944 (55).
Bishop, Ann, actress; d. Feb. 27, 1948 (40).
Bishop, Chester, actor; d. May 23, 1937 (79).
Bishop, Fayette, actor; d. Mar., 1927.
Bishop, Richard, actor; d. May 28, 1956 (58).
Bishop, Stark, Jr., actor; d. July 9, 1945 (13).
Bishop, William, actor; b. July 16, 1918, Oak Park, Ill.; d. Oct. 3, 1959 (41).
Bistagne, Emile, actor; d. May 21, 1950 (76).
Bittner, William, actor; d. July 5, 1918.
Bitzer, G.W. "Billy," cinematographer; b. Apr. 21, 1870, Boston, Mass.; d. Apr. 29, 1944 (74).
Bjoerling, Jussi, opera singer; b. Feb. 2, 1911, Stora Tuna, Sweden; d. Sept. 8, 1960 (49).
Bjorne, Hugo, actor; d. Feb. 14, 1966 (80).
Blache, Herbert, director; b. London, England; d. Oct. 23, 1953.
Black, Maurice, actor; b. Jan. 14, 1891, Warsaw, Poland; d. Jan. 18, 1938 (47).
Blackford, Mary, actress; d. Sept. 24, 1937 (23).
Blackley, Douglas (see Kent, Robert)
Blackman, Don, actor; d. Sept. 11, 1977 (65).
Blackmer, Sidney, actor; b. July 13, 1895, Salisbury, N.C.; d. Oct. 5, 1973 (78).
Blackton, J. Stuart, executive & producer; b. Jan. 5, 1875, Sheffield, England; d. Aug. 13, 1941 (66).
Blackwell, Carlyle, actor; b. Troy, Pa.; d. June 17, 1955 (71).
Blackwell, Carlyle, Jr., actor; b. May 22, 1913, California; d. Sept. 19, 1974 (61).
Blackwell, Jim, actor; b. June 6, 1876, Richmond, Mo.; d. Sept. 27, 1932 (56).
Blackwood, Bonnie, actress; d. Feb. 18, 1949 (40).
Blackwood, Diana, actress; d. Mar., 1961.
Blackwood, Helen, actress; d. Feb. 27, 1956 (80).
Blade, Augusta, actress; d. Nov. 9, 1953 (82).
Blagoi, George, actor; d. June 23, 1971 (73).
Blaha, Ludwig, actor; b. Feb. 9, 1903, Vienna, Austria; d. Feb. 26, 1978 (75).
Blaine, Joan, actress; d. Apr. 18, 1949.
Blair, David, ballet dancer; b. July 27, 1932, Halifax, N.S., Canada; d. Apr. 1, 1976 (43).
Blair, Ella S., actress; d. Dec. 11, 1917 (22).
Blair, George, director; d. Apr. 20, 1970 (64).
Blair, Mary, actress; b. Pittsburgh, Pa.; d. Sept. 17, 1947 (52).
Blaisdell, Charles, actor; d. May 10, 1930 (56).
Blaise, Pierre, actor; d. Aug. 31, 1975 (24).
Blake, Al, author & actor; b. Mar. 31, 1887, Colorado; d. Nov. 5, 1966 (79).
Blake, Madge, actress; b. May 31, 1899, Kansas; d. Feb. 19, 1969 (69).

Blake, Marie (see Rock, Blossom)
Blake, Paul, actor, d. Jan. 28, 1960.
Blakeley, James, actor; b. Hull, England; d. Oct. 19, 1915 (42).
Blakelock, Alban, actor; d. Dec. 6, 1966.
Blakeney, Olive, actress; b. Aug. 21, 1894, Kentucky; d. Oct. 21,
   1959 (65).
Blakeslee, Louise, actress; d. Aug. 5, 1920 (15).
Blakiston, Clarence, actor; b. Apr. 23, 1864, Giggleswick, England;
   d. Mar. 23, 1943 (78).
Blanc, Elizabeth L., actress; d. Dec. 13, 1932 (68).
Blancard, Rene, actor; b. Mar. 12, 1897, Paris, France; d. Nov. 7,
   1965 (68).
Blanchar, Pierre, actor; b. June 30, 1892, Philippeville, Algeria;
   d. Nov. 21, 1963 (71).
Blanchard, Frederic, actor; d. Aug. 29, 1948 (70).
Blanchard, Harry, actor; d. Apr. 27, 1944 (68).
Blanchard, Mari, actress; b. Apr. 13, 1932, Long Beach, Calif.;
   d. May 10, 1970 (38).
Blanche, Francis, actor; b. 1921, Paris, France; d. July 6, 1974 (52).
Blancke, Kate, actress; d. June 24, 1942 (82).
Blanco, Rafael, actor; b. 1866, Madrid, Spain; d. Jan. 10, 1952 (85).
Bland, Joyce, actress; b. May 10, 1906, Caerleon, England; d. Aug. 24,
   1963 (57).
Bland, R. Henderson, actor; d. Aug. 20, 1941.
Blandick, Clara, actress; b. June 4, 1881, American ship, Hong Kong,
   China; d. Apr. 15, 1962 (80).
Blankman, George, actor; d. Mar. 13, 1925 (48).
Blatchford, William O., actor; b. May 17, 1886, Pittsburgh, Pa.;
   d. Dec. 30, 1936 (50).
Bledsoe, Jules, actor; b. Dec. 29, 1898, Waco, Tex.; d. July 14,
   1943 (44).
Bleibtreu, Hedwig, actress; b. Dec. 23, 1868, Linz, Austria; d. Jan.
   24, 1958 (89).
Bletcher, Billy, actor; b. Sept. 24, 1894, Lancaster, Pa.; d. Jan. 5,
   1979 (84).
Blich, Mrs. Catto, actress; d. June 9, 1926.
Blick, Newton, actor; b. Bristol, England; d. Oct. 14, 1965 (66).
Blinn, Benjamin F., actor; b. Apr. 3, 1872, Allentown, Pa.; d. Apr.
   28, 1941 (69).
Blinn, Genevieve, actress; d. July 20, 1956 (82).
Blinn, Holbrook, actor; b. Jan. 23, 1872, San Francisco, Calif.;
   d. June 24, 1928 (56).
Blocker, Dan, actor; b. Dec. 10, 1928, Texas; d. May 13, 1972 (43).
Blomfield, Derek, actor; b. Aug. 31, 1920, London, England; d. July
   23, 1964 (43).
Blondell, Joan, actress; b. Aug. 30, 1906, New York City; d. Dec. 25,
   1979 (73).
Blore, Eric, actor; b. Dec. 23, 1887, London, England; d. Mar. 1,
   1959 (71).
Blount, James L. (r.n. James Leonard Blount), actor; b. June 23,
   1896, Iowa; d. June 8, 1973 (76).
Blue, Ben, actor; b. Sept. 12, 1901, Montreal, Canada; d. Mar. 7,
   1975 (73).
Blue, Jean, actress; d. July 10, 1972.
Blue, Monte, actor; b. Jan. 11, 1890, Indianapolis, Ind.; d. Feb. 18,
   1963 (73).

Blue Eagle, Chief (Lloyd C. Keith), actor; d. May 15, 1958 (54).
Bluette, Isa, actress; d. Nov. 10, 1939 (41).
Bluhm, Walter, actor; b. Aug. 5, 1907; d. Dec., 1976 (69).
Blum, Max, actor; d. Jan. 10, 1944 (70).
Blum, Sam, actor; b. May 25, 1889, New York City; d. May 30, 1945
    (56).
Blumner, Rudolf, actor; b. 1874; d. Sept. 2, 1945 (71).
Blyden, Larry, actor; b. June 23, 1925, Houston, Tex.; d. June 6,
    1975 (49).
Blystone, John G., director; d. Aug. 6, 1938 (45).
Blystone, Stanley, actor; b. Aug. 1, 1894, Wisconsin; d. July 16,
    1956 (61).
Blythe, Betty, actress; b. Sept. 1, 1893, Los Angeles, Calif.;
    d. Apr. 7, 1972 (78).
Boardman, Claude, actor; d. Dec. 10, 1928 (57).
Boardman, Thelma, actress; d. Apr. 21, 1978.
Boardman, True (r.n. William True Boardman), actor; b. Apr. 21, 1882,
    California; d. Sept. 28, 1918 (36).
Boardman, Virginia True (Virginia Eames), actress; b. May 23,
    1889, Ft. Davis, Tex.; d. June 10, 1971 (82).
Bobrik, Gunther, actor; b. Feb. 5, 1888; d. Sept., 1957 (69).
Boddey, Martin, actor; d. Oct. 24, 1975.
Bodel, Burman, actor; b. May 21, 1911, Missouri; d. July 17, 1969 (58).
Boesen, William, actor; d. Mar. 25, 1972 (48).
Boettiger, Julia, actress; d. Oct. 22, 1938 (85).
Bogart, Humphrey, actor; b. Dec. 25, 1899, New York City; d. Jan. 14,
    1957 (57).
Bogeaus, Benedict, producer; b. Chicago, Ill.; d. Aug. 23, 1968 (64).
Bohn, Merritt, actor; d. Dec. 11, 1978 (73).
Bohnen, Michael, opera singer & actor; b. May 2, 1887, Koln, Germany;
    d. Apr. 26, 1965 (77).
Bohnen, Roman, actor; b. Nov. 24, 1901, St. Paul, Minn.; d. Feb. 24,
    1949 (47).
Boland, Eddie, actor; b. Dec. 27, 1885, San Francisco, Calif.;
    d. Feb. 3, 1935 (49).
Boland, Mary, actress; b. Jan. 28, 1880, Philadelphia, Pa.; d. June
    23, 1965 (85).
Bold, Davey, actor; d. July 16, 1978 (55).
Bolder, Robert, actor; b. London, England; d. Dec. 10, 1937 (78).
Boles, Jim, actor; b. Feb. 28, 1914, Lubbock, Tex.; d. May 26, 1977
    (63).
Boles, John, actor & singer; b. Oct. 27, 1895, Greenville, Tex.;
    d. Feb. 27, 1969 (73).
Boleslawski, Richard, actor & stage director; b. Feb. 4, 1889,
    Warsaw, Poland; d. Jan. 17, 1937 (47).
Boley, May, actress; b. May 29, 1881, Washington, D.C.; d. Jan. 7,
    1963 (81).
Bolyard, Lewis E., actor; d. Jan. 23, 1977.
Bonanova, Fortunio, actor & opera singer; b. Jan. 13, 1895, Palma de
    Mallorca, Spain; d. Apr. 2, 1969 (74).
Bonavita, Capt. Jack, actor; b. Pennsylvania; d. Mar. 19, 1917 (51).
Bond, Frank G., actor; d. Oct. 4, 1929 (43).
Bond, Jack, actor; d. Apr. 29, 1952 (53).
Bond, Johnny, musician, actor, & composer; d. June 12, 1978 (63).
Bond, Raymond, actor; b. Apr. 21, 1885, Iowa; d. Feb. 13, 1972 (86).

Bond, Ward, actor; b. Apr. 9, 1903, Bendelmen, Neb.; d. Nov. 5, 1960
   (57).
Bondhill, Gertrude, actress; d. Sept. 15, 1960 (80).
Boniface, Symona, actress; b. Mar. 5, 1895, New York; d. Sept. 2,
   1950 (55).
Bonifant, Carmen, actress; d. Aug. 1, 1957 (67).
Bonillas, Myrta, actress; b. Nov. 3, 1890, Massachusetts; d. Nov. 13,
   1959 (69).
Bonini, Julio, actor; d. Jan. 15, 1953 (56).
Bonn, Ferdinand, actor; b. Dec. 20, 1861, Donauworth, Germany;
   d. Sept. 24, 1933 (71).
Bonn, Frank, actor; d. Mar. 4, 1944 (71).
Bonn, Walter, actor; b. Sept. 20, 1888, Germany; d. Sept. 4, 1953
   (64).
Bonnard, Mario, actor & director; b. June 21, 1889, Rome, Italy;
   d. Mar. 22, 1965 (75).
Bonner, Isabel, actress; b. Pittsburgh, Pa.; d. July 1, 1955 (47).
Bonner, Joe, actor; d. Apr. 13, 1959 (77).
Bonomo, Joe, actor; d. Mar. 28, 1978 (76).
Bonstelle, Helen, actress; d. July 26, 1979 (61).
Bonucci, Alberto, actor; b. May 19, 1918, Campobasso, Italy; d.
   Apr. 5, 1969 (50).
Booker, Harry, actor; d. June 28, 1924 (74).
Boone, Frederick, extra; d. Mar. 28, 1962 (53).
Booth, Charles G., writer; b. Feb. 12, 1896, England; d. May 22, 1949
   (53).
Booth, Elmer, actor; d. June 16, 1915.
Booth, Helen, actress; d. Feb. 5, 1971.
Booth, Nesdon, actor; b. Sept. 1, 1918, Baker, Ore.; d. Mar. 25,
   1964 (45).
Booth, Sydney Barton, actor; b. Jan. 29, 1873, Boston, Mass.; d. Feb.
   5, 1937 (64).
Boots, dog; d. Nov. 14, 1947 (16).
Borden, Eddie, actor; b. May 1, 1888, Deer Lodge, Tenn.; d. June 30,
   1955 (67).
Borden, Eugene, actor; b. Mar. 22, 1897, Paris, France; d. July 21,
   1971 (74).
Borden, Olive, actress; b. July 20, 1906, Richmond, Va.; d. Oct. 1,
   1947 (41).
Bordoni, Irene, actress; b. Jan. 16, 1895, France; d. Mar. 19, 1953
   (58).
Borell, Louis, actor; b. Oct. 6, 1906; Amsterdam, Netherlands;
   d. Apr., 1973 (66).
Borelli, Lyda, actress; b. Genoa, Italy; d. June 1, 1959 (71).
Boreo, Emile, actor; b. Poland; d. July 27, 1951 (66).
Borg, Veda Ann, actress; b. Jan. 11, 1919, Boston, Mass.; d. Aug. 16,
   1973 (54).
Borgato, Agostino, actor; b. June 30, 1871, Venice, Italy; d. Mar. 14,
   1939 (67).
Borghese, Viglione (r.n. Domenico Viglione Borghese), actor; b. July
   3, 1877, Mondoni, Italy; d. Oct. 26, 1957 (80).
Borgstrom, Hilda, actress; d. Jan. 2, 1953 (82).
Boring, Edward, actor; d. June 18, 1923.
Boris, Anthony H., actor; b. 1915; d. Aug. 12, 1954 (39).
Borland, Barlowe, actor; b. Aug. 6, 1877, Greenack, Scotland; d.
   Aug. 31, 1948 (71).

Boros, Ferike (r.n. Ferike Weinstock), actress; b. Aug. 2, 1880, Nagyvarad, Hungary; d. Jan. 16, 1951 (70).

Borzage, Dan, actor; b. Dec. 24, 1896, Utah; d. June 17, 1975 (78).

Borzage, Frank, director, producer, & actor; b. Apr. 23, 1893, Salt Lake City, Utah; d. June 19, 1962 (69).

Bos, Annie, actress; d. Aug. 3, 1975 (88).

Bosan, Alonso, actor; d. June 30, 1959 (70).

Bose, Joachim, actor; b. Apr. 30, 1932; d. Apr. 23, 1971 (38).

Boshell, Ada, actress; d. Mar. 31, 1924 (71).

Bosse, Harriet, actress; d. Nov., 1961 (83).

Bossick, Bernard B., director, actor, & producer; d. Nov. 10, 1975 (57).

Bostock, Evelyn, actress & author; b. Mar. 8, 1917, London, England; d. Nov. 28, 1944 (27).

Boswell, Connee, singer & recording artist; b. New Orleans, La.; d. Oct. 11, 1976 (68).

Bosworth, Hobart (r.n. Hobart Van Zandt Bosworth), actor; b. Aug. 11, 1867, Marietta, Ohio; d. Dec. 30, 1943 (76).

Boteler, Wade, actor; b. Oct. 3, 1888, Santa Ana, Calif.; d. May 7, 1943 (54).

Bothwell, John F. (Freckles), actor; d. Mar. 7, 1967 (46).

Bottomley, Roland, actor; b. Liverpool, England; d. Jan. 5, 1947 (67).

Botz, Gustav, actor; b. May 17, 1857; d. Apr. 6, 1932 (74).

Boucher, Victor, actor; b. 1877, Rouen, France; d. Feb. 22, 1942 (64).

Bouchey, Willis, actor; b. May 24, 1907, Michigan; d. Sept. 27, 1977 (70).

Boucicault, Nina, actress; b. Feb. 27, 1867, Marylebone, England; d. Aug. 2, 1950 (83).

Bouckou, Ralph H. (see Bucko, Buck)

Bouckou, Roy (see Bucko, Roy)

Boucot, Louis, actor; d. Mar. 30, 1949 (60).

Boulton, Matthew, actor; b. Jan. 20, 1883, England; d. Feb. 10, 1962 (79).

Bour, Armand, actor; b. 1868, Lille, France; d. 1945 (77).

Bourbon, Diana, actress; d. Mar. 19, 1978 (78).

Bourchier, Arthur, actor; b. June 22, 1863, Berkshire, England; d. Sept. 14, 1927 (64).

Bourke, Fan, actress; d. Mar. 9, 1959 (73).

Bourneuf, Philip, actor; b. Somerville, Mass.; d. Mar. 23, 1979 (71).

Bourvil (r.n. Andre Raimbourg), actor; b. July 27, 1917, France; d. Sept. 23, 1970 (53).

Bovy, Berthe, actress; b. Liege, France; d. Feb., 1977 (90).

Bow, Clara, actress; b. Aug. 5, 1906, Brooklyn, N.Y.; d. Sept. 27, 1965 (59).

Bowers, John, actor; d. Nov. 15, 1936 (41).

Bowers, Lyle, actor; b. May 22, 1895, Iowa; d. Mar. 8, 1943 (47).

Bowes, Cliff, actor; b. Nov. 14, 1894, Colorado; d. July 6, 1929 (34).

Bowker, Aldrich, actor; b. 1875, Massachusetts; d. Mar. 21, 1947 (72).

Bowman, Laura, actress; d. Mar. 29, 1957 (76).

Bowman, Lee, actor; b. Dec. 28, 1914, Cincinnati, Ohio; d. Dec. 25, 1979 (64).

Bowman, Palmer, producer & actor; d. Sept. 25, 1933 (50).

Bowman, Rudy, actor; b. Dec. 15, 1890, Kansas; d. Oct. 29, 1972 (81).

Bowman, William J., director; d. Jan. 1, 1960 (83).

Bowser, Charles, actor; d. Mar. 17, 1917.

Boyce, George, choreographer & actor; d. Feb. 4, 1977 (77).
Boyd, Ada, actress; d. Mar. 25, 1978 (87).
Boyd, Betty, actress; b. May 11, 1908, Kansas City, Mo.; d. Sept. 16,
    1971 (63).
Boyd, Bill (Cowboy Rambler), actor; d. Dec. 7, 1977 (67).
Boyd, Mary, actress; b. Dec. 11, 1883, Kentucky; d. Feb. 12, 1970
    (86).
Boyd, Stephen, actor; b. July 4, 1928, Belfast, Ireland; d. June 2,
    1977 (48).
Boyd, William, actor; b. New York City; d. Mar. 20, 1935 (45).
Boyd, William, actor; b. June 5, 1895, Cambridge, Ohio; d. Sept. 12,
    1972 (77).
Boyer, Charles, actor; b. Aug. 28, 1899, Figeac Lot, France; d. Aug.
    26, 1978 (78).
Boyer, Jean, director; b. Jan. 26, 1901, Paris, France; d. Mar. 10,
    1965 (64).
Boylan, Malcolm Stuart, writer; b. Apr. 13, 1897, Chicago, Ill.;
    d. Apr. 3, 1967 (69).
Boyle, Charles P., cinematographer; b. July 26, 1892, Illinois;
    d. May 28, 1968 (75).
Boyle, Jack G., actor & dancer; b. Oct. 9, 1916, Illinois; d. Oct. 15,
    1965 (49).
Boyle, Jack T., actor; b. Dec. 11, 1916, New York; d. Nov. 30,
    1969 (52).
Boyle, John, actor; d. Mar. 8, 1918 (45).
Boyle, John, cinematographer; d. Sept. 28, 1959 (78).
Boyne, Clifton, actor; b. 1874; d. Dec. 16, 1945 (71).
Boyne, Eva Leonard, actress; d. Apr. 12, 1960 (74).
Boyne, Hazel (Sunny), actress; d. Aug. 27, 1966 (83).
Boytler, Arcady (r.n. Arcadij Bojtler), director; b. Aug. 31, 1890,
    Russia; d. Nov. 23, 1965 (75).
Bozenhard, Albert, actor; b. Feb. 14, 1860, Ulm, Germany; d. Jan. 13,
    1939 (78).
Bozyk, Max, actor; d. Apr. 5, 1970 (71).
Brabin, Charles, actor & director; b. 1883, Liverpool, England;
    d. Nov. 3, 1957 (74).
Braccini, Lola, actress; b. Mar. 28, 1898, Pisa, Italy; d. Mar. 19,
    1969 (70).
Brace, Norman C., actor; d. June 20, 1954 (62).
Bracho, Julio, director; d. Apr. 26, 1978 (69).
Bracken, Bertram, director; d. Nov. 1, 1952 (72).
Brackett, Charles, producer & writer; b. Nov. 28, 1892, Saratoga
    Springs, N.Y.; d. Mar. 9, 1969 (76).
Brackett, Leigh, writer; d. Mar. 18, 1978 (60).
Bracy, Clara T., actress; d. Feb. 22, 1941 (94).
Bracy, Sidney, actor; b. Dec. 18, 1877, Melbourne, Australia;
    d. Aug. 5, 1942 (64).
Bradbury, James, Jr., actor; b. Oct. 5, 1894, New York; d. June 21,
    1936 (41).
Bradbury, James, Sr., actor; b. Oct. 12, 1857, Old Towne, Me.; d.
    Oct. 12, 1940 (83).
Bradbury, Saxe, actress; d. Nov. 13, 1976 (33).
Bradford, Lane, actor; d. June 7, 1973 (50).
Bradford, Marshall, actor; b. Jan. 19, 1895, New York; d. Jan. 11,
    1971 (75).

Bradley, Amanda, actress; d. Dec. 13, 1916.
Bradley, Benjamin R., actor; d. Sept. 29, 1950 (52).
Bradley, Harry C., actor; b. Apr. 15, 1869, San Francisco, Calif.; d. Oct. 18, 1947 (78).
Bradley, Lovyss, actress; d. June 21, 1969 (63).
Bradley, Russell F., actor; b. Mar. 27, 1894, Palo Alto, Calif.; d. Dec. 17, 1952 (58).
Bradley, Truman, actor; b. Feb. 8, 1905, Missouri; d. July 28, 1974 (69).
Bradshaw, Lionel, actor; d. Dec. 31, 1918 (26).
Brady, Alice, actress; b. Nov. 2, 1892, New York City; d. Oct. 28, 1939 (47).
Brady, Edwin J., actor; b. Dec. 6, 1889, New York City; d. Mar. 31, 1942 (52).
Brady, Fred (r.n. Frederick Kress), actor & author; b. Nov. 29, 1912, New York; d. Nov. 11, 1961 (48).
Brady, Pat, actor; b. Dec. 31, 1914, Toledo, Ohio; d. Feb. 27, 1972 (57).
Brady, Veronica, actress; d. Jan. 19, 1964 (73).
Brady, William J., actor; d. Dec. 26, 1936 (66).
Braga, Eurico, actor; b. Rio de Janeiro, Brazil; d. Nov. 19, 1962 (68).
Bragaglia, Arturo, actor; b. Jan. 7, 1893, Frosinone, Italy; d. Jan. 21, 1962 (69).
Braham, Harry, actor; b. London, England; d. Sept. 21, 1923 (73).
Braham, Horace, actor; b. July 29, 1892, London, England; d. Sept. 7, 1955 (63).
Braham, Lionel, actor; b. Apr. 1, 1879, Yorkshire, England; d. Oct. 6, 1947 (68).
Braidon, Thomas, actor; b. Mar. 1, 1870, England; d. June 22, 1950 (80).
Braithwaite, Dame Lilian, actress; b. Ramsgate, England; d. Sept. 17, 1948 (77).
Brandeis, Madeleine, actress; d. June 27, 1937 (39).
Branden, Michael (see Twitchell, Archie)
Brandon, Dolores, actress; d. Aug. 9, 1959 (42).
Brandon, Florence, actress; d. Oct. 11, 1961 (82).
Brandon, Francis, actor; d. Oct. 3, 1924 (38).
Brandon-Thomas, Amy, actress; b. Mar. 9, 1890, London, England; d. May, 1974 (84).
Brandt, Charles, actor; d. June 9, 1924 (60).
Brandt, Louise, actress; d. July 13, 1959 (82).
Branner, Per-Axel, director; b. Jan. 25, 1899, Linkoping, Sweden; d. Aug., 1975 (76).
Brannigan, Owen, opera singer; b. Mar. 10, 1908, Northumberland, England; d. May, 1973 (65).
Brannon, Fred C., director; d. Apr. 6, 1953 (51).
Brasfield, Rod, actor & country comic; b. Aug. 22, 1910, Smithville, Miss.; d. Sept. 12, 1958 (48).
Brasseur, Pierre, actor; b. Dec. 22, 1905, Paris, France; d. Aug. 14, 1972 (66).
Braswell, Charles, actor; b. Sept. 7, 1924, McKinney, Tex.; d. May 17, 1974 (49).
Braun, Dr. Harald, director; d. Sept. 24, 1960 (59).
Braun, Viktor, actor; b. July 21, 1899, Vienna, Austria; d. Dec., 1971 (72).

36                                    International Film Necrology

Braune, Marga, actress; d. May 22, 1974 (83).
Brausewetter, Hans, actor; b. May 27, 1900, Malaga, Spain; d. Apr.
  29, 1945 (44).
Braut, Frigga, actress; b. Hamburg, Germany; d. Feb. 13, 1975 (85).
Bravo, Jaime, actor & matador; d. Feb. 2, 1970 (38).
Brawn, Jack, actor; d. June 16, 1943 (74).
Bray, John F., actor; d. May 3, 1955 (49).
Brazeal, Hal (r.n. Russell Harold Brazeal), actor & film editor;
  b. Jan. 15, 1915, Missouri; d. May 2, 1973 (58).
Breakston, George, actor; b. Jan. 22, 1920, Paris, France; d. May
  21, 1973 (53).
Breamer, Sylvia, actress; d. June 7, 1943 (40).
Brecher, Egon, actor; b. Feb. 16, 1880, Olmeretz, Austria; d. Aug. 12,
  1946 (66).
Breeden, John, actor; b. May 3, 1904, San Francisco, Calif.; d. Sept.
  9, 1977 (73).
Breen, Hurley (Red), stuntman; d. Sept. 8, 1963 (54).
Breen, Margaret, actress; b. Feb. 3, 1907, Missouri; d. Dec. 5, 1960
  (53).
Breese, Edmund, actor; b. June 18, 1871, Brooklyn, N.Y.; d. Apr. 6,
  1936 (64).
Brel, Jacques, actor & composer; d. Oct. 9, 1978 (49).
Brendel, El, actor; b. Mar. 25, 1891, Philadelphia, Pa.; d. Apr. 9,
  1964 (73).
Brendlin, Andre, actor; d. Oct. 6, 1934 (23).
Breneman, Tom, actor & showman; d. Apr. 28, 1948 (46).
Brengk, Ernest, actor; b. Mar. 14, 1881, Germany; d. Dec. 5, 1961
  (80).
Brennan, Barney, actor; d. June 6, 1938 (26).
Brennan, Frederick Hazlett, writer; d. June 30, 1962 (60).
Brennan, Jay, actor & author; b. Baltimore, Md.; d. Jan. 14, 1961
  (78).
Brennan, Johnny, actor; d. Dec. 27, 1940 (75).
Brennan, Joseph D., actor; d. Dec. 10, 1940 (81).
Brennan, Joseph H., actor; d. Feb. 28, 1949.
Brennan, Robert, actor; d. Apr. 17, 1940 (48).
Brennan, Walter, actor; b. July 25, 1894, Swampscott, Mass.;
  d. Sept. 21, 1974 (80).
Brennen, Claire, actress; d. Nov. 27, 1977 (43).
Brenon, Herbert, director & actor; b. Jan. 13, 1880, Dublin, Ireland;
  d. June 21, 1958 (78).
Brent, Evelyn, actress; b. Oct. 20, 1899, Tampa, Fla.; d. June 4,
  1975 (75).
Brent, George, actor; b. Mar. 15, 1904, Dublin, Ireland; d. May 26,
  1979 (75).
Brent, Janet, actress; b. Dec. 15, 1920, California; d. Mar. 23,
  1974 (53).
Brent, Romney (r.n. Romulo Larralde), actor; b. Jan. 26, 1902,
  Saltillo, Mexico; d. Sept. 24, 1976 (74).
Brereton, Tyrone, actor; b. Dublin, Ireland; d. Apr. 25, 1939 (45).
Bressart, Felix, actor; b. Mar. 2, 1895, Eydtkuhnen, Germany;
  d. Mar. 17, 1949 (54).
Bretherton, Howard, director; b. Feb. 13, 1896, Tacoma, Wash.;
  d. Apr. 12, 1969 (73).
Breuer, Siegfried, actor; b. June 24, 1906, Vienna, Austria; d. Feb.
  1, 1954 (47).

Brewer, Monte, actor; d. Apr. 21, 1942 (8).
Breyer, Margarette, actress; d. Mar. 11, 1931 (86).
Brian, Donald, actor & singer; b. Feb. 17, 1875, St. John's, New-
  foundland, Canada; d. Dec. 22, 1948 (73).
Briant, Roy, actor & author; d. Dec. 16, 1927 (39).
Brice, Betty, actress; d. Feb. 15, 1935 (39).
Brice, Fanny, actress & singer; b. Oct. 29, 1891, New York City;
  d. May 29, 1951 (59).
Brice, Monte, author, director, & actor; d. Nov. 8, 1962 (71).
Bricker, Betty, actress; d. Feb. 15, 1954 (64).
Bricker, George, writer; b. July 18, 1899, St. Mary's, Ohio; d. Jan.
  22, 1955 (55).
Brickert, Carlton, actor; d. Dec. 23, 1943 (52).
Bridge, Alan, actor; b. Feb. 26, 1891, Pennsylvania; d. Dec. 27,
  1957 (66).
Bridge, Loie, actress; b. Oct. 16, 1889, Pennsylvania; d. Mar. 9, 1974
  (84).
Bridges, John A., actor; b. Oct. 24, 1888, Alabama; d. July 11, 1973
  (84).
Brierre, Maurice, actor; b. Feb. 10, 1885, Louisiana; d. Nov. 4,
  1959 (74).
Briggs, Harlan, actor; b. Aug. 17, 1879, Blissfield, Mich.; d. Jan.
  26, 1952 (72).
Briggs, Matt, actor; d. June 10, 1962 (79).
Briggs, Oscar, actor; d. Jan. 17, 1928 (51).
Brill, Patti, actress; d. Jan. 18, 1963.
Brinckman, Elsie, actress; d. Apr. 22, 1950 (57).
Brindley, Madge, actress; d. Aug. 28, 1968.
Brindmour, George, actor; d. July 31, 1941 (71).
Brinkman, Ernest, actor; d. Dec. 28, 1938 (66).
Brinley, Charles, actor; b. Nov. 15, 1880, Yuma, Ariz.; d. Feb. 17,
  1946 (65).
Briscoe, Lottie, actress; b. St. Louis, Mo.; d. Mar. 19, 1950 (69).
Brisson, Carl, actor & singer; b. Dec. 24, 1893, Copenhagen, Denmark;
  d. Sept. 26, 1958 (64).
Brister, Robert S., actor; b. Apr. 5, 1888, Hitchcock, S.D.; d. Feb.
  28, 1945 (56).
Britt, Elton, actor & recording artist; b. June 17, 1913, Marshall,
  Ark.; d. June 23, 1972 (59).
Britton, Barbara, actress; b. Sept. 26, 1920, Long Beach, Calif.;
  d. Jan. 16, 1980 (59).
Britton, Edna, actress; d. Aug. 5, 1960.
Britton, Ethel, actress; d. Feb. 26, 1972 (57).
Britton, Mozell, actress; d. May 18, 1953 (41).
Britton, Pamela, actress; d. June 17, 1974 (51).
Broadley, Edward, actor; d. Nov. 24, 1947 (72).
Brochard, Jean, actor; b. Mar. 12, 1893, Nantes, France; d. June,
  1972 (79).
Brock, George Thompson, actor; b. Jan. 8, 1890, Vermont; d. Apr. 29,
  1942 (52).
Brockbank, Harrison, actor; b. Liverpool, England; d. Nov. 30, 1947
  (80).
Brockwell, Gladys, actress; b. Sept. 26, 1894, Brooklyn, N.Y.; d.
  July 2, 1929 (34).
Brod, Max, author & actor; d. July 28, 1959 (79).

Broderick, Helen, actress; b. Aug. 11, 1891, Philadelphia, Pa.;
    d. Sept. 25, 1959 (68).
Broderick, Johnny, actor; d. Apr. 14, 1977 (83).
Brodie, Buster, actor; d. Apr. 9, 1948 (62).
Brody, Ann (r.n. Ann Brody Goldstein), actress; b. Aug. 29, 1884,
    Poland; d. July 16, 1944 (59).
Brogan, Harry, actor; d. May 20, 1977 (72).
Brokaw, Charles, actor; d. Oct. 23, 1975 (77).
Bromberg, J. Edward, actor; b. Dec. 25, 1903, Temesvar, Hungary;
    d. Dec. 6, 1951 (47).
Bromley-Davenport, A. (see Davenport, A. Bromley)
Bronson, Betty, actress; b. Nov. 17, 1906, New Jersey; d. Oct. 19,
    1971 (64).
Brook, Clive, actor; b. June 1, 1887, London, England; d. Nov. 17,
    1974 (87).
Brooke, Claude, actress; d. Dec. 14, 1933 (80).
Brooke, Clifford, actor & director; b. Mar. 31, 1873, England; d.
    Dec. 29, 1951 (78).
Brooke, Michael, actor; d. Jan. 10, 1978 (73).
Brooke, Myra, actress; d. Feb. 9, 1944 (79).
Brooke, Tyler, actor; b. 1886, New York City; d. Mar. 2, 1943 (57).
Brooke, Van Dyke, actor; d. Sept. 17, 1921 (62).
Brooker, Tom, actor; b. July 25, 1886, New York; d. Jan. 29, 1929
    (42).
Brookes, Olwen, actress; d. Oct., 1976 (74).
Brook-Jones, Elwyn, actor; b. Dec. 11, 1911, Sarawak; d. Sept. 4,
    1962 (50).
Brooks, Geraldine, actress; b. Oct. 29, 1925, New York City; d. June
    19, 1977 (51).
Brooks, Hank, actor; d. Dec. 3, 1925.
Brooks, Jess Lee, actor; d. Dec. 13, 1944 (50).
Brooks, Laura Kasley, actress; b. Mar. 31, 1887, West Virginia;
    d. Dec. 22, 1974 (87).
Brooks, Pauline, actress; d. June 7, 1967 (54).
Brooks, Ralph, actor & author; d. Dec. 4, 1963 (43).
Brophy, Edward, actor; b. Feb. 27, 1895, New York City; d. May 27,
    1960 (65).
Brosig, Egon, actor; b. Oct. 25, 1889, Ohlan; d. May 23, 1961 (71).
Broske, Octavia, actress; b. June 4, 1886, Pennsylvania; d. Mar. 19,
    1967 (80).
Brott, Robert, actor; b. 1881; d. Aug. 15, 1933 (52).
Brough, Arthur, actor; d. May 28, 1978 (73).
Brough, Mary, actress; b. Apr. 16, 1863, London, England; d. Sept.
    30, 1934 (71).
Brower, Otto, actor & director; d. Jan. 25, 1946 (55).
Brower, Robert, actor; b. July 14, 1850, Point Pleasant, N.J.;
    d. Dec. 8, 1934 (84).
Brower, Thomas L., actor; b. Feb. 20, 1878, Birmingham, Ala.;
    d. July 19, 1937 (59).
Brown, A.J. (r.n. Alfred John Brown), actor; d. Jan. 29, 1978 (80).
Brown, Barbara, actress; d. July 7, 1975.
Brown, Barry, actor; b. Apr. 19, 1951, San Jose, Calif.; d. June 25,
    1978 (27).
Brown, Bly, actress; d. Dec. 19, 1950 (52).
Brown, Charles D., actor; b. July 1, 1887, Council Bluffs, Iowa;
    d. Nov. 25, 1948 (61).

Brown, Earle, actor; b. Sept. 7, 1872, Vallejo, Calif.; d. Nov. 26, 1944 (72).
Brown, Everett, actor; b. Jan. 1, 1902, Texas; d. Oct. 14, 1953 (51).
Brown, Halbert, actor; d. Oct. 24, 1942 (77).
Brown, Harry, actor; b. Sept. 22, 1891, New York; d. Jan. 8, 1966 (74).
Brown, Harry Joe, producer; b. Sept. 22, 1893, Pittsburgh, Pa.; d. Apr. 28, 1972 (78).
Brown, Helen, actress; b. Dec. 24, 1917, Washington; d. Sept. 9, 1974 (56).
Brown, Horace, actor; b. Oct. 10, 1905, Virginia; d. Nov. 9, 1972 (67).
Brown, Joe E., actor; b. Sept. 22, 1892, Pittsburgh, Pa.; d. July 6, 1973 (80).
Brown, Josephine, actress; d. Apr. 26, 1976 (84).
Brown, John, actor; d. May 16, 1957 (53).
Brown, Johnny Mack, actor; b. Sept. 1, 1904, Dothan, Ala.; d. Nov. 14, 1974 (70).
Brown, Lee, actor; d. Mar. 9, 1957 (76).
Brown, Melville, director, author, & actor; b. Portland, Ore.; d. Jan. 31, 1938 (50).
Brown, Morgan, actor; b. Dec. 4, 1884, New York; d. Jan. 4, 1961 (76).
Brown, Pamela, actress; b. July 8, 1917, London, England; d. Sept. 18, 1975 (58).
Brown, Raymond, actor; b. Aug. 16, 1874, Champaign, Ill.; d. July 29, 1939 (64).
Brown, Reed, Jr., actor; b. Texas; d. July 26, 1962 (63).
Brown, Ronald C., dancer; d. Oct. 27, 1962 (51).
Brown, Rowland C., director & writer; b. Nov. 6, 1900, Akron, Ohio; d. May 6, 1963 (62).
Brown, Russ, actor; b. May 30, 1892, Philadelphia, Pa.; d. Oct. 19, 1964 (72).
Brown, Sedley, actor; d. Sept. 18, 1928 (72).
Brown, Troy, actor; d. Nov. 18, 1944.
Brown, Wally, actor; b. Oct. 9, 1904, Malden, Mass.; d. Nov. 13, 1961 (57).
Browne, Bothwell, actor & female impersonator; d. Dec. 12, 1947.
Browne, Irene, actress; b. June 29, 1896, England; d. July 24, 1965 (69).
Browne, Laidman, actor; b. Sept. 13, 1896, Newcastle-on-Tyne, England; d. Sept. 11, 1961 (64).
Browne, Lucile, actress; d. May 10, 1976 (69).
Browne, W. Graham, actor; b. Jan. 1, 1870, Ireland; d. Mar. 11, 1937 (67).
Browne-Decker, Kathryn, actress; d. Feb. 11, 1919.
Browning, Alan, actor; d. Sept. 7, 1979 (53).
Browning, Alice (see Houghton, Alice)
Browning, Tod, director & actor; b. July 12, 1882, Louisville, Ky.; d. Oct. 6, 1962 (80).
Browning, William E., actor; d. Dec. 21, 1930.
Brownlee, Frank, actor; b. Oct. 11, 1874, Dallas, Tex.; d. Feb. 10, 1948 (73).
Bruce, Belle, actress; d. June 15, 1960.
Bruce, Betty, dancer; d. July 18, 1974 (54).
Bruce, Beverly, actress; d. July, 1925.

Bruce, Clifford, actor; d. Aug. 27, 1919 (34).
Bruce, David (r.n. Andrew McBroom), actor; b. Jan. 6, 1914, Kankakee, Ill.; d. May 3, 1976 (62).
Bruce, Edgar K., actor; b. Oct. 21, 1893, Eyam, Derbyshire, England; d. Nov. 1, 1971 (78).
Bruce, George Mario (see Cory, Victor)
Bruce, Kate, actress; d. Apr. 2, 1946 (88).
Bruce, Nigel, actor; b. Feb. 14, 1895, Baja, Mexico; d. Oct. 8, 1953 (58).
Bruce, Paul, actor; b. Dec. 12, 1917, Pennsylvania; d. May 2, 1971 (53).
Bruce, Tony, actor; d. Mar. 3, 1937 (27).
Bruckman, Clyde, director & writer; d. Jan. 4, 1955 (60).
Bruggeman, George, actor; b. Nov. 1, 1904, Belgium; d. June 9, 1967 (62).
Brulatour, Jules, executive; d. Oct. 26, 1946 (76).
Brule, Andre, actor & director; d. Feb. 14, 1953 (74).
Brumage, Edward M., actor; d. July 8, 1945 (65).
Brundage, Mathilde, actress; d. May 6, 1939 (79).
Brunette, Fritzi, actress; b. May 27, 1895, Savannah, Ga.; d. Sept. 28, 1943 (48).
Brunetti, Miro, actor; b. Jan. 15, 1908, New York; d. July 1, 1966 (58).
Brunius, Jacques-Bernard, actor; b. Sept. 16, 1906, Paris, France; d. Apr. 24, 1967 (60).
Brunius, Pauline, actress; b. 1881; d. 1954 (73).
Brunnel, Joseph, actor; d. Apr. 25, 1943 (68).
Bruno, Frank, actor; d. June 20, 1945.
Brunot, Andre, actor; d. Oct. 3, 1879, Premery, France; d. Aug. 6, 1973 (93).
Bruns, Edna, actress; d. July 25, 1960 (80).
Brunton, William, actor; b. Mar. 13, 1883, Canada; d. Feb. 19, 1965 (81).
Bruyere, Gaby, actress; d. Aug. 31, 1978 (54).
Bryan, Arthur Q., actor; b. May 8, 1899, New York; d. Nov. 30, 1959 (60).
Bryan, Gerald E., assistant director; b. Nov. 21, 1917, Kansas; d. Oct. 18, 1970 (52).
Bryan, Jackson Lee (Jack), actor; b. Dec. 9, 1908, Illinois; d. Sept. 15, 1964 (55).
Bryant, Charles, actor & director; b. England; d. Aug. 7, 1948 (67).
Bryant, Marguerite, actress; d. Jan., 1951.
Bryant, Marie, actress; d. May 23, 1978 (59).
Bryant, Nana, actress; b. Nov. 23, 1888, Cincinnati, Ohio; d. Dec. 24, 1955 (67).
Bryant, Robin, actress; d. Jan. 18, 1976 (50).
Bryson, James, actor; d. Dec. 31, 1935.
Buccola, Guy, actor; b. June 7, 1899, Italy; d. Dec. 22, 1962 (63).
Buchanan, Edgar, actor; b. Mar. 30, 1903, Humansville, Mo.; d. Apr. 4, 1979 (76).
Buchanan, Jack, actor; b. Apr. 2, 1891, Helensburgh, Scotland; d. Oct. 20, 1957 (66).
Buchanan, Stuart, actor; d. Feb. 4, 1974 (79).
Buchman, Sidney, scenarist; b. Mar. 27, 1902, Duluth, Minn.; d. Aug. 23, 1975 (73).

Buck, Elizabeth, dancer; d. Mar. 21, 1934 (22).
Buck, Frank, director & actor; b. Gainesville, Tex.; d. Mar. 25, 1950 (66).
Buck, Inez, actress; b. South Dakota; d. Sept. 6, 1957 (67).
Buck, Nell Roy, actress; d. Feb. 28, 1962 (51).
Buck, Richard A., actor; b. May 28, 1909, Butte, Mont.; d. Dec. 9, 1948 (39).
Buckingham, Tom, writer & director; d. Sept. 7, 1934 (39).
Buckland, Veda, actress; b. Aug. 25, 1882, Montreal, Canada; d. May 20, 1941 (58).
Buckland, Wilfred, Sr., art director; d. July 18, 1946 (80).
Buckler, Hugh, actor; b. Sept. 9, 1881, Southampton, England; d. Oct. 30, 1936 (55).
Buckler, John, actor; b. Apr. 1, 1906, Capetown, South Africa; d. Oct. 30, 1936 (30).
Buckley, Floyd, actor; b. Chatham, N.Y.; d. Nov. 14, 1956 (82).
Buckley, Joseph, actor; d. Dec. 2, 1930 (55).
Buckley, Richard (Lord), actor; d. Nov. 12, 1960 (54).
Buckner, Robert L., writer & producer; b. May 28, 1903, Crewe, Va.; d. Jan. 24, 1961 (57).
Bucko, Buck (Ralph H. Bouckou), actor; d. Aug. 6, 1962 (70).
Bucko, Roy (Roy F. Bouckou), actor; b. Aug. 22, 1893, California; d. Aug. 6, 1954 (60).
Bucquet, Harold Spencer, director; d. Feb. 13, 1946 (54).
Budlong, Jack, actor; b. Feb. 22, 1913, New York City; d. Aug. 5, 1941 (28).
Buehler, Arthur, actor; b. June 26, 1894, Ohio; d. Dec. 1, 1962 (68).
Buel, Keenan, actor; d. Nov. 5, 1948 (75).
Buffalo Bill, Jr. (see Wilsey, Jay)
Buffington, Adele, writer; b. Feb. 12, 1900, St. Louis, Mo.; d. Nov. 23, 1973 (73).
Buffington, Sam, actor; b. Oct. 12, 1931, Massachusetts; d. May 15, 1960 (28).
Buhler, Richard, actor; b. Washington, D.C.; d. Mar. 27, 1925 (48).
Bulgakov, Leo, actor; b. Mar. 22, 1889, Tula, Russia; d. July 20, 1948 (59).
Bull, Charles Edward, actor; b. Feb. 26, 1881, Texas; d. Sept. 9, 1971 (90).
Bullock, Boris (see Barrymore, William)
Bump, Edmond, actor; d. Nov. 6, 1938 (61).
Bumpas, H.W. (Bob), actor; d. Dec. 9, 1959 (48).
Bunce, Alan, actor; d. Apr. 27, 1965 (62).
Bunker, Ralph, actor; d. Apr. 28, 1966 (77).
Bunny, George, actor; b. July 13, 1867, New York City; d. Apr. 16, 1952 (84).
Bunny, John, actor; b. Sept. 1, 1863, New York City; d. Apr. 26, 1915 (51).
Bunston, Herbert, actor; b. Oct. 21, 1865, England; d. Feb. 27, 1935 (69).
Burani, Michelette, actress; b. Asnieres, Paris, France; d. Oct. 27, 1957 (75).
Burbank, Frank, actor; d. Feb. 23, 1950 (93).
Burbank, Goldie, actress; d. Mar. 1, 1954 (74).
Burch, Betty, actress; d. May 30, 1956 (68).
Burch, John, actor; b. Aug. 17, 1896, Chicago, Ill.; d. July 29, 1969 (72).

Burdick, Hal (r.n. Harold P. Burdick), author & actor; d. June 12,
    1978 (84).
Burford, Edna, actress; d. Dec. 10, 1929.
Burg, Eugen, actor; b. Jan. 6, 1871, Berlin, Germany; d. Nov., 1944
    (73).
Burgess, Dorothy, actress; b. Mar. 4, 1905, Los Angeles, Calif.;
    d. Aug. 20, 1961 (56).
Burgess, Earl, actor; d. Feb. 5, 1920.
Burgess, Gladys, actress; d. Jan. 22, 1933 (33).
Burgess, Harry, actor; b. Pennsylvania; d. Apr. 27, 1936 (77).
Burgess, Hazel, actress; d. Dec. 11, 1973 (63).
Burgess, Helen, actress; b. Apr. 29, 1916, Portland, Ore.; d. Apr. 7,
    1937 (20).
Burgher, Fairfax (Robert Fairfax), actor; d. Sept. 20, 1965 (70).
Burian, Vlasta, actor; d. Feb. 5, 1962 (71).
Burke, Annie, actress; d. Dec. 24, 1952 (82).
Burke, Billie, actress; b. Aug. 7, 1885, Washington, D.C.; d. May 14,
    1970 (84).
Burke, Caroline, actress; d. Dec. 5, 1964 (51).
Burke, J. Frank, actor; b. Apr., 1867, Vermont; d. Jan. 23, 1918 (50).
Burke, James, actor; b. Sept. 24, 1886, New York City; d. May 23,
    1968 (81).
Burke, Joseph, actor; d. Dec. 17, 1942 (58).
Burke, Kevin, actor; b. Sept. 21, 1943, California; d. Sept. 1, 1969
    (25).
Burke, Orrin, actor; b. July 24, 1872, Urbana, Ohio; d. Jan. 14,
    1946 (73).
Burke, Thomas, actor; d. Mar. 25, 1941.
Burke, Tom, actor; d. Sept. 13, 1969 (79).
Burkhardt, Harry, actor; b. Sept. 27, 1870, Boston, Mass.; d. Sept.
    18, 1943 (72).
Burlando, Claude, actor; d. Sept. 25, 1938 (20).
Burlando, Joseph, actor; b. Oct. 27, 1877, France; d. Feb. 20,
    1951 (73).
Burmeister, Augusta, actress; d. Mar. 28, 1934 (74).
Burnaby, Davy, actor; b. Apr. 7, 1881, Buckland, Herts., England;
    d. Apr. 17, 1949 (68).
Burne, Arthur, actor; b. Nov. 24, 1873, Sydenham, England; d. Oct.
    23, 1945 (71).
Burne, Nancy, actress; b. England; d. Mar. 25, 1954 (41).
Burne, Rosamond, actress; d. Aug. 10, 1975.
Burnette, Dorsey, singer; b. Dec. 28, 1932, Memphis, Tenn.; d. Aug.
    19, 1979 (46).
Burnette, Johnny, singer; b. Mar. 25, 1934, Memphis, Tenn.; d. Aug.
    14, 1964 (30).
Burnette, Smiley (Lester Burnette), actor; b. Mar. 18, 1911, Summum,
    Ill.; d. Feb. 16, 1967 (55).
Burney, Hal, actor; d. Nov. 11, 1933 (33).
Burnley, Fred, director; d. July 7, 1975 (41).
Burns, Bob (see Burns, Robert E.)
Burns, Bob (High Ghere), actor; b. Aug. 2, 1890, Van Buren, Ark.;
    d. Feb. 2, 1956 (65).
Burns, Clyde, actor; b. Sept. 3, 1885, Illinois; d. Oct. 29, 1964 (79).
Burns, David, actor; b. June 22, 1900, New York City; d. Mar. 12,
    1971 (70).

Burns, Fred, actor; b. Apr. 24, 1878, Ft. Keough, Mont.; d. July 18, 1955 (77).
Burns, Harry, actor; b. Philadelphia, Pa.; d. July 9, 1948 (63).
Burns, Harry, director; d. Jan. 9, 1939 (55).
Burns, Irving, actor; d. Sept. 21, 1968 (54).
Burns, Joseph, actor; d. Nov. 3, 1946 (57).
Burns, Nat, actor; b. Philadelphia, Pa.; d. Nov. 8, 1962 (75).
Burns, Neal, actor; b. June 26, 1890, Georgia; d. Oct. 3, 1969 (79).
Burns, Paul E., actor; b. Jan. 26, 1881, Philadelphia, Pa.; d. May 17, 1967 (86).
Burns, Robert, actor; d. June 8, 1955 (26).
Burns, Robert E. (Bob Burns), actor; b. Nov. 21, 1884, Montana; d. Mar. 14, 1957 (72).
Burns, Robert P., actor; b. Sept. 1, 1878, Philadelphia, Pa.; d. Jan. 16, 1966 (87).
Burnside, William Wesley, Jr., actor & stuntman; d. Mar. 25, 1976 (49).
Burr, Donald, actor; b. July 31, 1907, Cincinnati, Ohio; d. Feb. 27, 1979 (71).
Burr, Eugene, actor; b. Leavenworth, Kans.; d. June 7, 1940 (56).
Burress, William, actor; b. Aug. 19, 1867, New Cornerstone, Ohio; d. Oct. 30, 1948 (81).
Burrough, Tom, actor; b. 1869, Clinton Co., Ill.; d. Sept. 8, 1929 (60).
Burroughs, Clark, actor; b. Aug. 23, 1883, Danville, Ill.; d. Feb. 4, 1937 (53).
Burt, Frederic, actor; b. Feb. 12, 1876, Onarge, Ill.; d. Oct. 2, 1943 (67).
Burt, Laura, actress; b. Sept. 16, 1872, Ramsay, Isle of Man; d. Oct. 16, 1952 (80).
Burt, William P., actor; b. Feb. 11, 1867, St. Peter, Minn.; d. Feb. 23, 1955 (88).
Burtis, James, actor; b. May 12, 1893, Emporia, Kans.; d. July 24, 1939 (46).
Burton, Blanche, actress; d. July 24, 1934 (55).
Burton, Charlotte, actress; d. Mar. 28, 1942 (60).
Burton, Clarence, actor; b. May 10, 1881, Ft. Lyons, Mo.; d. Dec. 1, 1933 (52).
Burton, David, director & actor; d. Dec. 30, 1963 (86).
Burton, Frederick, actor; d. Oct. 20, 1871, Indiana; d. Oct. 23, 1957 (86).
Burton, George, actor; b. Sept. 17, 1898, Montana; d. Dec. 8, 1955 (57).
Burton, John W., actor; b. Jan. 7, 1853, Wisconsin; d. Mar. 25, 1920 (67).
Burton, Langhorne, actor; b. Dec. 25, 1872, Somersby, Lincolnshire, England; d. Dec. 6, 1949 (77).
Burton, Martin, actor; b. Mitchell, Ind.; d. Aug. 4, 1976 (71).
Burton, Ned, actor; d. Dec. 11, 1922 (72).
Burton, Robert, actor; b. Aug. 13, 1895, Georgia; d. Sept. 29, 1962 (67).
Burton, Sam A. (r.n. Sam Augustus Burton), actor; b. Sept. 10, 1889, San Francisco, Calif.; d. July 16, 1946 (56).
Burton, Thomas, actor; d. Dec. 16, 1943 (69).
Burton, Tom, actor; d. Oct. 13, 1955 (36).

Burton, William H., actor; d. Mar. 15, 1926 (81).
Burtwell, Frederick, actor; d. Nov. 16, 1948.
Buscaglione, Fred, actor; d. Feb. 3, 1960 (39).
Busch, Mae, actress; b. Melbourne, Australia; d. Apr. 19, 1946 (44).
Bush, Anita, actress; d. Feb. 16, 1974.
Bush, George, actor; d. Nov. 23, 1937 (79).
Bush, Pauline, actress; b. May 22, 1886, Lincoln, Neb.; d. Nov. 1, 1969 (83).
Bush, Robert Finlay, actor; d. Apr. 2, 1929 (41).
Bushman, Francis X., actor; b. Jan. 10, 1883, Baltimore, Md.; d. Aug. 23, 1966 (83).
Busley, Jessie, actress; b. Mar. 10, 1869, Albany, N.Y.; d. Apr. 20, 1950 (81).
Busquets, Joaquin, actor; d. Dec. 4, 1942 (67).
Bussey, Hank, actor; d. Jan. 14, 1971 (80).
Buster, Budd L., actor; b. June 14, 1891, Colorado Springs, Colo.; d. Dec. 22, 1965 (74).
Butcher, Ernest, actor; b. Apr. 7, 1885, England; d. June 8, 1965 (80).
Buti, Carlo, singer; d. Nov. 16, 1963 (61).
Butler, Charles, actor; d. Aug. 17, 1920 (64).
Butler, David, director & actor; b. Dec. 17, 1895, San Francisco, Calif.; d. June 14, 1979 (83).
Butler, Eddie, actor; b. July 5, 1888, New York City; d. May 21, 1944 (55).
Butler, Frank, author & actor; b. Dec. 28, 1890, Oxford, England; d. June 10, 1967 (76).
Butler, Fred J., actor & director; b. Oct. 22, 1867, Idaho; d. Feb. 22, 1929 (61).
Butler, Hugo, writer; b. May 4, 1914, Calgary, Alberta, Canada; d. Jan. 7, 1968 (53).
Butler, Jimmy, actor; d. Feb. 18, 1945 (24).
Butler, John A., actor; b. May 1, 1884, Canada; d. Oct. 9, 1967 (83).
Butler, John K., writer; d. Sept. 18, 1964 (56).
Butler, Louise, actress; d. Dec. 8, 1958.
Butler, Roy E. (Edwin Richey), actor; b. May 4, 1893, Atlanta, Ga.; d. July 28, 1973 (80).
Butler, William J., actor; d. Jan. 27, 1927 (67).
Butt, Bob (see Bentley, Robert)
Butt, W. Lawson, actor; b. 1883; d. Jan. 14, 1956 (72).
Butterfield, Herbert, actor; d. May 2, 1957 (61).
Butterfield, Walton, actor & author; d. Aug. 22, 1966 (68).
Butterworth, Charles, actor; b. July 26, 1899, South Bend, Ind.; d. June 13, 1946 (46).
Butterworth, Peter, actor; d. Jan. 16, 1979 (59).
Butterworth, Walter T., actor; b. Apr. 4, 1892, Indiana; d. Mar. 10, 1962 (69).
Buxbaum, Edward F., actor; d. Jan. 21, 1951 (58).
Byford, Roy, actor; b. Jan. 12, 1873, London, England; d. Jan. 31, 1939 (66).
Byington, Spring, actress; b. Oct. 17, 1886, Colorado Springs, Colo.; d. Sept. 7, 1971 (84).
Byles, Bobby, actor; d. Aug. 26, 1969 (38).
Byram, Ronald, actor; d. 1919.
Byrd, Ralph, actor; b. Apr. 29, 1909, Dayton, Ohio; d. Aug. 18, 1952 (43).

Byrens, Myer, actor; d. June 29, 1933 (93).
Byrne, Cecily, actress; b. Birmingham, England; d. June 30, 1975 (85).
Byrne, John, actor; d. Feb. 14, 1924 (62).
Byron, Allan (see Randall, Jack)
Byron, A.S. (Pop) (r.n. Aquilla Stewart Byron), actor; b. Jan. 30,
    1876, Barnesville, Ohio; d. Feb. 5, 1943 (67).
Byron, Arthur, actor; b. Apr. 3, 1872, Brooklyn, N.Y.; d. July 16,
    1943 (71).
Byron, Paul, actor; d. May 12, 1959 (68).
Byron, Royal James, actor; d. Mar. 4, 1943 (56).
Byron, Walter, actor; b. June 11, 1899, Leicester, England; d. Mar. 2,
    1972 (72).


Cabanne, William Christy, director; b. St. Louis, Mo.; d. Oct. 15,
    1950 (62).
Cabot, Bruce, actor; b. Apr. 20, 1904, Coresheo, N.M.; d. May 3,
    1972 (68).
Cabot, Eliot, actor; b. June 22, 1899, Boston, Mass.; d. June 17,
    1938 (39).
Cabot, Sebastian, actor; b. July 6, 1918, London, England; d. Aug.
    23, 1977 (59).
Cadell, Jean, actress; b. Sept. 13, 1884, Edinburgh, Scotland;
    d. Sept. 24, 1967 (83).
Cady, Jerry, writer; d. Nov. 8, 1948 (40).
Caesar, Arthur, writer; b. Mar. 9, 1892, Rumania; d. June 20, 1953
    (61).
Cahill, Lily, actress; b. Texas; d. July 20, 1955 (69).
Cahill, Marie, actress; b. Brooklyn, N.Y.; d. Aug. 23, 1933 (63).
Cahn, Edward L., director; b. Feb. 12, 1899, Brooklyn, N.Y.;
    d. Aug. 25, 1963 (64).
Cahoon, William Benedict, actor; d. Jan. 28, 1951 (91).
Cain, Robert, actor; d. Apr. 27, 1954 (67).
Caine, Georgia, actress; b. Oct. 30, 1876, California; d. Apr. 4,
    1964 (87).
Caine, Henry, actor; b. Jan. 19, 1888, Leamington Spa, England;
    d. July 9, 1962 (74).
Caire, Reda, actor; b. Feb. 11, 1908, Cairo, Egypt; d. Sept. 22,
    1963 (55).
Cairns, Sally, actress; d. Feb. 9, 1965 (45).
Caits, Joseph, actor; d. Mar. 9, 1957 (68).
Caldara, Orme, actor; d. Oct. 21, 1925 (40).
Calder, King, actor; b. Apr. 21, 1898, Maryland; d. June 28, 1964
    (66).
Caldwell, Orville, actor; b. Feb. 8, 1896, California; d. Sept. 24,
    1967 (71).
Calhern, Louis, actor; b. Feb. 19, 1895, Brooklyn, N.Y.; d. May 12,
    1956 (61).
Calhoun, Alice, actress; b. Nov. 21, 1900, Cleveland, Ohio; d. June
    3, 1966 (65).
Cali, Giulio, actor; d. Jan. 20, 1967.
Call, John, actor; d. Apr. 3, 1973 (64).
Callahan, Charles S. (Chuck), actor & dancer; d. Nov. 12, 1964 (73).
Callahan, Robert, actor; d. May 15, 1938 (42).

Calleia, Joseph, actor; b. Aug. 4, 1897, Malta; d. Oct. 31, 1975 (78).
Calles, Guillermo, actor; d. Feb. 28, 1958.
Calley, Robert S., extra; d. May 6, 1977 (88).
Calliga, George, actor; b. Jan. 2, 1897, Rumania; d. Jan. 18, 1976
    (79).
Callis, David, actor; d. Sept. 10, 1934 (46).
Calthrop, Donald, actor; b. Apr. 11, 1888, London, England; d. July
    15, 1940 (52).
Calvert, Catherine, actress; b. Baltimore, Md.; d. Jan. 18, 1971 (80).
Calvert, E.H. (r.n. Elisha Helm Calvert), actor & director; b. June 27,
    1863, Alexandria, Va.; d. Oct. 5, 1941 (78).
Calvert, Eddie, band leader & recording artist; d. Aug. 7, 1978 (56).
Calvin, Henry, actor; d. Oct. 6, 1975 (57).
Calvin, Lester, extra; d. May 30, 1978 (88).
Calvo, Juan, actor; d. Mar., 1962.
Cambridge, Godfrey, actor; b. Feb. 26, 1933, New York City; d. Nov.
    29, 1976 (43).
Cameron, Bruce, actor; d. Apr. 10, 1959 (49).
Cameron, Donald, actor; b. Canada; d. July 11, 1955 (66).
Cameron, Gene, actor; d. Nov. 16, 1927.
Cameron, Hugh, actor; b. Duluth, Minn.; d. Nov. 9, 1941 (62).
Cameron, Rudolph, actor; d. Feb. 17, 1958 (63).
Camp, Shep, actor; b. July 16, 1882, West Point, Ga.; d. Nov. 20,
    1929 (47).
Campana, Nina, actress; d. June 21, 1950 (53).
Campbell, Alan, writer; d. June 14, 1963 (58).
Campbell, Alexander, actor; d. Dec. 25, 1970.
Campbell, Argyle, actor; d. Apr. 4, 1940 (53).
Campbell, Colin, director; b. Oct. 11, 1859, Scotland; d. Aug. 26,
    1928 (68).
Campbell, Colin, actor; b. Mar. 20, 1883, Falkirk, Scotland; d. Mar.
    25, 1966 (83).
Campbell, Eric, actor; d. Dec. 20, 1917 (37).
Campbell, Frank G., actor; d. Apr. 30, 1934 (87).
Campbell, Margaret, actress; b. Apr. 24, 1883, St. Louis, Mo.;
    d. June 27, 1939 (56).
Campbell, May, actress; d. Jan. 6, 1951.
Campbell, Mrs. Patrick, actress; b. Feb. 9, 1865, London, England;
    d. Apr. 9, 1940 (75).
Campbell, Webster (r.n. William Webster Campbell), actor; b. Kansas
    City, Kans.; d. Aug. 28, 1972 (79).
Campeau, Frank, actor; b. Dec. 14, 1864, Detroit, Mich.; d. Nov. 5,
    1943 (78).
Camron, Rocky (Gene Alsace), actor; b. Aug. 4, 1902, Colorado; d.
    June 16, 1967 (64).
Cane, Charles, actor; b. Apr. 18, 1899, Missouri; d. Nov. 30, 1973
    (74).
Canfield, William F., actor; d. Feb. 14, 1925 (64).
Cann, Alexander, actor; d. Dec. 21, 1977 (74).
Cannon, Norman, actor; d. Dec. 13, 1934.
Cannon, Raymond, actor & director; b. Sept. 1, 1892, Long Hollow,
    Tenn.; d. June 7, 1977 (84).
Cansino, Eduardo, dancer; d. Dec. 23, 1968 (73).
Cansino, Eduardo, Jr., actor; b. Oct. 13, 1919, New York; d. Mar. 11,
    1974 (54).

Cantor, Charles, actor; b. Sept. 4, 1898, USSR; d. Sept. 11, 1966
    (68).
Cantor, Eddie, actor & singer; b. Jan. 31, 1892, New York City;
    d. Oct. 10, 1964 (72).
Cantor, Herman, actor; d. Oct. 12, 1953 (57).
Cantor, Nat, actor; d. Mar. 15, 1956 (59).
Cantway, Fred R., actor; d. Mar. 12, 1939 (56).
Cantzen, Conrad, actor; d. June 28, 1945 (78).
Canzoneri, Tony, actor; d. Dec. 10, 1959 (51).
Capellani, Paul, actor; d. 1914.
Capozzi, Alberto A., actor; b. July 8, 1886, Genes; d. June 27, 1945
    (58).
Caprice, June, actress; b. Boston, Mass.; d. Nov. 9, 1936 (37).
Card, Kathryn, actress; b. Oct. 4, 1892, Montana; d. Mar. 1, 1964
    (71).
Cardwell, James, actor; b. Nov. 21, 1921, Camden, N.J.; d. Feb. 1,
    1954 (32).
Carell, Annette, actress; d. Oct. 20, 1967.
Carette (Julien Carette), actor; b. Dec. 23, 1897, Paris, France;
    d. July 20, 1966 (68).
Carew, James, actor; b. Feb. 5, 1876, Goshen, Ind.; d. Apr. 4, 1938
    (62).
Carewe, Arthur Edmund, actor; b. Dec. 30, 1884, Trebizond, Armenia;
    d. Apr. 21, 1937 (52).
Carewe, Edwin, director & actor; b. Mar. 5, 1881, Gainesville, Tex.;
    d. Jan. 22, 1940 (58).
Carewe, Ora, actress; d. Oct. 26, 1955 (62).
Carewe, Rita, actress; b. Sept. 9, 1909, New York City; d. Oct. 23,
    1955 (46).
Carey, Edward F., actor; d. Oct. 30, 1979 (74).
Carey, Harry, Sr., actor; b. Jan. 16, 1878, New York City; d. Sept.
    21, 1947 (69).
Carey, Leonard, actor; b. Feb. 25, 1887, England; d. Sept. 11, 1977
    (90).
Carl, Renee, actress; d. 1954.
Carle, Richard, actor; b. July 7, 1871, Somerville, Mass.; d. June
    28, 1941 (69).
Carles, Romeo, actor; d. Sept., 1971 (75).
Carleton, Claire, actress; d. Dec. 11, 1979 (66).
Carleton, George, actor; b. Oct. 28, 1885, New York; d. Sept. 23,
    1950 (64).
Carleton, Harry, actor; d. Jan. 31, 1922 (62).
Carleton, W.T., actor; d. Sept. 26, 1922 (73).
Carleton, Will C., author; b. Sept. 24, 1872, New York; d. Sept. 21,
    1941 (68).
Carleton, William P., actor; b. Oct. 3, 1872, London, England;
    d. Apr. 5, 1947 (74).
Carleton, William T., actor; d. Sept. 28, 1930.
Carlie, Edwin, actor; d. Nov. 25, 1938 (59).
Carlini, Paolo, actor; d. Nov., 1979 (53).
Carlisle, Alexandra, actress; b. Jan. 15, 1886, London, England;
    d. Apr. 21, 1936 (50).
Carlsen, Traute, actress; d. Nov. 22, 1968 (82).
Carlson, Ernest, actor; d. Feb. 7, 1940 (13).
Carlson, Richard, actor; b. Apr. 29, 1912, Albert Lee, Minn.; d.
    Nov. 25, 1977 (65).

Carlyle, Francis, actor; d. Sept. 15, 1916 (48).
Carlyle, Helen, actress; b. Oct., 1892; d. June 30, 1933 (40).
Carlyle, Richard, actor; b. May 21, 1876, Guelph, Ont., Canada;
    d. June 12, 1942 (66).
Carlyle, Rita, actress; b. Feb. 23, 1869, Mississippi; d. Aug. 24,
    1949 (80).
Carmel, Eddie, actor; d. July 30, 1972 (36).
Carmen, Sybil, actress; d. Apr. 15, 1929 (28).
Carmi, Maria, actress; b. Mar. 3, 1880, Florence, Italy; d. Aug.,
    1957 (77).
Carmi, Vera, actress; b. Nov. 23, 1917, Torino, Italy; d. Sept. 7,
    1969 (51).
Carminati, Tullio, actor; b. Sept. 21, 1894, Zara, Dalmatia, Italy;
    d. Feb. 26, 1971 (76).
Carnabuci, Piero, actor; b. Sept. 6, 1895, Santa Teresa Riva, Italy;
    d. 1957 (62).
Carnahan, Suzanne (see Peters, Susan)
Carnera, Primo, boxer, wrestler, & actor; b. Oct. 26, 1906, Sequals,
    Italy; d. June 29, 1967 (60).
Carney, Alan (r.n. David Boughal), actor; b. Dec. 22, 1909, Brooklyn,
    N.Y.; d. May 2, 1973 (63).
Carney, Don, actor; d. Jan. 14, 1954 (57).
Carney, George, actor; b. Nov. 21, 1887, Bristol, England; d. Dec. 9,
    1947 (60).
Carney, James, actor; d. Aug. 25, 1955 (44).
Carol, Martine, actress; b. May 16, 1920, France; d. Feb. 6, 1967
    (46).
Carpenter, Gloria, actress; d. Sept. 11, 1958 (31).
Carpenter, Horace B., actor & director; b. Jan. 31, 1875, Grand Rapids,
    Mich.; d. May 21, 1945 (70).
Carpenter, Paul, actor; b. Dec. 8, 1921, Montreal, Canada; d. June
    12, 1964 (42).
Carpentier, Georges, light heavyweight champion & actor; d. Oct. 27,
    1975 (81).
Carr, Alexander, actor; b. Mar. 7, 1878, Rumni, Russia; d. Sept. 19,
    1946 (68).
Carr, George, actor; d. Aug. 24, 1962 (69).
Carr, Geraldine, actress; d. Sept. 2, 1954 (37).
Carr, Ginna, actress; d. July 13, 1972 (35).
Carr, Gladys M., actress; d. Sept. 26, 1940 (50).
Carr, Jack, actor; b. May 17, 1906, New Jersey; d. Feb. 2, 1967 (60).
Carr, Jane, actress; b. Aug. 1, 1909, Whitley Bay, England; d. Sept.
    29, 1957 (48).
Carr, Luella, actress; d. Jan., 1937.
Carr, Mary, actress; b. Mar. 14, 1874, Philadelphia, Pa.; d. June
    24, 1973 (99).
Carr, Mildred Dolly, actress; d. Feb. 26, 1949 (52).
Carr, Nat, actor; b. Aug. 12, 1886, Poltava, Russia; d. July 6,
    1944 (57).
Carr, Percy, actor; b. England; d. Nov. 22, 1926 (51).
Carr, Sade, actress; d. Nov. 17, 1940 (51).
Carr, Thomas, actor; d. Aug. 18, 1946.
Carr, Trem, director; d. Aug. 18, 1946 (54).
Carr, William, actor; b. May 6, 1891, New York; d. Mar. 19, 1945 (53).
Carr, William C.D., director & actor; d. Feb. 13, 1937 (70).

Carre, Bart, actor, assistant director, & production manager;
  b. July 10, 1897, Melrose, Mass.; d. Apr. 26, 1971 (73).
Carre, Ben, art director; d. May 28, 1978 (94).
Carrigan, Thomas J., actor; b. Lapeer, Mich.; d. Oct. 2, 1941 (55).
Carrillo, Leo, actor; b. Aug. 6, 1881, Los Angeles, Calif.; d. Sept.
  10, 1961 (80).
Carrington, Evelyn Carter, actress; d. Nov. 21, 1942 (66).
Carrington, Frank, actor; d. July 3, 1975 (73).
Carrington, Helen, actress; d. Oct. 22, 1963 (68).
Carroll, Francis J., director; d. June 5, 1944 (65).
Carroll, John, actor; b. July 17, 1906, New Orleans, La.; d. Apr.
  24, 1979 (72).
Carroll, Leo G., actor; b. Oct. 25, 1886, Weedon, England; d. Oct.
  16, 1972 (85).
Carroll, Nancy, actress; b. Nov. 19, 1904, New York City; d. Aug. 6,
  1965 (60).
Carroll, Richard, writer; b. Oct. 27, 1898, Cambridge, Mass.;
  d. Mar. 11, 1959 (60).
Carroll, Richard F., actor & author; b. Oct. 27, 1865, Boston, Mass.;
  d. June 26, 1925 (59).
Carroll, William A., actor; b. 1876, New York; d. Dec. 26, 1927 (51).
Carron, George, actor; b. Canada; d. Apr. 23, 1970 (40).
Carruthers, Bruce C., actor; d. Jan. 1, 1954 (53).
Carsey, Mary, actress; d. Aug. 27, 1973 (35).
Carson, Charles, actor; b. Aug. 16, 1885, London, England; d. Aug. 5,
  1977 (91).
Carson, Jack, actor; b. Oct. 27, 1910, Carman, Man., Canada; d. Jan.
  2, 1963 (52).
Carson, James B., actor; b. Dec. 22, 1886, Missouri; d. Nov. 18,
  1958 (71).
Carson, Kit (r.n. Eldridge Franklin Carson), actor; d. Feb. 11, 1978
  (69).
Carson, Kit (see also Barrymore, William)
Carson, Robert S., actor; d. June 2, 1979 (69).
Carstairs, John Paddy, director; d. Dec. 12, 1970 (60).
Carstens, Lina, actress; b. Dec. 6, 1892, Wiesbaden, Germany;
  d. Sept. 22, 1978 (85).
Carter, Ben, actor; b. Feb. 10, 1911, Fairfield, Iowa; d. Dec. 10,
  1946 (35).
Carter, Calvert (r.n. Charles Calvert Carter), actor; b. Oct. 23,
  1858, Virginia; d. Aug. 26, 1932 (73).
Carter, Hubert, actor; d. Mar. 26, 1934 (65).
Carter, Mrs. Leslie, actress; b. June 10, 1862, Lexington, Ky.;
  d. Nov. 12, 1937 (75).
Carter, Lillian, actress; d. June 5, 1956 (75).
Carter, Louise, actress; b. Mar. 17, 1875, Iowa; d. Nov. 10, 1957
  (82).
Carter, Monte, actor; d. Nov. 14, 1950 (66).
Cartier, Inez Gibson, stunt flyer; d. Aug. 4, 1970 (52).
Carton, Pauline, actress; d. June 17, 1974 (89).
Caruso, Enrico, opera singer & actor; b. Feb. 25, 1873, Naples,
  Italy; d. Aug. 2, 1921 (48).
Caruso, Maria, actress; d. June 13, 1979 (56).
Caruth, Burr, actor; b. June 15, 1865, Illinois; d. June 2, 1953 (87).
Carver, Kathryn, actress; b. New York City; d. July 18, 1947 (41).

Carver, Louise, actress; b. June 9, 1868, Davenport, Iowa; d. Jan. 19, 1956 (87).
Carver, Lynne, actress; d. Aug. 12, 1955 (38).
Carvill, Henry, actor; d. Mar. 11, 1941 (74).
Casadesus, Mathilde, actress; b. May 5, 1921, Paris, France; d. Aug. 30, 1965 (44).
Casaleggio, Giovanni, actor; d. Nov. 11, 1955 (75).
Casaleggio, Mario, actor; b. Dec. 15, 1877, Torino, Italy; d. Feb. 8, 1953 (75).
Case, Paul, actor; d. Mar. 29, 1933 (38).
Caserini, Mario, director; b. 1874, Rome, Italy; d. Nov. 17, 1920 (46).
Casey, Jack, actor & stuntman; b. Aug. 15, 1888, Ireland; d. Aug. 30, 1956 (68).
Casey, Kenneth, actor; d. Aug. 10, 1965 (66).
Casey, Leslie, actor, author, & producer; d. Feb. 18, 1942 (50).
Casey, Lew J., actor; b. Dec. 6, 1899, Philadelphia, Pa.; d. Nov. 23, 1942 (42).
Casey, Stuart F., actor; d. Jan. 23, 1948 (52).
Cashman, Harry, actor; d. Apr. 14, 1912.
Casimir, Golda, actress; d. Jan., 1976 (74).
Cason, John, actor; b. July 30, 1918, Texas; d. July 7, 1961 (42).
Caspar, Horst, actor; b. Jan. 20, 1913, Badegast, Germany; d. Dec. 27, 1952 (39).
Cass, Francis, actor; d. June, 1927.
Cass, Guy, actor; d. Sept. 28, 1959 (38).
Cass, Lou, actor; d. July 27, 1942 (39).
Cass, Maurice, actor; b. Oct. 12, 1884, Vilna, Lithuania; d. June 9, 1954 (69).
Cassady, James, actor; d. Mar. 23, 1928 (58).
Cassel, Sid, actor; b. July 24, 1897, England; d. Jan. 17, 1960 (62).
Cassidy, Bill, actor; d. Apr. 6, 1943 (67).
Cassidy, Edward (r.n. Edward Bottomly Cassidy), actor; b. Mar. 21, 1893, Illinois; d. Jan. 19, 1968 (74).
Cassidy, Jack, actor; b. Mar. 5, 1927, Richmond Hill, N.Y.; d. Dec. 12, 1976 (49).
Cassidy, Ted, actor; b. July 31, 1932, Pittsburgh, Pa.; d. Jan. 16, 1979 (46).
Casson, Sir Lewis, actor; b. Oct. 26, 1875, England; d. May 16, 1969 (93).
Casson, Louis, actor; d. Jan. 23, 1950.
Castagna, Joe, actor & stuntman; d. Aug. 15, 1970 (36).
Castiglioni, Iphigenie, actress; b. Aug. 23, 1901, Austria; d. July 30, 1963 (61).
Castile, Lynn, actress; b. Jan. 11, 1898, Missouri; d. Mar. 27, 1975 (77).
Castle, Don, actor; b. Sept. 29, 1918, Texas; d. May 25, 1966 (47).
Castle, Irene, dancer & actress; b. Apr. 7, 1893; d. Jan. 25, 1969 (75).
Castle, Lillian, actress; d. Apr. 24, 1959 (94).
Castle, Peggie, actress; b. Dec. 22, 1927, Appalachia, Va.; d. Aug. 10, 1973 (45).
Castle, Vernon, dancer & actor; b. England; d. Feb. 15, 1918 (32).
Castle, William, director, producer, & actor; b. Apr. 24, 1914, New York City; d. May 31, 1977 (63).

Castro, Steven, actor; d. Nov. 19, 1952 (88).
Catlett, Walter, actor; b. Feb. 4, 1889, San Francisco, Calif.;
    d. Nov. 14, 1960 (71).
Catrani, Catrano, director; b. Italy; d. Oct. 19, 1974 (61).
Caulkins, Rufus, actor; d. July 15, 1935 (22).
Cavalieri, Gianni, actor; b. Mar. 7, 1908, Padova, Italy; d. July 5,
    1955 (47).
Cavalieri, Lina, actress & opera singer; b. Dec. 25, 1874, Rome,
    Italy; d. Feb. 8, 1944 (69).
Cavan, Allan, actor; b. Mar. 25, 1880, Concord, Calif.; d. Jan. 20,
    1941 (60).
Cavan, Taylor, writer; d. Mar. 23, 1949 (51).
Cavanagh, Paul, actor; b. Dec. 8, 1888, Chislehurst, England; d. Mar.
    15, 1964 (75).
Cavanaugh, Hobart, actor; b. Sept. 22, 1886, Virginia City, Nev.;
    d. Apr. 25, 1950 (63).
Cavanna, Elise, actress; b. Jan. 30, 1902, Pennsylvania; d. May 12,
    1963 (61).
Cavender, Glenn, actor; b. Sept. 19, 1883, Arizona; d. Feb. 9, 1962
    (78).
Cavendish, David (Dennis D'Auburn), actor; b. Oct. 29, 1893,
    England; d. Oct. 9, 1960 (66).
Cavendish, June, extra; d. Feb. 22, 1976.
Cavens, Fred, actor & fencing master; b. Aug. 30, 1882, Belgium;
    d. Apr. 30, 1962 (79).
Cavett, Frank, writer; b. Dec. 27, 1907, Jackson, Ohio; d. Mar. 25,
    1973 (65).
Cavin, Jess, actor; b. May 5, 1885, Indiana; d. July 20, 1967 (82).
Cawthorn, Joseph, actor; b. Mar. 29, 1868, New York City; d. Jan.
    21, 1949 (80).
Cazale, John, actor; b. Boston, Mass.; d. Mar. 12, 1978 (42).
Cazenuve, Paul, director & actor; d. June 22, 1925.
Cebotari, Maria, opera singer; b. Feb. 10, 1910, Kischinev, Rumania;
    d. June 9, 1949 (39).
Cecil, Edward, actor; b. Sept. 13, 1878, San Francisco, Calif.;
    d. Dec. 13, 1940 (62).
Cecil, Mary, actress; d. Dec. 21, 1940 (55).
Cedar, Ivan, stuntman; d. Nov., 1937.
Cedar, Ralph, writer & director; b. Feb. 2, 1898, Marinette, Wisc.;
    d. Nov. 29, 1951 (53).
Celeste, Olga, stuntwoman; d. Aug. 31, 1969 (82).
Celis, Claudia, actress; d. Mar. 15, 1958.
Cellier, Frank, actor; b. Feb. 23, 1884, Surbiton, Surrey, England;
    d. Sept. 27, 1948 (64).
Cennerazzo, Armando, actor; d. Jan. 10, 1962 (75).
Cerf, Kurt, actor; d. Oct. 27, 1979 (69).
Cerval, Claude, actor; d. July, 1972 (51).
Cervi, Gino, actor; b. May 3, 1901, Bologna, Italy; d. Jan. 3,
    1974 (72).
Cesana, Renzo, actor; b. Oct. 30, 1907, Italy; d. Nov. 8, 1970
    (63).
Chabrier, Marcel, actor; d. Aug. 18, 1946 (53).
Chadwick, Helene, actress; b. Nov. 25, 1898, Chadwick, N.Y.; d.
    Sept. 5, 1940 (41).
Chaibancha, Mitr, actor; d. Oct. 8, 1970 (36).

Chaillie, Joseph, actor; d. Dec. 17, 1924 (73).
Chaliapin, Feodor, actor & opera singer; b. Feb. 13, 1873, Kazan,
    Russia; d. Apr. 12, 1938 (65).
Challenger, Percy, actor; b. Sept. 3, 1858, England; d. July 23,
    1932 (73).
Chalmers, Thomas, actor & opera singer; b. Oct. 20, 1884, New York
    City; d. June 11, 1966 (81).
Chalzel, Leo, actor; b. Dayton, Ohio; d. July 16, 1953 (52).
Chamberlain, Cyril, actor; b. 1909; d. Apr. 30, 1974 (65).
Chamberlain, Riley, actor; d. Jan. 16, 1917 (62).
Chamberlin, Frank, actor; d. Aug. 29, 1935 (65).
Chamberlin, J. Raymond, actor; d. Dec. 2, 1957 (71).
Chambers, Lyster, actor; b. Michigan; d. Jan. 27, 1947 (71).
Chambers, Margaret, actress; b. Oct. 16, 1896, Kentucky; d. Oct. 6,
    1965 (68).
Chambers, Marie, actress; d. Mar. 21, 1933 (44).
Chambers, Ralph, actor; d. Mar. 16, 1968 (76).
Chambers, Wheaton (r.n. James Wheaton Chambers), actor; b. Oct. 13,
    1887, Philadelphia, Pa.; d. Jan. 31, 1958 (70).
Champion, horse; d. Jan. 24, 1947 (17).
Chan, George, actor; b. Jan. 18, 1876, China; d. Sept. 30, 1957 (81).
Chan, Oie, actress; d. Feb. 5, 1967 (81).
Chan, Mrs. Pon Y., actress; d. Apr. 1, 1958 (88).
Chan, Thomas F., actor; b. Nov. 26, 1897, San Francisco, Calif.;
    d. Nov. 2, 1942 (44).
Chance, Anna, actress; b. Oct. 25, 1879, Oxford, Md.; d. Sept. 10,
    1943 (63).
Chandlee, Harry, writer; b. Dec. 7, 1882, Washington, D.C.; d. Aug.
    3, 1956 (73).
Chandler, Anna, actress; d. July 10, 1957 (70).
Chandler, Eddy, actor; b. Mar. 12, 1894, Wilton Junction, Iowa;
    d. Mar. 23, 1948 (54).
Chandler, Helen, actress; b. Feb. 1, 1909, Charleston, S.C.;
    d. Apr. 30, 1965 (56).
Chandler, Jeff, actor; b. Dec. 15, 1918, Brooklyn, N.Y.; d. June 17,
    1961 (42).
Chandler, Joan, actress; d. May 11, 1979 (55).
Chandler, Lane (r.n. Robert C. Oakes), actor; b. June 4, 1899,
    North Dakota; d. Sept. 14, 1972 (73).
Chandler, Robert, actor; d. Mar. 17, 1950 (90).
Chaney, Creighton (see Chaney, Lon, Jr.)
Chaney, Lon, Jr. (Creighton Chaney), actor; b. Feb. 10, 1906,
    Oklahoma City, Okla.; d. July 12, 1973 (67).
Chaney, Lon, Sr., actor; b. Apr. 1, 1883, Colorado Springs, Colo.;
    d. Aug. 26, 1930 (47).
Chaney, Norman (Chubby), actor; b. Jan. 18, 1918, Baltimore, Md.;
    d. May 29, 1936 (18).
Chanslor, Roy, writer; b. Aug. 25, 1899, Liberty, Mo.; d. Apr. 16,
    1964 (64).
Chantal, Marcelle, actress; b. 1903; d. 1960 (57).
Chapin, Alice, actress; b. 1858; d. July 6, 1934 (76).
Chapin, Anne Morrison, writer; d. Apr. 7, 1967.
Chapin, Benjamin, actor; b. Bristolville, Ohio; d. June 2, 1918 (43).
Chapin, Harold, actor; b. Brooklyn, N.Y.; d. Sept. 26, 1915 (29).
Chaplin, Charles, actor, director, author, & composer; b. Apr. 16,
    1889, London, England; d. Dec. 25, 1977 (88).

Chaplin, Charles, Jr., actor; d. Mar. 20, 1968 (42).
Chaplin, Sydney, actor; b. Mar. 17, 1885, Capetown, South Africa;
  d. Apr. 15, 1965 (80).
Chapman, Blanche, actress; b. Covington, Ky.; d. June 7, 1941 (90).
Chapman, Edward, actor; b. Oct. 13, 1901, Harrogate, England;
  d. Aug. 9, 1977 (75).
Chapman, Edythe, actress; b. Oct. 8, 1863, Rochester, N.Y.; d. Oct.
  15, 1948 (85).
Chapman, Nina, actress; d. Oct. 18, 1956 (86).
Chapman, Maj. Gen. Thomas H., flyer; d. June 7, 1969 (73).
Charbeneau, Oscar, actor; d. Sept., 1915.
Charell, Erik, director & producer; d. July 15, 1974 (80).
Charles, John, actor; d. Nov. 7, 1921 (86).
Charles, Lewis, actor; d. Nov. 9, 1979 (63).
Charleson, Mary, actress; d. Dec. 3, 1961 (71).
Charleston, Helen, dancer; d. Dec. 22, 1978.
Charlesworth, John, actor; b. England; d. Apr. 2, 1960 (25).
Charlot, Andre, actor & producer; b. July 26, 1882, Paris, France;
  d. May 20, 1956 (73).
Charon, Jacques, actor & director; d. Oct. 15, 1975 (55).
Charpin, Fernand, actor; b. June 1, 1887, Marseilles, France;
  d. Nov. 6, 1944 (57).
Charsky, Boris, actor; b. May 28, 1893, Petrograd, Russia; d. June
  1, 1956 (63).
Charters, Jimmy, actor; d. Mar. 19, 1975.
Charters, Spencer, actor; b. Mar. 25, 1875, Duncannon, Pa.; d. Jan.
  25, 1943 (67).
Chase, Borden, writer; d. Mar. 8, 1971 (71).
Chase, Charley (Charles Parrott), actor; b. Oct. 20, 1893, Baltimore,
  Md.; d. June 20, 1940 (46).
Chase, Clarence, actor; b. Dec. 7, 1900, California; d. June 5,
  1964 (63).
Chase, Colin, actor; d. Apr. 24, 1937 (51).
Chase, Ilka, actress; b. Apr. 8, 1905, New York City; d. Feb. 15,
  1978 (72).
Chasen, Dave, actor; b. July 18, 1898, Odessa, Russia; d. June 16,
  1973 (74).
Chatterton, Ruth, actress; b. Dec. 24, 1893, New York City; d. Nov.
  24, 1961 (67).
Chatterton, Thomas, actor; b. Feb. 12, 1881, Geneva, N.Y.; d. Aug.
  17, 1952 (71).
Chatterton, Vivienne, actress; d. Jan. 1, 1974.
Chatton, Syd, actor; b. May 6, 1918, England; d. Oct. 6, 1966 (48).
Chaudet, Louis William, director; d. May 10, 1965 (81).
Chauffard, Rene-Jacques, actor; d. Nov., 1972 (52).
Chautard, Emile, actor & director; b. Avignon, France; d. Apr. 24,
  1934 (69).
Chauvel, Charles, director, writer, & producer; d. Nov. 11, 1959 (62).
Chavez, Marcelo, actor; d. Feb. 14, 1970 (58).
Cheatham, Jack, actor; b. Dec. 28, 1894, Mississippi; d. Mar. 30,
  1971 (76).
Checchi, Andrea, actor; b. Oct. 21, 1916, Firenze, Italy; d. Mar. 31,
  1974 (57).
Cheeseman, Martin, actor; d. June 9, 1924 (65).
Chefe, Jack, actor; b. Apr. 1, 1894, Kiev, Russia; d. Dec. 1, 1975
  (81).

Cheirel, Jeanne, actress; b. France; d. Nov. 2, 1934 (66).
Chekhov, Michael, actor; b. Aug. 29, 1891, Russia; d. Sept. 30, 1955 (64).
Cherkassov, Nikolai, actor; b. July 27, 1903, Petersburg, Russia; d. Sept. 14, 1966 (63).
Cheron, Andre (r.n. Andre Louis Duval), actor; b. Aug. 24, 1880, France; d. Jan. 26, 1952 (71).
Cherry, Charles, actor; b. Nov. 19, 1872, Greenwich, England; d. Sept. 2, 1931 (59).
Cherryman, Rex, actor; b. California; d. Aug. 10, 1928 (30).
Chesebro, George, actor; b. July 29, 1888, Minneapolis, Minn.; d. May 28, 1959 (70).
Chesney, Arthur, actor; b. London, England; d. Aug. 27, 1949 (67).
Cheshire, Harry V. "Pappy," actor; b. Aug. 16, 1891, Kansas; d. June 16, 1968 (76).
Chester, Alma, actress; d. Jan. 22, 1953 (82).
Chester, Betty, actress; d. Jan. 11, 1943 (47).
Chester, Virginia, actress; b. Aug. 27, 1896, San Francisco, Calif.; d. July 28, 1927 (30).
Chevalier, Albert, actor; b. Mar. 21, 1861, London, England; d. July 11, 1923 (62).
Chevalier, Albert, actor; d. Nov. 11, 1959 (60).
Chevalier, Maurice, actor & singer; b. Sept. 12, 1888, Paris, France; d. Jan. 1, 1972 (83).
Childers, Naomi, actress; b. Nov. 15, 1892, Pennsylvania; d. May 8, 1964 (71).
Childs, Monroe, actor; b. Nov. 18, 1890, California; d. Nov. 7, 1963 (72).
Chirello, George (Shorty), actor; d. Feb. 9, 1963 (66).
Chisholm, Robert, actor & vocalist; b. Apr. 18, 1898, Melbourne, Australia; d. Nov. 4, 1960 (62).
Chitty, Erik, actor; d. July 22, 1977 (70).
Chivvis, Frederick W. (Chic), stuntman; b. Dec. 2, 1884, New York; d. Oct. 26, 1963 (78).
Chkheidze, Nina P., actress; b. Oct. 12, 1881; d. Aug. 15, 1963 (81).
Chmara, Gregor, actor; b. 1893, Portava; d. Feb. 3, 1970 (77).
Chola, Sebastian, actor; d. Feb. 7, 1950.
Chorre, Gertrude, actress; b. Apr. 30, 1885, California; d. Sept. 3, 1972 (87).
Christian, John (r.n. Harry Albert Pihl), actor; b. Oct. 30, 1883, Massachusetts; d. Aug. 29, 1950 (66).
Christians, Mady, actress; b. Jan. 19, 1900, Vienna, Austria; d. Oct. 28, 1951 (51).
Christians, Rudolf (r.n. Broekern Rudolph Christians), actor; b. Jan. 15, 1869, Germany; d. Feb. 2, 1921 (52).
Christiansen, Arthur, actor & newspaper editor; d. Sept. 27, 1963 (59).
Christie, Al, producer; b. London, Ont., Canada; d. Apr. 14, 1951 (69).
Christie, Charles H., producer; b. Apr. 13, 1880; d. Oct. 1, 1955 (75).
Christie, George, actor; b. Feb. 27, 1873, Philadelphia, Pa.; d. May 20, 1949 (76).
Christie, Ivan, actor; d. May 9, 1949 (61).
Christie, Kim, actress; d. Aug. 8, 1979 (20).

Christy, Bill, actor; d. Feb. 25, 1946 (21).
Christy, Floyd, actor; b. Jan. 4, 1907, New York; d. May 21, 1962 (55).
Christy, Ken, actor; b. Nov. 23, 1894, Pennsylvania; d. July 23, 1962 (67).
Church, Billy, actor; d. Dec. 26, 1942 (50).
Church, Esme, actress; b. Feb. 10, 1893; d. May 31, 1972 (79).
Churchill, Berton, actor; b. Dec. 9, 1876, Toronto, Canada; d. Oct. 10, 1940 (63).
Churchill, Frank, composer; d. May 14, 1942 (41).
Cialente, Renato, actor; b. Feb. 2, 1897, Treviglio, Italy; d. Nov. 25, 1943 (46).
Ciannelli, Eduardo, actor; b. Aug. 30, 1889, Ischia, Italy; d. Oct. 8, 1969 (80).
Cichy, Martin, actor; b. Nov. 9, 1892, New York; d. Apr. 26, 1962 (69).
Cierkes, Vincent, extra; d. Mar. 14, 1979 (73).
Cifariello, Antonio, actor; b. May 19, 1930, Naples, Italy; d. Dec. 12, 1968 (38).
Cimara, Luigi, actor; b. July 19, 1897, Rome, Italy; d. Jan. 26, 1962 (64).
Ciolli, Augusta, actress; d. Feb. 2, 1967 (65).
Cirillo, Michael, actor; b. Apr. 20, 1903, Massachusetts; d. Aug. 29, 1968 (65).
Cirillo, Tony, actor; b. Nov. 14, 1910, Massachusetts; d. Nov. 16, 1968 (58).
Clair, Denise, actress; d. Nov., 1970.
Claire, Gertrude, actress; b. July 16, 1852, Illinois; d. Apr. 28, 1928 (75).
Clarance, Arthur, actor; d. Oct. 26, 1956 (73).
Clare, Madelyn, actress; d. Sept. 20, 1975 (81).
Clare, Mary, actress; b. July 17, 1894, London, England; d. Aug. 29, 1970 (76).
Clare, Phyllis, actress; b. London, England; d. Nov. 1, 1947 (42).
Clarence, O.B., actor; b. Mar. 25, 1870, London, England; d. Oct. 2, 1955 (85).
Clarendon, Jean (r.n. Jean B. Smith), actor; b. Sept. 22, 1878, Vermont; d. Nov. 23, 1952 (74).
Clarens, Elsie, actress; d. 1917.
Clarens, Henry F., actor; d. Dec. 19, 1928 (68).
Clarges, Verner, actor; d. Aug. 11, 1911 (65).
Clariond, Aime, actor; d. Jan. 1, 1960 (65).
Clark, Andy, actor; b. Mar., 1903, New York City; d. Nov. 16, 1960 (57).
Clark, Betty Ross, actress; b. Apr. 19, 1896, Pittsburgh, Pa.; d. Jan. 31, 1947 (50).
Clark, Bobby, actor; b. June 16, 1888, Springfield, Ohio; d. Feb. 12, 1960 (71).
Clark, Buddy, singer; b. July 26, 1911, Boston, Mass.; d. Oct. 1, 1949 (38).
Clark, Charles Dow, actor; b. St. Albans, Vt.; d. Mar. 26, 1959 (89).
Clark, Cliff, actor; b. June 10, 1889, New York; d. Feb. 8, 1953 (63).
Clark, Daniel B., cinematographer; b. Apr. 28, 1890; d. Dec. 14, 1961 (71).
Clark, Davison (r.n. George Davison Clark), actor; b. Jan. 15, 1881, California; d. Nov. 4, 1972 (91).

Clark, E. Holman, actor; b. Apr. 22, 1864, East Hothley, Sussex,
    England; d. Sept. 7, 1925 (61).
Clark, Edward, actor; b. May 6, 1878, Russia; d. Nov. 18, 1954 (76).
Clark, Ethel, actress; d. Feb. 18, 1964 (48).
Clark, Frank, actor; b. Dec. 22, 1857, Cincinnati, Ohio; d. Apr. 10,
    1945 (87).
Clark, Fred, actor; b. Mar. 19, 1914, Lincoln, Calif.; d. Dec. 5,
    1968 (54).
Clark, Harry, actor; d. Feb. 28, 1956 (45).
Clark, Harvey, actor; b. Oct. 4, 1885, Chelsea, Mass.; d. July 19,
    1938 (52).
Clark, Jimmy, actor; d. Mar. 18, 1972.
Clark, John J. (Jack), actor; d. Apr. 12, 1947 (70).
Clark, Johnny, actor, singer, & composer; b. Aug. 10, 1916, Hampton,
    Iowa; d. July 3, 1967 (50).
Clark, Les, actor; d. Mar. 24, 1959 (52).
Clark, Marguerite, actress; b. Feb. 22, 1887, Cincinnati, Ohio;
    d. Sept. 25, 1940 (53).
Clark, Paul, actor; d. May 20, 1960 (33).
Clark, Rose F.L., actress; b. Sept. 4, 1882, Wisconsin; d. Jan. 27,
    1962 (79).
Clark, Steve, actor; b. Feb. 26, 1891, Indiana; d. June 29, 1954 (63).
Clark, Wallace, actor; d. Aug. 24, 1960 (63).
Clark, Wallis, actor; b. Mar. 2, 1882, Essex, England; d. Feb. 14,
    1961 (78).
Clark, Wally, actor; d. Jan. 30, 1920.
Clarke, Downing, actor; d. Aug. 17, 1930 (71).
Clarke, Frank, actor & stuntman; b. Dec. 29, 1898, Paso Robles,
    Calif.; d. June 12, 1948 (49).
Clarke, Gage, actor; b. Mar. 3, 1900, Michigan; d. Oct. 23, 1964 (64).
Clarke, George, actor; d. Dec. 21, 1946 (58).
Clarke, Gordon B., actor; d. Jan. 11, 1972 (65).
Clarke, Nigel, actor; d. July, 1976 (84).
Clarke, Redfield, actor; d. Oct. 23, 1928.
Clarke, Westcott B., actor; b. Sept. 27, 1886, Jersey City, N.J.;
    d. Jan. 26, 1959 (72).
Clarke, Wilfred, actor; b. Philadelphia, Pa.; d. Apr. 27, 1945 (77).
Clarke-Smith, D.A., actor; b. Aug. 2, 1888, Montrose, N.B., Canada;
    d. Mar. 12, 1959 (70).
Clary, Charles, actor; b. Mar. 24, 1873, Charleston, Ill.; d. Mar.
    24, 1931 (58).
Claudis, Dane, actor; d. Apr. 27, 1946 (75).
Clawson, Elliott, writer; b. Salt Lake City, Utah; d. July 21, 1942
    (51).
Clayton, Bob, actor; d. Nov. 1, 1979 (57).
Clayton, Donald, actor; b. Oct. 27, 1889, Missouri; d. Jan. 18, 1964
    (74).
Clayton, Ethel, actress; b. Nov. 8, 1883, Missouri; d. June 11, 1966
    (82).
Clayton, Gilbert, actor; b. Jan. 18, 1859, Polo, Ill.; d. Mar. 1,
    1950 (91).
Clayton, Hazel (Mrs. Mack Hilliard), actress; d. Mar. 8, 1963 (77).
Clayton, Lou, actor; b. New York City; d. Sept. 12, 1950 (63).
Clayton, Marguerite, actress; b. Apr. 12, 1891, Ogden, Utah; d. Dec.
    20, 1968 (77).

International Film Necrology                                    57

Cleary, Leo, actor; b. June 15, 1894, Massachusetts; d. Apr. 11,
    1955 (60).
Cleary, Peggy, actress; b. Dec. 29, 1892, Michigan; d. Jan. 10,
    1972 (79).
Clegg, Valce V., actor; b. Feb. 27, 1888, Minnesota; d. July 29,
    1947 (59).
Clemens, Charles D., actor; d. Aug. 30, 1947 (73).
Clement, Andree, actress; b. Aug. 17, 1918; d. June 1, 1954 (35).
Clement, Clay, actor; b. May 19, 1888, Greentree, Ky.; d. Oct. 20,
    1956 (68).
Clement, Donald, actor; d. July 28, 1970 (29).
Clemento, Steve, actor; b. Nov. 22, 1885, Mexico; d. May 7, 1950 (64).
Clements, Dudley, actor; b. New York City; d. Nov. 4, 1947 (58).
Clements, Roy S., director & actor; b. Jan. 12, 1877, Sterling, Ill.;
    d. July 15, 1948 (71).
Clemons, James, actor; b. Jan. 14, 1883, Pennsylvania; d. June 5,
    1950 (67).
Clerget, Paul, actor; d. Dec. 4, 1935 (68).
Clermonto, Etta Miner, actress; d. Apr. 12, 1929 (48).
Cleveland, George, actor; b. Sept. 17, 1885, Sydney, Nova Scotia,
    Canada; d. July 15, 1957 (71).
Cliff, Laddie, actor; b. Sept. 3, 1891, Bristol, England; d. Dec. 8,
    1937 (46).
Cliffe, H. Cooper, actor; b. July 19, 1862; d. May 1, 1939 (76).
Clifford, Jack, actor; d. Nov. 10, 1956 (76).
Clifford, Jefferson, actor; d. Apr. 20, 1959 (66).
Clifford, Kathleen, actress; b. Feb. 14, 1894, England; d. Jan. 11,
    1963 (68).
Clifford, William, actor; b. June 27, 1877, Cincinnati, Ohio; d.
    Dec. 23, 1941 (64).
Clifford, William H., author; d. Oct. 9, 1938 (64).
Clift, Denison, director & author; d. Dec. 17, 1961 (76).
Clift, Montgomery, actor; b. Oct. 17, 1920, Omaha, Neb.; d. July 23,
    1966 (45).
Clifton, Bobby, actor; d. Feb. 5, 1924 (38).
Clifton, Elmer, actor & director; b. Mar. 14, 1890, Chicago, Ill.;
    d. Oct. 15, 1949 (59).
Clifton, Emma, actress & author; b. Nov. 1, 1874, Pennsylvania;
    d. Aug. 3, 1922 (47).
Clifton, Herbert, actor; b. Oct. 19, 1885, London, England; d. Sept.
    26, 1947 (61).
Clifton, Ray D., director & writer; d. Apr. 25, 1940 (62).
Cline, Eddie, director & actor; b. Nov. 7, 1892, Kenosha, Wisc.;
    d. May 22, 1961 (68).
Cline, Robert, cinematographer; d. Nov. 30, 1946 (50).
Clive, Colin, actor; b. Jan. 20, 1900, St. Malo, France; d. June 25,
    1937 (37).
Clive, E.E., actor; b. Aug. 28, 1883, Monmouthshire, Wales; d. June
    6, 1940 (56).
Clive, Henry, actor; b. Oct. 3, 1881, Melbourne, Australia; d. Dec.
    12, 1960 (79).
Clive, Vincent, actor; d. Apr. 11, 1943.
Cloninger, Ralph, actor; b. Apr. 20, 1888, Texas; d. June 17, 1962
    (74).
Close, Ivy, actress; d. Dec. 4, 1968 (78).

Cloud, Mabel, actress; d. June, 1921.
Clouzot, Henri-Georges, director; b. Nov. 20, 1907, Niort, France;
    d. Jan. 12, 1977 (69).
Clouzot, Vera, actress; d. Dec. 15, 1960.
Clovelly, Cecil, actor; d. Apr. 25, 1965 (74).
Clugston, H.N. (r.n. Howard Newkirk Clugston), actor; b. Oct. 18,
    1881, Scotland; d. Apr. 5, 1944 (62).
Clunes, Alec, actor; b. May 17, 1912, London, England; d. Mar. 13,
    1970 (57).
Clute, Chester, actor; b. Feb. 18, 1891, New Jersey; d. Apr. 2,
    1956 (65).
Clyde, Andy, actor; b. Mar. 25, 1892, Blairgowrie, Scotland;
    d. May 18, 1967 (75).
Clyde, David, actor; b. May 27, 1887. Blairgowrie, Scotland;
    d. May 16, 1945 (57).
Clymer, Beth, actress; d. Jan. 14, 1952 (65).
Clymer, John, writer; d. May 24, 1937 (50).
Coates, Albert, symphony orchestra conductor; d. Dec. 11, 1953
    (71).
Coats, Tommy, actor; d. June 6, 1954 (53).
Cobb, Edmund, actor; b. June 23, 1892, Albuquerque, N.M.; d. Aug. 15,
    1974 (82).
Cobb, Irvin S., actor & author; b. June 23, 1876, Paducah, Ky.;
    d. Mar. 11, 1944 (67).
Cobb, Lee J., actor; b. Dec. 8, 1911, New York City; d. Feb. 11,
    1976 (64).
Cobo, Alejandro, actor; d. 1951.
Coborn, Charles, actor; d. Nov. 22, 1945 (93).
Coburn, Charles, actor; b. June 19, 1877, Macon, Ga.; d. Aug. 30,
    1961 (84).
Coby, Fred (r.n. Frederick G. Beckner, Jr.), actor; b. Mar. 1, 1916,
    California; d. Sept. 27, 1970 (54).
Cochran, Steve, actor; b. May 25, 1917, Eureka, Calif.; d. June 15,
    1965 (48).
Cochrane, Frank, actor; b. Oct. 28, 1882, Durham, England; d. May 21,
    1962 (79).
Cocteau, Jean, director; b. July 5, 1889, Maisons-Laffitte, France;
    d. Oct. 11, 1963 (74).
Code, Grant Hyde, actor; b. Mar. 2, 1896, LaCrosse, Wisc.; d. June
    28, 1974 (78).
Codee, Ann, actress; b. Mar. 5, 1890, Belgium; d. May 18, 1961 (71).
Cody, Bill (r.n. William F. Cody), actor; b. Jan. 5, 1891, St. Paul,
    Minn.; d. Jan. 24, 1948 (57).
Cody, Harry, actor; b. May 10, 1896, Lebanon, Tenn.; d. Oct. 22,
    1956 (60).
Cody, Lew, actor; b. Feb. 22, 1888, Waterville, Me.; d. May 31,
    1934 (47).
Coedel, Lucien, actor; b. 1899, Paris, France; d. Sept. 28, 1947 (48).
Coffer, Jack, stuntman; b. Apr. 1, 1938, California; d. Feb. 18,
    1967 (28).
Coffey, John, actor; b. June 17, 1909, Hoisington, Kans.; d. Mar. 25,
    1944 (34).
Coffin, C. Hayden, actor; b. Apr. 22, 1862, Manchester, England;
    d. Dec. 8, 1935 (73).
Coffin, Hank, stunt pilot; d. Sept. 17, 1966 (62).

Cogan, Fanny Hay, actress; b. Philadelphia, Pa.; d. May 17, 1929 (63).
Cogdell, Josephine, actress; d. May 2, 1969 (68).
Coghlan, Charles F., actor; d. Mar. 18, 1972.
Coghlan, Gertrude, actress; b. Feb. 1, 1876, Hertfordshire, England; d. Sept. 11, 1952 (76).
Coghlan, Katherine, actress; b. Sept. 3, 1889, Connecticut; d. Sept. 20, 1965 (76).
Coghlan, Rose, actress; b. Mar. 18, 1851, Peterborough, England; d. Apr. 2, 1932 (81).
Cogley, Nick, actor; d. May 20, 1936 (67).
Cohan, George M., actor, singer, dancer, producer, & author; b. July 3, 1878, Providence, R.I.; d. Nov. 5, 1942 (64).
Cohen, Octavus Roy, writer; d. Jan. 6, 1959 (67).
Cohn, Alfred A., writer; b. Freeport, Ill.; d. Feb. 3, 1951 (71).
Cohn, Harry, producer & executive; b. July 23, 1891, New York City; d. Feb. 27, 1958 (66).
Cohn, Jack, producer & executive; b. New York City; d. Dec. 8, 1957 (67).
Coit, Sam, actor; d. Jan. 1, 1933 (60).
Coke, Richard, actor; d. Oct. 13, 1955 (63).
Colbourne, Maurice, actor; b. Sept. 24, 1894, Cuddington, England; d. Sept. 22, 1965 (70).
Colburn, Carrie, actress; d. May 23, 1932 (73).
Colby, Barbara, actress; d. July 24, 1975 (36).
Colcord, Mabel, actress; b. San Francisco, Calif.; d. June 6, 1952 (80).
Cole, Fred, actor; b. May 21, 1901, California; d. Sept. 19, 1964 (63).
Cole, Jack, dancer & choreographer; d. Feb. 17, 1974 (60).
Cole, Lester, actor & singer; d. May 4, 1962 (62).
Cole, Nat (King), actor, singer, & recording artist; b. Mar. 17, 1919, Alabama; d. Feb. 15, 1965 (45).
Colean, Chuck, stuntman & assistant director; d. Jan. 8, 1971 (63).
Colee, Forest Ralph, actor; b. Dec. 2, 1909, Colorado; d. Feb. 10, 1962 (52).
Coleman, Charles, actor; b. Dec. 22, 1885, Sydney, Australia; d. Mar. 7, 1951 (65).
Coleman, Claudia, actress; b. July 7, 1886, Hyram, Ga.; d. Aug. 18, 1938 (52).
Coleman, Emil, bandleader; b. Russia; d. Jan. 26, 1965 (71).
Coleman, Warren, actor & director; d. Jan. 13, 1968 (67).
Coleridge, Ethel, actress; b. Jan. 14, 1883, South Moulton, England; d. Aug. 15, 1976 (93).
Coles, Russell, actor; b. May 14, 1909, Tennessee; d. Sept. 23, 1960 (51).
Colin, Georges (Georges Randax; Gustave Colin), actor; d. Jan. 30, 1979 (81).
Colin, Julia, actress; d. Apr. 10, 1975 (73).
Coll, Owen Griffith, actor; d. Feb. 7, 1960 (81).
Colleano, Bonar, actor; b. Mar. 14, 1923, New York City; d. Aug. 17, 1958 (35).
Collier, Constance, actress; b. Jan. 22, 1878, Windsor, England; d. Apr. 25, 1955 (77).
Collier, Sherlee, actress; d. Feb. 19, 1972.
Collier, William, Sr., actor; b. Nov. 12, 1866, New York City; d. Jan. 13, 1944 (77).

Collinge, Patricia, actress; b. Sept. 20, 1892, Dublin, Ireland;
    d. Apr. 10, 1974 (81).
Collings, Pierre, writer; d. Dec. 21, 1937 (35).
Collins, C.E., actor; b. July 23, 1873, Missouri; d. Apr. 15, 1951
    (77).
Collins, Eddie, actor; b. Jan. 30, 1883, Jersey City, N.J.; d. Sept.
    1, 1940 (57).
Collins, G. Pat (r.n. George Percy Collins), actor; b. Dec. 16, 1895,
    New York; d. Aug. 5, 1959 (63).
Collins, Jose, actress; b. May 23, 1887, London, England; d. Dec. 6,
    1958 (71).
Collins, Lewis D., director & writer; b. Jan. 12, 1899, Baltimore,
    Md.; d. Aug. 24, 1954 (55).
Collins, May, actress; d. May 6, 1955 (49).
Collins, Monte, Jr., actor; d. Aug. 4, 1929 (73).
Collins, Monte, actor; b. Dec. 3, 1898, New York City; d. June 1,
    1951 (52).
Collins, Ray, actor; b. Dec. 10, 1889, Sacramento, Calif.; d. July
    11, 1965 (75).
Collins, Richard (Dick), actor; d. June 19, 1939 (78).
Collins, Russell, actor; b. Oct. 11, 1897, Indiana; d. Nov. 13, 1965
    (68).
Collo, Alberto, actor; b. July 6, 1883, Torino, Italy; d. May 7,
    1955 (71).
Collum, John, actor; b. June 29, 1926, Illinois; d. Aug. 28, 1962
    (36).
Collyer, June, actress; b. Aug. 19, 1906; d. Mar. 16, 1968 (61).
Colman, Ronald, actor; b. Feb. 9, 1891, Richmond, Surrey, England;
    d. May 19, 1958 (67).
Colmans, Edward, actor; b. Aug. 31, 1908, England; d. May 25, 1977
    (68).
Colson, Kate, actress; d. Sept. 6, 1944 (83).
Colton, John, writer; d. Dec. 28, 1946 (60).
Columbo, Russ, actor & singer; b. Jan. 14, 1908, Philadelphia, Pa.;
    d. Sept. 2, 1934 (26).
Colvig, Vance "Pinto," actor & voice for "Pluto" and "Goofy";
    b. Sept. 11, 1892, Oregon; d. Oct. 3, 1967 (75).
Colvin, William, actor; b. July 20, 1877, Ireland; d. Aug. 8, 1930
    (53).
Coman, Morgan, actor; d. Mar., 1947.
Comanche, Laurence "Tex," actor; d. Oct. 10, 1932 (24).
Comber, Bobbie, actor; b. Jan. 8, 1886, Bury St. Edmunds, England;
    d. Mar. 2, 1942 (56).
Comfort, Lance, director; b. London, England; d. Aug. 25, 1966 (58).
Comingore, Dorothy (Linda Winters), actress; b. Aug. 24, 1913, Los
    Angeles, Calif.; d. Dec. 30, 1971 (58).
Commerford, Thomas, actor; d. Feb. 17, 1920 (64).
Comont, Mathilde, actress; b. Sept. 9, 1886, Bordeaux, France;
    d. June 21, 1938 (51).
Compson, Betty, actress; b. Mar. 19, 1897, Beaver, Utah; d. Apr. 18,
    1974 (77).
Compson, John, actor; d. Mar. 15, 1913 (45).
Compton, Fay, actress; b. Sept. 18, 1894, London, England; d. Dec.
    12, 1978 (84).
Compton, Francis, actor; b. May 4, 1885, Malvern, England; d. Sept.
    17, 1964 (79).

Compton, Viola, actress; b. 1886, London, England; d. Apr. 7, 1971 (85).

Comstock, Clark, actor; b. Jan. 7, 1862, Yukatan, Minn.; d. May 24, 1934 (72).

Conde, Johnny, actor; b. Aug. 11, 1895, California; d. Dec. 3, 1960 (65).

Condon, Jackie (r.n. John Michael Condon), actor (Our Gang); b. Mar. 24, 1918, California; d. Oct. 13, 1977 (59).

Cone, Mike (Zets), actor; d. Jan. 4, 1969 (59).

Conibear, Elizabeth Jenkins, actress; d. Jan. 18, 1965 (86).

Conklin, Chester, actor; b. Jan. 11, 1886, Oskaloosa, Iowa; d. Oct. 11, 1971 (85).

Conklin, Frances, actress; d. June 28, 1935 (41).

Conklin, Frank, actor; b. Apr. 15, 1886, Atchison, Kans.; d. June 6, 1945 (59).

Conklin, Frederick Meade, actor; d. Jan. 22, 1929 (55).

Conklin, Heinie (r.n. Charles John Conklin), actor; b. July 16, 1880, San Francisco, Calif.; d. July 30, 1959 (79).

Conklin, William, actor; b. Dec. 25, 1872, Brooklyn, N.Y.; d. Mar. 21, 1935 (62).

Conlan, Frank, actor; d. Aug. 24, 1955 (81).

Conley, Harry J., actor; d. June 23, 1975 (90).

Conley, Lige (Lige Crommie) (r.n. Elijah A. Crommie), actor; b. Dec. 5, 1899, Los Angeles, Calif.; d. Dec. 11, 1937 (38).

Conley, William (Bing), actor & boxer; b. Aug. 16, 1901, Maine; d. July 23, 1962 (60).

Conlin, Jimmy, actor; b. Oct. 14, 1884, Camden, N.J.; d. May 7, 1962 (77).

Connell, Richard, writer; b. Oct. 17, 1893, Poughkeepsie, N.Y.; d. Nov. 22, 1949 (56).

Connelly, Bobby, actor; d. July 5, 1922 (13).

Connelly, Edward, actor; b. Dec. 30, 1859, New York City; d. Nov. 20, 1928 (68).

Connelly, Erwin, actor; b. May, 1879, Chicago, Ill.; d. Feb. 12, 1931 (51).

Connelly, Jane, actress; b. May 2, 1883, Port Huron, Mich.; d. Oct. 25, 1925 (42).

Conners, Barry, actor & author; b. May 31, 1883, Oil City, Pa.; d. Jan. 5, 1933 (49).

Conness, Robert, actor; b. La Salle Co., Ill.; d. Jan. 15, 1941 (73).

Connolly, Myles, writer; b. Oct. 7, 1897, Boston, Mass.; d. July 15, 1964 (66).

Connolly, Walter, actor; b. Apr. 8, 1887, Cincinnati, Ohio; d. May 28, 1940 (53).

Connor, Edric, actor; b. Trinidad; d. Oct. 16, 1968 (54).

Connor, Zack (r.n. Jack O'Connor), extra; b. Athens, Tex.; d. Mar. 25, 1939 (48).

Conrad, Eddie, actor; b. New York City; d. Apr. 27, 1941 (50).

Conrad, Eugene J., writer; b. New York City; d. Jan. 28, 1964 (69).

Conroy, Frank, actor; b. Oct. 14, 1890, Derby, England; d. Feb. 24, 1964 (73).

Conroy, Susan, actress; d. Apr. 15, 1968 (61).

Conroy, Thom, actor; b. Feb. 12, 1911, Rhode Island; d. Nov. 16, 1971 (60).

Conselman, William, writer; b. July 10, 1896, Brooklyn, N.Y.; d. May 25, 1940 (43).

Constanduros, Mabel, actress; d. Feb. 8, 1957 (77).
Constant, Max, actor; d. May, 1943.
Conte, Richard (r.n. Richard Nicholas Peter Conte), actor; b. Mar.
24, 1910, New Jersey; d. Apr. 15, 1975 (65).
Conti, Albert, actor; b. Jan. 29, 1887, Trieste, Austria; d. Jan. 18,
1967 (79).
Conti, Patricia, actress; d. Aug. 3, 1929 (24).
Contreras, Mariano "Pugo," actor; d. Jan., 1979 (68).
Contreras, Miguel, actor; d. Dec. 30, 1956 (52).
Conway, Curt, actor; b. May 4, 1915, Boston, Mass.; d. Apr. 11,
1974 (58).
Conway, Jack, director & actor; b. July 17, 1887, Graceville, Minn.;
d. Oct. 11, 1952 (65).
Conway, Lizzie, actress; d. May 4, 1916.
Conway, Tom, actor; b. Sept. 15, 1904, St. Petersburg, Russia; d. Apr.
22, 1967 (62).
Conway, William, actor; d. Oct. 13, 1924 (48).
Coogan, Gene B., actor & stuntman; d. Jan. 26, 1972.
Coogan, Robert, actor; d. May 12, 1978 (54).
Cook, Al, actor; d. July 6, 1935 (53).
Cook, Donald, actor; b. Sept. 26, 1901, Portland, Ore.; d. Oct. 1,
1961 (60).
Cook, Joe, actor; b. Evansville, Ind.; d. May 15, 1959 (69).
Cook, Ken, actor; b. Aug. 17, 1914, New Jersey; d. Dec. 28, 1963
(49).
Cook, Lester M., actor; d. Apr. 23, 1953 (63).
Cook, Lillian, actress; d. Mar. 14, 1918 (19).
Cook, Lucius, actor; b. July 23, 1891, New York; d. Jan. 2, 1952 (60).
Cook, Warren, actor; d. May 2, 1939 (60).
Cooke, Baldwin G., actor; d. Dec. 31, 1953 (65).
Cooke, John J., actor; b. Oct. 1, 1876, New York; d. Oct. 2, 1921
(45).
Cooke, Stanley, actor; d. Jan. 6, 1931 (62).
Cooke, Stephen Beach, actor; d. Sept. 16, 1948 (50).
Cooksey, Curtis, actor; b. Dec. 9, 1891, Indiana; d. Apr. 19, 1962
(70).
Cookson, S.A., actor; d. Feb. 27, 1947 (78).
Cooley, Charles, actor; b. Mar. 29, 1902, Italy; d. Nov. 15, 1960
(58).
Cooley, Frank, actor; b. Natchez, Miss.; d. July 6, 1941 (71).
Cooley, Hallam, actor; b. Feb. 8, 1895, Brooklyn, N.Y.; d. Mar. 20,
1971 (76).
Cooley, James, actor; d. Nov. 5, 1948 (68).
Cooley, Spade (r.n. Donnell Cooley), singer; d. Nov. 23, 1969 (59).
Coolidge, Philip, actor; b. Aug. 25, 1908, Concord, Mass.; d. May
23, 1967 (58).
Coombe, Carol, actress; b. 1911, Sydney, Australia; d. Oct. 4, 1966 (55).
Coon, Gene L., writer & producer; d. July 8, 1973 (49).
Coontz, Willard, actor; d. Apr. 7, 1978 (62).
Coop, Franco, actor; b. Sept. 27, 1891, Naples, Italy; d. Mar. 27,
1962 (70).
Cooper, Ashley, actor; b. Sydney, Australia; d. Jan. 3, 1952 (70).
Cooper, Clancy, actor; b. July 23, 1906, Idaho; d. June 14, 1975 (68).
Cooper, Claude, actor; d. July 20, 1932 (51).
Cooper, Edward, actor; d. Jan. 13, 1945 (40).
Cooper, Edward, actor; d. July, 1956 (73).

Cooper, Edwin (Bozo the Clown), actor & clown; d. Aug. 14, 1961 (41).
Cooper, Frederick, actor; b. London, England; d. Jan., 1945 (55).
Cooper, Gary, actor; b. May 7, 1901, Helena, Mont.; d. May 13, 1961 (60).
Cooper, George, actor; d. Dec. 9, 1943 (51).
Cooper, Georgie (Georgie Cooper Stevens), actress; b. July 31, 1882, Michigan; d. Sept. 3, 1968 (86).
Cooper, Gladys, actress; b. Dec. 18, 1888, Lewisham, England; d. Nov. 17, 1971 (82).
Cooper, Harry, stuntman; d. Aug. 28, 1957 (75).
Cooper, Isabel Rosario, actress; d. June 29, 1960.
Cooper, Lillian Kemble, actress; b. Mar. 21, 1898, England; d. May 4, 1977 (79).
Cooper, Melville, actor; b. Oct. 15, 1896, Birmingham, England; d. Mar. 29, 1973 (76).
Cooper, Merian C., director & producer; b. Oct. 24, 1894, Jacksonville, Fla.; d. Apr. 21, 1973 (78).
Cooper, Olive, actress; d. June 15, 1950 (58).
Cooper, Richard, actor; b. July 16, 1893, Harrow-on-the-Hill, England; d. June 18, 1947 (53).
Cooper, Tex (r.n. Judge Thomas Cooper), actor; b. Apr. 21, 1876, Texas; d. Mar. 29, 1951 (74).
Cooper, Violet Kemble, actress; b. London, England; d. Aug. 17, 1961 (75).
Cooper, Wyllis, writer & director; d. June 22, 1955 (56).
Coote, Bert, actor; b. London, England; d. Sept. 1, 1938 (70).
Copeau, Jacques, actor & writer; d. Oct. 20, 1949 (70).
Copeland, Nick, actor; b. Oct. 14, 1894, Omaha, Neb.; d. Aug. 17, 1940 (45).
Coppen, Hazel, actress; d. Apr. 8, 1975 (50).
Corbaley, Kate, writer; d. Sept. 23, 1938 (60).
Corbett, Ben, actor; b. Feb. 6, 1892, Ohio; d. May 19, 1961 (69).
Corbett, James J., actor & prizefighter; b. Sept. 1, 1866, San Francisco, Calif.; d. Feb. 18, 1933 (66).
Corbett, Jean, actress; d. Feb. 22, 1978 (66).
Corbett, Leonora, actress; b. June 28, 1908, London, England; d. July 29, 1960 (52).
Corbett, Mary, actress; d. Apr. 28, 1974 (48).
Corbin, Virginia Lee, actress; b. Dec. 5, 1910, Prescott, Ariz.; d. June 4, 1942 (31).
Corday, Ben, actor; d. Feb. 20, 1938 (63).
Cordell, Frank, actor; b. Feb. 3, 1898, Oklahoma; d. Oct. 25, 1977 (79).
Corder, Leeta, actress; d. Aug. 10, 1956 (66).
Cording, Harry, actor; b. Apr. 26, 1891, England; d. Sept. 1, 1954 (63).
Cordner, Blaine, actor; b. Aug. 21, 1901, Jacksonville, Fla.; d. Mar. 29, 1971 (69).
Cordy, Henry, singer; d. Nov. 27, 1965 (57).
Cordy, Raymond, actor; b. Dec. 9, 1898, Vitry-sur-Seine, France; d. Apr., 1956 (57).
Corey, Arthur H., actor; d. Mar. 26, 1950 (61).
Corey, Joseph, actor; d. Aug. 30, 1972 (45).
Corey, Milton, actor; d. Oct. 23, 1951 (72).
Corey, Wendell, actor; b. Mar. 20, 1914, Dracut, Mass.; d. Nov. 8, 1968 (54).

Corley, Robert A., actor; d. Nov. 18, 1971.
Cormack, Bartlett, author; d. Sept. 16, 1942 (44).
Cornelius, Henry, director & producer; b. Aug. 18, 1913, South
    Africa; d. May 2, 1958 (44).
Cornell, Katharine, actress; b. Feb. 16, 1893, Berlin, Germany;
    d. June 9, 1974 (81).
Corner, James, actor; d. Dec. 2, 1944 (25).
Corner, Sally, actress; d. Mar. 5, 1959 (65).
Correll, Charles ("Andy"), actor; b. Feb. 2, 1890, Peoria, Ill.;
    d. Sept. 26, 1972 (82).
Corrigan, Charles, actor; d. Apr. 4, 1966 (72).
Corrigan, D'Arcy, actor; b. Jan. 2, 1870, County Cork, Ireland; d.
    Dec. 25, 1945 (75).
Corrigan, Emmett, actor; b. June 5, 1868, Holland; d. Oct. 29, 1932
    (64).
Corrigan, James, actor; b. Oct. 17, 1867, Ohio; d. Feb. 28, 1929 (61).
Corrigan, Lloyd, actor & director; b. Oct. 16, 1900, San Francisco,
    Calif.; d. Nov. 5, 1969 (69).
Corrigan, Ray (Crash) (Raymond Benard), actor; b. Feb. 14, 1902,
    Milwaukee, Wisc.; d. Aug. 10, 1976 (74).
Cortazar, Ernesto, actor, composer, author, & producer; d. Nov. 30,
    1953.
Cortes, Armand, actor; b. Aug. 16, 1880, France; d. Nov. 19, 1948
    (68).
Cortez, Leon, actor; b. England; d. Dec. 31, 1970 (72).
Cortez, Ricardo, actor; b. Sept. 19, 1899, Brooklyn, N.Y.; d. Apr.
    28, 1977 (77).
Corthell, Herbert, actor; b. Jan. 20, 1878, Boston, Mass.; d. Jan.
    23, 1947 (69).
Cory, Robert, actor; d. Nov. 9, 1955 (72).
Cory, Victor (George Mario Bruce; George Kilbi), actor; b. Mar. 18,
    1902, Italy; d. Dec. 16, 1964 (62).
Cosgrave, Jack, actor; b. Sept. 29, 1875, Pennsylvania; d. Jan. 27,
    1925 (49).
Cosgrave, Luke, actor; b. Aug. 6, 1862, Ballaghdreen, Ireland; d.
    June 28, 1949 (86).
Cosgrove, Charles, extra; b. Nov. 17, 1865, Delaware, Iowa; d. Dec.
    12, 1943 (78).
Cosgrove, Robert, actor; d. Sept. 18, 1960 (59).
Cosmo, Tom, actor; d. Oct. 16, 1978 (63).
Coss, Joaquin, actor; d. Feb. 24, 1948.
Cossaeus, Sophie, actress; b. Wiesbaden, Germany; d. Sept. 23, 1965
    (72).
Cossar, John Hay, actor; b. Jan. 2, 1858, London, England; d. Apr.
    28, 1935 (77).
Cossart, Ernest, actor; b. Sept. 24, 1876, Cheltenham, England;
    d. Jan. 21, 1951 (74).
Cossy, Hans, actor; b. Oct. 4, 1911, Koln, Germany; d. July 31, 1972
    (60).
Costa, Sebastiano, actor; d. July 18, 1935 (59).
Coste, Maurice R., actor; d. Mar. 22, 1963 (88).
Costello, Delmar, actor; b. Oct. 1, 1905; d. May 15, 1961 (55).
Costello, Dolores, actress; b. Sept. 17, 1905, Pittsburgh, Pa.;
    d. Mar. 1, 1979 (73).
Costello, Don, actor; b. Sept. 5, 1901, Louisiana; d. Oct. 25, 1945
    (44).

Costello, Helene, actress; b. June 21, 1903, New York City; d. Jan. 26, 1957 (53).
Costello, John, actor; d. Jan. 29, 1946 (67).
Costello, Lou, actor; b. Mar. 6, 1906, Paterson, N.J.; d. Mar. 3, 1959 (52).
Costello, Mae, actress; d. Aug. 2, 1929.
Costello, Maurice, actor; b. Feb. 22, 1877, Pennsylvania; d. Oct. 29, 1950 (73).
Costello, Tom, actor; d. Nov. 8, 1943 (80).
Costello, William A., actor (voice of "Popeye"); d. Oct. 9, 1971 (73).
Coster, Naum, singer; d. Sept. 10, 1957 (69).
Cotsworth, Staats, actor; b. Feb. 17, 1908, Oak Park, Ill.; d. Apr. 9, 1979 (71).
Cotter, Louise, actress; d. July 11, 1930 (46).
Cotton, Lucy, actress; d. Dec. 12, 1948 (57).
Cotton, Richardson, actor; d. Sept. 24, 1916.
Cotts, Campbell, actor; d. Feb. 19, 1964 (61).
Coughlin, Kevin, actor; d. Jan. 19, 1976 (30).
Coulson, Roy, actor; b. Sept. 13, 1890, Streator, Ill.; d. May 10, 1944 (53).
Coulter, Frazer, actor; b. Aug. 20, 1848, Smith Falls, Ont., Canada; d. Jan. 26, 1937 (88).
Court, Alfred C., actor; d. Dec. 31, 1953 (67).
Courtenay, William, actor; b. June 19, 1875, Worcester, Mass.; d. Apr. 20, 1933 (57).
Courtleigh, Stephen, actor; b. Jan. 15, 1913, New York; d. Dec. 15, 1967 (54).
Courtleigh, William, actor; b. June 28, 1867, Guelph, Ont., Canada; d. Dec. 27, 1930 (63).
Courtleigh, William, Jr., actor; d. Mar. 13, 1918 (26).
Courtney, Inez, actress; b. Mar. 12, 1908, New York City; d. Apr. 5, 1975 (67).
Courtney, Oscar Willis, actor; d. June 18, 1962 (85).
Courtright, Clyde C., actor & stand-in; b. Dec. 1, 1889, California; d. Oct. 2, 1967 (82).
Courtright, William (r.n. Theodore Courtright), actor; b. Feb. 10, 1848, New Milford, Ill.; d. Mar. 6, 1933 (85).
Coventry, Florence, actress; d. Nov. 22, 1939 (65).
Covert, Earl L., actor; b. Aug. 10, 1909, California; d. Mar. 8, 1975 (65).
Covington, Z. Wall, actor & author; b. Jan. 21, 1876, Bon Terre, Mo.; d. Sept. 25, 1941 (65).
Cowan, Jerome, actor; b. Oct. 6, 1897, New York City; d. Jan. 24, 1972 (74).
Cowan, Sada, writer; d. July 31, 1943 (60).
Coward, Noel, actor, author, & director; b. Dec. 16, 1899, Teddington, England; d. Mar. 26, 1973 (73).
Cowl, George, actor; b. Feb. 24, 1878, Blackpool, England; d. Apr. 4, 1942 (64).
Cowl, Jane, actress; b. Dec. 14, 1884, Boston, Mass.; d. June 22, 1950 (65).
Cowles, Jules, actor; b. Oct. 7, 1877, Farmington, Conn.; d. May 22, 1943 (65).
Cowper, William C., actor; d. June 13, 1918 (65).

Cox, Morgan, writer; d. Oct. 23, 1968 (68).
Cox, Robert, actor; d. Sept. 8, 1974 (79).
Cox, Wally, actor; b. Dec. 6, 1924, Minnesota; d. Feb. 15, 1973 (48).
Coxen, Ed (r.n. Albert Edward Coxen), actor; b. Aug. 8, 1884,
    England; d. Nov. 21, 1954 (70).
Coy, Johnny, actor & dancer; d. Nov. 4, 1973 (52).
Coy, Walter, actor; b. Jan. 31, 1909, Montana; d. Dec. 11, 1974 (65).
Coyan, Betty, actress; d. Feb. 10, 1935 (34).
Coyle, Walter V., actor; d. Aug. 3, 1948 (60).
Coyne, Jeanne, actress; b. Feb. 28, 1923, Pennsylvania; d. May 10,
    1973 (50).
Cozens, Peter, actor; b. 1907, London, England; d. Mar. 19, 1968 (60).
Craddock, Claudia, actress; b. Feb. 16, 1889, Warsaw, Ind.; d. Dec.
    15, 1945 (56).
Craft, William James, director; d. June 30, 1931 (41).
Crafts, Griffin, actor; d. Aug. 7, 1973 (73).
Craig, Alec, actor; b. Mar. 30, 1885, Dunfermline, Scotland; d.
    June 25, 1945 (60).
Craig, Blanche, actress; b. Jan. 6, 1866, Cutler, Me.; d. Sept. 23,
    1940 (74).
Craig, Carolyn, actress; b. Oct. 27, 19--, Long Island, N.Y.;
    d. Dec. 11, 1970.
Craig, Edith, actress; b. Dec. 9, 1869, England; d. Mar. 27, 1947
    (77).
Craig, Edith, actress; d. Mar. 2, 1979 (71).
Craig, Frances B., actress; b. Oct. 10, 1866, Oregon; d. July 21,
    1925 (58).
Craig, Godfrey, actor; b. Jan. 20, 1915, Copper Cliff, Ont., Canada;
    d. May 26, 1941 (26).
Craig, May, actress; d. Feb. 8, 1972 (83).
Craig, Nell, actress; b. June 13, 1891, New Jersey; d. Jan. 5, 1965
    (73).
Craig, Richy, Jr., actor; d. Nov. 28, 1933 (31).
Crain, Ethel Gordon, actress; b. 1877, Illinois; d. Oct. 13, 1930
    (53).
Crain, Roy W., actor; d. Apr. 10, 1947 (40).
Cramer, Edd, actor; d. Dec. 21, 1963 (39).
Cramer, Howard B., stuntman; d. Feb. 28, 1956 (46).
Cramer, Richard, actor; b. July 3, 1890, Bryan, Ohio; d. Aug. 9,
    1960 (70).
Cramer, Susanne, actress; d. Jan. 7, 1969 (31).
Crampton, Howard, actor; b. Dec. 12, 1865, New York; d. June 15,
    1922 (56).
Crandall, Edward, actor; d. May 9, 1968 (64).
Crane, Bob, actor; b. July 13, 1928, Waterbury, Conn.; d. June 29,
    1978 (49).
Crane, Dixie, actress; d. Nov. 18, 1936 (48).
Crane, Frank H., actor; b. 1873, San Francisco, Calif.; d. Aug. 31,
    1948 (75).
Crane, Mrs. Gardner (Madge Crane) (r.n. Margaret T. Crane), actress;
    b. Feb. 19, 1875, Missouri; d. Mar. 7, 1963 (88).
Crane, James L., actor; b. Aug. 9, 1889, Rantolul, Ill.; d. June 3,
    1968 (78).
Crane, Madge (see Crane, Mrs. Gardner)
Crane, Mae, actress; d. Apr. 15, 1969 (44).

Crane, Norma, actress; b. Nov. 10, 1928, New York; d. Sept. 28, 1973 (44).
Crane, Richard, actor; b. June 6, 1918, Newcastle, Ind.; d. Mar. 9, 1969 (50).
Crane, Ward, actor; d. July 21, 1928 (37).
Crane, William H., actor; b. Apr. 30, 1845, Leicester, Mass.; d. Mar. 7, 1928 (82).
Crane, William H., actor; d. Jan. 22, 1957 (65).
Cravat, Noel, actor; b. Dec. 11, 1909, Pennsylvania; d. Feb. 20, 1960 (50).
Craven, Frank, actor; b. Boston, Mass.; d. Sept. 1, 1945 (65).
Crawford, Anne, actress; b. Nov. 22, 1920, Haifa, Palestine; d. Oct. 17, 1956 (35).
Crawford, Bessie, actress; d. Nov. 11, 1943 (61).
Crawford, Joan, actress; b. Mar. 23, 1908, San Antonio, Tex.; d. May 10, 1977 (69).
Crawford, Lester, actor; b. Dec. 25, 1882, Massachusetts; d. Nov. 24, 1962 (79).
Crawley, Constance, actress; b. Mar. 30, 1879, England; d. Mar. 17, 1919 (39).
Crawley, Sayre, actor; d. Mar. 7, 1948.
Creagh, George, actor; d. May, 1962 (60).
Creamer, Charles, extra; d. July 22, 1971 (77).
Creed, Catherine, actress; d. Nov. 20, 1978 (87).
Cregar, Laird (r.n. Samuel Laird Cregar), actor; b. July 28, 1913, Philadelphia, Pa.; d. Dec. 9, 1944 (31).
Crehan, Joseph, actor; b. July 12, 1884, Baltimore, Md.; d. Apr. 15, 1966 (81).
Cremonesi, Paul, actor; b. Jan. 8, 1872, Milan, Italy; d. Aug. 29, 1939 (67).
Creste, Rene, actor; b. 1875; d. 1924 (49).
Crews, Kay C., actress; d. Nov. 29, 1959 (58).
Crews, Laura Hope, actress; b. 1880, San Francisco, Calif.; d. Nov. 13, 1942 (62).
Crimmins, Dan (r.n. Alexander M. Lyon), actor; b. May 18, 1863, Liverpool, England; d. July 12, 1945 (82).
Criner, Lawrence (r.n. John Lawrence Criner), actor; b. July 19, 1898, Texas; d. Mar. 8, 1965 (66).
Crinley, William A., director & actor; d. Jan. 1, 1927.
Crino, Isa, actress; b. Sept. 15, 1930, New York; d. Apr. 6, 1976 (45).
Cripps, Kernan, actor; b. July 8, 1886, Connecticut; d. Aug. 12, 1953 (67).
Crisa, Erno, actor; b. Mar. 10, 1924, Bizerte, Tunisia; d. Apr. 4, 1968 (44).
Crisman, Arline C., actress; d. May 10, 1956.
Crisp, Donald, actor & director; b. July 27, 1882, Aberfeddy, Scotland; d. May 25, 1974 (91).
Cristina, Olinto, actor; b. Feb. 5, 1888, Firenze, Italy; d. June 17, 1962 (74).
Criswell, Floyd, actor; b. June 17, 1899, Texas; d. Dec. 28, 1974 (75).
Crittenden, Trockwood Dwight, actor; b. Sept. 27, 1878, Oakland, Calif.; d. Feb. 17, 1938 (59).
Crocker, Harry, actor; d. May 23, 1958 (64).

Crocker, May B., actress; d. Nov. 1, 1930.
Crockett, Charles, actor; b. Dec. 29, 1870, Baltimore, Md.; d. June
    12, 1934 (63).
Crockett, Dick, actor & stuntman; b. 1916; d. Jan. 25, 1979 (63).
Crockett, John, actor; d. Feb. 21, 1922 (40).
Crockett, Lute (r.n. Henry Luther Crockett), actor (character); b. Sept.
    3, 1890, Missouri; d. Apr. 6, 1952 (61).
Croker-King, Charles, actor; b. Apr. 30, 1873, Rock Holme, Yorks.,
    England; d. Oct. 25, 1951 (78).
Crolius, Gladys, actress; b. Sept. 6, 1892, Illinois; d. Apr. 5,
    1972 (79).
Crolla, Henri, actor; d. Nov., 1960 (40).
Crommie, Lige (see Conley, Lige)
Cromwell, John, actor & author; d. Sept. 1, 1979 (65).
Cromwell, John, director & actor; b. Dec. 23, 1887, Toledo, Ohio;
    d. Sept. 26, 1979 (91).
Cromwell, Richard (r.n. LeRoy Melvin Radabaugh), actor; b. Jan. 8,
    1910, Los Angeles, Calif.; d. Oct. 11, 1960 (50).
Cronjager, Edward, cinematographer; d. June 15, 1960 (56).
Cronjager, Henry, cinematographer; d. Aug. 1, 1967 (91).
Cronjager, Jules, cinematographer; d. Dec. 28, 1934 (62).
Crosby, Bing, actor & recording artist; b. May 2, 1904, Tacoma, Wash.;
    d. Oct. 14, 1977 (73).
Crosby, Juliette, actress; d. May 1, 1969 (73).
Crosby, Marshall, actor; d. Jan. 3, 1954 (71).
Crosby, Wade, actor; b. Aug. 22, 1905, Iowa; d. Oct. 2, 1975 (70).
Crosland, Alan, director; d. July 16, 1936 (42).
Crosman, Henrietta, actress; b. Sept. 2, 1861, Wheeling, W. Va.;
    d. Oct. 31, 1944 (83).
Cross, Alfred Francis, actor; d. Jan. 28, 1938 (47).
Cross, Larry (Russ Titus), actor; d. June 29, 1976.
Cross, Oliver, actor; b. July 18, 1894, New York; d. Feb. 19, 1971
    (76).
Crosse, Rupert, actor; d. Mar. 5, 1973 (45).
Crossland, Marjorie, actress; d. Nov. 15, 1954.
Crossley, Syd, actor; b. Nov. 18, 1885, London, England; d. Nov.,
    1960 (75).
Crosthwaite, Ivy, actress; d. Nov. 8, 1962 (64).
Crouch, Worth, actor & stuntman; b. Dec. 19, 1915, Texas; d. Feb. 6,
    1943 (27).
Crouse, Russel, writer; d. Apr. 3, 1966 (73).
Crowe, Eileen, actress; d. May 8, 1978 (79).
Crowell, Josephine, actress; d. July 27, 1932.
Crowley, Jane, actress; b. Nov. 28, 1888, Ohio; d. Aug. 7, 1970 (81).
Crume, Camilla, actress; d. Mar. 20, 1952 (78).
Crummit, Frank, actor; b. Jackson, Ohio; d. Sept. 7, 1943 (54).
Cruster, Aud, actor; d. May 18, 1938 (49).
Crute, Sally, actress; b. 1893, Chattanooga, Tenn.; d. Aug. 12,
    1971 (78).
Cruze, James, director & actor; b. Mar. 27, 1894, Ogden, Utah;
    d. Aug. 3, 1942 (58).
Cruze, Mae, actress; b. May 24, 1881, Utah; d. Aug. 16, 1965 (84).
Cuccia, Mae Ruth, actress; d. Sept. 28, 1952 (50).
Cuenca, Carlos Fernandez, actor & director; d. Nov. 25, 1977 (73).
Culley, Frederick, actor; b. Mar. 9, 1879, Plymouth, England; d. Nov.
    3, 1942 (63).

Cullington, Margaret, actress; b. Massachusetts; d. July 18, 1925 (39).

Cully, Zara, actress; b. Worcester, Mass.; d. Feb. 28, 1978 (86).

Cumming, Dorothy, script supervisor; b. Nov. 13, 1913, North Carolina; d. Apr. 22, 1975 (61).

Cumming, Ruth, actress; d. Aug. 11, 1967 (63).

Cummings, George F., actor; b. July 4, 1880, Richmond, Va.; d. Mar. 11, 1946 (66).

Cummings, Irving, director & actor; b. Oct. 9, 1888, New York City; d. Apr. 18, 1959 (70).

Cummings, Katherine, actress; d. July 8, 1950 (79).

Cummings, Richard H. (r.n. Richard Henry Cummings), actor; b. Aug. 20, 1858, New Haven, Conn.; d. Dec. 25, 1938 (80).

Cummings, Robert, actor; b. Feb. 8, 1865, Massachusetts; d. July 22, 1949 (84).

Cummings, Roy R., actor; d. Sept. 30, 1940 (51).

Cummings, Vicki, actress; b. Feb. 15, 1919, Northampton, Mass.; d. Nov. 30, 1969 (50).

Cumpson, John R., actor; d. Mar. 15, 1913 (45).

Cunard, Grace, actress; b. Apr. 8, 1893, Columbus, Ohio; d. Jan. 19, 1967 (73).

Cunard, Myna, actress; d. Aug. 9, 1978 (83).

Cuneo, Lester, actor; b. Oct. 25, 1888, Chicago, Ill.; d. Nov. 1, 1925 (37).

Cuningham, Philip, actor; d. Jan. 10, 1928 (62).

Cunningham, Aloysius, actor; d. July 27, 1936.

Cunningham, Cecil, actress; b. Aug. 2, 1888, Missouri; d. Apr. 17, 1959 (70).

Cunningham, George R., choreographer, stage director, & actor; b. Feb. 11, 1904, New York; d. Apr. 30, 1962 (58).

Cunningham, Jack, writer; b. Apr. 1, 1882, Ionia, Iowa; d. Oct. 4, 1941 (59).

Cunningham, Jack, actor; d. Jan. 13, 1967 (54).

Cunningham, Joseph, actor & author; b. June 22, 1890, Philadelphia, Pa.; d. Apr. 3, 1943 (52).

Cunningham, Zamah, actress; d. June 2, 1967 (74).

Cuny, Louis, director; b. Nov. 24, 1907, Paris, France; d. July 27, 1962 (54).

Curci, Gennaro, actor; b. Sept. 19, 1888, Italy; d. Apr. 13, 1955 (66).

Curiel, Gonzalo, actor; d. July 4, 1958.

Curley, Leo, actor; b. Apr. 12, 1878, New York; d. Apr. 11, 1960 (81).

Curran, J.P., actor; d. Jan. 11, 1919.

Curran, Tom, actor; b. 1879, Australia; d. Jan. 24, 1941 (61).

Currie, Clive, actor; b. Mar. 26, 1877, Birmingham, England; d. May 25, 1935 (58).

Currie, Finlay, actor; b. Jan. 20, 1878, Edinburgh, Scotland; d. May 9, 1968 (90).

Currier, Frank, actor; b. Sept. 4, 1857, Norwich, Conn.; d. Apr. 22, 1928 (70).

Curry, Elizabeth, dancer; d. Aug. 25, 1935 (17).

Curry, Nathan, actor; b. Jan. 2, 1897, Texas; d. Dec. 14, 1964 (67).

Curtis, Alan, actor; b. July 24, 1909, Chicago, Ill.; d. Feb. 1, 1953 (43).

Curtis, Beatrice, actress; b. Sept. 23, 1906, New York; d. Mar. 26, 1963 (56).

Curtis, Dick, actor; b. May 11, 1902, Newport, Ky.; d. Jan. 3, 1952 (49).

Curtis, Howard, stuntman; d. Sept. 2, 1979 (52).

Curtis, Jack, actor; b. May 28, 1880, California; d. Mar. 16, 1956 (75).

Curtis, John W., actor; d. July 21, 1925 (79).

Curtis, Spencer, actor; d. July 13, 1921 (63).

Curtis, Willa Pearl, actress; b. Mar. 21, 1896, Texas; d. Dec. 19, 1970 (74).

Curtiz, David, assistant director & film editor; b. Budapest, Hungary; d. May 23, 1962 (68).

Curtiz, Michael, director; b. Dec. 24, 1888, Budapest, Hungary; d. Apr. 10, 1962 (73).

Curwen, Patric, actor; b. Dec. 14, 1884, London, England; d. May 31, 1949 (64).

Curzon, George, actor; b. Oct. 18, 1898, Amersham, England; d. May 10, 1976 (77).

Cusack, Maureen, actress; d. Dec. 18, 1977 (57).

Cusanelli, Peter, actor; b. Apr. 12, 1898, Connecticut; d. Apr. 10, 1954 (55).

Cuscaden, Sarah D., actress; d. Oct. 18, 1954 (81).

Cuscaden, William H., actor; d. Jan. 6, 1955 (79).

Cushman, Nancy, actress; d. Sept. 26, 1979 (65).

Custer, Bob (Raymond Glenn) (r.n. Raymond Anthony Glenn), actor; b. Oct. 18, 1898, Frankfort, Ky.; d. Dec. 27, 1974 (76).

Cutler, Kate, actress; b. Aug. 14, 1870, London, England; d. May 14, 1955 (84).

Cutting, Richard, actor; b. Oct. 31, 1912, Massachusetts; d. Mar. 7, 1972 (59).

Cutts, Graham, director; b. 1885, Brighton, England; d. Oct., 1958 (73).

Cutts, Patricia (Patricia Wayne), actress; b. July 20, 1927, London, England; d. Sept. 6, 1974 (47).

Cybulski, Zbigniew, actor; b. Nov. 3, 1927, Kniaze, Poland; d. Jan. 8, 1967 (39).

Czepa, Friedl, actress; b. Sept. 3, 1905, Niederosterr; d. June, 1973 (67).

Czinner, Paul, director; b. Hungary; d. June 22, 1972 (82).


Dade, Frances, actress; d. Jan. 21, 1968 (60).

Dae, Frank E., actor; b. May 15, 1882, Wisconsin; d. Aug. 29, 1959 (77).

Daggett, Robert True, actor; d. Aug. 6, 1975 (71).

Daghofer, Fritz, actor; b. July 5, 1872, Vienna, Austria; d. Jan. 25, 1936 (63).

D'Agostino, Albert S., art director; b. Dec. 27, 1893, New York City; d. Mar. 14, 1970 (76).

Dagover, Lil, actress; b. Sept. 30, 1897, Madiven, Java; d. Jan. 23, 1980 (82).

Dahl, Diane, dancer; b. Sept. 18, 1914, Empire, Ore.; d. Mar. 10, 1946 (31).

Dai, Lin, actress; d. July 17, 1964 (33).
Dailey, Dan, actor; b. Dec. 14, 1915, New York; d. Oct. 16, 1978 (62).
Dailey, Joseph, actor; d. Sept. 23, 1940 (78).
Dalbert, Suzanne, actress; b. May 12, 1927, France; d. Dec., 1970 (43).
d'Albie, Julian, actor; b. Dublin, Ireland; d. Apr. 6, 1978 (86).
D'Albrew, William V., dancer; d. Oct. 20, 1962 (57).
D'Albrook, Sidney, actor; b. May 3, 1886, Chicago, Ill.; d. May 30, 1948 (62).
Dalby, Amy, actress; b. England; d. Mar. 10, 1969 (80).
Dale, Charlie (r.n. Charles Marks), actor; b. Sept. 6, 1881, New York City; d. Nov. 16, 1971 (90).
Dale, Dorothy, actress; d. Aug. 1, 1937 (12).
Dale, Dorothy, actress; d. May 13, 1957 (75).
Dale, Esther, actress; b. Nov. 10, 1885, Beaufort, S.C.; d. July 23, 1961 (75).
Dale, Margaret (Peggy), actress; b. Dec. 25, 1903, New York; d. June 6, 1967 (63).
Dale, Margaret, actress; b. Mar. 6, 1876, Philadelphia, Pa.; d. Mar. 23, 1972 (96).
Daley, Cass, actress; b. July 17, 1915, Philadelphia, Pa.; d. Mar. 22, 1975 (59).
Daley, Jack (r.n. John Almorin Daley), actor; b. Aug. 31, 1883, Massachusetts; d. Aug. 30, 1967 (83).
Daley, Mabel, actress; d. July 16, 1942 (48).
D'Algy, Tony, actor; d. Apr. 29, 1977 (72).
Dall, John, actor; b. New York; d. Jan. 15, 1971 (50).
Dalleu, Gilbert, actor; b. 1890; d. 1931 (41).
Dalley, Ted, actor; d. Aug. 30, 1952 (64).
Dallimore, Maurice, actor; b. June 23, 1912, England; d. Feb. 20, 1973 (60).
Dalroy, Harry (Rube), actor; d. Mar. 8, 1954 (75).
Dalton, Charles, actor; b. Aug. 29, 1864, England; d. June 11, 1942 (77).
Dalton, Dorothy, actress; b. Sept. 22, 1894, Chicago, Ill.; d. Apr. 13, 1972 (77).
Dalton, Irene, actress; d. Aug. 15, 1934 (33).
D'Alvarez, Marguerite, actress & opera singer; d. Oct. 18, 1953 (69).
Daly, Arnold, actor; b. Oct. 4, 1875, Brooklyn, N.Y.; d. Jan. 13, 1927 (51).
Daly, Herbert Gerard (Bill), actor; d. May 12, 1940 (38).
Daly, Jack (r.n. John Russell Daly), actor; b. Sept. 28, 1914, Massachusetts; d. June 2, 1968 (53).
Daly, James, actor; b. Oct. 23, 1918, Wisconsin; d. July 3, 1978 (59).
Daly, James L., actor; d. Nov. 9, 1933 (80).
Daly, Mark, actor; b. Aug. 23, 1887, Edinburgh, Scotland; d. Sept. 27, 1957 (70).
Daly, Pat, actor; d. Nov. 19, 1947 (56).
d'Ambricourt, Adrienne, actress; d. Dec. 6, 1957 (69).
Damerel, Donna, actress (Myrt and Marge); d. Feb. 15, 1941 (29).
Damia (r.n. Marie-Louise Damien), singer; d. Jan. 30, 1978 (88).
Damon, Les, actor; b. May 31, 1908, Rhode Island; d. July 21, 1962 (54).
Dampier, Claude, actor; d. Jan. 1, 1955 (76).
Damroth, George, actor & director; d. Feb. 10, 1939 (45).

Dana, Clara L., actress; d. June 23, 1956 (78).
Dana, Dick, actor; d. July 10, 1976 (75).
Dandridge, Dorothy, actress; b. Nov. 9, 1922, Cleveland, Ohio;
    d. Sept. 8, 1965 (42).
Dandy, Ned, writer & actor; d. Aug. 8, 1948 (60).
Dane, Clemence, writer; b. Blackheath, England; d. Mar. 28, 1965
    (77).
Dane, Karl, actor; b. Oct. 12, 1886, Copenhagen, Denmark; d. Apr. 14,
    1934 (47).
Danegger, Theodor, actor; b. Aug. 31, 1891; d. Oct. 11, 1959 (68).
Daneri, Julio, actor; d. Aug. 28, 1957 (43).
Danforth, William, actor; b. May 13, 1867, Syracuse, N.Y.; d. Apr. 16,
    1941 (73).
Daniell, Henry, actor; b. Mar. 5, 1894, London, England; d. Oct. 31,
    1963 (69).
Daniels, Bebe, actress; b. Jan. 14, 1901, Dallas, Tex.; d. Mar. 16,
    1971 (70).
Daniels, Billy, dancer, actor, & choreographer; b. July 4, 1912,
    Ft. Worth, Tex.; d. May 15, 1962 (49).
Daniels, Frank, actor; b. Dayton, Ohio; d. Jan. 12, 1935 (74).
Daniels, Hank (Henry H. Daniels, Jr.), actor; b. Jan. 27, 1919, New
    Jersey; d. Dec. 21, 1973 (54).
Daniels, Harold, director; b. June 25, 1903, New York; d. Dec. 27,
    1971 (68).
Daniels, Walter, actor; d. Mar. 30, 1928 (53).
Danilo, Don (Elmer Dewey), actor; d. Oct. 28, 1954 (70).
Dansey, Herbert, actor; d. May 30, 1917 (47).
Dante, actor & magician; d. June 15, 1955 (71).
Dante, Lionel, actor; d. July 30, 1974 (67).
Darbaud, Monique, actress; d. Feb., 1971 (47).
Dar Boggia, Henry P., actor; b. Mar. 27, 1904, New York; d. Jan. 11,
    1976 (71).
Darby, John J., actor; b. Aug. 27, 1893, Long Beach, Calif.; d. Dec.
    13, 1946 (53).
D'Arcy, Camille, actress; d. Sept. 27, 1916.
D'Arcy, Hugh Antoine, actor; b. France; d. Nov. 11, 1925 (82).
D'Arcy, Roy (r.n. R. Francis Guisti), actor; b. Feb. 10, 1894, San
    Francisco, Calif.; d. Nov. 15, 1969 (75).
Darden, Anne, actress; d. Nov. 29, 1977 (45).
Dare, Dorris, actress; d. Aug. 16, 1927 (28).
Dare, Helena, actress; d. Aug. 3, 1972.
Dare, Phyllis, actress; b. Aug. 15, 1890; d. Apr. 27, 1975 (84).
Dare, Virginia, actress; b. Aug. 6, 1882, Pennsylvania; d. July 8,
    1962 (79).
Dare, Zena, actress; b. Feb. 4, 1887; d. Mar. 11, 1975 (88).
Darien, Frank, actor; b. Mar. 18, 1876, Louisiana; d. Oct. 20, 1955
    (79).
Darin, Bobby, actor & recording artist; b. May 14, 1936, New York
    City; d. Dec. 20, 1973 (37).
Dark, Christopher, actor; b. Apr. 21, 1920, New York; d. Oct. 10,
    1971 (51).
Darkcloud, Beulah, actress; d. Jan. 2, 1946.
Darley, Brian, actor; d. Feb., 1924 (66).
Darling, Ida, actress; d. June 5, 1936 (61).
Darling, Ruth, actress; d. Sept. 11, 1918.

Darling, W. Scott, writer & director; b. May 28, 1898, Toronto, Ont.,
   Canada; d. Oct. 29, 1951 (53).
Darmond, Grace, actress; b. Toronto, Canada; d. Oct. 7, 1963 (65).
Darmour, Larry, producer; d. Mar. 17, 1942 (47).
Darnell, Jean, actress; d. Jan. 19, 1961 (72).
Darnell, Linda, actress; b. Oct. 16, 1921, Dallas, Tex.; d. Apr. 10,
   1965 (43).
D'Arno, Albert, actor; d. Dec. 19, 1977.
Darnold, Blaine A., actor; d. Mar. 11, 1926 (39).
D'Arrast, Henry D'Abbadie, director; d. Mar. 17, 1968 (71).
Darrell, Steve (r.n. J. Stevan Darrell), actor; b. Nov. 19, 1904,
   Iowa; d. Aug. 14, 1970 (65).
Darro, Frankie, actor; b. Dec. 22, 1918, Chicago, Ill.; d. Dec. 25,
   1976 (58).
Darrow, John, actor; b. July 17, 1907, New York City; d. Feb. 24,
   1980 (72).
Darvas, Charles, actor; b. Mar. 2, 1880, Hungary; d. Apr. 14, 1930 (50).
   (50).
Darvas, Lili, actress; b. Apr. 10, 1902, Budapest, Hungary; d. July
   22, 1974 (72).
Darvi, Bella (r.n. Bayla Wegier), actress; b. Oct. 23, 1928,
   Sosnowiec, Poland; d. Sept. 10, 1971 (42).
D'Arville, Camille, actress; b. June 21, 1863, Holland; d. Sept. 10,
   1932 (69).
Darwell, Jane, actress; b. Oct. 15, 1879, Palmyra, Mo.; d. Aug. 13,
   1967 (87).
Dash, Pauly, actor; d. Feb. 2, 1974 (55).
Dashiell, Willard, actor; b. 1868; d. Apr. 19, 1943 (76).
DaSilva, Henry, actor; d. June 6, 1947 (66).
Date, Keshavrao, actor; d. Sept. 13, 1971 (32).
Dattel, Paul, actor; d. Feb., 1968 (62).
Daube, Belle, actress; d. May 25, 1959 (71).
D'Auburn, Dennis (see Cavendish, David)
Daufel, Andre (r.n. David Van Offel), actor; d. Apr. 22, 1975 (56).
Daugherty, Jack (r.n. Virgil A. Dougherty), actor; b. Nov. 16,
   1895, Bowling Green, Mo.; d. May 16, 1938 (42).
Daumery, Carrie, actress; b. Mar. 25, 1863, Holland; d. July 1, 1938
   (75).
Daunt, William, actor; b. Aug. 21, 1893, Dublin, Ireland; d. Oct. 1,
   1938 (44).
Dauphin, Claude, actor; b. Aug. 19, 1903, Corbell, France; d. Nov.
   16, 1978 (75).
Davenport, A. Bromley, actor; b. Oct. 29, 1867, Baginton, Warwick-
   shire, England; d. Dec. 15, 1946 (79).
Davenport, Alice, actress; b. Feb. 29, 1864, New York; d. June 24,
   1936 (72).
Davenport, Blanche, actress; b. London, England; d. Oct. 17, 1921.
Davenport, Dorothy, actress; d. Oct. 12, 1977 (81).
Davenport, Edgar Loomis, actor; d. July 25, 1918.
Davenport, Harry, actor; b. Jan. 19, 1866, New York City; d. Aug. 9,
   1949 (83).
Davenport, Harry J., actor; b. May 7, 1857; d. Feb. 20, 1929 (71).
Davenport, Havis, actress; d. July 23, 1975 (42).
Davenport, Kate, actress; b. June 7, 1896, New York; d. Dec. 7, 1954
   (58).
Davenport, Milla, actress; b. Feb. 4, 1871, Zurich, Switzerland;
   d. May 17, 1936 (65).

Davenport, William, actor; d. May 11, 1941 (74).
Daves, Delmer, director, actor, & author; b. July 24, 1904, San Francisco, Calif.; d. Aug. 17, 1977 (73).
David, Thayer, actor; b. Mar. 4, 1927, Medford, Mass.; d. July 17, 1978 (51).
David, William, actor; b. Vicksburg, Miss.; d. Apr. 10, 1965 (83).
Davidoff, Frances Mack, actress; b. Sept. 4, 1906, Washington; d. Sept. 26, 1967 (61).
Davidson, Dore, actor; d. Mar. 7, 1930 (80).
Davidson, J.B. (Bing), actor; b. Dec. 17, 1940, Nebraska; d. July 18, 1965 (25).
Davidson, John, actor; d. July 27, 1957 (43).
Davidson, John, actor; b. Dec. 25, 1887, New York City; d. Jan. 15, 1968 (80).
Davidson, Max, actor; b. May 23, 1875, Berlin, Germany; d. Sept. 4, 1950 (75).
Davidson, Ronald A., writer; b. July 13, 1899, California; d. July 28, 1965 (66).
Davidson, William B., actor; b. June 16, 1888, Dobbs Ferry, N.Y.; d. Sept. 28, 1947 (59).
Davidt, Michael, actor; d. Mar. 15, 1944 (67).
Davies, Betty Ann, actress; b. Dec. 24, 1910, London, England; d. May 14, 1955 (44).
Davies, George, actor; d. Mar., 1960 (69).
Davies, Howard, actor; b. May 18, 1879, Liverpool, England; d. Dec. 30, 1947 (68).
Davies, Lillian, actress; b. Jan. 18, 1895, Lynmouth, N. Devon, England; d. Mar. 3, 1932 (37).
Davies, Marion, actress; b. Jan. 3, 1897, Brooklyn, N.Y.; d. Sept. 22, 1961 (64).
Davies, Reine (r.n. Reine Douras), actress; b. June 6, 1892, Montclair, N.J.; d. Apr. 2, 1938 (45).
Davies, Rosemary (r.n. Rose Douras), actress; b. June 15, 1903, New York; d. Sept. 20, 1963 (60).
Davies, Rupert, actor; b. Liverpool, England; d. Nov. 22, 1976 (59).
Davies, Valentine, writer & director; b. Aug. 25, 1905, New York City; d. July 23, 1961 (55).
Davis, Alan, actor; d. Dec. 11, 1943 (42).
Davis, Anna, actress; d. May 5, 1945 (55).
Davis, Bob (Alabam), actor; d. Sept. 22, 1971 (61).
Davis, Boyd, actor; b. June 19, 1885, California; d. Jan. 25, 1963 (77).
Davis, Conrad, actor; d. Dec. 22, 1969 (54).
Davis, Danny, actor; d. Feb. 10, 1970 (41).
Davis, Edwards (r.n. Cader Edwards Davis), actor; b. June 17, 1867, Santa Clara Co., Calif.; d. May 17, 1936 (68).
Davis, Freeman (Brother Bones), entertainer; d. June 14, 1974 (71).
Davis, George, actor; b. Nov. 7, 1889, Holland; d. Apr. 19, 1965 (75).
Davis, Gunnis (r.n. James Gunnis Davis), actor; b. Dec. 21, 1873, Sunderland, England; d. Mar. 22, 1937 (63).
Davis, Hal, actor; b. Oct. 6, 1909, Ohio; d. Jan. 4, 1960 (50).
Davis, Harry, actor; d. Apr. 4, 1929 (55).
Davis, Joan, actress; b. June 29, 1912, St. Paul, Minn.; d. May 23, 1961 (48).

Davis, Karl "Killer," actor & wrestler; b. Apr. 16, 1908, Ohio;
    d. July 1, 1977 (69).
Davis, Mildred, actress; b. Feb. 22, 1901, Pennsylvania; d. Aug. 18,
    1969 (68).
Davis, Morgan, actor & cowboy; b. May 2, 1890, Ethel, Mo.; d. Sept.
    2, 1941 (51).
Davis, Owen, Jr., actor; b. Oct. 6, 1907, New York City; d. May 21,
    1949 (41).
Davis, Rufe, actor; b. Dec. 2, 1908, Oklahoma; d. Dec. 13, 1974 (66).
Davis, Spencer, actor; d. Sept. 13, 1976.
Davis, Stringer (r.n. James Buckley Stringer Davis), actor; b. Aug.
    29, 1973 (74).
Daw, Evelyn, actress; b. Nov. 16, 1912, South Dakota; d. Nov. 29,
    1970 (58).
Dawkins, Irma L., actress; b. Mar. 25, 1892, Columbia, S.C.; d. Oct.
    14, 1972 (80).
Dawkins, Paul, actor; d. June 26, 1979 (59).
Dawley, Herbert M., author & producer; d. Aug. 15, 1970 (90).
Dawley, J. Searle, director; d. Mar. 29, 1949 (71).
Dawn, Gloria, actress; d. Apr. 2, 1978 (49).
Dawn, Isabel, actress & author; d. June 29, 1966 (62).
Dawn, Norman, director; b. May 25, 1884, Argentina; d. Feb. 2, 1975
    (90).
Dawson, Doris, actress; d. Nov. 14, 1950 (56).
Dawson, Frank, actor; b. July 4, 1870, England; d. Oct. 11, 1953 (83).
Dawson, Hazel, actress & stuntwoman; d. Aug. 30, 1948 (53).
Dawson, Ivo, actor; d. Mar. 7, 1934 (54).
Dawson, Marion, actress; d. Apr., 1975 (86).
Day, Edith, actress; d. May 1, 1971 (75).
Day, Josette, actress; b. July 31, 1914, Paris, France; d. June 29,
    1978 (63).
Day, Julietta, actress; d. Sept. 18, 1957 (63).
Day, Marie L., actress; d. Nov. 7, 1939 (84).
Daye, Dulce, actress; d. Dec. 1, 1954 (43).
Dayton, Frank, actor; d. Oct. 17, 1924 (59).
Daze, Mercedes, actress; d. Mar. 18, 1945 (53).
Deal, W.P. (Wally Dean) (r.n. Walter Perry Deal), actor; b. Dec. 26,
    1878, Pennsylvania; d. Oct. 1, 1955 (76).
de Alba, Carlos, actor; d. Oct., 1960 (35).
Dealy, James, director; d. Aug. 26, 1965 (85).
Dean, Basil, director, author, & producer; b. Sept. 27, 1888,
    Croyden, England; d. Apr. 22, 1978 (89).
Dean, Fabian (r.n. Fabian Dean Gibilaro), actor; b. Apr. 7, 1929,
    New York; d. Jan. 15, 1971 (41).
Dean, Helen, actress; d. June 19, 1930.
Dean, Ivor, actor; d. Aug. 10, 1974 (57).
Dean, Jack, actor; b. Bridgeport, Conn.; d. June 23, 1950 (75).
Dean, James, actor; b. Feb. 8, 1931, Marion, Ind.; d. Sept. 30,
    1955 (24).
Dean, Julia, actress; b. May 13, 1878, St. Paul, Minn.; d. Oct. 18,
    1952 (74).
Dean, Louis, actor; d. Apr. 8, 1933 (57).
Dean, Man Mountain, actor & wrestler; d. May 29, 1953 (63).
Dean, May, actress; d. Sept. 1, 1937.
Dean, Ruby, actress; d. Feb. 23, 1935 (48).

Dean, Wally (see Deal, W.P.)
de Anda, Agustin, actor; d. May 29, 1960 (25).
de Andrade, Fernando Freyre, actor; b. May 16, 1904, Avila, Spain;
    d. Oct. 16, 1946 (42).
Deane, Doris, actress; b. Jan. 20, 1900, Wisconsin; d. Mar. 24, 1974
    (74).
Deane, Ralph, actor & director; d. Feb. 4, 1955 (80).
de Angelis, Jefferson, actor; b. Nov. 30, 1859, San Francisco,
    Calif.; d. Mar. 20, 1933 (73).
Deans, Herbert, actor; b. Oct. 23, 1908, Canada; d. Oct. 8, 1967
    (58).
Dearden, Basil, director & author; b. Jan. 1, 1911, Westcliff-on-Sea,
    Essex, England; d. Mar. 23, 1971 (60).
Dearholt, Ashton (Richard Holt), actor & producer; b. Apr. 4, 1894,
    Milwaukee, Wisc.; d. Apr. 27, 1942 (48).
Dearing, Edgar, actor; b. May 4, 1893, Ceres, Calif.; d. Aug. 17,
    1974 (81).
Dearli, Bruno, actor; d. May 31, 1950 (73).
Dearly, Max, actor; d. June 2, 1943 (69).
Dease, John, actor; d. Feb. 1, 1979 (72).
De Aubry, Diane, actress; d. May 23, 1969 (79).
de Beauvolers, Maj. J.J. (r.n. Joseph J. de Beauvolers), actor;
    b. Nov. 30, 1881, Belgium; d. Apr. 20, 1960 (78).
De Becker, Harold, actor; b. June 8, 1889, London, England; d. July
    24, 1947 (58).
De Becker, Kate, actress; d. Apr. 7, 1946 (87).
De Becker, Marie, actress; b. June 13, 1880, London, England;
    d. Mar. 23, 1946 (65).
de Belleville, Frederic, actor; b. Feb. 17, 1857, Liege, Belgium;
    d. Feb. 25, 1923 (66).
de Beranger, Andre (see Beranger, George Andre)
de Blasio, Gene (Houston Savoy), actor; d. Nov. 3, 1971 (30).
De Bozoky, Barbara, actress; b. Nov. 10, 1871, Miskolcz, Hungary;
    d. Nov. 29, 1937 (66).
De Bray, Harold, actor; d. Oct. 31, 1932 (58).
de Bray, Henri, actor; d. Apr. 5, 1965 (75).
de Bray, Yvonne, actress; d. Feb. 1, 1954 (65).
de Breteuil, Gilberte, actress; d. Feb., 1972.
DeBriac, Jean, actor; b. Aug. 15, 1891, France; d. Oct. 18, 1970 (79).
de Brulier, Nigel, actor; b. July 8, 1877, Bristol, England; d. Jan.
    30, 1948 (70).
Debucourt, Jean, actor; b. Jan. 19, 1894, Paris, France; d. Mar. 22,
    1958 (64).
De Camp, Gayle S., stuntman; d. Dec. 30, 1976.
De Cardo, Walton Fay, actor; d. Jan. 26, 1953 (52).
De Carlos, Perla Granada, dancer; d. June 8, 1973 (70).
De Casalis, Jeanne, actress; b. May 22, 1897, Basutoland, South
    Africa; d. Aug. 19, 1966 (69).
de Castejon, Blanca, actress; d. Dec. 26, 1969 (53).
Dechamps, Charles, actor; b. 1890; d. 1958 (68).
De Cicco, Pat (r.n. Pasquale), actor; d. Oct. 24, 1978 (68).
De Coma, Eddie, actor & stuntman; d. July 30, 1938 (60).
Decomble, Guy, actor; b. Nov., 1910; d. Aug. 14, 1964 (53).
De Cordoba, Pedro, actor; b. Sept. 28, 1881, New York City; d. Sept.
    16, 1950 (68).

de Cordova, Arturo (r.n. Arturo Garcia Rodriguez), actor; b. May 8, 1908, Merida, Mexico; d. Nov. 3, 1973 (65).

De Cordova, Leander, actor; b. Dec. 5, 1878, Jamaica; d. Sept. 19, 1969 (90).

de Cordova, Rudolph, actor; b. Kingston, Jamaica; d. Jan. 11, 1941 (81).

de Corsia, Ted (r.n. Edward Gildea deCorsia), actor; b. Sept. 29, 1905, New York; d. Apr. 11, 1973 (67).

De Coureville, Albert, director & writer; b. London, England; d. Mar., 1960 (72).

Dectreaux, Evelyn, actress; d. Aug. 28, 1952 (50).

de Dios Muniz, Juan, actor; d. Oct., 1951 (45).

Dee, George (r.n. Georges de Gombert), actor; b. Apr. 11, 1901, France; d. Aug. 24, 1974 (73).

Deeley, Ben (r.n. N. Bernard Deely), actor; b. Jan. 22, 1878, California; d. Sept. 23, 1924 (46).

Deen, Nedra, actress; d. Dec. 28, 1975.

Deeping, Warwick, writer; d. Apr. 19, 1950 (73).

Deer, John J., actor; d. Mar. 31, 1940 (79).

Deering, Marda (Marda Browne Hartley), actress; d. Jan. 13, 1961 (49).

Deery, Jack, actor; b. July 31, 1893, Australia; d. May 5, 1965 (71).

de Feraudy, Maurice, actor; d. May 12, 1932 (73).

Deffon, Rusty, dancer; d. Oct., 1963 (51).

De Filippo, Peppino, actor; b. Aug. 24, 1903, Naples, Italy; d. Jan. 26, 1980 (76).

De Filippo, Titina, actress; b. Mar. 23, 1898, Naples, Italy; d. Dec. 26, 1963 (65).

de Foe, Annette, actress; d. Aug. 7, 1960 (71).

de Forest, Hal, actor; d. Feb. 16, 1938 (76).

de Fuentes, Fernando, director; b. Dec. 13, 1895, Vera Cruz, Mexico; d. 1958 (62).

Dega, Igor (Igor de Navrotsky), dancer; d. July 5, 1976.

De Grasse, Ida May, actress; b. Dec. 28, 1879, California; d. June 13, 1954 (74).

De Grasse, Joseph, director & actor; b. May 4, 1873, Bathurst, N.B., Canada; d. May 24, 1940 (67).

de Grasse, Robert, director; b. Feb. 9, 1900, New Jersey; d. Jan. 28, 1971 (70).

De Grasse, Sam, actor; b. June 20, 1875, Bathurst, N.B., Canada; d. Nov. 29, 1953 (78).

De Grey, Sydney, actor; b. June 16, 1866, Unn, England; d. June 30, 1941 (75).

de Grunwald, Anatole, writer & producer; b. Jan. 11, 1911, Leningrad, Russia; d. Jan. 13, 1967 (56).

de Guingand, Pierre, actor; b. June 6, 1885, Paris, France; d. June 10, 1964 (79).

De Haven, Carter, actor & assistant director; b. Oct. 5, 1886, Illinois; d. July 20, 1977 (90).

De Haven, Carter, Jr., assistant director; d. Mar. 1, 1979 (68).

De Haven, Flora, actress; d. Sept. 9, 1950 (67).

Dehelly, Jean, actor; b. 1896; d. 1964 (68).

Deighton, Marga Ann, actress; b. May 26, 1890, India; d. Apr. 10, 1971 (80).

de Kerekjarto, Duci, violinist & actor; d. Jan. 3, 1962 (61).

Dekker, Albert, actor; b. Dec. 20, 1905, Brooklyn, N.Y.; d. May 5,
   1968 (62).
de Kowa, Viktor, actor; b. Mar. 8, 1904, Hochkirch, Germany; d. Apr.
   8, 1973 (69).
De Lacey, John, actor; d. Dec. 18, 1924 (52).
De La Cruz, Joseph, actor; b. Mar. 19, 1892, Mexico; d. Dec. 14,
   1961 (69).
De La Cruz, Juan, actor; b. June 4, 1881, Copenhagen, Denmark;
   d. Nov. 12, 1953 (72).
De Lacy, Leigh (Jessie M. Williams), actress; b. Mar. 11, 1879,
   Kansas; d. Jan. 4, 1966 (86).
Delamare, Gil, stuntman; b. Oct. 14, 1924, Paris, France; d. May 31,
   1966 (41).
de La Mothe, Leon (see Kent, Leon)
De La Motte, Marguerite, actress; b. June 22, 1902, Duluth, Minn.;
   d. Mar. 10, 1950 (47).
de Landa, Juan, actor; b. Jan. 27, 1894, Matrico; d. Feb. 17, 1968
   (74).
Delaney, Charles, actor; b. Aug. 9, 1892, New York City; d. Aug. 31,
   1959 (67).
Delaney, Jere, actor; d. Jan. 2, 1954 (66).
Delaney, Leo, actor; d. Feb. 4, 1920 (38).
Delaney, Maureen, actress; b. Ireland; d. Mar. 27, 1961 (73).
Delannoy, Monique, actress; d. Apr. 25, 1979 (42).
Delano, Gwen, actress; d. Nov. 20, 1954 (72).
de La Plaza Griffin, Eva, actress; d. 1943.
Delargo, Celia, actress; d. Oct. 3, 1927 (26).
Delaro, Hattie, actress; d. Apr. 18, 1941 (80).
de la Torre, Raf, actor; d. July 15, 1975 (67).
de la Vega, Alfredo Gomez, actor; b. 1897, Mexico; d. Jan. 15,
   1958 (60).
del Diestro, Alfredo, actor; d. 1951.
De Leo, Don, actor; d. Aug. 14, 1979 (74).
De Leon, Aristides, actor; d. July 23, 1954 (50).
de Leon, Enedina Diaz, actress; d. Apr. 12, 1960.
DeLeon, Raoul, actor; b. June 19, 1905, New York; d. Jan. 6, 1972
   (66).
De Leon, Walter, writer; d. Aug. 1, 1947 (63).
Delevanti, Cyril, actor; b. Feb. 23, 1889, England; d. Dec. 13,
   1975 (86).
Del Frate, Renato, actor; b. Nov. 21, 1910, Rome, Italy; d. Aug. 28,
   1962 (51).
del Fuego, Luz, actress; d. July 19, 1967.
Delgado, Maria, actress; d. June 24, 1969 (63).
Delgado, Roger, actor; b. Mar., 1918, London, England; d. June 17,
   1973 (55).
del Giudice, Filippo, producer & actor; b. Trani, Italy; d. Dec. 31,
   1962 (70).
Delight, June, actress; d. Oct. 3, 1975 (77).
De Liguoro, Giuseppe, actor & director; b. Jan. 10, 1869, Naples,
   Italy; d. Mar. 19, 1944 (75).
de Liguoro, Rina, actress; b. July 24, 1892, Firenze, Italy; d. Apr.
   7, 1966 (73).
de Limur, Jean, director; d. June, 1976 (89).
De Linsky, Victor, actor; b. Mar. 18, 1883, Russia; d. May 9, 1951
   (68).

Dell, Claudia, actress; b. Jan. 10, 1909, San Antonio, Tex.; d. Sept. 5, 1977 (68).
Dell, Dorothy (r.n. Dorothy Goff), actress; b. Jan. 30, 1914, Hattiesburg, Miss.; d. June 8, 1934 (20).
Dell, Rupert L., actor; d. Oct. 25, 1945 (64).
della Santina, Bruno, actor; b. June 15, 1904, Italy; d. Sept. 1, 1968 (64).
del Llano, Amanda, actress; d. July 23, 1964.
Del Mar, Claire, actress; d. Jan. 10, 1959 (58).
Delmar, Eddie, actor; b. Aug. 17, 1885, Detroit, Mich.; d. Mar. 1, 1944 (58).
Delmar, Jack, actor; d. Mar. 24, 1954 (77).
Delmont, Edouard, actor; b. 1893; d. 1955 (62).
Delmonte, Jack, actor; d. June 8, 1973 (84).
Delmore, Ralph, actor; b. New York City; d. Nov. 21, 1923 (70).
Del Rio, Jack, actor; d. Mar. 8, 1978 (66).
Del Ruth, Hampton, director; b. Sept. 7, 1879, Delaware; d. May 15, 1958 (78).
Del Ruth, Roy, director; b. Oct. 18, 1893, Delaware; d. Apr. 27, 1961 (67).
Deltgen, Rene, actor; b. Apr. 30, 1909, Luxembourg; d. Jan. 28, 1979 (69).
Deltry, William, actor; d. Oct. 8, 1924.
Del Val, Jean (r.n. Jean Jacques Gauthier), actor; b. Nov. 17, 1891, France; d. Mar. 13, 1975 (83).
Del Valle, David G., actor; b. Nov. 22, 1875, St. Thomas, West Indies; d. May 7, 1934 (58).
del Valle, Luis Cotto, actor; d. Mar., 1971 (58).
Delysia, Alice, actress; d. Feb. 9, 1979 (90).
DeMain, Gordon (Gordon D. Wood; G.D. Wood), actor; b. Sept. 28, 1886, Iowa; d. Mar. 5, 1954 (67).
Demarest, Rubin, actor; b. Oct. 26, 1886, Minnesota; d. Sept. 20, 1962 (75).
de Marney, Derrick, actor; b. Sept. 21, 1906, London, England; d. Feb. 18, 1978 (71).
de Marney, Terence, actor; b. Mar. 1, 1909, London, England; d. May 25, 1971 (62).
de Max, Edouard, actor; d. Oct. 28, 1924 (55).
Demetrio, Anna, actress; b. Nov. 8, 1900, Italy; d. Nov. 8, 1959 (59).
De Mille, Cecil B., director, producer, & actor; b. Aug. 12, 1881, Ashfield, Mass.; d. Jan. 21, 1959 (77).
DeMille, William C., director & author; b. July 25, 1878, Washington, D.C.; d. Mar. 8, 1955 (76).
Demorest, Drew (r.n. Andrew J. Demorest), actor; b. Aug. 31, 1893, New York; d. Feb. 21, 1949 (55).
DeMott, John A., actor; d. Mar. 19, 1975 (63).
Dempsey, Clifford, actor; d. Sept. 4, 1938 (73).
Dempsey, Pauline, actress; d. 1923 (55).
Dempsey, Thomas, actor; b. Jan. 20, 1868, Philadelphia, Pa.; d. Oct. 6, 1947 (79).
De Navarro, Mary, actress; d. 1940.
de Navrotsky, Igor (see Dega, Igor)
Deniaud, Yves, actor; d. Dec. 1959 (58).
Denison, Edwin, actor; d. Jan. 26, 1928 (65).

Dennis, Crystal, actress; b. May 15, 1893, Kansas; d. Dec. 15, 1973
(80).
Dennis, Nadine, actress; d. Aug. 11, 1979 (83).
Denniston, Reynolds, actor; b. Dunedin, New Zealand; d. Jan. 29,
1943 (62).
Denny, Reginald, actor; b. Nov. 21, 1891, Richmond, Surrey, England;
d. June 16, 1967 (75).
De Normand, George, actor & stuntman; b. Sept. 22, 1903, New York
City; d. Dec. 23, 1976 (73).
Dent, Vernon, actor; b. Feb. 16, 1895, California; d. Nov. 4, 1963
(68).
Denton, Crahan, actor; b. Mar. 20, 1914, Seattle, Wash.; d. Dec. 4,
1966 (52).
Denton, George, actor; d. Mar. 12, 1918.
de Orduna, Juan, actor; d. Dec. 27, 1900, Madrid, Spain; d. Feb. 2,
1974 (73).
de Pomes, Felix, actor; b. Feb. 5, 1889, Barcelona, Spain; d. July 17,
1969 (80).
Depp, Harry, actor; b. Feb. 22, 1883, Missouri; d. Mar. 31, 1957 (74).
Deppe, Hans, director & actor; b. Nov. 12, 1897, Berlin, Germany;
d. Sept. 23, 1969 (71).
de Putti, Lya, actress; b. Jan. 10, 1900, Budapest, Hungary; d. Nov.
27, 1931 (31).
de Ravenne, Charline Marie, actress; b. May 13, 1882, France; d. May
8, 1962 (79).
De Ravenne, Raymond, actor; d. Oct. 14, 1950 (46).
Derba, Mimi, actress; b. Mexico; d. July 14, 1953 (59).
De Riso, Camillo, actor; b. 1854, Naples, Italy; d. Apr. 2, 1924 (70).
Dermo, Pierre (r.n. Leopold Molders), actor; d. June 15, 1976 (65).
Dermoz, Germaine, actress; b. 1889, Paris, France; d. Nov. 5, 1966
(77).
De Roche, Charles, actor; b. France; d. Feb. 2, 1952 (72).
de Rochemont, Louis, producer; b. Jan. 13, 1899, Boston, Mass.;
d. Dec. 23, 1978 (79).
De Rosas, Enrique, actor; b. July 14, 1888, Buenos Aires, Argentina;
d. Jan. 20, 1948 (59).
deRoulet, Yvonn, actress; d. May 17, 1950 (50).
Derwent, Clarence, actor; b. Mar. 23, 1884, London, England; d. Aug.
6, 1959 (75).
Des Autels, Van, actor & narrator; d. Sept. 2, 1968 (57).
de Segurola, Andreas, actor & opera singer; b. Madrid, Spain; d. Jan.
23, 1953 (78).
Desfis, Angelos, actor; b. Dec. 11, 1888, Greece; d. July 27, 1950
(61).
Desfontaines, Henri, actor & director; d. Jan. 7, 1931.
Deshon, Florence, actress; d. Feb. 4, 1922 (28).
De Sica, Vittorio, actor & director; b. July 7, 1901, Sora, Italy;
d. Nov. 13, 1974 (73).
De Silva, Frank, actor; d. Mar. 20, 1968 (78).
De Silva, Fred, actor; b. Feb. 7, 1885, Lisbon, Portugal; d. Feb. 16,
1929 (44).
Deslys, Gaby, actress; b. Marseilles, France; d. Feb. 11, 1920 (36).
Desmond, Ethel, actress; d. Feb. 5, 1949 (75).
Desmond, Lucille, actress; d. Nov. 20, 1936 (42).
Desmond, William, actor; b. Jan. 23, 1878, New York City; d. Nov. 2,
1949 (71).

Desmonde, Jerry, actor; b. July 20, 1908, Middlesbrough, England;
   d. Feb. 11, 1967 (58).
De Soto, Henri, actor; d. Sept. 9, 1963 (75).
Despres, Suzanne, actress; d. July, 1951 (76).
Deste, Luli, actress; b. Vienna, Austria; d. July 7, 1951 (42).
De Stefani, Helen, actress; d. Jan. 8, 1938 (58).
De Stefani, Joseph (Joseph Stefani), actor; b. Oct. 3, 1879,
   Venice, Italy; d. Oct. 26, 1940 (61).
Destinn, Emmy, actress & opera singer; b. Feb. 26, 1878, Prague,
   Czechoslovakia; d. Jan. 28, 1930 (51).
De Szemere, Julius, actor; d. Dec. 8, 1950 (61).
De Tellier, Mariette, actress; d. Dec. 9, 1957 (66).
de Tolly, Deena, actress; d. Jan. 23, 1976.
Deuel, Peter (see Duel, Pete)
Deutsch, Adolph, composer; b. Oct. 20, 1897, London, England; d.
   Jan. 1, 1980 (82).
Deutsch, Ernst (Ernest Dorian), actor; b. Sept. 16, 1890, Prague,
   Czechoslovakia; d. Mar. 22, 1969 (78).
Deutsch, Lou, actor; b. July 15, 1898, New York; d. Oct. 11, 1968
   (70).
Deval, Marguerite, actress; b. Sept. 19, 1868; d. Dec., 1955 (87).
de Valdez, Carlos, actor; b. Aug. 7, 1888, Peru, Chile; d. Oct. 30,
   1939 (51).
Devaull, William P., actor; b. Dec. 12, 1870, San Francisco, Calif.;
   d. June 4, 1945 (74).
de Vaux, Renee, actress; d. Mar. 29, 1961 (80).
de Vera, Cris (r.n. Cristobal Masilongan), actor; d. June 25, 1974
   (49).
Devere, Arthur, actor; d. Sept. 23, 1961 (78).
Devere, Francesca, actress; d. Sept. 11, 1952 (61).
DeVere, Harry, actor; b. Feb. 1, 1870, New York; d. Oct. 10, 1923
   (53).
Devereaux, Jack, actor; d. Jan. 19, 1958 (76).
Deverell, John W., actor; b. May 30, 1880; d. Mar. 2, 1965 (84).
DeVernon, Frank, actor; d. Oct. 19, 1923 (78).
De Vestel, Guy, actor; b. Oct. 12, 1896, France; d. Apr. 27, 1973
   (76).
Devine, Andy, actor; b. Oct. 27, 1905, Flagstaff, Ariz.; d. Feb. 18,
   1977 (71).
Devine, George, actor; b. Nov. 20, 1910, London, England; d. Jan.
   20, 1966 (55).
De Vinna, Clyde, cinematographer; d. July 26, 1953 (60).
Devlin, Joe (r.n. Christopher Joseph Devlin), actor; b. Feb. 7, 1894,
   New York; d. Oct. 1, 1973 (79).
Devoe, Bert, actor; d. Jan. 17, 1930 (45).
de Vogt, Carl, actor; b. Sept. 14, 1885; d. Feb., 1970 (84).
DeVol, Norman, cameraman; b. June 7, 1900, Marietta, Ohio; d. July
   31, 1933 (33).
Devore, Dorothy, actress; b. June 22, 1899, Ft. Worth, Tex.; d.
   Sept. 10, 1976 (77).
Dew, Eddie, actor; b. Jan. 29, 1909, Washington; d. Apr. 6, 1972
   (63).
Dew, Edward (see Dew, Eddie)
Dewan, Karan, actress; d. Aug. 2, 1979 (62).
De Warfaz, George, actor; b. Dec. 2, 1884, Spain; d. Oct. 14, 1959
   (74).

De Weese, Frank, actor; d. Apr. 15, 1928 (25).
Dewey, Anna, actress; b. Dec. 1, 1880, Missouri; d. June 24, 1967
    (86).
Dewey, Earle S., actor; b. June 2, 1881, Manhattan, Kans.; d. Feb. 5,
    1950 (68).
Dewhurst, William, actor; d. Oct. 26, 1937 (49).
De Wilde, Brandon, actor; b. Apr. 9, 1942, Brooklyn, N.Y.; d. July
    6, 1972 (30).
DeWitt, Alan, actor; d. June 2, 1976 (52).
De Wolfe, Billy, actor; b. Feb. 18, 1907, Massachusetts; d. Mar. 5,
    1974 (67).
Dexter, Aubrey, actor; b. Mar. 29, 1898, London, England; d. May,
    1958 (60).
Dexter, Donald A., photographer & actor; b. Dec. 19, 1909, Eaton,
    Colo.; d. Dec. 3, 1948 (38).
Dexter, Elliott, actor; d. June 23, 1941 (71).
Dexter, William, actor; d. Nov. 29, 1974.
Dhelia, France, actress; b. 1898, Saint-Lubin-in-Vergonnois, France;
    d. May 6, 1964 (66).
Dial, Patterson, actress; b. May 19, 1902, Madison, Fla.; d. Mar.
    23, 1945 (42).
Dicenta, Manuel, actor; d. Nov. 19, 1974 (70).
Dickerson, Dudley, actor; b. Nov. 27, 1906, Oklahoma; d. Sept. 23,
    1968 (61).
Dickerson, Jennie, actress & opera singer; d. Aug. 14, 1943 (88).
Dickey, Basil, writer; d. June 17, 1958 (77).
Dickey, Paul, actor & author; b. May 12, 1882, Chicago, Ill.; d.
    Jan. 8, 1933 (50).
Dickinson, Homer, actor; d. June 6, 1959 (69).
Dickson, Charles, actor; b. New York City; d. Dec. 11, 1927 (67).
Dickson, Gloria (r.n. Thais Dickerson), actress; b. Aug. 13, 1917,
    Pocatello, Ida.; d. Apr. 10, 1945 (27).
Dickson, John V., actor; b. Mar. 28, 1875, Bordentown, N.J.;
    d. Apr. 12, 1941 (66).
Dickson, Lamont, actor; d. May 7, 1944.
Dickson, Lydia, actress; b. Apr. 17, 1887, Missouri; d. Mar. 26,
    1928 (40).
Didway, Ernest, actor; d. Jan. 3, 1939 (67).
Diegelmann, Wilhelm, actor; b. Sept. 28, 1861, Worbeck, Germany;
    d. Mar. 1, 1934 (72).
Diehl, Karl Ludwig, actor; b. Aug. 14, 1896, Halle, Germany;
    d. Mar. 9, 1958 (61).
Dierkes, John, actor; b. Feb. 10, 1905, Ohio; d. Jan. 8, 1975 (69).
Diessl, Gustav, actor; b. Dec. 30, 1899, Vienna, Austria; d. Mar. 20,
    1948 (48).
Dieterle, William, director & actor; b. July 15, 1893, Ludwigshafen,
    Germany; d. Dec. 8, 1972 (79).
Dietl, Frank H., actor; b. Nov. 15, 1875, Lakeville, Ind.; d. Jan.
    24, 1923 (47).
Dieudonne, Albert, actor; d. Mar. 19, 1976 (84).
Di Gaetano, Adam, dancer; b. Nov. 6, 1906, Pennsylvania; d. Apr. 30,
    1966 (59).
Digges, Dudley, actor; b. 1879, Dublin, Ireland; d. Oct. 24, 1947
    (68).
Diggins, Eddie, actor; d. Mar. 26, 1927 (29).
Dignam, Basil, actor; b. 1905, Sheffield, England; d. Jan. 24, 1979 (73).

Di Golconda, Ligia, actress; d. Jan., 1942 (58).

Diky, Alexander, actor; d. 1955 (66).

Dill, Max M., actor; b. Cleveland, Ohio; d. Nov. 21, 1949 (71).

Dillard, Art (r.n. Charles A. Dillard), actor & stuntman; b. Feb. 20, 1907, Texas; d. Mar. 30, 1960 (53).

Dillard, Bert, actor; d. June 19, 1960 (51).

Dilligil, Avni, actor; d. June, 1971 (62).

Dillon, Dick, actor; d. Apr., 1961 (65).

Dillon, Edward, actor & director; b. Jan. 1, 1879, New York City; d. July 11, 1933 (54).

Dillon, George (Tim), actor; b. July 29, 1888, Georgia; d. Oct. 22, 1965 (77).

Dillon, John Francis, director & actor; b. Nov. 26, 1883, New York City; d. Apr. 4, 1934 (50).

Dillon, John T., actor; b. June 19, 1876, Deal Beach, N.J.; d. Dec. 29, 1937 (61).

Dillon, John Webb, actor; b. Feb. 6, 1877, England; d. Dec. 20, 1949 (72).

Dillon, Josephine, actress; b. Jan. 26, 1884, Colorado; d. Nov. 10, 1971 (87).

Dillon, Stella, actress; d. Apr. 28, 1934 (56).

Dillon, Thomas P., actor; d. Nov. 7, 1895, Ireland; d. Sept. 14, 1962 (66).

Dilson, Clyde, actor; b. May 7, 1899; d. Jan. 25, 1957 (57).

Dilson, John H., actor; b. Feb. 18, 1891, Brooklyn, N.Y.; d. June 3, 1944 (53).

Diltz, Charles B., editor, director, & author; d. Feb. 20, 1972 (76).

Dimock, Florence Irene, actress; d. Jan. 31, 1962 (72).

Dinehart, Alan, actor; b. St. Paul, Minn.; d. July 17, 1944 (58).

d'Ines, Denis, actor; b. Sept. 1, 1885, Paris, France; d. Oct. 25, 1968 (83).

Dingle, Charles, actor; b. Dec. 28, 1887, Wabash, Ind.; d. Jan. 19, 1956 (68).

Dione, Rose, actress; d. Jan. 29, 1936 (58).

Dippel, Andreas, producer & opera singer; b. Nov. 30, 1866, Kassel, Germany; d. May 19, 1932 (65).

di Sangro, Elena, actress; b. Sept. 5, 1901, Vasto d'Aimone, Italy; d. Jan. 26, 1969 (67).

Discipolo, Enrique Santos, actor; b. 1901; d. 1951 (50).

Disney, Roy, executive; d. Dec. 20, 1971 (78).

Disney, Walt, producer, director, & cartoonist; b. Dec. 5, 1901, Chicago, Ill.; d. Dec. 15, 1966 (65).

Ditt, Josephine, actress; b. Sept. 7, 1868, Chicago, Ill.; d. Oct. 18, 1939 (71).

Dix, Beulah Marie, writer; b. Kingston, Mass.; d. Sept. 25, 1970 (94).

Dix, Billy, actor; b. Sept. 4, 1911, Oklahoma; d. Mar. 22, 1973 (61).

Dix, Lillian, actress; d. Oct. 10, 1922 (58).

Dix, Richard (r.n. Ernest Carlton Brimmer), actor; b. July 18, 1893, St. Paul, Minn.; d. Sept. 20, 1949 (56).

Dix, Rollo (see Vallon, Michael)

Dixey, Henry E., actor; b. Jan. 6, 1859, Boston, Mass.; d. Feb. 25, 1943 (84).

Dixon, Charlotte Louise, actress; d. Oct., 1970.

Dixon, Conway, actor; d. Jan. 18, 1943 (69).

Dixon, Denver (r.n. Albert Adamson), actor & producer; b. Jan. 4, 1890, New Zealand; d. Nov. 9, 1972 (82).

Dixon, Emmett G., actor; b. Sept. 11, 1892, Texas; d. Jan. 17, 1969 (76).

Dixon, Henry, actor; b. Dec. 21, 1869, New York City; d. May 3, 1943 (73).

Dixon, Lee, actor; b. Jan. 22, 1910, Brooklyn, N.Y.; d. Jan. 8, 1953 (42).

Dobbins, Ben F., actor; d. July 22, 1930 (41).

Dobbins, Earl E., stuntman; d. Feb. 9, 1949 (38).

Doble, Frances, actress; b. 1902, Montreal, Canada; d. Dec., 1969 (67).

Doblin, Hugo, actor; d. Nov., 1960 (85).

Dockson, Evllyn, actress; b. Aug. 8, 1888, Missouri; d. May 20, 1952 (63).

Dockstader, Lew, actor; b. Hartford, Conn.; d. Oct. 26, 1924 (68).

Dodd, Claire, actress; b. Dec. 29, 1908, Arkansas; d. Nov. 23, 1973 (64).

Dodd, Elizabeth, actress; d. Nov. 19, 1928.

Dodd, Ellen, actress; d. Mar. 15, 1935 (65).

Dodd, Jimmie, actor; b. Cincinnati, Ohio; d. Nov. 10, 1964 (54).

Dodd, Neal, actor & minister; b. Sept. 6, 1879, Iowa; d. May 26, 1966 (86).

Dodds, Chuck, singer; b. May 6, 1935, California; d. Oct. 11, 1967 (32).

Dodds, Jack, dancer; b. May 22, 1928, Ohio; d. June 2, 1962 (34).

Dodge, Anna (Anna Hernandez), actress; b. Oct. 19, 1867, River Falls, Wisc.; d. May 4, 1945 (77).

Dodson, William T., stuntman; d. Sept. 17, 1933 (41).

Dodsworth, John, actor; b. Sept. 17, 1910, England; d. Sept. 11, 1964 (53).

Dohm, Will, actor; b. 1898, Koln, Germany; d. Nov. 28, 1948 (50).

Dolenz, George, actor; b. Jan. 5, 1908, Trieste, Yugoslavia; d. Feb. 8, 1963 (55).

Dolly, Jenny (Yancsi), actress; b. Oct. 25, 1890, Hungary; d. June 1, 1941 (50).

Dolly, Rosie (Roszika), actress; b. Oct. 25, 1890, Hungary; d. Feb. 1, 1970 (79).

Dolly, Lady, actress; d. Sept. 5, 1953 (77).

Domashyova, Mariya P., actress; b. Jan. 2, 1875; d. May 8, 1952 (77).

Dominguez, Beatrice, actress & dancer; b. Sept. 6, 1897, California; d. Feb. 27, 1921 (23).

Dominguez, Joe, actor; b. Mar. 19, 1894, Mexico; d. Apr. 11, 1970 (76).

Dominici, Mario, actor; b. Nov. 15, 1883, Italy; d. June 29, 1942 (58).

Dominique, Ivan, actor; b. Antwerp, Belgium; d. Apr. 3, 1973 (45).

Don, David L., actor; d. Oct. 27, 1949 (82).

Donadio, Giulio, actor; b. July 5, 1889, S. Maria Capua Vetere, Italy; d. June 15, 1951 (61).

Donahue, Jack, actor; b. Charlestown, Mass.; d. Oct. 1, 1930 (38).

Donahue, Vincent, actor; d. Feb. 10, 1976 (58).

Donaldson, Arthur, actor; b. Apr. 5, 1869, Norsholm, Sweden; d. Sept. 28, 1955 (86).

Donat, Robert, actor; b. Mar. 18, 1905, Withington, Manchester, England; d. June 9, 1958 (53).

Donath, Louis (see Donath, Ludwig)
Donath, Ludwig (Louis Donath), actor; b. Mar. 6, 1900, Vienna, Austria; d. Sept. 29, 1967 (67).
Donaz, Lyana (Lyn Donaldson Mittell), actress; b. Dec. 31, 1891, New York City; d. Mar. 2, 1966 (74).
Dondini, Ada, actress; b. Mar. 18, 1883, Cosenza, Italy; d. Jan. 3, 1958 (74).
Doner, Maurice, actor; d. Feb. 21, 1971 (66).
Doner, Rose, actress; d. Aug. 15, 1926 (21).
Donlan, James, actor; b. July 23, 1888, San Francisco, Calif.; d. June 7, 1938 (49).
Donlevy, Brian (r.n. Waldo Brian Donlevy), actor; b. Feb. 9, 1901, Ohio; d. Apr. 5, 1972 (71).
Donlin, Mike, actor; b. May 30, 1877, Peoria, Ill.; d. Sept. 24, 1933 (56).
Donnelley, Bill, actor; b. Mar. 15, 1900, Texas; d. Mar. 6, 1973 (72).
Donnelly, Dorothy, writer & actress; d. Jan. 3, 1928 (47).
Donnelly, James, actor; d. Apr. 13, 1937 (72).
Donnelly, Leo, actor; b. Philadelphia, Pa.; d. Aug. 20, 1935 (57).
Donohue, Joe, actor; d. Oct. 24, 1921 (37).
Donovan, Michael Patrick, actor; b. Nov. 29, 1878, Massachusetts; d. Nov. 11, 1960 (81).
Doolan, Toby, actor; d. Dec. 28, 1946 (79).
Dooley, Billy, actor; b. Feb. 8, 1893, Chicago, Ill.; d. Aug. 4, 1938 (45).
Dooley, J. Gordon, actor; d. Jan. 24, 1930 (31).
Dooley, Jed, actor; d. Sept. 4, 1973 (89).
Dooley, Johnny, actor & dancer; b. Glasgow, Scotland; d. June 7, 1928 (41).
Doonan, George, actor; d. Apr. 17, 1973 (76).
Doonan, Patric, actor; d. Mar. 10, 1958 (31).
Dora, Josefine, actress; d. May, 1944 (76).
Doraldina (r.n. Dora Saunders), b. San Francisco, Calif.; d. Feb. 13, 1936 (48).
Doran, Charles, actor; d. Apr. 5, 1964 (87).
Dorety, Charles R., actor; b. May 20, 1898, San Francisco, Calif.; d. Apr. 2, 1957 (58).
D'Orgaz, Elena, actress; d. Dec. 28, 1947.
Dorian, Charles W., director; d. Oct. 21, 1942 (49).
Dorian, Ernest (see Deutsch, Ernst)
Dorleac, Francoise, actress; b. Mar. 21, 1942, Paris, France; d. June 26, 1967 (25).
Dorn, Philip, actor; b. Sept. 13, 1901, Scheveningen, Holland; d. May 9, 1975 (73).
Doro, Marie, actress; b. May 25, 1882, Duncannon, Pa.; d. Oct. 9, 1956 (74).
Dorokhin, Nikolay I., actor; b. May 18, 1905; d. Dec. 31, 1953 (48).
Dorree, Bobbie (Babette), actress; d. Jan. 10, 1974 (68).
Dorsay, Edmund, actor; d. June 12, 1959 (62).
D'Orsay, Lawrence, actor; b. Aug. 19, 1853, Peterborough, Northamptonshire, England; d. Sept. 13, 1931 (78).
Dorsch, Kaethe, actress; b. Dec. 29, 1890, Neumarkt, Germany; d. Dec. 25, 1957 (66).
Dorsey, Jimmy, bandleader; b. Feb. 29, 1904, Shenandoah, Pa.; d. June 12, 1957 (53).

Dorsey, Tommy, bandleader; b. Nov. 19, 1905, Shenandoah, Pa.; d. Nov. 26, 1956 (51).
D'Orsi, Umberto, actor; b. 1929; d. Aug. 31, 1976 (47).
Dorville, actor; b. 1901; d. 1941 (40).
Dorziat, Gabrielle, actress; d. Nov. 30, 1979 (99).
Doscher, Doris, actress; d. Mar. 9, 1970 (88).
Dossett, Chappell, actor; b. Jan. 1, 1883, England; d. Dec. 19, 1961 (78).
Doty, Douglas, writer; d. Feb. 20, 1935 (60).
Doty, Weston, actor; b. Feb. 18, 1913, Malta, Ohio; d. Jan. 1, 1934 (20).
Doty, Winston, actor; b. Feb. 18, 1913, Malta, Ohio; d. Jan. 1, 1934 (20).
Doucet, Catherine, actress; b. Richmond, Va.; d. June 24, 1958 (83).
Dougherty, Joe, actor; d. Apr. 19, 1978 (80).
Douglas, Byron, actor; d. Apr. 21, 1935 (70).
Douglas, Don, actor; b. Aug. 24, 1905, Scotland; d. Dec. 31, 1945 (40).
Douglas, Frederick C., actor; d. July 17, 1929 (62).
Douglas, Gilbert, actor; d. Oct. 11, 1959.
Douglas, Keith (see Kennedy, Douglas)
Douglas, Maria, actress; d. Dec. 16, 1973 (50).
Douglas, Milton, actor; d. Sept. 5, 1970 (64).
Douglas, Paul, actor; b. Apr. 11, 1907, Philadelphia, Pa.; d. Sept. 11, 1959 (52).
Douglas, Royal, actor; d. June, 1924 (40).
Douglas, Tom, actor; d. May 4, 1978 (82).
Douglass, Kent (see Montgomery, Douglass)
Dovey, Alice, actress; d. Jan. 12, 1969 (84).
Dovzhenko, Alexander, director & actor; b. Sept. 11, 1894, Sosnitsy, Ukraine; d. Nov. 25, 1956 (62).
Dowlan, William C., actor & director; b. Sept. 21, 1882, St. Paul, Minn.; d. Nov. 6, 1947 (65).
Dowling, Constance, actress; b. New York City; d. Oct. 28, 1969 (49).
Dowling, Eddie, actor; b. Dec. 9, 1894, Woonsocket, R.I.; d. Feb. 18, 1976 (81).
Dowling, Eva, actress; d. Oct. 12, 1956.
Dowling, Joan, actress; b. Jan. 6, 1928, Laindon, Essex, England; d. May 31, 1954 (26).
Dowling, Joseph J. (r.n. Joseph Johnson Dowling), actor; b. Sept. 4, 1848, Pittsburgh, Pa.; d. July 8, 1928 (80).
Downing, Harry, actor; d. Jan. 9, 1972 (78).
Downing, Joseph, actor; b. June 26, 1903, New York; d. Oct. 16, 1975 (72).
Downing, Robert, actor & writer; b. Sioux City, Iowa; d. June 14, 1975 (61).
Downing, Walter, actor; b. Oct. 28, 1874, Rochester, N.Y.; d. Dec. 22, 1937 (63).
Downs, Cathy, actress; b. Mar. 3, 1926, New York; d. Dec. 8, 1976 (50).
Downs, Watson, actor; b. Apr. 10, 1879, West Virginia; d. May 26, 1969 (90).
Dowsey, Rose Walker, actress; d. July 29, 1951 (44).
Doyle, Billy, actor; d. Feb. 14, 1945 (53).
Doyle, Buddy, actor; d. Nov. 9, 1939 (38).

Doyle, John T., actor; b. St. Louis, Mo.; d. Oct. 16, 1935 (62).
Doyle, Maxine, actress; b. Jan. 1, 1915, California; d. May 7, 1973 (58).
Doyle, Mimi, actress; d. June 15, 1979 (64).
Doyle, Patricia, actress; d. Sept. 22, 1975 (60).
Doyle, Ray, actor; d. June 15, 1954 (56).
Doyle, Regina, actress; d. Sept. 30, 1931 (24).
Drago, Cathleen, actress; d. Dec. 24, 1938.
Drainie, John, actor; d. Oct. 30, 1966 (50).
Drake, Douglass (see Mitchell, Johnny)
Drake, Josephine Smart, actress; d. Jan. 7, 1929.
Drake, Steve (r.n. Dale Lawrence Fink), actor; b. Dec. 12, 1923,
    Wichita, Kans.; d. Dec. 19, 1948 (25).
Drake, Virgil, actor; b. Oct. 5, 1896, Hewins, Kans.; d. Feb. 12,
    1946 (49).
Dranem, actor; d. Oct. 13, 1935 (66).
Draper, Joseph, actor; d. Aug. 14, 1978 (61).
Dratler, Jay, writer; b. Sept. 14, 1911, New York City; d. Sept. 25,
    1968 (57).
Drayton, Alfred, actor; b. Nov. 1, 1881, Brighton, England; d. Apr.
    26, 1949 (67).
Dresdel, Sonia, actress; b. Hornsea, Yorks., England; d. Jan. 18,
    1976 (67).
Dresser, Louise, actress; b. Oct. 5, 1878, Evansville, Ind.; d. Apr.
    24, 1965 (86).
Dressler, Marie, actress; b. Nov. 9, 1869, Cobourg, Canada; d. July
    28, 1934 (64).
Drew, Ann, actress; b. New York City; d. Feb. 6, 1974 (83).
Drew, Lillian, actress; d. Feb. 4, 1924 (41).
Drew, Lowell, actor; b. Mar. 30, 1882, Pennsylvania; d. Oct. 14,
    1942 (60).
Drew, Lucille McVey, actress; d. Nov. 3, 1925 (35).
Drew, Philip Yale, actor; d. July 2, 1940 (60).
Drew, S. Rankin, actor; d. May 19, 1918 (27).
Drew, Sidney, actor; b. New York City; d. Apr. 9, 1919 (55).
Dreyer, Carl Th., director; b. Feb. 3, 1889, Copenhagen, Denmark;
    d. Mar. 20, 1968 (79).
Dreyfuss, Michael, actor; d. Mar. 30, 1960 (32).
Driggers, Donald Clayton, actor; d. Nov. 19, 1972 (79).
Driscoll, Bobby, actor; b. Mar. 3, 1937, Cedar Rapids, Iowa; d. Mar.
    30, 1968 (31).
Driscoll, Sam W., actor; d. Dec. 13, 1956 (88).
Driscoll, Tex (Frank Driscoll) (r.n. John W. Morris), actor; b. Sept.
    7, 1889, Indiana; d. June 1, 1970 (80).
Dromgold, George, actor & author; d. Apr. 9, 1948 (54).
Drouet, Robert, actor; b. Mar. 27, 1870, Clinton, Iowa; d. Aug. 17,
    1914 (44).
Drubin, Charles, actor; d. Sept. 23, 1976 (82).
Druce, Hubert, actor; b. May 20, 1870, Twickenham, England; d. Apr.
    6, 1931 (60).
Drum, Jim, actor; d. Nov. 28, 1976 (58).
Drumier, Jack, actor; d. Apr. 2, 1929 (60).
Dryden, Leo, actor; d. Apr. 21, 1939 (74).
Dryden, Wheeler, actor; b. Aug. 31, 1893, London, England; d. Sept.
    30, 1957 (64).
Duane, Jack (see Padjan, Jack)

Duarte, Eva (Eva Peron), actress & politician; d. July 26, 1952 (33).
Dubin, Al, composer & actor; b. Zurich, Switzerland; d. Feb. 11,
    1945 (54).
Dubois, Louis-Alexis, actor; d. Jan. 11, 1978 (44).
Dubosc, Andre, actor; b. 1865; d. 1935 (70).
Dubov, Paul, actor; b. Oct. 10, 1918, Illinois; d. Sept. 20, 1979 (60).
Du Cello, Countess (Mary Du Cello), actress; b. London, England;
    d. Nov. 20, 1921 (57).
Ducet, H. Paul, actor; d. Oct. 10, 1928 (42).
Duchin, Eddy, recording artist; b. Apr. 1, 1909, Cambridge, Mass.;
    d. Feb. 9, 1951 (41).
Du Count, George (George A. Gleboff), actor; b. Feb. 19, 1891, Russia;
    d. Feb. 7, 1960 (68).
Ducrow, Tote G., actor; b. Watsonville, Calif.; d. Dec. 12, 1927 (69).
Dudgeon, Elspeth, actress; b. Dec. 4, 1871, England; d. Dec. 11, 1955
    (84).
Dudley, Ethlyn (Ethyl Sloat Langley), actress; d. Apr. 28, 1977 (88).
Dudley, George, actor; d. Apr. 23, 1972 (91).
Dudley, John Stuart, actor; d. May 1, 1966 (72).
Dudley, Robert Y., actor; b. Sept. 13, 1869, Cincinnati, Ohio; d.
    Nov. 12, 1955 (86).
Dudow, Slatan, director; b. Jan. 30, 1903, Bulgaria; d. July 12, 1963
    (60).
Duel, Pete (Peter Deuel), actor; b. Feb. 24, 1940, Rochester, N.Y.;
    d. Dec. 31, 1971 (31).
Dufau, C.R., actor; b. Sept. 4, 1879, Mexico; d. Feb. 20, 1957 (77).
Duff, Warren, writer; b. May 17, 1904, San Francisco, Calif.; d.
    Aug. 5, 1973 (69).
Duffell, Bee, actress; d. Dec. 21, 1974.
Duffield, Brainerd, actor & author; d. Apr. 5, 1979 (62).
Duffield, Harry, actor; d. Oct. 31, 1921.
Duffy, Albert, writer; b. Feb. 3, 1903, Hartford, Conn.; d. Sept.
    15, 1976 (73).
Duffy, Jack, actor; b. Sept. 4, 1882, Pawtucket, R.I.; d. July 23,
    1939 (56).
Dufraine, Rosa, actress; d. Apr. 29, 1935 (34).
Dugan, Elsie M., actress; d. Apr., 1934 (25).
Dugan, Marie Engle, extra; d. Mar. 23, 1971 (69).
Dugan, Tom, actor; b. Jan. 1, 1889, Dublin, Ireland; d. Mar. 7, 1955
    (66).
Duggan, Jan (r.n. Genevieve Lelia Duggan), actress; b. Nov. 6, 1881,
    Missouri; d. Mar. 10, 1977 (95).
Duggan, Tom, actor & emcee; b. Chicago, Ill.; d. May 29, 1969 (53).
Duke, Michael (see Adlon, Louis)
Duke, Robert, actor; d. Mar. 8, 1979.
Dukelan, George W., actor; d. Jan. 9, 1933 (88).
Dulac, Arthur, actor; b. May 13, 1903, France; d. Sept. 18, 1962 (59).
Dulac, Germaine, director & producer; b. 1882, Amiens, France; d.
    July, 1942 (60).
Dullin, Charles, actor & director; b. Yenne, France; d. Dec. 11,
    1949 (64).
Dullzell, Paul, actor; b. June 15, 1879, Boston, Mass.; d. Dec. 21,
    1961 (82).
Du Maurier, Gerald, actor; b. Mar. 26, 1873, Hampstead, England;
    d. Apr. 11, 1934 (61).
Dumbrille, Douglass, actor; b. Oct. 13, 1889, Hamilton, Ont., Canada;
    d. Apr. 2, 1974 (84).

Dumcke, Ernst, actor; b. Nov. 13, 1887, Mannheim, Germany; d. June 21, 1940 (52).

Dumke, Ralph, actor; b. July 25, 1899, Indiana; d. Jan. 4, 1964 (64).

Dumont, Gordon (r.n. Raymond R. Bourgeois), actor; b. Apr. 24, 1894, Wisconsin; d. Mar. 7, 1966 (71).

Dumont, J.M. (J. Monte Dumont; George McNamara) (r.n. John Monte Dumont), actor; b. Feb. 7, 1879, Louisiana; d. Dec. 19, 1959 (80).

Dumont, Margaret, actress; b. Oct. 20, 1889, New York; d. Mar. 6, 1965 (75).

Dunbar, Blanche, actress; d. Mar. 7, 1932.

Dunbar, David, actor; b. Sept. 14, 1886, Australia; d. Nov. 7, 1953 (67).

Dunbar, Helen (r.n. Katheryn Burke Lackey), actress; b. Oct. 10, 1863, Philadelphia, Pa.; d. Aug. 28, 1933 (69).

Dunbar, Jack, actor & manager; d. Oct. 15, 1961 (65).

Dunbar, Robert, actor; b. July 1, 1858, Beaver, Pa.; d. Jan. 16, 1943 (84).

Duncan, Archie, actor; b. May 26, 1914, Glasgow, Scotland; d. July 24, 1979 (65).

Duncan, Bob, actor; b. Dec. 7, 1906, Topeka, Kans.; d. Mar. 13, 1967 (60).

Duncan, Bud (r.n. Albert Edward Duncan), actor; b. Oct. 31, 1883, New York; d. Nov. 26, 1960 (77).

Duncan, Charles, actor; d. Oct., 1942 (22).

Duncan, Evelyn, actress; b. Jan. 21, 1893, Los Angeles, Calif.; d. June 8, 1972 (79).

Duncan, Kenne (r.n. Kenneth D. MacLachlan), actor; b. Feb. 17, 1902, Chatham, Ont., Canada; d. Feb. 7, 1972 (69).

Duncan, Rosetta, actress; b. Los Angeles, Calif.; d. Dec. 4, 1959 (63).

Duncan, Tommy, singer; d. July 24, 1967 (57).

Duncan, William, actor; b. Dec. 16, 1879, Scotland; d. Feb. 7, 1961 (81).

Duncan, William Cary, author; b. Feb. 6, 1874, North Brookfield, Mass.; d. Nov. 21, 1945 (71).

Dundee, Jimmy, actor; b. Dec. 19, 1900, Missouri; d. Nov. 20, 1953 (52).

Dunham, Phil (r.n. Philip Gray Dunham), actor & director; b. Apr. 23, 1885, London, England; d. Sept. 5, 1972 (87).

Dunkinson, Harry, actor; b. Dec. 16, 1876, New York City; d. Mar. 14, 1936 (59).

Dunlap, Scott R., director & producer; b. June 20, 1892, Chicago, Ill.; d. Mar. 30, 1970 (77).

Dunn, Bobby (r.n. Robert V. Dunn), actor; b. Aug. 28, 1890, Milwaukee, Wisc.; d. Mar. 24, 1937 (46).

Dunn, Eddie, actor; b. Mar. 31, 1896, Brooklyn, N.Y.; d. May 5, 1951 (55).

Dunn, Emma, actress; b. Feb. 26, 1875, Cheshire, England; d. Dec. 14, 1966 (91).

Dunn, Harvey B., actor; b. Aug. 19, 1894, South Dakota; d. Feb. 21, 1968 (73).

Dunn, Herbert Stanley, actor; d. Apr. 14, 1979 (87).

Dunn, J. Malcolm, actor; b. London, England; d. Oct. 10, 1946 (70).

Dunn, Jack, actor & skater; b. Mar. 28, 1917, England; d. July 15, 1938 (21).

Dunn, James, actor; b. Nov. 2, 1901, New York City; d. Sept. 1, 1967 (65).
Dunn, John J., actor; d. Apr. 2, 1938 (32).
Dunn, Liam, actor; b. Nov. 12, 1916, New Jersey; d. Apr. 11, 1976 (59).
Dunn, Michael (r.n. Gary Neil Miller), actor; b. Oct. 20, 1934, Shattuck, Okla.; d. Aug. 29, 1973 (38).
Dunn, Ralph, actor; b. May 23, 1902, Titusville, Pa.; d. Feb. 19, 1968 (65).
Dunn, Robert H., actor; d. Feb. 11, 1960 (64).
Dunne, Charles, actor; d. Sept. 16, 1951.
Dunne, Elizabeth, actress; d. Nov. 12, 1954 (65).
Dunne, Michael (see Dunne, Steve)
Dunne, Steve (Michael Dunne) (r.n. Francis Michael Dunne), actor; b. Jan. 13, 1918, Northampton, Mass.; d. Sept. 28, 1977 (59).
Dunrobin, Lionel Claude, actor; d. Aug. 15, 1950 (75).
Dunskus, Erich, actor; b. July 27, 1890, Pillkallen; d. Nov. 25, 1967 (77).
Dunsmuir, Alexander, actor; d. July 3, 1938 (61).
Dunstan, Clifford, actor; b. July 18, 1906, Texas; d. Nov. 8, 1968 (62).
DuPea, Tatsumbie (Tatzumbia Dupea), actress; b. July 26, 1849, Lone Pine, Calif.; d. Feb. 26, 1970 (120).
Dupont, E.A., director; b. Dec. 25, 1891, Zeitz, Germany; d. Dec. 12, 1956 (64).
du Pont, Miss, actress; d. Feb. 6, 1973 (79).
Dupray, Gaston, actor; d. Dec. 12, 1976 (91).
Dupree, George, actor; d. July 29, 1951 (74).
Dupree, Minnie, actress; b. Jan. 19, 1875, La Crosse, Wisc.; d. May 23, 1947 (72).
Duprez, Fred, actor; b. Sept. 6, 1884; d. Oct. 27, 1938 (54).
Dupuis, Art, actor; b. Mar. 29, 1901, Canada; d. Apr. 18, 1952 (51).
Dupuis, Paul, actor; b. Aug. 11, 1913, Montreal, Canada; d. Jan. 23, 1976 (62).
Duran, Val, actor; d. Feb. 1, 1937 (41).
Durand, Edouard, actor; b. France; d. July 31, 1926 (55).
Durante, Checco, actor; b. Nov. 19, 1893, Rome, Italy; d. Jan. 5, 1976 (82).
Durante, Jimmy, actor; b. Feb. 10, 1893, New York City; d. Jan. 29, 1980 (86).
Du Rey, Peter, actor; b. June 5, 1903, Denmark; d. Apr. 6, 1943 (39).
Durfee, Minta, actress; d. Sept. 9, 1975 (85).
Durham, Lewis, actor; b. Aug. 19, 1852, New Oxford, Pa.; d. Oct. 16, 1937 (85).
Durieux, Tilla (r.n. Ottilie Godeffroy), actress; b. Aug. 18, 1880, Vienna, Austria; d. Feb. 21, 1971 (90).
Durkin, James, actor & director; b. May 21, 1879, Quebec, Canada; d. Mar. 12, 1934 (64).
Durkin, Junior (Trent Durkin), actor; d. May 4, 1935 (20).
Durkin, Trent (see Durkin, Junior)
Durning, Bernie, director; d. Aug. 29, 1923 (30).
Durst, Edward, actor; d. Mar. 10, 1945 (28).
Duryea, Dan, actor; b. Jan. 23, 1907, White Plains, N.Y.; d. June 7, 1968 (61).
Duryea, George (see Keene, Tom)
Duse, Carlo, actor; b. Jan. 5, 1899, Udine, Italy; d. Sept. 9, 1956 (57).

Duse, Eleonora, actress; b. Oct. 3, 1858, Italy; d. Apr. 21, 1924
(65).
d'Usseau, Leon, director & producer; d. June 6, 1963 (77).
Du Val, Joe, actor; b. Aug. 8, 1906, Wisconsin; d. Apr. 22, 1966
(59).
Duval, Juan, actor; b. Apr. 28, 1899, Spain; d. Apr. 1, 1954 (54).
Duvalles, Frederic, actor; d. Feb., 1971 (76).
Duvivier, Julien, director; b. Oct. 8, 1896, Lille, France; d. Oct.
29, 1967 (71).
Duxbury, Elspeth, actress; d. Mar. 10, 1967 (55).
Dvorak, Ann, actress; b. Aug. 2, 1912, New York City; d. Dec. 10,
1979 (67).
Dwiggins, Jay, actor; d. Sept., 1919.
Dwire, Earl, actor; b. Oct. 3, 1883, Rockport, Mo.; d. Jan. 16, 1940
(56).
Dwyer, Ruth, actress; d. Mar. 2, 1978 (80).
Dyall, Franklin, actor; b. Feb. 3, 1874, Liverpool, England; d. May
8, 1950 (76).
Dyas, Dave, actor; b. Apr. 11, 1895, Missouri; d. Nov. 5, 1929 (34).
Dyce, Hamilton, actor; d. Jan. 8, 1972.
D'yd, Jean, actor; b. May 17, 1880, Paris, France; d. May, 1964 (84).
Dyer, Bob, actor; d. Nov. 19, 1965 (65).
Dyer, John E., actor; d. Oct. 11, 1951 (67).
Dyer, William, actor; b. Mar. 11, 1881, Atlanta, Ga.; d. Dec. 22,
1933 (52).
Dyneley, Peter, actor; b. Apr. 13, 1921, Hastings, England; d. Aug.
19, 1977 (56).
Dyrenforth, James, actor; b. 1895, Chicago, Ill.; d. Dec. 26, 1973
(78).


Eagan, Evelyn, actress; d. July 17, 1946 (38).
Eagels, Jeanne, actress; b. Kansas City, Mo.; d. Oct. 3, 1929 (35).
Eager, Johnny (John Tanner), actor; b. Sept. 16, 1924, England;
d. Sept. 8, 1963 (38).
Eagle, James C., actor; b. Sept. 10, 1907, Virginia; d. Dec. 15,
1959 (52).
Eagle Eye (William Eagleye; William Ens), actor & stuntman;
b. Globe, Ariz.; d. Jan. 17, 1927 (50).
Eagles, Oscar, director; d. Mar. 14, 1930 (69).
Eames, Clare, actress; b. Hartford, Conn.; d. Nov. 8, 1930 (34).
Eames, Virginia (see Boardman, Virginia True)
Earl, Catherine, actress; d. Aug. 14, 1946 (60).
Earl, Kathleen, actress; d. May 21, 1954 (41).
Earl, Max, actor; d. July 29, 1954 (68).
Earlcott, Gladys, actress; d. May 18, 1939.
Earle, Blanche (Bonnie), actress; d. Jan. 22, 1952 (69).
Earle, Edward, actor; b. July 16, 1882, Toronto, Canada; d. Dec. 15,
1972 (90).
Earle, Josephine, actress; d. Aug., 1929 (37).
Earle, Richard Edmund, actor; b. Jan. 22, 1884, Illinois; d. Mar. 5,
1962 (78).
Earle, Virginia, actress; b. Aug. 6, 1875, Cincinnati, Ohio; d. Sept.
21, 1937 (62).

Earle, William P.S., producer; b. Dec. 28, 1882, New York City;
   d. Nov. 30, 1972 (89).
Early, Margo, actress; d. Jan. 13, 1936 (18).
Early, Pearl May, actress; b. Dec. 30, 1878, Ohio; d. June 17, 1960
   (81).
Eason, Breezy (r.n. Reaves Barnes Eason), actor; b. Nov. 19, 1914,
   California; d. Oct. 25, 1921 (6).
Eason, B. Reaves (r.n. William Reaves Eason), director; b. Oct. 2,
   1886, Pryors Point, Miss.; d. June 9, 1956 (69).
East, Ed, actor; d. Jan. 18, 1952 (56).
East, John, actor; d. Aug. 18, 1924 (63).
Eastman, George, pioneer & cameraman; b. July 12, 1854, Waterville,
   Me.; d. Mar. 14, 1932 (77).
Easton, Phillip, actor; d. June 25, 1975.
Eaton, Elwyn, actor; d. Apr. 30, 1937 (72).
Eaton, James, actor; b. Oct. 2, 1934, Ohio; d. May 8, 1964 (29).
Eaton, Jay, actor; b. Mar. 17, 1899, New Jersey; d. Feb. 5, 1970 (70).
Eaton, Mary, actress; b. Jan. 29, 1901, Norfolk, Va.; d. Oct. 10,
   1948 (47).
Eaton, Pearl, actress; b. Aug. 1, 1898, Virginia; d. Sept. 10, 1958
   (60).
Ebele, Edward, actor; b. May 22, 1861, Turkheim, France; d. Feb. 19,
   1936 (74).
Ebele, Edward, production manager; b. Oct. 14, 1896, Illinois;
   d. May 25, 1955 (58).
Eberg, Victor. actor; b. July 29, 1924, Mexico; d. Feb. 26, 1972 (47).
Eberle, Ray, singer & recording artist; d. Aug. 25, 1979 (60).
Ebert, Bernie, actor; d. Jan. 13, 1969 (54).
Eberty, Paula, actress; b. Sept. 8, 1869, Berlin, Germany; d. Feb.
   5, 1929 (59).
Eburne, Maude, actress; b. Nov. 10, 1875, Canada; d. Oct. 8, 1960
   (84).
Eby, Earl, actor; b. June 25, 1903, California; d. Jan. 24, 1973
   (69).
Eby-Rock, Helyn, actress; d. July 20, 1979 (83).
Eccles, Jane, actress; b. Aug. 19, 1895, Nafferton, England; d. July,
   1966 (70).
Echols, J. Kermit, actor; d. Jan. 4, 1978 (56).
Eckard, Fritz, actor; b. Oct. 16, 1908; d. Aug., 1970 (61).
Eckels, Lew, actor; d. Mar. 26, 1950 (62).
Eckerlein, John Elwood, actor; d. Sept. 9, 1926 (42).
Eckhardt, Oliver, actor; b. Sept. 14, 1873, Missouri; d. Sept. 15,
   1952 (79).
Ecklund, Carol, actress; d. Nov. 4, 1939 (5).
Eckstrom, Marta, actress; d. Jan. 26, 1952 (53).
Eddinger, Wallace, actor; b. July 14, 1881, Albany, N.Y.; d. Jan. 8,
   1929 (47).
Eddy, Leo, extra; d. July 3, 1978 (71).
Eddy, Nelson, actor & singer; b. June 29, 1901, Providence, R.I.;
   d. Mar. 6, 1967 (65).
Edelstein, "Dad," actor; d. June, 1927 (82).
Edeson, Arthur, cinematographer; b. Oct. 24, 1891, New York City;
   d. Feb. 14, 1970 (78).
Edeson, Robert, actor; b. Jan. 3, 1868, New Orleans, La.; d. Mar.
   24, 1931 (62).

Edgar, Marriott, actor; b. Oct. 5, 1880, Colvend, Kircudbright, Scotland; d. May 4, 1951 (70).

Edgar-Bruce, Tonie, actress; b. June 4, 1892, London, England; d. Mar. 28, 1966 (73).

Edison, Thomas A., producer & inventor; b. Feb. 11, 1847, Milan, Ohio; d. Oct. 18, 1931 (84).

Ediss, Connie, actress; b. Aug. 11, 1871, Brighton, England; d. Apr. 18, 1934 (62).

Edler, Charles, actor; b. Aug. 13, 1864, New Jersey; d. Mar. 29, 1942 (77).

Edlin, Theodore M., actor; b. Oct. 3, 1894, California; d. July 7, 1974 (79).

Edmonson, William, actor; d. May 28, 1979 (76).

Edney, Florence, actress; b. June 2, 1879, London, England; d. Nov. 24, 1950 (71).

Edstrom, Katherine, actress; d. June 2, 1973 (72).

Edthofer, Anton, actor; b. Sept. 18, 1883, Vienna, Austria; d. Feb. 21, 1971 (87).

Edward, Ted, actor; d. Sept. 29, 1945 (62).

Edwards, Alan, actor; b. June 3, 1892, New York City; d. May 8, 1954 (61).

Edwards, Cliff, actor; b. June 14, 1895, Hannibal, Mo.; d. July 17, 1971 (76).

Edwards, Edna Park, actress; b. Feb. 17, 1895, Pennsylvania; d. June 5, 1967 (72).

Edwards, Eleanor, actress; d. Oct. 22, 1968 (86).

Edwards, Harry J., actor & director; d. May 26, 1952 (63).

Edwards, Henry, actor; b. Sept. 18, 1883, Weston-super-Mare, England; d. Nov. 2, 1952 (69).

Edwards, J. Gordon, director; d. Dec. 31, 1925 (58).

Edwards, James, actor; b. Mar. 6, 1918, Muncie, Ind.; d. Jan. 4, 1970 (51).

Edwards, John, actor; d. Oct. 16, 1929 (60).

Edwards, Julia, actress; d. Apr. 16, 1976 (93).

Edwards, Mattie, actress; d. June 26, 1944 (78).

Edwards, Neely, actor; b. Sept. 16, 1883, Ohio; d. July 10, 1965 (81).

Edwards, Sarah, actress; b. Oct. 11, 1881, South Wales; d. Jan. 7, 1965 (83).

Edwards, Snitz, actor; b. Jan. 1, 1862, Hungary; d. May 1, 1937 (75).

Edwards, Virginia, actress; d. Mar. 7, 1964.

Effrat, John, actor; d. May 14, 1965 (57).

Egan, George, actor; d. Sept. 26, 1943 (60).

Egan, Mishka, actor; b. Nov. 28, 1888, USSR; d. Feb. 11, 1964 (75).

Eggenton, Joseph, actor; b. Feb. 29, 1871, Ponfert, Conn.; d. July 3, 1946 (75).

Egger, Josef, actor; d. Aug. 29, 1966 (78).

Eglevsky, Andre, dancer; d. Dec. 4, 1977 (60).

Egon, Joel, actor; d. Sept. 17, 1979 (38).

Ehfe, William C., actor; b. June 19, 1887, Payette, Idaho; d. Aug. 1, 1940 (53).

Ehn, Leonore, actress; b. Oct. 8, 1888, Langenlois; d. June 23, 1978 (89).

Eichberg, Richard, director; d. May 8, 1952 (64).

Eilers, Sally, actress; b. Dec. 11, 1908, New York City; d. Jan. 5, 1978 (69).

Eisenstein, Sergei, director; b. Jan. 23, 1898, Riga, Russia; d. Feb.
  11, 1948 (50).
Eissa, Mickey, actor; b. July 15, 1900, Asia; d. Aug. 14, 1962 (62).
Ekman, Goesta, actor; b. Dec. 28, 1890, Stockholm, Sweden; d. Jan.
  12, 1938 (47).
Elba, Marta, actress; d. Apr. 19, 1954 (34).
Elder, Dottie, actress; b. May 30, 1929, Arizona; d. Nov. 28, 1965
  (36).
Elder, Richard, singer; d. Oct. 4, 1963 (52).
Elder, Ruth, actress; d. Oct. 9, 1977 (73).
Eldredge, Frank E., extra; b. June 7, 1897, Ohio; d. Oct. 5, 1961
  (64).
Eldredge, Irene, actress; d. Aug. 19, 1950 (53).
Eldredge, John, actor; b. Aug. 30, 1904, San Francisco, Calif.;
  d. Sept. 23, 1961 (57).
Eldredge, Ruth, actress; d. Nov. 3, 1939.
Eldridge, Charles, actor; d. Oct. 29, 1922 (68).
Elgeti, Alexander, actor; d. July, 1977 (86).
Eliscu, Fernanda, actress; b. Apr. 24, 1880, Rumania; d. Sept. 27,
  1968 (88).
Elizondo, Joaquin, actor; d. June 15, 1952 (56).
Ellery, Arthur, actor; d. Aug. 27, 1945 (75).
Ellingford, William, actor; d. May 20, 1936 (73).
Ellington, Duke (r.n. Edward Kennedy Ellington), jazz artist;
  b. Apr. 29, 1899, Washington, D.C.; d. May 24, 1974 (75).
Ellingwood, Elmer (r.n. Helmert F. Ellingwood), actor; b. Oct. 14,
  1907, California; d. Oct. 13, 1971 (63).
Elliot, Del, actor; d. Jan. 22, 1945 (66).
Elliott, Bert, actor; b. Mar. 15, 1929, Michigan; d. July 3, 1972
  (43).
Elliott, Clyde E., director & writer; b. Ord, Neb.; d. June 12, 1959
  (74).
Elliott, Dick, actor; b. Apr. 30, 1886, Massachusetts; d. Dec. 22,
  1961 (75).
Elliott, Gertrude, actress; b. Dec. 14, 1874, Rockland, Me.; d. Dec.
  24, 1950 (76).
Elliott, Gordon (see Elliott, William)
Elliott, Heenan, actor; b. June 12, 1892, Ohio; d. Jan. 16, 1970 (77).
Elliott, John H., actor; b. July 5, 1876, Pella, Iowa; d. Dec. 12,
  1956 (80).
Elliott, Lester, actor; d. Nov. 9, 1954 (66).
Elliott, Lillian, actress; b. Apr. 24, 1874, Canada; d. Jan. 15,
  1959 (84).
Elliott, Marguerite, actress; d. 1951.
Elliott, Maxine, actress; b. Feb. 5, 1868, Rockland, Me.; d. Mar. 5,
  1940 (72).
Elliott, Milton, stuntman; d. Aug. 2, 1920.
Elliott, Robert, actor; b. Oct. 9, 1879, Ohio; d. Nov. 15, 1951 (72).
Elliott, Ruth Thorp, actress; b. Apr. 17, 1889, Connecticut; d. Feb.
  15, 1971 (81).
Elliott, William, actor; b. Dec. 4, 1879, Boston, Mass.; d. Feb. 5,
  1932 (52).
Elliott, William (Wild Bill; Gordon Elliott) (r.n. Gordon Nance),
  actor; b. Oct. 16, 1905, Pattonsburg, Mo.; d. Nov. 26, 1965 (60).
Ellis, Diane, actress; b. Dec. 20, 1909, Los Angeles, Calif.;
  d. Dec. 15, 1930 (20).

Ellis, Edith, writer; d. Dec. 27, 1960 (86).
Ellis, Edna Small, actress; d. July 14, 1917.
Ellis, Edward, actor; b. Nov. 12, 1870, Michigan; d. July 26, 1952
    (81).
Ellis, Edwin, actor; b. Nov. 27, 1895, London, England; d. Mar. 21,
    1958 (62).
Ellis, Evelyn, actress; d. June 5, 1958 (64).
Ellis, Frank (r.n. Frank Birney Ellis), actor; b. Feb. 26, 1897,
    Oklahoma; d. Feb. 23, 1969 (71).
Ellis, Houston, actor; d. Feb. 12, 1928.
Ellis, Johnny Charles, actor; b. Sept. 14, 1940, Texas; d. May 20,
    1968 (27).
Ellis, Lillian, actress; d. Feb. 21, 1951 (40).
Ellis, Patricia, actress; b. May 20, 1918, Birmingham, Mich.;
    d. Mar. 26, 1970 (51).
Ellis, Robert, actor; d. Nov. 23, 1973 (40).
Ellis, Robert J., art director; b. Sept. 5, 1888, Pasadena, Calif.;
    d. May 20, 1935 (46).
Ellis, Robert (r.n. Robert Ellis Reel), actor & writer; b. June 27,
    1892, New York City; d. Dec. 29, 1974 (82).
Ellison, Edith, actress; b. Oct. 31, 1864, Massachusetts; d. July
    29, 1944 (79).
Ellsler, Effie, actress; b. Cleveland, Ohio; d. Oct. 8, 1942 (87).
Ellsworth, Jack, actor; d. Aug. 19, 1949 (38).
Elmer, William (Billy), actor; b. Apr. 25, 1869, Council Bluffs,
    Iowa; d. Feb. 24, 1945 (75).
Elsholtz, Peter, actor; d. Aug. 30, 1977 (69).
Eltinge, Julian, actor & female impersonator; b. May 14, 1883, New-
    tonville, Mass.; d. Mar. 7, 1941 (57).
Elton, Edmund, actor; b. Feb. 5, 1871, England; d. Jan. 4, 1952 (80).
Elton, Margaret, actress; d. May 19, 1949 (62).
Elvey, Maurice, producer & director; b. Yorkshire, England; d. Aug.
    28, 1967 (79).
Elvidge, June, actress; d. May 1, 1965 (72).
Elwell, George, actor; d. Nov. 13, 1916.
Ely, Eleazer, actor; d. Feb. 9, 1929 (90).
Ely, Harry R., actor; d. July 15, 1951 (68).
Ely, S. Gilbert, actor; d. May, 1920 (62).
Elzy, Ruby, actress; d. June 27, 1943 (33).
Emerick, Besse, actress; d. Dec. 13, 1939 (64).
Emerson, Edward, actor; d. Apr. 11, 1975 (65).
Emerson, Hope, actress; b. Oct. 30, 1897, Iowa; d. Apr. 24, 1960 (62).
Emerson, John, author, director, & actor; b. May 28, 1871, Sandusky,
    Ohio; d. Mar. 7, 1956 (84).
Emerton, Roy, actor; b. Oct. 9, 1892, Burford, Oxfordshire, England;
    d. Nov. 30, 1944 (52).
Emery, Gilbert, actor; d. Dec. 31, 1934 (52).
Emery, Gilbert, actor; b. June 11, 1875, Naples, N.Y.; d. Oct. 28,
    1945 (70).
Emery, John, actor; d. Nov. 16, 1964 (59).
Emery, Katherine, actress; b. Birmingham, Ala.; d. Feb. 6, 1980 (73).
Emery, Pollie, actress; b. May 10, 1875, Bolton, England; d. Oct. 31,
    1958 (83).
Emmet, Joseph K., actor; d. Oct. 31, 1936 (70).
Emmet, Katherine, actress; b. San Francisco, Calif.; d. June 6, 1960
    (78).

Emmett, Fern, actress; b. Mar. 22, 1896, Oakland, Calif.; d. Sept. 3, 1946 (50).
Emmett, Katherine, actress; d. Mar. 19, 1927 (68).
Emmons, Louise, actress; d. Mar. 6, 1935 (85).
Emory, Carl, actor; d. Aug. 30, 1966 (59).
Empey, Guy, actor, author, director, & producer; d. Feb. 22, 1963 (79).
Empress, Marie, actress; d. 1919.
Encinas, Lalo, actor; b. June 27, 1886, Arizona; d. May 5, 1959 (72).
Endore, Guy, writer; b. July 4, 1900; d. Feb. 12, 1970 (69).
Endresse, Clara, actress; d. Dec. 2, 1979 (83).
Enfield, Hugh (see Reynolds, Craig)
Engel, Alexander, actor; b. June 4, 1902, Berlin, Germany; d. July, 1968 (66).
Engel, Erich B., actor; d. Oct. 7, 1955 (78).
Engel, Joseph W., director; d. Apr. 18, 1943 (60).
Engels, Virginia, actress; d. Dec. 5, 1956 (39).
England, Paul, actor; b. June 17, 1893, Streatham, England; d. Nov. 21, 1968 (75).
Engle, Billy, actor; b. May 28, 1889, Austria; d. Nov. 28, 1966 (77).
Englisch, Lucie, actress; b. Feb. 8, 1902, Baden, Germany; d. Oct., 1965 (63).
English, Elsa Granger, actress; d. Feb. 8, 1955 (51).
English, John, director; b. Cumberland, England; d. Oct. 11, 1969 (66).
English, Richard, writer; b. May 18, 1910, West Newton, Pa.; d. Oct. 2, 1957 (47).
Ennis, Skinnay, band leader & actor; b. Aug. 13, 1906, Salisbury, N.C.; d. June 2, 1963 (56).
Enright, Florence, actress; b. Dec. 4, 1883, New York; d. Apr. 3, 1961 (77).
Enright, Josephine, actress; b. Oct. 18, 1902, Illinois; d. Feb. 24, 1976 (73).
Enright, Ray, director; b. Mar. 25, 1896, Anderson, Ind.; d. Apr. 3, 1965 (69).
Ens, William (see Eagle Eye)
Enstedt, Howard, actor; b. May 7, 1906, Illinois; d. Dec. 13, 1928 (22).
Entratter, Jack, actor & nightclub manager; d. Mar. 11, 1971 (57).
Entwistle, Harold, actor; b. Sept. 5, 1865, London, England; d. Apr. 1, 1944 (78).
Entwistle, Peg, actress; d. Sept. 18, 1932 (24).
Epailly, Jules, actor; d. Apr. 28, 1967.
Ephron, Phoebe W., writer; d. Oct. 13, 1971 (57).
Epperson, Don, actor; d. Mar. 17, 1973 (35).
Epstein, Jean, director; b. Mar. 26, 1897, Warsaw, Poland; d. Apr. 2, 1953 (56).
Epstein, Philip G., writer; b. Aug. 22, 1909, New York City; d. Feb. 7, 1952 (42).
Erastoff, Edith, actress; b. 1887; d. 1945 (58).
Erby, Morris, actor; d. Jan. 8, 1978 (51).
Eric, Fred, actor; b. Peru, Ind.; d. Apr. 17, 1935 (61).
Erickson, Bob (r.n. Robert E. Erickson), actor & horseman; b. Oct. 10, 1898, Minneapolis, Minn.; d. Jan. 21, 1941 (42).
Erickson, Carl, writer; d. Aug. 29, 1935 (27).

Erickson, Knute, actor; b. May 27, 1870, Norrkoping, Sweden; d. Dec. 31, 1945 (75).

Eristoff, Nestor, actor; b. Nov. 15, 1875, USSR; d. Oct. 24, 1961 (85).

Ermelli, Claudio, actor; b. July 24, 1892, Torino, Italy; d. Oct. 29, 1964 (72).

Ermler, Friedrich, director; b. May 13, 1898, Lettonie; d. July, 1967 (69).

Errol, Leon, actor; b. July 3, 1881, Sydney, Australia; d. Oct. 12, 1951 (70).

Erskine, Wallace, actor; b. England; d. Jan. 6, 1943 (81).

Erwin, June, actress; d. Dec. 27, 1965 (47).

Erwin, Roy, actor; d. June 18, 1958 (33).

Erwin, Stuart, actor; b. Feb. 14, 1903, Squaw Valley, Calif.; d. Dec. 21, 1967 (64).

Escalante, Lalo, stuntman; d. Jan. 3, 1970 (60).

Escande, Maurice, actor; d. Feb. 11, 1973 (80).

Escoffier, Paul, actor; d. July 30, 1941.

Esdale, Charles, actor; d. July 10, 1937 (64).

Eshbaugh, Ted, animator & director; b. Feb. 5, 1906, Des Moines, Iowa; d. July 4, 1969 (63).

Esmelton, Fred, actor; b. June 22, 1872, Melbourne, Australia; d. Oct. 23, 1933 (61).

Esmond, Annie, actress; b. Sept. 27, 1873, Surrey, England; d. Jan. 4, 1945 (71).

Esmond, Henry V., writer; d. Apr. 17, 1922 (52).

Espantaleon, Juan (r.n. Juan Espantaleon Torres), actor; b. Mar. 12, 1885, Seville, Spain; d. Nov. 26, 1966 (81).

Esposito, Gianni, actor; b. Aug. 22, 1930, Paris, France; d. Jan., 1974 (43).

Essek, Rudolf, actor; b. Mar. 4, 1885, Wiesbaden, Germany; d. Jan. 11, 1941 (55).

Essel, Franz, actor; b. Jan. 31, 1909, Vienna, Austria; d. Oct., 1973 (64).

Esser, Peter, actor; b. Germany; d. June 23, 1970 (84).

Essler, Fred, actor; b. Feb. 13, 1895, Austria; d. Jan. 17, 1973 (77).

Estabrook, Howard, actor, director, & author; b. July 11, 1884, Detroit, Mich.; d. July 16, 1978 (94).

Estee, Adelyn, actress; d. June 3, 1941 (70).

Estudillo, Leo B., actor; d. Sept. 21, 1957 (57).

Etchepare, Pierre, actor; b. 1891; d. 1943 (52).

Ethier, Alphonz, actor; b. Dec. 10, 1874, Virginia City, Nev.; d. Jan. 5, 1943 (68).

Etting, Ruth, actress & singer; b. Nov. 23, 1896, David City, Neb.; d. Sept. 24, 1978 (81).

Ettlinger, Karl, actor; b. Jan. 22, 1882, Frankfurt, Germany; d. May 8, 1946 (64).

Eubank, Gene, actor; d. July 10, 1976 (81).

Euphrat, Augusta, actress; d. July 24, 1941 (79).

Eustrel, Antony, actor; b. Oct. 12, 1903; d. July 2, 1979 (75).

Evans, Bob (r.n. Rowley Dan Evans), actor; b. Aug. 17, 1903, Canada; d. Mar. 21, 1961 (57).

Evans, Brandon, actor; b. June 12, 1878, Ohio; d. Apr. 3, 1958 (79).

Evans, Bruce, actor; d. Feb. 9, 1978 (75).

Evans, Cecilia, actress; b. May 7, 1902, Oxford, Kans.; d. Nov. 11, 1960 (58).

Evans, Charles Evan, actor; b. Sept. 6, 1856, Rochester, N.Y.;
    d. Apr. 16, 1945 (88).
Evans, Douglas, actor; b. Jan. 26, 1904, Virginia; d. Mar. 25, 1968
    (64).
Evans, Edith, actress; d. Oct. 12, 1962 (68).
Evans, Dame Edith, actress; b. Feb. 8, 1888, London, England; d. Oct.
    14, 1976 (88).
Evans, Evan, singer; d. Jan. 3, 1954 (53).
Evans, Fred, actor; d. Oct. 31, 1909 (69).
Evans, Helen St. Clair, actress; d. June 6, 1927 (22).
Evans, Helena Phillips (Helena Phillips), actress; b. May 21, 1875,
    Massachusetts; d. July 24, 1955 (80).
Evans, Herbert, actor; b. Apr. 16, 1882, London, England; d. Feb.
    10, 1952 (69).
Evans, Jack, actor; b. Mar. 5, 1893, North Carolina; d. Mar. 7, 1950
    (57).
Evans, Joe, actor; d. Sept. 12, 1973 (57).
Evans, Margie, actress; d. July 29, 1960.
Evans, Nancy, actress; d. July 29, 1963 (53).
Evans, Pauline, actress; d. Jan. 22, 1952 (35).
Evans, Renee, actress & dancer; d. Dec. 22, 1971 (63).
Evans, Rex, actor; b. Apr. 13, 1903, England; d. Apr. 3, 1969 (65).
Evans, Will, actor; b. May 29, 1875, London, England; d. Apr. 11,
    1931 (55).
Evelyn, Judith, actress; b. Mar. 20, 1913, Seneca, S.D.; d. May 7,
    1967 (54).
Evelynne, May, actress; d. Apr. 3, 1943 (87).
Evennett, Wallace, actor; d. Oct., 1973 (84).
Everest, Barbara, actress; b. June 19, 1890, London, England; d. Feb.
    9, 1968 (77).
Everett, Timmy, actor & dancer; d. Mar. 4, 1977 (39).
Evers, Ernest P., actor; b. Sept. 12, 1874, Villa Ridge, Ill.;
    d. July 22, 1945 (70).
Everton, Paul, actor; b. Sept. 19, 1868, New York City; d. Feb. 26,
    1948 (79).
Ewald, Johanna, actress; d. Jan., 1961 (74).
Ewers, Hans Heinz, scenarist; b. Nov. 3, 1871, Dusseldorf, Germany;
    d. June 12, 1943 (71).
Eysoldt, Gertrude, actress; b. Nov. 11, 1870, Pirna, Germany; d. Jan.
    6, 1955 (84).
Eythe, William, actor; b. Apr. 7, 1918, Mars, Pa.; d. Jan. 26, 1957
    (38).
Eyton, Alice, actress; d. Nov., 1929.
Eyton, Charles F., producer; d. July 1, 1941 (70).


Faber, Leslie, actor; b. Aug. 30, 1879, Newcastle-on-Tyne, England;
    d. Aug. 5, 1929 (49).
Fabre, Saturnin, actor; d. Oct. 24, 1961 (77).
Fabregas, Virginia, actress; b. Mexico; d. Nov. 17, 1950 (80).
Fabrizi, Mario, actor; d. Apr. 5, 1963 (38).
Fagan, Barney, actor; b. Boston, Mass.; d. Jan. 12, 1937 (86).
Fahey, Myrna, actress; b. Mar. 12, 1933, South West Harbor, Me.;
    d. May 6, 1973 (40).
Fahrney, Milton H., director & actor; b. June 24, 1872, Dayton, Ohio;
    d. Mar. 26, 1941 (68).

Fain, John, actor; d. Jan. 9, 1970 (55).

Fair, Elinor, actress; b. Dec. 21, 1903, Richmond, Va.; d. Apr. 26, 1957 (53).

Fair, Virginia, actress; b. Aug. 23, 1899, Comstock, Tex.; d. Sept. 5, 1948 (49).

Fairbanks, Douglas, Sr., actor; b. May 23, 1883, Denver, Colo.; d. Dec. 12, 1939 (56).

Fairbanks, Flobelle, actress; d. Jan. 5, 1969 (60).

Fairbanks, Fred T., actor; d. May 15, 1927 (56).

Fairbanks, William (r.n. Carl Ullman), actor; b. May 24, 1894, St. Louis, Mo.; d. Apr. 1, 1945 (50).

Fairbrother, Sydney, actress; b. July 31, 1872, London, England; d. Jan. 10, 1941 (68).

Fairfax, Betty, actress; d. Nov. 3, 1962.

Fairfax, James, actor; d. May 8, 1961 (63).

Fairfax, Marian (Marian Tully Marshall), author; b. Oct. 24, 1875, Virginia; d. Oct. 2, 1970 (94).

Fairfax, Robert (see Burgher, Fairfax)

Fairman, Austin, actor; b. London, England; d. Mar. 26, 1964 (72).

Falconetti, Renee, actress; b. 1893, France; d. Dec. 12, 1944 (51).

Falconi, Armando, actor; d. Sept. 10, 1954 (82).

Falkenstein, Julius, actor; d. Dec. 9, 1933 (56).

Fallon, Charles, actor; b. Mar. 6, 1875, Antwerp, Belgium; d. Mar. 12, 1936 (61).

Fanck, Arnold, director & author; b. Mar. 6, 1889, Frankenthal, Germany; d. Sept. 27, 1974 (85).

Fanning, Frank, actor; b. Dec. 25, 1879, Los Angeles, Calif.; d. Mar. 1, 1934 (54).

Fanning, George Francis, actor; d. Jan. 8, 1946 (60).

Faragoh, Francis Edwards, writer; b. Hungary; d. July 25, 1966 (71).

Farebrother, Violet, actress; b. Aug. 22, 1888, Grimsby, Lincs., England; d. Sept. 27, 1969 (81).

Farfan, Marian (r.n. Marion Bancroft), actress; b. June 28, 1912, Kansas; d. Apr. 3, 1965 (52).

Farjeon, Herbert, actor; b. Oct. 27, 1879, San Francisco, Calif.; d. Nov. 3, 1972 (93).

Farley, Dot, actress; b. Feb. 6, 1881, Chicago, Ill.; d. May 21, 1971 (90).

Farley, James, actor; b. Jan. 8, 1882, Texas; d. Oct. 12, 1947 (65).

Farmer, Charles A., actor; d. Oct. 2, 1946 (63).

Farmer, Frances, actress; b. Sept. 19, 1914, Seattle, Wash.; d. Aug. 1, 1970 (55).

Farnum, Dustin, actor; b. May 27, 1874, Hampton Beach, N.H.; d. July 3, 1929 (55).

Farnum, Franklyn, actor; b. June 5, 1878, Boston, Mass.; d. July 4, 1961 (83).

Farnum, Marshall, director; d. Feb. 18, 1917.

Farnum, William, actor; b. July 4, 1876, Boston, Mass.; d. June 5, 1953 (76).

Farquharson, Robert, actor; b. Nov. 6, 1877, London, England; d. Jan. 11, 1966 (88).

Farr, Burton Cassius, actor; d. Feb. 9, 1930 (50).

Farr, Chick, actor; d. Feb. 28, 1948.

Farr, Frank E., actor; d. Mar. 20, 1953 (50).

Farr, Karl, actor & musician (Sons of the Pioneers); b. Apr. 25, 1909, Rochelle, Tex.; d. Sept. 20, 1961 (52).

Farr, Patricia, actress; b. Jan. 15, 1913, San Francisco, Calif.;
     d. Feb. 23, 1948 (35).
Farrar, Dorothy Margaret, actress; b. Apr. 8, 1901, Kansas City, Mo.;
     d. Aug. 9, 1925 (24).
Farrar, Geraldine, opera singer & actress; b. Feb. 28, 1882, Melrose,
     Mass.; d. Mar. 11, 1967 (85).
Farrar, Gwen, actress; b. July 14, 1899, London, England; d. Dec.
     25, 1944 (45).
Farrar, Stanley, actor; b. Oct. 4, 1910, California; d. Apr. 5,
     1974 (63).
Farrell, Charles (Skip), actor & singer; d. May 8, 1962 (43).
Farrell, Glenda, actress; b. June 30, 1904, Enid, Okla.; d. May 1,
     1971 (67).
Farrell, John W., actor; d. July 8, 1953 (68).
Farrell, Jon, actor; d. Dec. 21, 1971 (61).
Farrell, Paul, actor; d. June 12, 1975 (81).
Farrell, Skip, actor; b. Oct. 9, 1918, Illinois; d. May 8, 1962 (43).
Farrell, Vessie, actress; d. Sept. 30, 1935 (47).
Farren, George Francis, actor; b. Boston, Mass.; d. Apr. 21, 1935
     (74).
Farren, Mary, actress; d. May 9, 1977 (69).
Farrington, Adele, actress; d. Dec. 19, 1936 (69).
Farrington, Frank, actor; b. July 8, 1873, England; d. May 27, 1924
     (50).
Farrow, John, director & author; b. Feb. 10, 1904, Sydney, Australia;
     d. Jan. 27, 1963 (58).
Faure, Raymond, actor; d. Mar., 1972 (56).
Faussett, Jimmy, Jr., actor; d. Nov. 13, 1940.
Faust, Martin J., actor; b. Jan. 16, 1886, Germany; d. July 19,
     1943 (57).
Faversham, William, actor; b. Feb. 12, 1868, London, England; d. Apr.
     7, 1940 (72).
Fawcett, George, actor; b. Aug. 25, 1860, Fairfax Co., Va.; d. June
     6, 1939 (78).
Fawcett, James, actor; d. June 9, 1942 (35).
Fawcett, William (William F. Thompson), actor; b. Sept. 8, 1894,
     High Forest, Minn.; d. Jan. 25, 1974 (79).
Fax, Jesslyn, actress; b. Jan. 4, 1893, Canada; d. Feb. 16, 1975 (82).
Fay, Brendan, actor; d. Feb. 7, 1975 (54).
Fay, Elfie, actress; d. Sept. 18, 1927 (46).
Fay, Frank, actor; b. Nov. 17, 1897, San Francisco, Calif.; d. Sept.
     25, 1961 (63).
Fay, Jack, actor; d. Nov. 15, 1928 (25).
Fay, William G., actor; b. Nov. 12, 1872, Dublin, Ireland; d. Oct.
     27, 1947 (74).
Faye, Irma, actress; d. May 17, 1976 (63).
Faye, Julia, actress; b. Sept. 24, 1893, Richmond, Va.; d. Apr. 6,
     1966 (72).
Faylauer, Adolph, actor; b. Nov. 16, 1882, Ohio; d. Jan. 11, 1961
     (78).
Fazenda, Louise, actress; b. June 17, 1895, Lafayette, Ind.; d. Apr.
     17, 1962 (66).
Fealy, Margaret, actress; b. July, 1865, Memphis, Tenn.; d. Feb. 11,
     1955 (89).
Fealy, Maude, actress; b. Mar. 4, 1883, Tennessee; d. Nov. 9, 1971
     (88).

International Film Necrology . 101

Feicht, Georg, actor; b. May 3, 1892; d. Jan., 1964 (71).
Feiler, Herta, actress; b. Aug. 3, 1916, Vienna, Austria; d. Nov. 4,
1970 (54).
Feist, Felix, director & writer; b. Feb. 28, 1906, New York City;
d. Sept. 2, 1965 (59).
Feist, Harry, actor; b. 1903, Austria; d. May 25, 1963 (60).
Fejos, Paul, director; d. Apr. 23, 1963 (66).
Feldary, Eric, actor; b. Apr. 12, 1912, Budapest, Hungary; d. Feb.
25, 1968 (55).
Feldman, Andrea, actress; d. Aug. 8, 1972.
Feldman, Edythe A., actress; d. Feb. 28, 1971 (58).
Feldman, Gladys, actress; d. Feb. 12, 1974 (82).
Fellowes, Rockcliffe, actor; b. 1885, Ottawa, Canada; d. Jan. 28,
1950 (65).
Fells, George, actor; d. May 10, 1960 (58).
Felt, Edward, actor; d. July 7, 1928 (71).
Felton, Earl, writer; b. Oct. 16, 1910, Cleveland, Ohio; d. May 2,
1972 (61).
Felton, Felix, actor; d. Oct. 21, 1972 (60).
Felton, Happy, actor; d. Oct. 21, 1964 (56).
Felton, Verna, actress; b. July 20, 1890, Salinas, Calif.; d. Dec. 14,
1966 (76).
Fenimore, Ford, actor; d. Apr. 20, 1941.
Fenner, Walter, actor; b. Akron, Ohio; d. Nov. 7, 1947 (65).
Fenton, Frank, actor; b. Apr. 9, 1906, Hartford, Conn.; d. July 24,
1957 (51).
Fenton, Frank, writer; d. Aug. 23, 1971 (65).
Fenton, Leslie, actor & director; b. Mar. 12, 1903, Liverpool,
England; d. Mar. 25, 1978 (75).
Fenton, Lucille, actress; d. Oct. 17, 1966.
Fenton, Mark, actor; b. Nov. 11, 1866, Crestline, Ohio; d. July 29,
1925 (58).
Fenwick, Harry, actor; b. Aug. 1, 1880, Cincinnati, Ohio; d. Dec. 24,
1932 (52).
Fenwick, Irene, actress; b. Sept. 5, 1892, Chicago, Ill.; d. Dec. 24,
1936 (44).
Feodoroff, Leo, actor; b. Odessa, Russia; d. Nov. 23, 1949 (82).
Ferdl, Weiss, actor; b. June 28, 1883; d. June, 1949 (65).
Ferguson, Al, actor; b. Apr. 19, 1888, Rosslarre, Ireland; d. Dec. 4,
1971 (83).
Ferguson, Barney, actor; d. Aug. 28, 1924 (71).
Ferguson, Casson, actor; b. Louisiana; d. Feb. 12, 1929 (38).
Ferguson, Elsie, actress; b. Aug. 19, 1885, New York; d. Nov. 15,
1961 (76).
Ferguson, Frank, actor; b. Dec. 25, 1908, California; d. Sept. 12,
1978 (69).
Ferguson, George S., actor; d. Apr. 24, 1944 (60).
Ferguson, Helen, actress; b. July 23, 1901, Decatur, Ill.; d. Mar.
14, 1977 (75).
Ferguson, Lile, stuntman; d. Nov. 21, 1921.
Ferguson, William J., actor; d. May 4, 1930 (85).
Fern, Fritzie, actress; d. Sept. 20, 1932 (24).
Fernandel, actor; b. May 8, 1903, Marseille, France; d. Feb. 26,
1971 (67).
Fernandes, Nascimento, actor; d. Jan., 1956 (76).
Fernandez, Bijou, actress; b. New York City; d. Nov. 7, 1961 (84).

Fernandez, Felix (r.n. Felix Fernandez Garcia), actor; b. Sept. 21,
    1899, Cangas de Onis; d. July 5, 1966 (66).
Fernandez, Ramon S., actor; d. Sept. 22, 1962 (40).
Fernandez, Roy, actor; d. June 22, 1927 (39).
Ferniel, Dan, actor; b. Nov. 11, 1915; d. Oct. 15, 1975 (59).
Ferrand, Eula Pearl, actress; d. July 17, 1970.
Ferrandiz, Gloria, actress; b. Feb. 9, 1893, Montevideo, Uruguay;
    d. Sept. 12, 1970 (77).
Ferrari, Raquel, actress; d. Oct. 17, 1978 (25).
Ferreira, Procopio, actor; d. June 18, 1979 (80).
Ferrell, Jane, actress; d. June 3, 1952 (73).
Ferrers, Helen, actress; b. Cockham, Berks., England; d. Feb. 1, 1943
    (77).
Ferris, Dillon J., actor; d. Apr. 25, 1951 (37).
Ferriz, Miguel Angel, actor; d. Jan. 1, 1967.
Fetherston, Eddie, actor; b. Sept. 9, 1896, New York; d. June 12,
    1965 (68).
Feusier, Norman, actor; b. Mar. 24, 1886, San Francisco, Calif.;
    d. Dec. 27, 1945 (59).
Feussner, Alfred, actor; d. Aug. 25, 1969 (33).
Feyder, Jacques, director & writer; b. July 21, 1885, Brussels,
    Belgium; d. May 25, 1948 (62).
Fidler, Ben, actor; d. Oct. 19, 1932 (65).
Field, Alexander, actor; b. June 6, 1892, London, England; d. Aug.,
    1971 (79).
Field, Ben, actor; d. Oct. 21, 1939 (61).
Field, Betty, actress; b. Feb. 8, 1913, Boston, Mass.; d. Sept. 13,
    1973 (60).
Field, George, actor; b. Mar. 18, 1877, San Francisco, Calif.;
    d. Mar. 9, 1925 (47).
Field, Norman, actor; b. Jan. 4, 1881, Montreal, Canada; d. Sept. 11,
    1956 (75).
Field, Sid, actor; b. Apr. 1, 1904, Edgbaston, Birmingham, England;
    d. Feb. 3, 1950 (45).
Field, Capt. Walter, extra; b. Aug. 29, 1874; d. June 5, 1976 (101).
Fielding, Edward, actor; b. Brooklyn, N.Y.; d. Jan. 10, 1945 (65).
Fielding, Marjorie, actress; b. Gloucester, England; d. Dec. 28,
    1956 (64).
Fielding, Minnie, actress; d. July 22, 1936 (65).
Fielding, Romaine, actor & director; b. May 26, 1879, Kentucky;
    d. Dec. 15, 1927 (48).
Fields, Benny, actor; b. June 14, 1894, Milwaukee, Wisc.; d. Aug. 16,
    1959 (65).
Fields, Gracie, actress; b. Jan. 9, 1898, Rochdale, England; d. Sept.
    27, 1979 (81).
Fields, John, actor; d. Nov. 8, 1938 (62).
Fields, Lew, actor; b. Jan. 1, 1867, New York City; d. July 20, 1941
    (74).
Fields, Sidney, actor; d. Sept. 28, 1975 (77).
Fields, Stanley, actor; b. May 20, 1884, Allegheny, Pa.; d. Apr. 23,
    1941 (56).
Fields, W.C., actor; b. Apr. 9, 1879, Philadelphia, Pa.; d. Dec. 25,
    1946 (67).
Figman, Max, actor; b. Vienna, Austria; d. Feb. 13, 1952 (85).
Filauri, Antonio, actor; b. Mar. 9, 1889, Italy; d. Jan. 18, 1964 (74).

Fillmore, Clyde, actor; b. Sept. 25, 1875, McCannelsville, Ohio; d. Dec. 19, 1946 (71).
Fillmore, L., actor; d. July 17, 1933.
Fillmore, Russell, actor & director; b. Sept. 7, 1888, Tennessee; d. Aug. 18, 1950 (61).
Fils, Numes, actor; b. Nov. 9, 1896, Paris, France; d. Jan., 1972 (75).
Filson, Al W., actor; b. Jan. 27, 1857, Blufton, Ind.; d. Nov. 14, 1925 (68).
Finch, Flora, actress; b. Sussex, England; d. Jan. 4, 1940 (71).
Finch, Peter, actor; b. Sept. 28, 1916, London, England; d. Jan. 14, 1977 (60).
Finck, Werner, actor; d. July 31, 1978 (76).
Findlay, Ruth, actress; d. July 13, 1949 (45).
Findlay, Thomas B., actor; b. Guelph, Ont., Canada; d. May 29, 1941 (67).
Findon, Walter, actor; d. Mar. 9, 1957 (75).
Fine, Larry, actor; b. Oct. 5, 1902, Pennsylvania; d. Jan. 24, 1975 (72).
Fineman, Bernard P., producer; b. Feb. 23, 1895, New York; d. Sept. 28, 1971 (76).
Fink, Emma, actress; d. June 13, 1966 (56).
Finlayson, Alex, assistant director; b. Nov. 13, 1912, Scotland; d. Feb. 7, 1954 (41).
Finlayson, James H., actor; b. Aug. 27, 1887, Falkirk, Scotland; d. Oct. 9, 1953 (66).
Finley, Ned, actor; d. Sept. 27, 1920.
Finn, Adelaide, actress; d. Jan. 20, 1978 (84).
Finn, Elsie, writer & actress; d. Nov. 27, 1945 (42).
Finn, Sam, actor; d. Dec. 14, 1958 (65).
Finnegan, Walter, actor; d. May 30, 1943 (70).
Finnerty, Louis, actor; d. Aug. 4, 1937 (54).
Finnerty, Warren, actor; d. Dec. 22, 1974 (49).
Fiorenza, Alfredo, actor; d. Feb. 24, 1931 (63).
Fio Rito, Ted, orchestra leader; b. Dec. 20, 1900, Newark, N.J.; d. July 22, 1971 (70).
Fischer, David G., actor; d. Apr. 21, 1939 (48).
Fischer, Margarita, actress; b. Feb. 12, 1886, Iowa; d. Mar. 11, 1975 (89).
Fischer, Max, actor; b. Austria; d. Oct. 11, 1974 (65).
Fischer, Robert C. (r.n. Robert Carl Fischer), actor; b. May 28, 1881, Danzig, Germany; d. Mar. 11, 1973 (91).
Fischer-Koppe, Hugo, actor; b. Feb. 13, 1890; d. Dec. 31, 1937 (47).
Fischman, David, actor; d. Jan. 24, 1958 (48).
Fishell, Dick, actor; b. Sept. 19, 1909, New York; d. Aug. 12, 1972 (62).
Fisher, Alfred C., actor; b. Jan. 14, 1849, Bristol, England; d. Aug. 26, 1933 (84).
Fisher, Freddie, orchestra leader; d. Mar. 28, 1967 (63).
Fisher, George, actor; b. Aug. 10, 1891, Michigan; d. Aug. 13, 1960 (69).
Fisher, Harry, actor; d. 1917.
Fisher, Irving, actor; d. Feb. 4, 1959 (73).
Fisher, Larry, actor; b. Apr. 19, 1891, New York City; d. Dec. 6, 1937 (46).

Fisher, Maggie (see Halloway, Maggie)
Fisher, Sallie, actress; d. June 8, 1950 (69).
Fisher, William G., actor; d. Oct. 4, 1949 (66).
Fishman, Duke M., actor; d. Dec. 22, 1977 (71).
Fiske, Mrs. (Minnie Maddern), actress; b. Dec. 19, 1865, New Orleans,
    La.; d. Feb. 15, 1932 (66).
Fiske, Robert, actor; b. Oct. 20, 1889, Griggsville, Mo.; d. Sept.
    12, 1944 (54).
Fitz-Allen, Adelaide, actress; d. Feb. 26, 1935 (79).
Fitzgerald, Barry, actor; b. Mar. 10, 1888, Dublin, Ireland; d. Jan.
    4, 1961 (72).
Fitzgerald, Cissy, actress; b. England; d. May 5, 1941 (67).
Fitzgerald, Dallas M., director; b. Aug. 13, 1876, La Grange, Ky.;
    d. May 9, 1940 (63).
Fitzgerald, Edward P., actor; d. May 1, 1942 (59).
Fitzgerald, F. Scott, author; b. Sept. 24, 1896, St. Paul, Minn.;
    d. Dec. 21, 1940 (44).
Fitzgerald, James M., actor; b. Apr. 19, 1896, Mississippi; d. Jan.
    21, 1919 (22).
Fitzgerald, Lillian, actress; d. July 9, 1947.
Fitzgerald, Walter, actor; b. May 18, 1896, Keyham, Devonport,
    England; d. Dec. 20, 1976 (80).
Fitzhamon, Lewin, director; b. June 5, 1869, Aldingham, England;
    d. Oct. 10, 1961 (92).
Fitzharris, Edward, actor; b. England; d. Oct. 12, 1974 (84).
Fitzmaurice, George, director; b. Feb. 13, 1895, Paris, France;
    d. June 13, 1940 (45).
Fitzmaurice, Michael, actor; b. Apr. 28, 1908, Chicago, Ill.; d. Aug.
    31, 1967 (59).
Fitzroy, Emily, actress; b. May 24, 1860, London, England; d. Mar. 3,
    1954 (93).
Fitzroy, Louis, actor; b. Nov. 24, 1870, Sault Sainte Marie, Mich.;
    d. Jan. 26, 1947 (76).
Fitzsimmons, Cortland, writer; d. July 27, 1949 (56).
Flagstad, Kirsten, opera singer; b. July 12, 1895, Hamar, Norway;
    d. Dec. 8, 1962 (67).
Flaherty, Pat, actor; b. Mar. 8, 1903, Washington, D.C.; d. Dec. 2,
    1970 (67).
Flaherty, Robert, director; b. Feb. 16, 1884, Iron Mt., Mich.; d.
    July 23, 1951 (67).
Flanagan, Bud, actor; b. Oct. 14, 1896, Whitechapel, England;
    d. Oct. 20, 1968 (72).
Flanagan, Bud (see also O'Keefe, Dennis)
Flanagan, Edward J., actor; d. Aug. 18, 1925 (45).
Flanagan, Hugh, actor; d. Dec. 26, 1925.
Flanagan, Rebecca, actress; b. Feb. 10, 1878, Philadelphia, Pa.;
    d. Jan. 30, 1938 (59).
Flanders, Michael, actor; b. Mar. 1, 1922, London, England; d. Apr.
    14, 1975 (53).
Flateau, Georges, actor; d. Feb. 13, 1953 (71).
Flavin, James, actor; b. May 14, 1906, Portland, Me.; d. Apr. 23,
    1976 (69).
Flavin, Martin, scenarist; b. Nov. 2, 1883, San Francisco, Calif.;
    d. Dec. 27, 1967 (84).
Fleeson, Neville, actor; d. Sept. 13, 1945 (58).

Fleischer, Dave, animator; b. July 14, 1894, New York City; d. June 25, 1979 (84).

Fleischer, Max, animator; b. July 19, 1883, Austria; d. Sept. 11, 1972 (89).

Fleischmann, Harry, actor; b. Jan. 7, 1899, Segerstown, Pa.; d. Nov. 28, 1943 (44).

Fleming, Alice, actress; b. Brooklyn, N.Y.; d. Dec. 6, 1952 (70).

Fleming, Bob, actor; b. Feb. 19, 1878, Ontario, Canada; d. Oct. 4, 1933 (55).

Fleming, Claude, actor; b. Feb. 22, 1884, Camden, New South Wales; d. Mar. 23, 1952 (68).

Fleming, Eric, actor; d. Sept. 28, 1966 (41).

Fleming, Ian, actor; b. Sept. 10, 1888, Melbourne, Australia; d. Jan. 1, 1969 (80).

Fleming, John, actor; d. June, 1945 (70).

Fleming, Victor, director; b. Feb. 23, 1883, Pasadena, Calif.; d. Jan. 6, 1949 (65).

Flenn, Karl, actor; d. Apr. 9, 1978 (47).

Fletcher, Dusty, singer; d. Mar. 15, 1954 (57).

Fletcher, Lawrence M., actor; d. Feb. 11, 1970 (68).

Flick, Pat C., actor; d. Nov. 1, 1955 (57).

Flickenschildt, Elisabeth, actress; b. Mar. 16, 1905, Hamburg, Germany; d. Oct. 26, 1977 (72).

Flink, Hugo, actor; d. May, 1947.

Flint, Hazel, actress; d. Aug. 18, 1959 (66).

Flint, Helen, actress; b. June 14, 1898, Chicago, Ill.; d. Sept. 9, 1967 (69).

Flint, Joseph W., actor; d. May 5, 1933 (40).

Flippen, Jay C., actor; b. Mar. 6, 1899, Little Rock, Ark.; d. Feb. 3, 1971 (71).

Flood, James, director; b. July 31, 1895, New York City; d. Feb. 4, 1953 (57).

Florath, Albert, actor; b. Dec. 14, 1888, Bielefeld, Germany; d. Mar. 10, 1957 (68).

Florelle (r.n. Odette Rousseau), actress; b. Aug. 9, 1901, Sables d'Alonne; d. Oct. 1, 1974 (73).

Floresco, Michel, actor; d. Oct., 1925.

Florey, Robert, director & actor; b. Sept. 14, 1900, Paris, France; d. May 16, 1979 (78).

Flowerton, Consuelo, actress; d. Dec. 21, 1965 (65).

Fluker, Mack, actor; b. Apr. 22, 1903, Los Angeles, Calif.; d. Apr. 28, 1929 (26).

Flynn, Elinor, actress; d. July 4, 1938 (27).

Flynn, Emmett J., director & actor; b. Nov. 9, 1892, Denver, Colo.; d. June 4, 1937 (44).

Flynn, Errol, actor; b. June 20, 1909, Hobart, Tasmania; d. Oct. 14, 1959 (50).

Flynn, Jim, actor; d. Apr. 12, 1935 (55).

Flynn, Joe, actor; b. Nov. 8, 1925, Youngstown, Ohio; d. July 19, 1974 (48).

Flynn, John E. (Jack), actor; d. 1949.

Flynn, Maurice (Lefty), actor; d. Mar. 4, 1959 (66).

Fogel, Vladimir, actor; d. June 8, 1929.

Fogg, Orian, actor; d. May 24, 1923 (74).

Foley, Red, recording artist & actor; b. June 17, 1910, Blue Lick Springs, Ky.; d. Sept. 19, 1968 (58).

Fonss, Olaf, actor; d. Nov. 4, 1949 (67).
Fontaine, Frank, actor; d. Aug. 4, 1978 (58).
Fontaine, Lilian, actress; b. June 11, 1886, Reading, England;
    d. Feb. 20, 1975 (88).
Fontan, Gabrielle, actress; b. 1880; d. 1959 (79).
Foo, Lee Tung, actor; b. Apr. 23, 1875, California; d. May 1, 1966
    (91).
Foo, Wing, actor; d. Dec. 9, 1953 (43).
Fook, Monte, actor; d. Mar. 27, 1933 (25).
Foote, Courtenay, actor; d. Mar. 4, 1925.
Foote, John Taintor, writer; d. Jan. 28, 1950 (69).
Foran, Dick, actor; b. June 18, 1910, Flemington, N.J.; d. Aug. 10,
    1979 (69).
Forbes, Harry, cinematographer; d. Aug. 17, 1939 (52).
Forbes, Mary, actress; b. Dec. 30, 1883, Hornsey, England; d. July
    22, 1974 (90).
Forbes, Mary Elizabeth, actress; b. Nov. 8, 1879, Rochester, N.Y.;
    d. Aug. 20, 1964 (84).
Forbes, Ralph, actor; b. Sept. 30, 1905, London, England; d. Mar. 31,
    1951 (45).
Forbes, Richard S., actor; d. Sept. 12, 1979 (43).
Forbes-Robertson, Sir Johnston, actor; b. Jan. 16, 1853, London,
    England; d. Nov. 6, 1937 (84).
Forbstein, Leo F., musical director (Warner Brothers); b. Oct. 16,
    1892, St. Joseph, Mo.; d. Mar. 16, 1948 (55).
Force, Charles (r.n. Floyd Charles Force), actor; b. Mar. 22, 1876,
    South Line, Mich.; d. June 9, 1947 (71).
Ford, Claudette, actress; d. June 18, 1933.
Ford, Daisy, actress; d. Dec. 14, 1959 (53).
Ford, Fenton (Belford Forrest), actor; d. May 1, 1938 (60).
Ford, Francis, actor & director; b. Aug. 15, 1882, Portland, Me.;
    d. Sept. 5, 1953 (71).
Ford, Harrison, actor; b. Mar. 16, 1884, Kansas City, Mo.; d. Dec. 2,
    1957 (73).
Ford, John (r.n. Sean O'Feeney), director & actor; b. Feb. 1, 1894,
    Cape Elizabeth, Me.; d. Aug. 31, 1973 (79).
Ford, Lettie, actress; d. Sept. 26, 1936 (89).
Ford, Marty, actor; d. Nov. 12, 1954 (54).
Ford, Paul, actor; b. Nov. 2, 1901, Baltimore, Md.; d. Apr. 12, 1976
    (74).
Ford, Philip, actor & director; b. Oct. 16, 1900, Portland, Me.;
    d. Jan. 12, 1976 (75).
Ford, Wallace, actor; b. Feb. 12, 1898, Balton, England; d. June 11,
    1966 (68).
Forde, Eugenie, actress; b. June 22, 1879, New York City; d. Sept. 6,
    1940 (61).
Forde, Hal C., actor; b. Ireland; d. Dec. 4, 1955 (78).
Forde, Victoria, actress; b. Apr. 21, 1896, New York; d. July 24,
    1964 (68).
Forest, Bill, actor; d. Aug. 7, 1960 (39).
Forest, Frank, actor; b. St. Paul, Minn.; d. Dec. 23, 1976 (80).
Forest, Karl (r.n. Karl Obertimpfler), actor; b. Nov. 12, 1874,
    Vienna, Austria; d. June 3, 1944 (69).
Forman, Tom, actor & director; d. Nov. 7, 1926 (34).
Forman, Tom (r.n. Thomas B. Farmer), actor; b. Oct. 29, 1891,
    Minnesota; d. Nov. 16, 1951 (60).

Formby, George, actor; b. May 26, 1904, Wigan, England; d. Mar. 6, 1961 (56).
Formes, Carl, Jr., actor; b. July 3, 1841, London, England; d. Nov. 18, 1939 (98).
Forrest, Allan, actor; b. Brooklyn, N.Y.; d. July 25, 1941 (55).
Forrest, Arthur, actor; b. Bayreuth, Germany; d. May 14, 1933 (76).
Forrest, Belford (see Ford, Fenton)
Forrest, Mabel, actress; b. Nov. 5, 1894, Illinois; d. July 5, 1967 (72).
Forrester, Frederick C., actor; d. Oct. 14, 1952 (80).
Forsch, Robert, actor; d. Sept. 8, 1948.
Forshay, Harold, actor; d. Feb. 23, 1953 (69).
Forsman, Harry H., actor; d. May 20, 1933 (66).
Forster, Rudolf, actor; b. Oct. 30, 1884, Grobming, Austria; d. Oct. 25, 1968 (83).
Forsythe, Mimi, actress; d. Aug. 17, 1952 (30).
Fort, Garrett E., writer; d. Oct. 26, 1945 (47).
Forte, Joe, actor; b. June 14, 1893, England; d. Mar. 11, 1967 (73).
Fortier, Herbert, actor; d. Feb. 16, 1949 (82).
Fortune, Edmond, actor; b. Mar. 27, 1851, Geneva, N.Y.; d. Sept. 21, 1939 (88).
Foster, Arthur Turner, actor; b. Oct. 21, 1867, Brooklyn, N.Y.; d. July 4, 1947 (79).
Foster, Donald, actor; b. July 31, 1889, Pennsylvania; d. Dec. 23, 1969 (80).
Foster, Dudley, actor; d. Jan. 8, 1973 (48).
Foster, J. Morris, actor; b. Sept. 9, 1881, Pennsylvania; d. Apr. 24, 1966 (84).
Foster, Lewis R., director & author; d. June 10, 1974 (75).
Foster, Norman, actor, director, & author; b. Dec. 13, 1900, Richmond, Ind.; d. July 7, 1976 (75).
Foster, Preston, actor; b. Aug. 24, 1900, Ocean City, N.J.; d. July 14, 1970 (69).
Fouce, Frank, actor & executive; b. Oct. 26, 1899, Hawaii; d. Jan. 11, 1962 (62).
Fougez, Anna, actress; d. Sept., 1966 (71).
Foulger, Byron, actor; b. Aug. 27, 1899, Ogden, Utah; d. Apr. 4, 1970 (70).
Fowler, Art, actor; d. Apr. 4, 1953 (51).
Fowler, Bertie, actress; d. Aug. 8, 1941 (75).
Fowler, Brenda, actress; b. Feb. 16, 1883, Jamestown, N.D.; d. Oct. 27, 1942 (59).
Fowler, Gene, writer; b. Mar. 8, 1890, Denver, Colo.; d. July 2, 1960 (70).
Fowler, John C., actor; b. July 25, 1869, New York; d. June 27, 1952 (82).
Fox, Finis, writer; b. Oct. 8, 1884, Caddo, Okla.; d. Nov. 7, 1949 (65).
Fox, Franklyn, actor; d. Nov. 2, 1967 (73).
Fox, Fred, actor; b. Jan. 22, 1884, London, England; d. Dec. 1, 1949 (65).
Fox, Grace, actress; d. Apr. 27, 1946.
Fox, Harry, actor; b. May 25, 1882, New York; d. July 20, 1959 (77).
Fox, Jimmie (r.n. James T. Fox), actor; b. Mar. 22, 1891, Pennsylvania; d. June 16, 1974 (83).
Fox, Josephine, actress; d. Aug. 2, 1953 (84).

Fox, Sidney, actress; b. Dec. 10, 1911, New York City; d. Nov. 15, 1942 (30).
Fox, Wallace W., director; b. Mar. 9, 1895, Purcell, Okla.; d. June 30, 1958 (63).
Fox, William, executive; b. Jan. 1, 1879, Tulchva, Hungary; d. May 8, 1952 (73).
Foxe, Earle, actor; b. Dec. 25, 1891, Oxford, Ohio; d. Dec. 10, 1973 (81).
Foy, Bryan, producer; b. Chicago, Ill.; d. Apr. 20, 1977 (80).
Foy, Eddie, Sr., actor; b. Mar. 9, 1856, New York City; d. Feb. 16, 1928 (71).
Foy, Richard, actor; d. Apr. 4, 1947 (42).
Foyer, Eddie, actor; d. June 15, 1934 (51).
Fralick, Freddie, actor; d. May 13, 1958 (69).
France, C.V., actor; b. June 30, 1868, Bradford, England; d. Apr. 13, 1949 (80).
France, Charles H., director; d. June, 1940 (70).
France, Claude, actress; b. 1893, Austria; d. Jan. 4, 1928 (34).
Francen, Victor, actor; b. Aug. 5, 1888, Belgium; d. Nov. 18, 1977 (89).
Franchini, Teresa, actress; d. Aug., 1972 (95).
Francis, Alec B., actor; b. Dec. 2, 1867, London, England; d. July 6, 1934 (66).
Francis, Kay, actress; b. Jan. 13, 1905, Oklahoma City, Okla.; d. Aug. 26, 1968 (63).
Francis, Nicky, actor; d. Sept. 29, 1960 (40).
Francis, Noel, actress; b. Nov. 21, 1910, Temple, Tex.; d. Oct. 30, 1959 (48).
Francis, Olin, actor; b. Sept. 13, 1891, Mooreville, Miss.; d. June 30, 1952 (60).
Francis, Robert, actor; b. Feb. 26, 1930, Glendale, Calif.; d. July 31, 1955 (25).
Francisco, Betty (r.n. Elizabeth Bartman), actress; b. Sept. 26, 1900, Little Rock, Ark.; d. Nov. 25, 1950 (50).
Franck, John L., actor; b. July 31, 1852, Louisville, Ky.; d. Oct. 22, 1920 (68).
Franck, Walter, actor; b. Apr. 16, 1896, Huttensteinach, Germany; d. Aug. 10, 1961 (65).
Franey, Billy, actor; b. June 23, 1889, Chicago, Ill.; d. Dec. 6, 1940 (51).
Frank, Allan, actor; d. Aug. 9, 1979 (64).
Frank, Bruno, writer; d. June 2, 1945 (58).
Frank, Carl, actor; d. Sept. 23, 1972 (63).
Frank, Christian J., actor; b. Mar. 13, 1890, New York; d. Dec. 10, 1967 (77).
Frank, J. Herbert, actor; d. Mar. 11, 1926 (40).
Frank, John, actor; b. July 7, 1888, Missouri; d. Feb. 15, 1961 (72).
Frank, William, actor; d. Dec. 23, 1925 (45).
Frankau, Ronald, actor; b. Feb. 22, 1894, London, England; d. Sept. 11, 1951 (57).
Franke, Constant Louis, actor & director; b. May 5, 1893, Brussels, Belgium; d. Oct. 31, 1943 (50).
Frankel, Fanchon, actress; b. Apr. 28, 1874, St. Louis, Mo.; d. Aug. 12, 1937 (63).
Franklin, Alberta, actress; d. Mar. 14, 1976 (79).
Franklin, Chester M., director; d. Mar. 12, 1954 (64).

Franklin, Harry L., director; b. Sept. 5, 1880, St. Louis, Mo.;
d. July 3, 1927 (47).
Franklin, Irene, actress; b. June 13, 1876, New York City; d. June
16, 1941 (65).
Franklin, Martha (r.n. Martha Cohn), actress; b. Nov. 13, 1868,
Germany; d. Apr. 19, 1929 (60).
Franklin, Rupert, actor; d. Jan. 14, 1939 (77).
Franklin, Sidney, actor; d. Mar. 18, 1931 (61).
Franklin, Sidney, bullfighter; b. July 11, 1903, Brooklyn, N.Y.;
d. Apr. 26, 1976 (72).
Franklin, Sidney A., director; b. Mar. 21, 1893, San Francisco,
Calif.; d. May 18, 1972 (79).
Franklyn, Leo, actor; b. Apr. 7, 1897, London, England; d. Sept. 17,
1975 (78).
Franklyn, Milton, music director; d. Apr. 23, 1962 (64).
Franks, Dennis, actor; d. Oct. 14, 1967 (65).
Franks, Jerry, actor; d. June 19, 1971 (63).
Frantz, Dalies, actor & concert pianist; d. Dec. 1, 1965 (57).
Franz, Joseph J., actor & director; b. Oct. 12, 1884, Utica, N.Y.;
d. Sept. 9, 1970 (85).
Fraser, Constance, actress; d. May, 1973 (63).
Fraser, Harry, director; b. Mar. 31, 1889, California; d. Apr. 8,
1974 (85).
Fraser, Harry C., actor; b. Mar. 15, 1894, South Dakota; d. Aug. 2,
1949 (55).
Fraser, James S., actor; b. July 31, 1873, Dundee, Scotland; d. Oct.
19, 1943 (70).
Frausto, Antonio R., actor; d. Jan., 1954.
Frawley, William, actor; b. Feb. 26, 1887, Burlington, Iowa; d. Mar.
3, 1966 (79).
Frazer, Alex, actor; b. May 27, 1900, Scotland; d. July 30, 1958 (58).
Frazer, Robert, actor; b. June 29, 1889, Worcester, Mass.; d. Aug.
17, 1944 (55).
Frazin, Gladys, actress; d. Mar. 9, 1939 (38).
Frechette, Mark, actor; d. Sept. 27, 1975 (27).
Frederick, Pauline, actress; b. Aug. 12, 1885, Boston, Mass.; d.
Sept. 19, 1938 (53).
Frederick, William, actor; d. Mar. 2, 1931 (70).
Fredericks, Charles (r.n. Fred E. Cockerham), actor; b. Sept. 5,
1918, Columbus, Miss.; d. May 14, 1970 (51).
Freear, Louie, actor; d. Mar. 23, 1939 (62).
Freeborn, Henry F., actor; d. Mar. 2, 1957 (74).
Freed, Alan, disc jockey; b. Dec. 15, 1922, Johnstown, Pa.; d. Jan.
20, 1965 (42).
Freed, Arthur, producer; b. Sept. 9, 1894, Charleston, S.C.; d. Apr.
12, 1973 (78).
Freel, Aleta, actress; b. Jersey City, N.J.; d. Dec. 7, 1935 (28).
Freeman, Al, actor; d. Mar. 22, 1956 (72).
Freeman, Howard, actor; b. Dec. 9, 1899, Helena, Mont.; d. Dec. 11,
1967 (68).
Freeman, Maurice, actor; d. Mar. 26, 1953 (81).
Freeman, Stella, actress; b. Apr. 26, 1910, South Norwood, England;
d. May 13, 1936 (26).
Freeman, Y. Frank, executive; b. Dec. 14, 1890, Greenville, Ga.;
d. Feb. 5, 1969 (78).
Freeman-Mitford, Rupert, actor; d. Aug. 7, 1939 (44).

Fregoli, Leopoldo, actor; b. July 2, 1867, Rome, Italy; d. Nov. 26, 1936 (69).
Freil, Raymond A., actor, director, & author; d. May 24, 1939 (45).
Fremont, Al W., actor; b. Feb. 23, 1860, Cohoes, N.Y.; d. June 16, 1930 (70).
French, Charles K., actor & director; b. Jan. 17, 1860, Ohio; d. Aug. 2, 1952 (92).
French, George B., actor; b. Apr. 14, 1883, Storm Lake, Iowa; d. June 9, 1961 (78).
French, Helen, actress; d. Mar. 12, 1917.
French, Hugh, actor; b. England; d. Nov. 2, 1976 (66).
French, Lloyd, director & actor; b. Jan. 11, 1900, San Francisco, Calif.; d. May 24, 1950 (50).
Fresnay, Pierre, actor; b. Apr. 4, 1897, Paris, France; d. Jan. 9, 1975 (77).
Fresno, Fernando, actor; b. May 31, 1881, Madrid, Spain; d. Apr. 28, 1949 (67).
Freund, Karl, cinematographer, b. Jan. 16, 1890, Koeniginhof, Czechoslovakia; d. May 3, 1969 (79).
Frey, Arno, actor; b. Oct. 11, 1900, Munich, Germany; d. June 26, 1961 (60).
Frey, Callie, actress; d. Apr. 29, 1948 (72).
Frey, Nathaniel, actor; b. Aug. 3, 1913, New York City; d. Nov. 7, 1970 (57).
Friderici, Blanche, actress; b. 1878, Brooklyn, N.Y.; d. Dec. 23, 1933 (55).
Friebus, Theodore, actor; d. Dec. 26, 1917 (38).
Friedberger, Louis, actor; d. Feb. 16, 1924.
Friedkin, Joel, actor; b. May 15, 1885, Russia; d. Sept. 19, 1954 (69).
Friedlander, Louis (see Landers, Lew)
Friedlob, Bert, producer; d. Oct. 7, 1956 (49).
Friedmann, Shraga, actor; d. July, 1970 (47).
Fries, Otto H., actor; b. Oct. 28, 1887, St. Louis, Mo.; d. Sept. 15, 1938 (50).
Friganza, Trixie, actress; b. Nov. 29, 1870, Grenola, Kans.; d. Feb. 27, 1955 (84).
Frinton, Freddie, actor; d. Oct. 16, 1968 (56).
Fris, Maria, ballet dancer; d. May 27, 1961 (29).
Frisch, Lore, actress; b. May 4, 1925, Schwindegg, Germany; d. July, 1962 (37).
Frische, Axel, actor; b. Mar. 15, 1877, Tjele, Denmark; d. Feb. 2, 1956 (78).
Frisco, Joe, actor; b. Milan, Ill.; d. Feb. 16, 1958 (68).
Frith, J. Leslie, actor; d. Feb. 1, 1961 (77).
Frith, Thomas P., actor; d. Jan. 9, 1945 (62).
Fritsch, Willy, actor; b. Jan. 27, 1901, Kattowitz, Germany; d. July 12, 1973 (72).
Fritz, horse; d. Feb. 6, 1938.
Frizzell, Lou, actor; d. June 17, 1979 (59).
Froelich, Carl, director; b. Sept. 5, 1875, Berlin, Germany; d. Feb. 13, 1953 (77).
Froes, Wally "Froggie," actor; d. May 10, 1958 (36).
Froeschel, George, writer; b. Mar. 9, 1891, Vienna, Austria; d. Nov. 22, 1979 (88).

Frohman, Daniel, producer; b. Aug. 22, 1851, Sandusky, Ohio; d. Dec. 26, 1940 (89).

Frye, Dwight, actor; b. Feb. 22, 1899, Salina, Kans.; d. Nov. 7, 1943 (44).

Frye, Frank L., actor; b. Sept. 20, 1862, North Haven, Me.; d. June 23, 1935 (72).

Fuentes, Virginia, actress; d. Sept. 23, 1956 (72).

Fuerst, George David, stuntman; d. March, 1918.

Fuller, Clem, actor; b. July 6, 1908, California; d. May 24, 1961 (52).

Fuller, Edward (Eddie), narrator; d. Jan. 22, 1979 (67).

Fuller, Irene, actress; d. Mar. 20, 1945 (47).

Fuller, Jesse (Lone Cat), actor & jazz musician; b. Mar. 12, 1896, Jonesboro, Ga.; d. Jan. 29, 1976 (79).

Fuller, Leslie, actor; d. Apr. 24, 1948 (57).

Fulton, Maude, actress; b. May 14, 1881, Eldorado, Kans.; d. Nov. 9, 1950 (69).

Fung, Willie, actor; b. Mar. 3, 1896, Canton, China; d. Apr. 16, 1945 (49).

Fuqua, Charles, recording artist ("Ink Spots"); d. Dec. 21, 1971 (60).

Fuqua, Wilbur, actor; d. Jan. 31, 1953 (70).

Furey, Barney, actor; b. Sept. 7, 1886, Boise, Idaho; d. Jan. 18, 1938 (51).

Furey, James A., actor; b. May 10, 1865, Ogdenburg, N.Y.; d. July 7, 1930 (65).

Furse, Jill, actress; d. Nov. 27, 1944 (28).

Furse, Judith, actress; b. Mar. 4, 1912, Camberley, England; d. Aug. 29, 1974 (62).

Furthman, Charles, writer; b. Chicago, Ill.; d. Nov. 7, 1936 (56).

Furthman, Jules, writer; b. Mar. 5, 1888, Chicago, Ill.; d. Sept. 22, 1966 (78).

Furtner, Joe, actor; d. July, 1965 (71).

Fyffe, Will, actor; b. Feb. 16, 1885, Dundee, Scotland; d. Dec. 14, 1947 (62).


Gabin, Jean, actor; b. May 17, 1904, Villette, Paris, France; d. Nov. 15, 1976 (72).

Gable, Clark, actor; b. Feb. 1, 1901, Cadiz, Ohio; d. Nov. 16, 1960 (59).

Gabriel, Jean (r.n. Jean Gabriel Citarella), director & actor; d. Oct. 9, 1977 (79).

Gabrielsen, Holger, actor & director; b. Nov. 27, 1896, Copenhagen, Denmark; d. May 7, 1956 (59).

Gabrio, Gabriel, actor; b. 1888, Reims, France; d. Nov. 2, 1946 (58).

Gaby, Frank, actor; b. 1896; d. Feb. 12, 1945 (48).

Gad, Urban, director; d. Jan., 1948 (68).

Gade, Sven, director; b. Feb. 9, 1877, Copenhagen, Denmark; d. June 25, 1952 (75).

Gage, Ben, actor; d. Apr. 28, 1978 (63).

Gage, Erford, actor; d. Mar. 17, 1945 (32).

Gaige, Russell (Bruce Hamilton), actor; b. May 4, 1894, Iowa; d. Oct. 17, 1974 (80).

Gailing, Gretchen, actress; b. Aug. 30, 1915, Nebraska; d. June 18, 1961 (45).

Gaines, Richard, actor; b. July 23, 1904, Oklahoma City, Okla.; d. July 20, 1975 (70).

Gale, Alice, actress; d. Mar. 27, 1941 (82).

Gale, Gladys, actress; d. Sept., 1948 (55).
Gale, Lillian, actress; d. Apr. 2, 1972.
Gale, Marguerite H., actress; d. Aug. 20, 1948 (63).
Galeen, Henrik, director & writer; d. July 30, 1949 (57).
Galento, Tony, actor & boxer; b. Mar. 12, 1910, Orange, N.J.; d.
    July 22, 1979 (69).
Galindo, Nacho, actor; b. Nov. 7, 1908, Guadalajara, Mexico;
    d. June 22, 1973 (64).
Galitzine, Leo, actor; d. Dec. 19, 1969.
Galla, Tito, actor; d. Aug. 25, 1979 (43).
Gallagher, Ed, actor; d. May 28, 1929 (53).
Gallagher, Glen B., actor; b. May 12, 1908, Colorado; d. Mar. 31,
    1960 (51).
Gallagher, Ray, actor; b. Apr. 17, 1885, San Francisco, Calif.;
    d. Mar. 6, 1953 (67).
Gallagher, Richard "Skeets," actor; b. July 28, 1890, Terre Haute,
    Ind.; d. May 22, 1955 (64).
Galland, Jean, actor; b. Apr. 20, 1897, Laval, France; d. July 18,
    1967 (70).
Gallardo, Luis Rojas, actor; d. Mar. 5, 1957.
Gallatin, Alberta, actress; d. Aug. 25, 1948 (87).
Galli, Dina, actress; b. Dec. 6, 1877, Milan, Italy; d. 1951 (73).
Gallian, Ketti, actress; b. Dec. 25, 1913, Nice, France; d. Dec.,
    1972 (59).
Gallina, Mario (r.n. Mario Fedrico Gallina), actor; b. Mar. 23,
    1889, Trieste, Italy; d. Sept. 26, 1950 (61).
Gallone, Carmine, director; b. Sept. 18, 1886, Taggia, Italy; d.
    Mar. 11, 1973 (86).
Gallone, Soava, actress; b. 1880, Varsavia, Italy; d. May 30, 1957
    (77).
Galt, Galan (see Pingree, Earl M.)
Galvani, Ciro, actor; b. Apr. 10, 1867, Castel San Pietro, Italy;
    d. Jan. 28, 1956 (88).
Galvani, Dino, actor; b. Oct. 27, 1890, Milan, Italy; d. Sept. 14,
    1960 (69).
Gamble, Fred (r.n. Fred Gambold), actor; b. Oct. 26, 1868, Indianapo-
    lis, Ind.; d. Feb. 17, 1939 (70).
Gamble, Ralph, actor; d. Mar. 11, 1966 (64).
Gamble, Warburton, actor; d. Aug. 27, 1945 (62).
Gamboa, Elias, actor; b. July 20, 1895, Mexico; d. Dec. 9, 1959 (64).
Gamet, Kenneth, writer; d. Oct. 13, 1971 (67).
Gamlin, Lionel, actor; d. Oct. 16, 1967 (64).
Gan, Chester, actor; b. July 4, 1908, California; d. June 29, 1959
    (50).
Gandusio, Antonio, actor; b. July 29, 1875, Pola, Yugoslavia; d.
    May 23, 1951 (75).
Gangelin, Paul, writer; b. Milwaukee, Wisc.; d. Sept. 25, 1961 (64).
Gannon, John (Jack), stuntman; d. Nov. 8, 1969 (66).
Gant, Harry, actor; b. Feb. 11, 1881, Iowa; d. July 26, 1967 (86).
Gantvoort, Carl, actor; d. Sept. 28, 1935 (52).
Ganzhorn, Jack, actor; b. Mar. 21, 1881, Ft. Thomas, Ark.; d. Sept.
    19, 1956 (75).
Garasa, Angel, actor; d. Aug. 27, 1976 (71).
Garat, Henry, actor; b. Apr. 3, 1902, Paris, France; d. Aug. 13,
    1959 (57).
Garavaglia, Ferruccio, actor; b. May 1, 1868, San Zenone Po, Italy;
    d. Apr. 29, 1912 (43).

Garaveo, Onorato, actor; b. Dec. 2, 1888, Genoa, Italy; d. Mar. 31, 1956 (67).
Garber, Jan, orchestra leader; d. Oct. 5, 1977 (82).
Garbutt, Frank A., producer & actor; d. Nov. 19, 1947 (78).
Garcia, Allan, actor; b. Mar. 11, 1887, San Francisco, Calif.; d. Sept. 4, 1938 (51).
Garcia, Harry, actor; d. Nov. 3, 1970 (66).
Garcia, Humberto Rodriguez, actor; d. June 21, 1960 (45).
Gardel, Carlos, actor; d. June 24, 1935 (46).
Gardella, Tess, actress; b. Wilkes-Barre, Pa.; d. Jan. 3, 1950 (52).
Garden, Mary, actress & opera singer; b. Feb. 20, 1874, Aberdeen, Scotland; d. Jan. 3, 1967 (92).
Gardes, Renee, actress; d. Mar., 1972.
Gardin, Vladimir R., director & actor; b. Jan. 18, 1877, Russia; d. May 28, 1965 (88).
Gardiner, Patrick, actor; d. Sept. 30, 1970 (44).
Gardner, Cyril, director & actor; b. May 30, 1898, Paris, France; d. Dec. 30, 1942 (44).
Gardner, Ed, actor; b. June 29, 1901, New York; d. Aug. 17, 1963 (62).
Gardner, George, actor; d. May 12, 1929 (61).
Gardner, Helen, actress; d. Nov. 20, 1968.
Gardner, Hunter, actor; d. Jan. 16, 1952 (53).
Gardner, Jack, actor; d. Dec. 29, 1929 (53).
Gardner, Jack, actor; d. Sept. 30, 1950 (77).
Gardner, Jack, actor; d. Oct. 20, 1955 (40).
Gardner, Jack, actor; d. Feb. 13, 1977 (77).
Gardner, Peter, actor; d. Nov. 13, 1953 (55).
Gardner, Richard (Irish), actor; b. Sept. 26, 1915, Washington; d. July 1, 1972 (56).
Gardner, Shayle, actor; b. Aug. 22, 1890, Auckland, New Zealand; d. May 17, 1945 (55).
Garfield, John, actor; b. Mar. 4, 1913, New York City; d. May 21, 1952 (39).
Gargan, Edward, actor; d. Feb. 19, 1964 (62).
Gargan, Jack T., actor; b. Feb. 8, 1900, England; d. Sept. 30, 1958 (58).
Gargan, William, actor; b. July 17, 1905, Brooklyn, N.Y.; d. Feb. 16, 1979 (73).
Garibay, Emilio, actor; d. Aug. 31, 1965 (38).
Garland, Franklin, actor; d. May 5, 1945 (81).
Garland, Judy (r.n. Frances Gumm), actress; b. June 10, 1922, Grand Rapids, Mich.; d. June 22, 1969 (47).
Garland, Richard (r.n. Charles Richard Garland), actor; b. July 7, 1927, Texas; d. May 24, 1969 (41).
Garmes, Lee, cinematographer; b. May 27, 1898, Peoria, Ill.; d. Aug. 31, 1978 (80).
Garner, Erroll, jazz artist & composer; b. June 15, 1923, Pittsburgh, Pa.; d. Jan. 2, 1977 (53).
Garnett, Tay, director; b. June 13, 1894, Los Angeles, Calif.; d. Oct. 4, 1977 (83).
Garon, Norm, actor; d. Apr. 13, 1975 (41).
Garon, Pauline, actress; b. Sept. 9, 1904, Montreal, Canada; d. Aug. 27, 1965 (60).
Garr, Eddie, actor; b. Philadelphia, Pa.; d. Sept. 3, 1956 (56).
Garrett, Charlcie Hedge, actress; d. Apr., 1978 (75).

Garrett, Oliver H.P., writer; b. New Bedford, Mass.; d. Feb. 22, 1952 (58).

Garrett, Otis, director & writer; d. May 24, 1941 (36).

Garrick, Richard, actor; b. Dec. 27, 1878, Eire; d. Aug. 21, 1962 (83).

Garrity, Harry, actor; d. Dec. 13, 1928 (56).

Garry, Joseph R., actor; d. June 7, 1954 (77).

Garside, John, actor; b. Apr. 21, 1887, Salford, Manchester, England; d. Apr. 18, 1958 (70).

Garson, Harry, director; d. Sept. 21, 1938 (56).

Garth, Otis, actor; d. Dec. 21, 1955 (54).

Gaudio, Tony (r.n. Gaetano Gaudio), cinematographer; b. Rome, Italy; d. Aug. 9, 1951 (66).

Gaumont, Leon, producer; d. Aug. 11, 1946 (82).

Garvie, Edward, actor; b. Meriden, Conn.; d. Feb. 17, 1939 (73).

Garwood, William, actor; b. Apr. 28, 1884; d. Dec. 28, 1950 (66).

Garza, Eva, actress & recording artist; d. Nov. 1, 1966 (49).

Gaskell, Charles, actor & director; d. Dec. 9, 1943 (74).

Gasnier, Louis J., director; b. Sept. 26, 1875, France; d. Feb. 15, 1963 (87).

Gastrock, Phil, actor; b. Oct. 26, 1876, Louisiana; d. Apr. 10, 1956 (79).

Gateson, Marjorie, actress; b. Jan. 17, 1891, Brooklyn, N.Y.; d. Apr. 17, 1977 (86).

Gatzert, Nate, scenarist; b. Dec. 15, 1890, Illinois; d. Sept. 1, 1959 (68).

Gauge, Alexander, actor; b. July 29, 1914, China; d. Aug. 29, 1960 (46).

Gauguin, Lorraine, actress; d. Dec. 22, 1974 (50).

Gault, Mildred, actress; d. Sept. 15, 1938 (33).

Gaultier, Henry, actor; d. Mar., 1972.

Gauntier, Gene, actress & producer; d. Dec. 18, 1966.

Gaut, Lou (Slim), actor; b. July 8, 1893, Idaho; d. Apr. 17, 1964 (70).

Gavagan, Margaret, actress; d. July 19, 1949.

Gawthorne, Peter, actor; b. Sept. 1, 1884, Queens Co., Ireland; d. Mar. 17, 1962 (77).

Gaxton, William, actor; b. Dec. 2, 1893, San Francisco, Calif.; d. Feb. 2, 1963 (69).

Gay, Charles, actor & lion tamer; d. Feb. 23, 1950 (63).

Gay, Fred, actor; d. June 11, 1955 (73).

Gay, Maisie, actress; b. London, England; d. Sept. 13, 1945 (67).

Gay, Ramon, actor; d. May 27, 1960 (43).

Gay, Robby, dancer; d. Nov. 17, 1960 (32).

Gaye, Albie, actress; d. Nov. 26, 1965.

Gaye, Howard, actor; b. Hitchin, Hertfordshire, England; d. Dec. 26, 1955.

Gayer, Echlin, actor; d. Feb. 14, 1926 (48).

Gaynor, Ruth, actress; d. May 28, 1919.

Geary, Bud (Maine Geary), actor; b. Feb. 15, 1898, Salt Lake City, Utah; d. Feb. 22, 1946 (48).

Geary, Maine (see Geary, Bud)

Gebhardt, Frank, actor; d. May 23, 1951.

Gebhardt, George M., actor; d. May 2, 1919 (40).

Gebhart, Albert, actor; d. Jan. 4, 1950 (63).

Gebuhr, Otto, actor; b. May 29, 1877, Kettwig, Germany; d. Mar. 13, 1954 (76).
Gee, George, actor; d. Oct. 17, 1959 (64).
Geer, Will, actor; b. Mar. 9, 1902, Frankfort, Ind.; d. Apr. 22, 1978 (76).
Gehrig, Lou, baseball star & actor; b. June 19, 1903, New York City; d. June 2, 1941 (37).
Gehrman, Lucy, actress; d. May 8, 1954.
Gehrung, Jean, actor; d. Oct. 19, 1938 (55).
Geiger, Hermann, actor & pilot; d. Aug. 25, 1966 (53).
Geisendorfer, Julius, actor; b. Apr. 3, 1878, Karlsruhe, Germany; d. Mar., 1953 (74).
Geldert, Clarence, actor; b. June 9, 1867, St. John, N. Brunswick, Canada; d. May 13, 1935 (67).
Gellenbeck, Benno, actor; d. Sept. 6, 1974 (64).
Gemelli, Enrico, actor; b. 1841, Milan, Italy; d. May 7, 1926 (85).
Gemier, Firmin, actor; b. Feb. 13, 1865, Aubervilliers, France; d. Nov. 26, 1933 (68).
Gemora, Charles, actor; b. Aug. 15, 1903, Philippines; d. Aug. 19, 1961 (58).
Gendron, Pierre (r.n. Leon Pierre Gendron), actor; b. Mar. 4, 1896, Toledo, Ohio; d. Nov. 27, 1956 (60).
Geniat, Marcelle, actress; b. Petrograd, Russia; d. Sept. 28, 1959 (80).
Genina, Augusto, director & writer; b. Jan. 28, 1892, Rome, Italy; d. Sept. 28, 1957 (65).
Genn, Leo, actor; b. Aug. 9, 1905, London, England; d. Jan. 26, 1978 (72).
Genschow, Fritz, actor; b. May 15, 1905, Berlin, Germany; d. June 21, 1977 (72).
Gentilli, Olga Vittoria, actress; b. July 19, 1888, Naples, Italy; d. May 29, 1957 (68).
Gentle, Alice, actress & opera singer; b. Illinois; d. Feb. 28, 1958 (69).
George, Alice Latimer, actress; d. May 15, 1930.
George, George M., actor; d. Nov. 28, 1960 (72).
George, Gladys (r.n. Gladys Anna Clare), actress; b. Sept. 13, 1904, Patten, Me.; d. Dec. 8, 1954 (50).
George, Gorgeous (r.n. George Raymond Wagner), wrestler & actor; d. Dec. 26, 1963 (48).
George, Grace, actress; b. Dec. 25, 1879, New York City; d. May 19, 1961 (81).
George, Heinrich, actor; b. Oct. 9, 1893, Stettin, Poland; d. Sept. 26, 1946 (52).
George, John, actor; b. Jan. 21, 1898, Iraq; d. Aug. 25, 1968 (70).
George, Muriel, actress; b. Aug. 29, 1883, London, England; d. Oct. 22, 1965 (82).
George, Voya, actor; d. May 8, 1951 (56).
Georges, Katherine, actress; d. June, 1973.
Geraghty, Carmelita, actress; b. Mar. 21, 1901, Rushville, Ind.; d. July 7, 1966 (65).
Geraghty, Gerald, writer; b. Aug. 10, 1906, Rushville, Ind.; d. July 8, 1954 (47).
Geraghty, Tom C., author & actor; d. June 5, 1945 (62).
Gerald, Ara, actress; d. Apr. 2, 1957 (63).
Gerald, Jim, actor; b. 1889; d. 1962 (73).
Gerard, Teddie, actress; d. Aug. 31, 1942 (52).

Gerasch, Alfred, actor; b. Aug. 17, 1877, Berlin, Germany; d. Aug., 1955 (78).
Geray, Steven, actor; b. Nov. 10, 1904, Uzhored, Czechoslovakia; d. Dec. 26, 1973 (69).
Gering, Marion, director; d. Apr. 19, 1977 (73).
Germi, Pietro, actor, director, & author; b. Sept. 14, 1914, Genoa, Italy; d. Dec. 5, 1974 (60).
Gerold, Herman, actor; d. Nov. 19, 1920 (58).
Gerrard, Douglas, actor; b. Aug. 12, 1891, Dublin, Ireland; d. June 5, 1950 (58).
Gerrard, Gene, actor & director; b. Aug. 31, 1889, London, England; d. June 1, 1971 (81).
Gerron, Kurt, actor; b. 1897, Berlin, Germany; d. Oct., 1944 (47).
Gerson, Eva, actress; d. Sept. 5, 1959 (56).
Gerson, Paul, actor; d. June 5, 1957 (86).
Gersten, Berta, actress; d. Sept. 10, 1972 (78).
Gerstle, Frank, actor; b. Sept. 27, 1915, New York; d. Feb. 24, 1970 (54).
Gert, Valeska, actress; b. 1900, Berlin, Germany; d. Mar. 18, 1978 (78).
Gest, Inna, actress; d. Jan. 1, 1965 (43).
Gettinger, William (see Steele, William)
Ghere, High (see Burns, Bob)
Ghermanoff, George, actor; b. Aug. 2, 1888, Turkey; d. Sept. 17, 1965 (77).
Ghio, Antonio (Nino), actor; d. Jan. 13, 1956 (69).
Ghione, Emilio, actor; b. 1879, Turin, Italy; d. Jan. 7, 1930 (50).
Giachetti, Fosco, actor; b. Mar. 28, 1904, Livorno, Italy; d. Dec. 22, 1974 (70).
Giachetti, Gianfranco, actor; b. Sept. 17, 1888, Firenze, Italy; d. Nov. 29, 1936 (48).
Gibbons, Cedric, art director; b. Mar. 23, 1893, Brooklyn, N.Y.; d. July 26, 1960 (67).
Gibbons, Robert, actor; b. May 25, 1918, Illinois; d. Feb. 21, 1977 (58).
Gibbons, Rose, actress; d. Aug. 13, 1964 (73).
Gibbs, Irving, actor; d. Apr. 5, 1955 (79).
Gibbs, Joseph F., actor; d. Apr. 14, 1921.
Gibbs, Robert P., actor; b. Scranton, Pa.; d. Feb. 22, 1941 (81).
Giblyn, Charles, actor & director; b. Sept. 6, 1871, Watertown, N.Y.; d. Mar. 14, 1934 (62).
Gibson, Helen, actress; b. Aug. 27, 1894, Cleveland, Ohio; d. Oct. 10, 1977 (83).
Gibson, Hoot, actor; b. Aug. 6, 1892, Tekamah, Neb.; d. Aug. 23, 1962 (70).
Gibson, James, actor; b. Oct. 24, 1865, Indiana; d. Oct. 13, 1938 (72).
Gibson, James, actor; d. Sept., 1973 (79).
Gibson, John, actor; d. Sept. 14, 1971.
Gibson, Kenneth, actor; b. Jan. 17, 1898, Sandusky, Ohio; d. Nov. 26, 1972 (74).
Gibson, Margaret (Patricia Palmer), actress; b. Sept. 14, 1894, Colorado; d. Oct. 21, 1964 (70).
Gibson, Norman, actor; d. Sept. 29, 1976 (26).
Gideon, Melville, actor; b. May 21, 1884, New York; d. Nov. 11, 1933 (49).

Giehse, Therese, actress; b. Mar. 6, 1898, Munich, Germany; d. Mar. 3, 1975 (76).

Gigli, Beniamino, actor & opera singer; b. Mar. 20, 1890, Recanati, Italy; d. Nov. 30, 1957 (67).

Gigy, Mabel P., actress; d. July 18, 1952 (75).

Gilbert, Billy, actor; b. Sept. 15, 1891, California; d. Apr. 29, 1961 (69).

Gilbert, Billy, actor; b. Jan. 12, 1894, Louisville, Ky.; d. Sept. 23, 1971 (77).

Gilbert, Bobby, actor; b. Apr. 6, 1898, Pennsylvania; d. Sept. 19, 1973 (75).

Gilbert, Jody, actress; d. Feb. 3, 1979.

Gilbert, Joe, actor; d. May 26, 1959 (56).

Gilbert, John, actor; b. July 10, 1897, Logan, Utah; d. Jan. 9, 1936 (38).

Gilbert, Lou, actor; b. Aug. 1, 1909, Sycamore, Ill.; d. Nov. 6, 1978 (69).

Gilbert, Maude, actress; d. July 7, 1953 (70).

Gilbert, Oh Gran, actor; d. Sept. 12, 1971 (85).

Gilbert, Paul, actor; d. Feb. 12, 1976 (58).

Gilbert, Walter, actor; b. Brooklyn, N.Y.; d. Jan. 12, 1947 (60).

Giler, Berne, writer; b. Oct. 6, 1908, New York City; d. July 24, 1967 (58).

Giles, Anna, actress; b. Nov. 23, 1873, Illinois; d. Feb. 2, 1973 (99).

Gilfether, Daniel, actor; d. May 3, 1919 (70).

Gill, Basil, actor; b. Mar. 10, 1877, Birkenhead, Cheshire, England; d. Apr. 23, 1955 (78).

Gill, Florence, actress; b. July 27, 1877, England; d. Feb. 19, 1965 (87).

Gill, Tom, actor; b. July 26, 1916, Newcastle-on-Tyne, England; d. July 22, 1971 (54).

Gillespie, A. Arnold (Buddy), special effects executive; b. Oct. 14, 1899, El Paso, Tex.; d. May 3, 1978 (78).

Gillespie, Edward Charles, actor; d. July 23, 1918 (44).

Gillett, Elma, actress; b. July 3, 1874; d. July 9, 1941 (67).

Gillette, George William, Jr., actor; d. Mar. 10, 1957 (64).

Gillette, William, actor; b. July 24, 1855, Hartford, Conn.; d. Apr. 29, 1937 (81).

Gillie, Jean, actress; b. Oct. 14, 1915, London, England; d. Feb. 19, 1949 (33).

Gillingwater, Claude, actor; b. Aug. 2, 1870, Louisiana, Mo.; d. Nov. 1, 1939 (69).

Gillis, William S., actor; b. Nov. 17, 1867, Texas; d. Apr. 24, 1946 (78).

Gillmore, Frank, actor; b. May 14, 1867, New York City; d. Mar. 29, 1943 (75).

Gilman, Ada, actress; d. Dec. 18, 1921 (67).

Gilmore, Barney, actor; d. Apr. 19, 1949 (80).

Gilmore, Billie, actress & director; d. June 27, 1931.

Gilmore, Douglas, actor; b. June 25, 1903, Boston, Mass.; d. July 26, 1950 (47).

Gilmore, Helen, actress; d. Apr. 12, 1936 (35).

Gilmore, Lowell, actor; b. Dec. 20, 1906, Minnesota; d. Jan. 31, 1960 (53).

Gilmour, John H., actor; d. Nov. 24, 1922 (65).
Gilson, Tom, actor; b. Jan. 6, 1934, New York; d. Oct. 6, 1962 (28).
Gim, H.W., actor; b. Jan. 22, 1908, China; d. Mar. 16, 1973 (65).
Giniva, John, actor; d. Feb. 22, 1936 (68).
Ginn, Hayword J., actor; d. Feb. 14, 1926.
Ginn, Wells W., actor; d. Apr. 15, 1959 (68).
Gioi, Vivi, actress; b. Jan. 2, 1919, Livorno, Italy; d. July 12,
    1975 (56).
Giorda, Marcello, actor; b. Jan. 16, 1890, Rome, Italy; d. Apr. 22,
    1960 (70).
Girard, Joseph W., actor; b. Apr. 2, 1871, Williamsport, Pa.; d. Aug.
    21, 1949 (78).
Girardot, Etienne, actor; b. Feb. 22, 1856, London, England; d. Nov.
    10, 1939 (83).
Giraud, Octavio J., actor; b. Apr. 1, 1890, Cuba; d. June 3, 1958
    (68).
Girosi, Marcelo, producer & writer; d. Jan. 9, 1965 (62).
Gish, Dorothy, actress; b. Mar. 11, 1898, Massillon, Ohio; d. June
    4, 1968 (70).
Givney, Kathryn, actress; d. Mar. 16, 1978 (81).
Gladman, Anabelle, actress; d. Jan. 15, 1948 (49).
Glagolin, Boris S., actor; d. Dec. 12, 1948 (70).
Glaser, Lulu, actress; b. June 2, 1874, Allegheny, Pa.; d. Sept. 5,
    1958 (84).
Glaser, Vaughan, actor; b. Nov. 17, 1872, Ohio; d. Nov. 23, 1958 (86).
Glasmon, Kubec, writer; b. Poland; d. Mar. 13, 1938 (40).
Glass, Everett, actor; b. July 23, 1890, Maine; d. Mar. 22, 1966 (75).
Glass, Gaston, actor & assistant director; b. Dec. 31, 1899, Paris,
    France; d. Nov. 11, 1965 (65).
Glass, Myrtle, actress; d. May 13, 1945 (48).
Glassmire, Gus, actor; b. Aug. 29, 1879, Philadelphia, Pa.; d. July
    23, 1946 (66).
Glaum, Louise, actress; b. Sept. 4, 1900, Maryland; d. Nov. 25, 1970
    (70).
Glazer, Benjamin F., producer & writer; b. May 7, 1887, Belfast,
    Ireland; d. Mar. 18, 1956 (68).
Glazer, Eve F., actress; b. June 4, 1903, Pennsylvania; d. June 29,
    1960 (57).
Gleason, Adda, actress; b. Dec. 19, 1888, Illinois; d. Feb. 6, 1971 (82).
Gleason, Fred, actor; d. June 9, 1933 (79).
Gleason, James, actor, author, & director; b. May 23, 1882, New York
    City; d. Apr. 12, 1959 (76).
Gleason, Lucile Webster, actress; b. Feb. 6, 1888, Pasadena, Calif.;
    d. May 18, 1947 (59).
Gleason, Russell, actor; b. Feb. 6, 1908, Portland, Ore.; 'd. Dec. 26,
    1945 (37).
Gleboff, George A. (see Du Count, George)
Gleckler, Robert, actor; b. Jan. 11, 1887, Pierre, S.D.; d. Feb. 25,
    1939 (52).
Glendinning, Ernest, actor; b. Feb. 19, 1884, Ulverston, England;
    d. May 17, 1936 (52).
Glendon, J. Frank, actor; b. Oct. 25, 1886, Ohio; d. Mar. 17, 1937
    (50).
Glenn, Donald, actor; d. Mar. 11, 1958 (46).
Glenn, Forrest, actor; d. Aug. 24, 1954 (54).
Glenn, Raymond (see Custer, Bob)

International Film Necrology                                    119

Glenn, Roy, actor; d. Mar. 12, 1971 (56).
Glennon, Bert, cinematographer; b. Anaconda, Mont.; d. June 29, 1967
    (74).
Glessing, Molly, actress; d. Apr. 30, 1971.
Glick, Joseph, extra; d. Sept. 5, 1978 (72).
Gloeckner-Kramer, Pepi, actor; d. Jan. 17, 1954 (80).
Glori, Enrico, actor; b. Aug. 3, 1901, Naples, Italy; d. Apr. 20,
    1966 (64).
Glosz, Marie, actress & opera singer; d. Apr. 14, 1963 (83).
Glover, Edmund, actor; d. Nov. 25, 1978.
Glowner, M. Lee, actor; b. Oct. 21, 1866, California; d. July 9, 1923
    (56).
Glyn, Elinor, writer; d. Sept. 23, 1943 (78).
Glyn, Neva Carr, actress; d. Aug. 10, 1975.
Glynne, Mary, actress; b. Jan. 25, 1898, Peniarth, England; d. Sept.
    19, 1954 (56).
Gnass, Friedrich, actor; b. Bochum, Germany; d. May, 1958 (65).
Gobble, Henry A. (Hank), stuntman; b. Apr. 21, 1923, California;
    d. May 19, 1961 (38).
Goddard, Richard, actor; b. Mar. 1, 1878, England; d. Jan. 3, 1962
    (83).
Godden, Jimmy, actor; b. Aug. 11, 1879, Maidstone, England; d. Mar.
    5, 1955 (75).
Godden, Rudi, actor; b. 1908; d. Jan. 4, 1941 (32).
Godderis, Albert, actor; b. Nov. 4, 1880, Belgium; d. Feb. 2, 1971
    (90).
Godfrey, Michael, actor; d. Sept. 19, 1977.
Godfrey, Peter, actor & director; b. Oct. 16, 1899, London, England;
    d. Mar. 4, 1970 (70).
Godfrey, Renee (Renee Hall), actress; b. Sept. 1, 1919, New York;
    d. May 24, 1964 (44).
Godfrey, Sam, actor; b. Oct. 5, 1892, Brooklyn, N.Y.; d. Apr. 18,
    1935 (42).
Godowsky, Dagmar, actress; d. Feb. 13, 1975 (78).
Goettinger, William (see Steele, William)
Goetz, Curt, actor & author; b. Nov. 17, 1888, Mainz, Germany;
    d. Sept. 12, 1960 (71).
Goetz, Paul P. ("Pop"), actor; d. Sept. 26, 1929 (64).
Goetzke, Bernhard, actor; b. 1884, Danzig; d. Oct., 1964 (80).
Goff, Norris (Abner), actor; b. May 30, 1906, Cove, Ark.; d. June 7,
    1978 (72).
Goines, Betty, actress; d. Feb., 1929 (25).
Going, Frederica, actress; d. Apr. 11, 1959.
Gola, Jose, actor; b. 1905, La Plata, Argentina; d. Apr. 27, 1939
    (34).
Gold, Jimmy, actor, member of Crazy Gang; d. Oct. 7, 1967 (81).
Goldbeck, Willis, director; b. New York City; d. Sept. 17, 1979 (80).
Golden, Bob, actor; d. Nov. 5, 1979 (54).
Golden, Ruth Fuller, actress; b. May 19, 1901, New York; d. Aug. 15,
    1931 (30).
Goldenberg, Samuel, actor; d. Oct. 31, 1945 (59).
Goldie, F. Wyndham, actor; b. July 5, 1897, Rochester, Kent, England;
    d. Sept. 26, 1957 (60).
Goldin, Pat (r.n. Meyer Goldin), actor; b. Dec. 5, 1902, Russia;
    d. Apr. 24, 1971 (68).

Goldin, Sidney M., director & actor; d. Sept. 19, 1937 (57).
Goldman, Harold, writer; b. New York City; d. Jan., 1956 (66).
Goldman, Bernard, actor; d. Sept. 19, 1966 (43).
Goldner, Charles, actor; b. Dec. 7, 1900, Vienna, Austria; d. Apr. 15, 1955 (54).
Goldsworthy, John, actor; b. Apr. 28, 1884, England; d. July 10, 1958 (74).
Goldwyn, Samuel, producer; b. Aug. 27, 1882, Warsaw, Poland; d. Jan. 31, 1974 (91).
Golm, Ernest, actor; b. Dec. 21, 1885, Germany; d. May 29, 1962 (76).
Golm, Lisa, actress; d. Jan. 6, 1964.
Golubeff, Gregory, actor; b. Feb. 22, 1891, New York; d. Feb. 11, 1958 (66).
Gombell, Minna, actress; b. May 28, 1892, Baltimore, Md.; d. Apr. 14, 1973 (80).
Gomes, Eliezer, actor; d. Feb. 12, 1979 (58).
Gomez, Augie, actor; b. Aug. 10, 1889, Pennsylvania; d. Jan. 1, 1966 (76).
Gomez, Ralph, actor; d. Apr. 18, 1954 (57).
Gomez, Thomas (r.n. S. Thomas Gomez), actor; b. July 10, 1905, New York City; d. June 18, 1971 (65).
Gondi, Harry, actor; d. Nov., 1968 (68).
Gonzalez, Gilberto, actor; d. Mar. 21, 1954 (48).
Gonzalez, Mario Tecero, actor; d. Aug. 28, 1957 (38).
Gonzalez, Myrtle, actress; d. Oct. 22, 1918 (27).
Gonzalo, Maria Eduarda, actress; d. Jan. 24, 1955 (26).
Goodall, Grace, actress; b. June 12, 1889, San Francisco, Calif.; d. Sept. 27, 1940 (51).
Goode, Jack, actor; d. June 24, 1971 (63).
Goodliffe, Michael, actor; b. Oct. 1, 1914, Bebington, Cheshire, England; d. Mar. 20, 1976 (61).
Goodman, Gordon, actor & singer; d. Dec. 9, 1960 (49).
Goodrich, Charles W., actor; d. Mar. 20, 1931 (70).
Goodrich, Edna, actress; b. Dec. 22, 1883, Logansport, Ind.; d. May 26, 1971 (87).
Goodrich, Louis, actor; b. Sandhurst, England; d. Jan. 31, 1945 (80).
Goodwin, Bill, actor; b. July 10, 1910, San Francisco, Calif.; d. May 9, 1958 (47).
Goodwin, Nat C., actor; b. July 25, 1857, Boston, Mass.; d. Jan. 31, 1919 (61).
Goodwin, Ruby B., actress; b. Oct. 17, 1903, Illinois; d. May 31, 1961 (57).
Goodwins, Leslie, director; b. Sept. 17, 1899, London, England; d. Jan. 8, 1969 (69).
Gorcey, Bernard, actor; b. Russia; d. Sept. 11, 1955 (69).
Gorcey, Leo, actor; b. June 3, 1916, New York City; d. June 2, 1969 (52).
Gordon, A. George, actor; d. Dec. 27, 1953 (71).
Gordon, Bert (the Mad Russian), actor; b. Apr. 8, 1895, New York; d. Nov. 30, 1974 (79).
Gordon, C. Henry, actor; b. June 17, 1884, New York City; d. Dec. 3, 1940 (56).
Gordon, Charles (see Gordon, Glen C.)
Gordon, Colin, actor; b. Apr. 27, 1911, Ceylon; d. Oct. 4, 1972 (61).
Gordon, Edward, actor; d. Nov. 10, 1938 (52).

Gordon, G. Swayne, actor; b. Baltimore, Md.; d. June 23, 1949 (69).
Gordon, Glen C. (Charles Gordon), actor; b. Mar. 13, 1914, New York;
  d. Sept. 16, 1977 (63).
Gordon, Gloria, actress; d. Nov. 22, 1962.
Gordon, Grant, actor; d. Aug. 6, 1972 (64).
Gordon, Harold, actor; d. Jan. 19, 1959 (40).
Gordon, Harris, actor; b. July 4, 1884, Glenside, Pa.; d. Mar. 31,
  1947 (62).
Gordon, Harry, actor; d. Nov. 20, 1948 (64).
Gordon, Huntley, actor; b. Oct. 8, 1887, Montreal, Canada; d. Dec. 8,
  1956 (69).
Gordon, James, actor; b. Apr. 23, 1871, Pittsburgh, Pa.; d. May 12,
  1941 (70).
Gordon, Julia Swayne, actress; b. Oct. 29, 1878, Columbus, Ohio; d.
  May 28, 1933 (54).
Gordon, Kitty, actress; b. Apr. 22, 1878, Folkestone, England; d. May
  26, 1974 (96).
Gordon, Leon, producer, actor, & author; b. Jan. 12, 1884, Brighton,
  Sussex, England; d. Jan. 4, 1960 (75).
Gordon, Mary, actress; b. May 16, 1882, Scotland; d. Aug. 23, 1963
  (81).
Gordon, Maude Turner, actress; b. Nov. 10, 1868, Franklin, Indiana;
  d. Jan. 12, 1940 (71).
Gordon, Nora, actress; d. May 11, 1970 (76).
Gordon, Paul, actor; b. Brooklyn, N.Y.; d. May 3, 1929 (43).
Gordon, Peter, actor; d. May 25, 1943 (55).
Gordon, Richard, actor; d. Sept. 20, 1956 (63).
Gordon, Robert (r.n. Robert Gordon Duncan), actor; b. Mar. 3, 1895,
  Kansas; d. Oct. 26, 1971 (76).
Gordon, Roy, actor; b. Oct. 18, 1884, Ohio; d. July 23, 1972 (87).
Gordon, Roy, actor; d. Oct. 12, 1978 (82).
Gordon, Vera, actress; b. June 11, 1886, Russia; d. May 8, 1948 (61).
Gordoni, Arthur, actor; b. Mar. 17, 1893, New York; d. Aug. 10, 1966
  (73).
Gore, Rosa, actress; b. Sept. 15, 1866, New York City; d. Feb. 4,
  1941 (74).
Gorman, Charles, actor; d. Jan. 25, 1928 (63).
Gorman, Eddie, actor; d. June 28, 1919 (47).
Gorman, Eric (r.n. Frederick Eric Gorman), actor; d. Nov. 25, 1971
  (89).
Gorman, Tom, actor; b. Morgantown, W. Va.; d. Oct. 2, 1971 (63).
Gorss, Saul, actor & stuntman; b. Mar. 22, 1908, Ohio; d. Sept. 10,
  1966 (58).
Goryunov, Anatoliy I., actor; b. Dec. 17, 1902; d. July 10, 1951 (48).
Gosfield, Maurice, actor; d. Oct. 19, 1964 (51).
Gosford, Alice Peckham, actress; d. Jan. 23, 1919 (32).
Gosnell, Evelyn F., actress; d. Nov. 11, 1946 (51).
Goss, Jimmy, actor; d. Aug. 20, 1976 (74).
Gott, Barbara, actress; d. Nov. 18, 1944.
Gottler, Archie, actor; d. June 24, 1959 (63).
Gottschalk, Ferdinand, actor; b. Feb. 28, 1858, London, England; d.
  Nov. 10, 1944 (86).
Gottschalk, Joachim, actor; b. Apr. 10, 1909, Calau, Germany; d. Nov.
  6, 1941 (32).
Goty, Mici, actress; b. Jan. 12, 1890, Budapest, Hungary; d. July
  24, 1946 (56).

Gough, John, actor; b. Sept. 22, 1894, Boston, Mass.; d. June 29,
    1968 (73).
Gould, Howard, actor; b. St. Anthony, Minn.; d. Feb. 3, 1938 (74).
Gould, Myrtle, actress; d. Feb. 25, 1941 (61).
Gould, Violet, actress; d. Mar. 29, 1962 (78).
Gould, William, actor; d. Mar. 29, 1960.
Gould, William "Billy," actor; d. Feb. 1, 1950 (81).
Goulding, Alf (r.n. Alfred John Goulding), director; b. Jan. 26,
    1896, Melbourne, Australia; d. Apr. 25, 1972 (76).
Goulding, Edmund, director; b. Mar. 20, 1891, London, England;
    d. Dec. 24, 1959 (68).
Gover, Mildred, actress; b. June 22, 1903, Dover, Maryland; d. Sept.
    11, 1947 (44).
Govi, Gilberto, actor; b. Oct. 22, 1885, Genova; d. Apr. 27, 1966
    (80).
Gowers, Sulky, actor; d. Mar., 1970.
Gowland, Gibson, actor; b. Jan. 4, 1877, England; d. Sept. 9, 1951
    (74).
Gowman, Milton J., actor; d. Aug. 17, 1952 (45).
Goya, Mona, actress; b. Nov. 25, 1912, Mexico; d. 1961 (49).
Grable, Betty, actress; b. Dec. 18, 1916, St. Louis, Mo.; d. July 2,
    1973 (56).
Grabley, Ursula, actress; d. Apr. 3, 1977 (68).
Grace, Charity, actress; d. Nov. 28, 1965 (81).
Grace, Dick, stunt flier & actor; b. Jan. 10, 1898, Minnesota;
    d. June 25, 1965 (67).
Grace, Dinah, actress; d. May 12, 1963.
Grady, James H., actor; d. Feb. 17, 1941 (72).
Graetz, Paul, actor; b. Aug. 4, 1889, Berlin, Germany; d. Feb. 16,
    1937 (47).
Graetz, Paul, producer & actor; d. Feb. 5, 1966 (66).
Graf, Otto, actor; b. Nov. 28, 1896, Haina; d. Feb., 1977 (80).
Graf, Peter, actor; d. Oct. 20, 1951 (79).
Graf, Robert, actor; b. Nov. 18, 1923, Witten, Germany; d. Feb. 4,
    1966 (42).
Graff, Wilton (r.n. Wilton Calvert Ratcliffe), actor; b. Aug. 13,
    1903, St. Louis, Mo.; d. Jan. 14, 1969 (65).
Graham, Charlie, actor; b. Feb. 16, 1895, Carthage, Miss.; d. Oct. 9,
    1943 (48).
Graham, Fred, actor & stuntman; d. Oct. 10, 1979 (61).
Graham, Frederick, actor; d. Sept. 26, 1947 (81).
Graham, Julia Ann, actress; d. July 15, 1935 (20).
Graham, Malcolm, actor; d. Jan., 1959 (62).
Graham, Morland, actor; b. Aug. 8, 1891, Partick, Glasgow, Scotland;
    d. Apr. 8, 1949 (57).
Graham, Ronald, actor; b. Scotland; d. July 4, 1950 (38).
Grahame, Bert, actor; d. Mar. 23, 1971 (79).
Gramatica, Emma, actress; b. Mar. 22, 1875, Parma, Italy; d. Nov. 8,
    1965 (90).
Gramatica, Irma, actress; b. Nov. 25, 1873, Fiume; d. Oct. 14, 1962
    (88).
Gran, Albert, actor; b. Aug. 4, 1862, Bergen, Norway; d. Dec. 16,
    1932 (70).
Granach, Alexander, actor; b. 1890, Ukraine, Russia; d. Mar. 14, 1945
    (54).

Granby, Joseph, actor; b. Mar. 24, 1885, U.S.S.R.; d. Sept. 22, 1965 (80).

Grandais, Suzanne, actress; b. July 14, 1893, Paris, France; d. Aug. 18, 1920 (27).

Grandin, Elmer, actor; d. May 19, 1933 (72).

Grandin, Francis, actor & director; d. July 11, 1929 (50).

Granger, Maude, actress; d. Aug. 17, 1928 (77).

Granger, William, actor; b. May 24, 1854, Philadelphia, Pa.; d. Dec. 23, 1938 (84).

Granowsky, Alexander, actor; b. Moscow, Russia; d. Mar. 11, 1937 (47).

Grant, A. Cameron (r.n. Alexander C. Grant), actor; b. Aug. 27, 1901, Canada; d. Jan. 18, 1972 (70).

Grant, Albert, actor; d. Nov. 20, 1968.

Grant, Earl, actor & recording artist; d. June 10, 1970 (39).

Grant, James Edward, writer; d. Feb. 19, 1966 (61).

Grant, Lawrence (r.n. Percy Reginald Lawrence-Grant), actor; b. Oct. 30, 1869, Bournemouth, England; d. Feb. 19, 1952 (82).

Grant, Sydney, actor; b. Feb. 20, 1873, Massachusetts; d. July 11, 1953 (80).

Grant, Valentine, actress; b. Feb. 14, 1881, Indiana; d. Mar. 12, 1949 (68).

Granville, Bernard, actor; b. July 4, 1886, Chicago, Ill.; d. Oct. 5, 1936 (50).

Granville, Charlotte, actress; b. May 9, 1860, London, England; d. July 8, 1942 (82).

Granville, Joan, actress; d. Jan. 3, 1974.

Granville, Louise, actress; b. Sept. 29, 1895, Sydney, Australia; d. Dec. 22, 1968 (73).

Granville, Sydney, actor & stage singer; b. Bolton, Lancashire, England; d. Dec. 27, 1959 (79).

Granville, Taylor, director & actor; d. Apr. 14, 1923 (50).

Grapewin, Charles, actor; b. Dec. 20, 1869, Xenia, Ohio; d. Feb. 2, 1956 (86).

Grassby, Bertram, actor; b. Dec. 23, 1880, Lincolnshire, England; d. Dec. 7, 1953 (72).

Grasso, Giovanni, actor; d. Oct. 13, 1930 (60).

Grauman, Sid, showman & impresario; b. Mar. 17, 1879, Indianapolis, Ind.; d. Mar. 4, 1950 (71).

Graumann, Karl, actor; b. Nov. 11, 1874, Goettingen, Germany; d. Apr. 20, 1948 (73).

Gravers, Steve, actor; d. Aug. 26, 1978 (56).

Graves, George, actor; b. Jan. 1, 1876, London, England; d. Apr. 2, 1949 (73).

Graves, Jesse A., actor; b. Mar. 11, 1879, Iowa; d. Mar. 4, 1949 (69).

Graves, Kathryn, actress; b. Dec. 1, 1899, Minnesota; d. Feb. 26, 1977 (77).

Graves, Ralph, actor; b. Jan. 23, 1900, Cleveland, Ohio; d. Feb. 18, 1977 (77).

Graves, Robert, Jr., actor; b. Oct. 22, 1888, New York City; d. Aug. 19, 1954 (65).

Gravet, Fernand (Fernand Gravey), actor; b. Dec. 25, 1904, Belgium; d. Nov. 2, 1970 (65).

Gray, Arnold (see Gregg, Arnold)

Gray, Betty, actress; d. June, 1919.

Gray, Billy, actor; d. Jan. 4, 1978 (73).

Gray, Donald, actor; d. Apr. 7, 1978 (64).
Gray, Dorothy, actress; b. Oct. 23, 1922, Hollywood, Calif.; d. May 9, 1976 (53).
Gray, Eddie "Monsewer," actor (Crazy Gang); d. Sept. 15, 1969 (71).
Gray, Gene, actor; d. Feb. 11, 1950 (68).
Gray, George, actor (Keystone Kop); d. Sept. 8, 1967 (73).
Gray, Gilda, actress & burlesque star; b. Poland; d. Dec. 22, 1959 (60).
Gray, Glen, bandleader; d. Aug. 23, 1963 (63).
Gray, Gloria, actress; d. Apr. 4, 1918 (18).
Gray, Jack, actor; b. Apr. 13, 1956 (76).
Gray, Jean, actress; d. Sept. 23, 1953 (51).
Gray, Jennifer, actress; d. Feb. 4, 1962 (45).
Gray, Joe, actor; b. May 5, 1912, New York; d. Mar. 15, 1971 (58).
Gray, Lawrence, actor; b. July 28, 1898, San Francisco, Calif.; d. Feb. 2, 1970 (71).
Gray, Leo Don, actor; b. Dec. 4, 1901, Greece; d. July 24, 1966 (64).
Gray, Linda, actress; b. Nov. 7, 1912, Missouri; d. Sept. 4, 1963 (50).
Gray, Roger, actor; b. May 26, 1887, Omaha, Neb.; d. Jan. 20, 1959 (71).
Grayson, Charles, writer; b. Los Angeles, Calif.; d. May 4, 1973 (69).
Grayson, Hal, bandleader; b. May 31, 1908, Los Angeles, Calif.; d. Oct. 30, 1959 (51).
Grayson, Jessie, actress; b. Mar. 7, 1886, Iowa; d. Feb. 27, 1953 (66).
Greaves, Edith, actress; b. Dec. 7, 1888, Wisconsin; d. Feb. 14, 1952 (63).
Greaza, Walter, actor; b. Jan. 1, 1897, St. Paul, Minn.; d. June 1, 1973 (76).
Green, Alfred E., director; b. July 11, 1889, Perris, Calif.; d. Sept. 4, 1960 (71).
Green, Denis, actor; b. Apr. 11, 1903, London, England; d. Nov. 6, 1954 (51).
Green, Dorothy, actress; d. Nov. 16, 1963 (71).
Green, Harry, actor; b. Apr. 1, 1892, New York City; d. May 31, 1958 (66).
Green, Kenneth, actor; d. Feb. 24, 1969 (61).
Green, Martyn, actor; b. Apr. 22, 1899, London, England; d. Feb. 8, 1975 (75).
Green, Mitzi, actress; b. Oct. 22, 1920, New York City; d. May 24, 1969 (48).
Green, Nigel, actor; b. Oct. 15, 1924, South Africa; d. May 15, 1972 (47).
Green, Reginald, actor; d. Feb., 1973 (70).
Green, Sue, actress; d. Aug. 12, 1939 (37).
Green, William B., actor; d. Apr. 10, 1926 (74).
Green, William E., actor; b. Mar. 16, 1893, New Jersey; d. Jan. 4, 1962 (68).
Greene, Angela, actress; d. Feb. 9, 1978 (56).
Greene, Billy M., actor; b. Jan. 6, 1897, New York; d. Aug. 24, 1973 (76).
Greene, Harrison, actor; b. Jan. 18, 1884, Portland, Ore.; d. Sept. 28, 1945 (61).
Greene, Helen, actress; d. Oct. 10, 1947 (43).

Greene, Victor Hugo, actor; b. Feb. 26, 1895, Georgia; d. Aug. 9, 1971 (76).

Greene, William, actor; d. Mar. 12, 1970 (43).

Greenleaf, Mace, actor; d. Mar. 23, 1912.

Greenleaf, Raymond, actor; b. Nov. 27, 1892, Massachusetts; d. Oct. 29, 1963 (70).

Greenstreet, Sydney, actor; b. Dec. 27, 1879, Sandwich, Kent, England; d. Jan. 18, 1954 (74).

Greenwood, Charlotte, actress; b. June 25, 1890, Philadelphia, Pa.; d. Jan. 18, 1978 (87).

Greenwood, Ethel, actress; d. June 10, 1888, Missouri; d. Dec. 9, 1970 (82).

Greenwood, Hubert F., actor; b. Apr. 1, 1884, England; d. Apr. 7, 1950 (66).

Greenwood, Winifred, actress; b. Jan. 1, 1885, New York; d. Nov. 23, 1961 (76).

Greer, Julian, actor; d. Apr. 15, 1928 (56).

Greet, Clara, actress; b. June 14, 1871, England; d. Feb. 14, 1939 (67).

Gregg, Arnold (Arnold Gray) (r.n. Arnold R. Samberg), actor; d. Apr. 20, 1899, Toledo, Ohio; d. May 3, 1936 (37).

Gregg, Everley, actress; b. Oct. 26, 1903, Bishop Stoke, Hants., England; d. June 9, 1959 (55).

Gregor, Nora, actress; d. Jan. 20, 1949.

Gregory, Bobby, performer & song writer; b. Apr. 24, 1900, Staunton, Va.; d. May 13, 1971 (71).

Gregory, Dora, actress; b. Sept. 2, 1872, Dulwich, England; d. Mar. 5, 1954 (81).

Gregory, Edna, actress; d. July 3, 1965 (56).

Gregory, Paul, actor; b. 1904; d. July 19, 1942 (38).

Gregson, John, actor; b. Mar. 15, 1919, Liverpool, England; d. Jan. 8, 1975 (55).

Greig, Robert, actor; b. Dec. 27, 1879, Australia; d. June 27, 1958 (78).

Gremillion, Jean, director; b. Oct. 3, 1902, Bayeux, France; d. Nov. 25, 1959 (57).

Grenfell, Joyce, actress; b. Feb. 10, 1910, London, England; d. Nov. 30, 1979 (69).

Gretler, Heinrich, actor; b. Oct. 1, 1897, Zurich, Switzerland; d. Sept. 30, 1977 (79).

Grey, Georges, actor; b. 1911; d. 1954 (43).

Grey, Gloria, actress; b. Oct. 23, 1909, Portland, Ore.; d. Nov. 22, 1947 (38).

Grey, Jane, actress; b. May 22, 1883, Middlebury, Vt.; d. Nov. 9, 1944 (61).

Grey, Jerry, dancer; d. June 7, 1954 (44).

Grey, John, writer; d. June 27, 1933 (60).

Grey, John W., writer; d. Dec. 11, 1964 (77).

Grey, Katherine, actress; b. Dec. 27, 1873, San Francisco, Calif.; d. Mar. 21, 1950 (76).

Grey, Leonard, actor; d. Aug. 4, 1918.

Grey, Madeline, actress; b. July 18, 1887, California; d. Aug. 16, 1950 (63).

Grey, Olga, actress; d. Apr. 25, 1973 (75).

Grey, Robert H., actor; d. Apr. 26, 1934 (40).

Gribbon, Eddie, actor; b. Jan. 3, 1890, New York City; d. Sept. 28, 1965 (75).

Gribbon, Harry, actor; b. June 9, 1885, New York City; d. July 28, 1961 (76).

Gribov, Alexei, actor; b. Jan. 31, 1902, Moscow; d. Dec., 1977 (75).

Gridoux, Lucas, actor; b. 1896; d. Apr. 22, 1952 (56).

Gries, Tom, director & author; d. Jan. 3, 1977 (54).

Grifell, Prudencia, actress; b. 1881, Lugo, Spain; d. June 7, 1970 (89).

Griffell, Jose Martinez, actor; d. Nov. 14, 1955 (50).

Griffen, Nannie, actress; d. July 17, 1925.

Griffies, Ethel, actress; b. Apr. 26, 1878, Sheffield, Yorks, England; d. Sept. 9, 1975 (97).

Griffin, Arthur, actor; b. Boston, Mass.; d. Feb. 6, 1953 (75).

Griffin, Carlton E., actor; b. May 23, 1893, New York City; d. July 24, 1940 (47).

Griffin, Charles, actor; b. Sept. 2, 1888, Pennsylvania; d. Aug. 17, 1956 (67).

Griffin, Gerald, actor; d. Mar. 16, 1919 (65).

Griffin, Robert E., actor; b. July 31, 1902, Kansas; d. Dec. 19, 1960 (58).

Griffith, Corinne, actress; b. Nov. 21, 1894, Texarkana, Tex.; d. July 13, 1979 (84).

Griffith, David W., director, producer, & actor; b. Jan. 22, 1875, La Grange, Ky.; d. July 23, 1948 (73).

Griffith, Edward H., director; b. Aug. 23, 1888, Illinois; d. Mar. 3, 1975 (86).

Griffith, Gordon, actor & director; b. July 4, 1907, Chicago, Ill.; d. Oct. 12, 1958 (51).

Griffith, Harry S. (r.n. Harry Sutherland Griffith), actor; d. July 19, 1866, Indiana; d. May 4, 1926 (59).

Griffith, Katherine, actress; b. Sept. 30, 1876, San Francisco, Calif.; d. Oct. 17, 1921 (45).

Griffith, Raymond, actor & director; d. Nov. 25, 1957 (70).

Griffith, William, actor; b. Dec. 18, 1897, Indiana; d. July 21, 1960 (62).

Griffiths, Jane, actress; b. Oct. 16, 1930, Peacehaven, Sussex, England; d. June, 1975 (44).

Griggs, John, actor; d. Feb. 25, 1967 (58).

Grimes, Tommy, actor; b. Nov. 4, 1887, Marysville, Kans.; d. Aug. 19, 1934 (46).

Grimwood, Herbert, actor; b. Mar. 7, 1875, Walthamstow, England; d. Dec. 1, 1929 (54).

Grinde, Harry A. "Nick," director; b. Jan. 12, 1894, Madison, Wisc.; d. June 19, 1979 (85).

Grisel, Louis R., actor; d. Nov. 19, 1928 (80).

Grissell, Wallace, director; b. Sept. 3, 1904, Hounslow, England; d. Apr. 5, 1954 (49).

Griswold, Grace, actress & author; b. Ashtabula, Ohio; d. June 14, 1927 (55).

Griswold, James, actor; b. Apr. 30, 1882, New Britain, Conn.; d. Oct. 4, 1935 (53).

Groat, Carlton, actor; d. Aug. 29, 1940 (44).

Grock, actor & clown; b. 1880; d. 1959 (79).

Gronau, Ernst, actor; b. Aug. 21, 1887, Memel, Germany; d. Aug. 11, 1938 (50).

Gronberg, Ake, actor; b. 1914; d. 1969 (55).

Grooney, Ernest G., actor; b. Nov. 1, 1880, London, England; d. Jan. 20, 1946 (65).

Grosskurth, Kurt, actor; b. May 11, 1909, Langenselbehn, Rhineland; d. May 29, 1975 (66).

Grossman, Irving, actor; d. Mar. 24, 1964 (63).

Grossmith, Ena, actress; b. Aug. 14, 1896, London, England; d. Mar. 20, 1944 (47).

Grossmith, George, actor; b. May 11, 1874, London, England; d. June 6, 1935 (61).

Grossmith, Lawrence R., actor; b. Mar. 29, 1877, London, England; d. Feb. 21, 1944 (66).

Grosso, Paul, stuntman; d. July 5, 1979 (82).

Grove, Myrtle, actress; d. June 10, 1970.

Groves, Charles, actor; b. Nov. 22, 1875, Manchester, England; d. May 23, 1955 (79).

Groves, Fred, actor; b. Aug. 8, 1880, London, England; d. June 4, 1955 (74).

Groves, Victor Lauvi, actor; b. Oct. 10, 1901, American Samoa; d. July 12, 1971 (69).

Grower, Russell G., actor; d. Feb. 21, 1958 (34).

Gruber, Frank, writer; b. Feb. 2, 1904; d. Dec. 9, 1969 (65).

Grund, Leo, actor; d. Mar. 8, 1978 (77).

Grundgens, Gustaf, actor & director; b. Dec. 22, 1899, Dusseldorf, Germany; d. Oct. 7, 1963 (63).

Grune, Karl, director; b. Jan. 22, 1890, Vienna, Austria; d. Oct. 2, 1962 (72).

Gruning, Ilka, actress; b. Sept. 4, 1876, Austria; d. Nov. 14, 1964 (88).

Guard, A. Sully, actor; d. Mar. 21, 1916.

Guard, Kit, actor; b. May 5, 1894, Denmark; d. July 18, 1961 (67).

Guazzoni, Enrico, actor & director; b. Sept. 18, 1876, Rome, Italy; d. Sept. 24, 1949 (73).

Gudgeon, Bertrand C., stuntman; d. Oct. 22, 1948.

Guelstorff, Max, actor; b. Mar. 23, 1882, Ostpreussen, Germany; d. Feb. 6, 1947 (64).

Guenste, F.F. (r.n. Ferdinand F. Guenste), actor; b. Feb. 16, 1862, Pittsburgh, Pa.; d. Mar. 28, 1936 (74).

Guenther, Ruth, actress; d. June 25, 1974 (64).

Guessford, George, actor; b. Feb. 14, 1908, California; d. Mar. 31, 1968 (60).

Guest, Edgar A., author & actor; b. Aug. 20, 1881, Birmingham, England; d. Aug. 5, 1959 (77).

Guhl, George, actor; b. Sept. 27, 1875, St. Louis, Mo.; d. June 26, 1943 (67).

Guilbert, Yvette, actress; b. Paris, France; d. Feb. 3, 1944 (79).

Guilfoyle, James A., actor; b. Apr. 18, 1892, Michigan; d. Nov. 13, 1964 (72).

Guilfoyle, Paul, actor & director; b. July 14, 1902, Jersey City, N.J.; d. June 27, 1961 (58).

Guinan, Texas, actress & singer; b. Waco, Tex.; d. Nov. 5, 1933 (48).

Guinart, Roque (r.n. Pascual Espelt), actor; b. July 13, 1889, Spain; d. Jan. 22, 1975 (85).

Guiol, Fred, director, producer, & author; d. May 23, 1964 (66).

Guise, Thomas, actor; d. 1930.

Guitry, Genevieve, actress; b. 1920; d. 1964 (44).

Guitry, Sacha, actor & director; b. Feb. 21, 1885, St. Petersburg, Russia; d. July 24, 1957 (72).
Guitty, Madeleine, actress; d. Apr. 12, 1936 (65).
Gullan, Campbell, actor; b. Glasgow, Scotland; d. Dec. 1, 1939.
Gunn, Charles, actor; b. July 31, 1883, Wisconsin; d. Dec. 6, 1918 (35).
Gunn, Earl, actor; b. May 8, 1901, Michigan; d. Apr. 14, 1963 (61).
Gunn, Thomas Patrick, actor; d. Dec. 4, 1943 (71).
Gunreth, Elizabeth, actress; b. Aug. 20, 1905, Brazil; d. Mar. 4, 1948 (42).
Gunther, Carl, actor; d. June, 1951 (66).
Gurie, Sigrid (r.n. Sigrid Gurie Haukelid), actress; b. May 18, 1911, Brooklyn, N.Y.; d. Aug. 14, 1969 (58).
Gurin, Ellen, actress; d. June 5, 1972 (24).
Gurney, Edmund, actor; d. Jan. 14, 1925 (73).
Gustine, Paul, actor; b. Dec. 8, 1893, Michigan; d. July 16, 1964 (70).
Guthrie, Charles W., actor; d. June 30, 1939 (68).
Guthrie, Tyrone, producer, director, & actor; b. July 2, 1900, Tunbridge Wells, England; d. May 15, 1971 (70).
Guy-Blache, Alice, director; b. July 1, 1875, Saint-Mande, France; d. Mar. 24, 1968 (92).
Guye, La Jean, actress; d. Oct. 11, 1959 (23).
Gwenn, Edmund, actor; b. Sept. 26, 1875, London, England; d. Sept. 6, 1959 (83).
Gwynn, Michael, actor; b. Nov. 30, 1916, Bath, England; d. Jan. 29, 1976 (59).
Gwynne, Harold William, actor; d. Aug., 1927.
Gys, Leda, actress; b. Mar. 10, 1892, Rome, Italy; d. Oct. 2, 1957 (65).


Haade, William, actor; b. Mar. 2, 1903, New York; d. Nov. 15, 1966 (63).
Haagen, Margarete, actress; b. Nov. 29, 1889, Nurnberg, Germany; d. Nov., 1966 (76).
Haal, Renee (see Godfrey, Renee)
Haas, Hugo, actor & director; b. Feb. 19, 1902, Brno, Czechoslovakia; d. Dec. 1, 1968 (66).
Haase, Alfred, actor; b. Nov. 29, 1887, Berlin, Germany; d. Dec., 1960 (73).
Hack, Herman, actor; d. Oct. 19, 1967 (68).
Hack, Signe, extra; d. Jan. 6, 1973 (74).
Hackathorne, George (r.n. George Hackthorne), actor; b. Feb. 13, 1896, Pendleton, Ore.; d. June 25, 1940 (44).
Hacker, Maria, actress; d. Feb. 20, 1963 (59).
Hackett, Florence, actress; d. Aug. 21, 1954 (72).
Hackett, Hal, actor; d. Dec. 4, 1967 (44).
Hackett, James K., actor; b. Sept. 8, 1869, Wolf Island, Ontario, Canada; d. Nov. 8, 1926 (57).
Hackett, Karl (Wm. K. Hackett) (r.n. Carl Ellsworth Germain), actor (villain, character); b. Sept. 5, 1893, Carthage, Mo.; d. Oct. 24, 1948 (55).
Hackett, Lillian, actress; b. Oct. 11, 1896, Chicago, Ill.; d. Feb. 28, 1973 (76).
Hackett, Raymond, actor; b. July 15, 1902, New York City; d. July 7, 1958 (55).

Haddock, William F. "Silent Bill," director & actor; b. Nov. 27, 1877,
Portsmouth, N.H.; d. June 30, 1969 (91).
Haddon, Peter, actor; b. Mar. 31, 1898, Rawtenstall, England; d. Sept.
7, 1962 (64).
Hadley, Reed, actor; b. June 25, 1911, Texas; d. Dec. 11, 1974 (63).
Haefeli, Charles (Jockey), stuntman; b. July 16, 1887, New York;
d. Feb. 12, 1955 (67).
Hafter, Robert, actor; b. Jan. 7, 1897, London, England; d. Aug. 9,
1955 (58).
Hageman, Richard, actor & composer; d. Mar. 6, 1966 (83).
Hagen, Charles F., actor; d. June 13, 1958 (86).
Hagen, Jean, actress; b. Chicago, Ill.; d. Aug. 29, 1977 (54).
Hagenbruch, Charlotte, actress; d. May 19, 1968 (72).
Hager, Clyde, actor; d. May 21, 1944 (57).
Haggard, Stephen, actor; b. Mar. 21, 1911, Guatemala City, Guatemala;
d. Feb., 1943 (31).
Hagney, Frank, actor; b. Mar. 20, 1884, Sydney, Australia; d. June
25, 1973 (89).
Hahn, Sally, actress; d. June 2, 1933 (25).
Haig, Raymond V., actor; d. Sept. 17, 1963 (46).
Haine, Horace, actor; d. Sept. 26, 1940 (72).
Haines, Rhea, actress; b. Oct. 2, 1894, Indiana; d. Mar. 12, 1964 (69).
Haines, Robert T., actor; b. Feb. 3, 1868, Muncie, Ind.; d. May 6,
1943 (75).
Haines, William, actor; b. Jan. 1, 1900, Staunton, Va.; d. Dec. 26,
1973 (73).
Hale, Alan, Sr. (r.n. Rufus Edward Mackahan), actor & director;
b. Feb. 10, 1892, Washington, D.C.; d. Jan. 22, 1950 (57).
Hale, Barnaby, actor; b. Jan. 1, 1927, New York; d. Nov. 5, 1964 (37).
Hale, Bobby (see Hale, Robert)
Hale, Creighton, actor; b. May 24, 1882, Cork, Ireland; d. Aug. 9,
1965 (83).
Hale, Dorothy, actress; d. Oct. 21, 1938 (23).
Hale, John, actor; d. May 4, 1947 (88).
Hale, Jonathan, actor; b. Mar. 21, 1891; d. Feb. 28, 1966 (74).
Hale, Louise Closser, actress; b. Oct. 13, 1872, Chicago, Ill.;
d. July 26, 1933 (60).
Hale, Robert, actor; d. Apr. 18, 1940 (66).
Hale, Robert (Bobby Hale), actor; b. May 27, 1886, England; d. Sept.
27, 1977 (91).
Hale, Sonnie, actor; b. May 1, 1902, London, England; d. June 9,
1959 (57).
Haley, Jack, actor; b. Aug. 10, 1899, Boston, Mass.; d. June 6, 1979
(79).
Hall, Alexander, director; d. July 30, 1968 (74).
Hall, Alfred H., actor; b. Dec. 2, 1881, Brockton, Mass.; d. Apr. 21,
1943 (61).
Hall, Arch, actor & author; d. Apr. 28, 1978 (69).
Hall, Charles, actor; b. Aug. 19, 1899, Birmingham, England; d. Dec.
7, 1959 (60).
Hall, Cliff, actor; d. Oct. 6, 1972 (78).
Hall, Donald, actor; d. July 25, 1948 (80).
Hall, Dorothy, actress; d. Feb. 3, 1953 (47).
Hall, Edna, actress; d. July 17, 1945 (59).
Hall, Ethel, actress; d. June 30, 1927.

Hall, Gabrielle, actress; b. Apr. 18, 1898, Missouri; d. Jan. 1,
    1967 (68).
Hall, Geraldine, actress; b. Jan. 31, 1905, Illinois; d. Sept. 18,
    1970 (65).
Hall, Henry, actor; b. Nov. 5, 1876, Missouri; d. Dec. 12, 1954 (78).
Hall, Howard, actor; b. May 30, 1867, Michigan; d. July 25, 1921 (54).
Hall, J. Albert, actor; d. Apr. 18, 1920.
Hall, James, actor; b. Oct. 22, 1900, Dallas, Tex.; d. June 7, 1940
    (39).
Hall, Jane, actress; b. 1800, Winona, Minn.; d. Oct. 13, 1975 (95).
Hall, Jefferson, actor; d. May 26, 1945 (70).
Hall, John, actor; d. Apr. 25, 1936 (58).
Hall, Jon (Charles Locher), actor; b. Feb. 26, 1913, Fresno, Calif.;
    d. Dec. 13, 1979 (66).
Hall, Juanita, actress & singer; b. Keyport, N.J.; d. Feb. 28, 1968
    (66).
Hall, Marion, actress; d. Feb. 14, 1960.
Hall, Nelson L., actor; d. July 28, 1944 (63).
Hall, Norman S., writer; b. July 21, 1896, New Milford, Conn.; d. Dec.
    12, 1964 (68).
Hall, Pauline, actress; d. Oct. 6, 1974 (83).
Hall, Porter (r.n. Clifford Porter Hall), actor; b. Sept. 19, 1888,
    Cincinnati, Ohio; d. Oct. 6, 1953 (65).
Hall, Thurston, actor; b. May 10, 1882, Boston, Mass.; d. Feb. 20,
    1958 (75).
Hall, Willard Lee, actor; b. 1863, Altoma, Pa.; d. Oct. 30, 1936 (73).
Hall, William H. "Swede," actor; d. Oct. 24, 1944 (70).
Hall, Winter, actor; b. June 21, 1872, New Zealand; d. Feb. 10, 1947
    (74).
Hallam, Henry, actor; b. 1867, London, England; d. Nov. 9, 1921 (54).
Hallard, C.M., actor; b. Oct. 26, 1865, Edinburgh, Scotland; d. Mar.
    21, 1942 (76).
Hallatt, Henry, actor; b. Feb. 1, 1888, Whitehaven, England; d. July
    24, 1952 (64).
Hall-Davis, Lilian, actress; d. Oct. 25, 1933 (36).
Halle, Cliff, actor; d. Apr. 3, 1976 (57).
Haller, Ernest, cinematographer; b. May 31, 1896, Los Angeles, Calif.;
    d. Oct. 21, 1970 (74).
Hallet, Agnes, actress; d. Nov. 19, 1954 (74).
Hallett, Albert, actor; d. Apr. 3, 1935 (65).
Halliday, Jackson, actor; b. c. 1902, New York; d. Sept. 6, 1966 (64).
Halliday, John, actor; b. Sept. 14, 1880, Brooklyn, N.Y.; d. Oct. 17,
    1947 (67).
Halliday, Lena, actress; d. Dec. 19, 1937.
Halligan, William, actor; b. Mar. 29, 1883, Illinois; d. Jan. 28,
    1957 (73).
Hallor, Edith, actress; b. Mar. 26, 1896, Washington, D.C.; d. May
    21, 1971 (75).
Hallor, Ray, actor; b. Jan. 11, 1900, Washington, D.C.; d. Apr. 16,
    1944 (44).
Halloway, Maggie (Maggie Halloway Fisher), actress; b. June 10, 1854,
    Manchester, England; d. Nov. 3, 1938 (84).
Halls, Ethyl May, actress; d. Sept. 16, 1967 (85).
Halop, Billy, actor; b. Feb. 11, 1920, New York City; d. Nov. 9,
    1976 (56).

Halpern, Gertrude (Trudy Lawrence), actress; d. Sept. 23, 1978 (51).
Halstan, Margaret, actress; b. Dec. 25, 1879; d. Jan. 8, 1967 (87).
Halstead, Byron C., actor; d. July 13, 1963 (62).
Haltiner, Fred, actor; d. Dec. 7, 1973 (37).
Halton, Charles, actor; b. Mar. 16, 1876, Washington, D.C.; d. Apr. 16, 1959 (83).
Halverson, Leslie Eugene, actor; d. Feb. 20, 1953 (49).
Ham, Harry, actor & director; d. July 27, 1943 (52).
Hamel, William R., actor; b. Mar. 14, 1906, Pennsylvania; d. Mar. 8, 1958 (51).
Hamelin, Clement, actor; d. July 4, 1957 (64).
Hamer, Gerald (r.n. Geoffrey Earl Watton), actor; b. Nov. 16, 1886, South Wales; d. July 6, 1972 (85).
Hamer, Robert, director; b. Mar. 31, 1911, Kidderminster, England; d. Dec. 4, 1963 (52).
Hamil, Lucille, actress; d. June 17, 1939 (37).
Hamilton, Betty, actress; d. Apr. 10, 1935 (21).
Hamilton, Bruce (see Gaige, Russell)
Hamilton, George Gordon, actor; d. Jan. 16, 1939 (55).
Hamilton, Hale, actor; b. Feb. 28, 1881, Fort Madison, Iowa; d. May 19, 1942 (61).
Hamilton, J. Frank (see Hamilton, John F.)
Hamilton, Jack (Shorty), actor; d. Mar. 7, 1925 (37).
Hamilton, John, actor; b. Jan. 16, 1887, Pennsylvania; d. Oct. 15, 1958 (71).
Hamilton, John F. (J. Frank Hamilton), actor; d. July 11, 1967 (73).
Hamilton, Joseph H., actor; b. Jan. 1, 1899, Washington, D.C.; d. Feb. 20, 1965 (66).
Hamilton, Karen Sue, actress; d. Sept. 3, 1969 (23).
Hamilton, Laurel Lee, actress; d. Dec. 15, 1955.
Hamilton, Lloyd, actor; b. Aug. 19, 1891, Oakland, Calif.; d. Jan. 18, 1935 (43).
Hamilton, Mahlon, actor; b. June 15, 1880, Virginia; d. June 20, 1960 (80).
Hamler, John E., dancer; d. Dec. 2, 1969 (78).
Hamlin, William H., actor; d. Sept. 27, 1951 (66).
Hammer, Fred, actor & director; d. Mar., 1939.
Hammerstein, Elaine, actress; d. Aug. 13, 1948 (50).
Hammond, C. Norman (r.n. Charles Norman Hammond), actor; b. San Jose, Calif.; d. June 5, 1941 (63).
Hammond, Charles N. (see Hammond, C. Norman)
Hammond, Frank, actor; b. Nov. 11, 1872, Meadville, Pa.; d. Nov. 14, 1941 (69).
Hammond, Virginia, actress; d. Apr. 6, 1972 (78).
Hampden, Walter, actor; b. June 30, 1879, Brooklyn, N.Y.; d. June 11, 1955 (75).
Hamper, Genevieve, actress; d. Feb. 13, 1971 (82).
Hampton, Crystal, actress & director; d. June 17, 1922.
Hampton, Faith, actress; d. Apr. 1, 1949 (40).
Hampton, Grayce, actress; d. Dec. 20, 1963 (87).
Hampton, Louise, actress; d. Feb. 10, 1954 (73).
Hampton, Myra, actress; d. July 19, 1945 (44).
Hamrick, Burwell, actor; d. Sept. 21, 1970 (64).
Hancock, Don, director & producer; b. Oct. 21, 1888, London, England; d. Jan. 5, 1951 (62).

Hancock, Tony, actor; b. May 12, 1924, Birmingham, England; d. June
   25, 1968 (44).
Handforth, Ruth, actress; b. July 11, 1882, Springfield, Mass.;
   d. Sept. 10, 1965 (83).
Handley, Tommy, actor; b. Liverpool, England; d. Jan. 9, 1949 (55).
Handyside, Clarence, actor; d. Dec. 20, 1931 (77).
Haney, Carol, actress & dancer; b. Dec. 24, 1924, New Bedford, Mass.;
   d. May 10, 1964 (39).
Hanft, Jules (r.n. Julian O. Hanft), actor; b. Sept. 16, 1859,
   Jersey City, N.J.; d. Aug. 6, 1936 (76).
Hanley, Jimmy, actor; b. Oct. 22, 1918, Norwich, Norfolk, England;
   d. Jan. 13, 1970 (51).
Hanlon, Bert, actor & composer; b. Aug. 19, 1895, New York City;
   d. Jan. 1, 1972 (76).
Hanlon, Edward, actor; d. Mar. 15, 1931 (84).
Hanlon, Tom, actor & announcer; b. Nov. 7, 1907, Kansas; d. Sept. 29,
   1970 (62).
Hanna, Franklyn, actor; b. 1875, Missouri; d. Jan. 19, 1931 (55).
Hannah, James D., actor; d. Sept. 11, 1978 (72).
Hanneford, Poodles, actor & clown; d. Dec. 9, 1967 (75).
Hannen, Nicholas (r.n. Nicholas James Hannen), actor; b. May 1, 1881,
   London, England; d. June 25, 1972 (91).
Hannen, Peter, actor; d. 1932 (24).
Hanofer, Frank, actor & stuntman; d. Dec. 16, 1955 (58).
Hanray, Lawrence, actor; b. May 16, 1874, London, England; d. Nov. 28,
   1947 (73).
Hansen, Hans, actor; d. June 18, 1962 (76).
Hansen, Juanita, actress; b. Mar. 3, 1895, Iowa; d. Sept. 26, 1961
   (66).
Hansen, Max, actor; b. Dec. 22, 1887, Mannheim, Germany; d. Nov. 13,
   1961 (73).
Hansen, William, actor; b. Mar. 2, 1911, Washington; d. June 23, 1975
   (64).
Hanson, Einar, actor; b. June 15, 1899, Stockholm, Sweden; d. June 3,
   1927 (27).
Hanson, Gladys, actress; d. Feb. 23, 1973 (89).
Hanson, Lars, actor; d. Apr. 8, 1965 (78).
Hanson, Paul, actor; b. Kent, England; d. Oct. 4, 1940 (46).
Harbaugh, Carl, actor; b. Nov. 10, 1886, Washington, D.C.; d. Feb. 26,
   1960 (73).
Harbaugh, William, stuntman; d. Oct. 19, 1924 (25).
Harben, Hubert, actor; b. July 12, 1878, London, England; d. Aug. 24,
   1941 (63).
Harcourt, James, actor; b. Apr. 20, 1873, Headingly, England; d. Feb.
   18, 1951 (77).
Harcourt, Peggy, actress; d. July 31, 1916.
Hardie, Russell, actor; b. May 20, 1904, Buffalo, N.Y.; d. July 21,
   1973 (69).
Harding, Gilbert, actor & announcer; b. June 5, 1907, Hereford,
   England; d. Nov. 16, 1960 (53).
Harding, Lyn, actor; b. Oct. 12, 1867, Newport, Mon., Wales; d. Dec.
   26, 1952 (85).
Hardt, Ludwig, actor; d. 1947.
Hardtmuth, Paul, actor; d. Feb. 5, 1962 (73).

Hardwicke, Sir Cedric, actor; b. Feb. 19, 1893, Stourbridge, England; d. Aug. 6, 1964 (71).
Hardy, Oliver, actor; b. Jan. 18, 1892, Atlanta, Ga.; d. Aug. 7, 1957 (65).
Hardy, Sam, actor; b. Mar. 21, 1883, New Haven, Conn.; d. Oct. 16, 1935 (52).
Hare, Ernest, actor; d. Mar. 9, 1939 (55).
Hare, Sir John, actor; b. May 16, 1844, Giggleswick, Yorkshire, England; d. Dec. 28, 1921 (77).
Hare, Lumsden, actor; b. Apr. 27, 1875, Ireland; d. Aug. 28, 1964 (89).
Hare, Robertson, actor; b. Dec. 17, 1891, London, England; d. Jan. 25, 1979 (87).
Hare, Thomas, actor; d. Aug. 25, 1975 (51).
Harford, Alec, actor; b. Sept. 7, 1888, England; d. Mar. 31, 1955 (66).
Harford, Harry, actor; d. Sept. 20, 1925 (74).
Harker, Gordon, actor; b. Aug. 7, 1885, London, England; d. Mar. 2, 1967 (81).
Harkness, Alan, actor; d. Mar. 2, 1952.
Harkins, Dixie, actress; d. Sept. 1, 1963 (57).
Harlam, Macey, actor; d. Apr. 9, 1924.
Harlan, Kenneth, actor; b. July 26, 1895, Boston, Mass.; d. Mar. 6, 1967 (71).
Harlan, Otis, actor; b. Dec. 29, 1865, Zanesville, Ohio; d. Jan. 20, 1940 (74).
Harlan, Russell, cinematographer; d. Feb. 28, 1974 (70).
Harlan, Veit, director & actor; b. Sept. 22, 1899, Berlin, Germany; d. Apr. 13, 1964 (64).
Harley, Edwin, actor; d. Oct. 29, 1933 (85).
Harline, Leigh, composer-conductor; b. Mar. 26, 1907, Salt Lake City, Utah; d. Dec. 10, 1969 (62).
Harlow, Claudia, actress; d. Feb. 18, 1940 (53).
Harlow, Jean, actress; b. Mar. 3, 1911, Kansas City, Kans.; d. June 7, 1937 (26).
Harlow, John B., director; d. May 15, 1945.
Harmer, Lillian, actress; d. May 15, 1946 (60).
Harmon, Pat, actor; d. Nov. 26, 1958 (70).
Harned, Virginia, actress; d. Apr. 29, 1946 (74).
Harolde, Ralf, actor; b. May 17, 1899, Pittsburgh, Pa.; d. Nov. 1, 1974 (75).
Harout, Yeghishe (r.n. Eghiche Nerses Harout), actor; b. Oct. 1, 1898, Armenia; d. June 7, 1974 (75).
Harr, Silver (r.n. Arlie Silver Harr), actor; b. Sept. 21, 1892, Idaho; d. Sept. 19, 1968 (75).
Harradine, Archie, actor; b. Mar. 19, 1898, London, England; d. Aug. 10, 1974 (76).
Harrigan, William, actor; b. Mar. 27, 1894, New York City; d. Feb. 1, 1966 (71).
Harrington, Buck (r.n. Cyril J. Harrington), actor; b. Mar. 18, 1897, Iowa; d. Feb. 2, 1971 (73).
Harrington, John (r.n. John Daniel Harrington), actor; b. July 23, 1882, Riverside Co., Calif.; d. Sept. 9, 1945 (63).
Harrington, Kate, actress; b. Dec. 8, 1903, Boise, Idaho; d. Nov. 23, 1978 (74).
Harris, Arlene, actress; d. June 12, 1976 (79).
Harris, Averell, actor; d. Sept. 25, 1966.

Harris, Buddy (r.n. Emil Harris Birnkrant), cameraman; b. Mar. 28, 1891; d. Sept. 5, 1971 (80).
Harris, Elsie Lowe, actress; d. May 17, 1953 (61).
Harris, Joe, actor; b. Jan. 11, 1870, Maine; d. June 11, 1953 (83).
Harris, Katherine Corri, actress; d. May 2, 1927.
Harris, Kay, actress; b. Aug. 18, 1919, Elkhorn, Wisc.; d. Oct. 23, 1971 (52).
Harris, Leonore, actress; d. Sept. 27, 1953 (74).
Harris, Mabel, actress; d. Mar. 6, 1930 (36).
Harris, Major Sam, actor; b. Jan. 11, 1877, Australia; d. Oct. 22, 1969 (92).
Harris, Marion, actress; d. Apr. 23, 1944 (38).
Harris, Mildred, actress; b. Nov. 29, 1902, Cheyenne, Wyo.; d. July 20, 1944 (41).
Harris, Mitchell, actor; d. Nov. 16, 1948 (65).
Harris, Sibyl, actress; b. July 22, 1883, Twickenham, England; d. May 20, 1940 (56).
Harris, Stacy, actor; b. July 26, 1918, Washington; d. Mar. 13, 1973 (54).
Harris, Val (r.n. Valle E. Harris), actor; b. Feb. 14, 1882, Illinois; d. Mar. 17, 1961 (79).
Harris, Wadsworth, actor; b. Oct. 9, 1864, Boston, Mass.; d. Nov. 1, 1942 (78).
Harrison, Carey, actor; d. Mar. 25, 1957 (67).
Harrison, James, actor; b. May 26, 1908, Texas; d. Nov. 9, 1977 (69).
Harrison, June, actress; d. Mar. 10, 1974 (48).
Harrison, Mark, actor; d. June 1, 1952 (88).
Harrison, Nell, actress; d. Dec. 4, 1973 (93).
Harron, John, actor; b. Mar. 31, 1903, New York City; d. Nov. 24, 1939 (36).
Harron, Robert, actor; b. Apr. 24, 1893, New York City; d. Sept. 5, 1920 (27).
Harron, Theresa, actress; d. Nov. 8, 1918.
Hart, Albert, actor; b. Dec. 6, 1875, Liverpool, England; d. Jan. 10, 1940 (64).
Hart, Billy, actor; d. June 18, 1942 (78).
Hart, Florence, actress; d. Mar. 30, 1960.
Hart, Gordon, actor; b. Nov. 26, 1884, England; d. Dec. 27, 1973 (89).
Hart, James T., actor; d. Aug. 12, 1926 (58).
Hart, Lewis O., actor; d. Jan. 9, 1920 (73).
Hart, Louis, actor; b. Jan. 27, 1917, Texas; d. Apr. 25, 1972 (55).
Hart, Mabel, actress; b. Apr. 29, 1886, Illinois; d. June 9, 1960 (74).
Hart, Neal (r.n. Cornelius Augustus Neal Hart), actor; b. Apr. 7, 1879, Richmond, N.Y.; d. Apr. 2, 1949 (69).
Hart, Richard, actor; b. Apr. 14, 1915, Providence, R.I.; d. Jan. 2, 1951 (35).
Hart, Ruth, actress; d. May 2, 1952.
Hart, Sunshine, actress; b. July 6, 1886, Indiana; d. Jan. 3, 1930 (43).
Hart, Teddy, actor; b. Sept. 25, 1897, New York City; d. Feb. 17, 1971 (73).
Hart, William S., actor; b. Dec. 6, 1864, New Burgh, N.Y.; d. June 23, 1946 (81).
Hart, William V. "Pop," actor & director; d. Oct. 14, 1925 (60).
Harte, Betty, actress; d. Jan. 3, 1965 (82).

Hartford, David, actor; b. Jan. 11, 1873, Michigan; d. Oct. 30, 1932 (59).
Hartigan, Patrick C., actor; b. Dec. 21, 1881, New York; d. May 8, 1951 (69).
Hartley, Charles, actor; d. Oct. 13, 1930 (78).
Hartley, Helen, actress & circus performer; b. 1892; d. Oct. 30, 1954 (62).
Hartman, Don, writer & producer; b. Nov. 18, 1900, Brooklyn, N.Y.; d. Mar. 23, 1958 (57).
Hartman, Ferris, actor & director; d. Sept. 1, 1931 (70).
Hartman, Grace, actress; d. Aug. 8, 1955 (48).
Hartman, Gretchen, actress; b. Aug. 28, 1897, Chicago, Ill.; d. Jan. 27, 1979 (81).
Hartman, Jonathan William (Pop), actor; d. Oct. 19, 1965 (93).
Hartman, Marie, actress; d. Sept. 21, 1940 (51).
Hartman, Paul, actor; d. Oct. 2, 1973 (69).
Hartman, Ruth, actress; b. Apr. 3, 1893, Illinois; d. July 9, 1956 (63).
Hartmann, Paul, actor; b. Jan. 8, 1889, Furth (Bayern), Germany; d. June 30, 1977 (88).
Hartnell, William, actor; b. Jan. 8, 1908, London, England; d. Apr. 24, 1975 (67).
Harvey, Clarence, actor; d. May 3, 1945 (80).
Harvey, Don C., actor; b. Dec. 12, 1911, Kansas; d. Apr. 24, 1963 (51).
Harvey, Donald, actor; d. Feb. 1, 1931 (68).
Harvey, Edward, actor; d. Aug. 5, 1975 (82).
Harvey, Fletcher, actor; d. Sept. 8, 1931 (66).
Harvey, Forrester, actor; b. June 27, 1884, Cork, Ireland; d. Dec. 14, 1945 (61).
Harvey, Georgette, actress; b. St. Louis, Mo.; d. Feb. 17, 1952 (69).
Harvey, Hank, actor; d. Dec. 4, 1929 (80).
Harvey, Harry, Jr., actor & director; d. Dec. 8, 1978.
Harvey, Jean, actress; b. Nov. 17, 1900, Ohio; d. Dec. 14, 1966 (66).
Harvey, John, actor; d. Dec. 25, 1970 (53).
Harvey, John M. "Jack," actor; d. Nov. 10, 1954 (73).
Harvey, Laurence, actor; b. Oct. 1, 1928, Lithuania; d. Nov. 25, 1973 (45).
Harvey, Lee F., actor; d. Apr. 20, 1950 (55).
Harvey, Lew, actor; b. Oct. 6, 1887, Wisconsin; d. Dec. 19, 1953 (66).
Harvey, Lilian, actress; b. Jan. 19, 1907, Edmonton, England; d. July 27, 1968 (61).
Harvey, Lottie, actress; d. Aug. 2, 1948 (58).
Harvey, Marilyn, actress; d. Mar. 29, 1973 (44).
Harvey, Morris, actor; b. Sept. 25, 1877, London, England; d. Aug. 24, 1944 (66).
Harvey, Paul, actor; b. Sept. 10, 1882, Illinois; d. Dec. 5, 1955 (73).
Harwood, John, actor; b. Feb. 29, 1876, London, England; d. Dec. 26, 1944 (68).
Hascall, Lon, actor; d. Dec. 13, 1932 (60).
Hashim, Edmund, actor; d. July 2, 1974 (42).
Haskel, Leonhard, actor; d. Dec. 30, 1923.
Haskell, Al (r.n. Albert B. Haskell), actor; b. Dec. 4, 1886, California; d. Jan. 6, 1969 (82).
Haskin, Charles Wilson, actor; d. June 10, 1927 (59).
Haskin, Harry R., actor; d. Feb. 7, 1953 (82).

Hasee, Clemens, actor; b. Apr. 13, 1908; d. July, 1959 (51).
Hasse, O.E. (r.n. Otto Eduard Hasse), actor; b. July 11, 1903, Posen, Poland; d. Sept. 12, 1978 (75).
Hassell, George, actor; b. May 4, 1881, Birmingham, England; d. Feb. 17, 1937 (55).
Hastings, Henry, actor; b. May 19, 1879, Notchosis, La.; d. Feb. 21, 1963 (83).
Hastings, Victoria, actress; d. May 24, 1934.
Haswell, Percy, actress; d. June 14, 1945 (74).
Hatch, William Riley, actor; d. Sept. 6, 1925 (63).
Hathaway, Jean (r.n. Lillie de Fiennes), actress; b. June 15, 1876, Hungary; d. Aug. 23, 1938 (62).
Hathaway, Lillian, actress; d. Jan. 12, 1954 (78).
Hathaway, Rhody, actor; b. Oct. 5, 1868, San Francisco, Calif.; d. Feb. 18, 1944 (75).
Hattie, Hilo (r.n. Clara Haili), actress; b. Honolulu, Hawaii; d. Dec. 12, 1979 (78).
Hatton, Bradford, actor; d. Aug. 11, 1969 (63).
Hatton, C. Edward (see Hatton, Dick)
Hatton, Dick (C. Edward Hatton) (r.n. Clarence Hatton), actor; b. Kentucky; d. July 9, 1931 (40).
Hatton, Fanny, writer; d. Nov. 27, 1939 (69).
Hatton, Frances, actress; b. Oct. 19, 1886, Nebraska; d. Oct. 16, 1971 (84).
Hatton, Raymond, actor; b. July 7, 1887, Red Oak, Iowa; d. Oct. 21, 1971 (84).
Hatton, Rondo, actor; b. Apr. 22, 1894, Hagerstown, Md.; d. Feb. 2, 1946 (51).
Haubenreisser, Karl, actor; b. Nov. 11, 1903, Leipzig, Germany; d. Apr. 26, 1945 (41).
Hauber, William C., actor; b. Wisconsin; d. July 17, 1929 (38).
Hauck, Earl, actor; d. Feb., 1976.
Haught, Al, actor; d. Nov. 1, 1936.
Haupt, Ulrich, actor; b. Aug. 8, 1887, Prussia; d. Aug. 5, 1931 (43).
Hauser, Heinrich, actor; b. 1891; d. Dec., 1956 (65).
Haussler, Richard, actor; b. Oct. 26, 1908; d. Sept., 1964 (55).
Haver, Phyllis, actress; b. Jan. 6, 1899, Douglas, Kans.; d. Nov. 19, 1960 (61).
Havier, J. Alex (r.n. Jose Alex Havier), actor; b. Jan. 10, 1911, Philippine Islands; d. Dec. 18, 1945 (34).
Haviland, Rena, actress; d. Feb. 20, 1954 (76).
Hawke, Rohn Olin, actor; d. Feb. 15, 1967 (43).
Hawkins, Jack, actor; b. Sept. 14, 1910, London, England; d. July 18, 1973 (62).
Hawks, Charles Monroe, actor; d. Dec. 15, 1951 (77).
Hawks, Frank, actor & aviator; d. Aug. 23, 1938 (41).
Hawks, Howard, director; b. May 30, 1896, Goshen, Ind.; d. Dec. 26, 1977 (81).
Hawks, Kenneth, director; b. Aug. 12, 1898, Goshen, Ind.; d. Jan. 2, 1930 (31).
Hawley, H. Dudley, actor; d. Mar. 29, 1941 (62).
Hawley, Ormi, actress; d. June 3, 1942 (52).
Hawley, Wanda, actress; b. July 30, 1895, Scranton, Pa.; d. Mar. 18, 1963 (67).
Hawley, William E., actor; d. Aug. 22, 1976 (66).

Hawn, John Allen (Happy Jack), actor; b. May 4, 1882, California;
d. Feb. 12, 1964 (81).
Haworth, Vinton (see Hayworth, Vinton)
Hawthorne, David, actor; d. June 18, 1942.
Hawtrey, Sir Charles, actor; b. Sept. 21, 1858, Eton, England;
d. July 30, 1923 (64).
Hay, George D., actor & radio announcer; b. Nov. 9, 1895, Attica,
Ind.; d. May 8, 1968 (72).
Hay, Mary, actress; b. Aug. 22, 1901, Fort Bliss, Tex.; d. June 4,
1957 (55).
Hay, Will, actor; b. Dec., 1888, Stockton-on-Tees, England; d. Apr.
18, 1949 (60).
Hayakawa, Sessue, actor; b. June 10, 1889, Chiba, Japan; d. Nov. 23,
1973 (84).
Hayden, Harry, actor; b. Nov. 8, 1882, Canada; d. July 23, 1955 (72).
Hayden, J. Charles, actor & producer; d. Oct., 1943 (67).
Haydock, John, actor; d. Jan. 19, 1918.
Haydock, Ron (Vin Saxon), actor; d. Aug. 14, 1977 (37).
Haye, Helen, actress; b. Aug. 28, 1874, Assam, India; d. Sept. 1,
1957 (83).
Hayes, Allison, actress; b. Mar. 6, 1930, Charleston, W. Va.; d. Feb.
27, 1977 (46).
Hayes, Carrie, actress; d. Dec. 22, 1954 (76).
Hayes, Catherine, actress; d. Jan. 4, 1941 (55).
Hayes, Frank, actor; b. May 17, 1871, California; d. Dec. 28, 1923 (52).
Hayes, George, actor; b. Nov. 13, 1888, London, England; d. July 13,
1967 (78).
Hayes, George "Gabby" (r.n. George Francis Hayes), actor; b. May 7,
1885, Wellsville, N.Y.; d. Feb. 9, 1969 (83).
Hayes, Margaret, actress; b. Dec. 5, 1923, Baltimore, Md.; d. Jan.
25, 1977 (53).
Hayes, Reginald, actor; d. June 27, 1953.
Hayes, Sam, actor & announcer; b. Nov. 2, 1904, Illinois; d. July
28, 1958 (53).
Hayes, Sidney, actor; d. May 2, 1940 (75).
Hayes, William, actor; d. July 13, 1937 (50).
Hayle, Grace, actress; d. Mar. 20, 1963 (74).
Haynes, Arthur, actor; d. Nov. 19, 1966 (52).
Haynes, Daniel, actor; d. July 28, 1954 (60).
Haysel, A.R. (r.n. Arthur Richard Haysel), actor; b. Dec. 16, 1887,
Lincoln, Neb.; d. July 28, 1954 (66).
Haytipper, Nita, actress; d. Apr. 1, 1930.
Hayward, Lillie C., scenarist; b. Sept. 12, 1891, Minnesota; d. June
29, 1977 (85).
Hayward, Susan, actress; b. June 30, 1918, Brooklyn, N.Y.; d. Mar. 14,
1975 (56).
Haywood, Billie, recording artist; d. July 8, 1979 (75).
Hayworth, Vinton (Jack Arnold), actor; b. June 4, 1906, Washington,
D.C.; d. May 21, 1970 (63).
Hazell, Hy, actress; b. Oct. 4, 1922, Streatham, England; d. May 10,
1970 (47).
Hazelton, Joseph, actor; d. Oct. 8, 1936 (83).
Hazlett, William (Chief Many Treaties), actor; d. Feb. 29, 1948 (73).
Healy, Dan, actor; d. Aug. 31, 1969 (80).
Healy, Ted, actor; b. Oct. 1, 1896, Houston, Tex.; d. Dec. 21, 1937
(41).

Hearn, Edward, actor; b. Sept. 6, 1888, Dayton, Wash.; d. Apr. 15, 1963 (74).
Hearn, Fred G., actor; b. Dec. 20, 1871, Kentucky; d. Jan. 20, 1923 (51).
Hearn, Guy Edward (see Hearn, Edward)
Hearn, Sam, actor; b. Mar. 5, 1888, Austria; d. Oct. 28, 1964 (76).
Hearne, Richard, actor; b. Jan. 30, 1909, Norfolk, England; d. Aug. 25, 1979 (70).
Heath, Percy, writer; d. Feb. 9, 1933 (48).
Heatherley, Clifford, actor; b. Oct. 8, 1888, Preston, Lancs., England; d. Sept. 15, 1937 (48).
Heatter, Gabriel, newsman; d. Mar. 30, 1972 (81).
Heazlet, Eva. (Eva B. McKenzie), actress; b. Nov. 5, 1889, Toledo, Ohio; d. Sept. 15, 1967 (77).
Hebert, Helen, actress; b. Apr. 6, 1873, Brooklyn, N.Y.; d. Oct. 27, 1946 (73).
Hebert, Henry J., actor; b. Nov. 12, 1879, Providence, R.I.; d. Jan. 18, 1956 (76).
Hecht, Ben, author, producer, actor, & director; b. Feb. 28, 1894, New York City; d. Apr. 18, 1964 (70).
Hecht, Ted, actor; b. Feb. 17, 1906, New York; d. June 24, 1969 (61).
Heck, Stanton, actor; b. Jan. 8, 1877, Wilmington, Del.; d. Dec. 16, 1929 (52).
Hedlund, Guy, actor; b. Aug. 21, 1884, Connecticut; d. Dec. 29, 1964 (80).
Heflin, Van, actor; b. Dec. 13, 1910, Walters, Okla.; d. July 23, 1971 (60).
Heggie, O.P. (r.n. Otto Peters Heggie), actor; b. Sept. 16, 1876, Angaston, S. Australia; d. Feb. 7, 1936 (59).
Heidemann, Paul, actor; b. Oct. 26, 1884, Koln, Germany; d. June 20, 1968 (83).
Heimanns, Hannelore, actress; d. Dec., 1956 (20).
Heindorf, Ray, composer & conductor; d. Feb. 3, 1980 (71).
Heine, Albert, actor; d. Apr. 13, 1949 (81).
Heinz, Gerard, actor; b. Hamburg, Germany; d. Nov. 20, 1972 (68).
Heisler, Charles James, actor; d. Sept. 22, 1933 (21).
Heisler, Stuart R., director; d. Aug. 21, 1979 (82).
Held, Anna, actress; b. Mar. 18, 1873, Paris, France; d. Aug. 13, 1918 (45).
Heller, Fritz, actor; d. Dec. 30, 1966 (73).
Hellinger, Mark, producer; b. Mar. 21, 1903, New York City; d. Dec. 21, 1947 (44).
Hellman, Sam, writer; b. July 4, 1885, San Francisco, Calif.; d. Aug. 11, 1950 (65).
Hellmer, Karl, actor; b. Mar. 11, 1896, Vienna, Austria; d. May, 1974 (78).
Hellum, Barney, actor; b. Jan. 1, 1895, Seavyanv, Norway; d. Dec. 22, 1935 (40).
Helm, Christa, actress; d. Feb. 12, 1977 (27).
Helmers, Peter O. (r.n. Peter Otto Helmers), b. Feb. 16, 1901, Austria; d. Jan. 2, 1976 (74).
Helms, Ruth, actress; d. Oct. 27, 1960.
Helmuth, Osvald, actor; b. July 14, 1894, Copenhagen, Denmark; d. Mar. 18, 1966 (71).
Helton, Percy, actor; b. Jan. 31, 1894, New York; d. Sept. 11, 1971 (77).

Hemsley, Estelle E., actress; b. May 5, 1887, Boston, Mass.; d. Nov. 4, 1968 (81).
Henabery, Joseph E., director & actor; b. Jan. 15, 1888, Omaha, Neb.; d. Feb. 18, 1976 (88).
Henckels, Paul, actor; b. Sept. 9, 1885, Hurth, Germany; d. May 27, 1967 (81).
Hendee, Harold F., actor & cinema researcher; d. June 24, 1966 (87).
Henderson, Betty, actress; d. Aug., 1979 (71).
Henderson, Dell (r.n. George Delbert Henderson), actor & director; b. July 5, 1877, St. Thomas, Canada; d. Dec. 2, 1956 (79).
Henderson, Dick, actor; d. Oct. 15, 1958 (67).
Henderson, Douglas, actor; d. Apr. 5, 1978 (59).
Henderson, Grace, actress; d. Oct. 30, 1944 (84).
Henderson, Jack, actor; d. Jan. 1, 1957 (79).
Henderson, Lucius J., actor & director; d. Feb. 18, 1947 (86).
Henderson, Sephanie Le Beau, actress; d. June 5, 1967.
Henderson, Ted (Theodore) (r.n. Haines Theodore Henderson), actor; b. July 6, 1888, California; d. July 19, 1962 (74).
Henderson, V. Talbot, actor; b. Feb. 9, 1879, Phelps Mills, N.Y.; d. May 24, 1946 (67).
Hendrian, Dutch (see Hendrian, Oscar G.)
Hendrian, Oscar G., actor; b. Jan. 19, 1896, Michigan; d. Dec. 13, 1953 (57).
Hendricks, Arch, actor; b. Feb. 21, 1888, New York; d. May 10, 1964 (76).
Hendricks, Ben, Jr., actor; b. Nov. 2, 1893, New York City; d. Aug. 15, 1938 (44).
Hendricks, Ben, Sr., actor; d. Apr. 30, 1930 (65).
Hendricks, Dudley C., actor; b. Aug. 3, 1870, LaGrange, Ky.; d. Feb. 3, 1942 (71).
Hendricks, John B. (Jack), actor; d. Feb. 26, 1949 (76).
Hendrix, Noah "Shorty," actor; b. Dec. 20, 1889, Missouri; d. Mar. 4, 1973 (83).
Hendry, Anita, actress; d. Apr. 15, 1940.
Henie, Sonja, actress & figure skater; b. Apr. 8, 1913, Oslo, Norway; d. Oct. 12, 1969 (56).
Henker, Paul R., actor; b. Feb. 21, 1898, Suhl, Germany; d. June, 1960 (62).
Henley, Hobart, director, producer, & actor; d. May 22, 1964 (77).
Hennecke, Clarence, actor; b. Sept. 16, 1894, Omaha, Neb.; d. Aug. 28, 1969 (74).
Hennessey, David, actor; d. Mar. 24, 1926 (74).
Hennessey, John A., actor; d. May 16, 1920 (67).
Henning, Pat, actor; d. Apr. 28, 1973 (62).
Henry, Frank, actor; d. Oct. 3, 1963 (69).
Henry, Gale, actress; b. Apr. 15, 1893, Bear Valley, Calif.; d. June 17, 1972 (79).
Henry, Jay, actor; d. Dec. 23, 1951.
Henry, John, actor; d. Aug. 12, 1958 (76).
Henry, Robert Dee "Buzz," actor; b. Sept. 4, 1931, Colorado; d. Sept. 30, 1971 (40).
Henson, Leslie, actor; b. Aug. 3, 1891, London, England; d. Dec. 2, 1957 (66).
Hepburn, Barton, actor; b. Feb. 28, 1906, Minneapolis, Minn.; d. Oct. 9, 1955 (49).
Herald, Heinz, author; d. July 22, 1964 (77).
Herbert, Cliff, actor; d. Jan. 28, 1953 (73).

Herbert, Doris, actress; b. July 22, 1875, Memphis, Tenn.; d. Sept.
    19, 1945 (70).
Herbert, Hans (r.n. Hans Hausknecht), actor; b. June 11, 1882, Poland;
    d. June 21, 1957 (75).
Herbert, Henry, actor; d. Feb. 20, 1947 (68).
Herbert, Holmes, actor; b. July 30, 1882, Mansfield, England; d. Dec.
    26, 1956 (74).
Herbert, Hugh, actor; b. Aug. 10, 1885, Binghamton, N.Y.; d. Mar. 12,
    1952 (66).
Herbert, Joseph W., actor; d. Oct. 7, 1960 (73).
Herbert, Lew, actor; d. July 30, 1968 (55).
Herbert, Sidney, actor; d. Dec. 24, 1927.
Herbert, Tom, actor; b. Nov. 25, 1888, New York City; d. Apr. 3,
    1946 (57).
Heremans, Jean, actor & fencer; b. Jan. 31, 1914, Belgium; d. Aug. 2,
    1970 (56).
Herford, William, actor; b. May 5, 1853, Yorkshire, England; d. Dec.
    27, 1934 (81).
Heriat, Philippe, actor; b. Sept. 15, 1898, Paris, France; d. Oct.,
    1971 (73).
Herking, Ursula, actress; b. Jan. 28, 1912, Dessau, Germany; d. Nov.
    17, 1974 (62).
Herlein, Lilian, actress; d. Apr. 13, 1971 (70).
Herman, Al, director; b. Feb. 22, 1894, New York; d. Sept. 28, 1958
    (64).
Herman, Al, actor; b. Feb. 25, 1887, Scotland; d. July 2, 1967 (80).
Herman, Jill Kraft, actress; d. June 25, 1970 (39).
Herman, Milton C., actor; d. Jan. 21, 1951 (55).
Hernandez, Albert, actor; d. Jan. 2, 1948 (49).
Hernandez, Anna (see Dodge, Anna)
Hernandez, George F., actor; d. Dec. 31, 1922 (59).
Hernandez, Joe, actor; b. June 3, 1909, California; d. Feb. 2, 1972
    (62).
Hernandez, Juano (r.n. Juan G. Hernandez), actor; b. San Juan, Puerto
    Rico; d. July 17, 1970 (74).
Herne, Chrystal, actress; d. Sept. 19, 1950 (67).
Herrand, Marcel, actor & producer; b. Oct. 8, 1897, Paris, France;
    d. June 11, 1953 (55).
Herreros, Enrique, Sr., actor; d. Sept. 17, 1977 (73).
Herrick, Jack, actor; b. Feb. 4, 1891, Hungary; d. June 18, 1952 (61).
Herrick, Joseph, actor; b. Apr. 4, 1889, Hungary; d. Apr. 16, 1966
    (77).
Herring, Aggie, actress; b. Feb. 4, 1876, San Francisco, Calif.;
    d. Oct. 28, 1939 (63).
Herring, Jess, actor; b. Oct. 29, 1895, Missouri; d. Mar. 5, 1953 (57).
Herrmann, Bernard, composer & conductor; b. June 29, 1911, New York
    City; d. Dec. 24, 1975 (64).
Hersholt, Jean, actor; b. July 12, 1886, Copenhagen, Denmark; d. June
    2, 1956 (69).
Hertel, Adolph R., actor; d. Mar. 14, 1958 (80).
Herts, E.J., actor; b. May 27, 1883, New York; d. Dec. 26, 1951 (68).
Hervey, Harry, author & actor; d. Aug. 12, 1951 (50).
Herz, Ralph, actor; b. Mar. 25, 1878, Paris, France; d. July 12, 1921
    (43).
Herzfeld, Guido, actor; b. 1865, Berlin, Germany; d. Nov. 16, 1923
    (58).

Herzinger, Charles W., actor; b. Aug. 10, 1864, San Francisco, Calif.;
d. Feb. 18, 1953 (88).
Herzog, Frederic, actor; b. 1868; d. Mar. 2, 1928 (59).
Heslewood, Tom, actor; b. Apr. 8, 1868, Hessle, Yorkshire, England;
d. Apr. 28, 1959 (91).
Heslop, Charles, actor; b. June 8, 1883, Thames Ditton, England;
d. Apr. 13, 1966 (82).
Hesse, Baron William, actor; b. July 22, 1885, Moscow, Russia;
d. Apr. 4, 1936 (50).
Hessenland, Werner, actor; b. Mar. 14, 1909, Hochst, Germany;
d. June 10, 1979 (70).
Hesterberg, Trude, actress; b. May 2, 1892, Berlin, Germany; d. Aug.,
1967 (75).
Hewitt, Henry, actor; b. Dec. 28, 1885, London, England; d. Aug. 23,
1968 (82).
Hewston, Alfred, actor; b. Sept. 12, 1882, San Francisco, Calif.;
d. Sept. 6, 1947 (64).
Heyburn, Weldon, actor; b. Sept. 19, 1904, Selma, Ala.; d. May 18,
1951 (46).
Heydt, Louis Jean, actor; b. Apr. 17, 1905, Montclair, N.J.; d. Jan.
29, 1960 (54).
Heyes, Herbert, actor; b. Aug. 3, 1889, Vader, Wash.; d. May 31,
1958 (68).
Heywood, Herbert, actor; b. Feb. 1, 1881, Illinois; d. Sept. 15,
1964 (83).
Hibbert, Geoffrey, actor; b. June 2, 1920, Hull; d. Feb. 3, 1969 (48).
Hibbert, Jack, actor; d. May 27, 1958.
Hibler, Winston, producer & author (Disney) & narrator; d. Aug. 8,
1976 (65).
Hiby, Charles, actor; d. Feb. 15, 1947 (66).
Hickey, Howard L., actor; d. Mar. 25, 1942 (45).
Hickman, Alfred, actor; b. Feb. 25, 1872, England; d. Apr. 9, 1931
(59).
Hickman, Charles H., director; d. Sept. 19, 1938 (62).
Hickman, Howard, actor; b. Feb. 9, 1880, Columbia, Mo.; d. Dec. 30,
1949 (69).
Hickok, Rodney, actor; d. Mar. 9, 1942 (50).
Hicks, Bert (r.n. Edmond Burdell Hicks), actor; b. Aug. 3, 1920,
Illinois; d. Jan. 8, 1965 (44).
Hicks, Don, actor; b. Mar. 2, 1891, Ohio; d. Dec. 31, 1964 (73).
Hicks, Eleanor, actress; d. July 11, 1936 (50).
Hicks, Leonard M., actor; d. Aug. 8, 1971 (53).
Hicks, Russell, actor; b. June 4, 1895, Baltimore, Md.; d. June 1,
1957 (61).
Hicks, Sir Seymour, actor; b. Jan. 30, 1871, St. Heliers, England;
d. Apr. 6, 1949 (78).
Hiers, Walter, actor; b. July 18, 1893, Cordele, Ga.; d. Feb. 27,
1933 (39).
Higby, Wilbur (r.n. Wilbur Higby Jones), actor; b. Aug. 21, 1867,
Meridian, Miss.; d. Dec. 1, 1934 (67).
Higgin, Howard, director; d. Dec. 16, 1938 (47).
Higgins, David, actor; d. June 30, 1936 (78).
Hightower, Eloyce, actress; d. Dec. 12, 1939.
Hignett, H.R., actor; b. Jan. 29, 1870, Ringway, Cheshire, England;
d. Dec. 17, 1959 (89).

Hildebrand, Lo, actor; d. Sept. 11, 1936 (42).
Hildebrand, Rodney, actor; b. Mar. 22, 1892, Illinois; d. Feb. 22,
    1962 (69).
Hilforde, Mary, actress; d. Dec. 12, 1927 (74).
Hill, Al, actor; b. July 14, 1892, New York; d. July 14, 1954 (62).
Hill, Arthur, actor; d. Apr. 9, 1932 (57).
Hill, C.S. Ramsay (see Ramsay-Hill, C.S.)
Hill, Charles J., actor; d. Nov. 2, 1938 (50).
Hill, Dudley Sloan, actor; d. Jan. 7, 1960 (79).
Hill, Ethel, writer; b. Sacramento, Calif.; d. May 17, 1954 (56).
Hill, George, actor & stand-in; d. Mar. 2, 1945 (73).
Hill, George W., director; d. Aug. 10, 1934 (40).
Hill, Gus, producer & actor; d. Apr. 20, 1937 (78).
Hill, Hallene, actress; b. Sept. 12, 1876, Missouri; d. Jan. 6, 1966
    (89).
Hill, Howard, actor & archer; d. Feb. 4, 1975 (76).
Hill, Jack (see Keefe, Cornelius)
Hill, Jack Y., actor; b. Sept. 12, 1891, Virginia; d. Nov. 22, 1963
    (72).
Hill, Marcia, actress; d. June 18, 1947 (79).
Hill, Raymond, actor; d. Apr. 16, 1941 (50).
Hill, Robert F., director, actor, & author; b. Apr. 14, 1886, Port
    Rohen, Canada; d. Mar. 18, 1966 (79).
Hill, Thelma, actress; d. May 11, 1938 (32).
Hilliard, Ernest, actor; b. Jan. 31, 1890, New York City; d. Sept. 3,
    1947 (57).
Hilliard, Harry S., actor; b. Cincinnati, Ohio; d. Apr. 21, 1966.
Hillias, Margaret (Peg), actress; d. Mar. 18, 1960.
Hillyer, Lambert, director; b. July 8, 1893, South Bend, Ind.;
    d. July 5, 1969 (75).
Hilpert, Heinz, actor & director; b. Mar. 1, 1890, Berlin, Germany;
    d. Nov. 25, 1967 (77).
Hilton, Daisy, actress; b. Feb. 5, 1908, Brighton, England; d. Jan.,
    1969 (60).
Hilton, Frank, actor; d. Feb. 16, 1932 (61).
Hilton, Haran, actor; d. Aug., 1930 (30).
Hilton, Violet, actress; b. Feb. 5, 1908, Brighton, England;
    d. Jan., 1969 (60).
Hinckley, William L., actor; d. May, 1918.
Hinds, Samuel S., actor; b. Apr. 4, 1875, Brooklyn, N.Y.; d. Oct. 13,
    1948 (73).
Hines, Harry, actor; b. Mar. 28, 1889, New York; d. May 2, 1967 (78).
Hines, Johnny, actor; b. July 25, 1898, Golden, Colo.; d. Oct. 24,
    1970 (72).
Hines, Samuel E., actor; d. Nov. 17, 1939 (58).
Hinton, Ed, actor; b. Mar. 26, 1919, North Carolina; d. Oct. 12,
    1958 (39).
Hinzelmann, Helmuth, actor; b. Aug. 6, 1907, Oldenburg, Germany;
    d. May, 1972 (64).
Hippe, Lew, actor; d. July 19, 1952 (72).
Hirst, Alan, actor; d. Jan. 16, 1937 (6).
Hiscott, Leslie, director; d. May, 1968 (74).
Hislop, Joseph, opera singer; b. Apr. 5, 1884, Edinburgh, Scotland;
    d. May 6, 1977 (93).
Hitchcock, Keith (Keith Kenneth), actor; b. May 29, 1887, England;
    d. Apr. 11, 1966 (78).

Hitchcock, Raymond, actor; b. Oct. 22, 1865, Auburn, N.Y.; d. Nov. 24, 1929 (64).
Hitchcock, Walter, actor; d. June 23, 1917 (45).
Hively, Georgenia, stuntwoman & actress; d. May 21, 1977 (86).
Hix, Don (see Hicks, Don)
Hoagland, Harland, actor; d. Jan. 9, 1971 (75).
Hobbes, Halliwell, actor; b. Nov. 16, 1877, Stratford-on-Avon, England; d. Feb. 20, 1962 (84).
Hobbs, Carleton, actor; b. June 18, 1898, Farnborough, England; d. July 31, 1978 (80).
Hobbs, Jack, actor; b. Sept. 28, 1893, London, England; d. June 4, 1968 (74).
Hoch, Emil, actor; b. Oct. 27, 1866, Pforzheim, Germany; d. Oct. 13, 1944 (77).
Hoch, Winton C., cinematographer; d. Mar. 20, 1979 (73).
Hochuli, Paul, critic & extra; d. Mar. 24, 1964 (60).
Hock, Richard, stuntman; b. Jan. 30, 1933, Colorado; d. July 12, 1961 (28).
Hoctor, Harriet, dancer; d. June 9, 1977 (74).
Hodge, Al, actor; d. Mar. 19, 1979 (66).
Hodges, Horace, actor; b. Dec. 19, 1865; d. July 6, 1951 (85).
Hodges, William Cullen, actor; d. July 27, 1961 (85).
Hodgins, Earl, actor; b. Oct. 6, 1893, Utah; d. Apr. 14, 1964 (70).
Hodgins, Leslie, actor; d. Sept., 1927 (42).
Hodgson, Leyland (r.n. John Leyland Hodgson), actor; b. Oct. 5, 1892, London, England; d. Mar. 16, 1949 (56).
Hodiak, John, actor; b. Apr. 16, 1914, Pittsburgh, Pa.; d. Oct. 19, 1955 (41).
Hoeflich, Lucie, actress; b. Feb. 20, 1883, Hanover, Germany; d. Oct. 9, 1956 (73).
Hoerl, Arthur, writer; b. New York City; d. Feb. 6, 1968 (76).
Hoey, Dennis, actor; b. Mar. 30, 1893, London, England; d. July 25, 1960 (67).
Hoey, George J., actor; d. Feb. 17, 1955 (70).
Hoey, Iris, actress; b. July 17, 1885, London, England; d. May, 1979 (93).
Hoey, John, actor; d. Aug. 11, 1978 (59).
Hofer, Chris, actor; d. Feb. 11, 1964 (44).
Hoffe, Monckton, actor; b. Dec. 26, 1880, Connemara, Ireland; d. Nov. 4, 1951 (70).
Hoffenstein, Samuel, writer; b. Russia; d. Oct. 6, 1947 (57).
Hoffman, Bern, actor; d. Dec. 15, 1979 (66).
Hoffman, Charles H., writer; b. Sept. 28, 1911, San Francisco, Calif.; d. Apr. 8, 1972 (60).
Hoffman, David, actor; b. Feb. 2, 1904, Russia; d. June 19, 1961 (57).
Hoffman, Eberhard, actor; d. June 16, 1957 (74).
Hoffman, Gertrude, actress; d. June 3, 1955 (57).
Hoffman, Howard R., actor; b. Nov. 4, 1893, Ohio; d. June 26, 1969 (75).
Hoffman, Leonard, writer & assistant director; d. Aug. 24, 1969 (56).
Hoffman, M.H. (r.n. Maurice Henry Hoffman), producer; b. Mar. 21, 1881, Chicago, Ill.; d. Mar. 6, 1944 (62).
Hoffman, Max, Jr., actor; d. Mar. 31, 1945 (43).
Hoffman, Otto, actor; b. May 2, 1879, New York; d. June 23, 1944 (65).
Hoffmann, Gertrude W., actress; b. May 7, 1871, Heidelburg, Germany; d. Feb. 13, 1968 (96).
Hoffmann, Hermine H., juggler; d. Dec. 7, 1971 (47).

Hogan, Dan, actor; d. June 22, 1978 (54).
Hogan, James P., director; d. Nov. 6, 1943 (52).
Hogan, Pat, actor; b. Feb. 3, 1920, Oklahoma; d. Nov. 21, 1966 (46).
Hogan, Society Kid (Salvatore de Lorenzo), actor & prizefighter;
     d. Apr. 10, 1962 (63).
Hogarth, Lionel, actor; b. Apr. 16, 1874, Quincy, Mass.; d. Apr. 15,
     1946 (72).
Hogg, Jack (Curly) (The Singing Cowboys), singer; d. Sept. 4, 1974
     (57).
Hogue, Roland (r.n. John Roland Hogue), actor; d. Oct. 7, 1958 (76).
Hohl, Arthur, actor; b. May 21, 1889, Pittsburgh, Pa.; d. Mar. 10,
     1964 (74).
Holcombe, Herbert, actor; d. Oct. 15, 1970.
Holden, Fay, actress; b. Sept. 26, 1893, Birmingham, England;
     d. June 23, 1973 (79).
Holden, Harry, actor; d. Feb. 4, 1944 (76).
Holden, William, actor; d. Mar. 2, 1932 (57).
Holding, Thomas, actor; d. May 4, 1929.
Holdren, Judd, actor; b. Oct. 16, 1915, Iowa; d. Mar. 11, 1974 (58).
Holger-Madsen, F. (r.n. Forrest Holger-Madsen), director & actor;
     b. Apr. 11, 1878, Copenhagen, Denmark; d. Nov. 30, 1943 (65).
Holland, C. Maurice, actor; d. Nov. 14, 1974.
Holland, Cecil, actor; b. May 29, 1887, Gravesend, Kent, England;
     d. June 29, 1973 (86).
Holland, Mildred, actress; b. Apr. 9, 1869, Chicago, Ill.; d. Jan.
     27, 1944 (74).
Holland, Miriam, actress; d. Sept. 24, 1948 (31).
Holland, Ralph, actor; d. Dec. 7, 1939 (51).
Hollander, Friedrich, composer; d. Jan. 18, 1976 (79).
Hollander, Mildred, actress; d. July 19, 1937.
Holles, Anthony, actor; b. Jan. 17, 1901, London, England; d. Mar. 4,
     1950 (49).
Holliday, Frank, Jr., actor; d. Aug. 3, 1948 (35).
Holliday, Harry, actor; d. Feb. 3, 1942 (86).
Holliday, Judy, actress; b. June 21, 1923, New York City; d. June 7,
     1965 (41).
Holliday, Marjorie (r.n. Marjorie St. Angel), actress; d. June 16,
     1969 (49).
Hollingshead, Gordon, producer; d. July 8, 1952 (60).
Hollingsworth, Alfred, actor; b. Nebraska; d. June 19, 1926 (52).
Hollingsworth, Harry, actor; b. Sept. 3, 1888; d. Nov. 5, 1947 (59).
Hollis, T. Beresford (Jack), actor; d. Dec. 15, 1940 (81).
Hollister, Alice, actress; b. Sept. 28, 1886, Worcester, Mass.;
     d. Feb. 24, 1973 (86).
Hollister, Leonard, actor; d. Dec. 4, 1946 (62).
Hollmann, Werner, actor; b. 1882, Berlin, Germany; d. Mar. 3, 1933
     (50).
Holloway, Baliol, actor; b. Feb. 28, 1883, Brentwood, England;
     d. Apr. 15, 1967 (84).
Holloway, William Edwyn, actor; b. Sept. 18, 1885, Adelaide, S.
     Australia; d. June 30, 1952 (66).
Holly, Mary, actress; d. May 17, 1976 (89).
Hollywood, Jimmie, actor; b. Jan. 1, 1895, Massachusetts; d. July 2,
     1955 (60).
Holman, Dick, actor; d. Aug., 1955 (55).

Holman, Harry, actor; b. Mar. 15, 1862, Lebanon, Mo.; d. May 3, 1947
    (85).
Holman, Libby, actress & singer; d. June 18, 1971 (65).
Holman, Vincent, actor; d. Apr. 7, 1962.
Holmes, Ben, director & writer; d. Dec. 2, 1943 (53).
Holmes, Burton, producer; b. Jan. 8, 1870, Chicago, Ill.; d. July 22,
    1958 (88).
Holmes, Edward, actor; d. July 12, 1977 (66).
Holmes, Gilbert (Pee Wee), actor; b. June 15, 1895, Miles City,
    Mont.; d. Aug. 17, 1936 (41).
Holmes, Helen, actress; d. July 8, 1950 (58).
Holmes, Jack (J. Merrill), actor; b. July 21, 1889, Pennsylvania;
    d. Feb. 27, 1950 (60).
Holmes, Pee Wee (see Holmes, Gilbert)
Holmes, Phillips, actor; b. July 22, 1907, Grand Rapids, Mich.;
    d. Aug. 12, 1942 (35).
Holmes, Ralph, actor; d. Nov. 20, 1945 (30).
Holmes, Rapley, actor; d. Jan. 11, 1928 (60).
Holmes, Robert, actor; d. July 10, 1945 (46).
Holmes, Stuart (r.n. Joseph Liebchen), actor; b. Mar. 10, 1884,
    Chicago, Ill.; d. Dec. 29, 1971 (87).
Holmes, Taylor, actor; b. May 16, 1878, Newark, N.J.; d. Sept. 30,
    1959 (81).
Holmes, Wendell, actor; d. Apr. 26, 1962 (47).
Holmes, William J., actor; b. Mar. 17, 1877, Watertown, N.Y.; d.
    Dec. 1, 1946 (69).
Holmes-Gore, Arthur, actor; d. Aug. 12, 1915 (44).
Holt, Edwin, actor; d. July 5, 1920.
Holt, Helen, actress; d. Jan. 17, 1927 (37).
Holt, Jack (r.n. Charles John Holt), actor; b. May 31, 1888, New
    York; d. Jan. 18, 1951 (62).
Holt, Nat, producer; b. May 15, 1894, Vacaville, Calif.; d. Aug. 3,
    1971 (77).
Holt, Nick, actor; d. Oct. 6, 1979 (45).
Holt, Richard (see Dearholt, Ashton)
Holt, Seth, director; d. Feb. 14, 1971 (47).
Holt, Tim (r.n. Charles John Holt, Jr.), actor; b. Feb. 5, 1918,
    Beverly Hills, Calif.; d. Feb. 15, 1973 (55).
Holtz, Tenen (r.n. Elihu Tenenholtz), actor; b. Feb. 17, 1887,
    Russia; d. July 1, 1971 (84).
Holubar, Allan, actor; b. Aug. 3, 1889, California; d. Nov. 20,
    1923 (34).
Homans, Robert, actor; b. Nov. 8, 1877, Malden, Mass.; d. July 27,
    1947 (69).
Homes, Geoffrey (r.n. Daniel Mainwaring), writer; b. July 22, 1902,
    Oakland, Calif.; d. Jan. 31, 1977 (74).
Homolka, Oscar, actor; b. Aug. 12, 1898, Vienna, Austria; d. Jan. 27,
    1978 (79).
Honda, Frank K., actor; d. Feb. 7, 1924 (40).
Hood, Darla, actress (Our Gang); d. June 13, 1979 (48).
Hood, Joseph B., Sr., actor; d. June 26, 1965 (69).
Hood, Tom, actor; d. Dec. 8, 1950 (31).
Hooker, Son (r.n. Stanford Graham Hooker), actor; b. Nov. 11, 1939,
    Tenaha, Tex.; d. Oct. 18, 1974 (34).
Hoops, Arthur, actor; d. Sept. 16, 1916 (46).
Hoose, Fred, actor; b. Mar. 4, 1868, Vermont; d. Mar. 12, 1952 (84).

Hope, Diana, actress; d. Nov. 20, 1942 (70).
Hope, Jim (r.n. Francis James Hope), actor; d. July 27, 1975 (84).
Hope, Vida, actress; b. Dec. 16, 1918, Liverpool, England; d. Dec.
    23, 1963 (45).
Hopkins, Arthur, director & writer; d. Mar. 22, 1950 (71).
Hopkins, Ben, actor; b. May 9, 1870, Buffalo, N.Y.; d. Feb. 8, 1941
    (70).
Hopkins, Bob, actor; b. Apr. 23, 1918, Iowa; d. Oct. 5, 1962 (44).
Hopkins, Charles, producer & stage actor; d. Jan. 1, 1953 (69).
Hopkins, Miriam, actress; b. Oct. 18, 1902, Bainbridge, Ga.;
    d. Oct. 9, 1972 (69).
Hopper, De Wolf, actor; b. Mar. 30, 1858, New York City; d. Sept.
    23, 1935 (77).
Hopper, DeWolfe (see Hopper, William)
Hopper, E. Mason, director; b. Dec. 6, 1885, Enosberg, Vt.; d. Jan.
    3, 1967 (81).
Hopper, Frank, actor; d. Jan. 10, 1941 (68).
Hopper, Hedda, actress & columnist; b. June 2, 1890, Hallidaysburg,
    Pa.; d. Feb. 1, 1966 (75).
Hopper, William (DeWolfe Hopper), actor; b. Jan. 26, 1915, New York
    City; d. Mar. 6, 1970 (55).
Hopton, Russell, actor; b. Feb. 18, 1900, New York City; d. Apr. 7,
    1945 (45).
Horan, James, actor; b. Oct. 23, 1907, Minnesota; d. May 4, 1967
    (59).
Horgan, Betty, actress; d. Apr. 6, 1956 (81).
Horkheimer, Herbert M., producer; d. Apr. 25, 1962 (80).
Horn, Leonard, director; b. Aug. 1, 1926, Massachusetts; d. May 25,
    1975 (48).
Hornblow, Arthur, Jr., producer; b. Mar. 15, 1893, New York City;
    d. July 17, 1976 (83).
Hornbrook, Charles (Gus), actor; d. May 8, 1937 (63).
Horne, David, actor; b. July 14, 1898, Balcome, Sussex, England;
    d. Mar. 15, 1970 (71).
Horne, Edna, actress; d. July 17, 1945 (59).
Horne, James W., director; b. Dec. 14, 1881, San Francisco, Calif.;
    d. June 29, 1942 (60).
Horne, William T., actor; b. June 4, 1869, Batavia, Ill.; d. Dec. 15,
    1942 (73).
Horsley, David, director; d. Feb. 23, 1933 (60).
Horton, Benjamin, actor; d. Aug. 6, 1952 (80).
Horton, Clara (Baby Clara Marie Horton), actress; b. July 29, 1904,
    Brooklyn, N.Y.; d. Dec. 4, 1976 (72).
Horton, Edward Everett, actor; b. Mar. 18, 1886, Brooklyn, N.Y.;
    d. Sept. 29, 1970 (84).
Horvath, Charles, actor; d. July 23, 1978 (57).
Horwitz, Kurt, actor; b. Dec. 21, 1897, Neuruppin, Germany; d. Feb.
    14, 1974 (76).
Hossenfeldt, Vera, actress; d. Oct. 16, 1967 (57).
Hoster, Anne, actress; d. Aug. 9, 1954 (41).
Hostetter, Roy, actor; d. Sept. 22, 1951 (66).
Hotaling, Arthur D., actor; b. Feb. 3, 1873, New York; d. July 13,
    1938 (65).
Hotaling, Frank, art director; d. Apr. 13, 1977 (77).
Hotaly, Mae, actress; b. Oct. 7, 1872, Maryland; d. Apr. 6, 1954 (81).
Houdini, Harry, actor & magician; b. Mar. 24, 1874, Budapest, Hungary;
    d. Oct. 31, 1926 (52).

Houghton, Alice (Alice Browning), actress; b. June 14, 1887, Offalan, Mo.; d. May 12, 1944 (56).
House, Billy, actor; b. May 7, 1890, Minnesota; d. Sept. 23, 1961 (71).
House, Jack, actor & stuntman; b. Feb. 18, 1887, Texas; d. Nov. 20, 1963 (76).
House, Newton, actor & cattleman; b. Jan. 10, 1865, Texas; d. Dec. 16, 1948 (83).
Houser, Lionel, writer; b. Apr. 16, 1908, New York City; d. Nov. 12, 1949 (41).
Housman, Arthur, actor; b. Oct. 10, 1889, New York City; d. Apr. 8, 1942 (52).
Houston, George, actor; b. Jan. 11, 1896, Hampton, N.J.; d. Nov. 12, 1944 (48).
Houston, Jean, singer; d. Jan., 1965.
Houston, Renee, actress; b. July 24, 1902, Johnstone, Scotland; d. Feb. 9, 1980 (77).
Hovick, Louise (see Lee, Gypsy Rose)
Howard, Art, actor; b. Jan. 1, 1887, Massachusetts; d. May 28, 1963 (76).
Howard, Bert, actor; b. Aug. 7, 1878, Salmon Falls, N.H.; d. Oct. 27, 1958 (80).
Howard, Booth, actor; d. Oct. 4, 1936 (47).
Howard, Charles, actor; d. June 28, 1947 (65).
Howard, David, director & actor; d. Dec. 21, 1941 (45).
Howard, Edward M., actor; b. Sept. 2, 1910, Tuscaloosa, Ala.; d. Sept. 16, 1946 (36).
Howard, Esther, actress; b. Apr. 4, 1892, Montana; d. Mar. 9, 1965 (72).
Howard, Eugene, actor; b. July 7, 1881, Neustadt, Germany; d. Aug. 1, 1965 (84).
Howard, Florence, actress; d. Aug. 11, 1954 (66).
Howard, Frances, actress; d. July 2, 1976 (73).
Howard, George W., actor; d. Aug. 25, 1928 (55).
Howard, Gertrude, actress; b. Oct. 2, 1893, Hot Springs, Ark.; d. Sept. 30, 1934 (40).
Howard, Harold, actor; b. Aug. 22, 1870, Rutland, N.Y.; d. Dec. 9, 1944 (74).
Howard, Helen, actress; d. Mar. 13, 1927.
Howard, Jerome (Curly), actor; b. Oct. 22, 1903, New York; d. Jan. 18, 1952 (48).
Howard, Kathleen, actress & opera singer; b. July 27, 1884, Canada; d. Aug. 15, 1956 (72).
Howard, Leslie, actor; b. Apr. 3, 1893, London, England; d. June 1, 1943 (50).
Howard, Lewis, actor; d. Sept. 29, 1951 (32).
Howard, Lisa, actress; d. July 4, 1965 (35).
Howard, May, actress; d. Feb. 1, 1935 (65).
Howard, Moe, actor; b. June 19, 1897, New York; d. May 4, 1975 (78).
Howard, Norah, actress; b. Dec. 12, 1901; d. May 2, 1968 (66).
Howard, Peter, actor; d. Mar. 14, 1969 (91).
Howard, Shemp, actor; b. Mar. 4, 1895, Brooklyn, N.Y.; d. Nov. 22, 1955 (60).
Howard, Sidney, writer; d. Aug. 23, 1939 (48).
Howard, Sydney, actor; b. Aug. 7, 1885, Yeadon, England; d. June 12, 1946 (60).
Howard, Tom, actor; b. June 16, 1885, Ireland; d. Feb. 27, 1955 (69).

Howard, Vincent, actor; b. July 19, 1869, Los Angeles, Calif.;
    d. Nov. 2, 1946 (77).
Howard, Warda, actress; d. Mar. 17, 1943 (63).
Howard, William, actor; d. Jan. 23, 1944 (60).
Howard, William K., director; b. June 16, 1899, St. Mary's, Ohio;
    d. Feb. 21, 1954 (54).
Howard, Willie, actor; b. Apr. 13, 1886, Neustadt, Germany; d. Jan.
    14, 1949 (62).
Howdy, Clyde, actor; d. Oct. 3, 1969 (49).
Howe, Eliot, director; b. Dec. 23, 1886, Boston, Mass.; d. Dec. 18,
    1921 (34).
Howe, James Wong, cinematographer; b. Aug. 28, 1899, Kwangtung, China;
    d. July 12, 1976 (76).
Howe, Ronald, actor; d. Mar. 16, 1961 (33).
Howe, Walter L., actor; d. July 31, 1957 (78).
Howell, Alice, actress; b. May 5, 1888, New York; d. Apr. 12, 1961
    (72).
Howerton, Clarence "Major Mite," actor; d. Nov. 18, 1975 (62).
Howes, Bobby, actor; b. Aug. 4, 1895, Battersea, England; d. Apr. 27,
    1972 (76).
Howes, Reed, actor; b. July 5, 1900, Washington, D.C.; d. Aug. 6,
    1964 (64).
Howland, Jobyna, actress; b. Mar. 31, 1880, Indianapolis, Ind.;
    d. June 7, 1936 (56).
Howlin, Olin (r.n. Olin Howland), actor; b. Feb. 10, 1886, Denver,
    Colo.; d. Sept. 19, 1959 (73).
Hoxie, Hart (see Hoxie, Jack)
Hoxie, Jack (Hart Hoxie), actor; b. Jan. 24, 1885, Oklahoma; d. Mar.
    28, 1965 (80).
Hoyt, Arthur, actor; b. Mar. 19, 1874, Georgetown, Colo.; d. Jan. 4,
    1953 (78).
Hoyt, Clegg, actor; b. Dec. 10, 1910, Connecticut; d. Oct. 6, 1967
    (56).
Hoyt, Julia, actress; d. Oct. 31, 1955 (58).
Hoyt, Leo, actor; d. Jan. 3, 1937.
Hruby, Margarete, actress; d. July, 1948.
Hubbard, Lucien, writer; b. Dec. 25, 1889, Ft. Thomas, Ky.; d. Dec.
    31, 1971 (82).
Hubbard, Tom (r.n. Thomas G. Hubbard), actor & author; d. June 4,
    1974 (55).
Huber, Harold, actor; d. Sept. 29, 1959 (49).
Huber, Juanita (Billie), dancer; d. May 22, 1965 (60).
Hubert, Frank, actor; d. June, 1966.
Hubert, Harold, actor; d. Mar. 31, 1916 (57).
Hubner, Herbert, actor; b. Feb. 6, 1889, Breslau, Germany; d. Jan.
    27, 1972 (82).
Hudd, Walter, actor; b. Feb. 20, 1898, London, England; d. Jan. 20,
    1963 (64).
Hudman, Wesley, actor; d. Feb. 29, 1964 (48).
Hudson, Larry, actor; d. Jan. 8, 1961 (41).
Hudson, Rochelle, actress; b. Mar. 6, 1916, Claremore, Okla.; d. Jan.
    17, 1972 (55).
Hudson, William, actor; b. Jan. 24, 1925, California; d. Apr. 5, 1974
    (49).
Huestis, Russell, actor; d. Dec. 1, 1964 (70).
Hueston, Frederic, actor; b. Feb. 8, 1880, Canada; d. Feb. 25, 1961
    (81).

Huff, Louise, actress; b. Columbus, Ga.; d. Aug. 22, 1973 (77).
Huggins, George, actor; b. Nov. 8, 1901, Canada; d. Apr. 5, 1959 (57).
Hugh, Edwin Charles, actor; d. Dec. 3, 1979 (60).
Hughes, David Hillary (r.n. Thomas Joseph Keenan), actor; b. May 22, 1901, New York; d. Feb. 5, 1974 (72).
Hughes, Gareth, actor; b. Aug. 23, 1894, Llanelly, Wales; d. Oct. 1, 1965 (71).
Hughes, Hazel, actress; b. Apr. 21, 1913, Transvaal, South Africa; d. Nov. 16, 1974 (61).
Hughes, Howard, director & producer; b. Dec. 24, 1905, Houston, Tex.; d. Apr. 5, 1976 (70).
Hughes, J. Anthony (r.n. Joseph Anthony Hughes), actor; b. May 2, 1904, New York; d. Feb. 11, 1970 (65).
Hughes, Lloyd, actor; b. Oct. 21, 1897, Arizona; d. June 6, 1958 (60).
Hughes, Roy, actor; b. Jan. 11, 1894, Kinmundy, Ill.; d. Jan. 12, 1928 (34).
Hughes, Rupert, producer & writer; b. Jan. 31, 1872, Lancaster, Mo.; d. Sept. 9, 1956 (84).
Hughes, T. Arthur (r.n. Thomas Arthur Hughes), actor; d. Nov. 25, 1953 (66).
Hughes, Yvonne Evelyn, actress; d. Dec. 26, 1950 (50).
Hugo, Mauritz, actor; b. Jan. 12, 1909, Sweden; d. June 16, 1974 (65).
Hulbert, Claude, actor; b. Dec. 25, 1900, London, England; d. Jan. 22, 1964 (63).
Hulbert, Jack, actor; b. Apr. 24, 1892, Ely, England; d. Mar. 25, 1978 (85).
Huley, Pete (Klondike Pete), actor; d. Feb. 6, 1973 (80).
Hull, Arthur Stewart, actor; b. May 8, 1878, Pennsylvania; d. Feb. 28, 1951 (72).
Hull, Henry, actor; b. Oct. 3, 1890, Louisville, Ky.; d. Mar. 8, 1977 (86).
Hull, Josephine, actress; b. Jan. 3, 1886, Newtonville, Mass.; d. Mar. 12, 1957 (71).
Hull, Shelley, actor; b. Louisville, Ky.; d. Jan. 14, 1919 (33).
Hull, Warren, actor; b. Jan. 17, 1903, Gasport, N.Y.; d. Sept. 14, 1974 (71).
Human, Bob, actor; d. Apr. 5, 1979 (57).
Humbert, George, actor; b. July 29, 1880, Florence, Italy; d. May 8, 1963 (82).
Hume, Benita, actress; b. Oct. 14, 1906, London, England; d. Nov. 1, 1967 (61).
Hume, Cyril, scenarist; b. Mar. 16, 1900, New York; d. Mar. 26, 1966 (66).
Hume, Ilean, actress; d. Nov. 20, 1978 (82).
Hummel, Mary Rockwell, actress; d. Feb. 16, 1946 (57).
Humphrey, Bessie, actress; d. Mar. 8, 1933.
Humphrey, Harry, actor; b. Dec. 15, 1873, San Francisco, Calif.; d. Apr. 1, 1947 (73).
Humphrey, Orral (r.n. Thomas Orral Humphrey), actor; b. Apr. 3, 1880, Louisville, Ky.; d. Aug. 12, 1929 (49).
Humphrey, William J., actor & director; b. Jan. 2, 1875, Chicopee Falls, Mass.; d. Oct. 4, 1942 (67).
Humphreys, Cecil, actor; b. July 21, 1883, Cheltenham, England; d. Nov. 6, 1947 (64).
Humphries, Bee (r.n. Bertha A. Humphreys), actress; b. Feb. 3, 1885, Ohio; d. May 11, 1970 (85).

Hun, Hadi, actor; d. Dec., 1969 (69).
Hunnicutt, Arthur, actor; b. Feb. 17, 1911, Gravelly, Ark.; d. Sept. 26, 1979 (68).
Hunt, Jay, actor; b. Aug. 4, 1855, Philadelphia, Pa.; d. Nov. 18, 1932 (77).
Hunt, Madge, actress; b. Nov. 27, 1875, New York City; d. Aug. 2, 1935 (59).
Hunt, Martita, actress; b. Jan. 30, 1900, Argentina; d. June 13, 1969 (69).
Hunt, Rea M., actor & director; b. Nov. 5, 1892, New Mexico; d. June 21, 1961 (68).
Hunter, Colin, actor; b. July 20, 1892, South Africa; d. July 14, 1968 (75).
Hunter, Edna, actress; b. 1876; d. Feb. 5, 1920 (43).
Hunter, George F., actor; d. 1945.
Hunter, Glenn, actor; d. Dec. 30, 1945 (49).
Hunter, Ian, actor; b. June 13, 1900, Capetown, South Africa; d. Sept. 23, 1975 (75).
Hunter, Jackie, actor; d. Nov. 21, 1951 (50).
Hunter, Jeffrey, actor; b. Nov. 25, 1925, New Orleans, La.; d. May 27, 1969 (43).
Hunter, Kenneth, actor; b. Feb. 19, 1882, South Africa; d. Dec. 21, 1961 (79).
Hunter, Maurice, actor; d. Feb. 26, 1966 (80).
Hunter, Richard, actor; b. Apr. 21, 1875, California; d. Dec. 22, 1962 (87).
Hunter, T. Hayes, director; d. Apr. 14, 1944 (62).
Hunter, Todd, actor; b. June 1, 1903, Washington; d. Oct. 7, 1968 (65).
Huntley, Chet, actor & news commentator; d. Mar. 20, 1974 (62).
Huntly, Fred W. (r.n. Frederic William Huntly), actor; b. Aug. 29, 1864, London, England; d. Nov. 1, 1931 (67).
Huntress, Mary, actress; d. Dec. 11, 1933.
Hurley, Julia, actress; d. June 4, 1927 (80).
Hurn, Douglas, actor; d. Oct. 22, 1974 (49).
Hurst, Brandon, actor; b. Nov. 30, 1866, London, England; d. July 15, 1947 (80).
Hurst, Paul, actor & director; b. Oct. 15, 1888, Traver, Calif.; d. Feb. 27, 1953 (64).
Hurt, Mary, actress; d. Oct. 6, 1976 (87).
Hussenot, Olivier, actor; b. Sept. 10, 1913, Paris, France; d. Aug. 25, 1978 (64).
Huston, Walter, actor; b. Apr. 6, 1884, Toronto, Canada; d. Apr. 7, 1950 (66).
Huszar, Karoly (see Puffy, Charles H.)
Hutcheons, Bobbie (see Hutchins, Bobby)
Hutcheson, David, actor; b. June 14, 1905, Isle of Bute, Scotland; d. Feb. 18, 1976 (70).
Hutchins, Bobby "Wheezer" (Bobby Hutcheons), actor; b. Mar. 29, 1925, Tacoma, Wash.; d. May 17, 1945 (20).
Hutchins, George C., actor; d. Oct. 10, 1952 (83).
Hutchins, Richard, actor; d. Sept. 5, 1950 (74).
Hutchinson, Charles (see Hutchison, Charles)
Hutchison, Charles, actor & director; b. Dec. 3, 1879, Pittsburgh, Pa.; d. May 30, 1949 (69).

Hutchison, Muriel, actress; d. Mar. 24, 1975 (60).
Hutchison, Percy, actor; b. 1875, Stratford, England; d. Apr. 18, 1945 (69).
Huth, Harold, actor & director; b. Jan. 20, 1892, England; d. Oct. 26, 1967 (75).
Hutton, Jim, actor; b. May 31, 1934, Binghamton, N.Y.; d. June 2, 1979 (45).
Hutton, June, singer & recording artist; b. Aug. 11, 1923, Illinois; d. May 2, 1973 (49).
Hutton, Leona, actress; d. Apr. 1, 1949 (57).
Huxham, Kendrick (r.n. Frank Kendrick Huxham), actor; b. Feb. 22, 1898, England; d. July 24, 1967 (69).
Hyams, John, actor; b. July 6, 1869, Syracuse, N.Y.; d. Dec. 9, 1940 (71).
Hyams, Leila, actress; b. May 1, 1905, New York City; d. Dec. 4, 1977 (72).
Hyatt, Clayton, actor; d. June, 1932.
Hyatt, Herman, actor; d. Jan. 24, 1968 (62).
Hydes, David (see Wood, Victor)
Hylan, Donald, actor; d. June 20, 1968 (69).
Hyland, Augustin Allen, actor & stand in; b. Nov. 23, 1904, Massachusetts; d. Feb. 8, 1963 (58).
Hyland, Diana, actress; b. Jan. 25, 1936, Cleveland Hts., Ohio; d. Mar. 27, 1977 (41).
Hylton, Jack, actor; d. Jan. 29, 1965.
Hylton, Jane, actress; b. July 16, 1927, London, England; d. Feb. 28, 1979 (51).
Hylton, Richard, actor; b. Dec. 11, 1920, Oklahoma; d. May 12, 1962 (41).
Hyman, Bernard H., producer; b. Aug. 20, 1895, Grofton, W. Va.; d. Sept. 7, 1942 (47).
Hyman, Robert, actor; d. Mar. 30, 1934 (49).
Hymer, Elinor Kent, actress; d. Sept. 15, 1957.
Hymer, Warren, actor; b. Feb. 25, 1906, New York City; d. Mar. 25, 1948 (42).
Hynes, John E., actor; d. Apr. 12, 1931 (78).
Hytten, Olaf, actor; b. Mar. 3, 1888, Scotland; d. Mar. 11, 1955 (67).


Ibbotson, Frank, actor; b. Apr. 12, 1871, Quebec, Canada; d. Dec. 7, 1944 (73).
Ihnat, Steve, actor & director; b. Aug. 7, 1934, Czechoslovakia; d. May 12, 1972 (37).
Ikonnikoff, Alexander, actor; b. Kiev, Russia; d. Nov. 17, 1936 (52).
Ikonnikoff, Lois Logan, actress; b. Feb. 2, 1908, Seattle, Wash.; d. Sept. 15, 1943 (35).
Illing, Peter, actor; b. Mar. 4, 1905, Vienna, Austria; d. Oct. 29, 1966 (61).
Illington, Margaret, actress; b. July 23, 1881, Bloomington, Ill.; d. Mar. 11, 1934 (52).
Imboden, David, actor; d. Mar. 18, 1974 (87).
Imboden, Hazel Bourne, actress; d. Oct. 8, 1956.
Imhof, Marcelle, actress; d. Jan. 15, 1977 (88).
Imhof, Roger, actor; b. Apr. 15, 1875, Rock Island, Ill.; d. Apr. 15, 1958 (83).

Imhoff, Fritz, actor; b. Jan. 6, 1891; b. Feb. 24, 1961 (70).
Imperio, Pastora, actress; d. Sept. 14, 1979 (90).
Impolito, John, actor; b. Sept. 1, 1886, Italy; d. May 1, 1962 (75).
Ince, Ethel Jackson, actress; b. July 31, 1883, New York; d. July 27, 1952 (68).
Ince, John E., actor & director; b. Aug. 29, 1878, New York City; d. Apr. 10, 1947 (68).
Ince, Ralph, actor & director; b. Jan. 16, 1882, Boston, Mass.; d. Apr. 11, 1937 (55).
Ince, Thomas H., producer, director, actor, & writer; b. Nov. 16, 1882, Newport, R.I.; d. Nov. 19, 1924 (42).
Inclan, Miguel, actor; d. July 25, 1956 (56).
Indira, Princess, actress; d. Sept., 1979 (67).
Indrisano, John, actor & boxer; b. Nov. 1, 1905, Massachusetts; d. July 7, 1968 (62).
Inescort, Frieda, actress; b. June 29, 1901, Edinburgh, Scotland; d. Feb. 21, 1976 (74).
Infante, Pedro, actor; d. Apr. 15, 1957 (39).
Inge, William, author & actor; b. May 3, 1913, Independence, Kans.; d. June 10, 1973 (60).
Ingersoll, William, actor; d. May 7, 1936 (76).
Ingraham, Lloyd, actor & director; b. Nov. 30, 1874, Illinois; d. Apr. 4, 1956 (81).
Ingram, Jack (r.n. John Samuel Ingram), actor; b. Nov. 15, 1902, Illinois; d. Feb. 20, 1969 (66).
Ingram, Rex, director & actor; b. Jan. 15, 1893, Ireland; d. July 21, 1950 (57).
Ingram, Rex, actor; b. Oct. 20, 1895, nr. Cairo, Ill.; d. Sept. 19, 1969 (73).
Ingram, William D., actor; d. Feb. 2, 1926 (69).
Ingster, Boris, director & author; d. July 2, 1978 (74).
Inness, Jean, actress; d. Dec. 27, 1978 (76).
Ipsen, Bodil, director & actor; b. Aug. 30, 1889; d. Nov., 1964 (75).
Ireland, Anthony, actor; b. Feb. 5, 1902, Peru; d. Dec. 4, 1957 (55).
Irgat, Cahit, actor; d. June, 1971 (55).
Iris, Esperanza, actress; d. Nov. 8, 1962 (74).
Irvine, Robin, actor; b. Dec. 21, 1901, London, England; d. Apr. 28, 1933 (31).
Irving, Ethel, actress; b. Sept. 5, 1869; d. May 3, 1963 (93).
Irving, George, actor & director; b. Oct. 5, 1874, New York; d. Sept. 11, 1961 (86).
Irving, Paul, actor; b. Aug. 24, 1877, Massachusetts; d. May 8, 1959 (81).
Irving, William, actor; b. May 17, 1893, Hamburg, Germany; d. Dec. 25, 1943 (50).
Irwin, Boyd, actor; b. Mar. 12, 1880, England; d. Jan. 22, 1957 (76).
Irwin, Charles, actor; b. Jan. 31, 1887, Ireland; d. Jan. 12, 1969 (81).
Irwin, May, actress; b. June 27, 1862, Whitby, Ontario, Canada; d. Oct. 22, 1938 (76).
Isbert, Jose (Pepe) (r.n. Jose Isbert Alvarruiz), actor; b. Mar. 3, 1886, Madrid, Spain; d. Nov. 28, 1966 (80).
Isham, Gyles, actor; b. Oct. 31, 1903; d. Jan. 29, 1976 (72).
Ishii, Kan, actor; d. Apr. 29, 1972 (71).
Isik, Ayhan, actor; d. July, 1979 (50).

Ivan, John, actor; d. Apr. 19, 1947 (66).
Ivan, Rosalind, actress; b. London, England; d. Apr. 6, 1959 (75).
Ivers, Julia Crawford, writer; d. May 7, 1930 (59).
Ives, Anne, actress; d. May 15, 1979 (92).
Ives, Douglas, actor; d. Mar. 6, 1969.
Ivins, Perry, actor; b. Nov. 19, 1894, New Jersey; d. Aug. 22, 1963 (68).
Izvitskaya, Isolda, actress; d. Mar., 1971 (38).

Jaccard, Jacques, director; b. Sept. 11, 1886, New York; d. July 24, 1960 (73).
Jack, Chief, actor; d. Jan. 9, 1943 (66).
Jack, T.C., actor; d. Oct. 4, 1954 (72).
Jackie, William, actor; d. Sept. 19, 1954 (64).
Jackman, Fred W., cinematographer; d. Aug. 27, 1959 (78).
Jackson, Andrew, IV, actor; d. May 23, 1953 (66).
Jackson, Dale, actor; d. Aug. 9, 1961 (65).
Jackson, Elizabeth, actress; b. Sept. 26, 1920, Washington; d. June 30, 1972 (51).
Jackson, Frederick, writer & producer; b. Sept. 21, 1886, Pittsburgh, Pa.; d. May 22, 1953 (66).
Jackson, Horace, writer; d. Jan. 26, 1952 (53).
Jackson, Jenie, actress; b. Nov. 27, 1921, California; d. Mar. 14, 1976 (54).
Jackson, Joe, actor; b. Vienna, Austria; d. May 14, 1942 (67).
Jackson, Mahalia, recording artist & singer; b. Oct. 26, 1911, New Orleans, La.; d. Jan. 27, 1972 (60).
Jackson, Selmer, actor; b. May 7, 1888, Lake Mills, Iowa; d. Mar. 30, 1971 (82).
Jackson, Thomas E., actor; b. July 4, 1886, New York City; d. Sept. 7, 1967 (81).
Jackson, Warren, actor; b. Feb. 12, 1892, Paris, Tex.; d. May 10, 1950 (58).
Jacob, Naomi, actress; d. Aug. 27, 1964 (80).
Jacob, P. Walter, actor; b. Jan. 26, 1905, Duisburg, Germany; d. July 20, 1977 (72).
Jacobini, Maria, actress; b. Feb. 17, 1890, Rome, Italy; d. Nov. 20, 1944 (54).
Jacobs, Angela, actress; d. Feb. 7, 1951 (58).
Jacobs, Harrison, writer; d. Apr. 9, 1968 (85).
Jacobson, Irving, actor; d. Dec. 17, 1978 (80).
Jaffe, Carl, actor; b. Mar. 21, 1902, Hamburg, Germany; d. Apr. 12, 1974 (72).
Jahr, Adolf, actor; d. Apr. 19, 1964 (70).
James, Alan (Alvin J. Neitz) (r.n. Alvin James Neitz), director; b. Mar. 23, 1890, Washington; d. Dec. 30, 1952 (62).
James, Alfred P., actor; b. Oct. 12, 1865, Australia; d. Oct. 9, 1946 (80).
James, Eddie, actor & director; d. Dec. 22, 1944 (64).
James, Gardner, actor; b. Mar. 16, 1903, New York City; d. June 23, 1953 (50).
James, Gladden, actor; b. Zanesville, Ohio; d. Aug. 28, 1948 (56).
James, Horace D., actor; b. Baltimore, Md.; d. Oct. 16, 1925 (72).

James, Jesse, Jr. (r.n. Jesse E. James), actor; d. Mar. 26, 1951 (75).
James, John, actor; d. May 20, 1960.
James, M.E. Clifton, actor; d. May 8, 1963 (65).
James, Rian, writer; b. Oct. 3, 1899, Eagle Pass, Tex.; d. Apr. 26,
    1953 (53).
James, Sidney, actor; b. May 8, 1913, Johannesburg, South Africa;
    d. Apr. 26, 1976 (62).
James, Walter, actor; b. June 3, 1882, Chattanooga, Tenn.; d. June 27,
    1946 (64).
Jameson, House, actor; b. Dec. 17, 1902, Austin, Tex.; d. Apr. 23,
    1971 (68).
Jameson, Jessie H., actress; d. Aug. 2, 1957 (80).
Jamin, Georges, actor; d. Feb. 23, 1971 (64).
Jamis, Bill, actor; d. July 10, 1977 (52).
Jamison, Ann, singer; d. Apr. 16, 1961 (51).
Jamison, Bud, actor; b. Feb. 15, 1894, Vallejo, Calif.; d. Sept. 30,
    1944 (50).
Jamois, Marguerite, actress; b. Mar. 8, 1901, Paris, France; d. Nov.
    20, 1964 (63).
Jana, La, actress; b. Feb. 24, 1905, Berlin, Germany; d. Mar. 13,
    1940 (35).
Janis, Elsie, actress; b. Mar. 16 1889, Columbus, Ohio; d. Feb. 27,
    1956 (66).
Jannings, Emil, actor; b. July 26, 1886, Brooklyn, N.Y.; d. Jan. 2,
    1950 (63).
Jans, Harry, actor; b. June 6, 1898, Connecticut; d. Feb. 4, 1962 (63).
Janson, Victor, actor & director; b. Sept. 25, 1884, Riga, U.S.S.R.;
    d. July, 1960 (75).
Janssen, David (r.n. David Meyer), actor; b. Mar. 27, 1930, Naponee,
    Neb.; d. Feb. 13, 1980 (49).
Janssen, Walter, actor; b. Feb. 7, 1887, Krefeld, Germany; d. Jan. 1,
    1976 (88).
Jaque-Catelain, actor; b. Feb. 9, 1897, France; d. Mar. 5, 1965 (68).
Jaquet, Frank, actor; b. Mar. 16, 1885, Wisconsin; d. May 11, 1958
    (73).
Jarrett, Arthur L., actor & author; b. Feb. 5, 1884, Marysville,
    Calif.; d. June 12, 1960 (76).
Jarrett, Dan, author & actor; d. Mar. 13, 1938 (44).
Jarvis, Bobby (r.n. Robert C. Jarvis), actor; d. Nov. 13, 1971 (79).
Jarvis, Jean, actress; b. May 23, 1903, Denver, Colo.; d. Mar. 16,
    1933 (29).
Jarvis, Laura E., actress; d. Mar. 9, 1933 (67).
Jarvis, Maurice H., actor; d. Apr. 24, 1960 (75).
Jarvis, Sydney, actor; b. Jan. 11, 1878, Toronto, Canada; d. June 6,
    1939 (61).
Jason, Leigh, director; b. July 26, 1904, New York City; d. Feb. 19,
    1979 (74).
Jason, Will, director; d. Feb. 9, 1970 (60).
Javor, Pal, actor; b. Jan. 31, 1902, Arad, Hungary; d. Aug. 14, 1959
    (57).
Jay, Ernest, actor; b. Sept. 18, 1893, London, England; d. Feb. 8,
    1957 (63).
Jay, Griffin, writer; b. Mar. 29, 1905, Richmond, Ind.; d. Mar. 30,
    1954 (49).
Jayson, Paul, actor; d. Sept., 1979 (54).
Jeans, Desmond, actor; d. Dec., 1974 (71).

Jeans, Ursula, actress; b. May 5, 1906, Simla, India; d. Apr. 21, 1973 (66).
Jeayes, Allan, actor; b. Jan. 19, 1885, London, England; d. Sept. 20, 1963 (78).
Jefferies, Douglas, actor; b. Apr. 21, 1884, Hampstead, England; d. Dec. 27, 1959 (75).
Jeffers, George (Tex), actor; d. Nov. 1, 1979 (75).
Jeffers, John S., actor; d. Jan. 3, 1939 (65).
Jeffers, William L., actor; d. Apr. 18, 1959 (61).
Jefferson, Thomas, actor; b. 1857, New York; d. Apr. 2, 1932 (75).
Jefferson, William Winter, actor; b. London, England; d. Feb. 10, 1946 (70).
Jeffrey, Michael, actor; b. June 14, 1895, Illinois; d. Sept. 30, 1960 (65).
Jeffreys, Ellis, actress; b. May 17, 1872, Ceylon; d. Jan. 21, 1943 (70).
Jeffries, James J., actor & boxer; b. Apr. 15, 1875, Carroll, Ohio; d. Mar. 3, 1953 (77).
Jenkins, Allen (r.n. Al McConegal), actor; b. Apr. 9, 1900, Staten Island, N.Y.; d. July 20, 1974 (74).
Jenks, Frank, actor; b. Nov. 4, 1902, Des Moines, Iowa; d. May 13, 1962 (59).
Jenks, Lulu Burns, actress; d. Apr. 15, 1939 (69).
Jenks, Si (r.n. Howard H. Jenkins), actor; b. Sept. 23, 1876, Norristown, Pa.; d. Jan. 6, 1970 (93).
Jenner, George, actor; d. Dec. 16, 1946 (70).
Jennings, Al, actor & western badman; b. Nov. 25, 1863, Virginia; d. Dec. 26, 1961 (98).
Jennings, Claudia, actress; d. Oct. 3, 1979 (29).
Jennings, DeWitt, actor; b. June 21, 1872, Cameron, Mo.; d. Feb. 28, 1937 (64).
Jennings, S.E. (r.n. Sylvester Ennis Jennings), actor & make-up artist; b. Apr. 8, 1880, Chicago, Ill.; d. Feb. 3, 1932 (51).
Jensen, Eulalie, actress; b. Dec. 24, 1884, St. Louis, Mo.; d. Oct. 7, 1952 (67).
Jerome, Edwin, actor; b. Dec. 30, 1885, New York; d. Sept. 10, 1959 (73).
Jerome, Elmer, actor; b. Jan. 30, 1872, Illinois; d. Aug. 10, 1947 (75).
Jerome, Peter, actor; d. July 9, 1967 (74).
Jerrold, Mary, actress; b. Dec. 4, 1877, London, England; d. Mar. 3, 1955 (77).
Jeske, George, actor; d. Oct. 28, 1951 (60).
Jessel, Patricia, actress; d. June 8, 1968 (47).
Jessner, Leopold, director; b. Mar. 3, 1878, Konigsberg, Russia; d. Dec. 13, 1945 (67).
Jessup, Stanley, actor; b. Chester, N.Y.; d. Oct. 26, 1945 (67).
Jett, Sheldon, actor; d. Feb. 1, 1960 (59).
Jewell, Isabel, actress; b. July 15, 1909, Shoshone, Wyo.; d. Apr. 5, 1972 (62).
Jiggs, chimp; d. Feb. 28, 1938.
Jimenez, George W., actor; b. Nov. 29, 1877, Key West, Fla.; d. Sept. 14, 1945 (67).
Jiminez, Soledad, actress; b. Mar. 10, 1874 (or Feb. 28, 1874), Santander, Spain; d. Oct. 17, 1966 (92).
Job, Thomas, writer; d. July 31, 1947 (46).

Jobson, Edward (r.n. Edwin C. Jobson), actor; b. Feb. 29, 1861,
    Philadelphia, Pa.; d. Feb. 7, 1925 (63).
Joby, Hans, actor; b. Aug. 3, 1884, Kronstadt, Hungary; d. May 1,
    1943 (58).
John, Alice, actress; b. Llanelly, Wales; d. Aug. 9, 1956 (75).
Johns, Bertram, actor; b. England; d. May 9, 1934 (60).
Johnson, A. Martyn, actor & author; d. Jan. 22, 1934.
Johnson, Arthur V., actor; d. Jan. 17, 1916 (39).
Johnson, Chic (r.n. Harold Johnson), actor; b. Mar. 5, 1891,
    Chicago, Ill.; d. Feb. 26, 1962 (70).
Johnson, Chubby (r.n. Charles Randolph Johnson), actor; b. Aug. 13,
    1903, Terre Haute, Ind.; d. Oct. 31, 1974 (71).
Johnson, Edith, actress; b. Aug. 10, 1894, New York; d. Sept. 5,
    1969 (75).
Johnson, Emilie, writer; d. Sept. 23, 1941 (75).
Johnson, Emory, actor & director; d. Apr. 18, 1960 (66).
Johnson, Frances, actress; d. Jan. 1, 1933 (21).
Johnson, Fred, actor; d. Dec. 4, 1971 (72).
Johnson, Hall, choir leader; d. Apr. 30, 1970 (82).
Johnson, Hugh A. (Hackberry), actor; d. Dec. 3, 1979 (91).
Johnson, J. Louis, actor; b. Mar. 20, 1878, Indiana; d. Apr. 29,
    1954 (76).
Johnson, Jason, actor; b. Jan. 16, 1907, Pennsylvania; d. Nov. 24,
    1977 (70).
Johnson, Jay, actor; d. June 13, 1954 (26).
Johnson, Katie, actress; d. May 4, 1957 (78).
Johnson, Kay, actress; b. Nov. 29, 1904, Mt. Vernon, N.Y.; d. Nov. 17,
    1975 (70).
Johnson, Lydia, actress; b. Jan. 6, 1896, Rostov, Russia; d. Apr. 3,
    1969 (73).
Johnson, Marilyn, actress; d. July 19, 1960.
Johnson, Martin, producer; b. Oct. 9, 1884, Rockford, Ill.; d. Jan.
    13, 1937 (52).
Johnson, Nunnally, author & producer; b. Dec. 5, 1897, Columbus,
    Ga.; d. Mar. 25, 1977 (79).
Johnson, Orrin, actor; d. Nov. 24, 1943 (78).
Johnson, Osa, producer; d. Jan. 7, 1953 (58).
Johnson, Ray, actor; d. Jan. 25, 1976.
Johnson, Rita, actress; b. Aug. 13, 1913, Massachusetts; d. Oct. 31,
    1965 (52).
Johnson, S. Kenneth, actor; d. Nov. 1, 1974 (62).
Johnson, Tefft, actor & director; b. Washington; d. Oct., 1956.
Johnson, Tor, actor; b. Oct. 19, 1903, Sweden; d. May 12, 1971 (67).
Johnson, Walter, actor; b. Feb. 25, 1906, Chicago, Ill.; d. June 28,
    1946 (40).
Johnson, William, actor; d. Mar. 6, 1957 (38).
Johnston, Agnes Christine, writer; b. Swissvale, Pa.; d. July 19,
    1978 (82).
Johnston, Barry, actor; b. Dec. 24, 1869, England; d. Oct. 22, 1953
    (83).
Johnston, Caroline K., actress; b. Dec. 29, 1875, Illinois; d. July
    8, 1962 (86).
Johnston, J.W. (r.n. John William Johnston), actor; b. Oct. 2, 1876,
    Kilkee Co. Clain, Ireland; d. July 29, 1946 (69).
Johnston, Johnny, actor; d. Jan. 4, 1931 (62).

Johnston, Lorimer, actor; b. Nov. 2, 1858, Maysville, Ky.; d. Feb. 20, 1941 (82).
Johnston, Mac, dancer; d. Mar. 22, 1977 (71).
Johnston, Moffat, actor; b. Aug. 18, 1886, Scotland; d. Nov. 3, 1935 (49).
Johnston, Oliver, actor; d. Dec. 22, 1966 (78).
Johnstone, Lamar, actor; d. May 21, 1919 (34).
Joiner, Patricia, actress; d. Oct. 30, 1978 (49).
Jolley, I. Stanford, actor; b. Oct. 24, 1900, Elizabeth, N.J.; d. Dec. 6, 1978 (78).
Jolson, Al, actor & singer; b. May 26, 1886, St. Petersburg, Russia; d. Oct. 23, 1950 (64).
Jonay, Roberta, actress; d. Apr. 19, 1976 (55).
Jones, Billy, actor; d. Nov. 23, 1940 (51).
Jones, Bobby, golfer; b. Mar. 17, 1902, Atlanta, Ga.; d. Dec. 18, 1971 (69).
Jones, Buck, actor; b. Dec. 4, 1889, Vincennes, Ind.; d. Nov. 30, 1942 (52).
Jones, Chester, actor; b. Jan. 22, 1899, Kentucky; d. June 26, 1975 (76).
Jones, Clarence Y. (Fat), stuntman; b. Sept. 21, 1892, New York; d. Feb. 24, 1963 (70).
Jones, Curt, actor; d. Dec., 1956 (83).
Jones, Elizabeth "Tiny," actress; b. Nov. 25, 1875, Wales; d. Mar. 21, 1952 (76).
Jones, Emrys, actor; b. Sept. 22, 1915, Manchester, England; d. July 10, 1972 (56).
Jones, F. Richard, director; b. Sept. 7, 1893, Missouri; d. Dec. 14, 1930 (37).
Jones, Freda M., actress; d. Oct. 24, 1976 (79).
Jones, Gordon, actor; b. Apr. 5, 1912, Iowa; d. June 20, 1963 (51).
Jones, Grover, director & writer; d. Sept. 24, 1940 (52).
Jones, Harmon C. (r.n. Harmon Clifford Jones), director; b. June 3, 1911, Canada; d. July 10, 1972 (61).
Jones, Hazel, actress; d. Nov. 13, 1974 (79).
Jones, J. Parks (see Jones, James Parks)
Jones, James Parks (J. Parks Jones; Parks Jones); b. Aug. 22, 1890, Cincinnati, Ohio; d. Jan. 11, 1950 (59).
Jones, Mark, actor; b. Dec. 9, 1889, California; d. Apr. 14, 1965 (75).
Jones, Morgan, actor; d. Sept. 21, 1951 (72).
Jones, Norman, actor; d. Mar. 26, 1963 (35).
Jones, Orville "Hoppy," recording artist ("Ink Spots"); d. Oct. 17, 1944 (42).
Jones, Parks (see Jones, James Parks)
Jones, R.D., actor; d. June 12, 1925.
Jones, Rozene Kemper, actress; b. Aug. 21, 1892, Ohio; d. July 9, 1964 (71).
Jones, Spike, recording artist; b. Dec. 14, 1911, Long Beach, Calif.; d. May 1, 1965 (53).
Jones, Stan, actor & composer; b. June 5, 1914, Arizona; d. Dec. 13, 1963 (49).
Jones, T.C. (r.n. Thomas Craig Jones), actor; b. Oct. 26, 1920, Pennsylvania; d. Sept. 25, 1971 (50).
Jones, Thaddeus, actor; b. Sept. 8, 1874, Kentucky; d. Dec. 19, 1960 (86).

Jones, Trefor, actor; b. Aug. 27, 1902, South Wales; d. Jan. 22,
  1965 (62).
Jones, Wallace, actor; d. Oct. 7, 1936 (53).
Jordan, Bobby, actor; b. Apr. 1, 1923, New York; d. Sept. 10, 1965
  (42).
Jordan, Egon, actor; b. Mar. 19, 1902, Dux; d. Dec. 27, 1978 (76).
Jordan, Jules, actor; d. July 22, 1925 (54).
Jordan, Louis, band leader; b. July 8, 1908, Brinkley, Ark.; d. Feb.
  4, 1975 (66).
Jordan, Marian, actress; b. Apr. 15, 1898, Peoria, Ill.; d. Apr. 7,
  1961 (62).
Jordan, Sid, actor; b. Aug. 12, 1889, Muskogee, Okla.; d. Sept. 30,
  1970 (81).
Jordon, Harry, actor; d. June, 1945 (43).
Jorge, Paul, actor; d. Dec. 31, 1928 (80).
Jorgensen, Emilius A., actor; b. Mar. 15, 1888, Denmark; d. Dec. 5,
  1963 (75).
Jose, Edward, actor & director; d. Dec. 18, 1930.
Jose, Richard, actor; d. Oct. 20, 1941 (71).
Josephson, Julien, writer; b. Roseburg, Ore.; d. Apr. 13, 1959 (75).
Joshi, Pravin, actor; d. Jan. 19, 1979 (45).
Joslin, Howard, actor; b. Oct. 8, 1907, Georgia; d. Aug. 1, 1975 (67).
Joslin, Margaret, actress; b. Aug. 6, 1883, Cleveland, Ohio; d. Oct.
  14, 1956 (73).
Jostyn, Jay, actor; b. Dec. 13, 1901, Wisconsin; d. June 25, 1976 (74).
Joube, Romuald, actor; b. 1876; d. 1949 (73).
Jouvet, Louis, actor; b. Crozon, France; d. Aug. 16, 1951 (63).
Joy, Ernest, actor; b. Jan. 20, 1878, Iowa; d. Feb. 12, 1924 (46).
Joy, Nicholas, actor; b. Jan. 31, 1884, Paris, France; d. Mar. 16,
  1964 (80).
Joy, William, actor; b. Oct. 1, 1886, Iowa; d. Aug. 8, 1951 (64).
Joyce, Alice, actress; b. Oct. 1, 1890, Kansas City, Mo.; d. Oct. 9,
  1955 (65).
Joyce, James, actor; b. June 9, 1920, Ohio; d. May 17, 1974 (53).
Joyce, Martin, actor; d. Jan. 2, 1937 (22).
Joyce, Peggy Hopkins, actress; b. Norfolk, Va.; d. June 12, 1957 (63).
Juarez, Lilia, actress; d. May 26, 1970.
Judd, John, actor; d. Oct. 7, 1950 (57).
Judels, Charles, actor; b. Aug. 17, 1881, Amsterdam, Holland; d. Feb.
  14, 1969 (87).
Judge, Arline, actress; b. Feb. 21, 1912, Bridgeport, Conn.; d. Feb.
  7, 1974 (61).
Jugert, Rudolf, director & writer; b. Sept. 30, 1907, Hannover,
  Germany; d. Apr. 14, 1979 (71).
Julian, Alexander, actor; b. May 27, 1897, Constantinople, Turkey;
  d. May 18, 1945 (47).
Julian, Rupert (r.n. Percival T. Hayes), actor & director; b. Jan.
  26, 1879, Auckland, New Zealand; d. Dec. 27, 1943 (64).
June, Mildred, actress; d. June 19, 1940 (34).
June, Ray, cinematographer; b. Ithaca, N.Y.; d. May 27, 1958 (60).
Junkermann, Hans, actor; b. Feb. 24, 1872, Stuttgart, Germany;
  d. June 12, 1943 (71).
Justice, James Robertson, actor; b. June 15, 1905, Wigtown, Scotland;
  d. July 2, 1975 (70).
Justin, Morgan (r.n. Claude Olin "Tex" Wurman), actor; b. Wichita
  Falls, Tex.; d. July 7, 1974 (47).
Juul, Ralph, actor; d. Nov. 5, 1955 (67).

Kaart, Hans, actor & singer; d. June, 1963 (39).
Kachalov, Vasily I., actor; b. Feb. 11, 1875, Vilnius, Lithuania;
    d. Sept. 30, 1948 (73).
Kadar, Jan, director; d. June 1, 1979 (61).
Kahanamoku, Duke, actor & swimmer; b. Aug. 24, 1890, Honolulu,
    Hawaii; d. Jan. 22, 1968 (77).
Kahn, Florence, actress; b. Mar. 3, 1878, Memphis, Tenn.; d. Jan. 13,
    1951 (72).
Kahn, William "Smitty," actor; d. May 14, 1959 (77).
Kaiser-Titz, Erich, actor; b. 1878; d. Nov. 22, 1928 (50).
Kalich, Bertha, actress & opera singer; b. May 17, 1874, Lemberg,
    Poland; d. Apr. 18, 1939 (64).
Kalich, Jacob, actor; b. Nov. 18, 1891, Rymanov, Poland; d. Mar. 16,
    1975 (83).
Kalionzes, Janet, actress; d. Aug. 10, 1961 (39).
Kaliz, Armand, actor; b. Oct. 23, 1887, Paris, France; d. Feb. 1,
    1941 (53).
Kalkhurst, Eric, actor; d. Oct. 13, 1957 (55).
Kallman, Richard, actor; b. July 7, 1933, Brooklyn, N.Y.; d. Feb. 22,
    1980 (46).
Kalser, Erwin, actor; b. Feb. 22, 1883, Berlin, Germany; d. Mar. 26,
    1958 (75).
Kalthoum, Um, singer; d. Feb. 3, 1975 (77).
Kamaryt, Joseph, actor; b. Jan. 19, 1890, Illinois; d. June 14, 1977
    (87).
Kamen, Milt, actor; b. Mar. 5, 1921, Hurleyville, N.Y.; d. Feb. 24,
    1977 (55).
Kamenzky, Elizer, actor; d. Mar., 1957 (68).
Kamiyama, Sojin, actor; b. Jan. 30, 1884, Sendai, Japan; d. July 28,
    1954 (70).
Kammer, Klaus, actor; b. Jan. 10, 1929, Hannover, Germany; d. May 9,
    1964 (35).
Kampers, Fritz, actor; b. July 14, 1891, Germany; d. Sept. 1, 1950
    (59).
Kane, Blanche, actress; d. Aug. 24, 1937 (48).
Kane, Diana, actress; b. Jan. 10, 1901, Alabama; d. Apr. 20, 1977
    (76).
Kane, Eddie, actor; b. Aug. 12, 1889, St. Louis, Mo.; d. Apr. 30,
    1969 (79).
Kane, Gail, actress; d. Feb. 17, 1966 (81).
Kane, Helen, actress; b. Aug. 4, 1904, New York City; d. Sept. 26,
    1966 (62).
Kane, John P., actor; d. Dec. 1, 1945 (60).
Kane, Johnny, actor; d. Mar. 15, 1969.
Kane, Joseph, director; b. May 19, 1894, San Diego, Calif.; d. Aug.
    25, 1975 (81).
Kane, Lida, actress; d. Oct. 7, 1955.
Kane, Marion, actress; d. June 21, 1943 (33).
Kane, Whitford, actor; b. Jan. 30, 1881, Larne, Ireland; d. Dec. 17,
    1956 (75).
Kann, Lilly, actress; b. Berlin, Germany; d. Nov. 2, 1978 (80).
Kapoor, Prithvi Raj, actor; d. May 29, 1972 (66).
Kappeler, Alfred, actor; b. Zurich, Switzerland; d. Oct. 29, 1945
    (69).
Karchow, Ernst, actor; b. Sept. 23, 1892; d. Oct. 7, 1953 (61).
Kardos, Leslie, director & author; d. Apr. 11, 1962 (56).

Karels, Harvey, actor; b. Mar. 4, 1905, Illinois; d. Nov. 17, 1975
    (70).
Karloff, Boris (r.n. William Henry Pratt), actor; b. Nov. 23, 1887,
    Dulwich, England; d. Feb. 2, 1969 (81).
Karlstadt, Liesl, actress; b. Dec. 12, 1892, Munich, Germany;
    d. July 27, 1960 (67).
Karlweis, Oscar, actor; b. June 10, 1894, Hinterbuhl bei Wein,
    Austria; d. Jan. 24, 1956 (61).
Karnes, Robert, actor; d. Dec. 4, 1979 (62).
Karns, Roscoe, actor; b. Sept. 7, 1891, San Bernardino, Calif.;
    d. Feb. 6, 1970 (78).
Karr, Darwin, actor; b. July 25, 1875, Almond, N.Y.; d. Dec. 31,
    1945 (70).
Kashey, Abe (King Kong), actor; b. Nov. 28, 1903, Syria; d. Sept. 24,
    1965 (61).
Kastner, Bruno, actor; b. Jan. 3, 1890, Soest, Germany; d. June 10,
    1932 (42).
Kasznar, Kurt, actor; b. Aug. 13, 1913, Vienna, Austria; d. Aug. 6,
    1979 (65).
Katch, Kurt, actor; b. Jan. 26, 1893, Poland; d. Aug. 14, 1958 (65).
Katterjohn, Monte, writer; b. Oct. 20, 1891, Boonville, Ind.; d. Sept.
    8, 1949 (57).
Katzman, Sam, producer; b. July 14, 1901, New York City; d. Aug. 4,
    1973 (72).
Kaufman, Joseph, actor; d. Feb. 1, 1918.
Kaufmann, Willy, actor; b. Oct. 10, 1891, Germany; d. Dec. 21, 1966
    (75).
Kaul, Avtar, director; d. July 21, 1974 (34).
Kay, Henry, actor; d. Dec. 9, 1968 (57).
Kay, Marjorie, actress; d. June 25, 1949.
Kaye, Albert P., actor; b. Ringwood, England; d. Sept. 7, 1946 (68).
Kaye, Phil, actor; d. Nov. 28, 1959 (47).
Kaye, Sparky, actor; d. Aug. 23, 1971 (65).
Kayser, Charles Willy, actor; b. Jan. 28, 1881, Metz, Germany;
    d. July 10, 1942 (61).
Kayssler, Christian, actor; b. June 14, 1898, Breslau, Germany;
    d. Mar. 10, 1944 (45).
Kayssler, Friedrich, actor; b. Apr. 7, 1874, Neurode, Germany;
    d. Apr. 24, 1945 (71).
Kean, Richard, actor; b. Jan. 1, 1881, England; d. Dec. 29, 1959 (78).
Keane, Doris, actress; b. Dec. 12, 1881, Michigan; d. Nov. 25, 1945
    (63).
Keane, Edward, actor; b. May 28, 1884, New York; d. Oct. 12, 1959
    (75).
Keane, Raymond, actor; b. Sept. 6, 1906, Denver, Colo.; d. Aug. 24,
    1973 (66).
Kearns, Allen, actor; b. 1893, Canada; d. Apr. 20, 1956 (62).
Kearns, Joseph, actor; b. Feb. 12, 1907, Utah; d. Feb. 17, 1962 (55).
Keatan, Harry, actor; b. May 26, 1896, Russia; d. June 18, 1966 (70).
Keating, Fred, actor & magician; b. Mar. 27, 1897, New York City;
    d. June 29, 1961 (64).
Keating, Larry, actor; b. Apr. 13, 1899, Minnesota; d. Aug. 26,
    1963 (64).
Keaton, Buster, actor; b. Oct. 4, 1895, Piqua, Kans.; d. Feb. 1,
    1966 (70).

Keaton, Joe, actor; d. Jan. 13, 1946 (79).
Keckley, Jane, actress; b. Sept. 10, 1876, Charleston, S.C.; d. Aug.
    14, 1963 (86).
Kedrov, Mikhail, actor; d. Mar. 22, 1972 (78).
Keefe, Cornelius (Jack Hill), actor; b. July 13, 1900, Boston, Mass.;
    d. Dec. 11, 1972 (72).
Keefe, Zena, actress; d. Nov. 16, 1977 (82).
Keegan, Barry, actor; b. 1922, Dublin, Ireland; d. Sept., 1977 (55).
Keeler, Anna May, actress; d. Mar. 31, 1935 (19).
Keeler, "Sugar" Willie, actor; b. Sept. 14, 1890, Colorado; d. Jan.
    17, 1964 (73).
Keen, Malcolm, actor; b. Aug. 8, 1887, Bristol, England; d. Jan. 30,
    1970 (82).
Keenan, Frank, actor; b. Apr. 8, 1858, Dubuque, Iowa; d. Feb. 24,
    1929 (70).
Keene, Elsie, actress; d. Dec. 29, 1973.
Keene, Mattie, actress; d. Sept. 1, 1944 (82).
Keene, Richard (r.n. Richard Dooley), actor; b. Sept. 16, 1899,
    Philadelphia, Pa.; d. Mar. 12, 1971 (71).
Keene, Tom (George Duryea; Richard Powers), actor; b. Dec. 30, 1896,
    Rochester, N.Y.; d. Aug. 4, 1963 (66).
Keesee, Oscar, actor; b. Philippines; d. Mar. 15, 1968 (49).
Keightley, Cyril, actor; b. Nov. 10, 1875, Wellington, Australia;
    d. Aug. 14, 1929 (53).
Keil, Arno, actor; b. Aug. 17, 1900; d. Apr., 1974 (73).
Keith, Eugene, actor; d. Feb. 6, 1955.
Keith, Ian, actor; b. Feb. 27, 1899, Boston, Mass.; d. Mar. 26,
    1960 (61).
Keith, Richard, actor; b. Jan. 1, 1905, New York; d. Sept. 16, 1976
    (61).
Keith, Robert, actor; b. Feb. 10, 1898, Fowler, Ind.; d. Dec. 23,
    1966 (68).
Keith, Sherwood (r.n. Sherwood Keith La Count), actor; b. May 19,
    1912, Massachusetts; d. Feb. 21, 1972 (59).
Keith-Johnston, Colin, actor; b. Oct. 8, 1896, London, England;
    d. Jan. 3, 1980 (83).
Kelcey, Herbert, actor; b. Oct. 10, 1855, London, England; d. July
    10, 1917 (61).
Kellard, John E., actor; b. May 14, 1863, London, England; d. June 8,
    1929 (66).
Kellard, Ralph, actor; d. Feb. 5, 1955 (83).
Kellaway, Cecil, actor; b. Aug. 22, 1890, Capetown, South Africa;
    d. Feb. 28, 1973 (82).
Keller, Gertrude, actress; d. July 12, 1951 (70).
Keller, Nell Clark, actress; d. Sept. 2, 1965 (89).
Kellerman, Annette, actress & swimmer; b. July 6, 1888, Sydney,
    Australia; d. Nov. 5, 1975 (87).
Kelley, Mary, actress; d. June 7, 1941 (46).
Kellogg, Cornelia, actress; d. Feb. 21, 1934 (57).
Kellogg, Ray, director; d. July 5, 1976 (70).
Kelly, Anthony Paul, writer; d. Sept. 26, 1932 (35).
Kelly, Dorothy, actress; b. Feb. 12, 1894, Philadelphia, Pa.; d. May
    31, 1966 (72).
Kelly, Dorothy, actress; d. Nov. 28, 1969 (51).
Kelly, Emmett ("Weary Willie"), circus clown & actor; b. Dec. 9,
    1898, Sedan, Kans.; d. Mar. 28, 1979 (80).

Kelly, Fannie, actress; d. Jan. 27, 1925 (49).
Kelly, Gregory, actor; d. July 9, 1927 (36).
Kelly, Harold E., actor; d. May 27, 1941.
Kelly, J. Gordon, actor; d. Dec., 1939 (55).
Kelly, James T., actor; b. July 10, 1854, Ireland; d. Nov. 12, 1933 (79).
Kelly, John, actor; b. June 29, 1901, Boston, Mass.; d. Dec. 9, 1947 (46).
Kelly, Kitty, actress; b. Apr. 27, 1902, New York City; d. June 29, 1968 (66).
Kelly, Lew, actor; b. Aug. 24, 1879, St. Louis, Mo.; d. June 10, 1944 (64).
Kelly, Maurice, actor; d. Aug. 28, 1974 (59).
Kelly, Nan (Nan Kelly Yorke), actress; d. Oct. 26, 1978 (83).
Kelly, Nell, actress; d. Dec. 16, 1939 (29).
Kelly, Patrick J., actor; b. July 18, 1891, Philadelphia, Pa.; d. Mar. 19, 1938 (46).
Kelly, Paul, actor; b. Aug. 9, 1899, Brooklyn, N.Y.; d. Nov. 6, 1956 (57).
Kelly, Robert Henry, general manager; b. July 11, 1884, Illinois; d. Aug. 12, 1968 (84).
Kelly, Seamus, actor & critic; b. Belfast, Ireland; d. June 10, 1979 (67).
Kelly, "Tiny" Jimmie, actor; b. July 22, 1914, New York; d. May 5, 1964 (49).
Kelly, Walter C., actor; b. Oct. 29, 1873, Mineville, N.Y.; d. Jan. 6, 1939 (65).
Kelly, William J., actor; b. June 16, 1875, Newburyport, Mass.; d. May 17, 1949 (73).
Kelsall, Moultrie, actor; d. Feb. 12, 1980 (78).
Kelsey, Fred, actor; b. Aug. 20, 1884, Sandusky, Ohio; d. Sept. 2, 1961 (77).
Kelso, Mayme, actress; b. Feb. 28, 1867, Columbus, Ohio; d. June 5, 1946 (79).
Kelt, John, actor; d. Mar. 9, 1935 (70).
Kelton, Frank C., actor; d. May 24, 1938 (49).
Kelton, Pert, actress; b. Oct. 14, 1907, Great Falls, Mont.; d. Oct. 30, 1968 (61).
Kelton, Richard, actor; d. Nov. 27, 1978 (34).
Kemp, Paul, actor; b. May 20, 1889, Bad Godesberg, Germany; d. Aug. 13, 1953 (64).
Kemper, Charles, actor; b. Sept. 6, 1900, Oklahoma; d. May 12, 1950 (49).
Kemper, Joe, actor; d. Aug. 3, 1948 (65).
Kendall, Cy, actor; b. Mar. 10, 1898, Missouri; d. July 22, 1953 (55).
Kendall, Henry, actor; b. May 28, 1897, London, England; d. June 9, 1962 (65).
Kendall, Kay, actress; b. May 21, 1927, Withernsea, England; d. Sept. 6, 1959 (32).
Kendrick, Bryan, actor; d. Mar. 11, 1970 (40).
Kenessey, Joseph, actor; b. Dec. 31, 1881, Hungary; d. Mar. 6, 1951 (69).
Kennedy, Charles Rann, actor & author; b. Feb. 14, 1871, Derby, England; d. Feb. 16, 1950 (79).
Kennedy, Douglas (Keith Douglas), actor; b. Sept. 14, 1915, New York; d. Aug. 10, 1973 (57).

Kennedy, Edgar, actor; b. Apr. 26, 1890, Monterey, Calif.; d. Nov. 9, 1948 (58).
Kennedy, Fred, actor & stuntman; d. Dec. 5, 1958 (48).
Kennedy, Jack, actor; d. Nov. 6, 1960.
Kennedy, Joseph C., actor; d. May 4, 1949 (59).
Kennedy, Joyce, actress; b. July 1, 1898, London, England; d. Mar. 12, 1943 (44).
Kennedy, King, actor; d. Nov. 1, 1974 (70).
Kennedy, Merna, actress; b. Sept. 7, 1908, Kankakee, Ill.; d. Dec. 20, 1944 (36).
Kennedy, Tom, actor; b. July 15, 1885, New York City; d. Oct. 6, 1965 (80).
Kenneth, Harry D., actor; d. Jan. 18, 1929 (75).
Kenneth, Keith (see Hitchcock, Keith)
Kenney, Jack, actor; b. Nov. 16, 1886, Illinois; d. May 26, 1964 (77).
Kenny, Bill, recording artist ("Ink Spots"), d. Mar. 23, 1978 (63).
Kenny, Colin (r.n. Oswald Joseph Collins), actor; b. Dec. 4, 1888, England; d. Dec. 2, 1968 (79).
Kent, Arnold (r.n. Lido Manetti), actor; b. Jan. 21, 1899, Florence, Italy; d. Sept. 28, 1928 (29).
Kent, Charles, actor; d. May 21, 1923 (69).
Kent, Craufurd, actor; b. Oct. 12, 1881, England; d. May 14, 1953 (71).
Kent, Gerald, actor; d. Nov. 5, 1944.
Kent, Kate, actress; d. Dec. 11, 1934 (70).
Kent, Keneth, actor; b. Apr. 20, 1892, Liverpool, England; d. Nov. 17, 1963 (71).
Kent, Larry (r.n. Henri W. Trumbull), actor; b. Sept. 15, 1900, California; d. Nov. 7, 1967 (67).
Kent, Leon (Leon de La Mothe), actor & director; b. Dec. 26, 1880, New Orleans, La.; d. June 12, 1943 (62).
Kent, Raymond, actor; d. Nov. 1, 1948 (62).
Kent, Robert (Douglas Blackley), actor; b. Dec. 3, 1908, Hartford, Conn.; d. May 4, 1955 (46).
Kent, Stapleton, actor; b. May 15, 1883, England; d. Apr. 3, 1962 (78).
Kent, Willard, actor; b. Mar. 17, 1882, Pennsylvania; d. Sept. 5, 1968 (86).
Kent, William, actor; b. St. Paul, Minn.; d. Oct. 5, 1945 (59).
Kenton, Erle C., director; b. Aug. 1, 1896, Norboro, Mo.; d. Jan. 28, 1980 (83).
Kenton, James B. (Pop), actor; b. Oct. 11, 1866, Missouri; d. Feb. 11, 1952 (85).
Kentuck, Joe, actor; d. Feb. 7, 1923.
Kenyon, Charles, writer; b. Nov. 2, 1880, San Francisco, Calif.; d. June 27, 1961 (80).
Kenyon, Doris, actress; b. Sept. 5, 1897, Syracuse, N.Y.; d. Sept. 1, 1979 (81).
Kenyon, Neil, actor; b. Scotland; d. June 1, 1946 (73).
Kenyon, Robert, actor; d. Dec. 19, 1928 (39).
Kerby, Marion, actress; d. Dec. 16, 1957 (79).
Kern, Earl, actor; d. Oct. 17, 1945 (64).
Kern, James V., writer; b. Sept. 22, 1909, New York City; d. Nov. 9, 1966 (57).
Kerr, Bob, director & actor; d. Sept. 5, 1960 (65).

Kerr, Donald, actor; b. Aug. 5, 1891, Eagle Grove, Iowa; d. Jan. 25, 1977 (85).
Kerr, Frederick, actor; b. Oct. 11, 1858, London, England; d. May 2, 1933 (74).
Kerr, Jane, actress; d. Nov. 19, 1954 (83).
Kerr, Lorence V., actor; d. Feb. 25, 1968.
Kerrick, Tom, actor; d. Apr. 27, 1927 (32).
Kerrigan, J.M., actor; b. Dec. 16, 1884, Ireland; d. Apr. 29, 1964 (79).
Kerrigan, J. Warren, actor; b. July 25, 1879, Louisville, Ky.; d. June 9, 1947 (67).
Kerrigan, Kathleen, actress; d. Jan. 27, 1957 (88).
Kerry, Norman, actor; b. June 16, 1894, Rochester, N.Y.; d. Jan. 12, 1956 (61).
Kerry, Pat X. (see Moriarty, Patrick)
Kershaw, Eleanor, actress; b. Nov. 19, 1884, Missouri; d. Sept. 13, 1971 (86).
Kershaw, Wilette, actress; d. May 4, 1960 (78).
Kerwood, Dick, actor & stuntman; b. Oct. 8, 1892, Virginia; d. Oct. 15, 1924 (32).
Ketchum, Robyna Neilson, actress; d. Nov. 9, 1972.
Key, Kathleen (Kitty Lanahan), actress; b. Apr. 1, 1907, New York; d. Dec. 22, 1954 (47).
Keyes, Johnny (Spaghetti Joe), actor; d. Aug. 28, 1966 (74).
Keys, Nelson, actor; b. Aug. 7, 1886, London, England; d. Apr. 26, 1939 (52).
Khayyam, Hassan, actor; b. May 5, 1900, W. Pakistan; d. Oct. 31, 1964 (64).
Kibbee, Guy, actor; b. Mar. 6, 1882, El Paso, Tex.; d. May 24, 1956 (74).
Kibbee, Milton (r.n. Milne Bryan Kibbee), actor; b. Jan. 27, 1896, New Mexico; d. Apr. 17, 1970 (74).
Kidd, Kathleen, actress; d. Feb. 23, 1961 (62).
Kidder, Hugh, actor; d. June 3, 1952 (72).
Kieffer, Phillip, actor; b. July 31, 1886, Pennsylvania; d. July 13, 1962 (75).
Kieffer, Ruth A. (r.n. Ruth Albrecht Kieffer), actress; b. Apr. 13, 1891, Washington; d. June 30, 1965 (74).
Kiepura, Jan, actor & singer; b. May 6, 1902, Warsaw, Poland; d. Aug. 15, 1966 (64).
Kiernan, James, actor; d. July 24, 1975 (35).
Kikume, Al (r.n. Elmer Kawelo Gozier), actor; b. Oct. 9, 1894, Kansas; d. Mar. 27, 1972 (77).
Kilbi, George (see Cory, Victor)
Kilbride, Percy, actor; b. July 16, 1888, San Francisco, Calif.; d. Dec. 11, 1964 (76).
Kilbride, Richard D., actor; d. June 20, 1967 (48).
Kilgallen, Dorothy, actress, tv panelist, & news columnist; b. July 3, 1913, Chicago, Ill.; d. Nov. 8, 1965 (52).
Kilgour, Joseph, actor; b. July 11, 1863, Ayr, Ontario, Canada; d. Apr. 20, 1933 (69).
Kilian, Victor, actor; b. Mar. 6, 1898, Jersey City, N.J.; d. Mar. 11, 1979 (81).
Kilpack, Bennett, actor; b. Feb. 6, 1883, England; d. Aug. 17, 1962 (79).

Kilpatrick, Tom, writer; b. Nov. 16, 1898, Helena, Mont.; d. Mar. 11, 1962 (63).

Kimball, Edward M., actor; b. June 26, 1859, Keokuk, Iowa; d. Jan. 4, 1938 (78).

Kimball, Pauline Garrett, actress; b. Mar. 15, 1860; d. Dec. 11, 1919 (59).

Kimmins, Anthony, director, author, & actor; b. Nov. 10, 1901, Harrow, England; d. May 19, 1964 (62).

King, Allyn, actress; d. Mar. 30, 1930 (31).

King, Anita, actress; d. June 10, 1963 (74).

King, Boyd, actor; d. Feb. 19, 1940 (34).

King, Burton, director & producer; b. Aug. 25, 1877, Cincinnati, Ohio; d. May 4, 1944 (66).

King, Carlton, actor & director; b. Dec. 15, 1881, St. Louis, Mo.; d. July 6, 1932 (50).

King, Charles, actor & singer; b. Oct. 31, 1891, New York City; d. Jan. 11, 1944 (52).

King, Charles, singer; d. Dec. 14, 1946 (59).

King, Charles, actor; b. Feb. 21, 1895, Texas; d. May 7, 1957 (62).

King, Claude, actor; b. Jan. 15, 1875, England; d. Sept. 18, 1941 (66).

King, Dennis, actor; b. Nov. 2, 1897, Coventry, England; d. May 21, 1971 (73).

King, Emmett C. (r.n. Emmett Carleton King), actor; b. May 31, 1865, Griffin, Ga.; d. Apr. 21, 1953 (87).

King, Eugene, actor; d. Nov.' 26, 1950 (66).

King, Henry, orchestra leader; d. Aug. 8, 1974 (68).

King, Joseph, actor; b. Feb. 9, 1883, Texas; d. Apr. 11, 1951 (68).

King, Leslie, actor; d. Oct. 10, 1947 (71).

King, Louis, director; b. June 28, 1898, Christianburg, Va.; d. Sept. 7, 1962 (64).

King, Lucille, actress; d. Aug., 1977 (91).

King, Nosmo, actor; d. Jan. 13, 1949 (63).

King, Stanley, actor; b. Feb. 6, 1904, England; d. Dec. 3, 1975 (71).

Kingdon, Dorothy, actress; d. Mar. 31, 1939 (45).

Kingdon, Frank, actor; b. Providence, R.I.; d. Apr. 9, 1937 (82).

Kingsford, Alison, actress; d. June 10, 1950 (51).

Kingsford, Walter, actor; b. Sept. 20, 1881, Redhill, England; d. Feb. 7, 1958 (76).

Kingsley, Florida, actress; d. Mar. 19, 1937 (70).

Kingston, Harry, actor; d. July 4, 1951 (37).

Kingston, Tom, actor; b. Mar. 15, 1901, New York; d. Jan. 26, 1959 (57).

Kingston, Winifred, actress; b. Nov. 11, 1894, England; d. Feb. 3, 1967 (72).

Kinnell, Murray, actor; b. July 24, 1889, London, England; d. Aug. 11, 1954 (65).

Kinney, Clyde (r.n. Robert Clyde Ruffner), actor; b. Oct. 6, 1892, Pennsylvania; d. May 15, 1962 (69).

Kinsella, Kathleen, actress; b. Liverpool, England; d. Mar. 25, 1961 (83).

Kinsella, Walter, actor; b. New York City; d. May 11, 1975 (74).

Kinsolving, Lee, actor; d. Dec. 4, 1974 (36).

Kipling, Richard, actor; b. Aug. 21, 1879, New York; d. Mar. 11, 1965 (85).

Kippen, Manart, actor; d. Oct. 12, 1947 (55).
Kirby, David D., actor; b. July 16, 1883, Missouri; d. Apr. 4, 1954
    (70).
Kirby, George, actor; b. Feb. 18, 1879, London, England; d. Dec. 2,
    1953 (74).
Kirby, John, actor; d. July 3, 1973 (41).
Kirby, Ollie (Ollie Kirkby), actress; b. Sept. 26, 1886, Pennsylvania;
    d. Oct. 7, 1964 (78).
Kirchhoff, Fritz, director & actor; b. Dec. 10, 1901, Hannover,
    Germany; d. July 25, 1953 (51).
Kirk, Bertha W., actress; d. Sept. 9, 1928 (50).
Kirk, Jack, actor; d. Sept. 3, 1948 (53).
Kirk, Joe (r.n. Joseph Kirk), actor; b. Oct. 1, 1903, New York;
    d. Apr. 16, 1975 (71).
Kirk, Joseph (see Kirk, Joe)
Kirke, Donald (r.n. William H.F. Kirk), actor; b. May 17, 1901,
    Jersey City, N.J.; d. May 18, 1971 (70).
Kirkland, David S. (r.n. David Henry Swim), director & actor;
    b. Nov. 26, 1878, San Francisco, Calif.; d. Oct. 27, 1964 (85).
Kirkland, Hardee (r.n. Noble Rarda Kirkland), actor; b. Georgia;
    d. Feb. 18, 1929 (63).
Kirkland, Jack, writer; b. St. Louis, Mo.; d. Feb. 22, 1969 (66).
Kirkland, Muriel, actress; b. Aug. 19, 1903, Yonkers, N.Y.; d. Sept.
    26, 1971 (68).
Kirkpatrick, Jess, actor; d. Aug. 9, 1976 (78).
Kirkwood, Jack, actor; b. Aug. 6, 1894, Scotland; d. Aug. 2, 1964
    (69).
Kirkwood, James, actor & director; b. Feb. 22, 1875, Grand Rapids,
    Mich.; d. Aug. 24, 1963 (88).
Kirkwood-Hackett, Mme. Eva, actress; d. Feb. 8, 1968 (91).
Kissen, Murray, actor; d. Feb. 16, 1958 (68).
Kitzmiller, John, actor; b. Dec. 4, 1913, Battle Creek, Mich.;
    d. Feb. 23, 1965 (51).
Klein, Al, actor; d. Sept. 5, 1951 (66).
Klein, Robert, actor; b. May 16, 1880, Paris, France; d. Dec. 21,
    1960 (80).
Kleinau, Willy A., actor; d. Oct. 23, 1957 (49).
Klein-Rogge, Rudolf, actor; b. Nov. 24, 1888, Cologne, Germany;
    d. 1955 (67).
Kline, Benjamin, cinematographer; b. July 11, 1894, Birmingham, Ala.;
    d. Jan. 7, 1974 (79).
Kline, Brady, actor; b. June 4, 1892, Tilton, Ohio; d. Nov. 18,
    1946 (54).
Klinger, Paul, actor; b. June 14, 1907, Essen, Germany; d. Nov.,
    1971 (64).
Klopfer, Eugene, actor; b. Mar. 10, 1886, Talheim, Germany; d. Mar.
    3, 1950 (63).
Knabb, Harry G., actor; d. Dec. 17, 1955 (64).
Knaggs, Skelton, actor; b. June 27, 1911, England; d. May 1, 1955 (43).
Knight, Charles, actor; b. Mar. 23, 1885, England; d. Jan. 24, 1979 (93).
Knight, Charlott, actress; d. May 16, 1977 (83).
Knight, Fuzzy (r.n. John Forrest Knight), actor; b. May 9, 1901,
    Fairmont, W. Va.; d. Feb. 23, 1976 (74).
Knight, Hank, actor; d. Apr. 21, 1930 (83).
Knight, Lillian, actress; d. May 16, 1946 (65).
Knight, Percy, actor; d. Nov. 27, 1923 (50).

Knoles, Harley, director & writer; d. June 6, 1936.
Knott, Adelbert, actor; d. May 3, 1933 (74).
Knott, Clara, actress; b. Jan. 19, 1871, Indiana; d. Nov. 11, 1926 (55).
Knott, Else, actress; d. Aug. 10, 1975 (63).
Knott, Lydia, actress; b. Oct. 1, 1866, Tyner, Ind.; d. Mar. 30, 1955 (88).
Knowland, Alice, actress; d. May 27, 1930 (51).
Knox, Teddy, actor (member of Crazy Gang); d. Dec. 1, 1974 (78).
Koch-Riehl, Rudolf, actor; b. 1900; d. Sept., 1956 (56).
Koenig, Josef, actor; d. Feb. 26, 1938 (62).
Koerber, Hilde, actress; d. June 1, 1969 (63).
Koerner, Hermine, actress; d. Dec. 14, 1960 (78).
Kohler, Fred, Sr., actor; b. Apr. 21, 1888, Dubuque, Iowa; d. Oct. 28, 1938 (50).
Kohlmar, Lee, actor; b. Feb. 27, 1873, Forth, Germany; d. May 14, 1946 (73).
Kolb, Clarence, actor; b. July 31, 1874, Ohio; d. Nov. 25, 1964 (90).
Kolb, Therese, actress; d. Aug. 19, 1935 (79).
Kolberg, William, actor; d. Aug. 1, 1970 (92).
Kolker, Henry, actor & director; b. Nov. 13, 1870, Quincy, Ill.; d. July 15, 1947 (76).
Kollmar, Richard, actor; b. Dec. 31, 1910, Ridgewood, N.J.; d. Jan. 7, 1971 (60).
Kolossy, Erika, actress; d. Aug. 14, 1963.
Komai, Tetsu, actor; b. Apr. 23, 1894, Kumamoto, Japan; d. Aug. 10, 1970 (76).
Konstam, Phyllis, actress; b. Apr. 14, 1907, London, England; d. Aug. 20, 1976 (69).
Konstantin, Leopoldine, actress; b. Mar. 12, 1886, Brunn, Czechoslovakia; d. Dec., 1965 (79).
Kooy, Pete, actor; b. Apr. 5, 1917, Canada; d. Apr. 20, 1963 (46).
Kopp, Erwin, actor; b. July 3, 1877, Berlin, Germany; d. Apr. 24, 1928 (50).
Kopp, Mila, actress; b. Nov. 20, 1904, Vienna, Austria; d. Jan. 14, 1973 (68).
Koppenhofer, Maria, actress; b. Dec. 11, 1901, Stuttgart, Germany; d. Nov. 29, 1948 (46).
Korayim, Mohamed, director & actor; d. May 27, 1972 (74).
Korda, Sir Alexander, director & producer; b. Sept. 16, 1893, Turkeve, Hungary; d. Jan. 23, 1956 (62).
Korda, Vincent, art director; d. Jan. 4, 1979 (81).
Korda, Zoltan, director; d. Oct. 14, 1961 (66).
Korff, Arnold, actor; b. Aug. 2, 1870, Vienna, Austria; d. June 2, 1944 (73).
Korngold, Erich Wolfgang, composer; b. May 29, 1897, Bruenn, Austria-Moravia; d. Nov. 29, 1957 (60).
Kornman, Mary, actress; b. Dec. 27, 1915, Idaho Falls, Idaho; d. June 1, 1973 (57).
Kortman, Robert, actor; b. Dec. 24, 1887, New York; d. Mar. 13, 1967 (79).
Kortner, Fritz, actor; b. May 12, 1892, Vienna, Austria; d. July 22, 1970 (78).
Koshetz, Nina, actress & singer; d. May 14, 1965 (73).
Kosloff, Theodore, actor; b. Jan. 22, 1882, Russia; d. Nov. 22, 1956 (74).

Kotsonaros, George, actor; b. Nauplie, Greece; d. July 13, 1933.
Kovacs, Ernie, actor; b. Jan. 23, 1919, New Jersey; d. Jan. 13, 1962
    (42).
Koval-Samborskiy, Ivan I., actor; b. Sept. 16, 1893; d. 1962 (69).
Kowal, Mitchell, actor; d. May 2, 1971 (55).
Krah, Marc (r.n. Max Krahmalkov), actor; b. Jan. 24, 1906, Russia;
    d. Sept. 25, 1973 (67).
Krahn, Maria, actress; d. Dec. 19, 1977 (81).
Kraly, Hans, writer; d. Nov. 11, 1950 (65).
Kramer, Ida, actress; d. Oct. 14, 1930 (52).
Kramer, Leopold, actor; b. Sept. 29, 1869, Prague, Czechoslovakia;
    d. Oct. 29, 1942 (73).
Kramer, Maria, actress; d. Feb. 8, 1980 (73).
Kramer, Phil, actor; d. Mar. 31, 1972 (72).
Kramer, Wright, actor; b. May 19, 1875, Somerville, Mass.; d. Nov.
    14, 1941 (66).
Kraus, Charles, actor; d. July 12, 1931 (66).
Krauss, Werner, actor; b. June 23, 1884, Gestungshausen, Germany;
    d. Oct. 20, 1959 (75).
Kraussneck, Arthur, actor; b. Apr. 9, 1856, Ostpreussen, Germany;
    d. Apr. 21, 1941 (85).
Krech, Warren (see William, Warren)
Kress, Gladys, actress; b. July 15, 1900, Roumania; d. Oct. 29, 1969
    (69).
Kretzberg, Hermann, actor; d. June, 1951 (72).
Krieger, Lee, actor; b. June 30, 1919, Maryland; d. Dec. 22, 1967
    (48).
Kroell, Adrienne, actress; d. Oct. 2, 1949 (57).
Krohner, Sarah, actress; d. June 9, 1959 (76).
Krona, Claire (r.n. Claire Klein-Rohden), actress; b. Jan. 28, 1866,
    Dresden, Germany; d. Mar. 15, 1949 (83).
Kronert, Max, actor; d. July 22, 1925.
Krueger, Bum (r.n. Willy Krueger), actor; b. Mar. 13, 1906; d. Mar.
    15, 1971 (65).
Kruger, Alma, actress; b. Sept. 13, 1871, Pittsburgh, Pa.; d. Apr. 5,
    1960 (88).
Kruger, Fred H., actor; b. Sept. 23, 1913, Connecticut; d. Dec. 5,
    1961 (48).
Kruger, Harold (Stubby), actor; b. Sept. 23, 1897, Hawaii; d. Oct. 7,
    1965 (68).
Kruger, Otto, actor; b. Sept. 6, 1885, Toledo, Ohio; d. Sept. 6,
    1974 (89).
Kruger, Paul (r.n. Henry Paul Krueger), actor; b. July 24, 1895, Eau
    Claire, Wisc.; d. Nov. 6, 1960 (65).
Krumschmidt, Eberhard, actor; b. Aug. 3, 1904, Berlin, Germany;
    d. June 3, 1956 (51).
Krupa, Gene, jazz drummer & musician; b. Jan. 15, 1909, Chicago,
    Ill.; d. Oct. 16, 1973 (64).
Kuckelmann, Gertrud, actress; b. Jan. 3, 1929, Munich, Germany;
    d. Jan. 17, 1979 (50).
Kuhne, Friedrich (r.n. Franz Michna), actor; d. Oct., 1958 (89).
Kuleshov, Lev, director; b. Jan. 1, 1899, Tambov, Russia; d. Mar.
    29, 1970 (71).
Kulky, Henry, actor; b. Aug. 11, 1911, Hastings-on-the-Hudson, N.Y.;
    d. Feb. 12, 1965 (53).

Kumari, Meena, actress; d. Mar. 31, 1972 (40).
Kun, Magda, actress; b. Feb. 7, 1912, Szaszregen, Hungary; d. Nov. 7, 1945 (33).
Kunath, Hellmuth, actor; d. July, 1961 (58).
Kunde, Al (r.n. Emil Joseph Kunde), actor; b. Nov. 19, 1887, California; d. Aug. 10, 1952 (64).
Kunde, Anne, actress; b. July 10, 1895, Nebraska; d. June 14, 1960 (64).
Kunkel, George, actor; d. Nov. 8, 1937 (70).
Kupcinet, Karyn, actress; b. Mar. 6, 1941, Illinois; d. Nov. 30, 1963 (22).
Kupfer, Margarethe, actress; b. Apr. 10, 1881, Freystadt, Germany; d. May 11, 1953 (72).
Kurnitz, Harry, writer; b. Jan. 5, 1909, New York City; d. Mar. 18, 1968 (59).
Kuuks Walks-Alone (see Oliver, Mary)
Kuwa, George (r.n. Keiichi Kuwahara), actor; b. Apr. 7, 1885, Japan; d. Oct. 13, 1931 (46).
Kuznetzoff, Adia, actor & opera singer; b. Russia; d. Aug. 10, 1954 (64).
Kyle, Austin C., actor; d. Nov. 10, 1916 (23).
Kyveli, Mme., actress; d. May 25, 1978 (92).


La Badie, Florence, actress; d. Oct. 13, 1917 (23).
LaBissoniere, Erin, actress; b. Aug. 5, 1901, Minnesota; d. Sept. 22, 1976 (75).
La Brake, Harrison, actor; d. Dec. 2, 1933 (45).
LaCava, Gregory, director & author; b. Mar. 10, 1892, Towanda, Pa.; d. Mar. 1, 1952 (59).
Lacey, Adele, actress; d. July 3, 1953 (39).
Lacey, Catherine, actress; b. May 6, 1904, London, England; d. Sept. 23, 1979 (75).
Lachman, Harry, director; b. June 29, 1886, La Salle, Ill.; d. Mar. 19, 1975 (88).
Lackaye, Helen, actress; d. Oct. 19, 1940.
Lackaye, James, actor; d. June 8, 1919 (52).
Lackaye, Richard, actor; d. Mar. 5, 1951 (75).
Lackaye, Wilton, actor; b. Sept. 30, 1862, Virginia; d. Aug. 22, 1932 (69).
Lackland, Ben, actor; d. Jan. 22, 1959.
Lackteen, Frank, actor; b. Aug. 29, 1895, Lebanon; d. July 8, 1968 (72).
Ladd, Alan, actor; b. Sept. 3, 1913, Hot Springs, Ark.; d. Jan. 29, 1964 (50).
Ladd, Ernest Howard, actor; d. Nov. 8, 1940 (65).
Ladd, Leora Middleton, actress; b. Jan. 21, 1915, New York; d. Jan. 7, 1960 (44).
Ladd, Schuyler, actor; d. Apr. 14, 1961 (75).
Ladmiral, Nicole, actress; d. Apr., 1958 (27).
Laemmle, Carl, executive & producer; b. Jan. 17, 1867, Laupheim, Germany; d. Sept. 24, 1939 (72).
Laemmle, Edward, director; b. Oct. 25, 1887, Chicago, Ill.; d. Apr. 2, 1937 (49).

Lafayette, Ruby, actress; d. Apr. 3, 1935 (90).
LaFleur, Joy (Victoria Ward), actress; d. Nov. 6, 1957 (43).
La Garde, Jocelyne, actress; d. Sept. 12, 1979 (55).
Lagrenee, Maurice, actor; b. 1893; d. 1955 (62).
Lahr, Bert, actor; b. Aug. 13, 1895, New York City; d. Dec. 4, 1967
    (72).
Lahtinen, Warner H. (Duke), extra; d. Dec. 12, 1968 (58).
Laidlaw, Ethan, actor; b. Nov. 25, 1899, Butte, Mont.; d. May 25,
    1963 (63).
Laidlaw, Roy, actor; b. Mar. 25, 1883, Comber, Ontario, Canada;
    d. Feb. 2, 1936 (52).
Laing, Alfred Benson, actor; d. Aug. 3, 1976 (86).
Lair, Grace, actress; d. Jan. 5, 1955.
Laire, Judson, actor; b. Aug. 3, 1902, New York City; d. July 5,
    1979 (76).
Lait, Jack, writer; d. Apr. 1, 1954 (72).
Lait, Jack, Jr., writer; b. Aug. 1, 1909, Chicago, Ill.; d. Aug. 18,
    1961 (52).
Lake, Alice, actress; b. Sept. 12, 1895, Brooklyn, N.Y.; d. Nov. 15,
    1967 (72).
Lake, Frank, actor; d. Apr. 19, 1936 (87).
Lake, Harry, actor; d. Mar. 4, 1947 (62).
Lake, Lew, actor; d. Nov. 5, 1939 (65).
Lake, Veronica (r.n. Constance Ockleman), actress; b. Nov. 14, 1919,
    Brooklyn, N.Y.; d. July 7, 1973 (53).
Lal Singh, Reginald, actor; b. Aug. 8, 1905, Guyana; d. Dec. 1, 1970
    (65).
La Marr, Barbara (r.n. Reatha Dale Watson), actress; b. July 28, 1896,
    Washington; d. Jan. 30, 1926 (29).
LaMarr, Richard, actor; b. Nov. 6, 1895, Italy; d. Apr. 24, 1975 (79).
Lamb, Florence, actress; d. May 9, 1966 (82).
Lambart, Ernest, actor; b. Ireland; d. June 27, 1945 (71).
Lambert, Clara, actress; d. 1921.
Lambert, Theophile (Toby) J. "Skinny," actor; b. Sept. 17, 1916,
    Edmonton, Alberta, Canada; d. June 14, 1972 (55).
Lambert, Victor, actor; b. Oct. 4, 1868, Charlotte, Mich.; d. Apr. 9,
    1940 (71).
Lamberti, Professor (Michael), actor; d. Mar. 13, 1950.
Lamont, Harry (r.n. Alfred Guibert), actor; b. June 17, 1882, New
    York City; d. May 8, 1957 (74).
Lamont, Jack, actor; d. Feb. 28, 1956 (63).
Lamont, Lillian, actress; d. June 22, 1953 (45).
Lamorisse, Albert, director & writer; d. June 2, 1970 (48).
Lampin, Georges, director & actor; d. May, 1979 (78).
Lampton, Dee, actress; d. Sept. 2, 1919 (21).
Lancaster, Ann, actress; d. Oct. 31, 1970 (50).
Lancaster, John, actor; d. Oct. 11, 1935 (78).
Lancaster, Tom, actor; d. Aug. 4, 1947 (74).
Landa, Max, actor; b. 1880, Vienna, Austria; d. Nov. 9, 1933 (53).
Landau, David, actor; b. Mar. 9, 1879, Philadelphia, Pa.; d. Sept.
    20, 1935 (56).
Landers, Lew (Louis Friedlander), director; b. Jan. 2, 1901, New
    York City; d. Dec. 15, 1962 (61).
Landers, Muriel, actress; d. Feb. 19, 1977 (55).
Landi, Elissa, actress; b. Dec. 6, 1904, Venice, Italy; d. Oct. 22,
    1948 (43).

Landin, Hope, actress; b. May 3, 1893, Minneapolis, Minn.; d. Feb. 22, 1973 (79).

Landis, Carole, actress; b. Jan. 1, 1919, Fairchild, Wisc.; d. July 5, 1948 (29).

Landis, Cullen, actor; b. July 9, 1895, Nashville, Tenn.; d. Aug. 26, 1975 (80).

Landis, Jessie Royce, actress; b. Nov. 25, 1904, Chicago, Ill.; d. Feb. 2, 1972 (67).

Landone, Avice, actress; b. Sept. 1, 1910, India; d. June 12, 1976 (65).

Landreth, Gertrude Griffith, actress; b. Feb. 26, 1897, New York; d. Nov. 25, 1969 (72).

Lane, A.B., actor; d. Jan. 2, 1968 (76).

Lane, Adele, actress; b. July 17, 1877; d. Oct. 24, 1957 (80).

Lane, Allan "Rocky" (r.n. Harry Albershart), actor; b. Sept. 22, 1909, Mishawaka, Ind.; d. Oct. 27, 1973 (64).

Lane, Charles, actor; b. Jan. 25, 1869, Madison, Ill.; d. Oct. 17, 1945 (76).

Lane, Grace, actress; b. Jan. 13, 1876, England; d. Jan. 14, 1956 (80).

Lane, Harry, actor; d. Oct. 27, 1943 (67).

Lane, Harry, actor; d. July, 1960 (50).

Lane, Leota, actress; b. Oct. 25, 1903, Iowa; d. July 25, 1963 (59).

Lane, Lupino, actor; b. June 16, 1892, London, England; d. Nov. 10, 1959 (67).

Lane, Pat, actor; d. July 4, 1953 (53).

Lane, Rosemary, actress; b. Apr. 4, 1913, Indianola, Iowa; d. Nov. 25, 1974 (61).

Lanfield, Sidney, director; b. Apr. 20, 1898, Chicago, Ill.; d. June 30, 1972 (74).

Lang, Eva Clara, actress; d. Apr. 6, 1933 (48).

Lang, Fritz, director & author; b. Dec. 5, 1890, Vienna, Austria; d. Aug. 2, 1976 (85).

Lang, Gertrude, actress & singer; d. July 14, 1971 (73).

Lang, Harold, actor; d. Nov. 16, 1970 (45).

Lang, Harry, actor; b. Dec. 29, 1894, New York; d. Aug. 3, 1953 (58).

Lang, Howard, actor; b. May 12, 1874, New Orleans, La.; d. Jan. 26, 1941 (66).

Lang, Matheson, actor; b. May 15, 1879, Montreal, Canada; d. Apr. 11, 1948 (68).

Lang, Melvin, actor; b. Dec. 29, 1894, New York City; d. Nov. 14, 1940 (45).

Lang, Peter, actor; d. Aug. 20, 1932 (65).

Lang, Walter, director; b. Aug. 10, 1898, Memphis, Tenn.; d. Feb. 7, 1972 (73).

Langdon, Harry, actor; b. June 15, 1884, Council Bluffs, Iowa; d. Dec. 22, 1944 (60).

Langdon, Lillian, actress; d. Feb. 8, 1943 (81).

Lange, Mary, actress; d. Apr. 20, 1973 (60).

Langford, Martha, actress; d. Apr. 21, 1935.

Langford, William, actor; b. Montreal, Canada; d. July 20, 1955 (35).

Langley, Herbert, actor & opera singer; d. Oct., 1967 (79).

Langton, Hal, actor; d. Jan. 13, 1956 (70).

Langtry, Lily, actress; b. Oct. 13, 1852, Isle of Jersey, England; d. Feb. 12, 1929 (76).

Lani, Maria, actress; d. Mar. 11, 1954 (48).

Lanning, Edward, actor; b. Sept. 21, 1870, Iowa; d. Sept. 20, 1918
    (48).
Lanning, Frank, actor; b. Aug. 14, 1872, Marion, Iowa; d. June 17,
    1945 (72).
Lanning, George, actor; b. Feb. 20, 1877, Marion, Iowa; d. June 5,
    1941 (64).
Lanphier, Faye, actress; d. June 21, 1959 (53).
Lanphier, James F., actor; b. Aug. 31, 1920, New York; d. Feb. 11,
    1969 (48).
Lansing, Joi, actress; b. Apr. 6, 1934, Salt Lake City, Utah; d. Aug.
    7, 1972 (38).
Lansing, Ruth Douglas, actress; d. Aug. 19, 1931 (50).
Lanza, Mario, actor & singer; b. Jan. 31, 1921, Philadelphia, Pa.;
    d. Oct. 7, 1959 (38).
La Pearl, Harry, actor; d. Jan. 13, 1946 (61).
La Planche, Rosemary, actress; d. May 6, 1979 (56).
La Reno, Dick, actor; b. Oct. 31, 1863, New York City; d. July 26,
    1945 (81).
Largay, Raymond, actor; b. Mar. 7, 1886, Wisconsin; d. Sept. 28, 1974
    (88).
Largay, Roy J. (see Largay, Raymond)
Larimore, Earle, actor; b. Portland, Ore.; d. Oct. 22, 1947 (48).
Larkin, George, actor; d. Mar. 27, 1946 (59).
Larkin, John, actor; d. Mar. 19, 1936 (63).
Larkin, John, writer; b. New York City; d. Jan. 6, 1965.
Larkin, John, actor; b. Apr. 11, 1912, California; d. Jan. 29, 1965
    (52).
La Rocque, Rod, actor; b. Nov. 29, 1898, Chicago, Ill.; d. Oct. 15,
    1969 (70).
La Rose, Rose, actress & singer; d. July 27, 1972 (59).
Larquey, Pierre, actor; d. Apr. 17, 1962 (78).
Larrimore, Francine, actress; b. Aug. 22, 1898, Verdun, France;
    d. Mar. 7, 1975 (76).
Larsen, Viggo, actor; b. Aug. 14, 1880, Copenhagen, Denmark; d. Jan.
    6, 1957 (76).
LaRue, Frank, actor; b. Dec. 5, 1878, Ohio; d. Sept. 26, 1960 (81).
La Rue, Grace, actress; b. Kansas City, Mo.; d. Mar. 12, 1956 (75).
LaRue, Jean (Eugene M. Bailey), actor; d. June, 1956 (55).
Lascoe, Henry, actor; b. May 30, 1912, New York; d. Sept. 1, 1964
    (52).
Laskowski, Ernst, actor; b. 1885; d. Mar. 26, 1935 (50).
Lasky, Jesse L., producer & executive; b. Sept. 13, 1880, San
    Francisco, Calif.; d. Jan. 13, 1958 (77).
La Sorrentina (Mary Frasca), actress; d. July 24, 1973.
Latell, Lyle, actor; b. Apr. 9, 1904, Iowa; d. Oct. 24, 1967 (63).
Latinovits, Zoltan, actor; d. June, 1976 (44).
Lauck, Chester (Lum), actor; b. Feb. 9, 1902, Allene, Ark.; d. Feb.
    21, 1980 (78).
Lauder, Sir Harry, actor & singer; b. Aug. 14, 1870, Portobello,
    Scotland; d. Feb. 26, 1950 (79).
Laufbahn, Ihre, actress; d. 1931 (30).
Laughlin, Anna, actress; b. Sacramento, Calif.; d. Mar. 6, 1937 (50).
Laughlin, Billy "Froggy," actor; b. July 5, 1932, San Gabriel, Calif.;
    d. Aug. 30, 1948 (16).
Laughton, Charles, actor; b. July 1, 1899, Scarborough, England;
    d. Dec. 15, 1962 (63).

Laughton, Edward, actor; b. Sheffield, England; d. Mar. 21, 1952 (49).
Launders, Perc, actor; b. Oct. 11, 1904, California; d. Oct. 2, 1952 (47).
Laurel, Stan, actor; b. June 16, 1890, Ulverson, England; d. Feb. 23, 1965 (74).
Laurell, Kay, actress; d. Jan. 31, 1927 (37).
Lauren, S.K., writer; d. Dec. 4, 1979 (87).
Laurenz, John, actor; d. Nov. 7, 1958 (49).
Laurier, Jay, actor; b. May 31, 1879, England; d. Apr., 1969 (89).
Lauri-Volpi, Giacomo, opera singer; d. Mar. 17, 1979 (86).
Lava, William, composer; b. Mar. 18, 1911, Minnesota; d. Feb. 20, 1971 (59).
Lavalle, Cleo, actress; d. Aug. 30, 1925 (17).
La Varre, Mert (see Merton, John)
La Velle, Kay, actress; d. Nov. 18, 1965 (76).
Laverne, Dorothy, actress; d. Dec. 29, 1940 (30).
Laverne, Henry, actor; b. 1888; d. 1953 (65).
LaVerne, Lucille, actress; b. Nov. 8, 1872, Memphis, Tenn.; d. Mar. 4, 1945 (72).
La Vernie, Laura, actress; b. Mar. 2, 1854, Jefferson City, Mo.; d. Sept. 18, 1939 (85).
La Vinder, Gracille, actress; d. Apr. 22, 1973.
Law, Betty, actress; d. Feb. 3, 1955 (72).
Law, Burton, actor; b. Oct. 22, 1877, Ouray, Colo.; d. Nov. 2, 1963 (86).
Law, Donald, actor; d. Feb. 5, 1959 (38).
Law, Walter, actor; b. Mar. 26, 1876, Farmersville, Ohio; d. Aug. 8, 1940 (64).
Lawford, Betty, actress; b. London, England; d. Nov. 20, 1960 (44).
Lawford, Ernest E., actor; b. England; d. Dec. 26, 1940 (89).
Lawford, Sydney, actor; d. Feb. 15, 1953 (87).
Lawrence, Del, actor; b. Sept. 16, 1874, Nevada; d. Apr. 1, 1965 (90).
Lawrence, Eddy, actor; d. Dec. 5, 1931 (50).
Lawrence, Florence, actress; b. Jan. 1, 1890, Hamilton, Ontario, Canada; d. Dec. 28, 1938 (48).
Lawrence, Gerald, actor; b. Mar. 23, 1873, London, England; d. May 16, 1957 (84).
Lawrence, Gertrude, actress; b. July 4, 1898, London, England; d. Sept. 6, 1952 (54).
Lawrence, Jeanne, actress; d. July 12, 1945 (44).
Lawrence, John, actor; b. July 16, 1910, Utah; d. June 26, 1974 (63).
Lawrence, Lillian, actress; b. Feb. 17, 1868, West Virginia; d. May 7, 1926 (58).
Lawrence, Marjorie, opera singer; b. Feb. 17, 1907, Melbourne, Australia; d. Jan. 13, 1979 (71).
Lawrence, Raymond (r.n. Raymond Francis Miles Atkinson), actor; b. Dec. 8, 1888, London, England; d. May 28, 1976 (87).
Lawrence, Trudy (see Halpern, Gertrude)
Lawrence, Vincent, writer; b. Nov. 20, 1890, Boston, Mass.; d. Nov. 24, 1946 (56).
Lawrence, Walter, actor; b. Sept. 3, 1901, Kentucky; d. Jan. 19, 1961 (59).
Lawrence, William E. (r.n. William Effingham Lawrence), actor; b. Aug. 22, 1896, Brooklyn, N.Y.; d. Nov. 28, 1947 (51).
Lawson, John, actor; d. Nov. 25, 1920 (55).

Lawson, John Howard, writer; b. Sept. 25, 1886, New York City; d.
    Aug. 11, 1977 (80).
Lawson, Kate Drain, actress & designer; b. July 27, 1894, Washington;
    d. Nov. 14, 1977 (83).
Lawson, Louise, actress; d. Feb. 8, 1924.
Lawson, Mary, actress; b. Aug. 30, 1910, Darlington, England;
    d. May 4, 1941 (30).
Lawson, Stan, actor; d. July 17, 1977 (68).
Lawson, Wilfrid, actor; b. Jan. 14, 1900, Bradford, Yorkshire,
    England; d. Oct. 10, 1966 (66).
Lawton, Charles (Bud), Jr., cinematographer; d. July 11, 1965 (61).
Lawton, Frank, actor; b. Sept. 30, 1904, London, England; d. June 10,
    1969 (64).
Lawton, Kenneth, actor; b. Dec. 13, 1875, New York; d. Mar. 10,
    1949 (73).
Lawton, Thais, actress; b. June 18, 1881, Louisville, Ky.; d. Dec. 18,
    1956 (75).
Lax, Frances, actress; d. May 6, 1975 (80).
Lay, Irving T., actor; d. Mar., 1932.
Laymon, Gene, actor; b. July 25, 1889, Michigan City, Ind.; d. June
    6, 1946 (56).
Leach, Susanne, actress; b. Aug. 17, 1865, Brompton, Ontario, Canada;
    d. Aug. 16, 1945 (79).
Leahy, Eugene, actor; b. Mar. 14, 1883; d. Mar., 1967 (83).
Leahy, Margaret, actress; b. Aug. 17, 1902, London, England; d. Feb.
    17, 1967 (64).
Leal, Milagros, actress; d. Mar. 1, 1975 (73).
Leane, Patrick Daniel, actor; d. July 4, 1953 (53).
Lease, Rex, actor; b. Feb. 11, 1903, Central City, W. Va.; d. Jan. 3,
    1966 (62).
Leavitt, Douglas "Abe," actor; d. Mar. 3, 1960 (77).
Le Bargy, Charles, actor; b. France; d. Feb. 5, 1936 (77).
LeBaron, Bert (r.n. Arthur Krieger), actor & stuntman; b. Dec. 10,
    1900, Wisconsin; d. Mar. 3, 1956 (55).
Le Baron, William, producer & writer; b. Elgin, Ill.; d. Feb. 9,
    1958 (75).
Lebedeff, Ivan, actor; b. June 18, 1894, Uspoliai, Lithuania;
    d. Mar. 31, 1953 (58).
Lebius, Aenderly, actor; b. Dec. 6, 1867, Tilsit, U.S.S.R.; d. Mar.
    5, 1921 (53).
Leblanc, Georgette, actress; b. Rouen, France; d. Oct. 26, 1941 (66).
Le Brandt, Gertrude, actress; d. Aug. 28, 1955 (92).
Le Brun, Mignon, actress; b. Jan. 4, 1888, New York City; d. Sept.
    20, 1941 (53).
Lederer, Charles, writer; d. Mar. 5, 1976 (65).
Lederer, Gretchen, actress; b. May 23, 1891, Cologne, Germany;
    d. Dec. 20, 1955 (64).
Lederer, Otto, actor; b. Apr. 17, 1886, Czechoslovakia; d. Sept. 3,
    1965 (79).
Lederman, D. Ross (r.n. David Ross Lederman), director; b. Dec. 12,
    1894, Pennsylvania; d. Aug. 24, 1972 (77).
Ledner, David, actor; d. Dec. 17, 1957 (57).
Leduc, Claudine, actress; d. Feb. 15, 1969.
Lee, Allen, actor; d. Feb. 5, 1951 (76).
Lee, Auriol, actress; b. Sept. 13, 1880, London, England; d. July 2,
    1941 (60).

Lee, Belinda, actress; b. June 15, 1935, Devon, England; d. Mar. 13, 1961 (25).

Lee, Bessie, actress; d. Nov. 9, 1931 (27).

Lee, Bruce, actor; d. July 20, 1973 (32).

Lee, Canada, actor; b. Mar. 3, 1907, New York City; d. May 9, 1952 (45).

Lee, Carolyn, actress; d. Jan. 11, 1920.

Lee, Charles T., actor; d. Mar. 14, 1927 (45).

Lee, Ching Wah, actor; d. Jan. 2, 1980 (78).

Lee, Cosette, actress; d. Sept. 19, 1976 (66).

Lee, Dixie, actress; b. Nov. 4, 1911, Harriman, Tenn.; d. Nov. 1, 1952 (40).

Lee, Duke R., actor; b. May 13, 1881, Virginia; d. Apr. 1, 1959 (77).

Lee, Earl, actor; d. June 2, 1955 (69).

Lee, Etta, actress; d. Oct. 27, 1956 (50).

Lee, Florence, actress; b. Mar. 12, 1888, Vermont; d. Sept. 1, 1962 (74).

Lee, Gwen, actress; b. Nov. 12, 1904, Hastings, Neb.; d. Aug. 20, 1961 (56).

Lee, Gypsy Rose (Louise Hovick) (r.n. Rose Louise Hovick), actress; b. Jan. 9, 1914, Seattle, Wash.; d. Apr. 26, 1970 (56).

Lee, Harry, actor; b. June 1, 1872, Richmond, Va.; d. Dec. 8, 1932 (60).

Lee, Jack, actor; b. June 12, 1907, England; d. Apr. 24, 1969 (61).

Lee, Jane, actress; d. Mar. 17, 1957 (45).

Lee, Jennie, actress; d. May 3, 1930 (84).

Lee, Jenny, actress; d. Aug. 4, 1925 (75).

Lee, Johnny, actor; b. July 4, 1898, Mississippi; d. Dec. 12, 1965 (67).

Lee, Joseph, actor; d. July 11, 1943 (37).

Lee, Kendall, actress; d. July 30, 1978.

Lee, Leonard, writer; b. Sept. 4, 1903, New York City; d. Aug. 24, 1964 (60).

Lee, Lila, actress; b. July 25, 1905, Union Hill, N.J.; d. Nov. 13, 1973 (68).

Lee, Lila Dean, actress; d. Nov. 3, 1959 (69).

Lee, Margo, actress; d. Oct. 8, 1951.

Lee, Raymond, actor; d. June 26, 1974 (64).

Lee, Richard Lawrence, actor; d. July 24, 1931 (61).

Lee, Rowland V., director; b. Sept. 6, 1891, Findlay, Ohio; d. Dec. 21, 1975 (84).

Lee, Ruth, actress; d. Aug. 3, 1975 (79).

Lee, Sammy, dancer & dance director; d. Mar. 30, 1968 (78).

Lee, Tommy H., actor; b. Feb. 19, 1900, China; d. June 19, 1976 (76).

Lee, Wendy, actress; d. Aug. 23, 1968 (45).

Leeds, Herbert I., director; d. May 16, 1954 (42).

Leeds, Marian, actress; d. June 26, 1961 (74).

Lefaur, Andre, actor; b. July 25, 1879, Paris, France; d. Dec. 4, 1952 (73).

Lefebvre, Rolf, actor; b. 1916, S.W. Africa; d. Dec. 9, 1974 (58).

LeFeuvre, Guy, actor; b. Oct. 17, 1883, Ottawa, Canada; d. Feb. 15, 1950 (66).

Le Feuvre, Philip, actor; d. Aug. 23, 1939 (68).

Lefevre, Ned (r.n. Leroy Ned Lefevre), actor; b. Mar. 9, 1912, Indiana; d. June 10, 1966 (54).

Leffler, Hermann, actor; b. Oct. 3, 1864, Quedlinburg, Germany;
    d. Nov. 21, 1929 (65).
Leffler, Robert, actor; b. Jan. 9, 1866, Aschersleben, Germany;
    d. Mar. 15, 1940 (74).
Leftwich, Alexander, actor & director; b. Dec. 24, 1885, Baltimore,
    Md.; d. Jan. 13, 1947 (61).
Legal, Ernst, actor; b. May 2, 1881, Schlieben, Germany; d. June 29,
    1955 (74).
Legare, Ovila, actor; d. Feb. 9, 1978 (76).
Legneur, Charles, actor; d. Feb. 14, 1956 (64).
Le Guere, George, actor; b. Memphis, Tenn.; d. Nov. 21, 1947 (76).
Lehmann, Beatrix, actress; b. July 1, 1903, Bourne End, England;
    d. Aug. 1, 1979 (76).
Lehmann, Lotte, opera singer; b. Feb. 27, 1888, Perleberg, Germany;
    d. Aug. 26, 1976 (88).
Lehr, Lew, actor; b. May 14, 1895, Philadelphia, Pa.; d. Mar. 6,
    1950 (54).
Lehrer, George J., actor; d. Aug. 25, 1966 (77).
Lehrman, Henry, director, producer, & actor; b. Mar. 30, 1886, Vienna,
    Austria; d. Nov. 7, 1946 (60).
Leiber, Fritz, actor; b. Jan. 31, 1882, Chicago, Ill.; d. Oct. 14,
    1949 (67).
Leigh, Andrew, actor; b. Nov. 30, 1887, Brighton, England; d. Apr.
    21, 1957 (69).
Leigh, Frank, actor; b. Apr. 18, 1876, London, England; d. May 9,
    1948 (72).
Leigh, Lisle, actress; d. May 18, 1927 (48).
Leigh, Rowland, writer; b. May 16, 1902, London, England; d. Oct. 8,
    1963 (61).
Leigh, Vivien, actress; b. Nov. 5, 1913, Darjeeling, India; d. July
    8, 1967 (53).
Leighton, Daniel, actor; d. June 20, 1917.
Leighton, Frank, actor; b. July 16, 1908, Sydney, Australia; d. Oct.
    17, 1962 (54).
Leighton, Harry, actor; d. May 30, 1926 (60).
Leighton, Lillian, actress; b. May 17, 1874, Auroraville, Wisc.;
    d. Mar. 19, 1956 (81).
Leighton, Margaret, actress; b. Feb. 26, 1922, Barnt Green, England;
    d. Jan. 13, 1976 (53).
Leisen, Mitchell (r.n. James Mitchell Leisen), director; b. Oct. 6,
    1898, Menominee, Mich.; d. Oct. 29, 1972 (74).
Leister, Frederick, actor; b. Dec. 1, 1885, London, England; d. 1970
    (84).
Le Maire, George, director; b. Ft. Worth, Tex.; d. Jan. 20, 1930 (46).
Le Maire, William, actor; b. Dec. 21, 1892, Fort Worth, Tex.; d. Nov.
    11, 1933 (40).
Le Mans, Marcel, actor; d. Jan. 9, 1946 (49).
Le May, Alan, writer & director; b. June 3, 1899, Indianapolis, Ind.;
    d. Apr. 27, 1964 (64).
Lemieux, Carrie, actress; d. Oct. 3, 1925 (44).
LeMoyne, Charles, actor; b. June 27, 1880, Illinois; d. Sept. 13,
    1956 (76).
Lemuels, William E., actor; d. Feb. 21, 1953 (62).
Lengbach, Georg, actor; b. Jan. 7, 1873, Vienna, Austria; d. May 3,
    1952 (79).

Leni, Paul A., director & actor; b. July 8, 1885, Stuttgart, Germany; d. Sept. 2, 1929 (44).
Lenihan, Winifred, actress; b. Brooklyn, N.Y.; d. July 27, 1964 (65).
Lennart, Isobel, writer; d. Jan. 25, 1971 (55).
Leno, Charles, actor; d. Oct., 1972 (64).
Leno, Dan, actor; b. Dec. 20, 1860; d. Oct. 31, 1904 (43).
Le Noir, Pass, actor; d. June 12, 1946 (72).
Lenschau, Hermann, actor; d. Aug. 14, 1977 (65).
Leon, Connie, actress; d. May 10, 1955 (75).
Leon, Pedro, actor; b. June 29, 1878, Tucson, Ariz.; d. July 14, 1931 (53).
Leon, Valeriano, actor; d. Jan., 1956 (63).
Leonard, Archie, actor; d. Feb. 7, 1959 (42).
Leonard, Benny, actor & boxer; d. Apr. 18, 1947 (51).
Leonard, David A., actor; b. Sept. 5, 1891, New York; d. Apr. 2, 1967 (75).
Leonard, Eddie, actor; b. Richmond, Va.; d. July 29, 1941 (70).
Leonard, Gus, actor; b. Marseilles, France; d. Mar. 27, 1939 (83).
Leonard, Jack, actor; d. Oct., 1921.
Leonard, Jack E., actor; d. May 10, 1973 (62).
Leonard, James, actor; d. July 4, 1930 (62).
Leonard, Marion, actress; b. June 9, 1881, Ohio; d. Jan. 9, 1956 (74).
Leonard, Minnie, actress; d. Jan. 2, 1940 (66).
Leonard, Murray, actor; b. Apr. 11, 1898, New York; d. Nov. 6, 1970 (72).
Leonard, Robert Z., director & actor; b. Oct. 7, 1889, Chicago, Ill.; d. Aug. 27, 1968 (78).
Leone, Henry, actor; d. June 9, 1922 (64).
Leone, Maude, actress; d. Mar. 13, 1930 (45).
Leong, James B., actor; b. Jan. 18, 1900, China; d. Oct. 24, 1963 (63).
Leonidov, Leonid M., actor; b. June 3, 1873, Odessa, Russia; d. Aug. 6, 1941 (68).
Leoning, John, actor; d. Mar. 23, 1977 (50).
Lepe (r.n. Jose Alvarez Jaudenes), actor; b. 1890, Madrid, Spain; d. July 7, 1967 (76).
LePere, Paul, director; d. Dec. 10, 1965 (53).
Lerner, Irving, director & producer; b. Mar. 7, 1909, New York City; d. Dec. 25, 1976 (67).
Le Roux, Carmen, actress; b. Sept. 4, 1909, Durango, Mexico; d. Aug. 24, 1942 (32).
LeSaint, Edward J., actor & director; b. Dec. 13, 1870, Cincinnati, Ohio; d. Sept. 10, 1940 (69).
LeSaint, Stella (Stella Razetto), actress; b. Dec. 17, 1881, San Diego, Calif.; d. Sept. 21, 1948 (66).
Lesley, Carole (r.n. Maureen Rippingale), actress; d. Feb. 28, 1974 (38).
Leslie, Arthur, actor; d. June 30, 1970 (68).
Leslie, Edith, actress; b. Jan. 17, 1905, Massachusetts; d. Apr. 9, 1973 (68).
Leslie, Elinor, actress; d. June 14, 1929 (55).
Leslie, Fred, actor; b. Aug. 29, 1880, England; d. Aug. 1, 1945 (64).
Leslie, Gene, actor; d. Feb. 20, 1953 (49).
Leslie, Gladys, actress; b. Mar. 5, 1899, New York City; d. Oct. 2, 1976 (77).

Leslie, J. Hubert, actor; d. Dec. 24, 1953.
Leslie, Jack, actor; d. Apr. 25, 1945 (70).
Leslie, Lilie, actress; b. 1892, Scotland; d. Sept. 8, 1940 (48).
Lessey, George, actor; d. June 3, 1947 (67).
Lessig, John E., actor; d. Feb. 23, 1958 (80).
Lester, Kate, actress; b. 1857, England; d. Oct. 12, 1924 (67).
Lester, Louise, actress; b. Aug. 8, 1867, Wisconsin; d. Nov. 17, 1952 (85).
L'Estrange, Dick (r.n. Gunther von Strensch), actor, assistant director, & director; b. Dec. 27, 1889, North Carolina; d. Nov. 19, 1963 (73).
L'Estrange, Julian, actor; b. Aug. 6, 1878; d. Oct. 22, 1918 (40).
Le Strange, Norme, actor; d. June 5, 1936.
LeSueur, Hal Hayes, actor; d. May 3, 1963 (59).
Letondal, Henri, actor; b. June 29, 1901, Canada; d. Feb. 15, 1955 (53).
Lettch, Raymond "Tobby," actor; d. 1946.
Lettieri, Al, actor; b. Feb. 24, 1928, New York City; d. Oct. 18, 1975 (47).
Lettinger, Rudolf, actor; b. Oct. 26, 1865; d. Mar. 21, 1937 (71).
Leubas, Louis, actor; d. Aug. 29, 1932 (62).
Leudesdorff, Ernst, actor; b. Mar. 28, 1885, Elberfeld-Wuppertal, Germany; d. Sept. 7, 1954 (69).
Leudesdorff-Tormin, Philine, actress; b. 1894; d. Apr. 30, 1924 (30).
Levant, Oscar, actor & pianist; b. Dec. 27, 1906, Pittsburgh, Pa.; d. Aug. 14, 1972 (65).
Levelle, Estelle, actress; d. Jan. 6, 1960.
Levesque, Marcel, actor; b. Dec. 6, 1877, Paris, France; d. Feb., 1962 (84).
Levien, Sonya, writer; b. Russia; d. Mar. 19, 1960 (71).
Le Vigan, Robert, actor; d. Oct., 1972 (73).
Levine, Harry, actor; b. Mar. 4, 1908, Passaic, N.J.; d. Nov. 13, 1947 (39).
Levine, Lucy, actress; d. Sept. 4, 1939 (32).
Le Viness, Carl, actor & director; b. July 6, 1885, New York; d. Oct. 15, 1964 (79).
LeVino, Margaret Prussing, author; b. Mar. 29, 1890, Highland Park, Ill.; d. Jan. 13, 1944 (53).
Levy, Raoul, director & writer; d. Dec. 31, 1966 (44).
Levy, Sylvan, actor; d. Oct. 30, 1962 (56).
Lewin, Albert, director, producer, & author; b. Sept. 23, 1894, Brooklyn, N.Y.; d. May 9, 1968 (73).
Lewin, Ike, actor; d. June 10, 1941 (51).
Lewis, Albert, producer & writer; d. Apr. 5, 1978 (93).
Lewis, Cathy, actress; d. Nov. 20, 1968 (50).
Lewis, Dorothy W., actress; d. June 16, 1952 (81).
Lewis, Ed (Strangler), wrestler & actor; d. Aug. 7, 1966 (76).
Lewis, Edgar, director; d. May 21, 1938 (63).
Lewis, Eva, actress; d. May 6, 1939 (58).
Lewis, Flo, actress; d. June 11, 1938 (40).
Lewis, Forrest, actor; b. Nov. 5, 1899, Indiana; d. June 2, 1977 (77).
Lewis, Fred, actor; b. Dec. 23, 1860, Kingston-on-Thames, England; d. Dec. 25, 1927 (67).
Lewis, Fred Irving, actor; d. July 28, 1960 (77).

Lewis, Frederick, actor; b. Feb. 14, 1873, Oswego, N.Y.; d. Mar. 19, 1946 (73).

Lewis, Gene, writer & producer; b. Nov. 3, 1888, Philadelphia, Pa.; d. Mar. 27, 1979 (90).

Lewis, George "Beetlepuss," actor; d. Apr. 8, 1955 (54).

Lewis, Gordon, actor; d. Mar. 17, 1933 (42).

Lewis, Harry, actor; d. Nov. 18, 1950 (64).

Lewis, Herbert Clyde, writer; d. Oct. 17, 1950 (41).

Lewis, Ida, actress; d. Apr. 21, 1935 (86).

Lewis, James H. (Daddy), actor; d. Nov. 3, 1928 (78).

Lewis, Joe E., actor & nightclub comedian; d. June 4, 1971 (69).

Lewis, Martin, actor; b. Sept. 8, 1888, Blackheath, England; d. Apr., 1970 (81).

Lewis, Mary, actress & opera singer; b. Hot Springs, Ark.; d. Dec. 31, 1941 (41).

Lewis, Mitchell, actor; b. June 26, 1880, Syracuse, N.Y.; d. Aug. 24, 1956 (76).

Lewis, Ralph (r.n. Ralph Percy Lewis), actor; b. Oct. 28, 1872, Englewood, Ill.; d. Dec. 4, 1937 (65).

Lewis, Randolph C., writer; d. Sept. 3, 1934 (72).

Lewis, Richard, actor; d. Apr. 30, 1935 (66).

Lewis, Sam, actor; d. Apr. 28, 1963 (85).

Lewis, Sheldon, actor; b. Apr. 20, 1869, Philadelphia, Pa.; d. May 7, 1958 (89).

Lewis, Ted (r.n. Theodore Friedman), singer & bandleader; b. June 6, 1891, Circleville, Ohio; d. Aug. 25, 1971 (80).

Lewis, Tom, actor; b. St. John, New Brunswick, Canada; d. Oct. 19, 1927 (63).

Lewis, Vera, actress; b. June 10, 1873, New York City; d. Feb. 8, 1956 (82).

Lewis, Walter P., actor; b. June 10, 1866, Albany, N.Y.; d. Jan. 30, 1932 (65).

Lewisohn, Victor, actor; b. Apr. 21, 1897, London, England; d. Nov. 13, 1934 (37).

Lewman, Hiram Wallingford (Highe), actor; d. Aug. 27, 1976 (72).

Lewton, Val, producer; b. May 7, 1904, Yalta, Russia; d. Mar. 14, 1951 (46).

Leyssac, Paul, actor; d. Aug. 20, 1946.

l'Herbier, Marcel, director & author; b. Apr. 23, 1890, Paris, France; d. Nov. 26, 1979 (89).

Licho, Edgar A., actor; d. Oct. 11, 1944 (68).

Lichtman, Al, producer & executive; b. Apr. 9, 1885, Hungary; d. Feb. 20, 1958 (72).

Liddy, James, actor; d. Feb. 18, 1936 (40).

Lieberman, Jacob, actor; d. Feb. 16, 1956 (77).

Liebmann, Hans H., actor; d. Jan. 24, 1960 (65).

Liechtenstein, Rosa, actress; d. Dec., 1955.

Liedtke, Harry, actor; b. Oct. 12, 1882, Konigsberg, Germany; d. Apr. 28, 1945 (62).

Lieven, Albert, actor; b. June 23, 1906, Hohenstein, Germany; d. Dec. 22, 1971 (65).

Ligero, Miguel, actor; b. Oct. 21, 1897, Madrid, Spain; d. Feb. 20, 1968 (70).

Liggett, Louis (r.n. Louis Ligaty), actor; b. May 30, 1884, Hungary; d. Nov. 27, 1928 (44).

Lightner, Winnie, actress; b. Sept. 17, 1899, Greenport, L.I., N.Y.;
    d. Mar. 5, 1971 (71).
Lighton, Louis D., producer & writer; b. Omaha, Neb.; d. Feb. 1,
    1963 (71).
Ligon, Grover, actor; b. Feb. 1, 1885, Missouri; d. Mar. 3, 1965
    (80).
Like, Ralph M., producer; b. Sept. 2, 1894, Iowa; d. Dec. 27, 1955
    (61).
Lillard, Charlotte, actress; d. Mar. 4, 1946 (62).
Lilley, Edward Clarke, director; d. Apr. 3, 1974 (86).
Limon, Jose, dancer & choreographer; d. Dec. 2, 1972 (64).
Lincoln, E.K., actor; b. Aug. 8, 1884, Pennsylvania; d. Jan. 9, 1958
    (73).
Lincoln, Elmo (r.n. Otto Elmo Linkenhelt), actor; b. Feb. 6, 1889,
    Rochester, Ind.; d. June 27, 1952 (63).
Lind, Emil, actor; b. Aug. 14, 1872; d. Apr. 7, 1948 (75).
Lind, Gus A., actor; d. June 4, 1951 (55).
Lind, Ilse, actress; d. Sept., 1955 (81).
Linder, Alfred, actor; b. June 27, 1902, Germany; d. July 4, 1957
    (55).
Linder, Max, actor; b. Dec. 16, 1883, Saint Loubes, France; d. Oct.
    31, 1925 (41).
Lindley, Bert, actor; b. Dec. 3, 1873, Chicago, Ill.; d. Sept. 12,
    1953 (79).
Lindo, Olga, actress; b. London, England; d. May 7, 1968 (69).
Lindroth, Helen, actress; d. Oct. 5, 1956.
Lindsay, Howard, actor, director, & author; b. Mar. 29, 1889,
    Waterford, N.Y.; d. Feb. 11, 1968 (78).
Lindsay, James, actor; b. 1871, London, England; d. June 9, 1928 (57).
Lindsay, Lex, actor; d. Apr. 24, 1971 (70).
Lindsey, Emily, actress; d. Mar. 3, 1944 (57).
Lindt, Karl (r.n. Karl Ludwig Lindt), actor; d. Oct. 17, 1971.
Lingen, Theo, actor; b. June 10, 1903, Hanover, Germany; d. Nov. 10,
    1978 (75).
Lingham, Thomas G., actor; b. Apr. 7, 1870, Indianapolis, Ind.;
    d. Feb. 19, 1950 (79).
Link, Adolf, actor; b. Budapest, Hungary; d. Sept. 24, 1933 (82).
Link, William, actor; d. Apr. 17, 1937 (70).
Link, William E., actor; d. Dec. 13, 1949 (52).
Linkmann, Ludwig, actor; d. June, 1963 (61).
Linley, Betty, actress; b. Malmesbury, England; d. May 9, 1951 (61).
Linn, Grafton, actor; b. Apr. 30, 1909, Indiana; d. July 31, 1968
    (59).
Lion, Leon M., actor; b. Mar. 12, 1879, London, England; d. Mar. 28,
    1947 (68).
Lippert, Robert L., producer; b. Mar. 11, 1909, San Francisco,
    Calif.; d. Nov. 16, 1976 (67).
Lipscomb, William P., writer; b. England; d. July 24, 1958 (70).
Lipson, Jack "Tiny," actor; b. Jan. 17, 1901, Colorado; d. Nov. 28,
    1947 (46).
Lipson, Melba, actress; d. July 1, 1953 (52).
Lipton, Lew, writer; b. Feb. 23, 1893, Chicago, Ill.; d. Dec. 27,
    1961 (68).
Lister, Francis, actor; b. Apr. 2, 1899, London, England; d. Oct. 28,
    1951 (52).

Litel, John, actor; b. Dec. 30, 1892, Albany, Wisc.; d. Feb. 3, 1972 (79).
Little, Jimmy, actor; d. Oct. 12, 1969 (62).
Little Billy (Billy Rhodes), actor; b. Feb. 1, 1894, Illinois; d. July 24, 1967 (73).
Littlefield, Lucien, actor; b. Aug. 16, 1895, Texas; d. June 4, 1960 (64).
Litvak, Anatole, director; b. May 10, 1902, Kiev, Russia; d. Dec. 15, 1974 (72).
Lively, William Edison, writer; b. June 27, 1907, Charleston, W. Va.; d. Sept. 29, 1973 (66).
Livesey, Jack, actor; b. June 11, 1901, Wales; d. Oct. 12, 1961 (60).
Livesey, Roger, actor; b. June 25, 1906, Barry, South Wales; d. Feb. 4, 1976 (69).
Livesey, Sam, actor; b. Oct. 14, 1873, Flintshire, England; d. Nov. 7, 1936 (63).
Livingstone, Frank H., actor & director; d. Nov. 26, 1932 (62).
Llewellyn, Fewlass, actor; b. Mar. 5, 1866, Hull, England; d. June 16, 1941 (75).
Lloyd, Alice, actress; d. Nov. 16, 1949 (76).
Lloyd, Charles M., actor; b. Virginia; d. Dec. 4, 1948 (78).
Lloyd, Doris (r.n. Hessy Doris Lloyd), actress; b. July 3, 1896, Liverpool, England; d. May 21, 1968 (71).
Lloyd, Ethel, actress; d. Jan. 12, 1923.
Lloyd, Frank, director & actor; b. Feb. 2, 1888, Glasgow, Scotland; d. Aug. 10, 1960 (72).
Lloyd, Frederick W., actor; b. Jan. 15, 1880, London, England; d. Nov. 24, 1949 (69).
Lloyd, Gaylord E., actor & director; d. Sept. 1, 1943 (55).
Lloyd, Gladys, actress; d. June 6, 1971 (75).
Lloyd, Harold, actor; b. Apr. 20, 1893, Burchard, Neb.; d. Mar. 8, 1971 (77).
Lloyd, Harold, Jr., actor; b. Jan. 25, 1931; d. June 8, 1971 (40).
Lloyd, Jack, actor & composer; d. May 21, 1976 (53).
Lloyd, Marie, actress; b. Feb. 12, 1870, London, England; d. Oct. 7, 1922 (52).
Lloyd, Rollo, actor; b. Mar. 22, 1883, Akron, Ohio; d. July 24, 1938 (55).
Loback, Marvin (r.n. Marvin Oscar Loback), actor; b. Nov. 21, 1896, Tacoma, Wash.; d. Aug. 18, 1938 (41).
Lochary, David, actor; d. July 29, 1977 (31).
Locher, Charles (see Hall, Jon)
Locher, Felix, actor; b. July 16, 1882, Switzerland; d. Mar. 13, 1969 (86).
Lockerbie, Beth, actress; d. Sept. 21, 1968 (53).
Lockhart, Gene, actor; b. July 18, 1891, London, Ontario, Canada; d. Mar. 31, 1957 (65).
Lockhart, Kathleen, actress; b. Southsea, England; d. Feb. 17, 1978 (84).
Lockin, Danny, actor; d. Aug. 21, 1977 (34).
Locklear, Omer, actor & stunt pilot; b. Oct. 28, 1891, Ft. Worth, Tex.; d. Aug. 2, 1920 (28).
Lockwood, Harold, actor; b. Apr. 12, 1887, Newark, N.J.; d. Oct. 19, 1918 (31).
Lockwood, King, actor; d. Feb. 23, 1971 (73).

Lodi, Theodore (r.n. Theodore Lodijensky), actor; b. Russia; d. Mar. 6, 1947 (71).

Loeb, Philip, actor; b. Philadelphia, Pa.; d. Sept. 1, 1955 (61).

Loedel, Adi, actor; b. Germany; d. June 2, 1955 (18).

Loeffler, Edward H., actor; d. Jan. 18, 1962 (79).

Loew, Marcus, executive & producer; b. May 7, 1870, New York City; d. Sept. 5, 1927 (57).

Loff, Jeanette, actress; b. Oct. 9, 1906, Cronno, Idaho; d. Aug. 4, 1942 (35).

Loft, Arthur, actor; b. May 25, 1897, Ouray, Colo.; d. Jan. 1, 1947 (49).

Loftus, Cecilia, actress; b. Oct. 22, 1876, Glasgow, Scotland; d. July 12, 1943 (66).

Logan, Ella, actress & singer; b. Mar. 6, 1913, Glasgow, Scotland; d. May 1, 1969 (56).

Logan, John, actor; b. Feb. 7, 1924, California; d. Dec. 7, 1972 (48).

Logan, Stanley, actor; b. June 12, 1885, Earlsfield, England; d. Jan. 30, 1953 (67).

Logothides, Basil, actor; d. Feb. 20, 1960 (62).

Logue, Charles A., writer; b. Feb. 8, 1889, Boston, Mass.; d. Aug. 2, 1938 (49).

Lohde, Sigurd, actor; d. July, 1977 (78).

Lohr, Marie, actress; b. July 28, 1890, Sydney, Australia; d. Jan. 21, 1975 (84).

Loja, Maria, actress; b. 1890; d. Jan. 3, 1953 (62).

Lomas, Herbert, actor; b. 1887, Burnley, England; d. Apr. 11, 1961 (74).

Lomas, Jack, actor; b. Mar. 23, 1911, New York; d. May 12, 1959 (48).

Lombard, Carole, actress; b. Oct. 6, 1909, Ft. Wayne, Ind.; d. Jan. 16, 1942 (32).

Lombardo, Guy, recording artist & orchestra leader; d. Nov. 5, 1977 (75).

London, Jack, actor; d. May 31, 1966 (61).

London, Tom, actor; b. Aug. 24, 1889, Louisville, Ky.; d. Dec. 5, 1963 (74).

Lonergan, Lester, actor; d. Aug. 13, 1931 (62).

Lonergan, Lester, Jr., actor; d. Dec. 23, 1959 (65).

Lonergan, Lloyd, writer; d. Apr. 6, 1937.

Long, Clyde Clement, actor; b. Sept. 25, 1886, La Crosse, Wisc.; d. Sept. 23, 1942 (55).

Long, Jack, stuntman; d. Aug. 7, 1938.

Long, Nick, Jr., actor; d. Aug. 31, 1949 (43).

Long, Richard, actor; b. Dec. 17, 1927, Chicago, Ill.; d. Dec. 21, 1974 (47).

Long, Robert, actor; b. Mar. 26, 1894, Indiana; d. July 5, 1972 (78).

Long, Walter, actor; b. Mar. 5, 1879, Nashua, N.H.; d. July 4, 1952 (73).

Longden, John, actor; b. Nov. 11, 1900, West Indies; d. May 26, 1971 (70).

Longman, Edward G., actor; b. 1881, Brooklyn, N.Y.; d. Apr. 14, 1969 (88).

Lono, Jimmie K., actor; d. Aug. 18, 1954 (64).

Lonsdale, Harry G., actor; d. July 12, 1923.

Lontoc, Leon, actor; b. Feb. 20, 1908, Philippines; d. Jan. 19, 1974 (65).

Loomes, Harry, actor; d. Mar. 17, 1946.
Loos, Theodor, actor; b. May 18, 1883, Zwingenberg, Germany; d. June 27, 1954 (71).
Loper, Don, dancer; d. Nov. 21, 1972 (65).
Lopez, Carlos (Chaflan), actor; b. Nov. 4, 1887, Durango, Mexico; d. Feb. 13, 1942 (54).
Lopez, Manuel, actor; d. Jan. 31, 1976.
Lopez, Sylvia, actress; d. Nov., 1959.
Lopez, Tony, actor; d. Sept. 23, 1949 (47).
Loraine, Oscar, actor; b. Oct. 11, 1877, Austria; d. May 7, 1955 (77).
Loraine, Robert, actor; b. Jan. 14, 1876, New Brighton, Cheshire, England; d. Dec. 23, 1935 (59).
Loraine, Violet, actress; b. July 26, 1886, London, England; d. July 18, 1956 (69).
Lorch, Theodore, actor; b. Sept. 29, 1880, Illinois; d. Nov. 11, 1947 (67).
Lord, Del, director; b. Oct. 7, 1894, Grimsley, Canada; d. Mar. 23, 1970 (75).
Lord, Marion, actress; d. May 25, 1942 (59).
Lord, Pauline, actress; b. Aug. 8, 1890, Hanford, Calif.; d. Oct. 10, 1950 (60).
Lord, Phillip F., actor; d. Nov. 25, 1968 (89).
Lord, Phillips H., actor & radio author; d. Oct. 19, 1975 (73).
Lord, Robert, writer; b. May 1, 1900, Chicago, Ill.; d. Apr. 5, 1976 (75).
Lorde, Athena, actress; b. Sept. 11, 1915, New York; d. May 23, 1973 (57).
Lorenz, John, actor; b. Buffalo, N.Y.; d. Apr. 30, 1972 (85).
Loring, Val, stuntman; d. Aug. 20, 1978 (38).
Lorne, Constance, actress; b. Apr. 26, 1914, Peebles, Scotland; d. Dec. 21, 1969 (55).
Lorne, Marion, actress; b. Aug. 12, 1888, Pennsylvania; d. May 9, 1968 (79).
Lorrain, Charles, actor; d. Jan. 4, 1933.
Lorraine, Harry, actor; d. Aug. 21, 1934 (44).
Lorraine, Jean, actress; d. Jan. 24, 1958 (51).
Lorraine, Leota, actress; b. Mar. 14, 1899, Kansas; d. July 9, 1974 (75).
Lorraine, Lillian, actress; b. Jan. 1, 1892, San Francisco, Calif.; d. Apr. 17, 1955 (63).
Lorraine, Victor, actor; d. Aug. 23, 1973 (84).
Lorre, Peter, actor; b. June 26, 1904, Rosenberg, Hungary; d. Mar. 23, 1964 (59).
Lory, Jacques (r.n. Jacques Laumonier), actor; b. July 16, 1904, France; d. July 1, 1947 (42).
Lorys, Denise, actress; d. Nov. 19, 1930.
Losch, Tilly, actress; b. Nov. 15, 1904, Vienna, Austria; d. Dec. 24, 1975 (71).
Losee, Frank, actor; b. Brooklyn, N.Y.; d. Nov. 14, 1937 (81).
Loskarn, Franz, actor; b. May 3, 1890, Munich, Germany; d. Apr. 23, 1978 (87).
Lothar, Hanns, actor; b. Apr. 10, 1929, Hannover, Germany; d. Mar. 11, 1967 (37).
Lotinga, Ernie, actor; b. Sunderland, England; d. Oct. 28, 1951 (75).

Lotto, Claire, actress; d. Aug., 1952 (59).
Lotto, Fred, actor; b. Oct. 11, 1854, England; d. Dec. 10, 1937 (83).
Louden, Thomas, actor; b. Sept. 3, 1874, Belfast, Ireland; d. Mar.
    15, 1948 (73).
Loughran, Lewis, actor; b. Aug. 2, 1914, Australia; d. Feb. 24, 1975
    (60).
Louis, Willard, actor; d. July 23, 1926 (40).
Louise, Anita, actress; b. Jan. 9, 1915, New York City; d. Apr. 25,
    1970 (55).
Loukes, Nicholas, actor; d. Apr. 18, 1976 (31).
Love, Clarence M., actor; d. Mar. 18, 1942 (74).
Love, Dorothea, actress; d. Nov. 27, 1979 (75).
Love, Montagu, actor; b. 1877, Portsmouth, England; d. May 17, 1943
    (66).
Love, Robert, actor; d. July 8, 1948 (34).
Lovejoy, Frank, actor; b. Mar. 28, 1912, New York City; d. Oct. 2,
    1962 (50).
Lovell, Leigh, actor; d. Aug. 8, 1935 (63).
Lovell, Raymond, actor; b. Apr. 13, 1900, Montreal, Canada; d. Oct.
    1, 1953 (53).
Lovering, Otho, director & film editor; b. Philadelphia, Pa.; d.
    Oct. 25, 1968 (79).
Lovsky, Celia, actress; b. Feb. 21, 1897, Czechoslovakia; d. Oct. 12,
    1979 (82).
Low, Jack, actor; b. Aug. 2, 1897, Colorado; d. Feb. 21, 1958 (60).
Lowe, Edmund, actor; b. Mar. 3, 1890, San Jose, Calif.; d. Apr. 20,
    1971 (81).
Lowe, Edward T., writer; b. June 29, 1890, Nashville, Tenn.; d. Apr.
    17, 1973 (82).
Lowe, Harry, actor; b. Dec. 29, 1902, California; d. Aug. 4, 1963
    (60).
Lowe, James B., actor; b. Oct. 12, 1879, Georgia; d. May 19, 1963
    (83).
Lowe, K. Elmo, actor; b. Aug. 27, 1899, San Antonio, Tex.; d. Jan.
    26, 1971 (71).
Lowe, Sherman, writer; b. Salt Lake City, Utah; d. Jan. 23, 1968
    (74).
Lowell, Dorothy, actress; d. July 1, 1944 (28).
Lowell, Helen, actress; b. June 2, 1866, New York City; d. June 28,
    1937 (71).
Lowell, Joan, actress; d. Nov. 7, 1967 (67).
Lowell, John (see Russell, John Lowell)
Lowenadler, Holger, actor; d. June 18, 1977 (73).
Lowery, Robert (r.n. Robert Lowery Hanks), actor; d. Oct. 17, 1916,
    Kansas City, Mo.; d. Dec. 26, 1971 (55).
Lowery, William A., actor; b. July 22, 1885, St. Louis, Mo.; d. Nov.
    15, 1941 (56).
Lowry, Judith, actress; b. July 27, 1890, Ft. Sill, Okla.; d. Nov.
    29, 1976 (86).
Lowry, Rudd, actor; d. Dec. 15, 1965 (73).
Loyd, Alison (see Todd, Thelma)
Lubin, Siegmund, producer; d. Sept. 11, 1923 (72).
Lubitsch, Ernst, director, producer, & actor; b. Jan. 28, 1892,
    Berlin, Germany; d. Nov. 30, 1947 (55).
Luby, Edna, actress; d. Oct. 1, 1928 (37).
Lucan, Arthur, actor; d. May 17, 1954 (67).
Lucas, Curt, actor; b. Jan. 20, 1888, Golzow; d. Sept., 1960 (72).

Lucas, Jimmy, actor; d. Feb. 21, 1949 (61).

Lucas, Sam, actor; d. Jan. 11, 1916 (76).

Lucas, Wilfred, actor; b. Jan. 30, 1871, Ontario, Canada; d. Dec. 13, 1940 (69).

Lucenay, Harry, actor; b. May 8, 1887, Marseilles, France; d. May 28, 1944 (57).

Luchaire, Corinne, actress; d. Jan. 22, 1950 (28).

Lucy, Arnold, actor; d. Dec. 15, 1945 (80).

Luddy, Barbara, actress; d. Apr. 1, 1979 (71).

Luden, Jack (r.n. John Benson Luden), actor; b. Feb. 8, 1902, Reading, Pa.; d. Feb. 15, 1951 (49).

Luders, Gunther, actor; b. Mar. 5, 1905, Lubeck, Germany; d. Mar. 1, 1975 (69).

Luff, William, actor; d. Mar. 15, 1960 (84).

Lufkin, Sam, actor; d. Feb. 19, 1952 (61).

Lugosi, Bela, actor; b. Oct. 20, 1882, Lugos, Hungary; d. Aug. 16, 1956 (73).

Luguet, Andre, actor; b. May 15, 1892, Fontenay-sous-Bois, France; d. May, 1979 (87).

Lukas, Paul, actor; b. May 26, 1894, Budapest, Hungary; d. Aug. 15, 1971 (77).

Lukin, Mrs. Cecil S., actress; d. Sept. 2, 1953 (48).

Lukyanov, Sergey V., actor; b. Oct. 27, 1910; d. Mar. 1, 1965 (54).

Lulli, Folco, actor; b. July 3, 1912, Firenze, Italy; d. May 24, 1970 (57).

Lumiere, Auguste, producer; d. Apr. 10, 1954 (92).

Lumiere, Louis, producer; d. June 6, 1948 (83).

Lumley, Molly, actress; d. Oct. 22, 1960.

Luna, Donyale, actress; d. May 17, 1979 (33).

Lund, Richard, actor; d. Sept. 17, 1960 (75).

Lundequist, Gerda, actress; d. Oct., 1959 (88).

Lundigan, William, actor; b. June 12, 1914, Syracuse, N.Y.; d. Dec. 20, 1975 (61).

Lung, Charlie (r.n. Bernard Clerc Davey), actor; b. May 3, 1897, England; d. June 22, 1974 (77).

Lunt, Alfred, actor; b. Aug. 19, 1892, Milwaukee, Wisc.; d. Aug. 3, 1977 (84).

Lupino, Barry, actor; b. Jan. 7, 1882, London, England; d. Sept. 25, 1962 (80).

Lupino, Stanley, actor; b. May 15, 1893, London, England; d. June 10, 1942 (49).

Lupino, Wallace, actor; b. Jan. 23, 1897, Edinburgh, Scotland; d. Oct. 11, 1961 (64).

Lupo, George G., actor; d. Aug. 8, 1973 (49).

Lusk, Freeman, actor; b. Sept. 11, 1905, California; d. Aug. 25, 1970 (64).

Lussier, Dane, writer; b. Dec. 23, 1909, Spokane, Wash.; d. Oct. 20, 1959 (49).

Luther, Anna, actress; b. July 7, 1897, New Jersey; d. Dec. 16, 1960 (63).

Luther, Johnny, actor; b. Aug. 3, 1908, Missouri; d. July 30, 1960 (51).

Luther, Lester, actor; b. Dec. 18, 1887, N.A.; d. Jan. 19, 1962 (74).

Luttringer, Al, actor; b. Nov. 16, 1878, California; d. June 9, 1953 (74).

Lydecker, Howard, Jr., special effects artist; d. Sept. 28, 1969 (58).

Lyel, Viola, actress; b. Dec. 9, 1900, Hill, Yorks., England; d. Aug. 14, 1972 (71).
Lygo, Mary, actress; d. June 1, 1927.
Lyle, Clinton, actor; b. Aug. 27, 1883, California; d. June 26, 1950 (66).
Lynch, Brid, actress; d. Oct. 27, 1969 (55).
Lynch, Helen, actress; b. Apr. 6, 1900, Billings, Mont.; d. Mar. 2, 1965 (64).
Lyndon, Alice, actress; d. July 9, 1949 (75).
Lyndon, Barre, scenarist; b. Aug. 12, 1896, London, England; d. Oct. 23, 1972 (76).
Lynn, Diana (r.n. Dolly Loehr), actress; b. Oct. 7, 1926, Los Angeles, Calif.; d. Dec. 17, 1971 (45).
Lynn, Emmett, actor; b. Feb. 14, 1897, Muscatine, Iowa; d. Oct. 20, 1958 (61).
Lynn, Hastings, actor; d. June 30, 1932 (53).
Lynn, Ralph, actor; b. Mar. 18, 1882, Manchester, England; d. Aug. 8, 1962 (80).
Lynn, Robert, actor; d. Dec. 18, 1969 (72).
Lynn, Sharon, actress; b. Apr. 9, 1910, Weatherford, Tex.; d. May 26, 1963 (53).
Lynn, William H., actor; b. Providence, R.I.; d. Jan. 5, 1952 (63).
Lyon, Ben, actor; b. Feb. 6, 1901, Atlanta, Ga.; d. Mar. 22, 1979 (78).
Lyon, Frank, actor; b. Bridgeport, Conn.; d. Jan. 6, 1961 (60).
Lyon, Therese, actress; b. Aug. 14, 1887, Missouri; d. Apr. 15, 1975 (87).
Lyons, Chester, cinematographer; d. Nov. 27, 1936 (51).
Lyons, Cliff (r.n. Clifford William Lyons), actor & stuntman; b. July 4, 1901, South Dakota; d. Jan. 6, 1974 (72).
Lyons, Eddie, actor; d. Aug. 30, 1926 (40).
Lyons, Gene, actor; b. Feb. 9, 1921, Pennsylvania; d. July 8, 1974 (53).
Lyons, Harry, actor; d. Mar. 13, 1919.
Lyons, Tex (see Lyons, Cliff)
Lysons, Sam, actor; d. Feb. 20, 1953.
Lytell, Bert, actor; b. Feb. 24, 1885, New York City; d. Sept. 28, 1954 (69).
Lytell, Wilfred, actor; d. Sept. 10, 1954 (62).
Lytton, Bart, writer; d. June 29, 1969 (56).
Lytton, L. Rogers, actor; b. 1867, New Orleans, La.; d. Aug. 9, 1924 (57).


MacAnnan, George Burr, actor; b. Nov. 30, 1887, Texas; d. Nov. 12, 1970 (82).
MacArthur, Charles, playwright, author, & actor; b. Nov. 5, 1895, Scranton, Pa.; d. Apr. 21, 1956 (60).
Macaulay, Richard, writer; b. Chicago, Ill.; d. Sept. 18, 1969 (60).
MacBride, Donald, actor; b. June 23, 1893, Brooklyn, N.Y.; d. June 21, 1957 (63).
MacColl, James A., actor; d. Apr. 18, 1956 (44).
MacDermott, Marc, actor; b. July 24, 1881, Australia; d. Jan. 5, 1929 (47).
MacDonald, Catherine R.D., actress; d. Apr. 4, 1929.
MacDonald, Donald, actor; b. Mar. 13, 1898, Denison, Tex.; d. Dec. 9, 1959 (61).

MacDonald, Edmund, actor; b. May 7, 1908, Massachusetts; d. Sept. 2, 1951 (43).

MacDonald, Harry, actor; d. June 2, 1943 (73).

MacDonald, J. Farrell, actor; b. Apr. 14, 1875, Waterbury, Conn.; d. Aug. 2, 1952 (77).

MacDonald, Jeanette, actress & singer; b. June 18, 1907, Philadelphia, Pa.; d. Jan. 14, 1965 (57).

MacDonald, Katherine, actress; b. Dec. 14, 1891, Pennsylvania; d. June 4, 1956 (64).

MacDonald, Kenneth (r.n. Kenneth Dollins), actor; b. Sept. 8, 1901, Portland, Ind.; d. May 5, 1972 (70).

MacDonald, Pauline, actress; b. Dec. 21, 1912, Iowa; d. Jan. 29, 1976 (63).

MacDonald, Wallace, actor & producer; b. May 5, 1891, Mulgrave, N.S., Canada; d. Oct. 30, 1978 (87).

MacDougall, James D., actor; d. May, 1932.

MacDougall, Allan Ross, actor; b. Scotland; d. July 19, 1956 (62).

MacDougall, Ranald, writer; d. Dec. 12, 1973 (58).

MacDowell, Melbourne, actor; b. South River, N.J.; d. Feb. 18, 1941 (84).

MacFadden, Gertrude "Mickey," actress; d. June 3, 1967 (67).

MacFarlane, Bruce, actor; b. July 11, 1913, Washington; d. Nov. 25, 1967 (54).

MacFarlane, George, actor; b. Montreal, Canada; d. Feb. 22, 1932 (55).

MacGill, Moyna, actress; b. Dec. 10, 1895, Belfast, No. Ireland; d. Nov. 25, 1975 (79).

Macgowan, Kenneth, producer; b. Nov. 30, 1888, Winthrop, Mass.; d. Apr. 27, 1963 (74).

MacGowran, Jack, actor; b. Oct. 13, 1918, Dublin, Ireland; d. Jan. 30, 1973 (54).

MacGregor, Harmon B., actor; d. Dec. 4, 1948 (70).

MacGregor, Lee, actor; d. June, 1961 (34).

MacGregor, Parke, actor; d. Dec. 5, 1962 (55).

Mack, Andrew, actor; b. Boston, Mass.; d. May 21, 1931 (67).

Mack, Arthur, actor; d. June 19, 1942 (65).

Mack, Cactus (see McPeters, Taylor)

Mack, Charles E., actor; b. Nov. 22, 1887, White Cloud, Kans.; d. Jan. 11, 1934 (46).

Mack, Charles Emmett (r.n. Charles Stewart McNerney), actor; b. Nov. 25, 1900, Scranton, Pa.; d. Mar. 17, 1927 (26).

Mack, Charles W., actor & producer; d. Nov. 29, 1956 (78).

Mack, Eddie, actor; d. Aug. 1, 1944 (65).

Mack, Gertrude, actress; b. Nov. 16, 1896, Pennsylvania; d. Mar. 11, 1967 (70).

Mack, Hayward, actor; b. New York; d. Dec. 24, 1921 (42).

Mack, Hughie, actor; d. Oct. 13, 1927 (43).

Mack, Hughie, actor; d. Apr. 3, 1952 (54).

Mack, James (Buck), actor; d. Sept. 19, 1959 (71).

Mack, James T., actor; d. Aug. 12, 1948 (77).

Mack, Joseph P., actor; b. May 4, 1878, Boleneva, Italy; d. Apr. 8, 1946 (67).

Mack, Lester, actor; d. Oct. 11, 1972 (66).

Mack, Max, director, actor, producer, & author; b. Oct. 21, 1884, Halberstadt, Germany; d. Mar., 1973 (88).

Mack, Nila, actress & radio producer; d. Jan. 20, 1953 (62).

Mack, Rose, actress; d. Oct. 9, 1927 (61).

Mack, Russell, director; b. Oneonta, N.Y.; d. June 1, 1972 (79).
Mack, Wilbur, actor; b. July 29, 1873, New York; d. Mar. 13, 1964 (90).
Mack, Willard, actor; b. Sept. 18, 1873, Morrisburg, Ontario, Canada;
     d. Nov. 18, 1934 (61).
Mack, William B., actor; d. Sept. 13, 1955 (83).
MacKay, Charles Donald, actor; d. Nov. 19, 1935 (68).
MacKay, Edward J., actor & director; d. Dec. 26, 1948 (74).
Mackay, Jock, actor; d. Apr. 11, 1961.
Mackay, Leonard, actor; d. Jan. 3, 1929 (60).
Mackaye, Dorothy, actress; d. Jan. 5, 1940 (37).
MacKaye, Norman, actor; d. Apr. 24, 1968 (62).
MacKenna, Kate, actress; d. June 14, 1957 (79).
MacKenna, Kenneth, actor; b. Aug. 19, 1899, Canterbury, N.H.; d. Jan.
     15, 1962 (62).
Mackenzie, Aeneas, writer; d. June 2, 1962 (72).
Mackenzie, Alexander, actor; d. Dec., 1965 (80).
Mackenzie, Donald, actor & director; b. 1879, Edinburgh, Scotland;
     d. July 21, 1972 (93).
Mackenzie, Mary, actress; d. Sept. 20, 1966 (44).
MacLane, Mary, actress & author; d. Aug., 1929.
MacLane, Barton, actor; b. Dec. 25, 1902, Columbia, S.C.; d. Jan. 1,
     1969 (66).
Mackintosh, Louise, actress; b. Dec. 24, 1864, Port Hastings, Great
     Britain; d. Nov. 1, 1933 (68).
MacLaren, Ian, actor; b. May 1, 1875, Lynmouth, England; d. Apr. 10,
     1952 (76).
MacLaren, Ivor, producer & actor; b. Wimbledon, England; d. Oct. 30,
     1962 (58).
MacLean, Douglas (r.n. Charles Douglas MacLean), actor, author, &
     producer; b. Jan. 10, 1890, Philadelphia, Pa.; d. July 9, 1967
     (77).
MacLean, R.D., actor; b. Mar. 7, 1859, New Orleans, La.; d. June 27,
     1948 (89).
MacLeod, Kenneth T., actor; b. Sept. 6, 1895, Massachusetts; d. Dec.
     6, 1963 (68).
MacLiammoir, Micheal, actor; b. Oct. 25, 1899, Cork, Ireland; d. Mar.
     6, 1978 (78).
MacMahon, John G., actor; b. July 18, 1890, Louisiana; d. Aug. 18,
     1968 (78).
MacMillan, Violet, actress; d. Dec. 28, 1953 (66).
MacNaughton, Tom, actor; d. Nov. 28, 1923 (57).
MacPhail, Angus, writer; b. Apr. 8, 1903, London, England; d. Apr.
     22, 1962 (59).
MacPherson, James Gladstone, actor; d. Dec. 14, 1932.
MacPherson, Jeanie, author & actress; b. Boston, Mass.; d. Aug. 26,
     1946 (59).
MacPherson, Quinton, actor; d. Jan. 2, 1940 (69).
MacQuarrie, Albert, actor; b. Jan. 8, 1882, California; d. Feb. 17,
     1950 (68).
MacQuarrie, Frank M. (r.n. Frank Mike MacQuarrie), actor; b. Jan. 27,
     1875, California; d. Dec. 25, 1950 (75).
MacQuarrie, Haven (r.n. Frank Haven MacQuarrie), actor; b. Apr. 10,
     1894, Massachusetts; d. Aug. 4, 1953 (59).
MacQuarrie, Murdock, actor; b. Aug. 25, 1878, San Francisco, Calif.;
     d. Aug. 20, 1942 (63).

Macrae, Arthur, actor; b. Mar. 17, 1908, London, England; d. Feb. 25, 1962 (53).
Macrae, Duncan, actor; b. Glasgow, Scotland; d. Mar. 23, 1967 (61).
Macrorie, Alma, actress & editor; d. June 28, 1970 (65).
MacSarin, Kenneth, actor; d. Jan. 17, 1967 (55).
MacVicar, Martha (see Vickers, Martha)
McAllister, Paul, actor; b. June 30, 1875, Brooklyn, N.Y.; d. July 8, 1955 (80).
McAlpine, Jane, actress; d. Oct. 19, 1947 (51).
McAtee, Ben, actor; b. Jan. 15, 1903, Alabama; d. Dec. 3, 1961 (58).
McAtee, Clyde, actor; d. Feb. 20, 1947 (66).
McAvoy, Charles, actor; b. Apr. 2, 1885, New York; d. Apr. 20, 1953 (68).
McAvoy, Jean, actress; d. May 18, 1934 (22).
McAvoy, Mai Lewerenz, actress; b. Dec. 25, 1878, Michigan; d. Nov. 27, 1960 (81).
McBride, Carl, actor; d. Dec. 16, 1937 (44).
McCabe, George F., actor; d. Dec. 17, 1917.
McCabe, Harry, actor; d. Feb. 11, 1925 (44).
McCabe, Joe, actor; b. Jan. 31, 1913, Hawaii; d. Nov. 3, 1960 (47).
McCabe, John, actor; d. June 19, 1929 (50).
McCabe, May North, actress; d. June 22, 1949 (76).
McCall, Rex, actor; d. Oct. 30, 1939 (58).
McCall, William, actor; b. May 19, 1870, Delavin, Ill.; d. Jan. 10, 1938 (67).
McCallin, Clement, actor; b. Mar. 6, 1913, London, England; d. Aug., 1977 (64).
McCallum, John A., actor; b. Mar. 1, 1863, England; d. Feb. 19, 1923 (59).
McCallum, Neil, actor; d. Apr. 26, 1976 (46).
McCann, Frances, opera singer; d. Mar. 14, 1963 (41).
McCarey, Leo, director & producer; b. Los Angeles, Calif.; d. July 5, 1969 (71).
McCarey, Ray, director; d. Dec. 1, 1948 (50).
McCarroll, Frank, actor; b. Sept. 5, 1892, Minnesota; d. Mar. 8, 1954 (61).
McCarthy, Charlie, dummy; d. Sept. 30, 1978 (64).
McCarthy, Denis, actor; d. May, 1977.
McCarthy, Earl, actor; b. Ft. Wayne, Ind.; d. May 28, 1933 (27).
McCarthy, Eugene, actor; b. Mar. 31, 1884, Chicago, Ill.; d. Jan. 20, 1943 (58).
McCarthy, John P., director & author; b. Mar. 17, 1885, San Francisco, Calif.; d. Sept. 4, 1962 (77).
McCarthy, Myles, actor; b. Toronto, Canada; d. Sept. 27, 1928 (54).
McClain, Billy, actor; b. Sept. 15, 1884, Indiana; d. Jan. 28, 1950 (65).
McClary, Clyde, actor; d. June 30, 1939 (44).
McCauley, Edna, actress; d. 1918.
McClellan, Hurd, stuntman; d. Apr. 20, 1933.
McClintock, Harry K., singer & recording artist; b. Oct. 8, 1882, Knoxville, Tenn.; d. Apr. 24, 1957 (74).
McCloskey, Elizabeth Hayward, actress; d. Jan. 8, 1942 (70).
McClung, Bob, actor; d. Jan. 27, 1945 (24).
McClure, Bud, actor; d. Nov. 2, 1942 (56).
McClure, Frank, actor; d. Jan. 23, 1960 (65).
McClure, Gladys, actress; d. Dec., 1933 (18).

McClure, Irene, actress; d. Sept. 4, 1928.
McCollum, H.H., actor; d. Dec. 19, 1938.
McComas, Carroll, actress; b. Albuquerque, N.M.; d. Nov. 9, 1962 (76).
McComas, Glenn, actor; d. June 10, 1959 (59).
McComas, Lila, actress; d. June 13, 1936 (30).
McComas, Ralph C., actor; b. Sept. 8, 1889, California; d. July 13, 1924 (34).
McConnell, Gladys, actress; b. Oct. 22, 1907, Oklahoma City, Okla.; d. Mar. 4, 1979 (71).
McConnell, Lulu, actress; b. Apr. 8, 1882, Missouri; d. Oct. 9, 1962 (80).
McConnell, Mollie, actress; b. Sept. 24, 1865, Indiana; d. Dec. 9, 1920 (55).
McCord, Mrs. Lewis, actress; d. Dec. 24, 1917.
McCormack, Blanche, actress; d. Jan. 31, 1935 (58).
McCormack, Frank, actor; b. Washington, D.C.; d. May 22, 1941 (65).
McCormack, John, actor & opera singer; b. June 14, 1884, Athlone, Ireland; d. Sept. 16, 1945 (61).
McCormick, Alyce, actress; d. Jan. 6, 1932 (30).
McCormick, F.J., actor; b. Skerries, Ireland; d. Apr. 24, 1947 (56).
McCormick, Merrill (William Merrill McCormick), actor; b. Feb. 5, 1892, Denver, Colo.; d. Aug. 19, 1953 (61).
McCormick, Myron, actor; b. Feb. 8, 1908, Albany, Ind.; d. July 30, 1962 (54).
McCormick, William (see McCormick, Merrill)
McCoy, George B., actor; b. Jan. 14, 1904, Florida; d. Dec. 22, 1976 (72).
McCoy, Gertrude, actress; b. June 30, 1890, Sugar Valley, Ga.; d. July 17, 1967 (77).
McCoy, Harry, actor; d. Sept. 1, 1937 (43).
McCoy, Horace, writer; d. Dec. 16, 1955 (58).
McCoy, Tim, actor; b. Apr. 10, 1891, Saginaw, Mich.; d. Jan. 29, 1978 (86).
McCracken, Joan, actress; b. Dec. 31, 1922, Philadelphia, Pa.; d. Nov. 1, 1961 (38).
McCue, Matthew, actor; b. Oct. 4, 1895, Illinois; d. Apr. 10, 1966 (70).
McCullough, Paul, actor; b. Springfield, Ohio; d. Mar. 25, 1936 (52).
McCullough, Ralph, actor; b. Sept. 2, 1895, Laramie, Wyo.; d. Dec. 25, 1943 (48).
McCutcheon, Wallace, actor; b. Dec. 23, 1894, New York; d. Jan. 27, 1928 (33).
McDaniel, Etta, actress; b. Dec. 1, 1890, Wichita, Kans.; d. Jan. 13, 1946 (55).
McDaniel, George, actor; d. Aug. 20, 1944 (58).
McDaniel, Hattie, actress; b. June 10, 1895, Wichita, Kans.; d. Oct. 26, 1952 (57).
McDaniel, Sam "Deacon," actor; b. Jan. 29, 1886, Kansas; d. Sept. 24, 1962 (76).
McDermid, Del A., actor; d. Mar. 1, 1941 (52).
McDermott, Aline L., actress; d. Feb. 16, 1951 (70).
McDermott, Hugh, actor; b. Mar. 20, 1908, Edinburgh, Scotland; d. Jan. 30, 1972 (63).
McDermott, John, actor & author; d. July 22, 1946 (53).
McDevitt, Ruth, actress; b. Sept. 13, 1895, Coldwater, Mich.; d. May 27, 1976 (80).
McDonald, Charles, actor; d. Aug. 7, 1953 (77).

McDonald, Charles B., actor; b. May 26, 1886, Springfield, Mass.;
    d. Dec. 29, 1964 (78).
McDonald, Francis, actor; b. Aug. 22, 1891, Bowling Green, Ky.;
    d. Sept. 18, 1968 (77).
McDonald, James, actor; d. Dec. 26, 1952 (66).
McDonald, Joseph, actor; d. Oct. 27, 1935 (74).
McDonald, Marie, actress; b. July 6, 1923, Burgin, Ky.; d. Oct. 21,
    1965 (42).
McDonald, Ray, actor & dancer; b. Boston, Mass.; d. Feb. 20, 1959
    (35).
McDonald, Samson (Death Valley Mack) (r.n. Sampson McDonald), actor;
    b. Aug. 24, 1887; d. Sept. 25, 1970 (83).
McDonough, Joseph A., actor; d. May 11, 1944.
McDonough, Michael, actor; d. Aug. 8, 1956 (80).
McDonough, Robert M., stuntman; d. Dec. 11, 1945 (45).
McDowell, Claire, actress; b. Nov. 2, 1877, New York City; d. Oct.
    23, 1966 (88).
McDowell, Nelson, actor; b. Aug. 14, 1870, Greenfield, Mo.; d. Nov. 3,
    1947 (77).
McDuff, James, actor; d. Mar. 31, 1937 (74).
McDunnough, Walter S., actor; b. Dec. 15, 1863, Montreal, Canada;
    d. July 1, 1942 (78).
McElroy, Bob (r.n. Robert F. McElroy), actor; b. Oct. 3, 1890, Ken-
    tucky; d. Jan. 29, 1976 (85).
McEvoy, Dorothea, actress; d. Feb. 6, 1976 (79).
McEvoy, Earl, director; d. Feb. 26, 1959.
McEvoy, Ernest Simon, actor; d. Apr. 14, 1953 (59).
McEwan, Isabelle, singer; d. Feb. 19, 1963 (66).
McFadden, Charles Ivor, actor; b. Aug. 6, 1887, San Francisco, Calif.;
    d. Aug. 14, 1942 (55).
McFadden, Ivor (see McFadden, Charles I.)
McGarry, Garry, actor; d. Oct. 17, 1927 (38).
McGaugh, Wilbur, actor & assistant director; b. Mar. 12, 1895,
    California; d. Jan. 31, 1965 (69).
McGee, James, actor, producer, & author; b. June 7, 1873, Browns-
    ville, Neb.; d. Feb. 15, 1936 (62).
McGehee, Gloria, actress; d. May 4, 1964 (42).
McGill, Barney, cinematographer; d. Jan. 11, 1942 (50).
McGinn, Walter, actor; b. July 6, 1936, Providence, R.I.; d. Mar. 31,
    1977 (40).
McGiveney, Owen, actor; b. May 4, 1884, England; d. July 31, 1967
    (83).
McGiver, John, actor; b. Nov. 5, 1912, New York City; d. Sept. 9,
    1975 (62).
McGlynn, Frank, Sr., actor; b. Oct. 26, 1866, San Francisco, Calif.;
    d. May 18, 1951 (84).
McGlynn, Frank, Jr., actor; b. July 9, 1904, Marin Co., Calif.;
    d. Mar. 29, 1939 (34).
McGowan, J.P., actor & director; b. Feb. 24, 1880, Australia;
    d. Mar. 26, 1952 (72).
McGowan, Oliver, actor; b. Aug. 22, 1907, Kipling, Ala.; d. Aug. 23,
    1971 (64).
McGowan, Robert F., director; d. Jan. 27, 1955 (72).
McGrail, Walter, actor; b. Oct. 19, 1888, Brooklyn, N.Y.; d. Mar. 19,
    1970 (81).

McGranary, Al, actor; b. Sept. 3, 1902, Pennsylvania; d. May 15, 1971 (68).
McGrath, Frank, actor & stuntman; b. Feb. 2, 1903, Missouri; d. May 13, 1967 (64).
McGrath, Larry, actor; b. Aug. 28, 1888, New York; d. July 6, 1960 (71).
McGrath, Michael, actor; d. Jan. 16, 1976.
McGrath, Paul, actor; b. Apr. 11, 1904, Chicago, Ill.; d. Apr. 13, 1978 (74).
McGrath, Thomas, actor; d. Apr. 22, 1937 (79).
McGregor, Malcolm, actor; b. Oct. 13, 1892, Newark, N.J.; d. Apr. 29, 1945 (52).
McGuinn, Joe, actor; b. Jan. 21, 1904, Brooklyn, N.Y.; d. Sept. 22, 1971 (67).
McGuinness, James K., writer & producer; b. Dec. 20, 1893, New York City; d. Dec. 4, 1950 (56).
McGuire, Frederick Clarence, actor; b. May 5, 1878, Ontario, Canada; d. Apr. 14, 1942 (63).
McGuire, Kathryn, actress; d. Oct. 10, 1978 (74).
McGuire, Tom (r.n. Thomas Maguire), actor; b. Sept. 1, 1873, England; d. May 6, 1954 (80).
McGuire, William Anthony, writer; d. Sept. 16, 1940 (59).
McGuirk, Charles J., actor; d. Dec. 4, 1943 (54).
McGuirk, Harriet E., skater; d. Dec. 19, 1975 (72).
McGurk, Bob, actor; d. May 30, 1959 (52).
McHugh, Catherine, actress; d. Mar. 25, 1954 (84).
McHugh, Charles, actor; b. July 20, 1870, Philadelphia, Pa.; d. Oct. 21, 1931 (62).
McHugh, Grace, actress; d. July 1, 1914.
McHugh, Matt, actor; b. Jan. 22, 1894, Connellsville, Pa.; d. Feb. 22, 1971 (77).
McIllwain, William A., actor; d. May 27, 1933 (70).
McIntosh, Burr, actor; b. Aug. 21, 1862, Wellsville, Ohio; d. Apr. 28, 1942 (79).
McIntyre, Duncan, actor; d. Nov., 1973 (66).
McIntyre, Frank, actor; b. Feb. 25, 1879, Ann Arbor, Mich.; d. June 8, 1949 (70).
McIntyre, Leila, actress; b. Dec. 20, 1882, New York; d. Jan. 9, 1953 (70).
McIntyre, Marion (Marion Gray), actress; d. Nov. 19, 1975 (90).
McIntyre, Molly, actress; d. Jan. 29, 1952 (65).
McIver, George, actor; d. Feb. 6, 1957 (40).
McIvor, Mary, actress; d. Feb. 28, 1941 (40).
McKay, George (Red), actor; b. Apr. 15, 1886, Salt Lake City, Utah; d. Dec. 3, 1945 (59).
McKechnie, James, actor; b. Glasgow, Scotland; d. May 7, 1964 (53).
McKee, Buck, actor; b. Claremore, Okla.; d. Mar. 1, 1944 (79).
McKee, Donald M., actor; d. June 27, 1968 (69).
McKee, John, actor; d. Dec. 28, 1953.
McKee, Lafe (r.n. Lafayette S. McKee), actor; b. Jan. 23, 1872, Morrison, Ill.; d. Aug. 10, 1959 (87).
McKee, Pat R. (r.n. Frank Robert Crandall), actor; b. Mar. 24, 1895, Texas; d. Jan. 7, 1950 (54).
McKee, Scott, actor; b. May 9, 1881, Scotland; d. Apr. 17, 1945 (63).
McKee, Tom, actor; b. May 30, 1917, New York; d. June 20, 1960 (43).

McKeen, Lawrence D. (Snookums), Jr., actor; d. Apr. 2, 1933 (8).
McKelvie, Harold, actor & stuntman; d. June 9, 1937 (27).
McKenna, Henry T., actor; d. June 17, 1958 (64).
McKentry, Elizabeth, actress; d. Sept. 3, 1920 (21).
McKenzie, Robert B., actor; b. Sept. 22, 1880, Bellymania, Ireland;
    d. July 8, 1949 (68).
McKibbon, Columbia, actress; d. Oct. 4, 1948 (52).
McKim, Robert, actor; b. Aug. 26, 1886, California; d. June 4, 1927
    (40).
McKimson, Robert, animator; b. Oct. 13, 1910, Colorado; d. Sept. 27,
    1977 (66).
McKinnell, Norman, actor; b. Feb. 10, 1870, Maxwelltown, N.B.,
    Canada; d. Mar. 29, 1932 (62).
McKinney, Florine, actress; b. Dec. 13, 1912, Mart, Tex.; d. July
    28, 1975 (62).
McKinney, Nina Mae, actress; b. June 12, 1913, Lancaster, S.C.;
    d. May 3, 1967 (53).
McKnight, Anne, actress; d. Mar. 25, 1930 (22).
McLaglen, Clifford, actor; d. Sept., 1978 (86).
McLaglen, Victor, actor; b. Dec. 10, 1886, London, England; d. Nov.
    7, 1959 (72).
McLarty, James E., actor & author; b. Texas; d. Apr. 16, 1979 (48).
McLaughlin, Gibb, actor; b. July 19, 1884, Sunderland, England;
    d. 1960 (76).
McLennan, Rod, actor; d. Nov. 27, 1973.
McLeod, Barbara, actress; d. May 26, 1940 (32).
McLeod, Helen, actress; d. Apr. 20, 1964 (40).
McLeod, Norman Z., director; b. Sept. 20, 1895, Michigan; d. Jan.
    26, 1964 (68).
McMahon, David, actor; b. Dec. 11, 1910, New York; d. Jan. 27, 1972
    (61).
McMahon, Horace, actor; b. May 17, 1907, S. Norwalk, Conn.; d. Aug.
    17, 1971 (64).
McManus, George, actor & comic artist; b. Jan. 23, 1884, St. Louis,
    Mo.; d. Oct. 22, 1954 (70).
McMillan, Roddy, actor; d. July 9, 1979 (56).
McMillan, Walter Kenneth, actor; d. Jan., 1945 (28).
McMurphy, Charles, actor; b. July 31, 1892, North Vernon, Ind.;
    d. Oct. 24, 1969 (77).
McNall, Orange, actor; b. Apr. 29, 1890, Nebraska; d. Mar. 11, 1963
    (72).
McNamara, Edward, actor; b. Paterson, N.J.; d. Nov. 9, 1944 (57).
McNamara, James E., actor; b. June 28, 1891, Hartford, Conn.;
    d. July 4, 1946 (55).
McNamara, Maggie, actress; b. June 18, 1928, New York; d. Feb. 18,
    1978 (49).
McNamara, Ted, actor; b. Australia; d. Feb. 3, 1928 (36).
McNamara, Thomas J., actor; d. May 21, 1953.
McNamara, Tom, director & author; d. May 19, 1964 (78).
McNamee, Graham, announcer; d. May 9, 1942 (53).
McNaughton, Charles, actor; b. Apr. 24, 1878, England; d. Dec. 4,
    1955 (77).
McNaughton, Gus, actor; b. July, 1881, London, England; d. Nov. 18,
    1969 (88).
McNaughton, Harry, actor; d. Feb. 27, 1967 (70).
McNear, Howard, actor; b. Jan. 27, 1905, California; d. Jan. 3, 1969
    (64).

McNeil, Norman, actor; b. Oct. 27, 1891, Charleston, S.C.; d. Dec. 17, 1938 (47).
McNulty, Harold, actor; d. June 6, 1978 (75).
McNutt, Patterson, writer & producer; b. Sept. 30, 1896, Urbana, Ill.; d. Oct. 22, 1948 (52).
McNutt, William Slavens, writer & director; b. Sept. 12, 1885, Urbana, Ill.; d. Jan. 25, 1938 (52).
McPeters, Taylor (Cactus Mack), actor; b. Aug. 8, 1899, Weed, N.M.; d. Apr. 17, 1962 (62).
McPhail, Douglas, actor & singer; b. Apr. 16, 1910, Los Angeles, Calif.; d. Dec. 7, 1944 (34).
McQuade, John, actor; d. Sept. 21, 1979 (63).
McQuary, Charles S., actor; d. Feb. 9, 1970 (62).
McQuoid, Edwin (Bud), actor; d. July 15, 1950 (40).
McQuoid, Rose Lee, actress; b. Oct. 26, 1886, Arizona; d. May 4, 1962 (75).
McRae, Bruce, actor; b. Jan. 15, 1867, India; d. May 7, 1927 (60).
McRae, Duncan, actor & producer; d. Feb. 4, 1931.
McRae, Henry, director & producer; d. Oct. 2, 1944 (68).
McShane, Kitty, actress; d. Mar. 24, 1964 (66).
McTaggart, Malcolm "Bud" (James Taggart), actor; b. May 23, 1910, Nebraska; d. May 29, 1949 (39).
McTurk, Joe, actor; d. July 19, 1961 (63).
McVeigh, Pat (see McVey, Patrick)
McVey, Lucille (see Drew, Lucille McVey)
McVey, Patrick (Pat McVeigh), actor; b. Mar. 17, 1910, Ft. Wayne, Ind.; d. July 6, 1973 (63).
McVicker, Julius, actor; d. Mar. 11, 1940 (84).
McWade, Edward, actor; b. Jan. 14, 1865, Washington, D.C.; d. May 17, 1943 (78).
McWade, Margaret, actress; b. Sept. 3, 1872, Illinois; d. Apr. 1, 1956 (83).
McWade, Robert, actor; b. June 17, 1872, Buffalo, N.Y.; d. Jan. 19, 1938 (65).
McWatters, Arthur J., actor; d. July 16, 1963 (92).
Mabley, Jackie (Moms), actress; d. May 23, 1975 (75).
Macchia, John, actor; b. Oct. 30, 1931, California; d. July 30, 1967 (35).
Mace, Fred, actor & director; d. Feb. 21, 1917 (39).
Mace, Wynn, actor; b. Aug. 3, 1890, South Pasadena, Calif.; d. Jan. 15, 1955 (64).
Machaty, Gustav, director; b. May 9, 1901, Prague, Czechoslovakia; d. Dec. 14, 1963 (62).
Maciste (Ernesto Pagani; Bartolomeo Pagano), actor; d. Sept., 1917.
Macken, Walter, actor & author; d. Apr. 22, 1967 (51).
Mackin, William, actor; d. Sept. 9, 1928 (45).
Mackley, Arthur J. (r.n. Arthur James Mackley), actor; b. July 3, 1865, Portsmouth, England; d. Dec. 21, 1926 (61).
Mackris, Orestes, actor; d. Jan. 30, 1975 (75).
Macollum, Barry, actor; b. Apr. 6, 1889, No. Ireland; d. Feb. 22, 1971 (81).
Macowan, Norman, actor & playwright; b. Jan. 2, 1877, St. Andrews, England; d. Dec. 31, 1961 (84).
Macready, George, actor; b. Aug. 29, 1899, Providence, R.I.; d. July 2, 1973 (73).
Macy, Carleton, actor; d. Oct. 18, 1946 (85).

Macy, Jack, actor; d. July 2, 1956 (70).
Madden, Peter, actor; d. Feb., 1976 (71).
Madeira, Humberto, actor; d. July 15, 1971 (50).
Madison, Cleo, actress; d. Mar. 11, 1964 (81).
Madison, Harry, actor; d. July 8, 1936 (59).
Madison, Helene, actress & swimmer; b. June 22, 1914, Madison, Wisc.; d. Nov. 25, 1970 (56).
Madison, Noel, actor; b. New York City; d. Jan. 6, 1975 (77).
Madsen, Harald, actor; b. Nov. 20, 1890; d. July 13, 1949 (58).
Mae, Jimsey (Charlotte Rowley), actress; d. Apr. 10, 1968 (74).
Mael, Aaron, actor; d. Mar. 26, 1948 (57).
Maertens, Willy, actor; b. Oct. 30, 1893, Braunschweig, Germany; d. Nov. 28, 1967 (74).
Magee, Harriett, actress; d. Apr. 19, 1954 (76).
Maggi, Luigi, actor; b. Dec. 21, 1867, Turin, Italy; d. Aug. 22, 1946 (78).
Magnani, Anna, actress; b. Apr. 11, 1908, Alexandria, Egypt; d. Sept. 26, 1973 (65).
Magrill, George, actor; b. Jan. 5, 1900, Brooklyn, N.Y.; d. May 30, 1952 (52).
Maguire, Charles J., actor; d. July 22, 1939 (57).
Maguire, Edward, actor; d. Apr. 10, 1925 (58).
Maguire, Tom, actor; b. Sept. 7, 1870, Milford, Conn.; d. June 21, 1934 (63).
Mahan, Vivian L., actress; d. Oct. 13, 1933 (31).
Maher, Wally, actor; b. Aug. 4, 1908, Ohio; d. Dec. 27, 1951 (43).
Mahnke, Hans, actor; b. Apr. 22, 1905, Stralsund, Germany; d. May 29, 1978 (73).
Mahoney, Francis X., actor; d. Jan. 27, 1948 (63).
Mahoney, Tom, actor; b. Feb. 13, 1890, New York; d. Nov. 5, 1958 (68).
Mahoney, Will, actor; d. Feb. 8, 1967 (73).
Maigne, Charles, director, author, & actor; b. Nov. 11, 1881, Richmond, Va.; d. Nov. 28, 1929 (48).
Mailes, Charles Hill, actor; b. May 25, 1870, Halifax, N.S., Canada; d. Feb. 17, 1937 (66).
Main, Marjorie, actress; b. Feb. 24, 1890, Acton, Ind.; d. Apr. 10, 1975 (85).
Maines, Don, actor; d. Jan. 2, 1934 (65).
Mainwaring, Bernerd, director & scenarist; b. Shropshire, England; d. July 30, 1963 (66).
Maire, Edward J., actor; d. Jan., 1948.
Maison, Edna, actress; b. Aug. 17, 1892, San Francisco, Calif.; d. Jan. 11, 1946 (53).
Maitland, Lauderdale, actor; b. London, England; d. Feb. 28, 1929 (52).
Maitland, Ruth, actress; d. Mar. 12, 1961 (81).
Majeroni, Giorgio, actor; d. Aug. 5, 1924 (47).
Majeroni, Mario, actor; d. Nov. 18, 1931 (61).
Makeham, Eliot, actor; b. Dec. 22, 1882, London, England; d. Feb. 8, 1956 (73).
Mala, Ray, actor; b. Dec. 27, 1906, Alaska; d. Sept. 23, 1952 (45).
Malan, William, actor; b. Nov. 2, 1867, New York City; d. Feb. 13, 1941 (73).
Malatesta, Fred, actor; b. Apr. 18, 1889, Italy; d. Apr. 8, 1952 (62).
Malcolm, Reginald, actor; d. Jan. 20, 1966 (82).

International Film Necrology

Malin, Edward, actor; d. Mar. 1, 1977 (82).

Malipiero, Luigi, actor; b. Apr. 5, 1901; d. Feb. 24, 1975 (74).

Malis, Cy, actor; b. Feb. 26, 1907, Pennsylvania; d. Jan. 12, 1971 (63).

Maljan, Abdul (Terrible Turk), actor; d. Sept. 7, 1944 (62).

Mallalieu, Aubrey, actor; b. June 8, 1873, Liverpool, England; d. May 28, 1948 (74).

Malleson, Miles, actor & author; b. May 25, 1888, Croydon, England; d. Mar. 15, 1969 (80).

Mallinson, Rory (r.n. Charles J. Mallinson), actor; b. Oct. 27, 1913, Georgia; d. Mar. 26, 1976 (62).

Mallon, Catherine, actress; b. Mar. 9, 1906; d. Feb. 13, 1929 (22).

Mallory, Patricia (Boots), actress; b. Oct. 22, 1913, New Orleans, La.; d. Dec. 1, 1958 (45).

Malloy, Francetta, actress; d. July 17, 1978 (71).

Malo, Gina, actress; b. June 1, 1906, Cincinnati, Ohio; d. Nov. 30, 1963 (57).

Malone, Dudley Field, actor; d. Oct. 5, 1950 (68).

Malone, Pat, actor; d. Oct. 5, 1963.

Malone, Pick, entertainer; d. Jan. 22, 1962 (69).

Maloney, Leo, actor & director; d. Nov. 2, 1929 (41).

Maltby, Henry F., actor; b. Nov. 25, 1880, Ceres, South Africa; d. Oct. 25, 1963 (82).

Malyon, Eily, actress; b. Oct. 30, 1879, London, England; d. Sept. 26, 1961 (81).

Mamelock, Emil, actor; d. May, 1954 (72).

Mandel, Mrs. Frances Wakefield, actress; d. Mar. 26, 1943 (52).

Mandell, Nathan (see Martell, Marty)

Mander, Miles, actor; b. May 14, 1888, Wolverhampton, England; d. Feb. 8, 1946 (57).

Mandeville, William C., actor; d. Apr. 19, 1917 (50).

Mandy, Jerry (r.n. Gerard Mandia), actor; b. June 5, 1892, Utica, N.Y.; d. May 1, 1945 (52).

Mangean, Teddy, actor & stuntman; d. Sept. 9, 1964 (63).

Mangini, Alda, actress; b. July 13, 1914, Milan, Italy; d. July 19, 1954 (40).

Mankiewicz, Herman J., writer; b. Nov. 7, 1897, New York City; d. Mar. 5, 1953 (55).

Manley, Charles "Daddy," actor; d. Feb. 26, 1916 (86).

Manley, Dave, actor; b. Dec. 25, 1883, Paris, France; d. June 8, 1943 (59).

Manly, Louis J., entertainer; b. Mar. 17, 1900, Missouri; d. Nov. 25, 1959 (59).

Mann, Anthony, director; b. June 30, 1906, San Diego, Calif.; d. Apr. 29, 1967 (60).

Mann, Bertha, actress; b. Oct. 21, 1893, Atlanta, Ga.; d. Dec. 20, 1967 (74).

Mann, Billy, singer (Yacht Club Boys); d. Apr. 14, 1974.

Mann, Cato, actor; d. Dec. 14, 1977 (90).

Mann, George (r.n. George Kline Mann), actor; d. Nov. 23, 1977 (72).

Mann, Gloria, actress; d. Apr. 21, 1961 (33).

Mann, Hank (r.n. David W. Lieberman), actor; b. May 28, 1887, New York City; d. Nov. 25, 1971 (84).

Mann, Helen R., actress; d. Apr. 20, 1947 (31).

Mann, Louis, actor; b. Apr. 20, 1865, New York City; d. Feb. 15, 1931 (65).

Mann, Margaret, actress; b. Apr. 4, 1868, Aberdeen, Scotland; d. Feb. 4, 1941 (72).

Mann, Ned H., actor, director, & special effects man; d. July 1, 1967 (74).

Mann, Stanley, actor; b. Aug. 30, 1883, England; d. Aug. 10, 1953 (69).

Mannering, Lewin, actor; b. Jan. 19, 1879, Poland; d. June 7, 1932 (53).

Manners, Dorothy, actress; d. July 5, 1949.

Mannes, Florence Vensen, actress; d. Oct. 30, 1964 (68).

Mannheim, Lucie, actress; b. Apr. 30, 1899, Berlin, Germany; d. July 28, 1976 (77).

Manni, Ettore, actor; b. May 6, 1927, Rome, Italy; d. July 27, 1979 (52).

Manning, Aileen, actress; b. Jan. 20, 1886, Boulder, Colo.; d. Mar. 25, 1946 (60).

Manning, Ambrose, actor; d. Mar. 22, 1940 (79).

Manning, Bruce, producer & writer; b. New York; d. Aug. 3, 1965 (65).

Manning, Joseph, actor; d. July 31, 1946.

Manning, Marbene, actress; d. Dec. 19, 1942 (34).

Manning, Mary Lee, actress; d. Dec. 7, 1937.

Manning, Philipp, actor; b. Nov. 23, 1869, Lewisham; d. Apr. 11, 1951 (81).

Manning, Tom, actor; d. Oct. 10, 1936 (56).

Manning, W.H. (Speed), stuntman; d. Sept. 10, 1933 (34).

Mansfield, Duncan, editor, author, & director; d. Sept. 15, 1971 (74).

Mansfield, Jayne, actress; b. Apr. 19, 1933, Bryn Mawr, Pa.; d. June 29, 1967 (34).

Mansfield, John, actor; d. Sept. 18, 1956 (37).

Mansfield, Martha, actress; d. Nov. 30, 1923 (23).

Mansfield, Rankin, actor; d. Jan. 22, 1969.

Manso, Juanita, actress; d. Feb. 25, 1957 (84).

Manson, Mrs. Isabel Merson, actress; d. May 19, 1952 (68).

Mantell, Bruce, actor; b. Atlantic Highlands, N.J.; d. Oct. 24, 1933 (24).

Mantell, Robert B., actor; b. Feb. 7, 1854, Irvine, Ayrshire, Scotland; d. June 27, 1928 (74).

Mantz, Paul, stunt pilot; b. Aug. 2, 1903, California; d. July 8, 1965 (61).

Manx, Kate, actress; b. Oct. 19, 1930, Ohio; d. Nov. 15, 1964 (34).

Many Treaties, Chief (see Hazlett, William)

Manzini, Italia Almirante, actress; b. 1890, Taranto, Italy; d. Oct., 1941 (51).

Manzo, Carlo, actor; d. June 21, 1955 (40).

Marba, Joseph, actor; b. Oct. 19, 1879, Peabody, Mass.; d. Sept. 7, 1938 (58).

Marble, John S., actor; d. June 23, 1919 (74).

Marburgh, Bertram, actor; b. May 17, 1875, New York; d. Aug. 22, 1956 (81).

March, Eve, actress; b. Sept. 27, 1910, California; d. Sept. 19, 1974 (63).

March, Fredric, actor; b. Aug. 31, 1897, Racine, Wisc.; d. Apr. 14, 1975 (77).

March, Hal, actor; b. Apr. 22, 1920, San Francisco, Calif.; d. Jan. 19, 1970 (49).

March, Iris, actress; d. Feb. 23, 1966.

March, Joseph Moncure, writer; b. July 27, 1899, New York City;
    d. Feb. 14, 1977 (77).
March, Linda, actress; d. Nov. 25, 1933.
March, Nadine, actress; d. Oct. 10, 1944 (54).
Marchat, Jean, actor; b. June 8, 1902, Grigny, France; d. Oct. 2,
    1966 (64).
Marchesini, Nino, actor; d. Jan. 13, 1961.
Marcin, Max, director & writer; d. Mar. 30, 1948 (68).
Marco, Raoul, actor; d. Apr., 1971.
Marconi, Jean, actor; b. June 1, 1906, Toulouse, France; d. Jan.,
    1972 (65).
Marcus, Bernie, actor; b. Mar. 13, 1888, Colorado; d. Nov. 19, 1971
    (83).
Marcus, James A., actor; b. Jan. 21, 1867, New York City; d. Oct.
    15, 1937 (70).
Marcuse, Theodore, actor; b. Aug. 2, 1920, Washington; d. Nov. 29,
    1967 (47).
Marden, Adrienne, actress; d. Nov. 9, 1978 (69).
Marese, Janie, actress; b. 1880; d. 1931 (51).
Maretskaya, Vera, actress; d. Aug., 1978 (72).
Mareuil, Simone, actress; b. 1890; d. 1954 (64).
Marfield, Dwight, actor; d. Aug. 15, 1978 (70).
Margetson, Arthur, actor; b. Apr. 27, 1897, London, England;
    d. Aug. 13, 1951 (54).
Mari, Febo, actor & director; b. Jan. 18, 1884, Messina, Italy;
    d. June 6, 1939 (55).
Marian, Ferdinand (r.n. Ferdinand Haschkowetz), actor; b. Aug. 14,
    1902, Vienna, Austria; d. Aug. 7, 1946 (43).
Mariani, Marcella, actress; b. Feb. 8, 1936; d. 1956 (19).
Mariano, Luis, actor & recording artist; d. July 14, 1970 (50).
Marievsky, Joseph, actor; b. Jan. 1, 1888, Russia; d. Apr. 27,
    1971 (83).
Marin, Edwin L., director; b. Feb. 21, 1901, Jersey City, N.J.;
    d. May 2, 1951 (50).
Marino, Art (r.n. Rudy Cotz), actor; d. June 1, 1979 (61).
Marino, Frank S., actor; d. Apr. 6, 1956 (69).
Marinoff, Fania, actress; b. Mar. 20, 1890, Odessa, Russia; d. Nov.
    16, 1971 (81).
Marion, Edna, actress; b. Dec. 12, 1906, Chicago, Ill.; d. Dec. 2,
    1957 (50).
Marion, Frances, scenarist & actress; b. Nov. 18, 1888, San Fran-
    cisco, Calif.; d. May 12, 1973 (84).
Marion, George, actor; b. July 16, 1860, San Francisco, Calif.;
    d. Nov. 30, 1945 (85).
Marion, Sid, actor; b. Sept. 14, 1900, Massachusetts; d. June 29,
    1965 (64).
Marion, William, actor; b. Jan. 12, 1880, California; d. Jan. 3,
    1957 (76).
Marion-Crawford, Howard, actor; b. 1914; d. Nov. 24, 1969 (55).
Mariott, Charles, actor; d. Dec. 7, 1917.
Marischka, Hubert, director & opera singer; d. Dec. 4, 1959.
Mark, Michael (r.n. Maurice L. Schulmann), actor; b. Mar. 15, 1886,
    Russia; d. Feb. 3, 1975 (88).
Markhoff-Walter, Maria, actress; d. Mar., 1948.
Marks, Joe E., actor; b. June 15, 1891; d. June 14, 1973 (81).
Marks, Willis, actor; b. Aug. 20, 1865, Minnesota; d. Dec. 6, 1952
    (87).

Marle, Arnold, actor; b. Sept. 15, 1887, Berlin, Germany; d. Feb. 21, 1970 (82).

Marle, Otto, actor; b. 1878, Dresden, Germany; d. June 12, 1943 (65).

Marley, Peverell, cinematographer; b. Aug. 14, 1901, San Jose, Calif.; d. Feb. 2, 1964 (62).

Marlo, Mary, actress; d. Feb. 25, 1960.

Marlowe, Anthony, actor & opera singer; d. June 29, 1962 (52).

Marlowe, Anthony, actor; b. Oct. 12, 1913, London, England; d. Dec., 1975 (62).

Marlowe, Frank, actor; b. Jan. 20, 1904, Massachusetts; d. Mar. 30, 1964 (60).

Marlowe, Nora, actress; d. Dec. 30, 1977 (62).

Marly, Florence, actress; b. Moravia, Czechoslovakia; d. Nov. 9, 1978 (59).

Marmont, Percy, actor; b. Nov. 25, 1883, London, England; d. Mar. 3, 1977 (93).

Marquet, Mary, actress; d. Aug. 29, 1979 (84).

Marr, Hans (r.n. Johann Julius Richter), actor; b. July 22, 1878, Breslau, Poland; d. Mar. 30, 1949 (70).

Marr, William, actor; d. May 15, 1960 (67).

Marriott, John, actor; b. Boley, Okla.; d. Apr. 5, 1977 (83).

Marriott, Moore, actor; b. Sept. 14, 1885, W. Drayton, England; d. Dec. 11, 1949 (64).

Marriott, Sande, actor; d. June 7, 1962 (60).

Marsh, Charles, actor; b. Oct. 4, 1893, Wisconsin; d. Mar. 8, 1953 (59).

Marsh, Della, actress; d. May 6, 1973.

Marsh, Mae, actress; b. Nov. 9, 1895, Madrid, N.M.; d. Feb. 13, 1968 (72).

Marsh, Marguerite (Lovey), actress; d. Dec. 8, 1925 (33).

Marsh, Oliver, cinematographer; d. May 5, 1941 (49).

Marsh, Risley Halsey, actor; d. Jan. 14, 1965 (38).

Marshal, Alan, actor; b. Jan. 29, 1909, Sydney, Australia; d. July 9, 1961 (52).

Marshall, Boyd, actor; d. Nov. 9, 1950 (65).

Marshall, George, director & actor; b. Dec. 29, 1891, Chicago, Ill.; d. Feb. 17, 1975 (83).

Marshall, Herbert, actor; b. May 23, 1890, London, England; d. Jan. 22, 1966 (75).

Marshall, Mort, actor; b. Aug. 17, 1918, New York City; d. Feb. 1, 1979 (60).

Marshall, Oswald, actor; d. Apr. 19, 1954 (79).

Marshall, Tully, actor; b. Apr. 10, 1864, Nevada City, Calif.; d. Mar. 10, 1943 (78).

Marshalov, Boris, actor; d. Oct. 16, 1967 (65).

Marson, Aileen, actress; d. May 5, 1939 (26).

Marstini, Rosita, actress; d. Apr. 24, 1948 (54).

Marston, Ann, actress; d. Mar. 6, 1971 (32).

Marston, John, actor; d. Sept. 2, 1962 (72).

Martell, Alphonse, actor; b. Mar. 27, 1890, Strasbourg, France; d. Mar. 18, 1976 (85).

Martell, Karl, actor; b. Mar. 16, 1928; d. Dec., 1966 (38).

Martell, Marty (Nathan Mandell), actor; d. May 7, 1979 (79).

Martin, Chris-Pin, actor; b. Nov. 19, 1893, Tucson, Ariz.; d. June 27, 1953 (59).

Martin, Cye, actor; d. Mar. 28, 1972 (57).

Martin, Edie, actress; b. Jan. 1, 1880, London, England; d. Feb. 22, 1964 (84).

Martin, Irene, actress; b. Sept. 1, 1891, Massachusetts; d. Dec. 12, 1973 (82).

Martin, J. Lockard (Lock Martin) (r.n. Joseph Lockard Martin), actor; b. Oct. 12, 1916, Pennsylvania; d. Jan. 19, 1959 (42).

Martin, John E., actor; d. Nov. 22, 1933 (78).

Martin, Lewis, actor; b. Nov. 1, 1894, California; d. Feb. 21, 1969 (74).

Martin, Lock (see Martin, J. Lockard)

Martin, Owen, actor; d. May 4, 1960 (71).

Martin, Townsend, author & actor; d. Nov. 22, 1951 (55).

Martindel, Edward B., actor; b. July 28, 1873, Ohio; d. May 4, 1955 (81).

Martinez, Conchita, actress; d. May, 1960 (48).

Martinez, Paco, actor; d. Feb. 20, 1956.

Martinez, Pedro, actor; d. Dec. 25, 1978 (33).

Martin-Harvey, Sir John, actor; b. Wyvenhoe, Essex, England; d. May 14, 1944 (80).

Martin-Harvey, Michael, actor; d. June 30, 1975.

Martini, Nino, actor & singer; b. Aug. 8, 1905, Verona, Italy; d. Dec. 9, 1976 (71).

Martyn, Jack, actor; d. Nov. 22, 1953.

Martyn, Peter, actor; b. Oct. 19, 1925, London, England; d. Feb. 15, 1955 (29).

Marvin, Jack, actor; b. Apr. 16, 1884, Michigan; d. Oct. 17, 1956 (72).

Marvin, Warren Leete, actor; d. Feb. 12, 1938 (67).

Marx, Chico (r.n. Leonard Marx), actor; b. Mar. 22, 1887, New York City; d. Oct. 11, 1961 (74).

Marx, Groucho (r.n. Julius Marx), actor; b. Oct. 2, 1890, New York City; d. Aug. 19, 1977 (86).

Marx, Harpo (r.n. Arthur Marx), actor; b. Nov. 23, 1888, New York City; d. Sept. 28, 1964 (75).

Marx, Samuel, extra; d. May 11, 1933 (72).

Marx, Zeppo (r.n. Herbert Marx), actor; b. Feb. 25, 1901; d. Nov. 30, 1979 (78).

Marzola, Joe, actor; b. July 16, 1936, Italy; d. Dec. 31, 1976 (40).

Maskell, Virginia, actress; b. Feb. 27, 1936, Shepherd's Bush, England; d. Jan. 25, 1968 (31).

Mason, Ann, actress; d. Feb. 6, 1948 (50).

Mason, Bertha N., actress; d. Nov. 9, 1950 (73).

Mason, "Smiling" Billy, actor; d. Jan. 24, 1941 (53).

Mason, Buddy C. (r.n. Bruce Cameron Mason), actor & stuntman; b. Oct. 30, 1902, Pennsylvania; d. Apr. 15, 1975 (72).

Mason, Charles, actor; d. Dec. 8, 1976 (53).

Mason, Dan, actor; d. July 6, 1929 (72).

Mason, Elliot, actress; b. Glasgow, Scotland; d. June 20, 1949 (52).

Mason, Haddon, actor; b. Feb. 21, 1898, London, Emgland; d. Apr. 30, 1966 (68).

Mason, Herbert, director; b. Moseley, England; d. May 20, 1960 (69).

Mason, Homer B., actor; d. Sept. 27, 1959 (80).

Mason, James, actor; b. Feb. 3, 1889, Paris, France; d. Nov. 7, 1959 (70).

Mason, John, actor; b. Oct. 28, 1857, Orange, N.J.; d. Jan. 12, 1919 (61).

Mason, LeRoy, actor; b. July 2, 1903, Larimore, N.D.; d. Oct. 13, 1947 (44).
Mason, Louis, actor; b. June 1, 1888, Danville, Ky.; d. Nov. 12, 1959 (71).
Mason, Reginald, actor; b. June 27, 1875, California; d. July 10, 1962 (87).
Mason, Roy (see Mason, LeRoy)
Mason, Shirley, actress; d. July 27, 1979 (79).
Mason, Sidney L., actor; d. Mar. 1, 1923 (36).
Mason, Sully, actor; d. Nov. 27, 1970 (64).
Mason, Sydney, actor; d. Apr. 11, 1976 (71).
Massalitinova, Varvara O., actress; b. July 29, 1878; d. Oct. 20, 1945 (67).
Massey, Ilona, actress & singer; b. June 16, 1912, Budapest, Hungary; d. Aug. 20, 1974 (62).
Massine, Leonide, ballet dancer & choreographer; b. Aug. 8, 1895, Moscow, Russia; d. Mar. 16, 1979 (83).
Massingham, Richard, director & actor; b. 1898; d. Apr. 1, 1953 (55).
Masters, Harry, stand-in; d. May 12, 1974 (79).
Masters, Ruth, actress; d. Sept. 21, 1969 (75).
Mata, Miguel P., actor; d. Jan., 1956 (42).
Mate, Rudolph, director & cinematographer; b. Jan. 21, 1898, Cracow, Poland; d. Oct. 27, 1964 (66).
Mateos, Hector, actor; d. Feb. 13, 1957 (56).
Mathe, Edouard, actor; b. 1886; d. 1934 (48).
Mather, Aubrey, actor; b. Dec. 17, 1885, Minchinhampton, England; d. Jan. 15, 1958 (72).
Mather, John (Jack), actor; d. Aug. 16, 1966 (58).
Mathew, Ann, actress; d. May 31, 1976 (65).
Mathews, Carl, actor; b. Feb. 19, 1899, Oklahoma; d. May 3, 1959 (60).
Mathews, Francis T., actor; d. Nov., 1947.
Mathews, George H., actor; d. June 7, 1952 (75).
Mathieson, Muir, conductor & actor; b. Jan. 24, 1911, Stirling, Scotland; d. Aug. 2, 1975 (64).
Mathis, June, writer; d. July 26, 1927 (38).
Mathis, Milly, actress; b. Sept. 8, 1901, Marseilles, France; d. Mar. 30, 1965 (63).
Mathison, Richard R., actor; d. Jan. 31, 1980 (60).
Mathot, Leon, actor & director; b. Mar. 5, 1896, France; d. Mar. 6, 1968 (72).
Matiesen, Otto, actor; b. Copenhagen, Denmark; d. Feb. 19, 1932 (38).
Matray, Ernst, actor & director; d. Nov. 12, 1978 (87).
Matsui, Suisei, actor; d. Aug. 1, 1973 (73).
Mattera, Gino, actor; b. Mar. 14, 1923, Taranto, Italy; d. Apr. 25, 1960 (37).
Matterstock, Albert, actor; d. June 30, 1960 (48).
Matthews, A.E., actor; b. Nov. 22, 1869, Bridlington, Yorks, England; d. July 25, 1960 (90).
Matthews, Beatrice, actress; d. Nov. 10, 1942 (52).
Matthews, Dorothy, actress; b. Feb. 13, 1912, New York City; d. May 18, 1977 (65).
Matthews, Forrest, actor; d. Nov. 2, 1951.
Matthews, Junius, actor; b. June 12, 1890, Illinois; d. Jan. 18, 1978 (87).

Matthews, Lester, actor; b. Dec. 3, 1900, Nottingham, England;
    d. June 6, 1975 (74).
Matthison, Edith Wynne, actress; d. Sept. 23, 1955 (83).
Mattioli, Raf, actor; b. Oct. 18, 1936, Naples, Italy; d. Oct. 12,
    1960 (23).
Matto, Sisto, actor; d. Feb. 20, 1934.
Mattox, Martha, actress; d. May 2, 1933 (54).
Mattraw, Scott, actor; b. Oct. 19, 1880, Evans Mills, N.Y.; d. Nov.
    9, 1946 (66).
Maturin, Eric, actor; b. May 30, 1883, India; d. Oct. 17, 1957 (74).
Matzenauer, Margaret, opera singer & actress; b. June 1, 1881,
    Hungary; d. May 19, 1963 (81).
Maude, Charles R., actor; d. Nov. 14, 1943 (61).
Maude, Cyril, actor; b. Apr. 24, 1862, London, England; d. Feb. 20,
    1951 (88).
Maude, Margery, actress; b. Apr. 29, 1889, Wimbledon, England;
    d. Aug. 7, 1979 (90).
Maunsell, Charles, actor; d. Aug. 1, 1968.
Maupi, Ernest, actor; b. 1881, Toulon, France; d. Jan. 10, 1949 (67).
Maurice, Mary, actress; d. Apr. 30, 1918 (73).
Maurus, Gerda, actress; b. Aug. 25, 1909, Vienna, Austria; d. Aug.,
    1968 (59).
Mawdesley, Robert, actor; d. Oct. 1, 1953 (53).
Mawson, Edward, actor; d. May 20, 1917 (55).
Max, Jean, actor; d. Jan., 1971 (74).
Maxam, Louella Modie, actress; b. June 10, 1896, Florida; d. Sept. 3,
    1970 (74).
Maxey, Paul, actor; b. Mar. 15, 1907, Illinois; d. June 3, 1963 (56).
Maxted, Stanley, actor; d. May 10, 1963 (63).
Maxwell, Edwin, actor & director; b. Dublin, Ireland; d. Aug. 13,
    1948 (62).
Maxwell, Elsa, actress & hostess; d. Nov. 1, 1963 (80).
Maxwell, Lucien Y., actor; b. Sept. 4, 1898, South Dakota; d. Sept.
    17, 1972 (74).
Maxwell-Willshire, Gerard, actor; d. Apr. 3, 1947 (54).
May, Ada, actress; d. Apr. 26, 1978 (80).
May, Edna, actress; b. Sept. 2, 1875, Syracuse, N.Y.; d. Jan. 1,
    1948 (72).
May, Evy, actress; d. Sept. 11, 1924 (23).
May, Harold R., actor; d. Sept. 16, 1973 (70).
May, James C., actor; b. Apr. 8, 1857, Dundee, Scotland; d. Aug. 23,
    1941 (84).
May, Joe, director; b. Nov. 7, 1880, Vienna, Austria; d. Apr. 29,
    1954 (73).
May, Marty, actor; d. Nov. 11, 1975 (77).
May, Samuel Roderick, singer; d. Aug. 9, 1963 (53).
Mayall, Herschel, actor; d. June 10, 1941 (78).
Mayer, Carl, director; b. Feb. 20, 1894, Graz, Austria; d. July 3,
    1944 (50).
Mayer, Edwin Justus, writer; b. Nov. 8, 1896, New York; d. Sept. 11,
    1960 (63).
Mayer, Louis B., producer & executive; b. July 4, 1885, Minsk,
    Russia; d. Oct. 29, 1957 (72).
Mayer, Ray, actor; b. Apr. 24, Lexington, Neb.; d. Nov. 21, 1948.
Mayhew, Kate, actress; b. Sept. 2, 1853, Indianapolis, Ind.;
    d. June 16, 1944 (90).
Maynard, Claire, actress; d. July 19, 1941 (29).

Maynard, Harry, actor; d. July 23, 1976 (78).
Maynard, Ken, actor; b. July 21, 1895, Vevay, Ind.; d. Mar. 23, 1973 (77).
Maynard, Kermit (Tex Maynard), actor; b. Sept. 20, 1897, Vevay, Ind.; d. Jan. 16, 1971 (73).
Maynard, Tex (see Maynard, Kermit)
Mayne, Eric, actor; b. Apr. 28, 1865, Dublin, Ireland; d. Feb. 9, 1947 (81).
Mayo, Albert, actor; d. May 20, 1933 (46).
Mayo, Archie, director; b. New York City; d. Dec. 4, 1968 (77).
Mayo, Edgar C., director; d. June 21, 1944 (86).
Mayo, Edna, actress; b. Mar. 23, 1895, Philadelphia, Pa.; d. May 5, 1970 (75).
Mayo, Frank, actor; b. June 28, 1889, New York City; d. July 9, 1963 (74).
Mayo, Harry, actor; b. Mar. 11, 1898, Helena, Mont.; d. Jan. 6, 1964 (65).
Mayo, Joseph Anthony, actor; b. June 9, 1930, New York; d. Nov. 12, 1966 (36).
Mayor, Agustin G., actor; d. Nov. 19, 1968 (33).
Mayring, Lothar (Philipp Lothar Mayring), actor & director; b. Sept. 19, 1879, Wurzburg, Germany; d. July 6, 1948 (68).
Mayring, Philipp Lothar (see Mayring, Lothar)
Mc: *For names beginning with Mc, see pp. 189-194*
Meade, Claire, actress; b. Apr. 2, 1883, New Jersey; d. Jan. 14, 1968 (84).
Meader, George, actor & singer; b. July 6, 1888, Minnesota; d. Dec. 17, 1963 (75).
Meadows, Denny (see Moore, Dennis)
Meakin, Charles, actor; b. Oct. 2, 1879, Utah; d. Jan. 17, 1961 (81).
Meakin, Ruth, actress; d. Nov. 3, 1939 (60).
Mears, Benjamin S., actor; d. Jan. 27, 1952 (80).
Mears, Marion, extra; d. Jan. 26, 1970 (71).
Measor, Beryl, actress; b. Apr. 22, 1906, Shanghai, China; d. Feb. 8, 1965 (58).
Medel, Felix, actor; d. 1951.
Medford, Harold, writer; d. Oct. 26, 1977 (66).
Medley, Edgar, actor; d. Jan. 2, 1959 (65).
Meech, Edward, actor; d. Mar. 2, 1952 (60).
Meehan, Barry, actor; d. June 28, 1974 (39).
Meehan, Danny, actor; d. Mar. 29, 1978 (47).
Meehan, John, author & director; b. May 8, 1890, Lindsay, Ontario, Canada; d. Nov. 12, 1954 (64).
Meehan, John, Jr., writer; d. Oct. 16, 1967 (59).
Meehan, Lew, actor; b. Sept. 7, 1890, Minnesota; d. Aug. 10, 1951 (60).
Meek, Donald, actor; b. July 14, 1878, Glasgow, Scotland; d. Nov. 18, 1946 (68).
Meek, Kate, actress; d. Sept. 4, 1925 (87).
Meeker, Alfred, actor; b. Feb. 24, 1901, Brooklyn, N.Y.; d. June 6, 1942 (41).
Mehaffey, Blanche, actress; b. July 28, 1908, Cincinnati, Ohio; d. Mar. 31, 1968 (59).
Mehaffey, Harry S., actor; d. Dec. 23, 1963 (56).
Mehnert, Lothar, actor; b. Feb. 21, 1875, Berlin, Germany; d. Nov. 30, 1926 (50).
Mehrmann, Helen, actress; b. Jan. 14, 1894, Oakland, Calif.; d. Sept. 23, 1934 (40).

Meighan, Margaret, actress; d. Sept. 29, 1961.
Meighan, Thomas, actor; b. Apr. 9, 1879, Pittsburgh, Pa.; d. July 8, 1936 (57).
Meinel, Ernest R., actor; b. Oct. 14, 1917, Oregon; d. Feb. 22, 1977 (59).
Meinhard, Karl, actor; b. 1886; d. Mar., 1949 (62).
Meins, Gus, director; b. Germany; d. Aug. 4, 1940 (47).
Meixner, Karl, actor; b. Feb. 13, 1903, Vienna, Austria; d. Dec. 29, 1976 (73).
Melato, Maria, actress; b. Oct. 16, 1885, Reggio Emilia, Italy; d. Aug. 24, 1950 (64).
Melchior, Frederic, actor; b. July 12, 1897, Berlin, Germany; d. May 2, 1956 (58).
Melchior, Lauritz, opera singer & actor; b. Mar. 20, 1890, Copenhagen, Denmark; d. Mar. 18, 1973 (82).
Melesh, Alex, actor; b. Oct. 28, 1890, Kiev, Russia; d. Mar. 4, 1949 (58).
Melford, Austin, author & stage actor; b. Alverstoke; d. Aug. 19, 1971 (86).
Melford, George, director & actor; b. Feb. 19, 1877, Rochester, N.Y.; d. Apr. 25, 1961 (84).
Melford, Jack, actor; b. Sept. 5, 1899, London, England; d. Oct. 22, 1972 (73).
Melford, Louise, actress; d. Nov. 15, 1942 (62).
Melies, George, director & pioneer; d. Jan. 21, 1938 (77).
Mell, Joseph, actor; d. Aug. 31, 1977 (62).
Meller, Harro, actor; b. Germany; d. Dec. 26, 1963 (56).
Meller, Raquel, actress & singer; b. Madrid, Spain; d. July 26, 1962 (74).
Mellinger, Max, actor; b. Mar. 18, 1906, Oregon; d. Feb. 25, 1968 (61).
Mellish, Fuller, actor; b. Jan. 3, 1865, England; d. Dec. 7, 1936 (71).
Mellish, Fuller, Jr., actor; d. Feb. 8, 1930 (35).
Mellor, William C., cinematographer; d. Apr. 30, 1963 (59).
Melton, Frank, actor; b. Dec. 6, 1907, Pineapple, Ala.; d. Mar. 19, 1951 (43).
Melton, James, actor & singer; b. Jan. 2, 1904, Moultrie, Ga.; d. Apr. 21, 1961 (57).
Melville, Emilie, actress; d. May 20, 1932 (82).
Melville, Jean-Pierre, producer; d. Aug. 2, 1973 (55).
Melville, Rose, actress; b. Jan. 30, 1873, Terre Haute, Ind.; d. Oct. 8, 1946 (73).
Membrives, Lola, actress; d. Nov., 1969 (86).
Menant, Paul, actor; d. Apr. 27, 1934 (42).
Menard, Michael M., actor; d. Apr. 27, 1949 (51).
Mendel, Jules, actor; d. Mar. 17, 1938 (63).
Mendelssohn, Eleonora, actress; b. Berlin, Germany; d. Jan. 24, 1951 (51).
Mendes, John Prince; actor & magician; d. Sept. 30, 1955 (36).
Mendes, Lothar, director & actor; b. May 19, 1894, Berlin, Germany; d. Feb. 25, 1974 (79).
Mendoza, Harry, actor & magician; b. Jan. 6, 1900, Laredo, Tex.; d. Feb. 15, 1970 (70).
Menhart, Alfred, actor; b. Feb. 24, 1899, Munich, Germany; d. Oct. 19, 1955 (56).

Menjou, Adolphe, actor; b. Feb. 18, 1890, Pittsburgh, Pa.; d. Oct. 29, 1963 (73).
Menjou, Henri, actor; b. June 2, 1891, Pittsburgh, Pa.; d. Jan. 27, 1956 (64).
Menken, Helen, actress; b. Dec. 12, 1901, New York City; d. Mar. 27, 1966 (64).
Menzies, William Cameron, art director & director; b. July 29, 1896, New Haven, Conn.; d. Mar. 5, 1957 (60).
Mera, Edith, actress; d. Feb. 24, 1935 (27).
Merande, Doro, actress; b. Columbia, Kans.; d. Nov. 1, 1975.
Mercanton, Jean, actor; b. May 17, 1920; d. Nov. 5, 1947 (27).
Mercanton, Louis, director & actor; d. Apr. 29, 1932.
Mercer, Beryl, actress; b. Aug. 13, 1882, Seville, Spain; d. July 28, 1939 (56).
Meredith, Charles, actor; b. Aug. 27, 1894, Pennsylvania; d. Nov. 28, 1964 (70).
Meredith, Cheerio, actress; b. July 12, 1890, Missouri; d. Dec. 25, 1964 (74).
Meredith, Iris, actress; b. June 3, 1915, Sioux City, Iowa; d. Jan. 22, 1980 (64).
Meredith, Nicholas, actor; d. Oct., 1963.
Meredyth, Bess, writer; b. Buffalo, N.Y.; d. July 13, 1969 (79).
Merivale, Philip, actor; b. Nov. 2, 1886, Rehutia, India; d. Mar. 12, 1946 (59).
Merkyl, John (see Merkyl, Wilmuth)
Merkyl, Wilmuth (John Merkyl), actor; b. June 2, 1885, Iowa; d. May 1, 1954 (68).
Merlo, Anthony, actor; b. Oct. 1, 1886, Italy; d. Apr. 25, 1976 (89).
Merrall, Mary, actress; b. Jan. 5, 1890, Liverpool, England; d. Aug. 31, 1973 (83).
Merriam, Harold A., actor; d. Dec. 21, 1937 (61).
Merrill, Frank, actor; b. Mar. 21, 1893, New Jersey; d. Feb. 12, 1966 (72).
Merrill, Lou, actor; b. Apr. 1, 1912, Canada; d. Apr. 7, 1963 (51).
Merriss, Dick (r.n. Charles Richard Merriss), actor; b. Feb. 9, 1920, Illinois; d. July 6, 1974 (54).
Merritt, George, actor; b. Dec. 10, 1890, London, England; d. Aug. 27, 1977 (86).
Merson, Billy, actor; b. Mar. 29, 1881, Nottingham, England; d. June 26, 1947 (66).
Merton, Colette, actress; b. Mar. 7, 1907, New Orleans, La.; d. July 24, 1968 (61).
Merton, John (Mert La Varre) (John Merton La Varre; Myrtland F. La Varre), actor; b. Feb. 18, 1901, Washington; d. Sept. 18, 1959 (58).
Mervyn, William, actor; b. Jan. 3, 1912, Nairobi, Kenya; d. Aug. 6, 1976 (64).
Meskill, Katherine C., actress; d. Jan. 8, 1979.
Meskin, Aharon, actor; d. Nov. 11, 1974 (77).
Messinger, Buddy, actor & assistant director; b. Oct. 26, 1907, San Francisco, Calif.; d. Oct. 25, 1965 (57).
Messiter, Eric, actor; d. Sept. 13, 1960 (68).
Messlein, John, actor; d. Aug., 1920 (21).
Mestel, Jacob, actor; b. Poland; d. Aug. 5, 1958 (74).
Metaxa, Georges, actor; b. Sept. 11, 1899, Bucharest, Rumania; d. Dec. 8, 1950 (51).
Metcalf, Earle, actor; b. Mar. 11, 1889, Newport, Ky.; d. Jan. 26, 1928 (38).

Metcalfe, Edward, actor; d. Apr. 2, 1951 (84).
Metcalfe, James, actor; d. Apr. 2, 1960 (59).
Methot, Mayo, actress; b. Mar. 3, 1904, Portland, Ore.; d. June 9,
    1951 (47).
Metz, Albert, actor; d. Aug. 20, 1940 (54).
Metz, Victor, stuntman & actor; d. Aug. 21, 1949 (53).
Metzetti, Otto, stuntman & actor; d. Jan. 31, 1949 (58).
Meurisse, Paul, actor; d. Jan. 19, 1979 (66).
Meyer, Eve, actress; d. Mar. 27, 1977 (44).
Meyer, Frederic, actor; d. Sept. 16, 1973 (63).
Meyer, Greta, actress; b. Germany; d. Oct. 8, 1965 (82).
Meyer, Harry W., actor; d. June 18, 1954.
Meyer, Johannes, director; b. Brieg, Silesia; d. Jan. 25, 1976.
Meyer, Torben, actor; b. Dec. 1, 1884, Copenhagen, Denmark; d. May
    22, 1975 (90).
Meyers, George W., actor; b. Apr. 15, 1889, Illinois; d. Feb. 17,
    1962 (72).
Meyn, Robert, actor; b. Jan. 16, 1897, Hamburg, Germany; d. Mar. 3,
    1972 (75).
Michael, Gertrude, actress; b. June 1, 1911, Talladega, Ala.;
    d. Dec. 31, 1964 (53).
Michael, Mickie, actress; d. Nov. 18, 1973 (30).
Michaels, Sully, actor; d. Jan. 4, 1966 (49).
Michelena, Beatriz, actress; b. Feb. 22, 1890, New York City; d. Oct.
    10, 1942 (52).
Michelena, Vera, actress & singer; d. Aug. 26, 1961 (77).
Middlemass, Robert, actor; b. Sept. 3, 1883, New Britain, Conn.;
    d. Sept. 11, 1949 (66).
Middleton, Charles B., actor; b. Oct. 7, 1879, Elizabethtown, Ky.;
    d. Apr. 22, 1949 (69).
Middleton, Guy, actor; b. Dec. 14, 1907, Hove, England; d. July 29,
    1973 (65).
Middleton, Josephine, actress; b. Sept. 2, 1886, Nashville, Tenn.;
    d. Apr. 8, 1971 (84).
Middleton, Leora, actress; d. Sept. 4, 1945 (54).
Middleton, Robert, actor; b. May 13, 1911, Cincinnati, Ohio;
    d. June 14, 1977 (66).
Midgeley, Florence, actress; d. Nov. 16, 1949 (59).
Midgley, Fanny (r.n. Fanny B. Frier), actress; b. Nov. 26, 1879, Cin-
    cinnati, Ohio; d. Jan. 4, 1932 (52).
Midgley, Richard, actor; d. Nov. 30, 1956 (46).
Migliari, Armando, actor; b. Apr. 19, 1887, Frosinone; d. June,
    1976 (89).
Mihail, Alexandra, actress; d. Dec. 17, 1975 (28).
Milam, Pauline, dancer; d. May 2, 1965 (53).
Milan, Frank, actor; d. Apr. 8, 1977 (71).
Milani, Chef (Joseph), actor; b. Jan. 5, 1892, Naples, Italy;
    d. Nov. 30, 1965 (73).
Milar, Adolph, actor; b. Apr. 19, 1886, Germany; d. May 25, 1950 (64).
Milasch, Bob, actor; b. Apr. 18, 1885, New York City; d. Nov. 14,
    1954 (69).
Milcrest, H.M., actor; d. Nov. 23, 1920 (28).
Miles, Arthur K., actor; d. Nov. 6, 1955 (54).
Miles, Lotta, actress; d. July 25, 1937 (38).
Miljan, John, actor; b. Nov. 8, 1893, Lead City, S.D.; d. Jan. 24,
    1960 (66).

Millar, Adelqui, actor & director; b. Aug. 5, 1891, Concepcion,
   Chile; d. Aug. 7, 1956 (65).
Millar, Lee C., actor; b. Feb. 20, 1888, Oakland, Calif.; d. Dec. 24,
   1941 (53).
Millard, Edward R. "Rocky," actor & singer; d. Dec. 13, 1963.
Millard, Harry Williams, actor & producer; d. Sept. 2, 1969 (41).
Millarde, Harry, actor & director; d. Nov. 2, 1931 (46).
Millen, Frank H., actor; d. Dec. 26, 1931 (70).
Miller, Alice Duer, author & actress; b. July 28, 1874, New York
   City; d. Aug. 22, 1942 (68).
Miller, Arthur C., cinematographer; d. July 13, 1970 (75).
Miller, Ashley, actor & director; d. Nov. 19, 1949 (82).
Miller, Ranger Bill (r.n. William J. Miller), actor; b. Mar. 5,
   1887, Kutztown, Pa.; d. Nov. 12, 1939 (52).
Miller, Carl, actor; d. Feb., 1979.
Miller, Charles B., actor; b. Mar. 16, 1891, California; d. June 5,
   1955 (64).
Miller, David, actor; b. Mar. 31, 1871, Glasgow, Scotland; d. Jan. 1,
   1933 (61).
Miller, Diana (Diana Miller (Melford)), actress; b. Mar. 18, 1902,
   Seattle, Wash.; d. Dec. 18, 1927 (25).
Miller, Edward G., actor; b. Dec. 22, 1881, Eastbourne, England;
   d. Dec. 1, 1948 (66).
Miller, Flournoy E. (r.n. Flournoy Eakin Miller), actor; b. Apr. 14,
   1887, Tennessee; d. June 6, 1971 (84).
Miller, Frank, actor; d. Nov. 2, 1933.
Miller, Glenn, orchestra leader & recording artist; b. Mar. 1, 1904,
   Clarinda, Iowa; d. Dec. 15, 1944 (40).
Miller, Gordon (r.n. Luke Aloysius Miller), actor; b. May 18, 1882,
   Pennsylvania; d. Apr. 9, 1962 (79).
Miller, Harold (r.n. Harold Edwin Kammermeyer), actor; b. May 31,
   1894, California; d. July 18, 1972 (78).
Miller, Hugh, actor; b. May 22, 1889, Berwick-on-Tweed, England;
   d. Nov. 1, 1976 (87).
Miller, Isabelle, actress; d. Mar. 23, 1957 (76).
Miller, Ivan, actor; b. Nov. 13, 1888, Nebraska; d. Sept. 27, 1967
   (78).
Miller, Jack, actor; d. Sept. 25, 1928 (40).
Miller, Jack "Shorty," actor; d. Feb. 28, 1941 (46).
Miller, John, actor; d. Aug., 1968.
Miller, Lorraine, actress; b. Jan. 5, 1929; d. Feb. 6, 1978 (49).
Miller, Lou, actor; d. May 2, 1941 (35).
Miller, Marilyn, actress; b. Sept. 1, 1898, Findlay, Ohio; d. Apr. 7,
   1936 (37).
Miller, Martin (r.n. Rudolph Muller), actor; b. Czechoslovakia;
   d. Aug. 26, 1969 (70).
Miller, Max, actor; d. May 7, 1963 (68).
Miller, Ralph A. (Daredevil), stuntman; d. July 9, 1966 (71).
Miller, Ruby, actress; b. July 14, 1889, London, England; d. Apr. 2,
   1976 (86).
Miller, Seton I., writer; b. May 3, 1902, Chehalis, Wash.; d. Mar.
   29, 1974 (71).
Miller, Tom, actor; b. Dec. 6, 1872; d. Dec. 6, 1942 (70).
Miller, W. Chrystie, actor; d. Sept. 23, 1922 (79).
Miller, Walter, actor; b. Mar. 9, 1892, Dayton, Ohio; d. Mar. 30,
   1940 (48).

Millett, Arthur, actor; b. Apr. 21, 1874, Pittsfield, Me.; d. Feb. 24, 1952 (77).
Millhauser, Bertram, writer; b. Mar. 25, 1892, New York City; d. Dec. 1, 1958 (66).
Millican, James, actor; b. Feb. 17, 1910, New Jersey; d. Nov. 24, 1955 (45).
Milligan, Maura (Min), actress; d. Mar. 10, 1966 (84).
Millington, Mary, actress; d. Aug. 19, 1979 (34).
Millman, William, actor; d. July 19, 1937 (54).
Millner, Marietta, actress; d. July, 1929.
Mills, Bob, actor; d. Oct. 16, 1934 (36).
Mills, Edith M., actress; b. Nov. 20, 1894, Arizona; d. May 16, 1962 (67).
Mills, Frank, actor; b. Kendal, Mich.; d. June 11, 1921 (51).
Mills, Frank (r.n. Frank C. Mills), actor; b. Jan. 26, 1891, Washington; d. Aug. 18, 1973 (82).
Mills, Freddie, actor & boxer; d. July 25, 1965 (46).
Mills, Grace, actress; b. Oct. 28, 1883, Illinois; d. Jan. 7, 1972 (88).
Mills, Grant, actor; d. Aug. 4, 1973.
Mills, Jay, actor; d. Mar. 6, 1951 (52).
Mills, Joseph S., actor; d. Oct. 19, 1935 (60).
Mills, Thomas R., actor; b. June 28, 1878, England; d. Nov. 29, 1953 (75).
Millsfield, Charles A. (Monsieur Pompon), actor; b. Nov. 6, 1876, Netherlands; d. Sept. 18, 1962 (85).
Milos, Milos, actor; d. Jan. 31, 1966 (25).
Miltern, John (r.n. John E. Sheehan), actor; b. July 13, 1870, New Britain, Conn.; d. Jan. 15, 1937 (66).
Milton, Ernest, actor; b. Jan. 10, 1890, San Francisco, Calif.; d. July 24, 1974 (84).
Milton, Georges (r.n. Georges Michaud), actor; b. 1888, Puteaux, France; d. Oct. 16, 1970 (82).
Milton, Harry, actor; b. June 26, 1900, London, England; d. Mar. 8, 1965 (64).
Milton, Louette, actress; d. Oct. 29, 1930 (23).
Milton, Maud, actress; b. Mar. 24, 1859, Gravesend, England; d. Nov. 19, 1945 (86).
Milton, Robert D., director; b. Jan. 24, 1885, Russia; d. Jan. 13, 1956 (70).
Milward, Dawson, actor; d. May 15, 1926 (60).
Mims, Luke, stuntman; d. Aug. 26, 1933 (32).
Minciotti, Esther, actress; b. Italy; d. Apr. 15, 1962 (74).
Minciotti, Silvio, actor; b. Italy; d. May 2, 1961 (78).
Mineo, Sal, actor; b. Jan. 10, 1939, New York City; d. Feb. 12, 1976 (37).
Miner, Daniel, actor; d. June 24, 1938 (58).
Minevitch, Borrah, actor & harmonica player; b. Kiev, Russia; d. June 25, 1955 (52).
Ming, Moy, actor; b. Jan. 10, 1863, China; d. July 26, 1964 (101).
Minner, Kathryn, actress; d. May 26, 1969 (77).
Minotti, Felice, actor; b. Nov. 19, 1887, Milan, Italy; d. Mar. 21, 1963 (75).
Minter, William Fred, actor; d. July 13, 1937 (45).
Minuti, Baldo, actor; b. May 23, 1883, Italy; d. July 22, 1958 (75).

Minzey, Frank, actor; d. Nov. 12, 1949 (70).
Miranda, Carmen, actress & singer; b. Feb. 9, 1909, Portugal;
    d. Aug. 5, 1955 (46).
Mirande, Yves, writer; d. Mar., 1957 (82).
Mirandy (r.n. Marjorie Bauersfeld), actress; b. Springfield, Mo.;
    d. July 21, 1974 (84).
Miroslava, actress; b. Czechoslovakia; d. Mar. 10, 1955 (25).
Mishima, Masao, actor; d. July 18, 1973 (67).
Mishima, Yukio, actor & scenarist; d. Nov. 25, 1970 (45).
Mistinguett (r.n. Jeanne-Marie Bourgeois), actress; d. Jan. 5, 1956
    (82).
Mistral, Jorge, actor; d. Apr. 20, 1972 (49).
Mitchell, Barbara, actress; d. Dec. 9, 1977 (48).
Mitchell, Belle, actress; d. Feb. 12, 1979 (90).
Mitchell, Bruce (r.n. James Bruce Mitchell), director & actor;
    b. Nov. 16, 1880, Freeport, Ill.; d. Sept. 26, 1952 (71).
Mitchell, Carolyn, actress; d. Jan. 31, 1966 (29).
Mitchell, Charles J., actor; b. May 17, 1879, New York; d. Dec. 13,
    1929 (50).
Mitchell, Charles Mason, actor; d. June 16, 1930 (71).
Mitchell, Dodson, actor; b. Jan. 23, 1868, Memphis, Tenn.; d. June
    2, 1939 (71).
Mitchell, Geneva, actress; b. Feb. 3, 1907, Medarysville, Ind.;
    d. Mar. 10, 1949 (42).
Mitchell, George, actor; b. Feb. 21, 1905, Larchmont, N.Y.; d. Jan.
    18, 1972 (66).
Mitchell, Grant, actor; b. June 17, 1874, Columbus, Ohio; d. May 1,
    1957 (82).
Mitchell, Howard, director & actor; b. Dec. 11, 1887, Pennsylvania;
    d. Oct. 4, 1958 (70).
Mitchell, Irving (r.n. James Irving Mitchell), actor; b. Mar. 18,
    1891, Oregon; d. Aug. 3, 1969 (78).
Mitchell, Johnny (Douglass Drake; Douglass Newland), actor; d. Jan.
    19, 1951 (32).
Mitchell, Julien, actor; b. Nov. 13, 1888, Glossop, Derbyshire,
    England; d. Nov. 4, 1954 (65).
Mitchell, Mrs. Langdon Elwyn, actress; d. June 7, 1944 (83).
Mitchell, Leslie (Les) Harold, actor; d. Oct. 25, 1965 (80).
Mitchell, Mary Ruth, actress; d. May 21, 1941 (35).
Mitchell, Millard, actor; b. Aug. 14, 1903, Havana, Cuba; d. Oct. 13,
    1953 (50).
Mitchell, Norma, author & actress; d. May 29, 1967.
Mitchell, Norval, actor; b. Nov. 6, 1904, Michigan; d. Apr. 28,
    1972 (67).
Mitchell, Rhea, actress; b. Dec. 10, 1893, Oregon; d. Sept. 16,
    1957 (63).
Mitchell, Thomas, actor; b. July 11, 1892, Elizabeth, N.J.;
    d. Dec. 17, 1962 (70).
Mitchell, Yvonne, actress; b. 1925, Cricklewood, England; d. Mar. 24,
    1979 (53).
Mix, Art (r.n. George Kesterson), actor; b. June 18, 1896, Illinois;
    d. Dec. 7, 1972 (76).
Mix, Ruth, actress; d. Sept. 21, 1977 (65).
Mix, Tom, actor; b. Jan. 6, 1880, DuBois, Pa.; d. Oct. 12, 1940 (60).
Mizoguchi, Kenji, director; b. May 16, 1898, Tokyo, Japan; d. Aug.
    24, 1956 (58).

Mock, Alice D., opera singer; d. Oct. 24, 1972 (75).
Mockridge, Cyril J., composer & writer; d. Jan. 18, 1979 (82).
Modeen, Thor, actor; d. May 28, 1950 (52).
Modley, Albert, actor; d. Feb. 23, 1979 (87).
Modot, Gaston, actor; b. Dec. 31, 1887, Paris, France; d. Feb. 20,
    1970 (82).
Moebis, Hans Joachim, actor; d. 1930.
Moebus, Hans, actor; b. Sept. 23, 1902, Germany; d. Apr. 3, 1976 (73).
Moehring, Kansas (r.n. Carl F. Moehring), actor; b. July 9, 1897,
    Ohio; d. Oct. 3, 1968 (71).
Moffat, Margaret, actress; b. Oct. 11, 1883, Scotland; d. Feb. 19,
    1942 (58).
Moffatt, Graham, actor; b. Dec. 6, 1919, London, England; d. July 2,
    1965 (45).
Mog, Aribert, actor; d. Nov., 1941.
Mogi, Max, actor; b. Jan. 16, 1897, Tennessee; d. Oct. 14, 1970 (73).
Moguy, Leonide, director; b. July 14, 1899, Leningrad, U.S.S.R.;
    d. Apr. 21, 1976 (76).
Mohan, Earl, actor; d. Oct. 15, 1928 (39).
Mohr, Gerald, actor; b. June 11, 1914, New York City; d. Nov. 9,
    1968 (54).
Mohr, Hal, cinematographer; b. Aug. 2, 1894, San Francisco, Calif.;
    d. May 10, 1974 (79).
Moissi, Alexander, actor; b. Apr. 2, 1879, Triest, Austria; d. Mar.
    22, 1935 (55).
Moja, Hella, actress; b. Jan. 18, 1896; d. Feb., 1937 (41).
Mojave, King, actor; d. Mar. 23, 1973.
Mojica, Jose (r.n. Francisco Mojica), actor; b. 1896, San Miguel de
    Allende, Mexico; d. Sept. 20, 1974 (78).
Molander, Gustav, director & author; b. Nov. 11, 1888, Helsinki,
    Finland; d. June, 1973 (84).
Molander, Olof, actor; b. 1892; d. 1966 (74).
Molina, Joe, actor; b. May 23, 1899, Arizona; d. Dec. 16, 1977 (78).
Molnar, Ferenc, writer & playwright; b. Jan. 12, 1878, Budapest,
    Hungary; d. Apr. 1, 1952 (74).
Moloney, John, actor; d. July 14, 1969 (58).
Momo, Alessandro, actor; d. Nov. 20, 1974 (20).
Monberg, George, actor; b. Aug. 9, 1890, Illinois; d. Mar. 7, 1925
    (34).
Monclova, Felix, actor; d. Apr. 15, 1977 (42).
Moncries, Edward, actor; d. Mar. 22, 1938 (79).
Mondose, Alex, actor; d. Jan. 8, 1972 (78).
Mong, William V., actor; b. June 25, 1875, Chambersburg, Pa.;
    d. Dec. 11, 1940 (65).
Monk, Alice K. (r.n. Alice Kemp Monk), actress; b. July 22, 1877,
    England; d. July 17, 1954 (76).
Monk, Thomas (r.n. John Thomas Monk), actor; b. Sept. 2, 1877,
    London, England; d. Oct. 28, 1956 (79).
Monkman, Phyllis, actress; b. Jan. 8, 1892, London, England; d. Dec.
    2, 1976 (84).
Monroe, Marilyn, actress; b. June 1, 1926, Los Angeles, Calif.;
    d. Aug. 5, 1962 (36).
Monroe, Tom, writer; d. Apr. 24, 1960 (56).
Monroe, Vaughn, actor, singer, & recording artist; b. Oct. 7,
    1911, Akron, Ohio; d. May 21, 1973 (61).

Montague, Fred, actor; b. 1864, England; d. July 3, 1919 (55).
Montague, Monte (r.n. Walter H. Montague), actor; b. Apr. 23, 1891,
    Somerset, Ky.; d. Apr. 6, 1959 (67).
Montague, Rita, actress; b. May 16, 1883, Illinois; d. May 5, 1962
    (78).
Montalvan, Celia, actress; d. Jan., 1958.
Montana, Bull (r.n. Lewis Montagna), actor; b. May 16, 1887,
    Vogliera, Italy; d. Jan. 24, 1950 (62).
Monteiro, Pilar, actress; d. Dec., 1962 (86).
Monter, Rudolph, producer; d. Dec. 5, 1953 (51).
Montez, Maria, actress; b. June 6, 1920, Santo Domingo, Dominican
    Republic; d. Sept. 7, 1951 (31).
Montgomery, Betty, actress; d. June 1, 1922.
Montgomery, Douglass (Kent Douglass), actor; b. Oct. 29, 1909, Los
    Angeles, Calif.; d. July 23, 1966 (56).
Montgomery, Earl, actor; b. May 24, 1894, California; d. Oct. 28,
    1966 (72).
Montgomery, Goodee, actress; d. June 5, 1978 (72).
Montgomery, Jack, actor; b. Nov. 14, 1891, Nebraska; d. Jan. 21,
    1962 (70).
Montgomery, James S., actor; d. Nov. 9, 1955 (57).
Montgomery, Marian (r.n. Marian Baxter), actress; d. Feb. 7, 1977
    (80).
Monthyl, Marcelle, actress; b. 1892; d. 1950 (58).
Montiel, Nelly, actress; d. Sept. 14, 1951.
Montoya, Alex, actor; b. Oct. 19, 1907, Texas; d. Sept. 25, 1970 (62).
Montoya, Felipe, actor; d. Dec. 8, 1955.
Montrose, Belle, actress; d. Oct. 25, 1964 (78).
Montt, Cristina, actress; d. Apr. 22, 1969 (72).
Moody, Ralph, actor; b. Nov. 5, 1886, St. Louis, Mo.; d. Sept. 16,
    1971 (84).
Mooers, De Sacia, actress; b. Nov. 19, 1888, Michigan; d. Jan. 11,
    1960 (71).
Moon, George, actor; d. June 4, 1961 (75).
Moon, Lorna, writer; d. May 1, 1930 (35).
Moore, Alice, actress; d. May 7, 1960 (44).
Moore, Carlyle, Jr., actor; b. Jan. 5, 1909, New York; d. Mar. 3,
    1977 (68).
Moore, Charles R., actor; b. Apr. 23, 1893, Chicago, Ill.; d. July
    20, 1947 (54).
Moore, Clarence J. (Duke), actor; d. Nov. 16, 1976 (63).
Moore, Cleo, actress; b. Oct. 31, 1924, Baton Rouge, La.; d. Oct. 25,
    1973 (48).
Moore, Cleve, actor; b. June 10, 1904, Huron, Mich.; d. Jan. 25,
    1954 (49).
Moore, Del, actor; d. Aug. 30, 1970 (53).
Moore, Dennis (Denny Meadows), actor; b. Jan. 26, 1908, Ft. Worth,
    Tex.; d. Mar. 1, 1964 (56).
Moore, Eva, actress; b. Feb. 9, 1870, Brighton, England; d. Apr. 27,
    1955 (85).
Moore, Florence, actress; d. Mar. 23, 1935 (49).
Moore, Frank F., actor; d. May 28, 1924 (43).
Moore, Gerald, actor; d. June 17, 1954 (55).
Moore, Grace, actress & opera singer; b. Dec. 5, 1901, Tennessee;
    d. Jan. 25, 1947 (45).

Moore, Hilda, actress; d. May 18, 1929 (43).
Moore, Ida, actress; b. Mar. 1, 1882, Ohio; d. Sept. 26, 1964 (82).
Moore, Joe, actor; d. Aug. 22, 1926 (30).
Moore, Mary, actress; d. 1918.
Moore, Mary, actress; d. Apr. 6, 1931 (70).
Moore, Matt, actor; b. Jan. 8, 1888, County Meath, Ireland; d. Jan.
    20, 1960 (72).
Moore, Monette, singer & actress; b. May 19, 1912, Gainesville, Tex.;
    d. Oct. 21, 1962 (50).
Moore, Owen, actor; b. Dec. 12, 1886, County Meath, Ireland; d. June
    9, 1939 (52).
Moore, Patti, actress; d. Nov. 26, 1972 (71).
Moore, Percy, actor; b. Montreal, Canada; d. Apr. 8, 1945 (67).
Moore, Scott, actor; d. Dec. 18, 1967 (78).
Moore, Sue, actress; b. Jan. 19, 1904, California; d. Apr. 10, 1966
    (62).
Moore, Tim (r.n. Harry R. Moore), actor; b. Dec. 9, 1887, Illinois;
    d. Dec. 13, 1958 (71).
Moore, Tom, actor; b. May 1, 1883, County Meath, Ireland; d. Feb. 12,
    1955 (71).
Moore, Victor, actor; b. Feb. 24, 1876, Hammonton, N.J.; d. July 23,
    1962 (86).
Moore, Vin, director & actor; d. Dec. 5, 1949 (71).
Moorehead, Agnes, actress; b. Dec. 6, 1906, Boston, Mass.; d. Apr.
    30, 1974 (67).
Moorehouse, Bert, actor; b. Nov. 20, 1894, Illinois; d. Jan. 26,
    1954 (59).
Moos, Trude, actress; d. Jan. 9, 1969 (63).
Morales, "Esy" (r.n. Ishmael Morales), orchestra leader; b. Puerto
    Rico; d. Nov. 2, 1950 (33).
Moran, Frank, actor & boxer; b. Mar. 18, 1887, Ohio; d. Dec. 14,
    1967 (80).
Moran, George, actor; b. Oct. 3, 1881, Elwood, Kans.; d. Aug. 1,
    1949 (67).
Moran, Lee, actor; b. June 23, 1888, Chicago, Ill.; d. Apr. 24, 1961
    (72).
Moran, Manolo, actor; b. Mar. 1, 1904, Pittsburgh, Pa.; d. Apr. 27,
    1967 (63).
Moran, Pat, actor; d. Aug. 9, 1965 (64).
Moran, Patsy, actress; b. Oct. 13, 1903, Pennsylvania; d. Dec. 10,
    1968 (65).
Moran, Polly, actress; b. June 28, 1883, Chicago, Ill.; d. Jan. 25,
    1952 (68).
Morane, Jacqueline, actress; d. Mar., 1972.
Morant, Frederick, actor; d. Jan. 7, 1956 (67).
Morante, Milburn, actor; b. Apr. 6, 1887, San Francisco, Calif.;
    d. Jan. 28, 1964 (76).
Morcillo, Jose, actor; d. May 15, 1949.
Mordant, Edwin, actor; b. Dec. 22, 1868, Baltimore, Md.; d. Feb. 16,
    1942 (73).
Mordinov, Nikolai, actor; d. Jan. 27, 1966 (64).
Moreland, Mantan, actor; b. Sept. 3, 1902, Monroe, La.; d. Sept. 28,
    1973 (71).
Morell, Andre, actor; b. Aug. 20, 1909, London, England; d. Nov. 28,
    1978 (69).

Morelli, Michael, actor; d. Aug. 14, 1976 (66).
Morelli, Rina, actress; b. Dec. 6, 1908, Naples, Italy; d. July 17, 1976 (67).
Morena, Sena, actress & director; d. Dec. 6, 1925 (29).
Morency, Robert "Buster," actor; d. Mar. 30, 1937 (5).
Moreno, Antonio, actor; b. Sept. 26, 1887, Madrid, Spain; d. Feb. 15, 1967 (79).
Moreno, Dario, actor & singer; b. Apr. 3, 1921, Smyrna, Turkey; d. Dec. 1, 1968 (47).
Moreno, Jose Elias, actor; b. Nov. 12, 1910, Jalisco, Mexico; d. July 15, 1969 (58).
Moreno, Marguerite, actress; b. Paris, France; d. July 14, 1948 (77).
Moreno, Paco, actor; d. Oct. 15, 1941 (56).
Moreno, Thomas B. (Skyball), actor & stuntman; d. Oct. 25, 1938 (43).
Moreno, Tony, stuntman; d. Dec. 18, 1978 (72).
Morey, Harry T., actor; b. Michigan; d. Jan. 24, 1936 (63).
Morey, Henry A., actor; d. Jan. 8, 1929 (81).
Morgan, Byron, writer; b. Oct. 24, 1889, Carthage, Mo.; d. May 22, 1963 (74).
Morgan, Claudia, actress; b. June 12, 1912, Brooklyn, N.Y.; d. Sept. 17, 1974 (62).
Morgan, Frank, actor; b. June 1, 1890, New York City; d. Sept. 18, 1949 (59).
Morgan, Gene, actor; b. Mar. 12, 1893, Racine, Wisc.; d. Aug. 15, 1940 (47).
Morgan, Guy, writer; d. July 21, 1964 (56).
Morgan, Helen, actress & singer; b. Danville, Ill.; d. Oct. 8, 1941 (41).
Morgan, Ira H., cinematographer; d. Apr. 10, 1959 (70).
Morgan, Lee (r.n. Raymond Lee Morgan), actor; b. June 12, 1902, Texas; d. Jan. 30, 1967 (64).
Morgan, Margaret, actress; d. Aug. 29, 1926.
Morgan, Margo, actress & singer; b. Jan. 27, 1897, Kentucky; d. May 16, 1962 (65).
Morgan, Mike, actor; d. June 5, 1958 (29).
Morgan, Paul, actor; b. Oct. 1, 1886, Vienna, Austria; d. Jan., 1939 (52).
Morgan, Ralph, actor; b. July 6, 1883, New York City; d. June 11, 1956 (72).
Morgan, Rena V., actress; d. Jan. 10, 1956 (62).
Morgan, Russ, orchestra leader & actor; b. Apr. 28, 1904, Scranton, Pa.; d. Aug. 7, 1969 (65).
Morgan, Sydney, actor; b. Oct. 21, 1885, Dublin, Ireland; d. Dec. 5, 1931 (46).
Morgan, Victor J., actor; d. Apr. 18, 1933 (27).
Morgan, William, actor; d. Jan. 2, 1944 (92).
Moriarty, Joanne, actress; d. Mar. 2, 1964 (25).
Moriarty, Marcus, actor; d. June 21, 1916.
Moriarty, Patrick (Pat X. Kerry), actor; b. Jan. 27, 1896, Ireland; d. Oct. 21, 1962 (66).
Morisi, Guido, actor; b. 1903, Bologna, Italy; d. Jan. 4, 1951 (48).
Morison, Lindsay, actor; d. Feb. 22, 1917.
Moriya, Shizu, actress; d. Mar. 11, 1961 (50).
Morlay, Gaby, actress; b. June 8, 1893, Angers; d. July 4, 1964 (71).
Morley, Jay, actor; b. July 14, 1890, Port Orange, Fla.; d. Nov. 9, 1976 (86).

Morley, John, actor; d. Apr. 1, 1949 (35).
Morley, Robert James, actor; d. Aug. 29, 1952 (51).
Morne, Maryland, actress; d. July 18, 1935 (35).
Morosco, Oliver, producer; b. Logan, Utah; d. Aug. 25, 1945 (69).
Morosco, Walter, producer; d. Dec. 30, 1948 (49).
Morphy, Lewis H., actor; d. Nov. 7, 1958 (54).
Morrell, David, actor; d. Dec. 5, 1974.
Morrell, George, actor; b. Apr. 10, 1872, California; d. Apr. 28, 1955 (83).
Morrell, Louis, actor; d. July 11, 1945 (72).
Morris, Adrian (Michael Morris), actor; b. Jan. 12, 1907, Mt. Vernon, N.Y.; d. Nov. 30, 1941 (34).
Morris, Barboura, actress; d. Oct. 23, 1975 (43).
Morris, Chester, actor; b. Feb. 16, 1901, New York City; d. Sept. 11, 1970 (69).
Morris, Corbett, actor; b. Dec. 31, 1881, Colorado; d. Mar. 10, 1951 (69).
Morris, Dave, actor; d. June 8, 1960 (63).
Morris, Diana, actress; b. July 21, 1906, California; d. Feb. 19, 1961 (54).
Morris, Glenn, actor; b. June 18, 1912, Missouri; d. Jan. 31, 1974 (62).
Morris, Gordon, actor & author; d. Apr. 7, 1940 (41).
Morris, Johnnie, actor; b. June 15, 1887, New York; d. Oct. 7, 1969 (82).
Morris, Lee, actor; b. June 23, 1863, Missouri; d. Feb. 6, 1933 (69).
Morris, Margaret, actress; b. Nov. 7, 1898, Minneapolis, Minn.; d. June 7, 1968 (69).
Morris, Mary, actress; b. June 24, 1895, Swampscott, Mass.; d. Jan. 16, 1970 (74).
Morris, Michael (see Morris, Adrian)
Morris, Philip (r.n. Frank Charles Morris), actor; b. Jan. 20, 1893, Duluth, Minn.; d. Dec. 18, 1949 (56).
Morris, Reginald, writer & director; d. Feb. 16, 1928 (41).
Morris, Stephen (see Ankrum, Morris)
Morris, W. Richard Stuart, actor; d. Oct. 11, 1924 (63).
Morris, Wayne, actor; b. Feb. 17, 1914, Los Angeles, Calif.; d. Sept. 14, 1959 (45).
Morris, William, actor; b. Jan. 1, 1861, Boston, Mass.; d. Jan. 11, 1936 (75).
Morris, William E., actor; d. Sept. 21, 1948 (70).
Morrison, Adrienne, actress; b. New York City; d. Nov. 20, 1940 (57).
Morrison, Ann, actress; d. Apr. 18, 1978 (62).
Morrison, Anna Marie, actress; d. July 5, 1972 (88).
Morrison, Arthur, actor; b. May 1, 1877, Missouri; d. Feb. 20, 1950 (72).
Morrison, Chick (r.n. Charles Pacific Morrison), actor; b. Apr. 3, 1878, Colorado; d. June 20, 1924 (46).
Morrison, Elizabeth, actress; b. Oct. 21, 1871, Indiana; d. Nov. 22, 1960 (89).
Morrison, James, actor; b. Nov. 15, 1888, Mattoon, Ill.; d. Nov. 15, 1974 (86).
Morrison, Lou, actor; b. Feb. 8, 1866, Portland, Md.; d. Apr. 22, 1946 (80).
Morrison, Pete (r.n. George D. Morrison), actor; b. Aug. 8, 1890, Denver, Colo.; d. Feb. 5, 1973 (82).

Morrissey, Betty, actress; d. Apr. 20, 1944 (36).
Morrissey, John F., actor; d. Oct. 6, 1941 (58).
Morros, Boris, producer; b. Jan. 1, 1895, Russia; d. Jan. 8, 1963 (68).
Morrow, Doretta, actress & singer; b. Jan. 27, 1927, New York City; d. Feb. 28, 1968 (41).
Morse, Karl, actor; b. Ohio; d. Jan. 22, 1936 (48).
Morse, Robin, actor; d. Dec. 11, 1958 (43).
Mortimer, Charles, actor; d. Apr. 1, 1964 (79).
Mortimer, Dorothy, actress; d. Feb. 15, 1950 (52).
Mortimer, Edmund, director & actor; d. May 21, 1944 (69).
Mortimer, Henry, actor; d. Aug. 20, 1952 (77).
Mortimer, Louise Bates (Louise Emerald Bates), actress; b. Dec. 28, 1886, Massachusetts; d. June 11, 1972 (85).
Morton, Charles, actor; b. Jan. 28, 1908, Illinois; d. Oct. 26, 1966 (58).
Morton, Clive, actor; b. Mar. 16, 1904, London, England; d. Sept. 24, 1975 (71).
Morton, Hank, actor; d. Jan. 4, 1963 (50).
Morton, James C., actor; b. Helena, Mont.; d. Oct. 24, 1942 (58).
Mosbacher, Peter, actor; b. Feb. 17, 1915, Mannheim, Germany; d. Oct. 9, 1977 (62).
Moscovich, Maurice, actor; b. Nov. 23, 1871, Odessa, Russia; d. June 18, 1940 (68).
Moscowitz, Mrs. Jennie, actress; b. Romania; d. July 26, 1953 (85).
Moser, Hans, actor; b. Aug. 6, 1880, Vienna, Austria; d. June 19, 1964 (83).
Mosjoukine, Ivan, actor; d. Jan. 18, 1939 (50).
Moskvin, Ivan M., actor; b. June 18, 1874, Moscow, Russia; d. Feb. 16, 1946 (71).
Mosley, Frederick C., actor; d. Mar. 9, 1927 (73).
Moss, Basil Geoffrey, actor; d. June 10, 1935 (26).
Moss, Gaylin, actress; d. Apr. 13, 1979 (20).
Moss, Maitland, actor; d. Aug. 19, 1967 (66).
Mostel, Zero, actor; b. Feb. 28, 1915, Brooklyn, N.Y.; d. Sept. 8, 1977 (62).
Moulan, Frank, actor; d. May 13, 1939 (67).
Moulder, Walter C., actor; d. July 1, 1967 (34).
Moulton, Edwin "Buck," actor; b. Apr. 8, 1891, New York; d. May 7, 1959 (68).
Mouvet, Maurice, actor; d. May 18, 1927 (41).
Movar, Dunja, actress; b. Germany; d. Mar. 30, 1963 (23).
Mowbray, Alan, actor; b. Aug. 18, 1896, London, England; d. Mar. 25, 1969 (72).
Mowbray, Henry (Harry E. Sweeney), actor; b. Sept. 5, 1882, Australia; d. July 9, 1960 (77).
Mower, Jack, actor; b. Sept. 5, 1890, California; d. Jan. 6, 1965 (74).
Mozart, George, actor; b. Feb. 15, 1864, Yarmouth, England; d. Dec. 10, 1947 (83).
Mudd, E. Virginia (E. Virginia Mudd Klumker), actress; d. May 21, 1979 (85).
Mudge, Augustine B., actress; d. Apr. 7, 1952 (79).
Mudie, Leonard, actor; b. Apr. 11, 1883, England; d. Apr. 14, 1965 (82).

Mueller, Gerda, actress; b. July 30, 1894, Fornienen, Germany;
    d. Apr. 26, 1951 (56).
Mueller, Renate, actress; b. Apr. 24, 1904, Munich, Germany; d. Oct.
    7, 1937 (33).
Mueller, Wolfgang, actor; b. Dec. 14, 1922, Berlin, Germany; d. Apr.
    26, 1960 (37).
Muir, Gavin, actor; b. Sept. 8, 1909, Chicago, Ill.; d. May 24, 1972
    (62).
Muir, Helen, actress; d. Dec. 2, 1934 (70).
Mulcaster, G.H., actor; b. June 27, 1891, London, England; d. Jan.
    19, 1964 (72).
Mulgrew, Thomas G., actor; d. Dec. 3, 1954 (65).
Mulhall, Jack, actor; b. Oct. 7, 1887, Wappingers Falls, N.Y.;
    d. June 1, 1979 (91).
Mulhauser, James, actor; b. Oct. 31, 1889, Brooklyn, N.Y.; d. June
    15, 1939 (49).
Mulle, Ida, actress; d. Aug. 5, 1934 (71).
Mullen, Barbara, actress; b. June 9, 1914, Boston, Mass.; d. Mar. 9,
    1979 (64).
Mullens, Johnnie, actor; d. Jan. 3, 1978 (93).
Muller, Robert, actor; b. Mar. 29, 1879, Vienna, Austria; d. Feb. 1,
    1968 (88).
Muller-Lincke, Anna, actress; b. Apr. 8, 1869, Berlin, Germany;
    d. Jan. 24, 1935 (65).
Mumby, Diana, actress; b. July 6, 1922, Detroit, Mich.; d. May 19,
    1974 (51).
Mundin, Herbert, actor; b. Aug. 21, 1898, London, England; d. Mar. 4,
    1939 (40).
Mundy, Edward (Cap), actor; b. May 11, 1888, Illinois; d. Feb. 25,
    1962 (73).
Muni, Paul, actor; b. Sept. 22, 1895, Lemberg, Austria; d. Aug. 25,
    1967 (71).
Munier, Ferdinand, actor; b. Dec. 3, 1889, San Diego, Calif.;
    d. May 27, 1945 (55).
Munro, Douglas, actor; d. Feb., 1924.
Munro, Janet, actress; d. Dec. 6, 1972 (38).
Munshin, Jules, actor; b. Feb. 22, 1915, New York City; d. Feb. 19,
    1970 (54).
Munson, Martha, actress; d. Sept. 30, 1949 (65).
Munson, Ona, actress; b. June 16, 1906, Portland, Ore.; d. Feb. 11,
    1955 (48).
Mura, Corinna, actress & singer; d. Aug. 1, 1965 (55).
Murat, Jean, actor; b. July 13, 1888, Perigueux, France; d. Jan. 5,
    1968 (79).
Muratore, Lucien, actor & opera singer; b. Aug. 29, 1878, Marseilles,
    France; d. July 16, 1954 (75).
Murdock, Ann, actress; b. Nov. 10, 1890, Port Washington, N.Y.;
    d. Apr. 22, 1939 (48).
Murfin, Jane, writer; b. Oct. 27, 1892, Quincy, Mich.; d. Aug. 10,
    1955 (62).
Murnane, Allan, actor & director; d. Apr. 2, 1950 (67).
Murnau, F.W., director; b. Dec. 28, 1888, Bielefeld, Germany;
    d. Mar. 11, 1931 (42).
Murphy, Ada, actress; b. Jan. 6, 1887, England; d. Aug. 25, 1961
    (74).
Murphy, Audie, actor; b. June 20, 1924, Kingston, Tex.; d. May 28,
    1971 (46).

Murphy, Bob, actor; b. Mar. 9, 1889, Webster, N.Y.; d. Aug. 5, 1948 (59).
Murphy, Charles B., actor; b. Dec. 12, 1881, Independence, Mo.; d. June 11, 1942 (60).
Murphy, Edna, actress; b. Nov. 17, 1899, New York City; d. Aug. 3, 1974 (74).
Murphy, George, actor; d. Aug. 15, 1941 (42).
Murphy, Horace (r.n. William Horace Murphy), actor; b. June 3, 1880, Finley, Tenn.; d. Jan. 20, 1975 (94).
Murphy, John Daly, actor; b. County Kildare, Ireland; d. Nov. 20, 1934 (61).
Murphy, John T., actor; b. Aug. 24, 1879, Helena, Mont.; d. July 7, 1955 (75).
Murphy, Joseph, actor; b. May 16, 1877, California; d. July 31, 1961 (84).
Murphy, Maurice, actor; b. Oct. 3, 1913, Seattle, Wash.; d. Nov. 23, 1978 (65).
Murray, Charlie, actor; b. June 22, 1872, Laurel, Ind.; d. July 29, 1941 (69).
Murray, Edgar, actor; d. Oct. 16, 1959 (67).
Murray, Elizabeth, actress; d. 1914.
Murray, Elizabeth, actress; d. Mar. 27, 1946 (75).
Murray, Fred, actor; d. Jan. 4, 1950 (51).
Murray, J. Harold, actor; b. Feb. 17, 1891, South Berwick, Me.; d. Dec. 11, 1940 (49).
Murray, Jack, actor; d. May 1, 1941.
Murray, James, actor; b. Feb. 9, 1901, New York City; d. July 11, 1936 (35).
Murray, John T., actor; b. Aug. 28, 1886, Australia; d. Feb. 12, 1957 (70).
Murray, Lola, actress; d. Nov. 11, 1961 (47).
Murray, Mae, actress; b. May 10, 1889, Portsmouth, Va.; d. Mar. 23, 1965 (75).
Murray, Marion, actress; d. Nov. 11, 1951 (66).
Murray, Tom, actor; b. Sept. 8, 1874, Stonefoot, Ill.; d. Aug. 27, 1935 (60).
Murray-Hill, Peter, actor; b. Apr. 20, 1908, Bushy Heath, England; d. Nov. 25, 1957 (49).
Murth, Florence, actress; b. Jan. 20, 1897, Boswell, Pa.; d. Mar. 29, 1934 (37).
Musco, Angelo, actor; d. Oct. 6, 1937.
Muse, Clarence, actor; b. Oct. 14, 1889, Baltimore, Md.; d. Oct. 13, 1979 (89).
Musidora (Jeanne Roques), actress; b. France; d. Dec., 1957 (68).
Musolino, Vincenzo, actor; b. 1930, Reggio di Calabria, Italy; d. May 9, 1969 (39).
Mussette, Charles, actor; b. 1876; d. Dec. 8, 1939 (63).
Mussey, Francine, actress; d. Mar. 26, 1933.
Musson, Bennet, actor; d. Feb. 17, 1946 (80).
Mustin, Burt, actor; b. Feb. 8, 1882, Pittsburgh, Pa.; d. Jan. 28, 1977 (94).
Muthel, Lothar, actor; b. Feb. 8, 1896; d. Sept. 4, 1964 (68).
Mutio, Ricardo, actor; b. 1888, Mexico City, Mexico; d. Apr. 2, 1957 (69).
Muzquiz, Carlos, actor; d. Feb., 1960 (54).
Myers, Harry C., actor; b. Sept. 5, 1882, New Haven, Conn.; d. Dec. 25, 1938 (56).

Myers, Mrs. Lenora, actress; d. Feb. 10, 1950 (46).
Myers, Seldy, actor; d. May 6, 1939 (73).
Myers, Zion, writer & director; b. June 26, 1898, San Francisco,
    Calif.; d. Feb. 24, 1948 (49).
Mylong, John (r.n. John Mylong-Muenz), actor; b. Sept. 27, 1892,
    Austria; d. Sept. 7, 1975 (82).
Myrtil, Odette, actress; b. June 28, 1898, Paris, France; d. Nov. 18,
    1978 (80).
Myton, Fred K., writer; d. June 6, 1955 (68).


Nadajan, actor; d. Sept. 20, 1974.
Nadherny, Ernst, actor; b. Dec. 28, 1885, Vienna, Austria; d. Feb.,
    1966 (80).
Nadi, Aldo, actor & fencing master; b. Apr. 23, 1899, Leghorn, Italy;
    d. Nov. 10, 1965 (66).
Nagel, Anne, actress; b. Sept. 29, 1915, Boston, Mass.; d. July 6,
    1966 (50).
Nagel, Beth, actress; d. Oct. 29, 1936 (59).
Nagel, Conrad, actor; b. Mar. 16, 1897, Keokuk, Iowa; d. Feb. 24,
    1970 (72).
Nagiah, V., actor; d. Dec. 30, 1973 (70).
Nagy, Bill, actor; b. Hungary; d. Jan. 19, 1973 (51).
Naidoo, Bobby, actor; d. July 6, 1967 (40).
Nainby, Robert, actor; b. June 14, 1869, Dublin, Ireland; d. Feb. 17,
    1948 (78).
Naish, J. Carrol, actor; b. Jan. 21, 1897, New York City; d. Jan. 24,
    1973 (76).
Naldi, Nita, actress; b. Apr. 1, 1897, New York City; d. Feb. 17,
    1961 (63).
Nally, William, actor; d. Mar., 1929.
Namara, Marguerite (r.n. Marguerite Banks), opera singer & actress;
    b. 1888; d. Nov. 3, 1974 (86).
Nanook (of the North), actor; d. Nov., 1925.
Nansen, Betty, actress; b. Mar. 19, 1873, Copenhagen, Denmark;
    d. Mar. 15, 1943 (69).
Nardelli, George (r.n. Achille Nardelli), actor; b. Oct. 21, 1895,
    France; d. Sept. 16, 1973 (77).
Nares, Anna, actress; d. Dec. 19, 1915 (46).
Nares, Owen, actor; b. Aug. 11, 1888, England; d. July 30, 1943 (54).
Narvaez, Sara, actress; d. Dec., 1935.
Nash, Florence, actress; b. Oct. 2, 1888, Troy, N.Y.; d. Apr. 2,
    1950 (61).
Nash, George F., actor; b. Philadelphia, Pa.; d. Dec. 31, 1944 (71).
Nash, June, actress; d. Oct. 8, 1979 (68).
Nash, Mary, actress; b. Aug. 15, 1885, Troy, N.Y.; d. Dec. 3, 1976
    (91).
Nash, Maxine, singer & dancer; d. Mar. 18, 1938 (19).
Nassour, Edward, executive; b. Los Angeles, Calif.; d. Dec. 15, 1962
    (45).
Nat, Lucien, actor; d. July, 1972 (77).
Nataro, Jimmy (r.n. James V. Notaro), actor; b. Feb. 10, 1907,
    Minneapolis, Minn.; d. Jan. 31, 1946 (38).
Natheaux, Louis (r.n. Louis F. Natho), actor; b. Dec. 10, 1894,
    Pine Bluff, Ark.; d. Aug. 23, 1942 (47).

Naughton, Charlie, actor (Crazy Gang); d. Feb. 11, 1976 (89).
Navarro, Carlos, actor; b. Feb. 24, 1921, Mexico City, Mexico;
  d. Feb. 12, 1969 (47).
Navarro, Jesus Garcia, actor; d. Oct., 1960 (47).
Nayfack, Nicholas, producer; d. Mar. 31, 1958 (49).
Nazarro, Cliff, actor; b. Jan. 31, 1904, New Haven, Conn.; d. Feb. 18,
  1961 (57).
Nazimova, Alla, actress; b. May 22 or June 4, 1879, Yalta, Crimea,
  Russia; d. July 13, 1945 (66).
Nazzari, Amedeo, actor; b. Dec. 10, 1907, Cagliari, Sardinia;
  d. Nov. 5, 1979 (71).
Neal, Frank, dancer; d. May 8, 1955 (38).
Neal, Lloyd, actor; b. Oct. 20, 1861, Michigan; d. Aug. 19, 1952 (90).
Neal, Tom, actor; b. Jan. 28, 1914, Evanston, Ill.; d. Aug. 7, 1972
  (58).
Neame, Derek, author; d. Dec. 27, 1979 (64).
Neason, Hazel, actress; d. Jan. 20, 1920.
Nebenzal, Seymour, producer; b. July 22, 1899, New York City;
  d. Sept. 25, 1961 (62).
Nedd, Stuart (r.n. Daniel Stuart Nedd), actor; b. Oregon; d. Mar. 15,
  1971 (57).
Nedell, Bernard, actor; b. Oct. 14, 1893, New York City; d. Nov. 23,
  1972 (79).
Neff, Ralph, actor; b. Aug. 16, 1907, Nebraska; d. Jan. 28, 1973 (65).
Neft, Else, actress; b. Mar. 11, 1884, Austria; d. July 11, 1968 (84).
Negin, Kolia, actor; d. Mar. 4, 1947 (61).
Negrete, Jorge, actor & singer; b. Nov. 30, 1911, Mexico; d. Dec. 5,
  1953 (42).
Negri-Pouget, Fernanda, actress; b. 1889; d. 1955 (66).
Neher, Carola, actress; b. Nov. 2, 1900, Munich, Germany; d. 1936
  (35).
Neidel, Charles G., Sr., actor; b. Apr. 29, 1893, Massachusetts;
  d. Jan. 31, 1962 (68).
Neilan, Marshall, actor & director; b. Apr. 11, 1891, California;
  d. Oct. 26, 1958 (67).
Neilendam, Sigrid, actress; d. Jan. 26, 1955 (86).
Neill, James, actor; b. Sept. 29, 1860, Savannah, Ga.; d. Mar. 15,
  1931 (70).
Neill, R. William, director; d. Dec. 14, 1946 (59).
Neill, Richard R., actor; b. Nov. 12, 1875, Philadelphia, Pa.;
  d. Apr. 8, 1970 (94).
Neilson-Terry, Dennis, actor; b. Oct. 21, 1895, London, England;
  d. July 14, 1932 (36).
Neilson-Terry, Phyllis, actress; b. Oct. 15, 1892, London, England;
  d. Sept. 25, 1977 (84).
Neitz, Alvin J. (see James, Alan)
Nelson, Anne, actress; d. July 6, 1948 (37).
Nelson, Bill, actor; d. Aug. 6, 1973.
Nelson, Billy, actor; d. June 12, 1979 (75).
Nelson, Eddie, actor; d. Dec. 5, 1940 (46).
Nelson, Evelyn, actress; d. June 16, 1923.
Nelson, Frank, actor; d. Nov. 27, 1932 (60).
Nelson, Gordon, actor; d. Feb. 19, 1956 (58).
Nelson, Harold, actor; b. Aug. 26, 1864, Boston, Mass.; d. Jan. 26,
  1937 (72).

Nelson, Lottie (Lottie O. Tompkins), actress; b. Mar. 13, 1875, California; d. May 8, 1966 (91).
Nelson, Ozzie, actor; b. Mar. 20, 1907, Jersey City, N.J.; d. June 3, 1975 (68).
Nelson, Sam, actor & assistant director; b. May 31, 1896, Whittier, Calif.; d. May 1, 1963 (66).
Nelson-Ramsey, John, actor; d. Apr. 5, 1929.
Nemetz, Max, actor; b. Oct. 19, 1884; d. July 2, 1971 (86).
Neri, Giulio, opera singer; d. Apr. 21, 1958 (49).
Nerking, Hans, actor; b. Dec. 10, 1888, Darmstadt, Germany; d. Apr. 26, 1964 (75).
Nero, Curtis, actor; b. Apr. 3, 1906, Muskogee, Okla.; d. Jan. 28, 1942 (35).
Nervo, Jimmy, actor (Crazy Gang); d. Dec. 5, 1975 (78).
Nesbit, Evelyn, actress; d. Jan. 17, 1967 (82).
Nesbitt, John, actor, producer, scenarist, & commentator; b. Aug. 23, 1910, Victoria, B.C., Canada; d. Aug. 10, 1960 (49).
Nesbitt, Miriam, actress; b. Sept. 14, 1873, Chicago, Ill.; d. Aug. 11, 1954 (80).
Nesbitt, Tom, actor; d. Mar. 31, 1927 (36).
Nesmith, Ottola, actress; b. Dec. 12, 1889, Washington, D.C.; d. Feb. 7, 1972 (82).
Ness, Ole M., actor; d. July 19, 1953 (65).
Nestell, Bill, actor; b. Mar. 3, 1893, California; d. Oct. 18, 1966 (73).
Neu, Oscar, director; b. June 22, 1886, Buffalo, N.Y.; d. Aug. 26, 1957 (71).
Neumann, Eugene, actor; d. July 8, 1956 (67).
Neumann, Harry C., cinematographer; d. Jan. 14, 1971 (79).
Neumann, Kurt, director & actor; b. Apr. 5, 1908, Germany; d. Aug. 21, 1958 (50).
Neuss, Karl Heinrich, actor; b. 1879, Koln-Deutz, Germany; d. Oct. 29, 1935 (56).
Neusser, Eric, actor & director; d. Aug. 30, 1957 (55).
Neville, George, actor; d. Aug. 18, 1932 (67).
Neville, Harry, actor; d. Jan. 25, 1945 (77).
Newall, Guy, actor; b. May 25, 1885, Isle of Wight, England; d. Feb. 25, 1937 (51).
Newberry, Hazard P., actor; d. May 27, 1952 (45).
Newburg, Frank, actor; b. Oct. 9, 1886, Pennsylvania; d. Nov. 4, 1969 (83).
Newcomb, Mary, actress; d. Dec. 26, 1966 (73).
Newcombe, Caroline, actress; d. Dec. 17, 1941 (69).
Newcombe, Jessamine, actress; d. Mar. 15, 1961.
Newell, David, actor; b. Jan. 23, 1905, Carthage, Mo.; d. Jan. 25, 1980 (75).
Newell, William, actor; b. Jan. 6, 1894, New Jersey; d. Feb. 21, 1967 (73).
Newfield, Sam (Sherman Scott; Peter Stewart), director; b. Dec. 6, 1899, New York City; d. Nov. 10, 1964 (64).
Newhall, Mayo, actor; b. Nov. 24, 1891, California; d. Dec. 11, 1958 (67).
Newill, James, actor; b. Aug. 12, 1911, Pittsburgh, Pa.; d. July 31, 1975 (63).

Newlan, Paul, actor; b. June 29, 1903, Nebraska; d. Nov. 23, 1973 (70).
Newlan, Tiny (see Newlan, Paul)
Newland, Douglass (see Mitchell, Johnny)
Newman, Alfred, composer & musical director; b. Mar. 17, 1901, New Haven, Conn.; d. Feb. 17, 1970 (68).
Newman, Candy, actress; d. June 19, 1966 (21).
Newman, Henry (Hank) (Georgia Crackers), singer; d. July 25, 1978 (73).
Newman, Jack, actor; b. June 4, 1894, Poland; d. July 29, 1966 (72).
Newman, John Koch, actor; d. Mar. 2, 1927 (63).
Newman, Nell, actress; d. Aug., 1931 (50).
Newman, Scott, actor; d. Nov. 20, 1978 (28).
Newton, Charles, actor; d. 1926.
Newton, Ralph, actor; d. Mar. 14, 1977 (76).
Newton, Robert, actor; b. June 1, 1905, Shaftsbury, Dorsetshire, England; d. Mar. 25, 1956 (50).
Newton, Theodore, actor; b. Aug. 4, 1904, New Jersey; d. Feb. 23, 1963 (58).
Niblo, Fred, actor & director; b. Jan. 6, 1874, York, Neb.; d. Nov. 11, 1948 (74).
Niblo, Fred, Jr., writer; b. Jan. 23, 1903, New York City; d. Feb. 18, 1973 (70).
Nicholls, Anthony, actor; b. Oct., 1907, Windsor, England; d. Feb. 22, 1977 (69).
Nichols, Barbara, actress; b. Dec. 10, 1928, New York; d. Oct. 5, 1976 (47).
Nichols, Dudley, author, director, & producer; b. Apr. 6, 1895, Wapakoneta, Ohio; d. Jan. 4, 1960 (64).
Nichols, George, actor; d. Sept. 20, 1927 (62).
Nichols, George, Jr., director; d. Nov. 13, 1939 (42).
Nichols, Marguerite, actress; d. Mar. 17, 1941 (41).
Nichols, Marjorie, actress; d. Sept. 26, 1970.
Nichols, Nellie V., actress; b. May 5, 1885, New Jersey; d. July 16, 1971 (86).
Nicholson, John, actor; b. Charleston, Ill.; d. June 24, 1934 (61).
Nicholson, Lillian, actress; d. Mar. 31, 1949 (68).
Nicholson, Nora, actress; b. Dec. 7, 1889, Leamington, England; d. Sept. 18, 1973 (83).
Nicholson, Paul, actor; b. Orange, N.J.; d. Feb. 2, 1935 (58).
Nickols, Walter, actor; d. Dec. 25, 1927 (74).
Nicodemi, Aldo, actor; b. 1924, Viterbo, Italy; d. Nov. 8, 1963 (39).
Nicoletti, Louis A., assistant director; b. Nov. 7, 1906, New York; d. Oct. 16, 1969 (63).
Nielsen, Asta, actress; b. Sept., 1881, Copenhagen, Denmark; d. May 24, 1972 (90).
Nielsen, Hans, actor; b. Nov. 30, 1911, Hamburg, Germany; d. Oct., 1965 (53).
Niemeyer, Joseph H., dancer; b. June 14, 1887, Texas; d. Sept. 27, 1965 (78).
Niese, Hansi (r.n. Hansi Jarno), actress; b. 1901; d. Mar. 20, 1933 (32).
Niesen, Gertrude, actress; b. July 8, 1911, New York; d. Mar. 27, 1975 (63).
Nigh, William, director; b. Oct. 12, 1881, Wisconsin; d. Nov. 27, 1955 (74).

Nigro, Beatrice, actress; d. Dec. 6, 1956 (71).
Nillson, Carlotta, actress; b. Sweden; d. Dec. 31, 1951 (73).
Nilsson, Anna Q. (r.n. Anna Quirentia Nilsson), actress; b. Mar. 30,
    1888, Ystad, Sweden; d. Feb. 11, 1974 (85).
Ninchi, Annibale, actor; b. Nov. 20, 1887, Corfu, Greece; d. Jan. 15,
    1967 (79).
Ninchi, Carlo, actor; b. May 31, 1897, Bologna, Italy; d. May 1,
    1974 (76).
Nixon, Arundel, actor; d. Apr. 4, 1949 (42).
Nixon, Clint, actor; d. Oct. 22, 1937 (31).
Nixon, Lester, actor; d. Aug. 29, 1962 (33).
Noa, Manfred, actor & director; b. Mar. 22, 1893; d. Dec. 5, 1930
    (37).
Noble, Ray, pianist & composer; b. Dec. 17, 1903, Brighton, Sussex,
    England; d. Apr. 3, 1978 (74).
Nobles, Dolly, actress; b. Cincinnati, Ohio; d. Oct. 6, 1930 (67).
Nobles, Milton, actor; b. Dec., 1843, Cincinnati, Ohio; d. June 14,
    1924 (80).
Noel, Bernard, actor; d. Sept., 1970 (44).
Noemi, Lea, actress; d. Nov. 6, 1973 (90).
Nolan, Mary (Imogene Wilson), actress; b. Dec. 18, 1905, Louisville,
    Ky.; d. Oct. 31, 1948 (42).
Noll, Karel, actor; b. 1880; d. Mar., 1928 (47).
Noll, Mrs. Louise M., actress; d. Nov. 1, 1944 (60).
Nomis, Leo, actor & stuntman; d. Feb. 5, 1932 (38).
Noon, Paisley, actor; d. Mar. 27, 1932 (35).
Noonan, Patrick, actor; b. Jan. 9, 1887, Dublin, Ireland; d. May 19,
    1962 (75).
Noonan, Tommy, actor; b. Apr. 29, 1922, Bellingham, Wash.; d. Apr. 24,
    1968 (45).
Noor, Lies, actress; d. Mar. 16, 1961 (23).
Norcross, Frank, actor; b. July 10, 1857, Massachusetts; d. Sept. 12,
    1926 (69).
Norcross, Hale, actor; b. San Francisco, Calif.; d. Oct. 15, 1947
    (70).
Norden, Cliff, actor; d. Sept. 23, 1949 (26).
Nordstrom, Clarence, actor; d. Dec. 13, 1968 (75).
Noriega, Manolo (Manuel Noriega), actor; d. Aug. 12, 1961 (81).
Noriega, Manuel (see Noriega, Manolo)
Norman, Amber, actress; b. June 6, 1901, Utah; d. Oct. 21, 1972 (71).
Norman, Gertrude, actress; b. May 19, 1848, London, England; d. July 20,
    1943 (95).
Norman, Josephine, actress; b. Nov. 12, 1904, Vienna, Austria;
    d. Jan. 24, 1951 (46).
Norman, Perry, actor; d. Aug. 27, 1945 (61).
Normand, Mabel, actress & director; b. Nov. 10, 1894, Boston, Mass.;
    d. Feb. 23, 1930 (35).
Norrie, Claude, actor; d. May 10, 1916.
Norris, William, actor; b. June 15, 1870, New York City; d. Mar. 20,
    1929 (58).
North, Bob, actor; d. Mar. 18, 1936 (55).
North, Charles, actor; b. Apr. 11, 1870, Kentucky; d. May 24, 1936
    (66).
North, Joseph, actor; b. Dec. 27, 1873, England; d. Jan. 8, 1945 (71).
North, Robert, actor & producer; b. Feb. 2, 1884, New York City;
    d. Aug. 13, 1976 (92).

North, Wilfred, actor & director; b. Jan. 16, 1863, London, England;
d. June 3, 1935 (72).
Northpole, John (r.n. John Kovacevich), actor; b. Dec. 23, 1892,
Yugoslavia; d. Feb. 26, 1964 (71).
Northrup, Harry, actor; b. July 31, 1875, Paris, France; d. July 2,
1936 (60).
Norton, Barry (r.n. Alfredo Carlos de Birben), actor; b. June 16,
1909, Buenos Aires, Argentina; d. Aug. 25, 1956 (47).
Norton, Cecil A., actor; d. Nov. 30, 1955 (60).
Norton, Edgar (r.n. Harry Mills), actor; b. Aug. 11, 1868, England;
d. Feb. 6, 1953 (84).
Norton, Elda, actress; b. Apr. 21, 1891, Ontario, Canada; d. Apr. 15,
1947 (55).
Norton, Field (r.n. Henry Field Norton), actor; b. Dec. 12, 1891,
Jeffersonville, Ind.; d. Aug. 10, 1945 (53).
Norton, Fletcher, actor; b. Aug. 4, 1877, San Francisco, Calif.;
d. Oct. 3, 1941 (64).
Norton, Frederic, actor & singer; d. Dec. 15, 1946.
Norton, Jack, actor; b. Brooklyn, N.Y.; d. Oct. 15, 1958 (69).
Norton, Ned (Clothes), actor; d. Mar. 26, 1961 (79).
Norwood, Eille, actor; b. Oct. 11, 1861, York, England; d. Dec. 24,
1948 (87).
Norworth, Jack, actor & singer; b. Jan. 5, 1879, Philadelphia, Pa.;
d. Sept. 1, 1959 (80).
Nosher, Edith, actress; d. July 13, 1929 (35).
Nosseck, Max (Alexander M. Norris), director & scenarist; b. Sept. 19,
1902, Nakel, Poland; d. Sept. 29, 1972 (70).
Notari, Guido, actor; b. May 10, 1893, Asti, Italy; d. Jan. 21, 1957
(63).
Novack, Shelly, actor; d. May 27, 1978 (30).
Novarro, Ramon, actor; b. Feb. 6, 1899, Durango, Mexico; d. Oct. 31,
1968 (69).
Novelli, Amleto, actor; b. Oct. 18, 1885, Bologna, Italy; d. Apr. 16,
1924 (39).
Novelli, Ermete, actor; b. May 5, 1851, Lucca, Italy; d. Jan. 30,
1919 (67).
Novello, Ivor, actor; b. Jan. 15, 1893, Cardiff, Wales; d. Mar. 6,
1951 (58).
Novinsky, Alex, actor; b. July 1, 1878, St. Petersburg, Russia;
d. June 30, 1960 (81).
Novis, Donald, actor & singer; b. Mar. 3, 1906, Hastings, England;
d. July 23, 1966 (60).
Nowell, Wedgewood, actor; b. Portsmouth, N.H.; d. June 17, 1957 (79).
Nowlin, Herman F., actor; b. Jan. 16, 1892, Illinois; d. Sept. 2,
1951 (59).
Nox, Andre, actor; b. 1889; d. 1946 (57).
Noyes, Joseph (Skeets), actor; b. Sept. 19, 1868, New Orleans, La.;
d. Apr. 18, 1936 (67).
Nuatjim, Chamroon, actor; d. May 9, 1979 (65).
Nuemann, Charles, actor; d. July 16, 1927 (44).
Nugent, Frank, author; b. May 27, 1908, New York City; d. Dec. 29,
1965 (57).
Nugent, J.C., actor & author; b. Apr. 6, 1868, Niles, Ohio; d. Apr. 21,
1947 (79).
Nunn, Wayne, actor; d. Dec. 17, 1947 (66).

Nurney, Fred (r.n. Fritz Nuernborger), actor; d. Sept. 9, 1973.
Nusser, James, actor; b. May 3, 1905, Ohio; d. June 9, 1979 (74).
Nye, Carroll, actor; b. Oct. 4, 1901, Canton, Ohio; d. Mar. 17,
   1974 (72).


Oakie, Jack, actor; b. Nov. 12, 1903, Sedalia, Mo.; d. Jan. 23,
   1978 (74).
Oakland, Vivien, actress; b. May 20, 1895, California; d. Aug. 1,
   1958 (63).
Oakley, Annie, actress & marksman; d. Nov. 4, 1926 (66).
Oakley, Florence, actress; d. Sept. 25, 1956 (65).
Oakley, Laura, actress; d. Jan. 30, 1957 (77).
Oakman, Wheeler, actor; b. Feb. 21, 1890, Washington, D.C.;
   d. Mar. 19, 1949 (59).
Oates, Cicely, actress; d. Dec. 23, 1934 (45).
Obeck, Ferd, actor & director; d. Jan. 31, 1929 (46).
Ober, Kirk, actor; d. May 31, 1939 (64).
Ober, Robert, actor; b. Sept. 3, 1881, Bunker Hill, Ill.; d. Dec. 7,
   1950 (69).
Oberle, Florence, actress; d. July 10, 1943 (73).
Oberon, Merle, actress; b. Feb. 19, 1911, Tasmania; d. Nov. 23, 1979
   (68).
O'Brien, Dave (David Barclay), actor; b. May 31, 1912, Big Springs,
   Tex.; d. Nov. 8, 1969 (57).
O'Brien, Donnell, actor; d. July 27, 1970.
O'Brien, Eugene, actor; b. Nov. 14, 1880, Boulder, Colo.; d. Apr. 29,
   1966 (85).
O'Brien, Fifi, actress; d. Apr. 1, 1941 (52).
O'Brien, Seamus, actor; d. May 14, 1977 (41).
O'Brien, "Shots" (r.n. Charles O'Brien), actor; b. Oct. 26, 1894,
   Missouri; d. Mar. 29, 1961 (66).
O'Brien, Terence, actor; d. Oct. 13, 1970 (82).
O'Brien, Tom, actor; b. July 25, 1890, San Diego, Calif.; d. June 8,
   1947 (56).
O'Brien, Willis H., cinematographer; b. Mar. 2, 1886, California;
   d. Nov. 8, 1962 (76).
O'Brien-Moore, Erin, actress; b. May 2, 1902, Los Angeles, Calif.;
   d. May 3, 1979 (77).
O'Byrne, Patsy, actress; b. July 28, 1884, Kansas; d. Apr. 18, 1968
   (83).
O'Callahan, Fox (r.n. Maxwell Holcomb), actor; b. Jan. 13, 1900, South
   Dakota; d. Apr. 14, 1976 (76).
Ochs, Al, actor; b. May 30, 1894, New Jersey; d. July 16, 1964 (70).
O'Connell, Hugh, actor; b. June 16, 1889, Wisconsin; d. Jan. 19,
   1943 (53).
O'Connor, Edward, actor; d. May 14, 1932 (70).
O'Connor, Frank, actor & director; b. Apr. 11, 1882, New York;
   d. Nov. 22, 1959 (77).
O'Connor, Harry M., actor; b. Apr. 27, 1873, Chicago, Ill.; d. July
   10, 1971 (98).
O'Connor, Herbert, actor; d. Nov. 7, 1933.
O'Connor, Jack, actor; d. Apr. 3, 1955 (49).
O'Connor, Kathleen, actress; b. July 7, 1894, Ohio; d. June 24, 1957
   (62).

O'Connor, Kathryn Kennedy, actress; d. Nov. 16, 1965 (71).
O'Connor, Louis J., actor; b. June 28, 1879, Providence, R.I.;
    d. Aug. 7, 1959 (80).
O'Connor, Robert Emmet, actor; b. Mar. 18, 1885, Wisconsin;
    d. Sept. 4, 1962 (77).
O'Connor, Una, actress; b. Oct. 23, 1880, Belfast, Ireland; d. Feb. 4,
    1959 (78).
O'Dare, Peggy (see O'Day, Peggy)
O'Day, Maginnis, actress; b. Feb. 26, 1917, New York; d. Apr. 11,
    1964 (47).
O'Day, Peggy, stuntwoman; b. June 19, 1900, Ohio; d. Nov. 25, 1964
    (64).
O'Dea, Denis, actor; b. Apr. 26, 1905, Dublin, Ireland; d. Nov. 5,
    1978 (75).
O'Dea, Jimmy, actor; d. Jan. 7, 1965 (66).
O'Dea, Joseph, actor; d. Mar. 1, 1968 (65).
O'Dell, Georgia, actress; d. Sept. 6, 1950 (57).
Odell, Maude, actress; b. Beaufort, S.C.; d. Feb. 27, 1937 (65).
O'Dell, Seymour H., actor; d. Apr. 3, 1937 (74).
Odemar, Fritz, actor; b. Jan. 31, 1890, Hanover, Germany; d. June 3,
    1955 (65).
Odets, Clifford, director & author; b. July 18, 1906, Philadelphia,
    Pa.; d. Aug. 14, 1963 (57).
O'Doherty, Mignon, actress; d. Mar. 12, 1961 (71).
O'Donnell, Cathy (r.n. Ann Steely), actress; b. July 6, 1923, Siluria,
    Ala.; d. Apr. 11, 1970 (46).
O'Donnell, Charles H., actor; d. Sept. 10, 1962 (76).
O'Dowd, Mike, actor; d. Sept. 5, 1977.
O'Dunn, Irvin, actor; d. Jan. 1, 1933 (34).
Oettly, Paul, actor; b. 1899; d. 1959 (60).
Offenbach, Joseph, actor; b. Dec. 28, 1904; d. Oct. 15, 1971 (66).
Offerman, George, actor; b. Apr. 29, 1879, Hoboken, N.J.; d. Mar. 5,
    1938 (58).
Offerman, George, Jr., actor; b. Mar. 14, 1917, Chicago, Ill.;
    d. Jan. 14, 1963 (45).
Ogden, Vivia, actress; d. Dec. 22, 1952.
Ogle, Charles, actor; b. June 5, 1865, Steubenville, Ohio; d. Oct. 11,
    1940 (75).
O'Grady, Tom, actor; d. Sept. 1, 1942 (41).
O'Hannession, Dick, actor; b. July 24, 1894, Turkey; d. Feb. 13,
    1966 (71).
O'Hara, Barry J., actor; d. Sept. 5, 1979 (53).
O'Hara, Fiske, actor; b. Ireland; d. Aug. 2, 1945 (67).
O'Hara, George, actor; b. Feb. 22, 1899, Idaho; d. Oct. 16, 1966 (67).
O'Hara, Shirley, actress; d. May 5, 1979 (68).
Ohardieno, Roger, dancer; d. July 14, 1959 (40).
Ojeda, Jesus (Chucho), actor; d. Dec., 1943 (51).
O'Keefe, Arthur J., actor; d. Mar. 29, 1959 (85).
O'Keefe, Dennis (Bud Flanagan), actor; b. Mar. 28, 1908, Ft. Madison,
    Iowa; d. Aug. 31, 1968 (60).
O'Keefe, Lawrence V., actor; d. Jan. 23, 1950 (66).
O'Keefe, Loraine, actress; d. Sept., 1924 (25).
Okhlopkov, Nikolay P., actor; b. May 15, 1900, Siberia; d. Jan. 8,
    1967 (66).
Oland, Warner, actor; b. Oct. 3, 1880, Umea, Vesterbotten, Sweden;
    d. Aug. 6, 1938 (57).

Olcott, Sidney, director & actor; b. Sept. 20, 1872, Toronto, Canada; d. Dec. 16, 1949 (77).

Oldfield, Barney, actor & driver; b. Jan. 29, 1878, York Township, Ohio; d. Oct. 4, 1946 (68).

Oldham, Derek, actor; b. Mar. 29, 1892; d. Mar. 20, 1968 (75).

O'Leary, Bill, actor; b. Aug. 24, 1887, New York; d. Jan. 24, 1954 (66).

Olga, Duchess (Eva Liminana Bohr), actress; d. 1953 (52).

Olin, Bob, actor; d. Dec. 16, 1956 (48).

Oliver, Edna May, actress; b. Nov. 9, 1883, Malden, Mass.; d. Nov. 9, 1942 (59).

Oliver, Frank, actor; d. Oct. 15, 1939 (64).

Oliver, Guy, actor; b. Sept. 25, 1878, Chicago, Ill.; d. Sept. 1, 1932 (53).

Oliver, Larry, actor; d. Jan. 22, 1973 (93).

Oliver, Mary (Kuuks Walks-Alone), actress; d. Sept. 14, 1938 (25).

Oliver, Ted (r.n. Virgil Kinley Oliver), actor; b. Feb. 2, 1892, Kentucky; d. June 30, 1957 (65).

Oliver, Vic, actor; b. July 8, 1898, Vienna, Austria; d. Aug. 15, 1964 (66).

Olivette, Marie, actress; d. Mar. 15, 1959 (67).

Olivette, Nina, actress; d. Feb. 21, 1971 (63).

Ollivier, Paul, actor; b. 1882; d. 1948 (66).

Olmstead, Gertrude, actress; b. Nov. 13, 1904, Chicago, Ill.; d. Jan. 18, 1975 (70).

Olsen, Irene, actress; d. Apr., 1931 (29).

Olsen, Lauritz, actor; b. Aug. 10, 1872, Copenhagen, Denmark; d. May 9, 1955 (82).

Olsen, Moroni, actor; b. June 27, 1889, Ogden, Utah; d. Nov. 22, 1954 (65).

Olsen, Ole (r.n. John S. Olsen), actor; b. Nov. 6, 1892, Peru, Ind.; d. Jan. 26, 1963 (70).

Olsen, Steve, actor; d. Dec. 14, 1946 (46).

O'Madigan, Isabel, actress; b. Oct. 16, 1871, Missouri; d. Jan. 23, 1951 (79).

O'Malley, Charles, actor & director; d. July 29, 1958 (61).

O'Malley, John F., actor; b. Apr. 24, 1904, Morris, Minn.; d. Feb. 27, 1945 (40).

O'Malley, John Patrick, actor; d. Aug. 26, 1959 (43).

O'Malley, Pat, actor; b. Sept. 3, 1890, Forest City, Pa.; d. May 21, 1966 (75).

O'Malley, Rex, actor; b. Jan. 2, 1901, London, England; d. May 1, 1976 (75).

O'Malley, Thomas E., actor; d. May 5, 1926 (70).

O'Neal, Anne, actress; b. Dec. 23, 1893, Missouri; d. Nov. 24, 1971 (77).

O'Neal, William J., actor; d. May 23, 1961 (63).

O'Neil, Barry, actor & director; d. Mar. 23, 1918 (53).

O'Neil, George, writer; d. May 24, 1940 (42).

O'Neil, Nance, actress; b. Oct. 8, 1874, Oakland, Calif.; d. Feb. 7, 1965 (90).

O'Neil, Robert A. (Bob), actor; b. June 3, 1911, Missouri; d. Oct. 8, 1951 (40).

O'Neil, Sally, actress; b. Oct. 23, 1910, Bayonne, N.J.; d. June 18, 1968 (57).

O'Neill, Henry, actor; b. Aug. 10, 1891, Orange, N.J.; d. May 18, 1961 (69).
O'Neill, Jack, director & actor; d. Aug. 20, 1957 (74).
O'Neill, James, actor; b. Nov. 15, 1847, Kilkenny, Ireland; d. Aug. 10, 1920 (72).
O'Neill, James "Tip," actor; d. Oct. 8, 1938 (75).
O'Neill, Johnny, actor; d. Sept. 14, 1930 (78).
O'Neill, Marie, actress; b. Dublin, Ireland; d. Nov. 2, 1952 (65).
O'Neill, Mickey, actor; d. May 14, 1932 (29).
O'Neill, Peggy, actress; d. Apr. 13, 1945 (21).
Ong, Dana De Moss, actor; b. July 3, 1874, Richmond, Ohio; d. Dec. 31, 1948 (74).
Onno, Ferdinand (r.n. Ferdinand Onowotschek), actor; b. Oct. 19, 1881, Czernowitz, Russia; d. 1970 (89).
Onodera, Sho, actor; d. Oct. 26, 1974 (59).
Onorato, Giovanni, actor; b. 1910, Palermo, Italy; d. 1960 (50).
Ophuls, Max, director & writer; b. May 6, 1902, Saarbrucken, Germany; d. Mar. 26, 1957 (54).
Opp, Julie, actress; b. Jan. 28, 1871, New York City; d. Apr. 8, 1921 (50).
Oppenheim, Menasha, actor; d. Oct. 23, 1973.
O'Ramey, Georgia, actress; b. Dec. 31, 1886, Mansfield, Ohio; d. Apr. 2, 1928 (41).
Orchard, Julian, actor; b. Wheatley, England; d. June 21, 1979 (49).
Orde, Beryl, actress; d. Sept. 10, 1966 (54).
Ordonovna, Hanka, actress; b. Aug. 11, 1904, Varsavia; d. Sept. 2, 1950 (46).
Orellana, Carlos, actor; d. Jan. 24, 1960 (59).
Orfaly, Alexander, actor; d. Jan. 22, 1979 (43).
Orla, Resel, actress; b. 1889; d. July 23, 1931 (42).
Orlamond, William, actor; b. Aug. 1, 1867, Denmark; d. Apr. 23, 1957 (89).
Orlebeck, Lester, director & film editor; b. June 26, 1907, Sheboygan, Wisc.; d. Aug. 2, 1970 (63).
Orlov, Dmitriy N., actor; b. May 8, 1892, Spassk, U.S.S.R.; d. Dec. 19, 1955 (63).
Orlova, Lyubov, actress; d. Jan. 26, 1975 (72).
Ormos, Laszlo Ede, writer; d. Mar. 19, 1948 (45).
Ornellas, Norman, actor; d. May 31, 1975 (36).
Ornitz, Samuel, writer; d. Mar. 10, 1957 (66).
Orona, Vicente, Jr., actor; d. Mar. 11, 1961 (30).
O'Rorke, Brefni, actor; b. June 26, 1889, Dublin, Ireland; d. Nov. 11, 1946 (57).
O'Rourke, J.A., actor; d. June 17, 1937 (55).
O'Rourke, Thomas, actor; d. Oct. 16, 1958 (86).
Orr, Forrest, actor; b. Dallas, Tex.; d. Apr. 20, 1963 (63).
Orr, Stanley W., actor; b. Apr. 7, 1887, Canada; d. May 19, 1968 (81).
Orraca, Juan, actor; d. Aug. 2, 1956 (50).
Orrick, David (r.n. David Orrick McDearmon), actor; d. Aug. 18, 1979 (65).
Ortega, Santos, actor; d. Apr. 10, 1976 (76).
Ortego, Artie, actor; b. Feb. 9, 1890, California; d. July 24, 1960 (70).
Orth, Frank, actor; b. Feb. 21, 1880, Philadelphia, Pa.; d. Mar. 17, 1962 (82).

Ortin, Leopoldo "Chato," actor; d. Aug. 3, 1953.
Ortiz, Thula, actress; d. July 30, 1961 (67).
Ory, Edward (Kid), jazz musician; b. Dec. 25, 1886, La Place, La.;
    d. Jan. 23, 1973 (86).
Orzazewski, Kasia, actress; b. Oct. 16, 1888, Pennsylvania; d. July
    17, 1956 (67).
Osborn, Lyn, actor; d. Aug. 30, 1958 (32).
Osborne, Bud, actor; b. July 20, 1884, Oklahoma; d. Feb. 2, 1964 (79).
Osborne, Jefferson, actor; d. June 11, 1932 (61).
Osborne, Rowland, actor; d. Apr. 19, 1920 (45).
Osborne, Vivienne, actress; b. Dec. 10, 1896, Des Moines, Iowa;
    d. June 10, 1961 (64).
Oscar, Henry, actor; b. July 14, 1891, London, England; d. Dec. 28,
    1969 (78).
Ose, Jay, actor; b. Nov. 6, 1911, Minnesota; d. Nov. 5, 1967 (55).
O'Shea, "Black" Jack (r.n. John Rellaford), actor; b. Apr. 6, 1906,
    California; d. Oct. 1, 1967 (61).
O'Shea, Michael, actor; b. Mar. 17, 1906, Hartford, Conn.; d. Dec. 4,
    1973 (67).
O'Shea, Oscar, actor; b. Oct. 8, 1881, Canada; d. Apr. 5, 1960 (78).
Oshins, Jules, actor; b. Brooklyn, N.Y.; d. May 9, 1956 (50).
Osmond, Hal, actor; d. Dec., 1959.
Osterman, Jack, actor; b. Toledo, Ohio; d. June 8, 1939 (37).
O'Sullivan, Michael, actor; d. July 24, 1971 (37).
O'Sullivan, Tony, actor; d. July 4, 1920.
Oswald, Richard, director, producer, & author; d. Sept. 11, 1963 (83).
Oswalda, Ossi, actress; b. Feb. 2, 1899, Berlin, Germany; d. Jan.,
    1948 (48).
Otho, Henry (Otho Wright) (r.n. Henry Otho Wright), actor; b. Feb. 6,
    1888, Brooklyn, N.Y.; d. June 6, 1940 (52).
Otis, Elita Proctor, actress; b. Cleveland, Ohio; d. Aug. 10, 1927
    (76).
Otkan, John P., actor; d. Aug. 10, 1942 (62).
Ott, Fred, actor; d. Oct. 24, 1936 (76).
Otte, Henry Rolph, actor; d. Dec. 17, 1930 (51).
Ottiano, Rafaela, actress; b. Mar. 4, 1888, Venice, Italy; d. Aug. 15,
    1942 (54).
Otto, Henry, actor & director; b. Aug. 8, 1877, Missouri; d. Aug. 3,
    1952 (74).
Otto, Paul, actor; d. Nov. 25, 1943.
Otton, William G., actor; d. Mar. 7, 1930 (78).
Oudart, Felix, actor; b. 1881; d. 1956 (75).
Oughton, Winifred, actress; d. Dec. 26, 1964 (74).
Ouspenskaya, Mme. Maria, actress; b. July 29, 1887, Tula, Russia;
    d. Dec. 3, 1949 (62).
Overman, Jack, actor; d. Jan. 4, 1950 (34).
Overman, Lynne, actor; b. Sept. 19, 1887, Maryville, Mo.; d. Feb. 19,
    1943 (55).
Overton, Frank, actor; b. Mar. 12, 1918, New York; d. Apr. 23, 1967
    (49).
Ovey, George, actor; b. Dec. 13, 1870; d. Sept. 23, 1951 (80).
Owen, Catherine Dale, actress; b. July 28, 1903, Louisville, Ky.;
    d. Sept. 7, 1965 (62).
Owen, Garry, actor; b. Dec. 18, 1897, Brookhaven, Miss.; d. June 1,
    1951 (53).

Owen, Milton A., actor; b. Sept. 27, 1891, Australia; d. Oct. 2, 1969 (78).
Owen, Reginald, actor; b. Aug. 5, 1887, Wheathampstead, England; d. Nov. 5, 1972 (85).
Owen, Seena, actress; b. Nov. 14, 1894, Spokane, Wash.; d. Aug. 15, 1966 (71).
Owen, Tudor, actor; b. Jan. 20, 1898, Wales; d. Mar. 13, 1979 (81).
Owens, Kimo, actor & stuntman; d. Oct. 13, 1979 (37).
Owens, William, actor; d. Aug. 20, 1926 (63).
Owsley, Monroe, actor; b. Aug. 11, 1900, Atlanta, Ga.; d. June 7, 1937 (36).
Oysher, Moishe, actor; b. Russia; d. Nov. 27, 1958 (51).
Ozep, Fedor, director & writer; b. Feb. 9, 1895, Moscow, Russia; d. June 20, 1949 (54).
Ozu, Yasujiro, director; b. Dec. 15, 1903, Tokyo, Japan; d. Dec. 12, 1963 (60).


Pabst, G.W., director; b. Aug. 27, 1885, Raudnitz, Bohemia; d. May 29, 1967 (81).
Pace, Max, actor; d. Aug. 3, 1942 (36).
Packard, Clayton L. (r.n. Clayton Lincoln Packard), actor; b. Mar. 6, 1887, Washington; d. Sept. 7, 1931 (44).
Packer, Netta, actress; d. Nov. 7, 1962 (65).
Padden, Sarah, actress; b. Oct. 16, 1881, England; d. Dec. 4, 1967 (86).
Paddock, Charles, actor; d. July 21, 1943 (43).
Paderewski, Ignace Jan, classical pianist; b. Kurilovka, Poland; d. June 29, 1941 (80).
Padgen, Jack (see Padjan, Jack)
Padilla, Ema, actress; d. July 2, 1966 (66).
Padjan, Jack (Jack Padgen; Jack Duane), actor; b. Dec. 14, 1887, Montana; d. Feb. 1, 1960 (72).
Padula, Marguerita, actress; b. 1891, Massachusetts; d. Feb. 22, 1957 (66).
Padula, Vincent, actor; b. 1900, Argentina; d. Jan. 16, 1967 (67).
Pagano, Bartolomeo, actor; b. Sept. 27, 1878, Nerva; d. June 24, 1947 (68).
Pagano, Ernest, writer; b. Florence, Colo.; d. Apr. 29, 1953 (53).
Pagay, Sofie, actress; b. Apr. 22, 1857, Berlin, Germany; d. Jan. 23, 1937 (79).
Pagden, Leonard, actor; d. Mar. 24, 1928 (66).
Page, Arthur (Arthur W. Wellington), actor; b. Aug. 2, 1885, Massachusetts; d. Feb. 8, 1968 (82).
Page, Bob, actor; d. July 23, 1943 (57).
Page, James, actor; d. Mar. 26, 1930.
Page, Norman, actor; d. July 4, 1935 (59).
Page, Paul (r.n. Campbell U. Hicks), actor; b. May 13, 1903, Birmingham, Ala.; d. Apr. 28, 1974 (70).
Page, Rita, actress; b. Aug. 5, 1906, London, England; d. Dec. 19, 1954 (48).
Pagnol, Marcel, writer, producer, & director; b. Feb. 28, 1895, Aubagne, France; d. Apr. 18, 1974 (79).
Paia, John (Hawkshaw), actor; d. Oct. 24, 1954 (46).

Paige, Mabel, actress; b. Dec. 19, 1880, New York City; d. Feb. 8, 1954 (73).
Paige, Peggy, actress; b. Mar. 23, 1899, North Carolina; d. Aug. 26, 1974 (75).
Paine, Harry, actor; b. Jan. 6, 1872, Guernsey, England; d. Feb. 22, 1941 (69).
Paiva, Nestor, actor; b. June 30, 1905, Fresno, Calif.; d. Sept. 9, 1966 (61).
Palange, Inez, actress; b. June 13, 1889, Italy; d. Oct. 16, 1962 (73).
Palasthy, Alexander, actor; b. 1877, Hungary; d. Mar. 16, 1948 (71).
Palau (Pierre Palau), actor; b. Aug. 13, 1885; d. Dec. 5, 1966 (81).
Pallenberg, Max, actor; b. Dec. 18, 1877, Vienna, Austria; d. June 20, 1934 (56).
Pallette, Eugene, actor; b. July 8, 1889, Winfield, Kans.; d. Sept. 3, 1954 (65).
Palmar, Lorna, actress; d. June 14, 1928 (21).
Palmer, Charles (Chuck), actor; d. Mar. 21, 1976 (46).
Palmer, Dawson, actor; d. Sept. 10, 1972 (35).
Palmer, Ernest G., cinematographer; d. Feb. 22, 1978 (92).
Palmer, Inda, actress; d. Nov. 10, 1923.
Palmer, Jack F., actor; d. Sept. 27, 1928.
Palmer, Patricia (see Gibson, Margaret)
Palmese, Ernesto, extra; b. Sept. 1, 1871, Italy; d. Dec. 20, 1960 (89).
Palmese, Rose Marie, actress; d. Mar. 21, 1953 (82).
Pandolfini, Turi, actor; b. Nov. 1, 1883, Catania, Italy; d. Mar. 7, 1962 (78).
Pangborn, Franklin, actor; b. Jan. 23, 1889, Newark, N.Y.; d. July 20, 1958 (69).
Pann, Peter, actor; d. Dec. 29, 1948 (76).
Pannaci, Charles, actor; d. Feb. 15, 1927 (23).
Panthulu, B.R., actor; d. Oct. 8, 1974 (64).
Panzer, Paul, actor; b. Nov. 3, 1872, Wurtzberg, Germany; d. Aug. 16, 1958 (85).
Papana, Alex, actor; d. Apr., 1946 (40).
Pape, Lionel, actor; b. Apr. 17, 1877, England; d. Oct. 21, 1944 (67).
Parain, Brice, actor; d. Mar., 1971 (74).
Paramore, Edward E., Jr., writer; b. Sept. 17, 1895, Manchester, England; d. May 1, 1956 (60).
Paranjpe, Raja, actor; d. Feb. 9, 1979 (69).
Pardave, Joaquin, actor & director; b. Mexico; d. July 20, 1955 (54).
Pardave, Jose, actor; d. May 26, 1970 (68).
Pardee, C.W. (Doc), actor; d. July 17, 1975 (90).
Paris, Manuel, actor; b. July 27, 1894, Spain; d. Nov. 19, 1959 (65).
Park, Ida May, director; d. June 13, 1954 (74).
Park, Josephine, actress; d. Jan. 12, 1931.
Park, Post (r.n. Custer B. Park), actor & stuntman; b. Nov. 4, 1899, Missouri; d. Sept. 18, 1955 (55).
Parke, Macdonald, actor; d. July, 1960 (68).
Parke, William, actor & director; d. July 28, 1941 (68).
Parker, Agnes Gust, dancer; d. 1935.
Parker, Albert, director; d. Aug. 10, 1974 (87).
Parker, Austin, writer; b. Sept. 11, 1892, Great Falls, Mont.; d. Mar. 20, 1938 (46).

Parker, Barnett, actor; d. Aug. 5, 1941 (52).
Parker, Cecil, actor; b. Sept. 3, 1897, Hastings, Sussex, England;
    d. Apr. 20, 1971 (73).
Parker, Eddie (see Parker, Edwin)
Parker, Edwin (Eddie Parker), actor; b. Dec. 12, 1900, Minnesota;
    d. Jan. 20, 1960 (59).
Parker, Flora (see De Haven, Flora)
Parker, Franklin, actor; b. Nov. 8, 1900, Fillmore, Mo.; d. June 12,
    1962 (61).
Parker, Lew, actor; b. Oct. 29, 1907, Brooklyn, N.Y.; d. Oct. 27,
    1972 (64).
Parker, Lucy, actress; d. Mar. 21, 1947 (84).
Parker, Marion, actress; d. 1920.
Parker, Mary, actress; b. 1915, London, England; d. June 1, 1966 (51).
Parker, Murray, actor; b. June 14, 1896, New York; d. Oct. 17, 1965
    (69).
Parker, Norton S., writer; d. July 5, 1969 (68).
Parker, Vivien, actress; d. Feb. 2, 1974 (77).
Parker, Warren, actor; d. July 31, 1976.
Parkhurst, Frances, actress; d. Dec. 31, 1969.
Parkington, Beulah, actress; d. Nov. 7, 1958 (59).
Parkinson, Cliff, actor & stuntman; b. Sept. 3, 1898, Kansas;
    d. Oct. 1, 1950 (52).
Parkison, Charles Arden, Jr., stuntman; d. Nov. 23, 1976 (31).
Parks, Gordon, Jr., director; d. Apr. 3, 1979 (44).
Parks, Larry, actor; b. Dec. 13, 1914, Olathe, Kans.; d. Apr. 13,
    1975 (60).
Parkyakarkus (Harry Einstein), actor; d. Nov. 24, 1958 (54).
Parlo, Dita, actress; b. 1907, Stettin, Poland; d. Dec. 13, 1971 (64).
Parnell, Emory, actor; b. Dec. 29, 1892, St. Paul, Minn.; d. June 22,
    1979 (86).
Parnell, James, actor; b. Oct. 9, 1923, Minnesota; d. Dec. 27, 1961
    (38).
Parravicini, Florencio, actor; d. Mar. 25, 1941 (67).
Parrish, Helen, actress; b. Mar. 12, 1924, Columbus, Ga.; d. Feb. 22,
    1959 (34).
Parrish, Laura, actress; d. Aug. 15, 1977 (90).
Parrish, Mary Catherine, actress; d. Sept. 13, 1951 (78).
Parrott, Charles (see Chase, Charley)
Parrott, James, actor; b. Aug. 2, 1898, Baltimore, Md.; d. May 10,
    1939 (40).
Parrott, Paul (see Parrott, James)
Parry, Charlotte, actress; d. Nov. 2, 1959 (86).
Parry, Florence Ella, actress; d. Apr. 23, 1956 (71).
Parry, Paul, actor, producer, & photographer; d. Dec. 4, 1966 (58).
Parson, Carol, actress; d. Dec. 18, 1958.
Parsonett, Marion, writer; d. Dec. 7, 1960 (54).
Parsons, Louella, columnist & actress; d. Dec. 9, 1972 (91).
Parsons, Percy, actor; b. June 12, 1878, Louisville, Ky.; d. Oct. 3,
    1944 (66).
Parsons, William "Smiling Bill," actor; d. Sept. 29, 1919 (41).
Partos, Frank F., writer; .b. July 2, 1901, Budapest, Hungary;
    d. Dec. 23, 1956 (55).
Pascal, Ernest, writer; b. Jan. 11, 1896, London, England; d. Nov. 4,
    1966 (70).
Pascal, Gabriel, director & producer; b. June 4, 1894, Arad, Romania;
    d. July 6, 1954 (60).

Pasch, Reginald (r.n. Reinhold Pasch), actor; b. Oct. 11, 1883,
    Wolgast/Pommern; d. Aug., 1965 (81).
Pasha, Kalla (r.n. Joseph T. Rickard), actor; b. 1879, Paris, France;
    d. June 10, 1933 (54).
Pasolini, Pier Paolo, director; d. Nov. 1, 1975 (53).
Pastorino, Franco, actor; b. Dec. 25, 1933, Milan, Italy; d. July 13,
    1959 (25).
Pastrone, Giovanni (Piero Fosco), director; b. Sept. 13, 1882, Asti,
    Italy; d. June 29, 1959 (76).
Patch, Wally, actor; b. Sept. 26, 1888, London, England; d. Oct. 27,
    1970 (82).
Paterson, Pat, actress; b. Apr. 7, 1910, Bradford, England;
    d. Aug. 24, 1978 (68).
Pathe, Charles, producer & executive; b. Dec. 25, 1863, Chevry-
    Cossigny, France; d. Dec. 25, 1957 (94).
Paton, Charles, actor; b. London, England; d. Apr. 10, 1970 (96).
Paton, Stuart, actor & director; b. July 23, 1883, Glasgow, Scotland;
    d. Dec. 16, 1944 (61).
Patric, Gil (r.n. Thomas Weston Gilpatrick), actor; b. Aug. 6, 1896,
    Minnesota; d. Feb. 21, 1971 (74).
Patrick, Ethel, actress; d. Sept. 18, 1944 (57).
Patrick, Jerome, actor; b. New Zealand; d. Sept. 26, 1923 (39).
Patricola, Tom, actor; b. Jan. 22, 1891, New Orleans, La.; d. Jan. 1,
    1950 (58).
Patston, Doris, actress; b. London, England; d. June 12, 1957 (53).
Patten, Dorothy, actress; d. Apr. 11, 1975 (70).
Patterson, Elizabeth, actress; b. Nov. 22, 1875, Savannah, Tenn.;
    d. Jan. 31, 1966 (90).
Patterson, Hank (r.n. Elmer C. Patterson), actor; b. Oct. 9, 1888,
    Alabama; d. Aug. 23, 1975 (86).
Patterson, James, actor; b. June 29, 1932, Derry, Pa.; d. Aug. 19,
    1972 (40).
Patterson, Joy W., actress; d. Mar. 23, 1959 (53).
Patterson, Troy (r.n. Ettore Corvino), actor; d. Nov. 1, 1975 (49).
Patton, Bill (r.n. William P. Patton), actor; b. June 2, 1894,
    Amarillo, Tex.; d. Dec. 12, 1951 (57).
Patzak, Julius, opera singer; d. Jan. 26, 1974 (75).
Paul, Logan, actor; d. Jan. 15, 1932 (83).
Paul, Rene, actor; d. Oct. 21, 1968.
Paul, Val, actor, producer, director, & author; b. Apr. 10, 1886,
    Denver, Colo.; d. Mar. 23, 1962 (75).
Pauley, Paul, actor; b. Feb. 18, 1886, Paris, France; d. May 13, 1938
    (52).
Paulig, Albert, actor; b. 1873, Saxony, Germany; d. Mar. 19, 1933
    (60).
Paulmuller, Herbert, actor; b. Nov. 30, 1858, Berlin, Germany;
    d. Oct. 25, 1939 (80).
Paulsen, Arno, actor; b. Jan. 3, 1900, Stettin, Poland; d. Sept. 17,
    1969 (69).
Paulsen, Harald, actor; b. Aug. 26, 1895, Elmshorn, Germany;
    d. Aug. 4, 1954 (58).
Paulsen, Lina, actress; d. Nov. 17, 1932.
Pauncefort, George, actor; d. Mar. 25, 1942 (72).
Pavanelli, Livio, actor; b. Sept. 7, 1881, Copparo; d. Apr. 29,
    1958 (76).

Pavlowa, Anna, ballet danseuse & actress; b. Jan. 31, 1882, Petrograd, Russia; d. Jan. 23, 1931 (48).
Pavon, Blanca Estela, actress; d. Sept. 26, 1949 (23).
Pawle, Lennox, actor; b. Apr. 27, 1872, London, England; d. Feb. 22, 1936 (63).
Pawley, William, actor; b. July 21, 1904, Kansas City; d. June 15, 1952 (47).
Pawson, Hargrave, actor; b. Dec. 6, 1902, England; d. Jan. 26, 1945 (42).
Paxinou, Katina, actress; b. Piraeus, Greece; d. Feb. 22, 1973 (73).
Paxton, George, actor; d. Feb. 19, 1914.
Paxton, Sidney, actor; b. June 25, 1860, London, England; d. Oct. 13, 1930 (70).
Payne, B. Iden (r.n. Ben Iden Payne), director; b. Sept. 5, 1881, Newcastle-on-Tyne, England; d. Apr. 6, 1976 (94).
Payne, Douglas, actor; d. Aug. 3, 1965 (90).
Payne, Edna, actress; b. Dec. 5, 1891, New York City; d. Jan. 31, 1953 (61).
Payne, Louis (William Louis Payne), actor; b. Jan. 13, 1873, Pennsylvania; d. Aug. 14, 1953 (80).
Payson, Blanche, actress; b. Sept. 20, 1881, California; d. July 4, 1964 (82).
Payton, Barbara, actress; b. Nov. 16, 1927, Cloquet, Minn.; d. May 8, 1967 (39).
Payton, Claude, actor; b. Mar. 30, 1882, Iowa; d. Mar. 1, 1955 (72).
Payton, Lou, actor; b. Sept. 27, 1874, Huntington, W. Va.; d. May 27, 1945 (70).
Peabody, Eddie, recording artist & entertainer; b. Feb. 19, 1902, Reading, Mass.; d. Nov. 7, 1970 (68).
Peacock, Keith, stuntman; d. Nov. 1, 1966 (35).
Peacock, Kim, actor; d. Dec. 26, 1966 (65).
Peacock, Lillian, actress; d. Aug. 18, 1918 (28).
Pearce, Al, actor; b. July 25, 1898, California; d. June 2, 1961 (62).
Pearce, Alice, actress; d. Mar. 3, 1966 (47).
Pearce, George, actor; b. June 26, 1865, New York City; d. Aug. 13, 1940 (75).
Pearce, Vera, actress; d. Jan. 18, 1966 (70).
Pearson, George, director; b. 1875; d. Feb. 8, 1973 (97).
Pearson, Lloyd, actor; b. Dec. 13, 1897, Bradford, Yorkshire, England; d. June 2, 1966 (68).
Pearson, Molly, actress; b. Edinburgh, Scotland; d. Jan. 26, 1959 (83).
Pearson, Ted, actor; d. Oct. 5, 1961 (58).
Pearson, Virginia, actress; b. Louisville, Ky.; d. June 6, 1958 (70).
Peck, J. Lydell, director; d. Jan. 25, 1957 (51).
Peckham, Frances Miles, actress; d. June 7, 1959 (66).
Peer, Heinrich, actor; b. Nov. 25, 1867, Vienna, Austria; d. May 13, 1927 (60).
Peer, Helen, actress; d. May 6, 1942 (44).
Peers, Donald, singer; d. Aug. 9, 1973 (64).
Peers, Joan, actress; b. Aug. 19, 1909, Chicago, Ill.; d. July 11, 1975 (65).
Pegg, Vester, actor; b. May 23, 1889, Appleton City, Mo.; d. Feb. 19, 1951 (61).
Peil, Edward, Jr. (Johnny Jones), actor; b. Nov. 18, 1907, Wisconsin; d. Nov. 7, 1962 (54).

Peil, Edward J., Sr., actor; b. Jan. 18, 1883, Racine, Wisc.;
    d. Dec. 29, 1958 (75).
Peile, Kinsey, actor; b. Dec. 20, 1862, India; d. Apr. 13, 1934 (71).
Peisley, Frederick, actor; b. Dec. 6, 1904, Finchley, England;
    d. Mar. 22, 1975 (70).
Pelletti, John V., actor; b. Sept. 27, 1913, California; d. Mar. 5,
    1960 (46).
Pellicer, Pina, actress; b. Apr. 3, 1937, Mexico City, Mexico;
    d. Dec. 10, 1964 (27).
Pelly, Farrell, actor; b. County Galway, Ireland; d. Apr. 23, 1963
    (72).
Pelt, Tim, actor; d. Sept. 6, 1977 (39).
Pemberton, Henry W., actor; d. July 26, 1952 (77).
Pemberton, Patricia, actress; d. Mar. 9, 1929.
Pembroke, George (r.n. George Prud'homme), actor; b. Dec. 27, 1900,
    Canada; d. June 11, 1972 (71).
Pembroke, Scott, director & writer; d. Feb. 21, 1951 (61).
Pena, Julio, actor; d. July 26, 1972 (60).
Pendleton, Nat (r.n. Nathaniel Greene Pendleton), actor; b. Aug. 9,
    1895, Davenport, Iowa; d. Oct. 11, 1967 (72).
Penman, Lea, actress; b. Red Cloud, Neb.; d. Oct. 12, 1962 (67).
Penn, Leonard, actor; b. 1907, Massachusetts; d. May 20, 1975 (68).
Pennell, Richard O., actor; b. Feb. 21, 1866, Jersey City, N.J.;
    d. Mar. 22, 1934 (68).
Penner, Joe, actor; b. Nov. 11, 1904, Nagechkereck, Hungary; d. Jan.
    10, 1941 (36).
Pennick, Jack, actor; b. Dec. 7, 1895, Portland, Ore.; d. Aug. 16,
    1964 (68).
Pennick, Ronald J. (see Pennick, Jack)
Pennington, Ann, actress & dancer; b. Dec. 23, 1894, Camden, N.J.;
    d. Nov. 4, 1971 (76).
Penny, Frank, actor; d. Apr. 20, 1946 (51).
Penrose, Charles, actor; d. Nov. 17, 1952 (76).
Penwarden, Duncan, actor; d. Sept. 13, 1930 (50).
Pepper, Barbara, actress; b. May 31, 1915, New York City; d. July 18,
    1969 (54).
Pepper, Jack, actor; d. Mar. 31, 1979 (76).
Pepper, Robert C., stuntman & actor; b. June 10, 1915, Pennsylvania;
    d. Oct. 27, 1964 (49).
Peralta, Gabriel, actor; b. Nov. 17, 1887, Arizona; d. Sept. 27,
    1977 (89).
Percival, Walter C., actor & author; b. Chicago, Ill.; d. Jan. 28,
    1934 (46).
Percy, Eileen, actress; b. Aug. 21, 1900, Belfast, Ireland;
    d. July 29, 1973 (72).
Percy, Esme, actor; b. Aug. 8, 1887, London, England; d. June 17,
    1957 (69).
Percy, W.S., actor; b. Dec. 23, 1872, Melbourne, Australia; d. June 19,
    1946 (73).
Perelman, S.J., writer; d. Oct. 17, 1979 (75).
Perez, Pepito, actor & musician; d. July 13, 1975 (79).
Periolat, George, actor; d. Feb. 20, 1940 (64).
Periot, Arthur, stuntman; d. Feb. 24, 1929 (30).
Periquin, actor; d. Nov. 6, 1957 (45).
Perkins, Jean, stuntwoman; d. Dec., 1922.

Perkins, Osgood, actor; b. May 16, 1892, West Newton, Mass.;
    d. Sept. 21, 1937 (45).
Perkins, Voltaire, actor; b. Apr. 1, 1894, Wisconsin; d. Oct. 10,
    1977 (83).
Perkins, Walter E., actor; b. Biddeford, Me.; d. June 3, 1925 (55).
Perlberg, William, producer; b. Oct. 22, 1899, New York City;
    d. Oct. 31, 1968 (69).
Perley, Anna, actress; d. Jan. 20, 1937 (88).
Perley, Charles, actor; d. Feb. 10, 1933 (47).
Perojo, Benito, director; b. 1894, Madrid, Spain; d. Nov. 11, 1974
    (80).
Peron, Eva (see Duarte, Eva)
Perret, Leonce, director & actor; b. May 13, 1880, Niort, France;
    d. Aug. 14, 1935 (55).
Perrin, Jack, actor; b. July 25, 1896, Michigan; d. Dec. 17, 1967
    (71).
Perrins, Leslie, actor; b. England; d. Dec. 13, 1962 (60).
Perry, Charles Emmett, actor; b. Dec. 26, 1901, New York; d. Feb. 26,
    1967 (65).
Perry, Ida, actress; b. Feb. 16, 1877; d. Sept., 1966 (89).
Perry, Jack, actor; d. Oct. 7, 1971.
Perry, Jessie, actress; b. Sept. 1, 1876, Aurora, Ind.; d. July 6,
    1944 (67).
Perry, Mary, actress; b. Gainesville, Ga.; d. Mar. 6, 1971 (83).
Perry, Pascale (r.n. Harvey Poirier), actor; b. Oct. 22, 1895,
    Arizona; d. July 11, 1953 (57).
Perry, Robert, actor; b. Dec. 26, 1878, New York; d. Jan. 8, 1962
    (83).
Perry, Sara, actress; d. Jan. 18, 1959 (87).
Perry, Vic, actor; d. Aug. 14, 1974 (54).
Perry, Walter, actor; b. Sept. 14, 1868, California; d. Jan. 22,
    1954 (85).
Perryman, Lloyd (Sons of the Pioneers) (The Singing Cowboys);
    b. Jan. 29, 1917, Ruth, Ark.; d. May 31, 1977 (60).
Persse, Thomas, actor & opera singer; b. Sept. 4, 1862, Lembrick,
    Ireland; d. Apr. 17, 1920 (57).
Persson, Edvard, actor; b. Sweden; d. Sept. 26, 1957 (70).
Pertwee, Roland, author & actor; b. May 15, 1885, Brighton,
    England; d. Apr. 26, 1963 (77).
Peters, Fred, actor; b. June 30, 1884, Waltham, Mass.; d. Apr. 23,
    1963 (78).
Peters, House (r.n. Robert House Peters), actor; b. Mar. 12, 1880,
    England; d. Dec. 7, 1967 (87).
Peters, John S., actor; b. Dec. 31, 1894, Ohio; d. Nov. 7, 1963 (68).
Peters, Page, actor; d. June 22, 1916 (26).
Peters, Peter, actor; b. Oct. 5, 1925, Mainz, Germany; d. Sept.,
    1955 (29).
Peters, Ralph, actor & extra; b. May 19, 1915, Canada; d. Apr. 12,
    1959 (43).
Peters, Ralph, actor; b. Aug. 3, 1902, Kansas; d. June 5, 1959 (56).
Peters, Susan (Suzanne Carnahan), actress; b. July 3, 1921, Spokane,
    Wash.; d. Oct. 23, 1952 (31).
Peters, Werner, actor; b. July 7, 1918, Werlitzsch, Germany;
    d. Mar. 31, 1971 (52).
Petersen, Peter (r.n. Max Paulsen), actor; b. Nov. 18, 1876, Hamburg,
    Germany; d. Mar. 11, 1956 (79).

Peterson, Marjorie, actress; b. Houston, Tex.; d. Aug. 19, 1974 (68).
Petit, Albert, actor; b. Jan. 20, 1886, Switzerland; d. Feb. 26,
    1963 (77).
Petley, Frank E., actor; b. Mar. 28, 1872, Old Charlton, England;
    d. Jan. 12, 1945 (72).
Petrie, D. Hay, actor; b. July 16, 1895, Dundee, Scotland;
    d. July 30, 1948 (53).
Petrie, Howard, actor; b. Nov., 1906, Beverly, Mass.; d. Mar. 24,
    1968 (61).
Petrolini, Ettore, actor; b. Jan. 13, 1886; d. June 28, 1936 (50).
Petrova, Olga, actress; b. England; d. Nov. 30, 1977 (93).
Pettingell, Frank, actor; b. Jan. 1, 1891, Liverpool, England;
    d. Feb. 17, 1966 (75).
Pettit, Wilfred, writer; d. Dec. 9, 1948 (38).
Peukert, Leo, actor; d. Jan., 1944 (58).
Peukert-Impekoven, Sabine, actress; d. May 5, 1970 (80).
Peyton, Lawrence, actor; d. Nov., 1918.
Pezzulo, Ted, actor; d. Nov. 10, 1979 (43).
Pharr, Frank (r.n. Frank Pharr Simms), actor; b. Aug. 25, 1890,
    Georgia; d. Mar. 10, 1969 (78).
Phelps, Fancher, Sr., actor; d. Nov. 2, 1972 (74).
Phelps, Lee (r.n. Napoleon Bonaparte Ku-Kuck), actor; d. May 15,
    1893, Pennsylvania; d. Mar. 19, 1953 (59).
Philbrick, William H., actor; d. Oct. 20, 1955.
Philipe, Gerard, actor; b. Dec. 4, 1922, Cannes, France; d. Nov. 27,
    1959 (37).
Philippe, Michele, actress; b. 1926, Paris, France; d. Oct., 1972
    (46).
Philips, Mary, actress; b. Jan. 23, 1900, Connecticut; d. Apr. 22,
    1975 (75).
Philliber, John, actor; b. Elkhart, Ind.; d. Nov. 6, 1944 (72).
Phillips, Adolph, actor; d. July 30, 1937 (72).
Phillips, Charles, actor; d. May 25, 1958 (54).
Phillips, Clement K., actor; d. Oct. 4, 1928.
Phillips, E.R., actor; d. Aug. 29, 1915.
Phillips, Eddie (see Phillips, Edward)
Phillips, Edna, actress; b. Feb. 26, 1878, Canada; d. Feb. 26, 1952
    (74).
Phillips, Edward, actor; d. Oct. 7, 1944 (76).
Phillips, Edward (Eddie Phillips), actor; b. Aug. 14, 1899, Phila-
    delphia, Pa.; d. Feb. 22, 1965 (65).
Phillips, Festus, actor; d. Sept. 5, 1955 (83).
Phillips, Helena (see Evans, Helena Phillips)
Phillips, Jean, actress; b. Sept. 22, 1914, Sioux Falls, S.D.;
    d. Dec. 15, 1970 (56).
Phillips, Joe E., actor; b. May 12, 1913, Montana; d. Oct. 19, 1972
    (59).
Phillips, Kember (Tubby), actor; d. Apr. 26, 1930.
Phillips, Minna, actress; d. Jan. 17, 1963 (91).
Phillips, Norma, actress; b. Baltimore, Md.; d. Nov. 12, 1931 (38).
Phillips, Norman, actor; d. Feb. 11, 1931 (39).
Phillips, Richard, actor; d. May 4, 1941 (115).
Phillips, William "Bill," actor; b. June 1, 1908, Washington, D.C.;
    d. June 27, 1957 (49).
Phipps, Charles, actor; b. Oct. 2, 1877, Fenton, Mich.; d. Feb. 12,
    1950 (72).

Phipps, Sally, actress; d. Mar. 17, 1978 (67).
Piaf, Edith, singer; b. Dec. 19, 1915, Paris, France; d. Oct. 11, 1963 (47).
Piazza, Dario, actor; d. Sept. 1, 1974 (70).
Pica, Tina, actress; b. Mar. 31, 1884, Naples, Italy; d. Aug. 16, 1968 (84).
Picha, Hermann, actor; b. 1865, Charlottenburg, Germany; d. June 7, 1936 (71).
Pichel, Irving, actor & director; b. June 24, 1891, Pittsburgh, Pa.; d. July 13, 1954 (63).
Pick, Lupu, director & actor; b. Jan. 2, 1886, Jassy, Rumania; d. Mar. 7, 1931 (45).
Pickard, Helena, actress; b. Oct. 13, 1900, Handsworth, England; d. Sept. 27, 1959 (58).
Pickard, Obed (Dad), actor; b. July 22, 1874, Tennessee; d. Sept. 24, 1954 (80).
Pickering, Alice Marie, actress; d. Sept. 11, 1938 (21).
Pickering, Sara Reed, actress; d. Dec. 11, 1977 (39).
Pickett, Ingram B. "Seven Foot," actor; d. Feb. 14, 1963 (64).
Pickford, Charlotte (Smith), actress; d. Mar. 22, 1928 (55).
Pickford, Jack, actor; b. Aug. 18, 1896, Toronto, Canada; d. Jan. 3, 1933 (36).
Pickford, Lottie, actress; b. Toronto, Canada; d. Dec. 9, 1936 (41).
Pickford, Mary (r.n. Gladys Smith), actress; b. Apr. 8, 1893, Toronto, Canada; d. May 29, 1979 (86).
Pickles, Wilfred, actor; b. Oct. 13, 1904, Halifax, N.S., Canada; d. Mar. 27, 1978 (73).
Picorri, John, actor; b. Aug. 4, 1895, England; d. July 1, 1976 (80).
Pidal, Jose, actor; d. Oct. 26, 1956 (60).
Piel, Harry, actor & director; b. July 12, 1892, Dusseldorf, Germany; d. Mar. 27, 1963 (70).
Pierce, Evelyn, actress; b. Feb. 5, 1908, Del Rio, Tex.; d. Aug. 9, 1960 (52).
Pierce, Frances, actress; d. Nov., 1913.
Pierce, Jack P., makeup executive & artist; d. July 19, 1968 (79).
Pierlot, Francis, actor; b. July 15, 1875, Massachusetts; d. May 11, 1955 (79).
Pierpont, Laura, actress; d. Dec. 11, 1972 (91).
Pierry, Marguerite, actress; b. 1888, Paris, France; d. Jan. 20, 1963 (74).
Pierson, Arthur, actor & director; b. June 6, 1891 or June 16, 1901, Oslo, Norway; d. Jan. 1, 1975 (83 or 73).
Piffle, John, actor; b. Nov. 22, 1886, Austria; d. May 26, 1951 (64).
Pigott, Tempe, actress; b. Feb. 2, 1884, England; d. Oct. 6, 1962 (78).
Pike, Harry J., actor; d. Dec. 18, 1919.
Pike, Nita, actress; d. May 11, 1954 (41).
Pila, Maximo, actor; b. Jan. 30, 1885, Santanda, Spain; d. Aug. 2, 1939 (54).
Pilcer, Harry, actor & dancer; b. New York City; d. Jan. 14, 1961 (75).
Pilkington, Paul, actor; d. Jan. 26, 1918 (40).
Pilotto, Camillo, actor; b. Feb. 6, 1890, Rome, Italy; d. May 27, 1963 (73).
Piltz, George E., actor; b. Sept. 24, 1908, Hawaii; d. Apr. 18, 1968 (59).

Pinchot, Rosamond, actress; b. Oct. 26, 1904, New York City; d. Jan. 24, 1938 (33).
Pine, Ed, actor; d. May 9, 1950 (46).
Pine, William H., producer; b. Feb. 15, 1896, Los Angeles, Calif.; d. Apr. 29, 1955 (59).
Pingree, Earl M. (Galan Galt), actor; b. Mar. 4, 1887, Illinois; d. July 12, 1958 (71).
Pinson, Lucile, actress; b. June 1, 1900, Illinois; d. Jan. 12, 1977 (76).
Pinza, Ezio, actor & opera singer; b. May 18, 1892, Rome, Italy; d. May 9, 1957 (64).
Pious, Minerva, actress; d. Mar. 16, 1979 (75).
Piovani, Pina, actress; b. 1897, Rome, Italy; d. Jan. 2, 1955 (57).
Piper, Frederick, actor; b. Sept. 23, 1902, London, England; d. Sept. 22, 1979 (76).
Pipkorn, Frank, actor; d. July, 1959.
Pipo (r.n. Gustave Sofman), actor; d. Aug. 6, 1970 (68).
Pisu, Mario, actor; b. May 21, 1910, Montecchio, Italy; d. July 17, 1976 (66).
Pitt, Archie, actor; d. Nov. 12, 1940 (55).
Pitti, Ben, actor; d. July 26, 1955 (62).
Pittman, Monte, author & actor; b. Mar. 1, 1917, Louisiana; d. June 26, 1962 (45).
Pittman, Tom, actor; b. Mar. 16, 1932, Phoenix, Ariz.; d. Nov. 19, 1958 (26).
Pitts, ZaSu, actress; b. Jan. 3, 1898, Parsons, Kans.; d. June 7, 1963 (65).
Pittschau, Ernst, actor; b. 1883; d. June 2, 1951 (68).
Pittschau, Werner, actor; d. Nov., 1928 (25).
Pivar, Ben, producer; b. Mar. 2, 1901, Manchester, England; d. Mar. 28, 1963 (62).
Pixley, Gus, actor; d. June 2, 1923 (58).
Pizani, Robert, actor; b. Apr. 26, 1896, Paris, France; d. June 17, 1965 (69).
Pizzo, John F., actor & clown; d. May 9, 1952 (45).
Planer, Franz, cinematographer; b. Mar. 29, 1894; d. Jan. 10, 1963 (68).
Platen, Karl, actor; b. Mar. 6, 1877; d. July, 1952 (75).
Platt, Edward, actor; b. Feb. 14, 1916, Staten Island, N.Y.; d. Mar. 19, 1974 (58).
Playfair, Sir Nigel, actor; b. July 1, 1874, London, England; d. Aug. 19, 1934 (60).
Playter, Wellington, actor; b. Dec. 9, 1879, Rawcliff, England; d. July 15, 1937 (57).
Plessow, Ellen, actress; b. Jan. 12, 1891, Oldenburg, Germany; d. Sept., 1967 (76).
Plowden, Roger S., actor; d. Sept. 26, 1960 (58).
Plowright, Hilda, actress; b. Nov. 29, 1890, England; d. Oct. 9, 1973 (82).
Plues, George L., actor; b. June 12, 1895, Washington; d. Aug. 16, 1953 (58).
Plumer, Lincoln, actor; b. Sept. 28, 1875, Maryland; d. Feb. 14, 1928 (52).
Plumer, Rose, actress; b. Jan. 19, 1876, California; d. Mar. 3, 1955 (79).

Po, Hung, actor; d. Nov. 17, 1968 (47).
Poff, Lon, actor; b. Feb. 8, 1870, Indiana; d. Aug. 8, 1952 (82).
Pogue, Tom, actor; d. Mar. 21, 1941 (65).
Pol, Talitha, actress; d. July 13, 1971 (31).
Polaire, Emilie, actress; b. May 13, 1879, Algeria; d. Oct. 14, 1939 (60).
Polan, Lou, actor; b. June 15, 1904, Ukraine, Russia; d. Mar. 3, 1976 (71).
Polanski, Goury, actor; d. Oct. 17, 1976 (83).
Poliakov, Nikolai (Coco the Clown), actor; b. Oct. 5, 1900, Besinowitz, Russia; d. Sept. 25, 1974 (73).
Polidor, actor; d. Feb. 16, 1920.
Polidor (Ferdinando Gillaume), actor; b. May 19, 1887, Bayonne, France; d. Dec., 1977 (90).
Polito, Sol, cinematographer; d. May 23, 1960 (68).
Polk, Gordon, actor; b. May 17, 1923, Idaho; d. June 10, 1960 (37).
Polla, Pauline M., actress; d. Apr. 9, 1940 (72).
Pollar, Gene, actor; d. Oct. 20, 1971 (79).
Pollard, Alexander (r.n. Wilfred Alexander Pollard), actor; b. Oct. 15, 1886, England; d. June 17, 1950 (63).
Pollard, Bud, director; b. May 12, 1886; d. Dec. 17, 1952 (66).
Pollard, Daphne, actress; b. Melbourne, Australia; d. Feb. 22, 1978 (85).
Pollard, Harry, actor & director; b. Jan. 23, 1879, Republic City, Kans.; d. July 6, 1934 (55).
Pollard, Snub, actor; b. Nov. 9, 1889, Melbourne, Australia; d. Jan. 19, 1962 (72).
Pollock, Nancy R., actress; b. Feb. 10, 1902, Brooklyn, N.Y.; d. June 20, 1979 (77).
Polo, Eddie, actor; b. Feb. 1, 1875; d. June 14, 1961 (86).
Polo, Robert, extra & stand-in; d. May 4, 1968.
Polo, Sam, actor; b. Nov. 7, 1872, California; d. Oct. 3, 1966 (93).
Pommer, Erich, producer & director; b. July 20, 1889, Hildesheim, Germany; d. May 8, 1966 (76).
Pompon, Monsieur (see Millsfield, Charles A.)
Pon, Mrs. Chew S., actress; d. Dec. 5, 1959 (63).
Poncin, Marcel, actor; d. June 8, 1953.
Ponder, Jack, actor; b. Nov. 20, 1903, Shreveport, La.; d. Aug. 5, 1970 (66).
Pongratz, Alfred, actor; b. Sept. 29, 1900, Munich, Germany; d. Oct., 1977 (77).
Pons, Lily, opera singer & actress; b. Apr. 12, 1904, Cannes, France; d. Feb. 13, 1976 (71).
Ponto, Erich, actor; b. Dec. 14, 1884, Lubeck, Germany; d. Feb. 4, 1957 (72).
Porcasi, Paul, actor; b. Jan. 1, 1879, Palermo, Sicily; d. Aug. 8, 1946 (67).
Porredon, Luis, actor; d. Apr. 7, 1958 (76).
Porten, Henny, actress; b. Jan. 7, 1890, Magdeburg, Germany; d. Oct. 15, 1960 (70).
Porter, Caleb, actor; b. Sept. 1, 1867, London, England; d. Mar. 13, 1940 (72).
Porter, Catherine, dancer; d. Dec. 10, 1929 (16).
Porter, Ed, actor; b. May 26, 1884, Columbus, Ind.; d. July 29, 1939 (55).

Porter, Edwin S., director; b. Apr. 21, 1870, Connellsville, Pa.;
    d. Apr. 30, 1941 (71).
Porter, Paul, actor; d. Oct. 17, 1957 (71).
Porter, Reed, actor; d. Aug. 12, 1979 (69).
Porter, Viola Adele, actress; d. Dec. 29, 1942 (63).
Porterfield, Robert, actor; b. Dec. 21, 1905, Virginia; d. Oct. 28,
    1971 (65).
Portman, Eric, actor; b. July 13, 1903, Yorkshire, England; d. Dec. 7,
    1969 (66).
Post, Charles A. (r.n. Charles Ashbrook Post), actor; b. Nov. 3,
    1897, Salt Lake City, Utah; d. Dec. 20, 1952 (55).
Post, Guy Bates, actor; b. Sept. 22, 1875, Seattle, Wash.; d. Jan. 16,
    1968 (92).
Post, Wiley, aviator & actor; b. Texas; d. Aug. 15, 1935.
Postance, William C.F., actor; d. Apr. 14, 1953 (78).
Potel, Victor, actor; b. Oct. 12, 1889, Lafayette, Ind.; d. Mar. 8,
    1947 (57).
Potter, H.C., director; b. Nov. 13, 1904, New York City; d. Aug. 31,
    1977 (73).
Potts, Walter L., actor; d. Feb. 25, 1943 (70).
Pouyet, Eugene, actor; b. Aug. 23, 1883, France; d. May 22, 1950 (66).
Powell, David, actor; d. Apr. 16, 1925 (40).
Powell, Dick, stuntman; d. Sept. 26, 1948 (46).
Powell, Dick, actor, director, & producer; b. Nov. 14, 1904, Mt. View,
    Ark.; d. Jan. 2, 1963 (58).
Powell, Lee, actor; b. May 15, 1908, Long Beach, Calif.; d. July 29,
    1944 (36).
Powell, Lee, actor; d. Feb. 3, 1954 (58).
Powell, Paul M., director; d. July 2, 1944 (63).
Powell, Richard, actor; d. Jan. 1, 1937 (40).
Powell, Russell, actor; b. Sept. 16, 1875, Indiana; d. Nov. 28, 1950
    (75).
Powell, W. Templar, actor; d. June 29, 1949.
Power, Hartley, actor; b. Mar. 14, 1894, New York City; d. Jan. 29,
    1966 (71).
Power, Paul (r.n. Luther Vestergard), actor; b. Dec. 7, 1902,
    Chicago, Ill.; d. Apr. 5, 1968 (65).
Power, Tyrone, actor; b. May 5, 1913, Cincinnati, Ohio; d. Nov. 15,
    1958 (45).
Power, Tyrone, Sr., actor; b. May 2, 1869, London, England; d. Dec.
    30, 1931 (62).
Powers, Francis, director & actor; b. June 4, 1865, Marner, Va.;
    d. May 10, 1940 (74).
Powers, John, actor; d. Sept. 25, 1951 (77).
Powers, Jule, actress; d. Feb. 14, 1932.
Powers, Leona, actress; b. Mar. 13, 1896, Salida, Colo.; d. Jan. 7,
    1970 (73).
Powers, Marie, opera singer; d. Dec. 28, 1973.
Powers, May, actress; d. July 24, 1961.
Powers, Richard (see Keene, Tom)
Powers, Tom, actor; b. July 7, 1890, Owensboro, Ky.; d. Nov. 9, 1955
    (65).
Powley, Bryan, actor; b. Sept. 16, 1871, Reading, England; d. Dec.,
    1962 (91).
Prada, Jose Maria, actor; d. Aug. 13, 1978 (53).

Prager, Stanley, actor & director; b. Jan. 8, 1917, New York City; d. Jan. 18, 1972 (55).
Prager, Willy, actor; d. Mar. 4, 1956 (79).
Praskins, Leonard, writer; d. Oct. 2, 1968 (70).
Prather, Lee (r.n. Oscar Lee Prather), actor; b. May 5, 1888, Nebraska; d. Jan. 3, 1958 (69).
Pratt, Jack, actor; b. Jan. 12, 1878, New Brunswick, Canada; d. Dec. 24, 1938 (60).
Pratt, Lynn, actor; d. Jan. 9, 1930 (67).
Pratt, Neil, actor; d. Jan. 3, 1934 (44).
Pratt, Purnell, actor; b. Oct. 20, 1885, Bethel, Ill.; d. July 25, 1941 (55).
Pray, Anna M., actress; d. June 30, 1971 (80).
Preer, Evelyn, actress; b. July 26, 1896, Chicago, Ill.; d. Nov. 17, 1932 (36).
Prejean, Albert, actor; b. Oct. 27, 1893; d. Nov. 1, 1979 (85).
Prentiss, Eleanor, actress; d. Aug. 14, 1979 (67).
Prentiss, Lewis R., actor; d. June 26, 1967 (62).
Presley, Elvis, actor & recording artist; b. Jan. 8, 1935, Tupelo, Miss.; d. Aug. 16, 1977 (42).
Press, Marvin, actor; b. Oct. 20, 1915, Connecticut; d. Mar. 17, 1968 (52).
Pressburger, Arnold, producer & director; d. Feb. 17, 1951 (65).
Preston, Edna, actress; d. Aug. 18, 1960 (68).
Pretty, Arline, actress; d. Apr. 14, 1978 (92).
Prevost, Frank (r.n. Frank Gregory), actor; b. July 13, 1895, New York City; d. Apr. 16, 1946 (50).
Prevost, Marie, actress; b. Nov. 6, 1899, Sarnia, Ontario, Canada; d. Jan. 20, 1937 (37).
Price, Alonzo, actor; b. Feb. 4, 1884, Massachusetts; d. June 4, 1962 (78).
Price, Dennis, actor; b. June 23, 1915, Twyford, England; d. Oct. 6, 1973 (58).
Price, Georgie, actor & singer; d. May 10, 1964 (64).
Price, Hal (r.n. Harry F. Price), actor; b. June 24, 1886, Ohio; d. Apr. 15, 1964 (77).
Price, Harry F. (see Price, Hal)
Price, Kate (r.n. Katherine Duffy Ludwig), actress; b. Feb. 13, 1872, Cork, Ireland; d. Jan. 4, 1943 (70).
Price, Mark, actor; d. Mar. 31, 1917.
Price, Nancy, actress; b. Feb. 3, 1880, Kinver, Worcestershire, England; d. Mar. 31, 1970 (90).
Price, Stanley L., actor; b. Dec. 31, 1892, Kansas; d. July 13, 1955 (62).
Prickett, Maudie, actress; d. Apr. 14, 1976 (61).
Prieto, Antonio, actor; d. Mar. 3, 1965 (50).
Prieto, Chula, actress; d. Oct. 1, 1960.
Prima, Louis, actor, musician, & recording artist; b. Dec. 7, 1911, New Orleans, La.; d. Aug. 24, 1978 (66).
Primrose, Daisy, actress; d. Nov. 19, 1927 (38).
Prince, John T., actor; b. Sept. 11, 1871, Boston, Mass.; d. Dec. 23, 1937 (66).
Pringle, John, actor; d. Aug. 12, 1929 (67).
Printemps, Yvonne, actress; b. July 25, 1895, Ermont; d. Jan. 18, 1977 (81).

Printzlau, Olga, writer; d. July 8, 1962 (69).
Prior, Herbert, actor; b. July 2, 1867, England; d. Oct. 3, 1954 (87).
Prockl, Ernst, actor; b. June 21, 1888, Vienna, Austria; d. Nov. 26, 1957 (69).
Proctor, Jessie, extra; d. July 6, 1975 (102).
Prohaska, Janos, actor; d. Mar. 13, 1974 (51).
Prohaska, Robert, actor; b. Oct. 2, 1946; d. Mar. 13, 1974 (27).
Promis, Flo, actress; d. Apr. 23, 1956 (72).
Prosser, Hugh, actor; d. Nov. 8, 1952 (46).
Prouty, Jed, actor; b. Apr. 6, 1879, Boston, Mass.; d. May 10, 1956 (77).
Prowse, Peter, actor; d. Dec., 1976 (52).
Prud'homme, Cameron, actor; b. Dec. 16, 1892, Auburn, Calif.; d. Nov. 27, 1967 (74).
Pryor, Ainslie (r.n. James Ainslie Pryor), actor; b. Feb. 1, 1921, Memphis, Tenn.; d. May 28, 1958 (37).
Pryor, Hugh, actor; d. Nov. 6, 1963 (38).
Pryor, Maureen, actress; d. May 5, 1977 (53).
Pryor, Roger, actor; b. Aug. 27, 1901, New York City; d. Jan. 31, 1974 (72).
Pryse, Hugh, actor; b. Nov. 11, 1910, London, England; d. Aug. 11, 1955 (44).
Psilander, Valdemar, actor; b. May 9, 1884, Copenhagen, Denmark; d. Mar. 16, 1917 (32).
Puck, Eva, actress; b. Nov. 27, 1892, Brooklyn, N.Y.; d. Oct. 25, 1979 (86).
Pudovkin, Vsevolod, director & actor; b. Feb. 28, 1893, Penza, Saratov, Russia; d. June 30, 1953 (60).
Puettjer, Gustav, actor; b. May 15, 1886, Hamburg, Germany; d. Aug. 11, 1959 (73).
Puffy, Charles H. (Karoly Huszar), actor; b. Nov. 3, 1884, Budapest, Hungary; d. 1942 (57).
Pugh, Jess M., actor; d. Jan. 22, 1962 (82).
Puglia, Frank, actor; b. Mar. 9, 1892, Sicily; d. Oct. 25, 1975 (83).
Puig, Eva, actress; b. Feb. 3, 1894, Mexico; d. Oct. 6, 1968 (74).
Pulaski, Lillian, actress; d. Jan. 29, 1977 (95).
Pully, B.S., actor; d. Jan. 6, 1972 (61).
Purcell, Charles, actor; d. Mar. 20, 1962 (78).
Purcell, Dick, actor; b. Aug. 6, 1905, Greenwich, Conn.; d. Apr. 10, 1944 (38).
Purcell, Ethel, actress; d. 1946.
Purcell, Gertrude, writer; b. New York City; d. May 1, 1963 (67).
Purcell, Irene, actress; b. Aug. 7, 1901, Hammond, Ind.; d. July 9, 1972 (70).
Purdell, Reginald, actor; b. Nov. 4, 1896, London, England; d. Apr. 21, 1953 (56).
Purdy, Constance, actress; b. Kansas; d. Apr. 1, 1960 (75).
Purviance, Edna, actress; b. Oct. 21, 1896, Lovelock, Nev.; d. Jan. 13, 1958 (61).
Putnam, George, actor & announcer; b. Jan. 21, 1914, New York; d. Apr. 8, 1975 (61).
Pyott, Keith, actor; d. Apr. 6, 1968.

Qualls, Teddy, dancer; d. Aug. 25, 1972 (53).
Qualters, Tot, actress; d. Mar. 27, 1974 (79).
Quartermaine, Charles, actor; b. Dec. 30, 1877, Richmond, Surrey, England; d. Aug., 1958 (80).
Quartermaine, Leon, actor; b. Sept. 24, 1876, Richmond, Surrey, England; d. June 25, 1967 (90).
Quigley, Charles, actor; b. Feb. 12, 1906, New Britain, Conn.; d. Aug. 5, 1964 (58).
Quillan, Joseph F., actor; b. Glasgow, Scotland; d. Nov. 16, 1952 (68).
Quimby, Fred, cartoonist & producer; d. Sept. 16, 1965 (79).
Quimby, Margaret, actress; d. Aug. 26, 1965 (60).
Quince, Louis Veda, actor; d. Sept. 24, 1954 (54).
Quinlivan, Charles, actor; b. Sept. 30, 1924, Jersey City, N.J.; d. Nov. 12, 1974 (50).
Quinn, Allen, actor; d. Jan. 23, 1944 (55).
Quinn, Jack, dancer; d. Dec. 10, 1929.
Quinn, James, actor; d. Nov. 30, 1919 (35).
Quinn, James, actor; b. July 17, 1885, New Orleans, La.; d. Aug. 21, 1940 (55).
Quinn, Joe, actor; d. Feb. 2, 1971 (54).
Quinn, Joe, actor; d. May 20, 1974 (75).
Quinn, Tony, actor; d. June 1, 1967 (62).
Quirk, Billy, actor; b. Mar. 29, 1873, Jersey City, N.J.; d. Apr. 20, 1926 (53).
Quiroz, Salvador, actor; d. Nov. 23, 1956 (75).


Rabagliati, Alberto, actor; b. June 26, 1906, Milan, Italy; d. Mar. 8, 1974 (67).
Rabasse, Marie, actress; b. June 9, 1878, France; d. Oct. 7, 1967 (89).
Rabe, John Earl, actor; b. Aug. 4, 1864, Smithfield, Ohio; d. Mar. 11, 1943 (78).
Rackin, Martin, writer & producer; b. July 31, 1913, New York City; d. Apr. 15, 1976 (62).
Radcliffe, Jack, actor; b. Sept. 18, 1900, Cleland, Scotland; d. Apr. 26, 1967 (66).
Radd, Ronald, actor; d. Apr. 23, 1976 (47).
Radford, Basil, actor; b. June 25, 1897, Chester, England; d. Oct. 20, 1952 (55).
Radha, M.R., actor; d. Oct., 1979.
Radilak, Charles H., actor; d. July 19, 1972 (65).
Rae, Claire, actress; d. July 7, 1938 (49).
Rae, Jack, actor; d. May 3, 1957 (58).
Rae, John, actor; b. 1896, Perth, Scotland; d. June, 1977 (81).
Raeburn, Frances, actress; b. Aug. 15, 1924, North Carolina; d. Dec. 26, 1976 (52).
Rafferty, Chips (r.n. John Goffage), actor; b. Mar. 26, 1909, Broken Hill, N.S.W., Australia; d. May 27, 1971 (62).
Raglan, James, actor; b. Jan. 6, 1901, Redhill, Surrey, England; d. Nov. 15, 1961 (60).
Ragland, Rags (r.n. John Morgan Lee Ragland), actor; b. Aug. 28, 1906, Louisville, Ky.; d. Aug. 20, 1946 (39).
Rahm, Knute Olaf, actor & cameraman; b. Mar. 20, 1876, Sweden; d. July 23, 1957 (81).

Raimu, Jules, actor; b. Dec. 17, 1883, Toulon, France; d. Sept. 20, 1946 (62).
Rainboth, Frank, actor; b. Mar. 23, 1874, Canada; d. Feb. 17, 1951 (76).
Raine, Jack, actor; b. May 18, 1897, London, England; d. May 30, 1979 (82).
Raine, Norman Reilly, writer; d. July 19, 1971 (76).
Rainey, Norman (r.n. William Morison), actor; b. Apr. 28, 1888, Ireland; d. Sept. 10, 1960 (72).
Rains, Claude, actor; b. Nov. 10, 1889, London, England; d. May 30, 1967 (77).
Rains, Fred, actor; d. Dec. 3, 1945 (85).
Raisa, Rosa, opera singer; b. May 30, 1893, Bialystok, Poland; d. Sept. 28, 1963 (70).
Raju (Raju Ahmed), actor; d. Dec. 12, 1972 (35).
Raker, Lorin, actor; b. May 8, 1891, Missouri; d. Dec. 25, 1959 (68).
Ralli, Paul, actor; b. Mar. 2, 1903, Greece; d. Sept. 4, 1953 (50).
Ralph, Jessie, actress; b. Gloucester, Mass.; d. May 30, 1944 (79).
Ralston, Jobyna, actress; b. Nov. 21, 1900, S. Pittsburgh, Tenn.; d. Jan. 22, 1967 (66).
Rambal, Enrique, actor; b. May 8, 1924, Madrid, Spain; d. Dec. 15, 1971 (47).
Rambeau, Marjorie, actress; b. July 15, 1889, San Francisco, Calif.; d. July 7, 1970 (80).
Rambo, Dirk (r.n. Orman Rambo), actor; b. Nov. 13, 1941, California; d. Feb. 5, 1967 (25).
Rambova, Natacha, actress; b. Jan. 19, 1897, Salt Lake City, Utah; d. June 5, 1966 (69).
Rameau, Emil, actor; b. Aug. 13, 1878, Berlin, Germany; d. Sept. 9, 1957 (79).
Ramirez, Pepita, actress; d. Dec. 27, 1927 (25).
Ramos, Carlos, singer; d. Nov. 6, 1969 (62).
Ramos, Fernando, dancer; b. July 6, 1913, Mexico; d. Nov. 21, 1969 (56).
Ramos, Jesus Maza, actor; d. Apr., 1955 (44).
Ramsay-Hill, C.S. (r.n. Cyril Seyes Ramsay-Hill), actor; b. Nov. 30, 1890, British Guiana; d. Feb. 3, 1976 (85).
Ranalow, Frederick, actor; b. Nov. 7, 1873, Dublin, Ireland; d. Dec. 8, 1953 (80).
Rand, John, actor; d. Jan. 25, 1940 (68).
Rand, Sally, actress & dancer; b. Jan. 2, 1904, Hickory Co., Mo.; d. Aug. 31, 1979 (75).
Randall, Addison (see Randall, Jack)
Randall, Bernard, actor; b. July 4, 1884, Odessa, Russia; d. Dec. 17, 1954 (70).
Randall, Brett, actor; d. July 3, 1963 (79).
Randall, Fred, actor; d. Aug., 1933 (34).
Randall, Jack (Addison Randall; Allan Byron), actor; b. May 12, 1906, San Fernando, Calif.; d. July 16, 1945 (39).
Randall, Larry, actor; d. Oct. 17, 1951 (31).
Randall, Rae, actress; d. May 7, 1934 (25).
Randall, William, actor; d. Apr. 22, 1939 (62).
Randi, Ermanno, actor; b. 1920, Arezzo, Italy; d. Nov. 1, 1951 (31).
Randle, Frank, actor; b. 1902, Wigan, England; d. July 7, 1957 (55).
Randolf, Anders, actor; b. Dec. 18, 1870, Denmark; d. July 2, 1930 (59).

Randolph, Amanda, actress; b. Sept. 22, 1896, Kentucky; d. Aug. 24, 1967 (70).
Randolph, Isabel, actress; b. Dec. 4, 1889, Illinois; d. Jan. 11, 1973 (83).
Randolph, May, actress; d. Apr. 13, 1956 (83).
Rangel, Arturo Soto, actor; b. Mar. 12, 1882, Leon, Mexico; d. May 25, 1965 (83).
Ranier, Richard, actor; b. Nov. 6, 1889, California; d. Aug. 25, 1960 (70).
Ranin, Helge, actor; d. Apr. 15, 1952 (55).
Rank, J. Arthur, executive; b. Dec. 23, 1888, Hull, England; d. Mar. 29, 1972 (83).
Rankin, Arthur, actor; d. Mar. 23, 1947 (51).
Rankin, Caroline "Spike," actress; b. Aug. 22, 1880, Pittsburgh, Pa.; d. Feb. 2, 1953 (72).
Rankin, Herbert, actor; b. Feb. 27, 1876, Chicago, Ill.; d. July 16, 1946 (70).
Ranson, Nellie Crawford, actress; d. Nov. 16, 1964 (88).
Ranous, William V., actor & director; b. Mar. 12, 1857; d. Apr. 1, 1915 (58).
Rao, S.V. Ranga, actor; d. July 19, 1974 (56).
Raphael, Enid, actress; d. Mar. 5, 1964.
Rappe, Virginia, actress; d. Sept. 9, 1921 (22).
Rapport, Fred, actor; b. June 23, 1895, New York; d. May 29, 1973 (77).
Rapport, Helena, actress; d. Dec. 5, 1954 (70).
Raquello, Edward, actor; b. Warsaw, Poland; d. Aug. 24, 1976 (76).
Rasp, Fritz, actor; b. May 13, 1891, Bayreuth, Germany; d. Nov. 30, 1976 (85).
Rasser, Alfred, actor; d. Aug. 18, 1977 (71).
Rasumny, Mikhail, actor; b. May 13, 1890, Odessa, Russia; d. Feb. 17, 1956 (65).
Ratcliffe, E.J. (r.n. Edward J. Ratcliffe), actor; b. Mar. 10, 1863, London, England; d. Sept. 28, 1948 (85).
Rathbone, Basil, actor; b. June 13, 1892, Johannesburg, Transvaal, South Africa; d. July 21, 1967 (75).
Ratner, Anna, actress; d. July 2, 1967 (75).
Ratoff, Gregory, actor, director, & author; b. Apr. 20, 1897, Petrograd, Russia; d. Dec. 14, 1960 (63).
Rattenberry, Harry, actor; b. Nov. 14, 1857, California; d. Dec. 9, 1925 (68).
Rattigan, Terence, writer; b. June 10, 1911, London, England; d. Nov. 30, 1977 (66).
Raucourt, Jules, actor; b. May 8, 1890, Brussels, Belgium; d. Jan. 30, 1967 (76).
Ravel, Sandra, actress; d. Aug. 13, 1954 (44).
Ravelle, Ray (r.n. Otto F. Wess), actor & dancer; d. Mar. 18, 1969 (55).
Ravenel, John, actor; d. Sept. 14, 1950 (38).
Ravenscroft, Ralph, actor; d. May, 1934 (63).
Rawlinson, Herbert, actor & director; b. Nov. 15, 1885, Brighton, England; d. July 12, 1953 (67).
Ray, Albert, director; d. Feb. 5, 1944 (60).
Ray, Barbara, actress; d. May 19, 1955 (41).
Ray, Bernard B., director, producer, author, & cameraman; d. Dec. 11, 1964 (66).
Ray, Carl, producer; d. July 22, 1949 (72).

Ray, Charles, actor; b. May 15, 1891, Jacksonville, Ill.; d. Nov. 23, 1943 (52).
Ray, Emma, actress; d. Jan. 3, 1935 (64).
Ray, Estelle Goulding, actress; d. Aug. 1, 1970 (82).
Ray, Helen, actress; d. Oct. 2, 1965 (86).
Ray, Jack, actor ("Freckles," Our Gang); d. Oct. 31, 1975 (58).
Ray, Johnny, actor; b. Wales; d. Sept. 4, 1927 (68).
Ray, Marjorie, actress; d. July 22, 1924 (34).
Ray, Naomi, actress; d. Mar. 13, 1966 (73).
Ray, Nicholas, director; b. Aug. 7, 1911, La Crosse, Wisc.; d. June 16, 1979 (67).
Ray, Ted, actor; d. Nov. 8, 1977 (71).
Ray, Terry (r.n. Edwin Lee Terry Ray), actor; d. July 22, 1978 (67).
Raya, Nick S., actor; d. Jan. 9, 1950 (89).
Raymaker, Herman, director & actor; b. Jan. 22, 1893, Oakland, Calif.; d. Mar. 6, 1944 (51).
Raymond, Cyril, actor; d. Mar., 1973 (75).
Raymond, Ford, actor; b. Apr. 23, 1899, Mississippi; d. Apr. 25, 1960 (61).
Raymond, Frances (Frankie Raymond), actress; b. May 24, 1869, Massachusetts; d. June 18, 1961 (92).
Raymond, Frankie (see Raymond, Frances)
Raymond, Jack (r.n. George Feder), actor; b. Dec. 14, 1902, Minneapolis, Minn.; d. Dec. 5, 1951 (48).
Raymond, Jack, director & actor; d. Mar. 20, 1953 (61).
Raymond, Pete, actor; b. 1871, Minneapolis, Minn.; d. Mar. 30, 1927 (56).
Raymond, Ray, actor; d. Apr. 19, 1927 (33).
Raymond, William, actor; d. Nov. 2, 1960 (87).
Raynaud, Fernand, actor; b. May 17, 1926, Clermont-Ferrand, France; d. Sept. 28, 1973 (47).
Rayner, Minnie, actress; b. May 2, 1869, London, England; d. Dec. 13, 1941 (72).
Razetto, Stella (see LeSaint, Stella)
Re, Gustavo, actor & singer; d. July, 1979 (71).
Rea, Mabel Lillian, actress; d. Dec. 24, 1968 (36).
Read, Barbara, actress; d. Dec. 11, 1963 (45).
Read, Didde, actress; d. Feb. 6, 1932 (33).
Readick, Frank M., actor; d. Aug. 27, 1924 (63).
Ready, Mike, actor; b. Aug. 21, 1858, Troy, N.Y.; d. Mar. 26, 1936 (77).
Real, Betty, actress; d. Sept. 9, 1969.
Reardon, Casper, jazz artist; d. Mar. 8, 1941 (33).
Reardon, Ned, actor; d. Feb. 4, 1916.
Redfield, William, actor; b. Jan. 26, 1927, New York City; d. Aug. 17, 1976 (49).
Red Fox, Chief William, actor; b. June 11, 1870, South Dakota; d. Mar. 1, 1976 (105).
Redmond, Edward, actor; b. Aug. 8, 1870, Illinois; d. Dec. 31, 1954 (84).
Redmond, Elmer E., actor & assistant director; b. May 5, 1887, Pennsylvania; d. July 18, 1955 (68).
Redwing, Rodd, actor; b. Aug. 24, 1904, New York; d. May 30, 1971 (66).
Reece, Brian, actor; d. Apr. 12, 1962 (48).

Reed, Alan, actor; b. Aug. 20, 1907, New York City; d. June 14, 1977
(69).
Reed, Sir Carol, director; b. Dec. 30, 1906, London, England;
d. Apr. 25, 1976 (69).
Reed, Dave, actor; d. Apr. 11, 1946 (74).
Reed, Donald, actor; b. July 23, 1901, Mexico City, Mexico; d. Feb.
28, 1973 (71).
Reed, Florence, actress; b. Jan. 10, 1883, Philadelphia, Pa.;
d. Nov. 21, 1967 (84).
Reed, George E., actor; d. June 11, 1952.
Reed, George H., actor; b. Nov. 27, 1866, Macon, Ga.; d. Nov. 6, 1952
(85).
Reed, Gus, actor; d. July 17, 1965 (85).
Reed, Julian, actor; d. May 28, 1934 (74).
Reed, Leslie, actor; d. 1915.
Reed, Luther, director & writer; b. July 14, 1888, Berlin, Wisc.;
d. Nov. 16, 1961 (73).
Reed, Maxwell, actor; b. Apr. 2, 1919, Larne, England; d. Oct. 31,
1974 (55).
Reed, Tom, writer; b. Dec. 24, 1901, Shelton, Wash.; d. Aug. 17, 1961
(59).
Rees, Arthur, actor; d. Sept. 18, 1960.
Rees, Edward, actor; d. Apr. 29, 1978.
Rees, Edward Randolph, actor; d. Mar. 19, 1976 (57).
Reese, W. James, actor; d. Feb. 19, 1960 (62).
Reeve, Ada, actress; b. Mar. 3, 1874, London, England; d. Sept. 25,
1966 (92).
Reeves, Billy, actor; b. England; d. Dec. 29, 1943 (79).
Reeves, George (r.n. George Lescher Bessolo), actor; b. Jan. 6, 1914,
Kentucky; d. June 16, 1959 (45).
Reeves, Jim, actor & country recording artist; b. Aug. 20, 1924,
Galloway, Texas; d. July 31, 1964 (39).
Reeves, Jim (r.n. James Albert Reeves), actor; b. Sept. 6, 1896,
Oklahoma; d. Mar. 20, 1971 (74).
Reeves, Kynaston, actor; b. May 29, 1893, London, England; d. Dec. 10,
1971 (78).
Reeves, Michael, director & author; b. 1944; d. Feb. 11, 1969 (24).
Reeves, Richard, actor; b. Aug. 10, 1912, New York; d. Mar. 17, 1967
(54).
Reeves, Robert, actor; b. Jan. 28, 1892, Marlin, Tex.; d. Apr. 13,
1960 (68).
Reeves-Smith, H., actor; b. England; d. Jan. 29, 1938 (75).
Regan, Barry, actor; d. Jan. 16, 1956 (52).
Regan, Edgar J., actor; d. June 21, 1938 (58).
Regan, Joseph Francis, actor; d. Aug. 18, 1933.
Regas, George, actor; b. Nov. 9, 1890, Sparta, Greece; d. Dec. 13,
1940 (50).
Regas, Pedro, actor; b. Apr. 18, 1897, Sparta, Greece; d. Aug. 10,
1974 (77).
Rehan, Mary, actress; d. Aug. 28, 1963 (76).
Rehfeld, Curt, actor; b. Feb. 11, 1881, Dresden, Germany; d. Mar. 24,
1934 (53).
Rehkopf, Paul, actor; d. June, 1949 (77).
Reicher, Frank, actor & director; b. Dec. 2, 1875, Munich, Germany;
d. Jan. 19, 1965 (89).

Reicher, Hedwiga, actress; b. June 12, 1884, Germany; d. Sept. 2, 1971 (87).
Reichers, Helene, actress; b. June 6, 1869; d. July 15, 1957 (88).
Reichert, Willy, actor; b. Aug. 30, 1896, Stuttgart, Germany; d. Dec., 1973 (77).
Reichow, Werner, actor; b. June 21, 1922, Germany; d. Aug. 17, 1973 (51).
Reid, Carl Benton, actor; b. Aug. 14, 1893, Lansing, Mich.; d. Mar. 15, 1973 (79).
Reid, Cliff, producer; d. Aug. 22, 1959 (69).
Reid, Hal, author & actor; d. May 22, 1920 (60).
Reid, Leslie, actor; d. 1917.
Reid, Mary, actress; d. July 18, 1979 (83).
Reid, Maxwell, actor; b. Aug. 22, 1903, Apia, Western Samoa; d. May 3, 1969 (65).
Reid, Trevor, actor; d. Apr. 19, 1965 (56).
Reid, Wallace, actor & director; b. Apr. 15, 1891, St. Louis, Mo.; d. Jan. 18, 1923 (31).
Reif, Rudolf, actor; b. Nov. 9, 1901, Leipzig, Germany; d. Apr., 1961 (59).
Reigbert, Claire, actress; b. Oct. 7, 1889; d. June 1, 1957 (67).
Reinhardt, John, actor & author; d. Aug. 6, 1953 (52).
Reinhardt, Wolfgang, writer & producer; d. July 28, 1979 (70).
Reis, Irving, director & writer; b. May 7, 1906, New York City; d. July 3, 1953 (47).
Reithe, Aloise D., actor; d. Sept. 5, 1943 (53).
Rejane, Mme. Gabrielle, actress; b. June 6, 1857, Paris, France; d. June 14, 1920 (63).
Relangi (r.n. Relangi Venkataramaya), actor; d. Dec., 1975 (65).
Relph, George, actor; b. Jan. 27, 1888, Cullercoats, England; d. Apr. 24, 1960 (72).
Remarque, Erich Maria (r.n. Erich Paul Remark), actor & author; b. June 22, 1898, Osnabrueck, Germany; d. Sept. 25, 1970 (72).
Remley, Ralph, actor; b. May 24, 1885, Cincinnati, Ohio; d. May 26, 1939 (54).
Remy, Albert, actor; b. Apr. 9, 1911, Sevres, France; d. Jan. 26, 1967 (55).
Renard, David, actor; b. July 22, 1921, Texas; d. Aug. 19, 1973 (52).
Renavent, Georges (r.n. Georges de Cheux), actor; b. Apr. 23, 1894, Paris, France; d. Jan. 2, 1969 (74).
Renfro, James Lige (Rennie Renfro) (r.n. James Leige Renfro), actor & stuntman; b. Sept. 30, 1892, Denison, Tex.; d. Mar. 2, 1962 (69).
Renn, Katharina, actress; d. Oct., 1975 (62).
Rennert, Guenther, director; d. Aug. 1, 1978 (67).
Rennie, James, actor; b. Apr. 18, 1890, Toronto, Canada; d. July 31, 1965 (75).
Rennie, Michael, actor; b. Aug. 25, 1909, Bradford, Yorkshire, England; d. June 10, 1971 (61).
Renno, Vincent, actor; d. Nov. 5, 1955 (41).
Renoir, Jean, director, actor, & author; b. Sept. 15, 1894, Paris, France; d. Feb. 12, 1979 (84).
Renoir, Pierre, actor; b. Mar. 21, 1885, Paris, France; d. Mar. 11, 1952 (66).
Repp, Stafford, actor; b. Apr. 26, 1918, California; d. Nov. 6, 1974 (56).
Requa, Charles, actor; b. Mar. 20, 1892, New York; d. Dec. 11, 1967 (75).

Reshaw, Selma Mary, actress; d. Oct. 2, 1955 (72).
Restivo, Georgio, actor; b. July 29, 1902, Italy; d. Dec. 23, 1953 (51).
Retford, Ella, actress; d. June 29, 1962 (76).
Revel, Mollie, actress; d. Dec. 31, 1932 (84).
Revelle, Hamilton, actor; b. Spain; d. Apr. 11, 1958 (85).
Revol, Max, actor; b. 1894, France; d. Dec. 23, 1967 (73).
Revy, Richard (Richard Ryen), actor; b. Sept. 13, 1885, Hungary; d. Dec. 22, 1965 (80).
Rex, Eugen, actor; b. July 8, 1884, Berlin, Germany; d. Feb. 21, 1943 (58).
Rey, Roberto, actor; d. May 30, 1972 (68).
Rey, Rosa, actress; b. Sept. 4, 1892, Spain; d. Apr. 7, 1969 (76).
Reyes, Eva, dancer; d. Mar. 20, 1970 (55).
Reyes, Lucha, actress; d. June 25, 1944 (36).
Reynolds, Abe, actor; d. Dec. 25, 1955 (71).
Reynolds, Adeline de Walt, actress; b. Sept. 19, 1862, Benton Co., Iowa; d. Aug. 13, 1961 (98).
Reynolds, Alan D., actor; b. Sept. 14, 1908, California; d. June 22, 1976 (67).
Reynolds, Benjamin A., actor; d. Jan. 28, 1950 (62).
Reynolds, Craig (Hugh Enfield), actor; b. July 15, 1907, Anaheim, Calif.; d. Oct. 22, 1949 (42).
Reynolds, E. Vivian, actor; b. June 24, 1866, London, England; d. May 13, 1952 (85).
Reynolds, Harold, actor; d. Sept. 21, 1972 (76).
Reynolds, Harrington (Harry) (r.n. Harrington Ford Reynolds), editor; b. Apr. 4, 1901, California; d. Dec. 22, 1971 (70).
Reynolds, Jack, actor; d. Aug. 7, 1977 (77).
Reynolds, Lake, actor; d. Feb. 9, 1952 (63).
Reynolds, Lynn F., director; b. May 7, 1891, Iowa; d. Feb. 25, 1927 (35).
Reynolds, Noah, actor; d. Sept. 19, 1948.
Reynolds, Peter, actor; d. Apr., 1975 (48).
Reynolds, Quentin, reporter & actor; b. Apr. 11, 1902, New York City; d. Mar. 17, 1965 (62).
Reynolds, Tom, actor; b. Aug. 9, 1866, London, England; d. July 25, 1942 (75).
Reynolds, Vera, actress; b. Nov. 25, 1899, Richmond, Va., or Nebraska; d. Apr. 22, 1962 (62).
Rhein, Mitchell, actor; b. June 16, 1900, New York; d. Sept. 23, 1977 (77).
Rhein-Schrading, Otto Franz, actor; d. Apr. 30, 1952.
Rhodes, Alfred (Dusty), actor & stuntman; b. Apr. 28, 1915, Arizona; d. Feb. 6, 1948 (32).
Rhodes, Dusty (see Rhodes, Alfred)
Rhodes, Marjorie, actress; b. Apr. 9, 1903, Hull, England; d. July 4, 1979 (76).
Rhudin, Fridolf, actor; d. Mar. 6, 1935 (40).
Riano, Renie, actress; b. Aug. 7, 1899, England; d. July 3, 1971 (71).
Riavme, Helen, actress; d. Nov. 1, 1924.
Ribeiro, Joy, actress; d. Dec. 19, 1972 (26).
Riccardo, Rick, Jr., actor; d. June 3, 1977 (47).
Ricci, Nora, actress; b. July 19, 1924, Viareggio, Italy; d. Apr. 16, 1976 (51).

Riccioli, Guido, actor; b. Oct. 5, 1883, Firenze, Italy; d. Mar. 28, 1958 (74).

Rice, Emmit B., executive & actor; d. Mar. 23, 1939.

Rice, Florence, actress; b. Feb. 14, 1911, Cleveland, Ohio; d. Feb. 22, 1974 (63).

Rice, Frank, actor; b. May 13, 1892, Muskegon, Mich.; d. Jan. 9, 1936 (43).

Rice, Jack, actor; b. May 14, 1893, Grand Rapids, Mich.; d. Dec. 14, 1968 (75).

Rice, John C., actor; d. June 5, 1915 (57).

Rice, Norman, actor & author; d. Nov. 12, 1957 (47).

Rice, Roy (r.n. Roy S. Munroe), actor; b. Apr. 4, 1887, New York; d. Dec. 29, 1966 (79).

Rice, Sam, actor; d. Mar. 12, 1946 (72).

Rich, Dick (r.n. Richard Lee Jossenberger), actor; b. Feb. 27, 1909, Kansas; d. Mar. 29, 1967 (58).

Rich, Helen, actress; d. Aug. 28, 1963 (66).

Rich, Lillian, actress; b. Jan. 1, 1900, London, England; d. Jan. 5, 1954 (54).

Rich, Myrtle May, actress; d. Oct., 1931.

Rich, Phil, actor; d. Feb. 22, 1956 (60).

Rich, Robert (see Trumbo, Dalton)

Rich, Vernon, actor; d. Feb. 7, 1978 (72).

Rich, Vivian, actress; b. May 26, 1893, Pennsylvania; d. Nov. 17, 1957 (64).

Richard, Frieda, actress; b. Nov. 1, 1873, Vienna, Austria; d. Sept. 12, 1946 (72).

Richard, Fritz, actor; b. 1870; d. Feb. 9, 1933 (62).

Richards, Addison, actor; b. Oct. 20, 1902, Zanesville, Ohio; d. Mar. 22, 1964 (61).

Richards, Cicely, actress; d. Apr. 8, 1933 (83).

Richards, Cully, actor; d. June 17, 1978 (68).

Richards, Eddie, actor; d. May 12, 1947 (52).

Richards, Gordon, actor; b. Oct. 27, 1893, Gillingham, Kent, England; d. Jan. 13, 1964 (70).

Richards, Grant, actor; b. Dec. 21, 1911, New York City; d. July 4, 1963 (51).

Richards, Paul, actor; b. Nov. 23, 1924, California; d. Dec. 10, 1974 (50).

Richardson, Frankie, actor & singer; b. Sept. 6, 1898, Philadelphia, Pa.; d. Jan. 30, 1962 (63).

Richardson, Jack, actor; d. Nov. 17, 1957 (73).

Richardson, William, actor; d. Nov. 8, 1937 (51).

Richey, Edwin (see Butler, Roy E.)

Richman, Al, actor; d. Apr. 20, 1936 (51).

Richman, Charles, actor; b. Jan. 12, 1870, Chicago, Ill.; d. Dec. 1, 1940 (70).

Richman, Harry (r.n. Harry Reichman), actor & singer; b. Aug. (or Oct.) 10, 1895, Cincinnati, Ohio; d. Nov. 3, 1972 (77).

Richmond, Kane (r.n. Frederick W. Bowditch), actor; b. Dec. 23, 1906, Minneapolis, Minn.; d. Mar. 22, 1973 (66).

Richmond, Leo C., actor; d. Apr. 21, 1979 (65).

Richmond, Susan, actress; b. Dec. 5, 1894, London, England; d. Jan., 1959 (64).

Richmond, Warner, actor; b. Jan. 11, 1886, Racine, Wisc.; d. June 19, 1948 (62).

Richter, Hans, director; b. Berlin, Germany; d. Feb. 1, 1976 (87).
Richter, Paul, actor; b. Apr. 1, 1895, Vienna, Austria; d. Dec. 30, 1961 (66).
Richter, Rotraut, actress; b. May 15, 1915, Berlin, Germany; d. Oct. 1, 1947 (32).
Rickelt, Gustav, actor; b. June 21, 1862, Dortmund, Germany; d. June 26, 1946 (84).
Ricketts, Tom, actor; b. Jan. 15, 1853, London, England; d. Jan. 19, 1939 (86).
Ricks, Archie, actor; b. Feb. 29, 1896, California; d. Jan. 10, 1962 (65).
Ricksen, Lucille (r.n. Lucille Ericksen), actress; b. Aug. 22, 1910, Illinois; d. Mar. 13, 1925 (14).
Rickson, Joe, actor; b. Sept. 6, 1880, Clearcreek, Mont.; d. Jan. 8, 1958 (77).
Ridge, Walter, actor; b. Dec. 28, 1898, Pennsylvania; d. Sept. 20, 1968 (69).
Ridgely, Cleo, actress; b. May 12, 1894, New York; d. Aug. 18, 1962 (68).
Ridgely, John (r.n. John Huntington Rea), actor; b. Sept. 6, 1909, Chicago, Ill.; d. Jan. 17, 1968 (58).
Ridges, Stanley C., actor; b. Southampton, England; d. Apr. 22, 1951 (59).
Ridgeway, Fritzi, actress; b. Missoula, Mont.; d. Mar. 29, 1961 (62).
Ridgwell, Audrey, actress; d. Oct. 27, 1968 (64).
Ridley, Arthur, actor; d. Mar. 11, 1978.
Ridley, Robert, actor; d. Nov. 19, 1958 (57).
Riemann, Johannes, actor & director; b. 1888, Berlin, Germany; d. Sept. 30, 1959 (71).
Riento, Virgilio, actor; b. Nov. 29, 1889, Rome, Italy; d. Sept. 7, 1959 (69).
Ries, William J., actor; d. Nov. 16, 1955 (60).
Riesner, Charles F. (Chuck), director, producer, & actor; b. Mar. 14, 1887, Minneapolis, Minn.; d. Sept. 24, 1962 (75).
Rietty, Victor, actor; b. Feb. 28, 1888, Ferrara, Italy; d. Dec. 3, 1963 (75).
Riga, Nadine, actress; d. Dec. 11, 1968 (59).
Rigas, George (see Regas, George)
Rigby, Arthur, actor; d. Apr. 17, 1944 (79).
Rigby, Arthur, actor; d. Apr. 24, 1971 (70).
Rigby, Edward, actor; b. Feb. 5, 1879, Ashford, Kent, England; d. Apr. 5, 1951 (72).
Riggio, Jerry, actor; d. Sept. 12, 1971.
Riggs, Ralph, actor; b. St. Paul, Minn.; d. Sept. 16, 1951 (62).
Riggs, Tommy, actor; b. Oct. 21, 1908, Pittsburgh, Pa.; d. May 21, 1967 (58).
Rihani, Neguib, actor; d. June 8, 1949 (58).
Riley, Adele, actress; d. Feb. 3, 1938 (48).
Riley, George, actor; b. Dec. 3, 1897, New York; d. May 30, 1972 (74).
Riley, Jack "Slim," actor; d. July 9, 1933 (38).
Riley, Mack (r.n. Maynard Cyril Stokes), actor; b. Feb. 15, 1886, Tennessee; d. Aug. 29, 1963 (77).
Rimoldi, Adriano, actor; b. Oct. 3, 1912, La Spezia, Italy; d. June 19, 1965 (52).
Ring, Blanche, actress; b. Apr. 24, 1878, Massachusetts; d. Jan. 13, 1961 (82).

Ring, Cyril, actor; b. Dec. 5, 1892, Massachusetts; d. July 17, 1967 (74).
Rin Tin Tin, dog; b. Sept. 12, 1918, France; d. Aug. 8, 1932 (13).
Riordan, Robert, actor & author; b. Dec. 11, 1911, Chicago, Ill.; d. Jan. 1, 1968 (56).
Rios, Lalo (r.n. Edward C. Rios), actor; b. Feb. 7, 1927, Mexico; d. Mar. 7, 1973 (46).
Ripley, Raymond, actor; d. Oct. 7, 1938 (47).
Rippert, Otto, actor; d. Jan., 1940 (71).
Riscoe, Arthur, actor; b. Nov. 19, 1896, Sherburn-in-Elmet, Yorkshire, England; d. Aug. 6, 1954 (57).
Risdon, Elisabeth, actress; b. Apr. 26, 1888, Wandsworth, England; d. Dec. 20, 1958 (70).
Rising, William S., actor; d. Oct. 5, 1930 (79).
Riskin, Robert, writer, director, & producer; b. New York City; d. Sept. 20, 1955 (58).
Riss, Dan, actor; b. Mar. 22, 1910, Illinois; d. Aug. 28, 1970 (60).
Rissone, Giuditta, actress; b. Aug. 28, 1895, Genoa, Italy; d. May 31, 1977 (81).
Ristelhueber, Joseph H., actor; d. Feb. 28, 1943 (96).
Ritchard, Cyril, actor; b. Dec. 1, 1897, Sydney, Australia; d. Dec. 18, 1977 (80).
Ritchey, William M., writer; d. Jan. 14, 1937 (55).
Ritchie, Adele, actress; b. Dec. 21, 1874, Philadelphia, Pa.; d. Apr. 24, 1930 (55).
Ritchie, Billy, actor; b. Sept. 14, 1878, Glasgow, Scotland; d. July 7, 1921 (42).
Ritchie, Franklin, actor; d. Jan. 25, 1918 (52).
Ritchie, Perry V., actor; d. Aug., 1918.
Ritchie, William A., actor; d. May 13, 1970.
Ritter, Esther, actress; d. Dec. 30, 1925 (23).
Ritter, George, actor; d. Dec., 1919.
Ritter, Paul J., producer & actor; d. Apr. 27, 1962.
Ritter, Rudolf, opera singer & actor; b. Jan. 19, 1878; d. June 3, 1966 (88).
Ritter, Tex (r.n. Woodward Maurice Ritter), actor & recording artist; b. Jan. 12, 1906, Murvaul, Tex.; d. Jan. 2, 1974 (67).
Ritter, Thelma, actress; b. Feb. 14, 1905, Brooklyn, N.Y.; d. Feb. 5, 1969 (63).
Ritterband, Gerhard, actor; d. Oct., 1959 (54).
Rittner, Rudolf, actor; b. June 30, 1869, Weissbach, Germany; d. Feb. 4, 1943 (73).
Ritz, Al, actor; b. Aug. 27, 1903, Newark, N.J.; d. Dec. 22, 1965 (62).
Riva, Mario, actor; b. Jan. 26, 1913, Rome, Italy; d. Sept. 1, 1960 (47).
Rivas, Jose Maria Linares, actor; d. Apr. 14, 1955.
Rivelles, Rafael (r.n. Rafael Rivelles Guillen), actor; b. 1899, Valencia, Spain; d. Dec., 1966 (67).
Rivero, Julian, actor; b. July 25, 1890, San Francisco, Calif.; d. Feb. 24, 1976 (85).
Rivers, Fernand, director & actor; d. Sept., 1960 (78).
Rivers, Victor, stuntman; d. July 8, 1977 (29).
Riviere, Fred (Curly), actor; d. Nov. 6, 1935 (60).
Rizzo, Carlo, stuntman & actor; b. June 29, 1925, California; d. Feb. 10, 1977 (51).
Roach, Bert (r.n. Egbert Roach), actor; b. Aug. 21, 1891, Washington, D.C.; d. Feb. 16, 1971 (79).

Roach, Margaret, actress; b. Mar. 15, 1921, Los Angeles, Calif.;
    d. Nov. 22, 1964 (43).
Roache, Viola, actress; b. Oct. 3, 1885, England; d. May 17, 1961
    (75).
Roadman, Betty, actress; b. Dec. 5, 1889, Missouri; d. Mar. 24,
    1975 (85).
Roanne, Andre, actor; b. Sept. 22, 1896, Paris, France; d. Sept.,
    1959 (63).
Roark, Counsellor F. (r.n. Charles Francis Roark), actor; b. Apr. 26,
    1860, Indiana; d. Nov. 15, 1929 (69).
Robards, Jason, Sr., actor; b. Dec. 31, 1892, Hillsdale, Mich.;
    d. Apr. 4, 1963 (70).
Robards, Willis, actor; b. Jan. 1, 1873, Texas; d. Nov. 3, 1921 (48).
Robb, Lotus, actress; d. Sept. 28, 1969.
Robbins, Archie, actor; d. Sept. 26, 1975 (62).
Robbins, Gale, actress; b. May 7, 1921, Mitchell, Ind.; d. Feb. 18,
    1980 (58).
Robbins, Marc (r.n. Mercus B. Robbins), actor; b. Jan. 3, 1868;
    d. Apr. 5, 1931 (63).
Robbins, Richard, actor; b. Boston, Mass.; d. Oct. 23, 1969 (50).
Robbins, Skeeter Bill (Roy R. Robbins), actor & superintendent,
    stock ranch; b. July 16, 1887, Glen Rock, Wyo.; d. Nov. 28, 1933
    (46).
Robeling, Albin, actor; b. June 25, 1901, Austria; d. Apr. 10, 1953
    (51).
Rober, Richard (r.n. Richard Rauber), actor; b. May 14, 1910, New
    York; d. May 26, 1952 (42).
Roberson, Lou, actor & stuntman; b. June 19, 1921, Texas; d. Nov. 21,
    1966 (45).
Roberti, Lyda, actress; b. May 20, 1912, Veromich, Russia; d. Mar. 12,
    1938 (25).
Roberts, A. Cledge, actor; d. June 14, 1957 (52).
Roberts, Albert G., actor & cameraman; b. Oct. 11, 1902, Blackfoot,
    Idaho; d. May 30, 1941 (38).
Roberts, Arthur, actor; b. Sept. 21, 1852, London, England; d. Feb.
    27, 1933 (80).
Roberts, Benjamin H., actor; d. Sept. 13, 1947 (62).
Roberts, Charles B. (Jack), actor; d. Sept. 14, 1927.
Roberts, Desmond, actor; b. Feb. 5, 1894, London, England; d. Jan. 11,
    1968 (73).
Roberts, Dick, banjoist; d. Nov. 1, 1966 (69).
Roberts, Edd J., actor; d. Jan. 23, 1953 (60).
Roberts, Edith, actress; d. Aug. 20, 1935 (36).
Roberts, Evelyn, actor; b. Aug. 28, 1886, Reading, Berks, England;
    d. Nov. 30, 1962 (76).
Roberts, Florence, actress; b. Feb. 14, 1871, New York City;
    d. July 17, 1927 (56).
Roberts, Florence, actress; b. Mar. 16, 1861, Frederick, Md.;
    d. June 6, 1940 (79).
Roberts, Glen (Leonard Freeman), actor, producer, & author; d. Jan. 20,
    1974 (53).
Roberts, J.H., actor; b. July 11, 1884, London, England; d. Feb. 1,
    1961 (76).
Roberts, John (Todd), actor; d. Dec. 14, 1979 (25).
Roberts, Joseph, actor; d. Oct. 28, 1923 (53).
Roberts, Leona, actress; d. Jan. 29, 1954 (74).

Roberts, Merrill, actor; d. Dec. 2, 1940 (55).
Roberts, Nancy, actress; d. June 25, 1962 (70).
Roberts, Ned, actor; b. Apr. 18, 1904, New York; d. Mar. 29, 1973
    (68).
Roberts, Ralph Arthur (r.n. Robert Arthur Schonherr), actor; b. Oct. 2,
    1884, Meerane, Germany; d. Mar. 12, 1940 (55).
Roberts, Ralph, actor; b. Shikapur, India; d. Oct. 31, 1944 (75).
Roberts, Roy, actor; b. Mar. 19, 1906, Florida; d. May 28, 1975 (69).
Roberts, Sara Jane, actress; d. Aug. 19, 1968 (44).
Roberts, Thayer, actor; b. June 21, 1902; d. Feb. 28, 1968 (65).
Roberts, Theodore, actor; b. Oct. 8, 1861, San Francisco, Calif.;
    d. Dec. 14, 1928 (67).
Roberts, Wilfred, actor; d. Feb. 24, 1954 (47).
Robertshaw, Jerrold, actor; b. Mar. 28, 1866, Allerton, England;
    d. Feb. 14, 1941 (74).
Robertson, Frances Jean, actress; d. June 29, 1942 (40).
Robertson, James, actor; d. Nov. 13, 1936 (77).
Robertson, James Francis, actor; d. May, 1942 (74).
Robertson, Jean, actress; d. Aug., 1967 (73).
Robertson, John S., director; b. June 14, 1878, Ontario, Canada;
    d. Nov. 5, 1964 (86).
Robertson, Orie O., actor & stuntman; b. Jan. 9, 1881, Illinois;
    d. Apr. 14, 1964 (83).
Robertson, Stuart, actor; b. Mar. 5, 1901, London, England;
    d. Dec. 26, 1958 (57).
Robertson, Willard, actor; b. Jan. 1, 1886, Runnels, Tex.; d. Apr. 5,
    1948 (62).
Robeson, Paul, actor & singer; b. Apr. 9, 1898, Princeton, N.J.;
    d. Jan. 23, 1976 (77).
Robey, Sir George, actor; b. Sept. 20, 1869, England; d. Nov. 29,
    1954 (85).
Robins, Edward H., actor; b. Oct. 15, 1880, Shamokin, Pa.; d. July 27,
    1955 (74).
Robinson, Bill, actor & dancer; b. May 25, 1878, Richmond, Va.;
    d. Nov. 25, 1949 (71).
Robinson, Casey, scenarist; b. Oct. 17, 1903, Logan, Utah; d. Dec. 6,
    1979 (76).
Robinson, Dewey, actor; b. New Haven, Conn.; d. Dec. 11, 1950 (51).
Robinson, Edward G., actor; b. Dec. 12, 1893, Bucharest, Rumania;
    d. Jan. 26, 1973 (79).
Robinson, Edward G., Jr., actor; d. Feb. 26, 1974 (40).
Robinson, Forrest, actor; b. Aug. 2, 1858, New York; d. Jan. 6, 1924
    (65).
Robinson, Frances (r.n. Marion Frances Ladd), actress; b. Apr. 26,
    1916, Ft. Wadsworth, N.Y.; d. Aug. 16, 1971 (55).
Robinson, Gertrude, actress; d. Mar. 19, 1962 (71).
Robinson, Harry T., actor; b. June 1, 1872, Des Moines, Iowa;
    d. Sept. 8, 1946 (74).
Robinson, John, actor; b. Nov. 11, 1908, Liverpool, England;
    d. Mar. 6, 1979 (70).
Robinson, Legal W., actor; d. Jan., 1919.
Robinson, Robert Hamilton, Jr., actor; b. Nov. 1, 1948, California;
    d. Oct. 9, 1976 (27).
Robinson, Ruth, actress; b. Aug. 18, 1887, Kansas; d. Mar. 17, 1966
    (78).

Robison, Arthur, director; b. June 25, 1888, Chicago, Ill.; d. Oct.
20, 1935 (47).
Robison, "Spike," actor; d. July 13, 1942 (58).
Robles, Richard, actor; b. June 14, 1902, El Paso, Tex.; d. Apr. 21,
1940 (37).
Robles, Rudy, actor; b. Apr. 28, 1910, Manila, Philippines;
d. Aug., 1970 (60).
Robson, Andrew, actor; d. Apr. 26, 1921 (52).
Robson, Mark, director & producer; b. Dec. 4, 1913, Montreal, Canada;
d. June 20, 1978 (64).
Robson, May, actress; b. Apr. 19, 1858, Melbourne, Australia;
d. Oct. 20, 1942 (84).
Robson, Philip, actor; d. May 6, 1919.
Robson, Mrs. Stuart (see Waldron, May)
Robyn, Gay, actress; d. July 25, 1942 (30).
Robyns, William, actor; d. Jan. 22, 1936 (80).
Roccardi, Albert, actor; b. May 9, 1864, Rome, Italy; d. May 14,
1934 (70).
Rocha, Miguel Faust, actor; d. Mar. 6, 1961.
Roche, Franklyn Dix, actor; b. Nov. 9, 1904, Maryland; d. Nov. 20,
1963 (59).
Roche, John, actor; b. May 6, 1893, Penn Yan, N.Y.; d. Nov. 10,
1952 (59).
Rochin, Paul, actor; b. May 9, 1890, Poland; d. May 5, 1964 (73).
Rock, Blossom (Marie Blake), actress; b. 1899; d. Jan. 14, 1978 (78).
Rock, Charles, actor; b. May 30, 1866, Vellore, India; d. July 12,
1919 (53).
Rock, Warren (r.n. Clarence Warren Rock), actor; b. Oct. 2, 1898,
California; d. July 14, 1960 (61).
Rockett, Al, producer; b. Vincennes, Ind.; d. Aug. 30, 1960 (68).
Rockne, Knute, actor & coach; b. Mar. 4, 1888, Voss, Norway;
d. Mar. 31, 1931 (43).
Rockwell, Florence, actress; b. St. Louis, Mo.; d. Mar. 24, 1964 (76).
Rockwell, Jack, actor; d. Nov. 10, 1947.
Roda, Roda (r.n. Sandor Friedrich Rosenfeld), actor; b. Apr. 13, 1872,
Puszta Zdenci; d. Aug. 20, 1945 (73).
Rode, Walter, actor; b. July 6, 1904, Russia; d. Feb. 8, 1973 (68).
Roderick, Leslie, dancer; d. Aug. 16, 1927 (20).
Rodgers, Eugene, actor; d. Mar. 9, 1919 (52).
Rodgers, Jimmie, singer & recording artist; b. Sept. 8, 1897,
Meridian, Miss.; d. May 26, 1933 (35).
Rodgers, Walter, actor; b. Aug. 31, 1886, Ohio; d. Apr. 24, 1951 (64).
Rodman, Victor, actor; b. Aug. 6, 1892, Arkansas; d. June 29, 1965
(72).
Rodney, Earle (r.n. Earle Rodney Hupp), actor; b. June 4, 1888,
Toronto, Canada; d. Dec. 16, 1932 (44).
Rodney, Jack, actor; d. Feb. 20, 1967 (51).
Rodriguez, Estelita, actress; b. July 2, 1928, Cuba; d. Mar. 12,
1966 (37).
Rodriguez, Tito, actor & singer; d. Feb. 28, 1973 (50).
Roels, Marcel, actor; b. Jan. 12, 1894, Anversa; d. Dec. 27, 1973
(79).
Rogell, Sid, producer; b. Jan. 16, 1900, St. Joseph, Mo.; d. Nov. 15,
1973 (73).
Rogers, Bessie, actress; d. Mar. 5, 1930 (46).

Rogers, Carl D., actor; d. Mar. 2, 1965 (63).
Rogers, Charles A., author; b. Jan. 15, 1887, England; d. Dec. 20, 1956 (69).
Rogers, Charles R., producer; b. July 15, 1892, New York City; d. Mar. 29, 1957 (64).
Rogers, Frank B., actor; d. Nov. 12, 1959 (82).
Rogers, George, actor; b. Jan. 5, 1898, Cleveland, Ohio; d. Dec. 10, 1942 (44).
Rogers, Howard Emmett, writer; b. July 13, 1890, New York City; d. Aug. 16, 1971 (81).
Rogers, John, actor; b. Aug. 28, 1888, England; d. July 31, 1963 (74).
Rogers, Joseph, actor; b. Apr. 10, 1871, Lebanon-Syria; d. Dec. 27, 1942 (71).
Rogers, Kent, actor; d. July 9, 1944.
Rogers, Lora, actress; d. Dec. 23, 1948 (74).
Rogers, Mildred, actress; b. Apr. 14, 1899, Nebraska; d. Apr. 14, 1973 (74).
Rogers, Rena, actress; b. June 7, 1900, Illinois; d. Feb. 19, 1966 (65).
Rogers, Ruth, actress; d. Oct. 9, 1953 (35).
Rogers, Will, actor; b. Nov. 4, 1879, Oologah, Okla.; d. Aug. 15, 1935 (55).
Rohrer, Kay, actress & softball player; d. Mar. 17, 1962 (39).
Roland, Frederic, actor; b. Nov. 12, 1885, Toronto, Canada; d. June 2, 1936 (50).
Roland, Marion (Marion Ross), actress; d. July 23, 1966 (68).
Roland, Ruth, actress; b. Aug. 26, 1894, San Francisco, Calif.; d. Sept. 22, 1937 (43).
Roldan, Enrique, actor; d. Feb. 4, 1954 (53).
Rolf, Erik, actor; b. June 1, 1911, Illinois; d. May 28, 1957 (45).
Rollan, Henri, actor; b. Mar. 23, 1888, Paris, France; d. June 23, 1967 (79).
Rolland, Jean-Claude, actor; d. Apr., 1967 (34).
Rollett, Raymond, actor; b. England; d. Dec. 19, 1961 (54).
Rollin, Georges, actor; b. Apr. 6, 1912, France; d. Mar. 2, 1964 (51).
Rollow, Preston J., actor; d. May, 1947 (76).
Roma, Clarice, actress; d. May 3, 1947 (27).
Romaine, George, actor; d. May 7, 1929.
Romano, John, actor; d. July 24, 1957 (61).
Romanoff, Prince Michael, actor; d. Sept. 1, 1971 (81).
Romanowsky, Richard, actor; d. July, 1968 (85).
Rome, Bert, actor; d. Aug. 25, 1946 (59).
Rome, Stewart, actor; b. Jan. 30, 1886, England; d. Feb. 26, 1965 (79).
Romea, Alberto, actor; d. Apr. 24, 1960 (77).
Romee, Marcelle, actress; d. Dec. 4, 1932 (29).
Romer, Tomi, actress; d. July 21, 1969 (45).
Romero, Florita, dancer; d. Feb. 6, 1961 (30).
Romeyn, Jane, actress; b. Dec. 7, 1900, Michigan; d. May 5, 1963 (62).
Rooke, Irene, actress; b. Bridport, England; d. June 14, 1958 (80).
Room, Abram, director & author; d. July, 1976 (80).
Rooner, Charles, actor; b. Vienna, Austria; d. Nov. 22, 1954 (53).
Rooney, Pat, actor; d. Jan. 15, 1933 (42).
Rooney, Pat, Sr., actor; b. July 4, 1880, New York City; d. Sept. 9, 1962 (82).

Rooney, Pat, 3d, actor; d. Nov. 5, 1979 (70).
Roope, Fay, actor; d. Sept. 13, 1961 (68).
Roosevelt, Buddy (Kent Sanderson), actor; b. June 25, 1898, Meeker, Colo.; d. Oct. 6, 1973 (75).
Roper, Jack, actor & boxer; b. Mar. 25, 1904, Mississippi; d. Nov. 28, 1966 (62).
Roquemore, Henry, actor; b. Mar. 13, 1886, Marshall, Tex.; d. June 30, 1943 (57).
Roquevert, Noel, actor; d. Nov., 1973 (81).
Rorke, Ina, actress; b. 1868, Portugal; d. Apr. 23, 1944 (76).
Rosanova, Rosa, actress; b. June 23, 1869, Odessa, Russia; d. May 29, 1944 (74).
Rosar, Annie, actress; b. May 17, 1888, Vienna, Austria; d. Aug. 1, 1963 (75).
Rosas, Fernando, actor; d. Mar., 1959 (44).
Rosay, Francoise, actress; b. Apr. 19, 1891, Paris, France; d. Mar. 28, 1974 (82).
Roscoe, Alan (Albert Roscoe), actor; b. Aug. 23, 1888, Memphis, Tenn.; d. Mar. 8, 1933 (44).
Roscoe, Albert (see Roscoe, Alan)
Rose, Blanche, actress; b. Detroit, Mich.; d. Jan. 5, 1953 (75).
Rose, Harry, actor; d. Dec. 10, 1962 (70).
Rose, Harry, actor; d. Apr. 20, 1975.
Rose, Jane, actress; d. June 29, 1979 (66).
Rose, Jewel, actress; d. Oct. 21, 1970.
Rose, Michael, actor; d. Oct. 26, 1974.
Rose, Polly, actress; d. Feb. 13, 1971.
Rose, Robert, actor; d. June 1, 1936 (68).
Rose, Veronica, actress; d. Jan. 25, 1968.
Rose, Willi, actor; d. June, 1978 (76).
Roseleigh, Jack, actor; d. Jan. 5, 1940 (53).
Roselle, William, actor; d. June 1, 1945 (67).
Rosemond, Clinton, actor; b. Nov. 1, 1882, South Carolina; d. Mar. 10, 1966 (83).
Rosen, Jimmy, actor; d. June 1, 1940 (55).
Rosen, Phil, director; b. May 8, 1888, Russia; d. Oct. 22, 1951 (63).
Rosenberg, Michel, actor; d. Nov. 18, 1972 (71).
Rosenberg, Sarah, actress; b. July 1, 1874, Poland; d. June 16, 1964 (89).
Rosenbloom, Maxie, actor & boxer; b. Sept. 6, 1904, New York City; d. Mar. 6, 1976 (71).
Rosenbluth, Nancy, actress & singer; d. June 15, 1962 (47).
Rosener, George, actor & author; b. May 23, 1879, Brooklyn, N.Y.; d. Mar. 29, 1945 (65).
Rosenthal, Harry, actor; b. May 15, 1900; d. May 10, 1953 (52).
Rosher, Charles, cinematographer; d. Jan. 15, 1974 (89).
Rosing, Bodil, actress; b. Dec. 27, 1877, Copenhagen, Denmark; d. Dec. 31, 1941 (64).
Rosley, Adrian, actor; b. Oct. 28, 1888, Rumania; d. Mar. 5, 1937 (48).
Rosmer, Milton, actor; b. Nov. 4, 1882, Southport, England; d. Dec. 7, 1971 (89).
Ross, Anthony, actor; b. New York; d. Oct. 26, 1955 (46).
Ross, Arthur S., actor; d. Feb. 17, 1955 (75).
Ross, Barney, prizefighter & actor; b. Dec. 23, 1909, Chicago, Ill.; d. Jan. 18, 1967 (57).

Ross, Charles J., actor; b. Feb. 18, 1859, Montreal, Canada;
    d. June 15, 1918 (59).
Ross, Chris, actor; d. May 5, 1970 (24).
Ross, Churchill, actor; b. Jan. 29, 1901, Lafayette, Ind.; d. May 23,
    1962 (61).
Ross, Corinne, actress; b. June 15, 1879, Illinois; d. June 21, 1965
    (86).
Ross, David, narrator; d. Nov. 12, 1975 (84).
Ross, Earle, actor; b. Mar. 29, 1888, Illinois; d. May 21, 1961 (73).
Ross, Eve McClure, actress; b. Feb. 18, 1922, Minnesota; d. July 31,
    1966 (44).
Ross, Herbert, actor; b. Oct. 3, 1865, Calcutta, India; d. July 18,
    1934 (70).
Ross, Mabel Fenton, actress; b. Michigan; d. Apr. 19, 1931 (63).
Ross, Myrna, actress; d. Dec. 26, 1975 (36).
Ross, Robert, actor; d. Feb. 23, 1954 (52).
Ross, Shirley, actress; b. Jan. 7, 1913, Omaha, Neb.; d. Mar. 9,
    1975 (62).
Ross, Thomas W., actor; b. Jan. 22, 1875, Boston, Mass.; d. Nov. 14,
    1959 (84).
Ross, William, actor; d. Feb. 25, 1963 (38).
Rossellini, Roberto, director; b. May 8, 1906, Rome, Italy; d. June 3,
    1977 (71).
Rossen, Robert, director & author; b. Mar. 16, 1908, New York;
    d. Feb. 18, 1966 (57).
Rosson, Arthur H., producer & director; b. London, England; d. June
    17, 1960 (73).
Rosson, Richard, director; b. New York City; d. May 31, 1953 (60).
Rosvaenge, Helge, opera singer; b. Aug. 29, 1897, Copenhagen,
    Denmark; d. June 19, 1972 (74).
Rota, Nino, composer; d. Apr. 10, 1979 (68).
Roth, Gene (Eugene Stutenroth), actor; b. Jan. 8, 1903, South Dakota;
    d. July 19, 1976 (73).
Roth, Murray, director & writer; d. Feb. 17, 1938 (44).
Roth, Sandy, actor & director; d. Nov. 4, 1943 (54).
Rothe, Anita, actress; d. Jan. 9, 1944 (77).
Rotmund, Ernst, actor; b. 1886, Thorn, Poland; d. Mar. 2, 1955 (68).
Roughwood, Owen, actor; b. June 9, 1870, London, England; d. May 30,
    1947 (76).
Roulien, Tosca, actress; d. Sept. 27, 1933 (23).
Rouverol, Aurania, writer; d. June 23, 1955 (69).
Rounseville, Robert, opera singer; b. Mar. 25, 1914, Attleboro,
    Mass.; d. Aug. 6, 1974 (60).
Roux, Tony, actor; b. May 7, 1901, Mexico; d. Nov. 9, 1976 (75).
Rovensky, Joseph, actor; b. Apr. 17, 1894; d. Nov. 5, 1937 (43).
Roveri, Ermanno, actor; b. Oct. 5, 1903, Milan, Italy; d. Dec. 28,
    1968 (65).
Rowan, Don, actor; d. Feb. 17, 1966 (60).
Rowan, Ernest, actor; d. Sept. 30, 1960 (74).
Rowland, Adele, actress; b. July 10, 1883, Washington, D.C.;
    d. Aug. 8, 1971 (88).
Rowland, James G., actor; d. Nov. 27, 1951.
Rowland, Richard A., director & producer; d. May 12, 1947 (66).
Rowlands, Art, actor; b. Aug. 26, 1897, Oakland, Calif.; d. May 25,
    1944 (46).

Roy, Jahar, actor; d. Aug. 11, 1977 (58).
Roy, John, stuntman; d. May 31, 1975 (77).
Royal, Charles (r.n. Charles Elliott Royal), actor & playwright;
    b. Jan. 27, 1880, Oregon; d. July 26, 1955 (75).
Royce, Brigham, actor; b. Memphis, Tenn.; d. Mar. 7, 1933 (66).
Royce, Frosty (r.n. Forest Royse), actor & stuntman; d. Dec. 20,
    1910, Oklahoma; d. May 15, 1965 (54).
Royce, Julian, actor; b. Mar. 26, 1870, Bristol, England; d. May 10,
    1946 (76).
Royce, Lionel, actor; b. Mar. 30, 1887, Dolina, Poland; d. Apr. 1,
    1946 (59).
Royce, Ruth, actress; b. Feb. 6, 1893, Versailles, Mo.; d. May 7,
    1971 (78).
Royce, Virginia, actress; d. July 8, 1962 (30).
Royer, Harry, actor; b. Oct. 6, 1890, Missouri; d. Aug. 1, 1951 (60).
Royle, William, actor; b. Mar. 22, 1887, Rochester, N.Y.; d. Aug. 9,
    1940 (53).
Royston, Julius, actor; d. July 1, 1935.
Royston, Roy, actor; d. Oct., 1976 (77).
Rozanska, Elektra, actress & opera singer; d. July 3, 1978 (87).
Rub, Christian, actor; b. Apr. 13, 1886, Austria; d. Apr. 14, 1956
    (70).
Ruben, Jose, actor; d. Apr. 28, 1969 (80).
Rubens, Alma, actress; b. Feb. 19, 1897, San Francisco, Calif.;
    d. Jan. 21, 1931 (33).
Rubin, Pedro, actor; d. Apr. 17, 1938.
Rubinstein, Ida, actress & dancer; b. 1883, Kharkov, Russia;
    d. Sept. 20, 1960 (77).
Rudami, Rosa, actress; d. Feb. 2, 1966 (67).
Rufart, Carlos, actor; d. Apr., 1957 (70).
Ruffini, Sandro, actor; b. Sept. 21, 1889, Rome, Italy; d. Nov. 29,
    1954 (65).
Ruggeri, Ruggero, actor; b. Nov. 14, 1871, Fano, Italy; d. July 20,
    1953 (81).
Ruggles, Charles, actor; b. Feb. 8, 1886, Los Angeles, Calif.;
    d. Dec. 23, 1970 (84).
Ruggles, Wesley, director & actor; b. June 11, 1889, Los Angeles,
    Calif.; d. Jan. 8, 1972 (82).
Ruhl, William, actor; b. Oct. 25, 1901, Oregon; d. Mar. 12, 1956 (54).
Ruick, Barbara, actress; b. Dec. 23, 1930, Pasadena, Calif.;
    d. Mar. 2, 1974 (43).
Ruick, Mel, actor; b. July 8, 1898, Idaho; d. Dec. 24, 1972 (74).
Ruiz, Jose Rivero, actor; d. Dec. 27, 1949 (53).
Ruman, Sig (Siegfried Rumann), actor; b. Oct. 11, 1884, Hamburg,
    Germany; d. Feb. 14, 1967 (82).
Rumsey, Bert, actor; b. Oct. 15, 1892, Montana; d. July 6, 1968 (75).
Ruskin, Harry, writer; b. Nov. 30, 1894, Cincinnati, Ohio; d. Nov. 16,
    1969 (74).
Ruskin, Shimen, actor; b. Feb. 25, 1907, Poland; d. Apr. 23, 1976 (69).
Russell, Albert, actor & director; b. Aug. 2, 1890, New York City;
    d. Mar. 4, 1929 (38).
Russell, Albert, actor; b. Sept. 6, 1876, Kentucky; d. Apr. 3,
    1946 (69).
Russell, Ann, actress; d. July 31, 1955 (24).
Russell, Billy, actor; d. Nov. 25, 1971.

Russell, Byron, actor; b. Ireland; d. Sept. 4, 1963 (79).
Russell, Edd X., actor; b. May 27, 1878, New York; d. Nov. 17, 1966
    (88).
Russell, Evangeline, actress; b. Aug. 18, 1902, New York; d. Feb. 22,
    1966 (63).
Russell, Evelyn, actress; d. Feb. 4, 1976 (49).
Russell, Gail, actress; b. Sept. 23, 1924, Chicago, Ill.; d. Aug. 26,
    1961 (36).
Russell, George, actor; b. Mar. 7, 1904, Oklahoma; d. Feb. 22, 1975
    (70).
Russell, J. Gordon, actor; b. Jan. 11, 1883, Alabama; d. Apr. 21,
    1935 (52).
Russell, John, writer; d. Mar. 6, 1956 (71).
Russell, John Lowell, actor; b. Apr. 22, 1875, Pleasant Valley, Iowa;
    d. Sept. 19, 1937 (62).
Russell, Lewis L., actor; b. Sept. 10, 1889, Illinois; d. Nov. 12,
    1961 (72).
Russell, Lillian, actress; b. Dec. 4, 1861, Clinton, Iowa; d. June 6,
    1922 (60).
Russell, Paul, actor; d. Dec. 26, 1979 (83).
Russell, Reb, actor; b. May 31, 1905, Osawatomie, Kans.; d. Mar. 16,
    1978 (72).
Russell, Rosalind, actress; b. June 4, 1907, Waterbury, Conn.;
    d. Nov. 28, 1976 (69).
Russell, William, actor; b. Apr. 12, 1886, New York City; d. Feb. 18,
    1929 (42).
Russell-Scott, R., actor; d. 1950 (58).
Rutan, Charles Hart, actor; b. July 6, 1892, Brooklyn, N.Y.;
    d. July 17, 1968 (76).
Ruth, George Herman (Babe), actor & baseball star; b. Feb. 6, 1895,
    Baltimore, Md.; d. Aug. 16, 1948 (53).
Ruth, Jean Noble, actress; d. Dec. 19, 1955 (57).
Ruth, Marshall, actor; b. Dec. 24, 1898, Marshalltown, Iowa;
    d. Jan. 17, 1953 (54).
Rutherford, Margaret, actress; b. May 11, 1892, London, England;
    d. May 22, 1972 (80).
Rutherfurd, Tom, actor; d. Jan. 6, 1973.
Ruttmann, Walter, director; b. Dec. 28, 1887, Frankfurt, Germany;
    d. July 15, 1941 (53).
Ruysdael, Basil, actor; b. July 24, 1888, New Jersey; d. Oct. 10,
    1960 (72).
Ryan, Annie, actress; d. Feb. 14, 1943 (78).
Ryan, Chet, actor; b. May 17, 1889, Spearfish, S.D.; d. Jan. 20,
    1943 (53).
Ryan, Dick, actor; b. Aug. 25, 1896, Connecticut; d. Aug. 12, 1969
    (72).
Ryan, Irene, actress; b. Oct. 17, 1902, El Paso, Tex.; d. Apr. 26,
    1973 (70).
Ryan, James E., actor; d. Jan. 6, 1976 (35).
Ryan, Joe, actor; b. May 23, 1887, Crook Co., Wyo.; d. Dec. 23, 1944
    (57).
Ryan, Mary, actress; d. Oct. 2, 1948 (68).
Ryan, Robert, actor; b. Nov. 11, 1909, Chicago, Ill.; d. July 11,
    1973 (63).
Ryan, Robert J., actor; b. Apr. 16, 1896, Pipestone, Minn.; d. Nov. 27,
    1958 (62).

Ryan, Sheila, actress; b. June 8, 1921, Topeka, Kans.; d. Nov. 4, 1975 (54).
Ryan, Tim, actor; b. July 27, 1899, New Jersey; d. Oct. 22, 1956 (57).
Ryen, Richard (see Revy, Richard)
Ryno, William H., actor; b. Oct. 8, 1864; d. Dec. 3, 1939 (75).
Rytjkov, Nikolaj, actor; d. Sept. 1, 1973 (60).


Sabato, Alfred, actor; b. Mar. 23, 1894, Italy; d. Feb. 10, 1956 (61).
Sabbatini, Ernesto, actor; b. Sept. 8, 1878, Padova, Italy; d. Oct. 5, 1954 (76).
Sabin, Mrs. Catherine J., actress; d. May 19, 1943 (54).
Sablon, Loulette, actress; b. July 16, 1897, France; d. Oct. 21, 1970 (73).
Sabouret, Marie, actress; b. 1924, France; d. July 23, 1960 (36).
Sabu (r.n. Sabu Dastagir), actor; b. Jan. 27, 1924, India; d. Dec. 2, 1963 (39).
Sacchetto, Rita, actress; b. 1879, Germania; d. Jan., 1959 (79).
Sack, Erna, opera singer; b. Feb. 6, 1898, Berlin, Germany; d. Mar. 2, 1972 (74).
Sack, Nathaniel, actor; d. July 2, 1966 (84).
Sackheim, Jerry, writer; d. May 13, 1979 (74).
Sackville, Gordon, actor; d. Aug. 6, 1926 (46).
Sada, Keiji, actor; b. 1926, Kyoto, Japan; d. July 22, 1964 (38).
Sadler, Charles R., actor & stuntman; d. Mar. 23, 1950 (75).
Sadler, Dudley, actor; d. Sept. 25, 1951 (33).
Sadler, Ian, actor; b. Glasgow, Scotland; d. July, 1971 (69).
Saenz, Eddie, stuntman; b. Sept. 21, 1922, California; d. Apr. 23, 1971 (48).
Sagar, Anthony, actor; b. 1920, Burnley, England; d. Jan., 1973 (52).
Sage, Frances, actress; b. Feb. 28, 1915, New York; d. Jan. 7, 1963 (47).
Sage, Willard (r.n. James Willard Sage), actor; b. Aug. 13, 1922, Canada; d. Mar. 17, 1974 (51).
Sahni, Balraj, actor; d. Apr. 13, 1973 (60).
Sainpolis, John (see St. Polis, John)
St. Alwyn, Harry, actor; b. July 24, 1883, Truro, Cornwall, England; d. Feb. 1, 1943 (59).
St. Clair, Lydia, actress; d. Jan. 1, 1970.
St. Clair, Malcolm, director & actor; b. May 17, 1897, Los Angeles, Calif.; d. June 1, 1952 (55).
St. Clair, Maurice, actor; b. Nov. 29, 1902, France; d. May 9, 1970 (67).
St. Clair, Yvonne, dancer; d. Sept. 22, 1971 (57).
St. Claire, Adah, actress; d. Aug. 16, 1928 (74).
St. Denis, Joe, actor; d. May 15, 1968 (40).
St. Helier, Ivy, actress; d. Nov. 8, 1971.
St. James, William, actor; d. July 23, 1931 (55).
St. John, Al, actor; b. Sept. 10, 1892, Santa Ana, Calif.; d. Jan. 21, 1963 (70).
St. John, Howard, actor; b. Oct. 9, 1905, Chicago, Ill.; d. Mar. 13, 1974 (68).
St. John, Marguerite, actress; b. London, England; d. Oct. 16, 1940 (79).

St. John, Richard, actor; d. Feb. 5, 1977.
St. Leo, Leonard, actor; b. May 1, 1894, England; d. Feb. 9, 1977 (82).
St. Maur, Adele, actress; d. Apr. 20, 1959 (71).
St. Pierre, Clara, actress; d. Jan. 30, 1942 (76).
St. Polis, John, actor; b. Nov. 24, 1873, New Orleans, La.; d. Oct. 8, 1946 (72).
Saintsbury, H.A., actor; b. Dec. 18, 1869, London, England; d. June 19, 1939 (69).
Sais, Marin, actress; b. Aug. 2, 1890, San Rafael, Calif.; d. Dec. 31, 1971 (81).
Sakall, S.Z. (r.n. Szoke Sakall), actor; b. Feb. 2, 1883, Budapest, Hungary; d. Feb. 12, 1955 (72).
Salas, Paco, actor; d. Dec. 24, 1964 (89).
Sale, Charles "Chic," actor; b. Aug. 25, 1885, Huron, S.D.; d. Nov. 7, 1936 (51).
Sale, Frances, actress; d. Aug. 6, 1969 (77).
Salfner, Heinz, actor; b. Dec. 31, 1877, Munich, Germany; d. Oct. 13, 1945 (67).
Salisbury, Monroe, actor; b. May 8, 1876, Angola, Erie Co., N.Y.; d. Aug. 6, 1935 (59).
Salou, Louis, actor; b. 1902, Quimper, France; d. Oct. 21, 1948 (46).
Salter, Harold "Hal," actor; b. Apr. 8, 1886, Atlanta, Ga.; d. May 9, 1928 (42).
Salter, Thelma, actress; d. Nov. 17, 1953 (44).
Salvaneschi, Mario, dancer; d. Apr. 26, 1977 (65).
Salvini, Alessandro, actor; b. Aug. 6, 1890, Pisa, Italy; d. July 24, 1955 (64).
Samberg, Anders W., director; b. May 22, 1887, Denmark; d. Mar. 27, 1938 (50).
Samper, Felix, actor; d. Sept. 23, 1957 (70).
Sampson, Teddy, actress; b. Aug. 8, 1898, New York; d. Nov. 24, 1970 (72).
Samson, Ivan, actor; b. Aug. 28, 1894, Brighton, England; d. May 1, 1963 (68).
Samuels, Maurice, actor; b. Jan. 13, 1885, Rumania; d. Aug. 1, 1964 (79).
Sanborn, Fred, actor; b. Nov. 23, 1899, Massachusetts; d. Mar. 9, 1961 (61).
Sande, Walter, actor; b. July 9, 1906, Denver, Colo.; d. Feb. 22, 1972 (65).
Sanders, George, actor; b. July 3, 1906, St. Petersburg, Russia; d. Apr. 25, 1972 (65).
Sanders, Hugh, actor; b. Mar. 13, 1911, Illinois; d. Jan. 9, 1966 (54).
Sanders, Scott, actor; d. Dec. 2, 1956 (68).
Sanderson, Julia, actress; b. Aug. 20, 1887, Springfield, Mass.; d. Jan. 27, 1975 (87).
Sanderson, Kent (see Roosevelt, Buddy)
Sandow, Eugene, circus strongman; b. Konigsberg, Germany; d. Oct. 14, 1925 (58).
Sandquist, Hans, actor; d. Feb. 23, 1935 (39).
Sandrich, Mark, director, producer, & author; b. Oct. 26, 1900, New York; d. Mar. 4, 1945 (44).
Sandrock, Adele, actress; b. Aug. 19, 1863, Rotterdam, Netherlands; d. Aug. 30, 1937 (74).

Sandrock, Wilhelmine, actress; b. Feb. 5, 1861, Rotterdam, Netherlands; d. Nov., 1948 (87).
Sands, Diana, actress; b. Aug. 22, 1934, New York City; d. Sept. 21, 1973 (39).
Sands, George, actor; d. Dec. 7, 1933 (33).
Sanford, Agnes, actress; d. Nov. 27, 1955 (46).
Sanford, Albert, actor; d. Feb. 10, 1953 (60).
Sanford, Erskine, actor; b. Nov. 19, 1885, Trinidad, Colo.; d. July 7, 1969 (83).
Sanford, Ralph, actor; b. May 21, 1899, Springfield, Mass.; d. June 20, 1963 (64).
Sanford, Stanley J., actor; b. Feb. 26, 1894, Osage, Iowa; d. Oct. 29, 1961 (67).
Sanger, Bert, actor; d. Aug., 1968 (74).
Sangster, Alfred, actor; b. June 15, 1880, Norwood, London, England; d. Aug., 1972 (92).
Sanquer, Dagmar Worth, actress; d. Dec. 31, 1957 (53).
Santamaria, Manuel, actor; d. 1960.
Santana, Vasco, actor; d. Aug., 1958 (68).
Santa Romano, Privitivo, actor; d. July, 1961.
Santley, Frederic, actor; b. Nov. 20, 1888; d. May 14, 1953 (64).
Santley, Joseph, actor & director; b. Jan. 10, 1889, Salt Lake City, Utah; d. Aug. 8, 1971 (82).
Santschi, Tom (r.n. Paul William Santschi), actor; b. Oct. 24, 1880, Missouri; d. Apr. 9, 1931 (50).
Sarecky, Barney, scenarist; b. May 7, 1895, New York City; d. Aug. 10, 1968 (73).
Sargent, Alfred Maxwell, actor; d. Jan., 1949 (68).
Sarner, Alexander, actor; b. Dec. 17, 1892, London, England; d. Jan. 6, 1948 (55).
Sarno, Hector V., actor; b. Apr. 24, 1880, Naples, Italy; d. Dec. 16, 1953 (73).
Sarrachini, Gerald, actor; d. Dec. 26, 1957 (30).
Sattler, Ernst, actor; b. Oct. 14, 1887, Munich, Germany; d. Jan. 3, 1974 (86).
Sauberlich, Lu, actress; b. Nov. 9, 1911, Bremen, Germany; d. Oct., 1976 (64).
Sauerman, Carl, actor; d. Apr. 9, 1924 (56).
Saum, Clifford, actor; b. Dec. 18, 1882, Columbus, Ohio; d. Mar. 5, 1943 (60).
Saunders, Alice, actress; b. Sept. 4, 1872, Holyoke, Mass.; d. July 25, 1953 (80).
Saunders, Jackie, actress; b. Oct. 6, 1897, Philadelphia, Pa.; d. July 14, 1954 (56).
Saunders, Mrs. Nellie Peck, actress; d. Mar. 3, 1942 (71).
Savage, May G., actress & opera singer; d. Apr. 18, 1963 (62).
Saville, Gus, actor; d. Mar. 25, 1934 (77).
Saville, Victor, director & producer; b. Sept. 25, 1895, Birmingham, England; d. May 8, 1979 (83).
Savitt, Jan, orchestra leader; d. Oct. 4, 1948 (35).
Savo, Jimmy, actor; d. Sept. 6, 1960 (64).
Savoie, Blanche, actress; d. Apr. 24, 1933 (45).
Savoy, Houston (see de Blasio, Gene)
Sawamura, Kunitaro, actor; d. Nov. 26, 1974 (69).
Sawyer, Laura, actress; d. Sept. 7, 1970 (85).

Saxe, Templar, actor; b. Redhill, Surrey, England; d. Apr. 17, 1935 (70).
Saxon, Hugh, actor; b. Jan. 14, 1869, New Orleans, La.; d. May 14, 1945 (76).
Saxon, Marie, actress; b. Lawrence, Mass.; d. Nov. 12, 1941 (37).
Saxon, Pauline, actress; d. Oct. 30, 1949 (65).
Saxon, Vin (see Haydock, Ron)
Sayles, Francis, actor; b. Nov. 22, 1891, Buffalo, N.Y.; d. Mar. 19, 1944 (52).
Saylor, Syd, actor; b. May 24, 1895, Chicago, Ill.; d. Dec. 21, 1962 (67).
Sayre, C. Bigelow (r.n. Chauncey Bigelow Sayre), actor; b. June 5, 1908, New Jersey; d. Sept. 14, 1975 (67).
Sayre, George Wallace, writer; d. Oct. 23, 1962 (59).
Sayre, Jeffrey, actor; d. Sept. 25, 1974 (73).
Sayre, Joel, writer; d. Sept. 9, 1979 (78).
Sayres, Margaret, actress; d. Apr. 17, 1937.
Sazarina, Maria, actress & dancer; d. Oct. 20, 1959 (45).
Scaduto, Joseph, actor; b. May 28, 1898, New York City; d. Oct. 19, 1943 (45).
Scala, Gia, actress; b. Mar. 3, 1935, Liverpool, England; d. Apr. 30, 1972 (37).
Scannell, William J., actor; b. Dec. 31, 1911, Massachusetts; d. July 8, 1963 (51).
Scardon, Paul, actor & director; b. May 6, 1874, Melbourne, Australia; d. Jan. 17, 1954 (79).
Schable, Robert, actor; b. Aug. 31, 1873, Hamilton, Ontario; d. July 3, 1947 (73).
Schacht, Gustave, actor; d. Oct. 8, 1943 (67).
Schade, Fritz, actor; b. 1880, Germany; d. June 17, 1926 (46).
Schaefer, Albert (r.n. Albert John Schaefer), actor; b. May 1, 1916, Galveston, Tex.; d. Oct. 26, 1942 (26).
Schaefer, Ann, actress; b. July 10, 1870, Missouri; d. May 3, 1957 (86).
Schaefer, Wilmo, actor; b. Sept. 28, 1917, Ludwigshafen, Germany; d. Nov. 24, 1941 (24).
Schaeffer, Charles N., actor; b. Feb. 12, 1863; d. Feb. 5, 1939 (75).
Schaeffers, Willi, actor; b. Sept. 2, 1884, Landsberg, Germany; d. Aug. 10, 1962 (77).
Schaffer, Sylvester, actor; d. June 20, 1949 (64).
Schafheitlin, Franz, actor; b. Aug. 9, 1895, Berlin, Germany; d. Feb. 6, 1980 (84).
Schallert, Edwin F., author; b. Apr. 16, 1890, Los Angeles, Calif.; d. Sept. 28, 1968 (78).
Scharff, Herman, actor; d. Apr. 8, 1963 (62).
Scharff, Lester (see Sharpe, Lester)
Scharpegge, Ernie, actor; d. Mar. 11, 1940 (42).
Schaufuss, Hans Joachim, actor; b. 1919; d. Oct. 27, 1941 (22).
Schauman, Runar, actor; d. Mar., 1977 (68).
Schayer, E. Richard, writer; d. Mar. 13, 1956 (75).
Scheff, Fritzi, actress & singer; b. Aug. 30, 1879, Vienna, Austria; d. Apr. 8, 1954 (74).
Schenck, Joe, actor; b. Brooklyn, N.Y.; d. June 28, 1930 (39).
Schenck, Joseph M., executive; b. Dec. 25, 1877, Russia; d. Oct. 22, 1961 (83).

Schenck, Nicholas, executive; b. Russia; d. Mar. 3, 1969 (87).
Schenstrom, Carl, actor; b. Nov. 13, 1881, Copenhagen, Denmark;
    d. Apr. 10, 1942 (60).
Scherman, Barbara, actress; d. Jan. 29, 1935.
Schertzinger, Victor, director; b. Apr. 8, 1890, Mahanoy City, Pa.;
    d. Oct. 26, 1941 (51).
Scheu, Just, actor; d. Aug. 9, 1956 (53).
Scheuer, Constance, actress; b. Nov. 5, 1910, Toledo, Ohio; d. Nov. 27,
    1962 (52).
Schier, Franz, opera singer; d. Jan. 14, 1954 (45).
Schieske, Alfred, actor; b. Sept. 6, 1908, Stuttgart, Germany;
    d. July 14, 1970 (61).
Schildkraut, Joseph, actor; b. Mar. 22, 1895, Vienna, Austria;
    d. Jan. 21, 1964 (68).
Schildkraut, Rudolph, actor; b. Apr. 27, 1862, Constantinople,
    Turkey; d. July 15, 1930 (68).
Schilling, Gus, actor; b. June 20, 1907, New York; d. June 16, 1957
    (49).
Schilling, Margaret, actress; d. July, 1976.
Schindel, Seymore, actor; d. Aug. 24, 1948 (41).
Schipa, Tito, opera singer & actor; b. Jan. 2, 1889, Lecce, Italy;
    d. Dec. 16, 1965 (76).
Schipper, Anna, extra; d. Oct. 16, 1978 (90).
Schlesinger, Leon, producer; b. Philadelphia, Pa.; d. Dec. 25, 1949
    (66).
Schluter-Weiner, Hilma, actress; b. Feb. 14, 1878, Munich, Germany;
    d. May, 1956 (78).
Schmidt, Albrecht, actor; b. Apr. 9, 1870, Copenhagen, Denmark;
    d. Mar. 5, 1945 (74).
Schmidt, Joseph, actor & opera singer; b. Mar. 4, 1904, Davidende,
    Rumania; d. Nov. 16, 1942 (38).
Schmidt, Robert, actor; b. Apr. 27, 1882, Copenhagen, Denmark;
    d. Nov. 17, 1941 (59).
Schmidt, Wolf, actor; d. Jan. 17, 1977 (64).
Schmitt, Joseph, actor; d. Mar. 25, 1935 (64).
Schmitz, Ludwig, actor; d. July, 1954 (70).
Schmitz, Sybille, actress; b. Dec. 2, 1909, Duren, Germany;
    d. Apr. 13, 1955 (45).
Schnee, Charles, writer; d. Nov. 29, 1962 (45).
Schneider, Hilde, actress; d. June, 1961.
Schneider, James, actor; b. Dec. 15, 1881, New York; d. Feb. 14,
    1967 (85).
Schneiderman, George, cinematographer; b. Sept. 20, 1894, New York;
    d. Nov. 19, 1964 (70).
Schoenhals, Albrecht, actor; b. Mar. 7, 1888, Mannheim, Germany;
    d. Dec. 4, 1978 (90).
Schofield, Johnnie, actor; b. 1889, London, England; d. Sept. 9,
    1955 (66).
Scholler, William F., actor; d. Sept. 12, 1946 (65).
Schonberg, Alexander, actor; d. Oct. 1, 1945 (59).
Schonberg, Ib, actor; b. Oct. 23, 1902, Copenhagen, Denmark;
    d. Sept. 24, 1955 (52).
Schopp, Herman, cinematographer & actor; d. Aug. 8, 1954 (55).
Schott, Werner, actor; b. Nov. 20, 1891; d. Sept., 1965 (73).
Schrader, Genevieve, actress; b. Mar. 4, 1889, Wisconsin; d. Sept. 5,
    1972 (83).

Schramm, Karla, actress; d. Jan. 17, 1980 (89).
Schramm, William, actor; d. Aug. 15, 1979 (74).
Schreck, Max, actor; b. Sept. 6, 1879, Berlin, Germany; d. Feb. 19, 1936 (56).
Schrecker, Frederick, actor; d. July 13, 1976 (83).
Schrock, Raymond L., writer; b. Goshen, Ind.; d. Dec. 12, 1950 (58).
Schroder-Schrom, Franz Wilhelm, actor; d. May, 1956 (77).
Schroff, William, actor; b. Feb. 25, 1889, Germany; d. Dec. 5, 1964 (75).
Schryver, Clinton, actor; d. Feb. 26, 1954 (72).
Schubert, Eddie (r.n. Edward Cizenowski), actor; b. July 11, 1894, Milwaukee, Wisc.; d. Jan. 23, 1937 (42).
Schulberg, B.P., producer; b. Jan. 19, 1892, Bridgeport, Conn.; d. Feb. 25, 1957 (65).
Schultz, Cecil E., actor; d. Sept. 2, 1953 (48).
Schultz, Harry, actor; b. Mar. 11, 1883, Germany; d. July 4, 1935 (52).
Schulz, Fritz, actor; d. May 9, 1972 (76).
Schumacher, Jerry, actor; b. Sept. 17, 1911, Minnesota; d. Jan. 11, 1975 (63).
Schumann-Heink, Ernestine, actress & opera singer; b. June 15, 1861, Lieben, Bohemia; d. Nov. 17, 1936 (75).
Schumann-Heink, Ferdinand, actor; b. Aug. 9, 1893, Hamburg, Germany; d. Sept. 15, 1958 (65).
Schumm, Harry W., actor; b. Sept. 27, 1877, Illinois; d. Apr. 4, 1953 (75).
Schunzel, Reinhold, actor & director; b. Nov. 7, 1886, Hamburg, Germany; d. Sept. 11, 1954 (67).
Schur, Willi, actor; b. Aug. 22, 1888, Breslau, Poland; d. Nov., 1940 (52).
Schutz, Maurice, actor; b. Aug. 4, 1866, Paris, France; d. Mar., 1955 (88).
Schwab, Laurence, director & writer; d. May 29, 1951 (57).
Schwamm, George S. (Tony), stuntman; d. Feb. 15, 1966 (63).
Schwannecke, Ellen, actress; d. June 16, 1972.
Schwartz, Maurice, actor; b. June 18, 1890, Sedikor, Russia; d. May 10, 1960 (69).
Schyberg, Robert, actor; b. July 8, 1872, Copenhagen, Denmark; d. Dec. 19, 1946 (74).
Scott, Adrian, writer & producer; b. Feb. 6, 1912, Arlington, N.J.; d. Dec. 25, 1972 (60).
Scott, Carrie, actress; b. 1870; d. Dec. 18, 1928 (58).
Scott, Cyril, actor; b. Feb. 9, 1866, Banbridge, Ireland; d. Aug. 16, 1945 (79).
Scott, Dick, actor; b. July 24, 1903, Indiana; d. Sept. 2, 1961 (58).
Scott, Frederick T., actor; d. Feb. 22, 1942.
Scott, Harold, actor; d. Apr. 15, 1964 (72).
Scott, Ivy, actress; d. Feb. 3, 1947 (61).
Scott, Kay, actress; b. Aug. 12, 1927, California; d. Jan. 1, 1971 (43).
Scott, Leslie, actor; d. Aug. 20, 1969 (48).
Scott, Mabel Julienne, actress; b. Nov. 2, 1892, Minneapolis, Minn.; d. Oct. 1, 1976 (83).
Scott, Markie, actor; d. July 4, 1958 (85).
Scott, Paul, actor; d. Nov. 24, 1944 (50).

Scott, Peggy, actress; d. Aug. 26, 1926.
Scott, Sherman (see Newfield, Sam)
Scott, Wallace, actor; b. Sept. 18, 1905, Australia; d. May 8, 1970
    (64).
Scott, Walter F., actor; d. Mar. 5, 1940 (61).
Scott, Zachary, actor; b. Feb. 24, 1914, Austin, Tex.; d. Oct. 3,
    1965 (51).
Scott-Gatty, Alexander, actor; b. Oct. 3, 1876, Ecclesfield,
    Yorkshire, England; d. Nov. 6, 1937 (61).
Scudamore, Margaret, actress; b. Nov. 13, 1884, Portsmouth, England;
    d. Oct. 5, 1958 (73).
Seabury, Forrest, actor; d. Feb. 15, 1944 (68).
Seabury, Inez, actress; b. June 26, 1907, Oregon; d. Apr. 11, 1973
    (65).
Seal, Peter, actor; d. Oct. 11, 1959 (67).
Sealy, Lewis A., actor; d. Mar. 19, 1931 (80).
Seaman, Earl, actor; b. Jan. 24, 1897, Wisconsin; d. Mar. 6, 1961
    (64).
Seaman, Marjorie, actress; b. June 21, 1900, Pennsylvania; d. Mar. 9,
    1923 (22).
Searle, Kamuela C. (r.n. Samuel Cooper Searle), actor; b. Aug. 29,
    1890, Hawaii; d. Feb. 14, 1924 (33).
Searles, Cora B., actress; d. Mar. 4, 1935 (73).
Sears, Allan (Alfred Sears), actor; b. Mar. 9, 1887, Texas;
    d. Aug. 18, 1942 (55).
Sears, Mrs. Blanche, actress; b. Aug. 29, 1870, Waterford, Pa.;
    d. Aug. 7, 1939 (68).
Sears, Eleanor, actress; b. Jan. 8, 1913, New York City; d. June 19,
    1936 (23).
Sears, Fred F. (r.n. Frederic Francis Sears), actor & director;
    b. July 7, 1912, Boston, Mass.; d. Nov. 30, 1957 (45).
Sears, Zelda, actress & author; b. Jan. 21, 1873, Brockway, Mich.;
    d. Feb. 19, 1935 (62).
Seastrom, Dorothy, actress; d. July, 1930.
Seastrom, Victor, director & actor; b. Sept. 20, 1879, Silbodal,
    Sweden; d. Jan. 3, 1960 (80).
Seaton, George, director & author; b. Apr. 17, 1911, South Bend,
    Ind.; d. July 28, 1979 (68).
Seaton, Scott (r.n. Horace Scott Seaton), actor; b. Mar. 11, 1871,
    Sacramento, Calif.; d. June 3, 1968 (97).
Seaton, Walter, director; d. Sept., 1952 (80).
Sebastian, Dorothy, actress; b. Birmingham, Ala.; d. Apr. 8, 1957
    (52).
Seberg, Jean, actress; b. Nov. 13, 1938, Marshalltown, Iowa;
    d. Aug. 30, 1979 (40).
Seddon, Margaret (r.n. Marguerite H.W. Sloan), actress; b. Nov. 18,
    1872, Washington, D.C.; d. Apr. 17, 1968 (95).
Sedgwick, Edie, actress; d. Nov. 16, 1971 (28).
Sedgwick, Edward, director & actor; b. Nov. 7, 1892, Galveston, Tex.;
    d. May 7, 1953 (60).
Sedgwick, Josie, actress; b. Mar. 13, 1898, Texas; d. Apr. 30, 1973
    (75).
Seeck, Adelheid, actress; b. Nov. 3, 1912, Berlin, Germany; d. Feb.,
    1973 (60).
Seed, David, actor; b. July 8, 1888, New York City; d. Nov. 3, 1960
    (72).

Seel, Jeanne N., actress; b. July 16, 1898, New York; d. Sept. 9, 1964 (66).

Seeley, Blossom, actress; b. July 16, 1891, San Francisco, Calif.; d. Apr. 17, 1974 (82).

Seff, Manuel, writer; b. June 6, 1895, Baltimore, Md.; d. Sept. 22, 1969 (74).

Sefton, Ernest, actor; d. Dec. 5, 1954 (71).

Segall, Harry, writer; b. Apr. 10, 1897, Chicago, Ill.; d. Nov. 25, 1975 (78).

Segarra, Consuelo, actress; d. Apr. 28, 1946 (70).

Seger, Lucia Backus, actress; d. Jan. 17, 1962 (88).

Segura, Leticia Espinosa, actress; d. Dec. 26, 1956.

Seidewitz, Marie, actress; d. Dec. 27, 1929.

Seidler, Alma, actress; d. Dec. 8, 1977 (78).

Seidner, Irene, actress; b. Dec. 10, 1880, Austria; d. Nov. 17, 1959 (78).

Seiler, Lewis, director; d. Jan. 8, 1964 (73).

Seiter, William A., director & actor; b. June 10, 1892, New York City; d. July 26, 1964 (72).

Seitz, George B., director & actor; b. Jan. 3, 1888, Boston, Mass.; d. July 8, 1944 (56).

Sekely, Steve, director; b. Feb. 25, 1899, Budapest, Hungary; d. Mar. 9, 1979 (80).

Selander, Lesley, director; d. Dec. 5, 1979 (79).

Selbie, Evelyn, actress; b. July 6, 1871, Ohio; d. Dec. 6, 1950 (79).

Selby, Norman, actor; b. Oct. 13, 1873, Rush Co., Ind.; d. Apr. 18, 1940 (66).

Selby, Sarah, actress; b. St. Louis, Mo.; d. Jan. 7, 1980 (74).

Self, Margaret Callahan, actress; d. Nov. 29, 1947 (57).

Selig, William N., executive & producer; d. July 16, 1948 (84).

Selk, George, actor; b. May 15, 1893, Nebraska; d. Jan. 22, 1967 (73).

Sellon, Charles, actor; b. Aug. 24, 1870, Boston, Mass.; d. June 26, 1937 (66).

Selpin, Herbert, director; d. July 31, 1942.

Selten, Morton, actor; b. Jan. 6, 1860; d. July 27, 1939 (79).

Selwyn, Edgar, actor, author, & producer; b. Oct. 20, 1875, Cincinnati, Ohio; d. Feb. 13, 1944 (68).

Selwyn, Ruth, actress; b. Nov. 6, 1905, Tazwell, Va.; d. Dec. 13, 1954 (49).

Selwynne, Clarissa, actress; b. London, England; d. June 13, 1948.

Selznick, David O., producer; b. May 10, 1902, Pittsburgh, Pa.; d. June 22, 1965 (63).

Selznick, Lewis J., producer; d. Jan. 25, 1933 (62).

Semels, Harry, actor; b. Nov. 20, 1887, New York City; d. Mar. 2, 1946 (58).

Semon, Larry, actor; b. July 16, 1889, West Point, Miss.; d. Oct. 8, 1928 (39).

Sennett, Mack, director, producer, & actor; b. Jan. 17, 1880, Danville, Quebec, Canada; d. Nov. 5, 1960 (80).

Seragnoli, Oreste, actor; b. July 10, 1883, Italy; d. Apr. 13, 1965 (81).

Serda, Julia, actress; d. Nov. 3, 1965 (90).

Serling, Rod, author; b. Dec. 25, 1924, Syracuse, N.Y.; d. June 28, 1975 (50).

Serrano, Vincent, actor; b. Feb. 17, 1866, New York City; d. Jan. 10, 1935 (68).

Serret, Virginia, actress; d. May 2, 1958.
Sertel, Necla, actress; d. Dec., 1969 (68).
Servaes, Dagny, actress; b. Mar. 10, 1897, Berlin, Germany; d. July, 1961 (64).
Servais, Jean, actor; b. Sept. 24, 1910, Angers, Belgium; d. Feb. 22, 1976 (65).
Servoss, Mary, actress; b. Chicago, Ill.; d. Nov. 20, 1968 (80).
Sessions, Almira, actress; b. Sept. 16, 1888, Washington, D.C.; d. Aug. 3, 1974 (85).
Seton, Bruce, actor; b. May 29, 1909, Simla, India; d. Sept. 27, 1969 (60).
Seton, Violet, actress; b. Mar. 25, 1882, Woodford, England; d. Jan. 28, 1970 (87).
Seval, Nevin, actress; d. Nov., 1958 (38).
Severin-Mars, M., actor; b. 1873, Bordeaux, France; d. July 17, 1921 (48).
Sevor, Alfred, actor; d. Mar. 26, 1953 (62).
Sewall, Allen D. (r.n. Allen Devereaux Sewall), actor; b. July 23, 1882, Massachusetts; d. Jan. 20, 1954 (71).
Sewall, Lucile, actress; d. Dec. 15, 1976 (88).
Seward, Edmond, writer; d. Feb. 12, 1954 (63).
Seyferth, Wilfried, actor; b. Apr. 21, 1908, Darmstadt, Germany; d. Oct. 9, 1954 (46).
Seymour, Clarine, actress; d. Apr. 25, 1920 (20).
Seymour, Harry, actor & composer; b. June 22, 1891, New York; d. Nov. 11, 1967 (76).
Seymour, Jane, actress; b. Hamilton, Ontario, Canada; d. Jan. 30, 1956 (57).
Shackelford, Floyd, actor; b. Sept. 7, 1905, Iowa; d. Dec. 17, 1972 (67).
Shackleton, Robert, actor; b. Lawrence, Mass.; d. June 21, 1956 (42).
Shade, Jamesson, actor; b. Nov. 23, 1895, New York; d. Apr. 17, 1956 (60).
Shadle, Jackson, actor; b. May 29, 1881; d. Feb. 5, 1969 (87).
Shadow, Bert, actor; d. Nov. 12, 1936 (46).
Shafer, Molly, actress; d. Nov. 19, 1940 (68).
Shaffner, Mrs. Lillian, actress; d. Jan. 10, 1930 (69).
Shaiffer, Charles, actor; d. Jan. 24, 1967 (49).
Shain, John Howard, actor; d. Dec. 6, 1979 (76).
Shall, Theo, actor; d. Oct. 4, 1955 (60).
Shamroy, Leon, cinematographer; b. July 16, 1901, New York City; d. July 7, 1974 (72).
Shank, Arthur (see Baker, Art)
Shanks, John, actor; d. Apr. 17, 1956 (60).
Shanley, Robert, actor; d. June 30, 1968.
Shannon, Cora, actress; b. Jan. 30, 1869, Illinois; d. Aug. 27, 1957 (88).
Shannon, Mrs. Dale, actress; d. June 1, 1923.
Shannon, Effie, actress; b. May 13, 1867, Cambridge, Mass.; d. July 24, 1954 (87).
Shannon, Ethel, actress; b. May 22, 1898, Colorado; d. July 10, 1951 (53).
Shannon, Frank, actor; b. July 27, 1874, Ireland; d. Feb. 1, 1959 (84).
Shannon, Harry, actor; b. June 13, 1890, Saginaw, Mich.; d. July 27, 1964 (74).

Shannon, Jack (r.n. Jack L. Tyler), actor & stuntman; b. Aug. 31,
    1892, Ohio; d. Dec. 27, 1968 (76).
Shannon, Peggy, actress; b. Jan. 10, 1907, Pine Bluff, Ark.;
    d. May 11, 1941 (34).
Shannon, Ray, actor; d. Jan. 1, 1971 (76).
Shanor, Peggy, actress; d. May 30, 1935 (39).
Sharland, Reginald, actor; b. Nov. 19, 1886, Southend-on-Sea,
    England; d. Aug. 21, 1944 (57).
Sharp, Henry, actor; d. Jan. 10, 1964 (77).
Sharp, Leonard, actor; d. Oct. 24, 1958 (68).
Sharp, Ramona, actress; d. Apr. 26, 1941 (39).
Sharpe, Lester, actor; b. Mar. 21, 1895, New York City; d. Nov. 30,
    1962 (67).
Sharplin, John, actor; d. Apr., 1961 (45).
Shattuck, Edward F., actor; d. Jan. 31, 1948 (58).
Shattuck, Ethel, actress; d. Jan. 25, 1963 (73).
Shattuck, Truly, actress; b. July 27, 1876, San Miguel, Calif.;
    d. Dec. 6, 1954 (78).
Shaw, Albert, actor; d. July 7, 1957 (66).
Shaw, Bud, actor; d. Aug. 29, 1976 (70).
Shaw, C. Montague (r.n. Charles Montague Shaw), actor; b. Mar. 23,
    1882, Adelaide, Australia; d. Feb. 6, 1968 (85).
Shaw, Denis, actor; b. Apr. 7, 1921, Dulwich; d. Feb. 28, 1971 (49).
Shaw, Frank M., actor; d. May 7, 1937 (43).
Shaw, Harold (r.n. Henry Marvin Shaw), actor & director; b. Nov. 3,
    1877, Tennessee; d. Jan. 30, 1926 (48).
Shaw, Oscar, actor; d. Mar. 6, 1967 (76).
Shaw, Robert, actor & author; b. Aug. 9, 1927, England; d. Aug. 28,
    1978 (51).
Shaw, Susan, actress; b. Aug. 29, 1929, London, England; d. Nov. 27,
    1978 (49).
Shawn, Philip (see Waltz, Patrick)
Shawzin, Barry, actor; d. Mar. 28, 1968 (38).
Shay, Dorothy, actress & singer; d. Oct. 22, 1978 (57).
Shay, Patricia, actress; b. June 10, 1922, Illinois; d. Aug. 9,
    1966 (44).
Shay, Rose Cecilia; d. June 4, 1929.
Shayne, Konstantin, actor; b. Nov. 29, 1888, Russia; d. Nov. 15,
    1974 (85).
Shchukin, Boris V., actor; b. Apr. 17, 1894, Moscow, Russia;
    d. Oct. 7, 1939 (45).
Shea, Bird, actress; d. Nov. 23, 1924.
Shea, Jack, actor; b. Apr. 24, 1913, Rockford, Ill.; d. July 17, 1972
    (59).
Shea, William J., actor; d. Nov. 5, 1918 (56).
Shean, Al, actor; b. May 12, 1868, Dornum, Germany; d. Aug. 12, 1949
    (81).
Shear, Barry, director; b. Mar. 23, 1923, New York City; d. June 13,
    1979 (56).
Shearer, Douglas, sound recorder; b. Westmount, Quebec, Canada;
    d. Jan. 5, 1971 (70).
Sheehan, Jack, actor; b. Oct. 22, 1890, Manchester, N.H.; d. Dec. 11,
    1958 (68).
Sheehan, John J., actor; b. Oct. 22, 1885, Oakland, Calif.; d. Feb. 15,
    1952 (66).

Sheehan, Perley Poore, writer; d. Sept. 30, 1943 (69).
Sheehan, Winfield R., producer; b. Sept. 24, 1883, New York City;
    d. July 25, 1945 (61).
Sheer, William A., actor; b. Birmingham, England; d. July 10, 1933.
Sheerer, Will, actor; d. Dec. 24, 1915.
Sheffield, Leo, actor; b. Nov. 15, 1873, Malton, Yorkshire, England;
    d. Sept. 3, 1951 (77).
Sheffield, Maceo Bruce, actor; b. Sept. 8, 1897, Texas; d. Aug. 20,
    1959 (61).
Sheffield, Reginald (r.n. Matthew Reginald Sheffield-Cassan), actor;
    b. Feb. 18, 1901, London, England; d. Dec. 8, 1957 (56).
Shelby, Margaret, actress; b. San Antonio, Tex.; d. Dec. 21, 1939
    (39).
Sheldon, Connie, actress; d. Jan. 10, 1947 (26).
Sheldon, Jerome, actor; b. Aug. 13, 1890, Ohio; d. Apr. 15, 1962 (71).
Sheldon, Jerry (Charles H. Patton), actor; b. Mar. 6, 1901, Missouri;
    d. Apr. 11, 1962 (61).
Sheldon, Kathryn, actress; b. Sept. 22, 1879, Cincinnati, Ohio;
    d. Dec. 25, 1975 (96).
Sheldon, Marion W., actress; b. May 3, 1885, Cambridge, Mass.;
    d. Feb. 28, 1944 (58).
Shelton, Don, actor; d. June 19, 1976 (64).
Shelton, George, actor; d. Feb. 12, 1971 (87).
Shelton, James, actor; d. Sept. 2, 1975 (62).
Shelton, John, actor; b. May 18, 1914, Los Angeles, Calif.;
    d. May 16, 1972 (57).
Shelton, Violet, actress; d. Jan. 3, 1970 (77).
Shepherd, William H., actor & film editor; d. July 10, 1979 (85).
Shepley, Michael, actor; b. Sept. 29, 1907, Plymouth, England;
    d. Sept. 28, 1961 (53).
Shepley, Ruth, actress; b. May 29, 1892, Providence, R.I.; d. Oct. 16,
    1951 (59).
Sheppard, Bert, actor; d. Aug. 18, 1929 (47).
Sheppard, Jim, stuntman; d. Aug. 18, 1977 (40).
Sherart, Georgia, actress; d. Jan. 24, 1929 (67).
Sheridan, Ann, actress; b. Feb. 21, 1915, Denton, Tex.; d. Jan. 21,
    1967 (51).
Sheridan, Cecil, actor; d. Jan. 4, 1980 (70).
Sheridan, Dan (r.n. Daniel M. Sheridan), actor; b. Sept. 3, 1916,
    Ireland; d. June 29, 1963 (46).
Sheridan, Frank, actor; b. June 11, 1869, Boston, Mass.; d. Nov. 24,
    1943 (74).
Sherman, Adah, actress; d. May 12, 1942 (81).
Sherman, Evelyn, actress; b. Dec. 13, 1882, Iowa; d. Apr. 19, 1974
    (91).
Sherman, Fred E., actor; d. May 20, 1969 (64).
Sherman, Harry, producer; b. Nov. 5, 1884, Boston, Mass.; d. Sept. 25,
    1952 (67).
Sherman, Lowell, actor & director; b. Oct. 11, 1888, San Francisco,
    Calif.; d. Dec. 28, 1934 (46).
Sherriff, Robert C., writer; b. June 6, 1896, Kingston-on-Thames,
    Sur., England; d. Nov. 13, 1975 (79).
Sherry, J. Barney, actor; d. Feb. 23, 1944 (72).
Sherwood, Clarence L., actor; b. Jan. 5, 1884, Shiloh, La.;
    d. Jan. 15, 1941 (57).

Sherwood, Millige G. (r.n. Millige Grassie Sherwood), actor;
    b. Apr. 24, 1876, Los Angeles, Calif.; d. Nov. 12, 1958 (82).
Sherwood, Robert E., writer & playwright; b. Apr., 1896, New
    Rochelle, N.Y.; d. Nov. 12, 1955 (59).
Sherwood, Yorke, actor; b. Dec. 14, 1873, England; d. Sept. 27, 1958
    (84).
Shields, Arthur, actor; b. Feb. 15, 1896, Dublin, Ireland; d. Apr. 27,
    1970 (74).
Shields, Ella, actress; d. Aug. 5, 1952 (72).
Shields, Frank (r.n. Francis X. Shields), actor; b. Nov. 18, 1910;
    d. Aug. 20, 1975 (64).
Shields, Helen, actress; d. Aug. 7, 1963.
Shields, Sandy, actor; d. Aug. 3, 1923 (50).
Shields, Sydney, actress; b. New Orleans, La.; d. Sept. 19, 1960 (72).
Shindo, Eitaro, actor; d. Dec. 24, 1977 (78).
Shine, Wilfred, actor; b. July 12, 1864, Manchester, England;
    d. Mar. 14, 1939 (74).
Shiner, Ronald, actor; b. June 8, 1903, London, England; d. June 30,
    1966 (63).
Shipman, Nell, actress, producer, & author; b. Oct. 25, 1892, British
    Columbia, Canada; d. Jan. 23, 1970 (77).
Shirley, Arthur, author & actor; b. Feb. 17, 1853, London, England;
    d. Aug. 22, 1925 (72).
Shirley, Florence, actress; b. June 5, 1892, New York; d. May 12,
    1967 (74).
Shirley, Tom, actor; d. Jan. 24, 1962 (62).
Shoemaker, Ann, actress; b. Jan. 10, 1891, Brooklyn, N.Y.; d. Sept. 18,
    1978 (87).
Shooting Star, actor; d. June 4, 1966 (76).
Shores, Byron L., actor; d. Nov. 13, 1957 (50).
Short, Antrim (r.n. Mark Antrim Short), actor; b. July 11, 1900,
    Ohio; d. Nov. 24, 1972 (72).
Short, Florence, actress; d. July 10, 1946 (57).
Short, Gertrude (r.n. Carmen Gertrude Short), actress; b. Apr. 6,
    1902, Cincinnati, Ohio; d. July 31, 1968 (66).
Short, Harry, actor; d. Aug. 17, 1943 (67).
Short, Hassard, director & actor; b. Oct. 15, 1877, Eddington,
    England; d. Oct. 9, 1956 (78).
Short, Lew, actor; b. Feb. 14, 1875, Dayton, Ohio; d. Apr. 26,
    1958 (83).
Shotwell, Marie, actress; b. New York City; d. Sept. 18, 1934 (54).
Shoulters, Mabelle, actress; b. Dec. 10, 1871, Crown Point, Indiana;
    d. July 11, 1942 (70).
Shtraukh, Maxim, actor; d. Jan. 3, 1974 (73).
Shukshin, Vasily, director; d. Oct. 2, 1974 (45).
Shuman, Roy, actor; d. July 30, 1973 (48).
Shumlin, Herman, director; d. June 4, 1979 (80).
Shumway, Lee, actor; b. Mar. 4, 1884, Salt Lake City, Utah; d. Jan. 4,
    1959 (74).
Shumway, Walter, actor; b. Aug. 26, 1884, Cleveland, Ohio; d. Jan. 13,
    1965 (80).
Shunmugham, T.K., actor; b. Apr. 26, 1911, Sudan; d. Mar., 1973 (61).
Shutta, Ethel, actress; d. Feb. 5, 1976 (79).
Shutta, Jack, actor; d. June 28, 1957 (58).
Shy, Gus, actor; b. May 28, 1903, Buffalo, N.Y.; d. June 15, 1945 (42).

Sidney, George, actor; b. Mar. 15, 1877, Nagynichal, Hungary;
    d. Apr. 29, 1945 (68).
Sidney, Mabel, actress; d. Oct. 18, 1969 (85).
Sidney, Scott, producer & actor; d. July 20, 1928 (56).
Siegel, Bernard, actor; b. Apr. 19, 1868, Austria; d. July 9, 1940
    (72).
Siegmann, George, actor; b. Feb. 8, 1882, New York; d. June 22, 1928
    (46).
Sielanski, Stanley, actor; d. Apr. 28, 1955.
Sierra, Margarita, actress; b. Dec. 31, 1936, Spain; d. Sept. 6,
    1963 (26).
Sigaloff, Eugene, actor; b. Feb. 24, 1887, Russia; d. Jan. 13, 1960
    (72).
Signoret, Gabriel, actor; d. Mar. 16, 1937 (64).
Signoret, Jean, actor; b. 1885, Cavaillon, France; d. Oct. 10, 1923
    (38).
Sigueiros, Placido (r.n. Placido Sicairios), actor; b. Oct. 10,
    1861, Sinaloa, Mexico; d. Dec. 19, 1946 (85).
Silbert, Lisa, actress; d. Nov. 29, 1965 (85).
Siletti, Mario, actor; b. July 22, 1903, Italy; d. Apr. 19, 1964 (60).
Sills, Milton, actor; b. Jan. 12, 1882, Chicago, Ill.; d. Sept. 15,
    1930 (48).
Silva, Antonio Joao, actor; d. Jan. 31, 1954 (84).
Silva, David, actor; d. Sept. 21, 1976 (60).
Silva, Simone, actress; d. Dec. 1, 1957 (29).
Silvani, Aldo, actor; b. Jan. 21, 1892, Torino, Italy; d. Nov. 12,
    1964 (72).
Silver, Christine, actress; d. Nov. 23, 1960 (75).
Silver, Pauline, actress; b. Feb. 13, 1888, South Dakota; d. Jan. 2,
    1969 (80).
Silvera, Frank, actor; b. July 24, 1914, Jamaica; d. June 11, 1970
    (55).
Silverheels, Jay, actor; d. Mar. 5, 1980 (62).
Silvern, Charles, actor; b. Sept., 1902; d. Apr. 1, 1979 (76).
Silvernail, Clarke, author & actor; d. Sept. 22, 1930 (37).
Silvers, Sid, actor & author; b. Jan. 1, 1904 (cert.: 1907),
    Brooklyn, N.Y.; d. Aug. 20, 1976 (72).
Silverwood, Don, actor; d. Jan. 10, 1928.
Sim, Alastair, actor; b. Oct. 9, 1900, Edinburgh, Scotland;
    d. Aug. 19, 1976 (75).
Sima, Oskar, actor; b. July 31, 1900; d. June, 1969 (68).
Simanek, Otto, actor; d. Oct. 15, 1967 (66).
Simon, Abe, actor & boxer; d. Oct. 24, 1969 (56).
Simon, Michel, actor; b. Apr. 9, 1895, Geneva, Switzerland;
    d. May 30, 1975 (80).
Simon, S. Sylvan, director & actor; b. Mar. 9, 1910, Chicago, Ill.;
    d. May 17, 1951 (41).
Simon, Sol S., actor; b. Dec. 15, 1864, Sacramento, Calif.; d. Apr.
    24, 1940 (75).
Simonds, Annette, actress; b. England; d. Oct. 28, 1959 (41).
Simon-Girard, Aime, actor; b. 1889, Paris, France; d. June, 1950 (61).
Simonov, Nikolai, actor; d. Apr., 1973 (71).
Simpson, Fanny, actress; d. Oct. 17, 1961.
Simpson, Grant M., actor; d. Jan. 5, 1932 (47).
Simpson, Ivan, actor; b. Feb. 4, 1875, Glasgow, Scotland; d. Oct. 12,
    1951 (76).
Simpson, Reginald, writer; d. Nov. 12, 1964 (68).

Simpson, Ronald, actor; b. Sept. 27, 1896, Acton, England; d. Sept. 23, 1957 (60).

Simpson, Russell, actor; b. June 17, 1880, California; d. Dec. 12, 1959 (79).

Sinaz, Guglielmo, actor; b. Nov. 20, 1885, Rome, Italy; d. Feb. 5, 1947 (61).

Sinclair, Arthur, actor; b. Aug. 3, 1883, Dublin, Ireland; d. Dec. 14, 1951 (68).

Sinclair, Daisy, actress; d. Jan. 14, 1929 (51).

Sinclair, Edward, actor; d. Aug. 29, 1977 (63).

Sinclair, Horace, actor; d. Feb. 19, 1949 (65).

Sinclair, Hugh, actor; b. May 19, 1903, London, England; d. Dec. 29, 1962 (59).

Sinclair, John W., actor & stuntman; b. Jan. 6, 1900, Memphis, Tenn.; d. Feb. 13, 1945 (45).

Sinclair, Robert B., director; b. Mar. 24, 1905, Ohio; d. Jan. 3, 1970 (64).

Singer, Campbell, actor; b. Mar. 16, 1909, London, England; d. Mar., 1976 (66).

Singh, Sarain, actor; d. Apr. 14, 1952 (64).

Singleton, Catherine, actress; d. Sept. 9, 1969 (65).

Sin-nui, Hung, actress; d. Sept., 1966 (46).

Sinoel, actor; b. France; d. Aug. 31, 1949 (81).

Siodmak, Robert, director; b. Aug. 8, 1900, Memphis, Tenn.; d. Mar. 10, 1973 (72).

Sipperley, Ralph, actor; d. Jan. 9, 1928 (38).

Sisson, Vera, actress; b. July 31, 1891, Colorado; d. Aug. 6, 1954 (63).

Sjostrand, Arnold, actor; b. June 30, 1903, Stockholm, Sweden; d. Feb. 1, 1955 (51).

Skelly, Hal, actor; b. May 31, 1891, Allegheny, Pa.; d. June 16, 1934 (43).

Skelly, James, actor; d. Apr. 19, 1969 (33).

Sketchley, Leslie, actor; b. Aug. 17, 1902, England; d. Oct. 14, 1972 (70).

Skillan, George, actor; b. Oct. 3, 1893, Woodford, Essex, England; d. Apr., 1975 (81).

Skinner, Cornelia Otis, actress; b. May 30, 1901, Chicago, Ill.; d. July 9, 1979 (78).

Skinner, Frank, composer; b. Dec. 31, 1898, Meredosia, Ill.; d. Oct. 8, 1968 (69).

Skinner, Otis, actor; b. June 28, 1858, Cambridge, Mass.; d. Jan. 4, 1942 (83).

Skipworth, Alison, actress; b. July 25, 1863, London, England; d. July 5, 1952 (88).

Skoda, Albin, actor; b. Sept. 29, 1909, Vienna, Austria; d. Sept. 22, 1961 (51).

Skouras, Spyros, executive; d. Aug. 16, 1971 (78).

Slack, Freddie, jazz pianist; b. Aug. 7, 1910, La Crosse, Wisc.; d. Aug. 10, 1965 (55).

Slade, Olga, actress; d. Apr. 24, 1949.

Slater, John, actor; b. Aug. 22, 1916, London, England; d. Jan. 9, 1975 (58).

Slater, Robert S. (Bob), actor; d. June 20, 1930 (61).

Slaughter, Tod, actor; b. Mar. 19, 1885, Newcastle-on-Tyne, England; d. Feb. 19, 1956 (70).

Slavin, John, actor; d. Aug. 27, 1940 (71).

Slavin, Jose, actor; d. Jan., 1978 (44).

Sleeman, Philip, actor; b. Feb. 28, 1891, England; d. Sept. 19, 1953 (62).

Sleep 'n' Eat (see Best, Willie)

Sleight, Orme (Sock), stuntman; d. Sept. 17, 1933 (16).

Slesinger, Tess, writer; d. Feb. 21, 1945 (39).

Slezak, Leo, actor & opera singer; b. Aug. 18, 1872, Moravia; d. June 6, 1946 (73).

Slezak, Margarete, actress & opera singer; d. Aug. 30, 1953 (52).

Sloan, William Hope, actor; d. Jan. 12, 1933 (69).

Sloane, Everett, actor; b. Oct. 1, 1909, New York City; d. Aug. 6, 1965 (55).

Sloane, Olive, actress; d. June 28, 1963 (67).

Sloane, Paul, director; b. Apr. 16, 1893, New York City; d. Nov. 15, 1963 (70).

Slocum, Tex, stuntman; d. Jan. 18, 1963 (61).

Sloman, Edward, director; b. July 19, 1883, London, England; d. Sept. 29, 1972 (89).

Sloman, Hylda Hallis, actress; b. July 10, 1891, Pennsylvania; d. Dec. 9, 1961 (70).

Slott, Nate D., assistant director & actor; d. Sept. 26, 1963 (58).

Small, Edward, producer; b. Feb. 1, 1891, Brooklyn, N.Y.; d. Jan. 25, 1977 (85).

Smalley, Phillips, actor & director; b. Aug. 7, 1865, Brooklyn, N.Y.; d. May 2, 1939 (73).

Smallwood, Ray, director; d. Feb. 23, 1964 (76).

Smart, H.F., actor; d. July 22, 1923 (78).

Smart, J. Scott, actor; d. Jan. 15, 1960 (57).

Smart, Jack (see Smart, J. Scott)

Smedley, Henry, actor; d. July 31, 1932.

Smelker, Mary, actress; d. June 2, 1933 (24).

Smeraldo, Ida, actress; b. Feb. 18, 1898, Italy; d. Sept. 20, 1964 (66).

Smiley, Joseph, actor & director; d. Dec. 2, 1945 (64).

Smiley, Ralph, actor; d. Sept. 14, 1977 (62).

Smirnova, Dina, actress; b. Feb. 24, 1889, Russia; d. Jan. 16, 1947 (57).

Smith, Albert E., director; d. Aug. 1, 1958 (83).

Smith, Albert J. (r.n. Albert Jones Smith), actor; b. Feb. 15, 1894, Chicago, Ill.; d. Apr. 11, 1939 (45).

Smith, Art, actor; d. Feb. 24, 1973 (73).

Smith, Arthur T., actor; d. Apr. 14, 1958 (79).

Smith, Beatrice Lieb, actress; d. Aug. 6, 1942 (80).

Smith, Bessie, singer; b. Apr. 15, 1895, Chattanooga, Tenn.; d. Sept. 26, 1937 (42).

Smith, Sir C. Aubrey, actor; b. July 21, 1863, London, England; d. Dec. 20, 1948 (85).

Smith, Charles H., actor; d. July 11, 1942 (76).

Smith, Charles Wilfred, singer; d. July 23, 1971 (74).

Smith, Clifford S., director; d. Sept. 17, 1937 (51).

Smith, Cyril, actor & singer; d. Jan. 8, 1950 (46).

Smith, Cyril, actor; b. Apr. 4, 1892, Peterhead, Scotland; d. Mar. 5, 1963 (70).

Smith, Dwight, actor; d. May 30, 1949 (92).

Smith, Edward I. "Gunboat," actor; b. Dec. 12, 1887, Philadelphia,
    Pa.; d. Feb. 16, 1934 (46).
Smith, Frederick Wilson, actor; d. July 13, 1944 (64).
Smith, G. Albert, actor; b. Louisville, Ky.; d. Sept. 3, 1959 (61).
Smith, George W., actor; d. Nov. 18, 1947 (48).
Smith, Gerald Oliver, actor; b. June 26, 1892, London, England;
    d. May 28, 1974 (81).
Smith, "Gunboat" (see Smith, Edward I.)
Smith, Harold Jacob, author; b. July 2, 1912, New York; d. Dec. 28,
    1970 (58).
Smith, Harry Walter, actor; d. Oct. 25, 1967 (56).
Smith, Howard, actor; b. Aug. 12, 1894, Attleboro, Mass.; d. Jan. 10,
    1968 (73).
Smith, J. Lewis, actor & standin; b. May 24, 1906, Ohio; d. Sept. 11,
    1964 (58).
Smith, Jack, actor; d. Jan. 14, 1944 (48).
Smith, Jess, actor; d. Apr. 11, 1965 (68).
Smith, Joe, actor; d. May 5, 1952 (52).
Smith, Leonard L., actor; d. May, 1942 (58).
Smith, Leonard R., actor; d. July 9, 1958.
Smith, Margaret M., actress; b. July 9, 1881, England; d. Dec. 9,
    1960 (79).
Smith, Mark, actor; d. May 10, 1944 (58).
Smith, Matthew, actor; d. Mar. 16, 1953 (48).
Smith, Oscar, actor; b. Oct. 28, 1885, Kansas; d. Mar. 18, 1956 (70).
Smith, Paul Gerard, writer; d. Apr. 4, 1968 (73).
Smith, Pete, producer; b. Sept. 4, 1892, New York City; d. Jan. 12,
    1979 (86).
Smith, Pleasant, actor & wrestler; d. Mar. 12, 1969 (83).
Smith, Queenie, actress; b. Sept. 8, 1902, New York City; d. Aug. 15,
    1878 (75).
Smith, Richard H., scenarist; b. Sept. 17, 1886, Cleveland, Ohio;
    d. Feb. 7, 1937 (50).
Smith, Roy, actor & stuntman; b. Oct. 30, 1889, Poland; d. Dec. 12,
    1944 (55).
Smith, Sebastian J., actor; b. Oct. 3, 1869, Southwell, Nottingham-
    shire, England; d. Jan. 15, 1948 (78).
Smith, Sid, actor; d. July 4, 1928 (36).
Smith, Solly G., actor; d. Aug. 28, 1933 (57).
Smith, Stanley (r.n. Joseph Stanley Smith), actor; b. Jan. 6, 1903,
    Kansas City, Mo.; d. Apr. 13, 1974 (71).
Smith, Sydney, actor; d. Mar. 4, 1978 (68).
Smith, Thomas, actor; d. Dec. 3, 1950 (58).
Smith, Tom, actor; b. Sept. 10, 1892, Oklahoma; d. Feb. 23, 1976 (83).
Smith, Verne B. (r.n. Verne Bryce Smith), actor & announcer;
    b. July 7, 1913, Nebraska; d. Apr. 23, 1968 (54).
Smith, Wallace, writer; b. Dec. 30, 1888, Chicago, Ill.; d. Jan. 31,
    1937 (48).
Smith, "Whispering" Jack, actor & singer; b. May 31, 1898, New York
    City; d. May 13, 1950 (51).
Smith, Winchell, writer & director; d. June 10, 1933 (61).
Smith, Wingate (r.n. Charles Edward Wingate Smith), assistant director
    & actor; b. Dec. 2, 1894, Washington, D.C.; d. July 22, 1974 (79).
Smithson, Laura, actress; b. Feb. 14, 1885, England; d. Dec. 20,
    1963 (78).

Smoller, Dorothy, actress; d. Dec. 10, 1926 (25).
Smythe, Florence, actress; b. Apr. 19, 1878, California; d. Aug. 29, 1925 (47).
Smythe, J. Anthony, actor; b. Dec. 18, 1885, California; d. Mar. 20, 1966 (80).
Snegoff, Leonid, actor; b. May 15, 1883, Russia; d. Feb. 22, 1974 (90).
Snell, Earle, writer; b. May 23, 1886, Santa Ana, Calif.; d. May 6, 1965 (78).
Snelling, Minnette, actress; d. Dec. 19, 1945 (67).
Snodgrass, Smythe, actor; d. Oct. 3, 1921.
Snow, Charmion, actress; b. Dec. 7, 1895, California; d. June 20, 1973 (77).
Snow, Marguerite, actress; d. Feb. 17, 1958 (69).
Snow, Mortimer, actor; d. June 20, 1935 (66).
Snowdon, Eric, actor; b. England; d. June 27, 1979 (90).
Snowflake (see Toomes, Fred)
Snyder, Earl "Spanky," actor; d. Jan. 16, 1973 (65).
Snyder, Matt, actor; d. Mar., 1917 (81).
Snyder, Samuel J., actor; d. Aug. 15, 1954 (94).
Soboloff, Arnold, actor; b. Nov. 11, 1930, New York City; d. Oct. 28, 1979 (48).
Sobotka, Ruth, actress; d. June 18, 1967 (42).
Sodders, Carl, actor; d. Dec. 18, 1958.
Soderling, Walter, actor; b. Apr. 13, 1872, Connecticut; d. Apr. 10, 1948 (75).
Sojin (see Kamiyama, Sojin)
Sokoloff, Vladimir, actor; b. Dec. 24, 1889, Moscow, Russia; d. Feb. 15, 1962 (72).
Soldan, Louis, actor; b. Mar. 19, 1920; d. Apr. 25, 1971 (51).
Soldani, Charles, actor; b. June 1, 1893, Oklahoma; d. Sept. 10, 1968 (75).
Soldevilla, Laly, actress; d. Sept. 12, 1979 (46).
Soldi, Steve, actor; b. Jan. 20, 1899, Italy; d. Nov. 14, 1974 (75).
Soler, Andres, actor; b. Nov. 18, 1898, Saltillo, Mexico; d. July 26, 1969 (70).
Soler, Domingo (r.n. Domingo Diaz Pavia), actor; b. Apr. 17, 1902, Guererro, Mexico; d. June 13, 1961 (59).
Soler, Julian, actor; d. May 5, 1977 (72).
Solis, Javier, actor & recording star; b. Nogales, Mexico; d. Apr. 19, 1966 (35).
Solovitch, Don, actor; d. Jan. 6, 1928.
Solow, Eugene, writer; b. July 19, 1904, Salem, Mass.; d. July 23, 1968 (64).
Soltz, Rose Posner, actress; b. Mar. 6, 1902, Austria; d. Sept. 18, 1973 (71).
Somers, Capt. Fred, actor; b. Apr. 27, 1893, New Jersey; d. Sept. 18, 1970 (77).
Somers, Julian, actor; d. Nov. 11, 1976 (72).
Somerset, Pat, actor; b. Feb. 28, 1897, London, England; d. Apr. 20, 1974 (77).
Sonnemann, Emmy, actress; d. June 8, 1973 (80).
Sonneveld, Wim, actor; d. Mar. 8, 1974 (56).
Soo, Jack, actor; d. Jan. 11, 1979 (63).
Sorano, Daniel, actor; b. Dec. 14, 1920, Toulouse, France; d. May 18, 1962 (41).

Sorel, Cecile, actress; d. Sept. 3, 1966 (93).
Sorel, George S., actor; b. Mar. 24, 1901, Odessa, Russia; d. Jan. 19, 1948 (46).
Sorin, Louis, actor; b. Sept. 23, 1893, New York City; d. Dec. 14, 1961 (68).
Sorter, Irma, actress; b. Nov. 3, 1904, Colorado; d. Sept. 3, 1968 (63).
Sosso, Pietro, actor; b. Nov. 20, 1869, Italy; d. Apr. 25, 1961 (91).
Sothern, E.H., actor; b. Dec. 6, 1859, New Orleans, La.; d. Oct. 28, 1933 (73).
Sothern, Ethel, actress; d. Feb. 20, 1957 (75).
Sothern, Harry, actor; b. Apr. 26, 1883, London, England; d. Feb. 22, 1957 (73).
Sothern, Hugh, actor; b. July 20, 1881, Missouri; d. Apr. 13, 1947 (65).
Sothern, Jean, actress; d. Jan., 1924 (25).
Sothern, Sam, actor; d. Mar. 21, 1920 (55).
Soto, Luchy, actress; b. 1920, Madrid, Spain; d. Oct. 5, 1970 (50).
Soto, Roberto, actor; d. July 18, 1960 (72).
Sotomayor, Jose, actor; d. Jan. 24, 1967 (62).
Souper, Kay, actor; d. Jan. 2, 1947.
Souplex, Raymond (Raymond Guillermain), actor; b. June 1, 1901, Paris, France; d. Nov. 22, 1972 (71).
Soussanin, Nicholas, actor; b. 1889, Yalta, Russia; d. Apr. 27, 1975 (86).
Soutar, J. Farren, actor; d. Jan. 23, 1962 (91).
Southard, Harry, actor; d. Apr. 27, 1939 (58).
Southwick, Albert P., actor; d. Jan. 19, 1929 (53).
Southwick, Dale, actor (Our Gang); d. Apr. 29, 1968 (55).
Sovern, Clarence, stuntman; d. Mar. 13, 1929 (29).
Sowards, Len (r.n. James Len Sowards), actor & stuntman; b. Oct. 17, 1892, Missouri; d. Aug. 20, 1962 (69).
Spaak, Charles, director & writer; d. Mar. 4, 1975 (71).
Spacey, John G., actor; d. Jan. 2, 1940 (45).
Spadaro, Odoardo, actor; b. Jan. 16, 1895, Firenze, Italy; d. June 26, 1965 (70).
Spalla, Erminio, actor; b. July 7, 1897, Borgo San Martino, Italy; d. Aug. 14, 1971 (74).
Sparks, Jola, dancer; d. Dec. 10, 1929 (16).
Sparks, Ned, actor; b. Nov. 19, 1883, Guelph, Ontario, Canada; d. Apr. 3, 1957 (73).
Sparks, Robert, producer & writer; b. Feb. 4, 1901, West Union, Ohio; d. July 22, 1963 (62).
Spaulding, George, actor; b. July 6, 1881, Colorado; d. Aug. 23, 1959 (78).
Speaight, Robert, actor; b. Jan. 14, 1904, St. Margaret-at-Cliffe, England; d. Nov. 4, 1976 (72).
Spear, Harry, actor; b. Dec. 25, 1912, New York; d. Feb. 11, 1969 (56).
Speelmans, Hermann, actor; b. Aug. 14, 1904, Urdingen, Germany; d. Feb., 1960 (55).
Spence, Ralph, writer; b. Nov. 4, 1890, Key West, Fla.; d. Dec. 21, 1949 (59).
Spencer, Douglas (r.n. William Henry Mesenkop), actor; b. Feb. 10, 1910, Illinois; d. Oct. 6, 1960 (50).

Spencer, Fred, actor; d. Oct. 13, 1952 (51).
Spencer, George Soule, actor; b. Sept. 25, 1874, Wisconsin;
    d. Aug. 7, 1949 (74).
Spencer, James, actor; d. July 28, 1943 (50).
Spencer, Kenneth, actor & singer; b. Los Angeles, Calif.; d. Feb. 25,
    1964 (51).
Spencer, Miles C., actor; d. Sept. 5, 1955 (71).
Spencer, Terry, actor & director; d. Oct. 3, 1954 (59).
Spencer, Tim (Sons of the Pioneers), actor & musician; b. July 13,
    1908, Webb City, Mo.; d. Apr. 26, 1974 (65).
Spencer, Walter, actor; b. Sept. 17, 1882, Murray, Utah; d. Sept. 8,
    1927 (44).
Spender, Frederick J., actor; d. Oct. 17, 1950 (65).
Spero, Kathy, actress; d. Jan. 25, 1979 (30).
Sperzel, Martin, actor; b. June 22, 1881, Pennsylvania; d. Jan. 18,
    1962 (80).
Spewack, Samuel, writer; d. Oct. 14, 1971 (72).
Spiker, Ray, actor; b. Jan. 6, 1902, Wisconsin; d. Feb. 23, 1964 (62).
Spinelly (r.n. Andree Faurier), actress; b. May 1, 1890, Paris,
    France; d. July 29, 1966 (76).
Spingler, Harry, actor; b. Buffalo, N.Y.; d. Apr. 22, 1953 (63).
Spira, Francoise, actress; b. 1928; d. Jan., 1965 (36).
Spivey, Victoria, actress & recording artist; b. Houston, Tex.;
    d. Oct. 3, 1976 (68).
Spivy, Madame (r.n. Spivy Le Voe), actress; d. Jan. 7, 1971 (64).
Spofford, Baby Charles, actor; b. Dec. 10, 1915, W. Los Angeles,
    Calif.; d. Sept. 29, 1935 (19).
Spong, Hilda, actress; b. May 14, 1875, London, England; d. May 16,
    1955 (80).
Spooner, Cecil, actress; d. May 13, 1953 (78).
Spooner, Edna May, actress; b. Centerville, Iowa; d. July 14, 1953
    (78).
Spoor, George K., director; d. Nov. 24, 1953 (81).
Spottswood, James, actor; b. Washington, D.C.; d. Oct. 11, 1940 (58).
Sprotte, Bert, actor; b. Dec. 9, 1870, Germany; d. Dec. 30, 1949 (79).
Squire, Jack, actor; d. June 21, 1938 (43).
Squire, Ronald, actor; b. Mar. 25, 1886, Tiverton, Devonshire,
    England; d. Nov. 16, 1958 (72).
Sritrange, Wandee, actress; d. Aug. 31, 1975 (25).
Stafford, Hanley, actor; b. Sept. 22, 1898, Staffordshire, England;
    d. Sept. 9, 1968 (69).
Stafford, Harry B., actor; d. Sept. 16, 1950 (76).
Stahl, John M., director & producer; b. Jan. 21, 1886, New York
    City; d. Jan. 12, 1950 (63).
Stahl, Walter O., actor; b. June 3, 1884, Bonn, Germany; d. Aug. 6,
    1943 (59).
Stahl-Nachbaur, Ernst, actor; b. Mar. 6, 1886, Munich, Germany;
    d. May 13, 1960 (74).
Stainton, Philip, actor; b. Apr. 9, 1908, Birmingham, England;
    d. Aug. 1, 1961 (53).
Stall, Karl, actor; d. June 14, 1947 (76).
Stalling, Carl W., composer & conductor; d. Nov. 29, 1972 (84).
Stallings, Laurence, writer; d. Feb. 28, 1968 (73).
Stamp-Taylor, Enid, actress; b. June 12, 1904, Monkseaton, England;
    d. Jan. 13, 1946 (41).

Stamper, F. Pope, actor; b. Nov. 20, 1880, Richmond, Surrey, England; d. Nov. 12, 1950 (69).
Standing, Charlene, dancer; d. Jan. 8, 1957 (36).
Standing, Gordon, actor; b. Nov. 24, 1887, London, England; d. May 21, 1927 (39).
Standing, Sir Guy, actor; b. Sept. 1, 1873, London, England; d. Feb. 24, 1937 (63).
Standing, Guy, Jr., actor; b. Apr. 12, 1904, New York; d. Nov. 14, 1954 (50).
Standing, Herbert, actor; b. Nov. 13, 1846, Peckham, England; d. Dec. 5, 1923 (77).
Standing, Herbert, actor; b. London, England; d. Sept. 23, 1955 (71).
Standing, Jack, actor; b. Feb. 10, 1886, England; d. Oct. 26, 1917 (31).
Standing, Joan, actress; d. Feb. 3, 1979 (76).
Standing, Wyndham, actor; b. Aug. 24, 1881, London, England; d. Feb. 1, 1963 (81).
Standing Bear, Chief (r.n. Chief Luther Standing Bear), actor; b. 1860, Ft. Robinson, Neb.; d. Feb. 20, 1939 (79).
Standish, Joseph W., actor; d. Oct. 27, 1943.
Stanhope, Adeline, actress; d. June, 1935.
Stanhope, Ted, actor; b. Jan. 30, 1902, New York; d. July 10, 1977 (75).
Stanitsyn, Viktor Y., actor; d. Dec. 24, 1976 (79).
Stanley, Edwin, actor; b. Nov. 22, 1880, Chicago, Ill.; d. Dec. 25, 1944 (64).
Stanley, Forrest, actor; b. Aug. 21, 1889, New York City; d. Aug. 27, 1969 (80).
Stanley, S. Victor, actor; b. Feb. 17, 1892, Clun, England; d. Jan. 29, 1939 (46).
Stanmore, Frank, actor; b. Mar. 10, 1877, London, England; d. Aug. 15, 1943 (66).
Stannard, Don, actor; b. 1916, Westcliff, England; d. July 9, 1949 (33).
Stantley, Ralph, actor; d. May 10, 1972 (58).
Stanton, Ernie (r.n. Ernest G. Stanton-Burch), actor; b. Aug. 23, 1890, London, England; d. Feb. 6, 1944 (53).
Stanton, Fred R., actor; d. May 27, 1925 (44).
Stanton, Harry, actor; b. Dec. 7, 1901, Washington; d. Feb. 7, 1978 (76).
Stanton, Larry T., actor; b. Oct. 22, 1893, Ohio; d. May 9, 1955 (61).
Stanton, Paul, actor; b. Dec. 21, 1884, Illinois; d. Oct. 9, 1955 (70).
Stanton, Will, actor; b. Sept. 18, 1885, London, England; d. Dec. 18, 1969 (84).
Stanwood, Rita, actress; b. Jan. 15, 1888, Massachusetts; d. Nov. 15, 1961 (73).
Starace-Sainati, Bella, actress; b. June 2, 1878, Naples, Italy; d. Aug. 4, 1958 (80).
Stark, Leighton, actor; d. July 20, 1924.
Starke, Pauline, actress; b. Jan. 10, 1901, Joplin, Mo.; d. Feb. 3, 1977 (76).
Starkey, Bert (Buckley Starkey), actor; b. Jan. 10, 1880, England; d. June 10, 1939 (59).
Starkey, Buckley (see Starkey, Bert)
Starling, Lynn, writer; b. Hopkinsville, Ky.; d. Mar., 1955 (67).
Starr, Frances, actress; b. June 6, 1881, Albany, N.Y.; d. June 11, 1973 (92).

Starr, Frederick, actor; b. 1878, San Francisco, Calif.; d. Aug. 20, 1921 (43).
Staub, Ralph, director & producer; b. July 21, 1899, Chicago, Ill.; d. Oct. 22, 1969 (70).
Steadman, Vera, actress; b. June 21, 1900, Monterey, Calif.; d. Dec. 14, 1966 (66).
Steckel, Leonhard, actor; b. Jan. 8, 1901, Ungarn; d. Feb. 9, 1971 (70).
Stedman, Lincoln, actor; d. Mar. 22, 1948 (41).
Stedman, Marshall, actor; d. Dec. 16, 1943 (69).
Stedman, Myrtle, actress; b. Mar. 3, 1885, Chicago, Ill.; d. Jan. 8, 1938 (52).
Steele, Agnes, actress; d. Mar. 3, 1949 (67).
Steele, Clifford, actor; d. Mar. 5, 1940 (62).
Steele, Minnie, actress; d. Jan. 5, 1949 (68).
Steele, Vernon, actor; b. Sept. 18, 1882, Chile; d. July 23, 1955 (72).
Steele, Vickie Fee, actress; d. Dec. 13, 1975 (28).
Steele, William (William Gettinger; William Goettinger), actor; b. Mar. 28, 1889, San Antonio, Tex.; d. Feb. 13, 1966 (76).
Steelman, Hosea, actor; b. Mar. 31, 1876, Cincinnati, Ohio; d. July 4, 1953 (77).
Steers, Larry, actor; b. Feb. 14, 1888, Indiana; d. Feb. 15, 1951 (63).
Stefan, Virginia, actress; d. May 5, 1964 (38).
Stefani, Joseph (see De Stefani, Joseph)
Stefford, Miriam, actress; d. Aug. 26, 1931.
Steger, Julius, actor; b. Vienna, Austria; d. Feb. 25, 1959.
Stehli, Edgar, actor; b. July 12, 1884, Lyons, France; d. July 25, 1973 (89).
Steibner, Hans, actor & director; b. Nov. 19, 1898, Vetschau; d. Mar. 27, 1958 (59).
Stein, Carol Eden, actress; d. Oct. 18, 1958 (31).
Stein, Sammy, actor; d. Mar. 30, 1966 (60).
Steinbeck, Walter, actor; b. Sept. 26, 1884; d. Aug. 27, 1942 (57).
Steiner, Elio, actor; b. Mar. 9, 1904, Stroa; d. Dec. 6, 1965 (61).
Steiner, Max, composer & musical director; b. May 10, 1888, Vienna, Austria; d. Dec. 28, 1971 (83).
Steinke, Hans, actor & wrestler; b. Germany; d. June 26, 1971 (78).
Steinmetz, Earl, actor; d. May 22, 1942 (27).
Steinruck, Albert, actor; b. May 20, 1872, Wetterburg-Waldeck, Germany; d. Feb. 2, 1929 (56).
Stelzer, Hannes, actor; d. Jan., 1945.
Stembridge, J.S. (r.n. James Sidney Stembridge), actor; b. Feb. 9, 1869, Milledgeville, Ga.; d. Oct. 31, 1942 (73).
Stenning, Arthur N., actor; b. Feb. 6, 1883, England; d. Dec. 24, 1972 (89).
Stephens, Jud, actor; d. Apr. 18, 1935 (47).
Stephens, Lewis, extra; d. Mar. 7, 1978 (77).
Stephenson, Henry, actor; b. Apr. 16, 1871, British West Indies; d. Apr. 24, 1956 (85).
Stephenson, James, actor; b. Apr. 14, 1889, Selby, Yorkshire, England; d. July 29, 1941 (52).
Stephenson, Robert (r.n. Robert Robinson Stephenson), actor; b. Feb. 7, 1901, Washington; d. Sept. 5, 1970 (69).
Steppat, Ilse, actress; b. Wuppertal, Germany; d. Dec. 22, 1969 (52).

Steppling, John, actor; b. Aug. 8, 1870, Essen, Germany; d. Apr. 6, 1932 (61).
Sterling, Edythe, actress; b. Oct. 29, 1892, Kansas; d. June 5, 1962 (69).
Sterling, Ford (r.n. George Ford Stich), actor; b. Nov. 3, 1884, La Crosse, Wisc.; d. Oct. 13, 1939 (54).
Sterling, Larry, actor; d. Aug. 25, 1958 (23).
Sterling, Lee, actor; d. Mar. 4, 1951 (47).
Sterling, Merta, actress; d. Mar. 14, 1944 (61).
Sterling, Richard, actor; b. Aug. 30, 1880, New York City; d. Apr. 15, 1959 (78).
Stern, Bill, sportscaster; b. July 1, 1907, Rochester, N.Y.; d. Nov. 19, 1971 (64).
Stern, George, producer; b. Apr. 7, 1904, Russia; d. May 3, 1972 (68).
Stern, Louis, actor; b. Jan. 10, 1860, New York City; d. Feb. 15, 1941 (81).
Sternroyd, Vincent, actor; b. Oct. 8, 1857, London, England; d. Nov. 3, 1948 (91).
Stevens, Byron Malcolm, actor; b. Feb. 26, 1905; d. Dec. 14, 1964 (59).
Stevens, Charles, actor; b. May 26, 1893, Solomonsville, Ariz.; d. Aug. 22, 1964 (71).
Stevens, Cy, actor; b. June 1, 1893, Pennsylvania; d. June 5, 1974 (81).
Stevens, Edwin, actor; b. Aug. 16, 1860, California; d. Jan. 1, 1923 (62).
Stevens, Emily, actress; b. Feb. 27, 1882, New York City; d. Jan. 2, 1928 (45).
Stevens, Evelyn, actress; d. Aug. 28, 1938 (47).
Stevens, George, director; b. Dec. 18, 1904, Oakland, Calif.; d. Mar. 8, 1975 (70).
Stevens, Inger, actress; b. Oct. 18, 1931, Stockholm, Sweden; d. Apr. 30, 1970 (38).
Stevens, Landers, actor; b. Feb. 17, 1877, San Francisco, Calif.; d. Dec. 19, 1940 (63).
Stevens, Leith, composer & actor; b. Sept. 13, 1909, Missouri; d. July 23, 1970 (60).
Stevens, Louis, writer; d. Sept. 29, 1963 (63).
Stevens, Lynn, actor; d. Mar. 28, 1950 (52).
Stevens, Morton L., actor; d. Aug. 5, 1959 (69).
Stevens, Onslow, actor; b. Mar. 29, 1902, Los Angeles, Calif.; d. Jan. 5, 1977 (73).
Stevens, Vi, actress; d. Mar. 22, 1967 (75).
Stevenson, Charles A., actor; b. Dublin, Ireland; d. July 2, 1929 (77).
Stevenson, Charles E. (Charles Ed. Hafner), actor; b. Oct. 13, 1887, Sacramento, Calif.; d. July 4, 1943 (55).
Stevenson, Houseley, Sr., actor; b. July 30, 1879, England; d. Aug. 6, 1953 (74).
Stevenson, John, actor; d. Aug. 10, 1922 (38).
Stevenson, Richard Wilson, actor; d. Apr. 17, 1967 (75).
Steward, Maynon, actor; d. Dec. 25, 1932 (52).
Stewart, Anita, actress; b. Feb. 17, 1895, New York; d. May 4, 1961 (66).
Stewart, Athole, actor; b. June 25, 1879, Ealing, England; d. Oct. 18, 1940 (61).

Stewart, Blanche, actress; d. July 25, 1952.

Stewart, Cray, actor; d. May 30, 1961 (37).

Stewart, Danny, actor & musician; d. Apr. 15, 1962 (55).

Stewart, David J., actor; b. Omaha, Neb.; d. Dec. 24, 1966 (52).

Stewart, Dona Jean, actress; b. July 16, 1939, Colorado; d. July 30, 1961 (22).

Stewart, Donald, actor; d. Mar. 1, 1966 (55).

Stewart, Eillen, actress; d. Feb. 7, 1931 (44).

Stewart, Etta, actress; d. Apr. 23, 1929.

Stewart, Fred, actor; b. Dec. 7, 1906, Atlanta, Ga.; d. Dec. 5, 1970 (63).

Stewart, Gene, actress; d. Nov. 23, 1926.

Stewart, George, actor; b. June 27, 1888, New York City; d. Dec. 24, 1945 (57).

Stewart, Jack, actor; d. Jan. 2, 1966 (52).

Stewart, Peter (see Newfield, Sam)

Stewart, Rex, actor & jazz musician; b. Feb. 22, 1907, Philadelphia, Pa.; d. Sept. 7, 1967 (60).

Stewart, Roy (r.n. John Roy Stewart), actor; b. Oct. 17, 1883, San Diego, Calif.; d. Apr. 26, 1933 (49).

Stewart, Sophie, actress; b. Mar. 5, 1908, Crieff, Perthshire, Scotland; d. June 6, 1977 (69).

Stieler, Kurt, actor; b. Oct. 28, 1877; d. Sept. 26, 1963 (85).

Stignani, Ebe, opera singer; d. Oct. 5, 1974 (70).

Still, Charles H., actor; d. Nov. 3, 1961 (55).

Stiller, Mauritz, director; b. July 17, 1883, Helsinki, Finland; d. Nov. 8, 1928 (45).

Stine, Charles J., actor; d. Jan. 5, 1934 (65).

Stinson, Mortimer E., actor; b. Dec. 25, 1871, New York; d. July 20, 1927 (55).

Stival, Giulio, actor; b. Mar. 4, 1903, Venezia, Italy; d. Apr. 1, 1953 (50).

Stock, Werner, actor; b. Oct. 20, 1903; d. Apr., 1972 (68).

Stockbridge, Henry, actor; b. May 29, 1871, Maine; d. Dec. 9, 1952 (81).

Stockdale, Carl, actor; b. Feb. 19, 1874, Worthington, Minn.; d. Mar. 15, 1953 (79).

Stockdale, Franklin E., actor; d. Dec. 31, 1950 (80).

Stockfield, Betty, actress; b. Jan. 15, 1905, Sydney, Australia; d. Jan. 26, 1966 (61).

Stoddard, Belle, actress; b. Sept. 13, 1869, Ohio; d. Dec. 13, 1950 (81).

Stoddard, Betsy, actress; d. Sept. 7, 1959 (75).

Stoeckel, Joe, actor; b. Sept. 27, 1894; d. June 14, 1959 (64).

Stoeckel, Otto, actor; b. Aug. 6, 1873; d. Nov. 17, 1958 (85).

Stoker, H.G. (Hew Gordon Dacre), actor; b. Feb. 2, 1885, Dublin, Ireland; d. Feb. 2, 1966 (81).

Stokes, Ernest L. (Mustard), actor; d. May 26, 1964 (57).

Stokes, Olive, actress; b. Apr. 10, 1887, Oklahoma; d. Nov. 1, 1972 (85).

Stokowski, Leopold, classical conductor; b. Apr. 18, 1882, London, England; d. Sept. 13, 1977 (95).

Stoloff, Ben, director; b. Philadelphia, Pa.; d. Sept. 7, 1960 (64).

Stolz, Robert, composer; b. Aug. 8, 1880, Graz, Austria; d. June 27, 1975 (94).

Stone, Arthur, actor; b. Nov. 28, 1883, St. Louis, Mo.; d. Sept. 4, 1940 (56).

Stone, Dorothy, actress; b. June 3, 1905, Brooklyn, N.Y.; d. Sept. 24, 1974 (69).

Stone, Eugene, actor; d. Feb. 21, 1947 (55).

Stone, Florence, actress; d. Aug. 25, 1950 (70).

Stone, Fred, actor; b. Aug. 19, 1873, Longmont, Colo.; d. Mar. 6, 1959 (85).

Stone, George E., actor; b. May 18, 1903, Lodz, Poland; d. May 26, 1967 (64).

Stone, James F., actor; b. Mar. 10, 1898, New York; d. Jan. 9, 1969 (70).

Stone, John, director, producer, & writer; b. Sept. 12, 1888, New York City; d. June 3, 1961 (72).

Stone, Lewis, actor; b. Nov. 15, 1879, Worcester, Mass.; d. Sept. 13, 1953 (73).

Stone, Maxine, actress; d. Nov. 20, 1964 (54).

Stone, Mrs. Robert E., actress; d. Nov. 5, 1916.

Stonehouse, Ruth, actress; b. Sept. 28, 1892, Denver, Colo.; d. May 12, 1941 (48).

Stoney, Jack, actor; b. Oct. 1, 1897, Pennsylvania; d. Jan. 29, 1978 (80).

Storey, Edith, actress; d. Sept. 23, 1955 (63).

Stossel, Ludwig, actor; b. Feb. 12, 1883, Austria; d. Jan. 29, 1973 (89).

Stothart, Herbert, composer; b. Sept. 11, 1885, Milwaukee, Wisc.; d. Feb. 1, 1949 (63).

Stout, Royal C., actor; d. Apr. 2, 1958 (84).

Stowe, Leslie, actor; d. July 16, 1949 (63).

Stowell, Clarence Warner, actor; d. Nov. 26, 1940 (62).

Stowell, William, actor; d. Dec., 1919 (34).

Stradner, Rose, actress; b. July 31, 1913, Vienna, Austria; d. Sept. 27, 1958 (45).

Strang, Harry (r.n. Howard Raymond Strain), actor; b. Dec. 13, 1892, Virginia; d. Apr. 10, 1972 (79).

Strang, Mae, actress; d. Aug. 18, 1941.

Strange, Glenn, actor; b. Aug. 16, 1899, Weed, N.M.; d. Sept. 20, 1973 (74).

Strange, Robert, actor; b. Nov. 26, 1881, New York; d. Feb. 22, 1952 (70).

Strangis, Jane, actress; b. Oct. 16, 1930, California; d. Jan. 25, 1966 (35).

Strassberg, Morris, actor; d. Feb. 8, 1974 (76).

Stratton, Chester, actor; b. July 31, 1910, New Jersey; d. July 7, 1970 (59).

Stratton, Harry, actor; d. Aug. 19, 1955 (57).

Straub, Agnes, actress; b. Apr. 2, 1890; d. July 8, 1941 (51).

Strauss, Robert, actor; b. Nov. 8, 1913, New York City; d. Feb. 20, 1975 (61).

Strauss, William H., actor; b. June 13, 1885, New York City; d. Aug. 5, 1943 (58).

Strayer, Frank R., director; b. Sept. 7, 1891, Altoona, Pa.; d. Feb. 3, 1964 (72).

Street, David, actor & singer; b. Dec. 13, 1917, California; d. Sept. 3, 1971 (53).

Street, George A., actor; d. May 30, 1956 (87).
Strickland, Helen, actress; b. Boston, Mass.; d. Jan. 11, 1938 (75).
Striker, Joseph, actor; b. New York; d. Feb. 24, 1974 (74).
Stromberg, Hunt, producer; b. Louisville, Ky.; d. Aug. 23, 1968 (74).
Strong, Carl E., rodeo rider; d. Jan. 14, 1965 (58).
Strong, Eugene K., actor; b. Aug. 9, 1893, Wisconsin; d. June 25, 1962 (68).
Strong, Jay, actor; d. Dec. 1, 1953 (57).
Strong, Porter, actor; d. June 11, 1923 (44).
Strongheart, Nipo, actor; b. May 15, 1891, Yakima, Wash.; d. Dec. 30, 1966 (75).
Stroud, Clarence, actor; d. Aug. 15, 1973 (66).
Stryker, Gustave, actor; d. June 3, 1943 (77).
Stuart, Donald, actor; b. Dec. 2, 1898, London, England; d. Feb. 22, 1944 (45).
Stuart, Gil (r.n. Gilchrist Stuart), actor; b. Jan. 19, 1919, London, England; d. June 8, 1977 (58).
Stuart, Jean (r.n. Margaret Eliz. Leisenring), actress; b. July 13, 1906, California; d. Nov. 23, 1926 (20).
Stuart, John (r.n. John Croall), actor; b. July 18, 1898, Edinburgh, Scotland; d. Oct. 17, 1979 (81).
Stuart, Nick, actor; b. Apr. 10, 1903, Romania; d. Apr. 7, 1973 (69).
Stuart, Ralph Ramsey, actor; d. Nov. 4, 1952 (62).
Stubbs, Harry, actor; b. Sept. 7, 1874, England; d. Mar. 9, 1950 (75).
Stuewe, Hans, actor; b. May 14, 1901, Marnitz/Meckl, Germany; d. May 13, 1976 (74).
Stumar, Charles, cinematographer; d. June 29, 1935 (44).
Sturges, Preston, director & writer; b. Aug. 29, 1898, Chicago, Ill.; d. Aug. 6, 1959 (60).
Sturgis, Edwin (r.n. Josef Edwin Sturgis), actor; b. Oct. 22, 1881, Washington, D.C.; d. Dec. 13, 1947 (66).
Stutenroth, Eugene (see Roth, Gene)
Styles, Edwin, actor; b. Jan. 13, 1899, London, England; d. Dec. 20, 1960 (61).
Styles, Patricia, actress; d. Dec. 13, 1948 (25).
Subject, Evelyn, actress; d. Apr. 22, 1975.
Suckmann, Erich, actor & singer; b. Jan. 1, 1892; d. May, 1970 (78).
Sudlow, Joan, actress; d. Feb. 1, 1970 (78).
Sues, Leonard, actor; d. Oct. 24, 1971 (50).
Suessenguth, Walther, actor; b. Feb. 7, 1903, Schleiz, Germany; d. Apr. 28, 1964 (61).
Sul Te Wan, Mme. (r.n. Nellie Conley), actress; b. Mar. 7, 1873, Kentucky; d. Feb. 1, 1959 (85).
Sulky, Leo (r.n. Leo Bernstein), actor; b. Dec. 6, 1874, Cincinnati, Ohio; d. June 3, 1957 (82).
Sullavan, Margaret, actress; b. May 16, 1911, Norfolk, Va.; d. Jan. 1, 1960 (48).
Sullivan, Billy, actor & author; d. May 23, 1946 (55).
Sullivan, Brian, opera singer; b. Aug. 9, 1919, Oakland, Calif.; d. June 17, 1969 (49).
Sullivan, Brick (r.n. John L. Scroggs), actor; b. July 28, 1899, South Dakota; d. Sept. 4, 1959 (60).
Sullivan, C. Gardner, writer; b. Sept. 18, 1884, Stillwater, Minn.; d. Sept. 4, 1965 (80).
Sullivan, Charles, actor; b. Apr. 24, 1899, Louisiana; d. June 25, 1972 (73).

Sullivan, Clayton, actor; d. Aug., 1931 (21).
Sullivan, Ed, film & television personality; d. Oct. 13, 1974 (73).
Sullivan, Elliott, actor; b. July 4, 1907, San Antonio, Tex.;
    d. June 2, 1974 (66).
Sullivan, Francis L., actor; b. Jan. 6, 1903, London, England;
    d. Nov. 19, 1956 (53).
Sullivan, Frederick, actor; b. July 18, 1872, London, England;
    d. July 24, 1937 (65).
Sullivan, John Maurice, actor; b. Sept. 24, 1875, Washington, D.C.;
    d. Mar. 8, 1949 (73).
Sully, Frank, actor; b. June 17, 1908, St. Louis, Mo.; d. Dec. 17,
    1975 (67).
Summer, Verlyn, actress; b. June 7, 1897, Lakefield, Minn.; d. Feb. 10,
    1935 (37).
Summers, Ann, actress; d. Jan. 15, 1974 (54).
Summers, Hope, actress; d. July 22, 1979 (78).
Summers, Leonora (r.n. Lillian Hill (Le) Callahan), actress;
    d. June 29, 1976 (78).
Summerville, Amelia, actress; b. Kildare, Ireland; d. Jan. 21, 1934
    (71).
Summerville, George (see Summerville, Slim)
Summerville, Slim, actor; b. June 10, 1892, Albuquerque, N.M.;
    d. Jan. 5, 1946 (53).
Sunderland, Nan, actress; d. Nov. 23, 1973.
Sundholm, Oscar W. (r.n. Oscar William Sundholm), actor; b. May 15,
    1898, British Columbia; d. Feb. 28, 1971 (72).
Sundholm, William (see Sundholm, Oscar W.)
Supple, Cuyler, actor & author; b. Feb. 13, 1894, Germantown, Pa.;
    d. May 3, 1944 (50).
Suratt, Valeska, actress; d. July 2, 1962 (80).
Sutch, Herbert, actor; b. June 29, 1884, London, England; d. Jan. 22,
    1939 (54).
Sutherland, A. Edward (r.n. Albert Edward Sutherland), director &
    actor; b. Jan. 5, 1897, London, England; d. Dec. 31, 1973 (76).
Sutherland, Annie, actress; b. Mar. 1, 1867, Washington, D.C.;
    d. June 22, 1942 (75).
Sutherland, Dick (r.n. Archie Thomas Johnson), actor; b. Dec. 23,
    1881, Benton, Ky.; d. Feb. 3, 1934 (52).
Sutherland, Victor, actor; b. Feb. 28, 1889, Paducah, Ky.; d. Aug. 29,
    1968 (79).
Sutton, Frank, actor; b. Oct. 23, 1922, Clarksville, Tenn.;
    d. June 28, 1974 (51).
Sutton, John, actor; b. Oct. 22, 1908, Rawalpindi, India; d. July 10,
    1963 (54).
Sutton, Paul, actor; d. Jan. 31, 1970 (58).
Sutton, William, actor; d. Sept. 10, 1955 (78).
Sverdlin, Lev N., actor; d. Aug. 30, 1969 (67).
Swain, Mack, actor; b. Feb. 16, 1876, Salt Lake City, Utah;
    d. Aug. 25, 1935 (59).
Swan, Paul, actor & dancer; b. 1883, Ashland, Ill.; d. Feb. 1, 1972
    (88).
Swanstrom, Karin, actress & producer; b. June 13, 1873, Norrkoping,
    Sweden; d. July 5, 1942 (69).
Swanwick, Peter, actor; d. Nov. 14, 1968 (46).
Swarthout, Gladys, opera singer & actress; b. Dec. 25, 1904, Deep-
    water, Mo.; d. July 7, 1969 (64).

Swartz, Sara, extra; d. Mar. 30, 1949 (50).

Sweatnam, Willis P., actor; b. Zanesville, Ohio; d. Nov. 25, 1930 (76).

Sweatt, A.W., actor; d. Jan. 11, 1944 (21).

Sweeney, Fred C., actor; d. Dec. 10, 1954 (60).

Sweeney, Jack, actor; d. Apr. 12, 1950 (61).

Sweeney, Joseph, actor; d. Nov. 25, 1963.

Sweet, Harry, actor; d. June 18, 1933 (32).

Sweet, Polly Louise, dancer; d. Jan. 17, 1935 (21).

Sweet, Tom, actor & stuntman; b. Aug. 23, 1931, California; d. Nov. 19, 1967 (36).

Swenson, Alfred G., actor; d. Mar. 28, 1941 (58).

Swenson, Karl, actor; d. Oct. 8, 1978 (70).

Swickard, Charles F., director & actor; b. Mar. 21, 1868, Germany; d. May 12, 1929 (61).

Swickard, Joseph, actor; b. June 26, 1866, Coblenz, Germany; d. Mar. 1, 1940 (73).

Swinley, Ion, actor; b. Oct. 27, 1891, Barnes, England; d. Sept. 16, 1937 (45).

Switzer, Carl (Alfalfa), actor; b. Aug. 7, 1927, Illinois; d. Jan. 21, 1959 (31).

Swoger, Harry, actor; b. Mar. 6, 1919, Ohio; d. June 14, 1970 (51).

Swor, Bert, actor; b. Paris, Tenn.; d. Nov. 30, 1943 (65).

Swor, James L., actor; d. July 3, 1954 (72).

Swor, John, actor; b. Paris, Tenn.; d. July 15, 1965 (87).

Sydney, Basil, actor; b. Apr. 23, 1894, St. Osyth, Essex, England; d. Jan. 10, 1968 (73).

Sydney, Bruce, actor; d. Oct. 18, 1942 (53).

Sylva, Marguerite, actress & opera singer; b. July 10, 1875, Brussels, Belgium; d. Feb. 21, 1957 (81).

Sylvani, Gladys, actress; b. 1886, England; d. Apr. 20, 1953 (67).

Sylvester, Clara, actress; d. Mar. 23, 1941 (70).

Sylvester, Frank L., actor; d. Dec. 17, 1931 (63).

Sylvester, Henry, actor; b. Sept. 2, 1881, Missouri; d. June 8, 1961 (79).

Sylvie (r.n. Louise Sylvain), actress; d. Jan., 1970 (88).

Sym, Igo, actor; b. July 3, 1896, Innsbruck, Austria; d. Mar. 7, 1941 (44).

Symon, Burk, actor; b. Nov. 18, 1888, Pittsburgh, Pa.; d. Feb. 20, 1950 (61).

Symonds, Augustin, actor; b. Nov. 24, 1868, New Castle, England; d. July 14, 1944 (75).

Szabo, Sandor, actor & wrestler; b. Jan. 4, 1906, Hungary; d. Oct. 13, 1966 (60).

Szold, Bernard, actor; d. Nov. 16, 1960 (66).


Taber, Richard, actor; b. Long Branch, N.J.; d. Nov. 16, 1957 (72).

Tabler, P. Dempsey, actor; b. Nov. 23, 1876, Tennessee; d. June 7, 1956 (79).

Taboada, Julio, Jr., actor; d. Sept. 15, 1962 (36).

Tabor, Joan, actress; d. Dec. 18, 1968 (34).

Tabor, Rose, actress; d. Sept. 19, 1925 (35).

Tackova, Jarmila, actress; b. Aug. 19, 1908, Illinois; d. Sept. 26, 1971 (63).

Tafler, Sydney, actor; b. July 31, 1916, London, England; d. Nov. 7,
    1979 (63).
Taft, Sara (Sara Taft Teschke), actress; b. July 5, 1893, California;
    d. Sept. 24, 1973 (80).
Taggart, Ben, actor; b. Apr. 5, 1889, New York, N.Y.; d. May 17,
    1947 (58).
Taggart, Hal, actor; b. Aug. 12, 1896, Arizona; d. Dec. 7, 1971 (75).
Taggart, James (see McTaggart, Malcolm "Bud")
Tahir, Mahmed, extra; d. Oct. 1, 1963 (60).
Taillon, Gus, actor; b. Oct. 11, 1887, Canada; d. May 8, 1953 (65).
Tait, Robert B., singer; d. May 28, 1950 (50).
Takada, Minoru, actor; d. Dec. 28, 1977 (78).
Talbot, Mae, actress; d. Aug. 4, 1942 (73).
Talbot, Slim (r.n. Jay Talbot), actor; b. Hamilton, Ill.; d. Jan. 25,
    1973 (77).
Talegalli, Alberto, actor; b. Oct. 2, 1913, Pincano, Italy;
    d. July 10, 1961 (48).
Taliaferro, Edith, actress; b. Dec. 21, 1893, Richmond, Va.;
    d. Mar. 2, 1958 (64).
Taliaferro, Hal (Wally Wales) (r.n. Floyd Taliaferro Alderson), actor;
    b. Nov. 13, 1895, Sheridan, Wyo.; d. Feb. 12, 1980 (84).
Taliaferro, Mabel, actress; b. May 21, 1887, New York City; d. Jan.
    24, 1979 (91).
Tallier, Armand, actor; b. Mar., 1887; d. Mar. 1, 1958 (70).
Tallman, Frank, stunt pilot; b. Apr. 17, 1919, Orange, N.J.;
    d. Apr. 16, 1978 (58).
Talmadge, Constance, actress; b. Apr. 19, 1900, Brooklyn, N.Y.;
    d. Nov. 23, 1973 (73).
Talmadge, Natalie, actress; b. Apr. 29, 1899, New York; d. June 19,
    1969 (70).
Talmadge, Norma, actress; b. May 26, 1897, Niagara Falls, N.Y.;
    d. Dec. 24, 1957 (60).
Talman, William, actor; b. Feb. 4, 1915, Michigan; d. Aug. 30, 1968
    (53).
Tamara (Swann), actress; b. Russia; d. Feb. 22, 1943 (32).
Tamarez, Tom (r.n. Gaber Tanos), actor; b. Feb. 27, 1901, Syria;
    d. Oct. 25, 1963 (62).
Tamblyn, Edward, actor; d. June 22, 1957 (50).
Tamiroff, Akim, actor; b. Oct. 29, 1899, Tiflis, Russia; d. Sept. 17,
    1972 (72).
Tamiya, Jiro, actor; d. Dec. 28, 1978 (43).
Tandy, Valerie, actress; b. England; d. Apr. 27, 1965 (42).
Tang, Frank, actor; b. Nov. 27, 1905, California; d. June 29, 1968
    (62).
Tanguay, Eva, actress & singer; b. Aug. 1, 1878, Marbleton, Canada;
    d. Jan. 11, 1947 (68).
Tannen, Beatrice, actress; b. Sept. 3, 1880, Indiana; d. Aug. 4,
    1960 (79).
Tannen, Julius, actor; b. May 16, 1880, New York; d. Jan. 3, 1965
    (84).
Tannen, William, actor; b. Nov. 17, 1911, New York City; d. Dec. 2,
    1976 (65).
Tanner, Jack, actor; d. Apr. 3, 1934 (61).
Tano, Guy, actor; d. Aug. 19, 1952 (38).
Tansey, Emma, actress; b. Sept. 12, 1870, Louisville, Ky.; d. Mar. 23,
    1942 (71).

Tansey, Robert Emmett, director, producer, & writer; b. June 28, 1897, Brooklyn, N.Y.; d. June 17, 1951 (53).
Tapley, Rose, actress; b. June 30, 1881, Massachusetts; d. Feb. 23, 1956 (74).
Tarasova, Alla, actress; d. Apr. 5, 1973 (75).
Tarbat, Lorna, actress; b. England; d. Apr., 1961 (45).
Tarkhanov, Mikhail, actor; d. Aug., 1948.
Tashlin, Frank, director, author, & animator; b. Feb. 19, 1913, New Jersey; d. May 5, 1972 (59).
Tashman, Kitty, actress; d. Nov. 6, 1931 (44).
Tashman, Lilyan, actress; b. Oct. 23, 1899, Brooklyn, N.Y.; d. Mar. 21, 1934 (34).
Tasker, Robert, writer; d. Dec. 7, 1944 (46).
Tata, Paul M., actor & fencer; d. Mar. 30, 1962 (79).
Tate, Cullen B., director; b. Mar. 10, 1896, Paducah, Ky.; d. Oct. 12, 1947 (51).
Tate, Harry, actor; b. July 4, 1872, Scotland; d. Feb. 14, 1940 (67).
Tate, John, actor; d. Mar. 20, 1979 (65).
Tate, Reginald, actor; b. Dec. 13, 1896, Garforth, Yorkshire, England; d. Aug. 23, 1955 (58).
Tate, Sharon, actress; b. Jan. 24, 1943, Dallas, Tex.; d. Aug. 8, 1969 (26).
Tatum, Buck, actor; d. Oct. 2, 1941 (44).
Taube, Robert, actor; b. Mar. 15, 1880, Riga; d. Aug. 18, 1964 (84).
Tauber, Richard, actor & opera singer; b. May 16, 1891, Linz, Austria; d. Jan. 8, 1948 (56).
Tavares, Arthur, actor; b. Jan. 10, 1884, California; d. May 27, 1954 (70).
Taylor, Al, actor; d. Oct. 10, 1947 (65).
Taylor, Albert, actor; b. 1868, Montgomery, Ala.; d. Apr. 9, 1940 (72).
Taylor, Alma, actress; b. Jan. 3, 1895, London, England; d. Jan., 1974 (79).
Taylor, Andy, actor; d. June 8, 1948 (53).
Taylor, Beth, actress; d. Mar. 1, 1951 (62).
Taylor, Colin Campbell, actor; d. Mar. 31, 1938 (73).
Taylor, Eric, writer; d. Sept. 8, 1952 (55).
Taylor, Estelle, actress; b. May 20, 1894, Delaware; d. Apr. 15, 1958 (63).
Taylor, Ferris, actor; b. Mar. 25, 1888, Texas; d. Mar. 6, 1961 (72).
Taylor, Floye, actress; d. Apr. 13, 1957 (77).
Taylor, Forrest, actor; b. Dec. 29, 1883, Bloomington, Ill.; d. Feb. 19, 1965 (81).
Taylor, George, actor; d. Nov. 2, 1939 (50).
Taylor, George, actor; b. Oct. 24, 1900, Ohio; d. Dec. 20, 1970 (70).
Taylor, Josephine, actress; d. Nov. 26, 1964 (73).
Taylor, Laurette, actress; b. Apr. 1, 1884, New York City; d. Dec. 7, 1946 (62).
Taylor, Louise, actress; d. Mar. 18, 1965 (57).
Taylor, Ray, director; b. Dec. 1, 1888, Perham, Minn.; d. Feb. 15, 1952 (63).
Taylor, Robert, actor; d. Dec. 9, 1936 (63).
Taylor, Robert (r.n. Spangler Arlington Brugh), actor; b. Aug. 5, 1911, Filley, Neb.; d. June 8, 1969 (57).
Taylor, Sam, director; d. Mar. 6, 1958 (62).

Taylor, Stanner E.V., author & director; b. Sept. 28, 1877, St. Louis,
    Mo.; d. Nov. 23, 1948 (71).
Taylor, Walter L. (r.n. Walter Lewis Taylor), actor; b. Mar. 22,
    1904, Utah; d. Nov. 24, 1971 (67).
Taylor, William Desmond, director & actor; b. Mar. 26, 1872, Ireland;
    d. Feb. 1, 1922 (49).
Taylor, William H. (Billy), actor; d. Dec. 26, 1930 (103).
Taylor, Wilton, actor; b. 1869; d. Jan. 24, 1925 (56).
Teachout, Arthur, actor; d. Mar. 5, 1939 (51).
Tead, Phil, actor; b. Sept. 29, 1893, Massachusetts; d. June 9, 1974
    (80).
Teagarden, Jack, jazz musician; b. Aug. 29, 1905, Vernon, Tex.;
    d. Jan. 15, 1964 (58).
Teague, Brian, actor; d. May 30, 1970 (33).
Teague, Guy, actor; d. Jan. 24, 1970.
Teal, Ray, actor; b. Jan. 12, 1902, Grand Rapids, Mich.; d. Apr. 2,
    1976 (74).
Teare, Ethel, actress; b. Jan. 11, 1894, Arizona; d. Mar. 4, 1959
    (65).
Tearle, Conway, actor; b. May 17, 1878, New York City; d. Oct. 1,
    1938 (60).
Tearle, Sir Godfrey, actor; b. Oct. 12, 1884, New York City;
    d. June 8, 1953 (68).
Teather, Ida, actress; d. Apr. 20, 1954.
Tedmarsh, William J., actor; b. Feb. 3, 1876, London, England;
    d. May 10, 1937 (61).
Tedro, Henrietta, actress; d. July 25, 1948 (63).
Teege, Joachim, actor; b. Feb., 1925, Spremberg, Germany; d. Nov. 23,
    1969 (44).
Telaak, Bill, actor; b. Jan. 9, 1898, New York; d. Dec. 21, 1963 (65).
Tell, Alma, actress; b. Mar. 27, 1898, New York City; d. Dec. 29,
    1937 (39).
Tell, Olive, actress; b. New York City; d. June 6, 1951 (55).
Tellegen, Lou, actor; b. Nov. 26, 1883, Holland; d. Oct. 29, 1934
    (50).
Tellegen, Mike, actor; b. Apr. 20, 1885, Russia; d. Aug. 16, 1970
    (85).
Tello, Alfonso Sanchez, actor; b. Mar. 8, 1905, Mexico; d. Apr. 18,
    1979 (74).
Tempest, Marie, actress; b. July 15, 1862, London, England;
    d. Oct. 15, 1942 (80).
Tempest, Tom, actor; d. Dec. 14, 1955 (81).
Templeton, Fay, actress; b. Dec. 25, 1865, Little Rock, Ark.;
    d. Oct. 3, 1939 (73).
Templeton, Olive, actress; d. May 29, 1979 (96).
Tenbrook, Harry, actor; b. Oct. 9, 1887, Norway; d. Sept. 14, 1960
    (72).
Tenenholtz, Elihu (see Holtz, Tenen)
Ten Eyck, Lillian, actress; b. Apr. 22, 1886, New Jersey; d. Dec. 6,
    1966 (80).
Tennant, Dorothy, actress; d. July 3, 1942 (77).
Tennberg, Jean-Marc, actor; b. May 12, 1924, Pantin, France;
    d. Aug. 12, 1971 (47).
Terhune, Max, actor; b. Feb. 12, 1891, Franklin, Ind.; d. June 5,
    1973 (82).

Terr, Albert R. (see Terry, Al)
Terranova, Dino (r.n. Corrado Vacirca), actor; b. Italy; d. Apr. 27, 1969 (65).
Terrell, Kenneth, actor; b. Apr. 29, 1904, Georgia; d. Mar. 8, 1966 (61).
Terriss, Ellaline, actress; b. Apr. 13, 1871, Falkland Islands; d. June 16, 1971 (100).
Terriss, Tom, actor & director; b. Sept. 28, 1872, London, England; d. Feb. 8, 1964 (91).
Terry, Al (Albert R. Terr), actor; b. May 22, 1893, New York; d. July 15, 1967 (74).
Terry, Ellen, actress; b. Feb. 27, 1848, Coventry, Warwickshire, England; d. July 21, 1928 (80).
Terry, Ethel Grey, actress; b. Oct. 2, 1891, California; d. Jan. 6, 1931 (39).
Terry, Fred, actor; b. Nov. 9, 1863, London, England; d. Apr. 17, 1933 (69).
Terry, Hazel, actress; b. Jan. 23, 1918, London, England; d. Oct. 12, 1974 (56).
Terry, Paul, animator; b. Feb. 19, 1887, San Francisco, Calif.; d. Oct. 25, 1971 (84).
Terry, Robert A. (r.n. Robert Anthony Terry), scenarist; b. Dec. 5, 1918, Nebraska; d. Aug. 14, 1975 (56).
Terry, Sheila, actress; d. Jan. 19, 1957 (46).
Terry-Lewis, Mabel, actress; b. Oct. 28, 1872, London, England; d. Nov. 28, 1957 (85).
Teschke, Sara Taft (see Taft, Sara)
Tesler, Jack, actor; b. May 13, 1898, New York; d. Sept. 8, 1976 (78).
Tetley, Walter, actor; b. June 2, 1915, New York City; d. Sept. 7, 1975 (60).
Tetzel, Joan, actress; b. June 21, 1921, New York City; d. Oct. 31, 1977 (56).
Tevis, Carol, actress; b. Mar. 6, 1907, Pennsylvania; d. May 15, 1965 (58).
Te Wiata, Inia, actor; d. June 26, 1971 (55).
Thalasso, Arthur, actor; b. Nov. 26, 1883, Ohio; d. Feb. 13, 1954 (70).
Thalberg, Irving, producer & executive; b. May 30, 1899, Brooklyn, N.Y.; d. Sept. 14, 1936 (37).
Thanhouser, Edwin, producer; d. Mar. 21, 1956 (90).
Tharnaes, Charles Sofus, actor; b. Mar. 9, 1900, Copenhagen, Denmark; d. Jan. 29, 1952 (51).
Thatcher, Billy, actor; b. Apr. 28, 1922, London, England; d. Oct., 1964 (42).
Thatcher, Evelyn, actress; b. Mar. 14, 1862, Omaha, Neb.; d. Sept. 28, 1942 (80).
Thawl, Evelyn, actress; d. Oct., 1945 (30).
Thayer, Donald, actor; b. Nov. 29, 1893, Minnesota; d. Dec. 4, 1953 (60).
Theis, Alfred, actor; d. Sept. 16, 1951 (52).
Thesiger, Ernest, actor; b. Jan. 15, 1879, London, England; d. Jan. 14, 1961 (81).
Thiele, Wilhelm J., director, actor, & author; b. Vienna, Austria; d. Sept. 7, 1975 (85).
Thiele, William J. (see Thiele, Wilhelm J.)

Thimig, Helene, actress; b. June 5, 1889, Austria; d. Nov. 6, 1974 (85).

Thoeren, Robert, writer; b. Apr. 21, 1903, Bruenn, Czechoslovakia; d. July 15, 1957 (54).

Thom, Norman, actor; b. Oct. 19, 1877, Greenup, Ky.; d. May 24, 1931 (53).

Thomas, A.E., writer; d. June 18, 1947 (74).

Thomas, Alfred, actor; b. Mar. 1, 1905, Hohenlimburg; d. Oct. 3, 1976 (71).

Thomas, Edna, actress; d. July 22, 1974 (88).

Thomas, Edward, actor; b. Dec. 20, 1884, Redbank, N.J.; d. Dec. 29, 1943 (59).

Thomas, Gretchen, actress; d. Nov. 1, 1964 (67).

Thomas, Jameson, actor; b. Mar. 24, 1888, London, England; d. Jan. 10, 1939 (50).

Thomas, John Charles, actor & opera singer; b. Sept. 6, 1889, Pennsylvania; d. Dec. 13, 1960 (71).

Thomas, Leslie (r.n. Ernest Leslie Thomas), actor; b. July 5, 1901, England; d. June 24, 1967 (65).

Thomas, Olive, actress; b. Oct. 16, 1898, Charleroi, Pa.; d. Sept. 9, 1920 (21).

Thomas, Powys, actor; d. June 22, 1977 (51).

Thomas, Ruth, actress; d. Mar. 23, 1970 (59).

Thompson, Al (Albert Thompson), actor; b. Sept. 21, 1884, Pennsylvania; d. Mar. 1, 1960 (75).

Thompson, Arthur L., Sr., actor; d. July 16, 1950 (62).

Thompson, Bill, actor; b. July 8, 1913, Terre Haute, Ind.; d. July 15, 1971 (58).

Thompson, David H., actor; d. May 20, 1957 (73).

Thompson, Frederick A., actor; d. Jan. 23, 1925 (55).

Thompson, George C., actor; b. Mar. 25, 1868, Iowa; d. May 29, 1929 (61).

Thompson, George L., actor; d. Dec., 1941.

Thompson, Jim, actor & author; d. Apr. 7, 1977 (70).

Thompson, Keene, writer; d. July 11, 1937 (51).

Thompson, Margaret, actress; b. Oct. 26, 1889, Trinidad, Colo.; d. Dec. 26, 1969 (80).

Thompson, Molly, actress; d. Feb. 14, 1928 (49).

Thompson, Ray, actor; d. June 29, 1927 (29).

Thompson, Raymond L., actor; b. Aug. 14, 1894, Salt Lake City, Utah; d. Dec. 9, 1937 (43).

Thompson, Dr. Ross, actor; d. Oct. 12, 1972.

Thompson, Walker, actor; d. Sept. 19, 1922 (34).

Thompson, William F. (see Fawcett, William)

Thompson, William H., actor; b. Apr. 24, 1852, Scotland; d. Feb. 4, 1923 (70).

Thompson, William H., actor; d. July 24, 1945 (72).

Thomson, Fred, actor; b. Feb. 26, 1890, Pasadena, Calif.; d. Dec. 25, 1928 (38).

Thomson, Kenneth (r.n. Charles Kenneth Thomson), actor; b. Jan. 7, 1899, Pittsburgh, Pa.; d. Jan. 26, 1967 (68).

Thor, Larry, actor; d. Mar. 15, 1976 (59).

Thorburn, June, actress; b. June 30, 1931, Kashmir; d. Nov. 4, 1967 (36).

Thordsen, Kelly, actor; b. Jan. 19, 1917, South Dakota; d. Jan. 23, 1978 (61).

Thorn, John, actor; d. Aug. 28, 1935 (55).

Thornby, Robert T., actor; b. Mar. 27, 1888, New York; d. Mar. 6, 1953 (64).

Thorndike, Oliver, actor; b. Sept. 12, 1918, Boston, Mass.; d. Apr. 14, 1954 (35).

Thorndike, Russell, actor; b. Feb. 6, 1885, Rochester, Kent, England; d. Nov. 7, 1972 (87).

Thorndike, Dame Sybil, actress; b. Oct. 24, 1882, Gainsborough, Yorkshire, England; d. June 9, 1976 (93).

Thorndyke, Lucyle, actress; b. Seattle, Wash.; d. Dec. 17, 1935 (70).

Thorne, Dick, actor; d. Jan. 31, 1957 (52).

Thorne, Frank A., Sr., actor; d. May 28, 1953 (71).

Thorne, Robert, actor; d. July 3, 1965 (84).

Thorne, William L., actor; b. Oct. 14, 1878, Fresno, Calif.; d. Mar. 10, 1948 (69).

Thornton, Gladys, actress; b. Mar. 8, 1899, Florida; d. Sept. 2, 1964 (65).

Thornton, Richard, actor; d. May 9, 1936 (63).

Thorpe, George, actor; b. Jan. 20, 1891, Croydon, Surrey, England; d. Dec. 24, 1961 (70).

Thorpe, Jim, actor & athlete; b. May 28, 1888, Prague, Okla.; d. Mar. 28, 1953 (64).

Thunderbird, Chief, actor; b. Aug. 6, 1866, Montana; d. Apr. 6, 1946 (79).

Thundercloud, Chief (Victor Daniels), actor; b. Apr. 12, 1899, Muskogee, Okla.; d. Dec. 1, 1955 (56).

Thurman, Mary, actress; d. Dec. 22, 1925 (25).

Thurn-Taxis, Alexis, director; d. July 26, 1979 (88).

Thursby, David, actor; b. Feb. 28, 1889, Scotland; d. Apr. 20, 1977 (88).

Thurston, Carol, actress; b. Sept. 27, 1923, Forsyth, Mont.; d. Dec. 31, 1969 (46).

Thurston, Charles, actor; b. Aug. 10, 1868, Oconto, Wisc.; d. Mar. 4, 1940 (71).

Thurston, Harry, actor; b. London, England; d. Sept. 2, 1955 (81).

Thurston, Muriel, actress; d. May 1, 1943 (68).

Tibbett, Lawrence, actor & opera singer; b. Nov. 16, 1896, Bakersfield, Calif.; d. July 15, 1960 (63).

Tickle, Frank, actor; b. June 25, 1893, London, England; d. Oct. 18, 1955 (62).

Tidblad, Inga, actress; b. May 29, 1901, Stockholm, Sweden; d. Sept. 12, 1975 (74).

Tidmarsh, Ferdinand, actor; d. Nov., 1922.

Tiedtke, Jakob, actor; b. June 23, 1875, Berlin, Germany; d. June 30, 1960 (85).

Tighe, Harry, actor & director; b. New Haven, Conn.; d. Feb. 10, 1935 (50).

Tilbury, Zeffie, actress; b. Nov. 20, 1863, London, England; d. July 22, 1950 (86).

Tilden, Bill, actor & tennis star; b. Feb. 10, 1893, Germantown, Pa.; d. June 4, 1953 (60).

Tilden, Milano C., actor & director; b. Paris, France; d. Sept. 30, 1951 (73).

Tilton, Edwin Booth, actor; b. Sept. 15, 1859, Illinois; d. Jan. 16, 1926 (66).

Timmons, Joanne, actress; b. Apr. 22, 1931, Kansas; d. May 5, 1962 (31).

Timmons, Joseph, stuntman; d. Mar. 29, 1933 (36).
Tindall, Loren, actor; b. May 23, 1921, Oklahoma; d. May 11, 1973
    (51).
Tinling, James, director; b. May 8, 1898, Seattle, Wash.; d. May 14,
    1967 (69).
Tiomkin, Dmitri, composer; b. May 10, 1899, Russia; d. Nov. 11, 1979
    (80).
Tirado, Romualdo, actor; b. Sept. 3, 1880, Spain; d. Oct. 17, 1963
    (83).
Tirella, Eduardo, actor; d. Oct. 7, 1966 (42).
Tisdale, Franklin M., director & actor; d. Feb. 14, 1947 (76).
Tisse, Eduard, cinematographer; b. Apr. 13, 1897, Lithuania;
    d. Nov. 18, 1961 (64).
Tissier, Jean, actor; b. Apr. 1, 1896, Paris, France; d. Apr., 1973
    (77).
Tissot, Alice, actress; d. May 5, 1971 (81).
Titheradge, Dion, actor; b. Mar. 30, 1889, Melbourne, Australia;
    d. Nov. 16, 1934 (45).
Titheradge, Madge, actress; b. July 2, 1887, Melbourne, Australia;
    d. Nov. 14, 1961 (74).
Titmuss, Phyllis, actress; b. 1901; d. Jan. 6, 1946 (44).
Titus, Lydia Yeamans, actress; b. at sea; d. Dec. 29, 1929 (63).
Tobias, George, actor; b. July 14, 1901, New York City; d. Feb. 27,
    1980 (78).
Todd, Harry, actor; b. Dec. 13, 1863, Allegheny, Pa.; d. Feb. 15,
    1935 (71).
Todd, Holbrook N., film editor; b. Feb. 10, 1906, New York; d. Aug. 7,
    1972 (66).
Todd, James, actor; b. July 8, 1908, Chicago, Ill.; d. Feb. 8, 1968
    (59).
Todd, Mike, producer; b. June 22, 1907, Minneapolis, Minn.;
    d. Mar. 22, 1958 (50).
Todd, Rufo Wesley, actor; d. Oct. 1, 1958 (76).
Todd, Thelma (Alison Loyd), actress; b. July 29, 1905, Lawrence,
    Mass.; d. Dec. 16, 1935 (30).
Tokar, Norman, director; d. Apr. 6, 1979 (59).
Tokatyan, Armand, opera singer; b. July 17, 1895, Bulgaria;
    d. June 12, 1960 (64).
Toland, Gregg, cinematographer; b. May 29, 1904, Charleston, Ill.;
    d. Sept. 28, 1948 (44).
Toler, Sidney, actor; b. Apr. 28, 1888, Warrensburg, Va.; d. Feb. 12,
    1947 (58).
Tollaire, August, actor; b. Mar. 7, 1866, France; d. Jan. 15, 1959
    (92).
Tollen, Otz, actor; b. Apr. 9, 1882, Berlin, Germany; d. July, 1965
    (83).
Tolly, Frank, stuntman; d. Nov. 26, 1924.
Tolnaes, Gunnar, actor; b. Feb. 7, 1879, Cristiania; d. Nov. 9, 1940
    (61).
Tomack, Sid, actor; b. Sept. 8, 1907, New York; d. Nov. 12, 1962 (55).
Tomamoto, Thomas, actor; d. Sept. 29, 1924 (45).
Tomarchio, Ludovico, actor; b. Jan. 6, 1886, Catania, Italy;
    d. June 25, 1947 (61).
Tomei, Luigi, actor; d. May 15, 1955 (45).
Tomich, Jean, stuntman; d. Aug. 11, 1969 (28).

Tone, Franchot, actor; b. Feb. 27, 1905, Niagara Falls, N.Y.;
    d. Sept. 18, 1968 (63).
Toney, Jim, actor; d. Jan. 1, 1884; d. Sept. 19, 1973 (89).
Tong, Kam, actor; b. Dec. 18, 1906, California; d. Nov. 8, 1969 (62).
Tong, Sammee, actor; b. Apr. 21, 1901, California; d. Oct. 27, 1964
    (63).
Tonge, H. Assheton, actor; d. Apr. 2, 1927 (55).
Tonge, Philip (r.n. Philip Asheton Tonge), actor; b. Apr. 26, 1897,
    England; d. Jan. 28, 1959 (61).
Tony, horse; d. Oct. 10, 1942 (40).
Tooker, William H., actor; b. Sept. 2, 1869, New York City; d. Oct.
    10, 1936 (67).
Toomes, Fred (Snowflake), actor; b. Jan. 5, 1906, North Carolina;
    d. Feb. 13, 1962 (56).
Topart, Lise, actress; d. Mar. 3, 1952 (22).
Topey, Lester, actor; d. Aug., 1920 (21).
Tordesillas, Jesus, actor; d. Mar. 24, 1973 (80).
Toren, Marta, actress; b. May 21, 1926, Stockholm, Sweden; d. Feb. 19,
    1957 (30).
Tornek, Jack, actor; b. Jan. 2, 1888, Russia; d. Feb. 18, 1974 (86).
Torrence, David, actor; b. Jan. 17, 1864, Scotland; d. Dec. 26, 1951
    (87).
Torrence, Ernest, actor; b. June 26, 1878, Edinburgh, Scotland;
    d. May 15, 1933 (54).
Torriani, Aimee, actress; d. July 18, 1963 (73).
Torruco, Miguel, actor; d. Apr. 22, 1956 (36).
Torvay, Jose, actor; d. 1973.
Toso, Otello, actor; b. Feb. 22, 1914, Padova, Italy; d. Mar. 15,
    1966 (52).
Totheroh, Dan, writer; d. Dec. 3, 1976 (82).
Totheroh, Roland (Rollie), cinematographer; d. June 18, 1967 (76).
Toto (Armando Novello), actor; d. Dec. 15, 1938 (50).
Toto, actor; b. Feb. 15, 1898, Naples, Italy; d. Apr. 15, 1967 (69).
Toto, Billie, actress; d. Dec. 24, 1928 (34).
Totten, Joseph Byron, director & actor; b. Brooklyn, N.Y.; d. Apr. 29,
    1946 (70).
Toulout, Jean, actor; b. Sept. 28, 1887, Paris, France; d. Oct. 18,
    1962 (75).
Tourel, Jennie, opera singer; d. Nov. 23, 1973 (63).
Tourjansky, Victor, director; d. Aug. 13, 1976 (85).
Tourneur, Jacques, director; b. Nov. 12, 1904, Paris, France;
    d. Dec. 19, 1977 (73).
Tourneur, Maurice, director; b. Feb. 2, 1873, Paris, France;
    d. Aug. 4, 1961 (88).
Toutain, Roland, actor; d. Oct., 1977 (72).
Tover, Leo, cinematographer; b. Dec. 6, 1902, New Haven, Conn.;
    d. Dec. 30, 1964 (62).
Tover, May, actress; d. Dec. 20, 1949 (38).
Towne, Gene, writer; b. Mar. 27, 1904, New York City; d. Mar. 17,
    1979 (74).
Townley, Jack, writer; b. Mar. 3, 1897, Kansas City, Mo.; d. Oct. 15,
    1960 (63).
Townsend, Anna, actress; b. Jan. 5, 1845, Utica, N.Y.; d. Sept. 11,
    1923 (78).
Tozere, Frederic, actor; b. June 19, 1901, Brookline, Mass.;
    d. Aug. 5, 1972 (71).

Tozzi, Fausto, actor; d. Dec. 10, 1978 (57).
Tracey, Thomas, actor & assistant director; d. Aug. 27, 1961 (81).
Tracy, Helen, actress; d. Sept. 5, 1924 (74).
Tracy, Lee, actor; b. Apr. 14, 1898, Atlanta, Ga.; d. Oct. 18, 1968 (70).
Tracy, Spencer, actor; b. Apr. 5, 1900, Milwaukee, Wisc.; d. June 10, 1967 (67).
Tracy, William (r.n. Clarence William Tracy), actor; b. Dec. 1, 1917, Pittsburgh, Pa.; d. June 18, 1967 (49).
Trader, George Henry, actor; d. Mar. 12, 1951 (85).
Trafton, Herbert (Curl), actor (Keystone Kop); d. Sept. 1, 1979 (86).
Train, Jack, actor; b. Plymouth, England; d. Dec. 19, 1966 (64).
Trainor, Leonard, actor; b. Feb. 24, 1879, Talaquah, Okla.;
    d. July 28, 1940 (61).
Tramel, actor; b. 1879, Toulon, France; d. Jan. 12, 1948 (68).
Trask, Wayland, actor; b. July 16, 1887, New York; d. Nov. 18, 1918 (31).
Traubel, Helen, opera singer & actress; b. June 20, 1899, St. Louis, Mo.; d. July 28, 1972 (73).
Trautman, Ludwig, actor; d. Jan. 24, 1957 (71).
Travers, Celia, actress; b. Apr. 10, 1915, New Hampshire; d. June 10, 1975 (60).
Travers, Henry, actor; b. Mar. 5, 1874, England; d. Oct. 18, 1965 (91).
Travers, Nat, actor; d. Dec. 22, 1958 (83).
Travers, Richard C., actor; b. Apr. 15, 1885, Hudson Bay Trading Post, Canada; d. Apr. 20, 1935 (50).
Travers, Tony, actor; d. Jan. 16, 1959 (39).
Travers, Vic, actor; b. Bradford, England; d. May 26, 1948 (61).
Traverse, Jean, actress; d. May 11, 1947 (70).
Traverse, Madlaine, actress; d. Jan. 7, 1964 (88).
Travis, Charles William, actor; d. Aug. 14, 1917 (56).
Traynor, John F., actor; d. Oct. 1, 1955 (81).
Treacher, Arthur, actor; b. July 23, 1894, Brighton, England;
    d. Dec. 14, 1975 (81).
Treacy, Emerson, actor; b. Sept. 7, 1900, Philadelphia, Pa.;
    d. Jan. 10, 1967 (66).
Treadway, Charlotte, actress; b. May 18, 1895, Louisiana; d. Feb. 26, 1963 (67).
Treadwell, Laura, actress; b. July 14, 1879, West Virginia; d. Nov. 22, 1960 (81).
Tree, Sir Herbert Beerbohm, actor; b. Dec. 17, 1853, London, England;
    d. July 2, 1917 (63).
Tree, Lady, actress; b. Oct. 5, 1858, London, England; d. Aug. 7, 1937 (78).
Tree, Viola, actress; b. July 17, 1884, London, England; d. Nov. 15, 1938 (54).
Trenholme, Helen, actress; b. June 23, 1911, Montreal, Canada;
    d. Jan. 30, 1962 (50).
Trent, Jack, actor; b. Aug. 24, 1896, Texas; d. Aug. 1, 1961 (64).
Trent, John (r.n. LaVerne W. Browne), actor; b. Dec. 9, 1906, Orange, Calif.; d. May 12, 1966 (59).
Trent, Sheila, actress; d. May 26, 1954 (46).
Treskoff, Olga, actress; d. Apr. 23, 1938 (36).
Tressler, Otto, actor; b. Apr. 13, 1871, Stuttgart, Germany;
    d. Apr. 27, 1965 (94).

Treumann, Paul, actor; d. Jan., 1951 (83).

Trevelyan, Hilda, actress; b. Feb. 4, 1880; d. Nov. 10, 1959 (79).

Trevelyan, Una, actress; d. May 14, 1948 (52).

Trevi, Christina, actress & opera singer; d. July 1, 1956 (26).

Trevor, Ann, actress; d. July, 1970.

Trevor, Austin, actor; b. Oct. 7, 1897, Belfast, N. Ireland; d. Jan. 22, 1978 (80).

Trevor, Hugh, actor; b. Oct. 28, 1903, New York; d. Nov. 10, 1933 (30).

Trevor, Norman, actor; b. June 23, 1877, Calcutta, India; d. Oct. 30, 1929 (52).

Trevor, Spencer, actor; b. May 29, 1875, Biarritz, France; d. May 22, 1945 (69).

Trexler, Lee Hill, actor; d. Sept. 15, 1957 (63).

Tricoli, Carlo, actor; b. Dec. 2, 1889, Italy; d. Apr. 11, 1966 (76).

Triesault, Ivan, actor; b. July 14, 1898, Estonia; d. Jan. 3, 1980 (81).

Trigger, horse; d. July 3, 1965 (33).

Triller, Armand, actor; b. Mar. 20, 1883, Bucharest, Rumania; d. Dec. 12, 1939 (56).

Trimble, Larry, director & actor; b. Feb. 15, 1885, Maine; d. Feb. 8, 1954 (68).

Trivas, Viktor, director; b. 1896, Russia; d. Apr., 1970 (73).

Trosper, Guy, writer; b. Mar. 27, 1911, Lander, Wyo.; d. Dec. 20, 1963 (52).

Trotti, Lamar, author & producer; b. Oct. 18, 1900, Georgia; d. Aug. 23, 1952 (51).

Trouncer, Cecil, actor; b. Apr. 5, 1898, Southport, Lancashire, England; d. Dec. 15, 1953 (55).

Trout, Francis "Dink," actor; b. June 18, 1898, Beardstown, Ill.; d. Mar. 26, 1950 (51).

Trow, William, actor; b. Oct. 19, 1890, Illinois; d. Sept. 2, 1973 (82).

Trowbridge, Charles, actor; b. Jan. 10, 1882, Vera Cruz, Mexico; d. Oct. 30, 1967 (85).

Troy, Elinor, actress; d. Nov. 29, 1949 (33).

Troy, Helen, actress; b. Dec. 23, 1903, San Francisco, Calif.; d. Nov. 1, 1942 (38).

Troy, Sidney Z., stuntman; d. June 10, 1978 (70).

Truax, Maude, actress; d. Sept. 6, 1939 (54).

True, Bessie, actress; d. July 9, 1947 (48).

Truesdale, Howard, actor; b. Jan. 3, 1861, Conneautville, Pa.; d. Dec. 8, 1941 (80).

Truesdell, Fred C., actor; d. May 9, 1929 (55).

Truesdell, George Frederick, actor; d. May 3, 1937 (64).

Truex, Ernest, actor; b. Sept. 19, 1889, Kansas City, Mo.; d. June 27, 1973 (83).

Trujillo, Lorenzo L., actor; d. Feb., 1962 (56).

Truman, Ralph, actor; b. May 7, 1900, London, England; d. Oct. 15, 1977 (77).

Trumbo, Dalton (Robert Rich), writer; b. Dec. 9, 1905, Montrose, Calif.; d. Sept. 10, 1976 (70).

Truppi, Daniel, actor; b. July 25, 1919, New York; d. July 6, 1970 (50).

Tryon, Glenn, actor & director; b. Sept. 14, 1899, Julietta, Idaho; d. Apr. 18, 1970 (70).

Tschepe, Kurt, actor; b. May 7, 1887, Berlin, Germany; d. Feb., 1967 (79).

Tsiang, H.T., actor; b. 1906, China; d. July 16, 1971 (65).

Tsukamoto, Raynum, actor; b. Mar. 1, 1889, Japan; d. Aug. 9, 1974 (85).

Tubbs, William, actor; d. Jan. 25, 1953 (45).

Tucker, Cy, actor; b. June 3, 1890, England; d. July 4, 1952 (62).

Tucker, Ethel, actress; d. May 14, 1926.

Tucker, George Loane, director & actor; b. Chicago, Ill.; d. June 20, 1921 (49).

Tucker, Harland, actor; b. Dec. 8, 1893, Ohio; d. Mar. 22, 1949 (55).

Tucker, John, actor; d. Aug., 1922 (62).

Tucker, Richard, actor; b. June 4, 1884, New York City; d. Dec. 5, 1942 (58).

Tucker, Sophie (r.n. Sophie Abuza), singer & actress; b. Jan. 13, 1888, Russia; d. Feb. 9, 1966 (78).

Tufts, Sonny (r.n. Bowen Charleston Tufts II), actor; b. July 16, 1911, Boston, Mass.; d. June 4, 1970 (58).

Tully, Ethel, actress; d. Oct. 1, 1968 (70).

Tully, Jim, author & actor; b. June 3, 1891, St. Marys, Ohio; d. June 22, 1947 (56).

Tunc, Irene, actress; d. Jan. 16, 1972 (34).

Tunis, Fay, actress; d. Dec. 4, 1967 (77).

Tunney, Gene, actor & boxer; b. May 25, 1898, New York City; d. Nov. 7, 1978 (80).

Turleigh, Veronica, actress; b. Jan. 14, 1903, Ireland; d. Sept. 3, 1971 (68).

Turnbull, John, actor; b. Nov. 5, 1880, Dunbar, Scotland; d. Feb. 23, 1956 (75).

Turnbull, Stanley, actor; b. Whitby, Yorkshire, England; d. May 8, 1924 (43).

Turner, Bowditch "Smoke," actor; b. 1878, Virginia; d. Sept. 12, 1933 (55).

Turner, Emanuel, actor; d. Dec. 13, 1941 (57).

Turner, Florence, actress; b. New York City; d. Aug. 28, 1946 (61).

Turner, Frank DeLauny (Pops), actor; d. Oct. 27, 1957 (76).

Turner, Fred A., actor; b. Oct. 12, 1858, New York; d. Feb. 13, 1923 (64).

Turner, George, actor; b. Apr. 27, 1877, Leavenworth, Kans.; d. Oct. 3, 1947 (70).

Turner, George K., author & actor; d. Feb. 15, 1952 (83).

Turner, Maidel, actress; b. Sherman, Tex.; d. Apr. 12, 1953 (72).

Turner, Martin, actor; b. Dec. 20, 1882, Texas; d. May 14, 1957 (74).

Turner, Col. Roscoe, stunt pilot; d. June 23, 1970 (74).

Turner, Smoke (see Turner, Bowditch "Smoke")

Turner, William H., actor; d. Sept. 27, 1942 (80).

Turpin, Ben, actor; b. Sept. 19, 1869, New Orleans, La.; d. July 1, 1940 (70).

Tutmarc, Paul H., singer; d. Sept. 23, 1972 (76).

Tuttle, Frank, director; b. Aug. 6, 1892, New York City; d. Jan. 6, 1963 (70).

Tweddell, Frank, actor; b. Mar. 15, 1895, Muree, India; d. Dec. 20, 1971 (76).

Tweed, Tommy, actor; d. Oct. 12, 1971 (64).

Twelvetrees, Helen (r.n. Helen Marie Jurgens), actress; b. Dec. 25, 1908, Brooklyn, N.Y.; d. Feb. 13, 1958 (49).

Twist, Derek, director; d. Aug. 15, 1979 (74).

Twist, John, writer; b. July 14, 1898, Albany, Mo.; d. Feb. 11, 1976 (77).

Twitchell, Archie (Michael Branden), actor; b. Nov. 28, 1906, Oregon; d. Jan. 31, 1957 (50).

Tyke, Johnny (r.n. Johnny Tyacke), actor; b. Oct. 20, 1894, Oregon; d. Feb. 23, 1940 (45).

Tyler, Harry, actor; b. June 13, 1888, New York City; d. Sept. 15, 1961 (73).

Tyler, Judy, actress; d. July 3, 1957 (24).

Tyler, Lelah, actress; d. Feb. 10, 1944 (66).

Tyler, Odette, actress; b. Sept. 26, 1869, Savannah, Ga.; d. Dec. 8, 1936 (67).

Tyler, T. Texas (r.n. David Luke Myrick), recording artist & actor; b. June 20, 1916, Mena, Ark.; d. Jan. 23, 1972 (55).

Tyler, Tom (r.n. Vincent Markowski), actor; b. Aug. 9, 1903, Port Henry, N.Y.; d. May 1, 1954 (50).

Tynan, Brandon, actor; b. Apr. 11, 1875, Dublin, Ireland; d. Mar. 19, 1967 (91).

Tyrrell, John, actor; b. Dec. 7, 1900; d. Sept. 19, 1949 (48).


Ucicky, Gustav, director; d. Apr. 28, 1961 (60).

Udet, Ernst, actor & flying ace; b. Apr. 26, 1896, Germany; d. Nov. 17, 1941 (45).

Uhlig, Max E., actor; d. May 28, 1958 (62).

Ullman, Daniel, author; d. Oct. 23, 1979 (61).

Ullman, Edward G., photographer; b. July 3, 1867, Natchez, Miss.; d. Feb. 9, 1940 (72).

Ullman, Frederic, Jr., producer & actor; b. Apr. 19, 1903, Buffalo, N.Y.; d. Dec. 26, 1948 (45).

Ulman, Ernst, actor; d. July 27, 1977.

Ulmer, Anna, actress; d. Oct. 28, 1928 (75).

Ulmer, Edgar G. (r.n. Edgar George Ulmer), director; b. Sept. 17, 1904, Vienna, Austria; d. Sept. 30, 1972 (68).

Ulmer, Friedrich, actor; b. Mar. 27, 1877; d. Apr. 26, 1952 (75).

Ulric, Lenore, actress; b. July 21, 1892, New Ulm, Minn.; d. Dec. 30, 1970 (78).

Underhill, John G., actor; b. Apr. 26, 1870, New York City; d. May 26, 1941 (71).

Underwood, Frances, actress; b. May 10, 1884, California; d. Apr. 21, 1961 (76).

Underwood, Franklyn, actor; b. Denver, Colo.; d. Dec. 22, 1940 (63).

Underwood, Lawrence, actor; b. Albion, Iowa; d. Feb. 2, 1939 (68).

Underwood, Loyal, actor; b. Aug. 6, 1893, Illinois; d. Sept. 30, 1966 (73).

Unger, Gladys B., writer; d. May 25, 1940 (55).

Unterkircher, Hans, actor; d. May, 1971.

Updegraff, Henry, actor; d. July 29, 1936 (47).

Urban, Dorothy Karroll, actress; d. Oct. 29, 1961 (92).

Urbansky, Yevgeny, actor; b. 1932, Russia; d. Nov. 5, 1965 (33).

Ure, Mary, actress; b. Feb. 18, 1933, Glasgow, Scotland; d. Apr. 3, 1975 (42).

Urecal, Minerva, actress; b. Sept. 22, 1884, California; d. Feb. 26, 1966 (81).

Urquhart, Alasdair, actor; b. Scotland; d. Aug. 25, 1954 (41).
Urquhart, Molly, actress; d. Oct. 6, 1977 (71).
Urson, Frank B., director; d. Aug. 16, 1928 (41).
Urzi, Saro, actor; b. Feb. 24, 1913, Catania; d. Nov. 2, 1979 (66).
Usher, Guy, actor; b. May 9, 1883, Mason City, Iowa; d. June 16,
    1944 (61).
Usher, Harry, actor; d. Oct. 28, 1950 (63).
Uttal, Fred, actor; d. Nov. 28, 1963 (55).


Vaccaro, Frank A., actor; d. July 6, 1948 (64).
Vadnay, Laszlo, writer; b. June 6, 1904, Budapest, Hungary; d. Apr.
    18, 1967 (62).
Vague, Vera (Barbara Jo Allen), actress; b. Sept. 2, 1908, New York;
    d. Sept. 14, 1974 (66).
Vail, Lester, actor; b. June 29, 1899, Colorado; d. Nov. 28, 1959
    (60).
Vail, Myrtle, actress (Myrt and Marge); d. Sept. 18, 1978 (90).
Vail, Olive, actress; d. June 14, 1951 (47).
Vajda, Ernest, writer; b. Hungary; d. Apr. 3, 1954 (67).
Vajda, Ladislao, director; b. Aug. 18, 1905, Budapest, Hungary;
    d. Apr., 1965 (59).
Valdemar, Tania, actress; d. Nov. 12, 1955 (61).
Valdes, Miguelito, singer; d. Nov. 9, 1978 (62).
Vale, Louise, actress; d. Oct. 29, 1918.
Vale, Travers, director; b. Jan. 31, 1865, England; d. Jan. 10, 1927
    (61).
Valentin, Karl, actor; b. June 4, 1882, Monaco; d. Feb. 9, 1948 (65).
Valentine, Elizabeth, actress; b. Mar. 16, 1877, New York City;
    d. July 23, 1971 (94).
Valentine, Grace, actress; d. Nov. 12, 1964 (80).
Valentine, Joseph, cinematographer; b. July 24, 1903, New York City;
    d. May 18, 1949 (45).
Valentino, Rudolph, actor; b. May 6, 1895, Italy; d. Aug. 23, 1926
    (31).
Valli, Romolo, actor; b. Feb. 7, 1925, Reggio Emilia, Italy;
    d. Feb. 1, 1980 (54).
Valerio, Albano, actor; d. Feb. 2, 1961 (72).
Valk, Frederick, actor; d. July 23, 1956 (55).
Valkyrien, Valda, actress; b. Sept. 30, 1895, Denmark; d. Oct. 22,
    1956 (61).
Vallentin, Herman, actor; d. Nov., 1945 (75).
Valli, Valli, actress; b. Feb. 11, 1882, Berlin, Germany; d. Nov. 4,
    1927 (45).
Valli, Virginia, actress; b. June 10, 1898, Chicago, Ill.; d. Sept. 24,
    1968 (70).
Vallin, Rick, actor; b. Sept. 24, 1919, Russia; d. Aug. 31, 1977 (57).
Vallis, Robert, actor; d. Dec. 19, 1932 (56).
Vallon, Michael (Rollo Dix) (r.n. Rolla D. Olin), actor; b. July 21,
    1897, Minnesota; d. Nov. 13, 1973 (76).
Valsted, Myrtle, actress; d. Sept. 19, 1928 (18).
Van, Billy (r.n. Vito Coppola), actor; d. Aug. 22, 1973 (61).
Van, Billy B., actor; b. Pottstown, Pa.; d. Nov. 16, 1950 (72).
Van, Connie, actress; d. July 16, 1961 (52).

Van, Gus, actor; b. Brooklyn, N.Y.; d. Mar. 13, 1968 (80).
Van, Wally, actor; b. Sept. 27, 1885, New Hyde Park, N.Y.; d. May 9, 1974 (88).
Van Antwerp, Albert, actor; b. 1898, Denver, Colo.; d. Oct. 30, 1946 (48).
Van Auker, Cecil K., actor; d. Feb. 18, 1938.
Van Beers, Stanley, actor; b. May 4, 1911, London, England; d. May 25, 1961 (50).
Vanbrugh, Dame Irene, actress; b. Dec. 2, 1872, Exeter, England; d. Nov. 30, 1949 (76).
Vanbrugh, Violet, actress; b. June 11, 1867, Exeter, England; d. Nov. 11, 1942 (75).
Van Buren, A.H. (r.n. Archimedes H. Van Buren), actor; b. Apr. 9, 1879, New Jersey; d. Aug. 1, 1965 (86).
Van Buren, Mabel, actress; b. July 17, 1878, Chicago, Ill.; d. Nov. 4, 1947 (69).
Vance, Lucille, actress; d. May 10, 1974.
Vance, Virginia, actress; d. Oct. 13, 1942 (40).
Vance, Vivian, actress; b. July 26, 1913, Cherryvale, Kans.; d. Aug. 17, 1979 (66).
Van Cortland, Jan, actor; d. July 21, 1928 (68).
Vandergrift, Monte (r.n. J. Monte Vandergrift), actor; b. Jan. 12, 1893, Pittsburgh, Pa.; d. July 29, 1939 (46).
Vanderic, Georges, actor; d. Aug. 1, 1979 (78).
Vanderveer, Ellinor, actress; d. May 27, 1976 (89).
Van Druten, John, writer; d. Dec. 19, 1957 (56).
Van Dyk, James, actor; d. Dec. 17, 1951 (56).
Van Dyke, W.S. (r.n. Woodbridge Strong Van Dyke), director; b. Mar. 21, 1890, San Diego, Calif.; d. Feb. 5, 1943 (52).
Vane, Denton, actor; d. Sept. 17, 1940 (50).
Vane, Myrtle, actress; d. Feb. 17, 1932 (62).
Van Eyck, Peter, actor; b. July 16, 1913, Steinwehr, Germany; d. July 15, 1969 (55).
Van Gyseghem, Andre, actor; b. Aug. 18, 1906, Eltham, Kent, England; d. Oct. 13, 1979 (73).
Van Haden, Anders, actor; d. June 19, 1936 (60).
Van Horn, James, actor & stuntman; b. Sept. 24, 1917, South Dakota; d. Apr. 20, 1966 (48).
Van Houten, Frankie, actor; d. July 19, 1978.
Vanin, Vasiliy V., actor; b. Jan. 13, 1898, Tambov, U.S.S.R.; d. May 12, 1951 (53).
Van Meter, Harry, actor; b. Mar. 29, 1871, Malta Bend, Mo.; d. June 2, 1956 (85).
Van Meter, Joseph, actor; b. Aug. 3, 1876, Missouri; d. Nov. 22, 1961 (85).
Vann, W.T., actor; d. Sept. 15, 1927.
Van Name, Elsie, actress; b. Staten Island, N.Y.; d. Nov. 4, 1934 (44).
Vanne, Marda, actress; d. Apr. 27, 1970.
Vanni-Marcoux, opera singer; b. July 12, 1877, Torino, Italy; d. Oct. 22, 1962 (85).
Vanoni, Cesar, actor; b. Dec. 1, 1890, Montevideo, Uruguay; d. Oct. 4, 1953 (62).
Van Riper, Kay, writer; d. Dec. 31, 1948 (40).
Van Rooten, Luis, actor; b. Nov. 29, 1906, Mexico City, Mexico; d. June 17, 1973 (66).

Van Sickel, Dale, actor & stuntman; b. Nov. 29, 1907, Georgia;
    d. Jan. 25, 1977 (69).
Van Sloan, Edward, actor; b. Nov. 1, 1882, Minnesota; d. Mar. 8,
    1964 (81).
Van Tassell, Marie, actress; d. 1946 (72).
Van Trees, James C., cinematographer; d. Apr. 11, 1973 (83).
Van Tress, Mabel, actress; b. Oct. 6, 1872, California; d. Mar. 16,
    1962 (89).
Van Trump, Jessalyn, actress; b. Jan. 16, 1887, St. Johns, Ohio;
    d. May 2, 1939 (52).
Van Tuyl, Hellen Marr, actress; b. Mar. 4, 1892, Iowa; d. Aug. 22,
    1964 (72).
Van Upp, Virginia, writer & producer; b. Chicago, Ill.; d. Mar. 25,
    1970 (68).
Van Vleck, Will, actor; b. June 20, 1886, San Antonio, Tex.;
    d. May 19, 1966 (79).
Van Zandt, Philip (r.n. Pinheiro), actor; b. Oct. 12, 1904, Amsterdam,
    Holland; d. Feb. 15, 1958 (53).
Varconi, Victor, actor; b. Mar. 31, 1891, Kisvard, Hungary; d. June
    16, 1976 (85).
Varden, Evelyn, actress; b. June 12, 1893, Adair, Okla.; d. July 11,
    1958 (65).
Varela, Alfredo, actor; d. Mar. 31, 1962.
Varennes, Jacques, actor; b. Nov. 8, 1895, Nantes, France; d. Sept.,
    1958 (62).
Varley, Beatrice, actress; b. July 11, 1896, Manchester, England;
    d. July 4, 1964 (67).
Varnel, Marcel, director; b. Oct. 16, 1894, Paris, France; d. July 13,
    1947 (53).
Varvaro, Gloria, actress; d. Apr. 8, 1976 (61).
Vas Dias, Zelma, actress; d. Sept., 1977 (65).
Vasiliev, Georgi, director & writer; b. Nov. 25, 1899; d. June 18,
    1946 (46).
Vasiliev, Sergei, director & writer; b. Nov. 4, 1900, Moscow, Russia;
    d. Dec. 16, 1959 (59).
Vass, Lulu, actress; d. May 6, 1952 (75).
Vassar, Queenie, actress; b. Glasgow, Scotland; d. Sept. 11, 1960 (89).
Vaughan, Dorothy, actress; b. Nov. 5, 1889, St. Louis, Mo.; d. Mar. 15,
    1955 (65).
Vaughn, Adamae, actress; b. Nov. 8, 1905, Ashland, Ky.; d. Sept. 11,
    1943 (37).
Vaughn, Hilda, actress; b. Dec. 27, 1898, Baltimore, Md.; d. Dec. 28,
    1957 (59).
Vaughn, Phyllis, dancer; d. Sept. 16, 1977 (63).
Vaughn, Vivian (Gypsy Gould), actress; d. Feb. 1, 1966 (64).
Vaughn, William (see Von Brincken, William)
Vaverka, Anton, actor; b. Czechoslovakia; d. July 2, 1937.
Vavitch, Michael, actor; b. Odessa, Russia; d. Oct. 5, 1930 (54).
Veasey, William, actor; d. Nov. 13, 1956 (54).
Vedder, William H., actor; b. Sept. 9, 1873, Ohio; d. Mar. 3, 1961
    (87).
Vegeres, Joe, actor; d. Mar. 31, 1977 (82).
Veidt, Conrad, actor; b. Jan. 22, 1893, Berlin, Germany; d. Apr. 3,
    1943 (50).
Veiller, Anthony, writer; b. June 23, 1903, New York City;
    d. June 27, 1965 (62).

Veiller, Bayard, writer; b. Brooklyn, N.Y.; d. June 16, 1943 (74).
Vejar, Harry J., actor; b. Apr. 24, 1889, Los Angeles, Calif.;
    d. Mar. 1, 1968 (78).
Vekroff, Perry, actor & director; b. June 3, 1880, Alexandria,
    Egypt; d. Jan. 4, 1937 (56).
Velez, Jorge (r.n. Jorge Velez Alatriste), actor; b. Puebla, Mexico;
    d. Feb. 11, 1970 (58).
Velez, Lupe, actress; b. July 18, 1910, San Luis Potosi, Mexico;
    d. Dec. 14, 1944 (34).
Veloise, Harry, actor; d. June 16, 1936 (59).
Veness, Amy, actress; d. Sept. 22, 1960 (84).
Verdi, Francis M., actor; d. Mar. 20, 1952 (71).
Verdi, Joseph, actor; d. Dec. 27, 1957 (72).
Verebes, Erno, actor; b. Dec. 6, 1902, New York City; d. June 13,
    1971 (68).
Verhoeven, Paul, director & actor; b. June 23, 1901, Unna, Germany;
    d. Mar. 22, 1975 (73).
Vermilyea, Harold, actor; b. Oct. 10, 1889, New York City; d. Jan. 8,
    1958 (68).
Vermoyal, Paul, actor; d. Nov., 1925.
Vernay, Annie, actress; b. 1922, Nice, France; d. Aug. 19, 1941 (19).
Verne, Kaaren, actress; b. Apr. 6, 1918, Berlin, Germany; d. Dec. 23,
    1967 (49).
Verneuil, Louis, writer; b. May 14, 1893, Paris, France; d. Nov. 3,
    1952 (59).
Verney, Guy, actor; b. 1915, London, England; d. Sept. 19, 1970 (55).
Verno, Jerry, actor; b. July 26, 1895, London, England; d. June 29,
    1975 (79).
Vernon, Bobby, actor; b. Mar. 9, 1897, Chicago, Ill.; d. June 28,
    1939 (42).
Vernon, Dorothy, actress; b. Nov. 11, 1875, Germany; d. Oct. 28,
    1970 (94).
Vernon, Isabel, actress; d. Apr. 21, 1930 (56).
Vernon, Lou, actor; d. Dec. 22, 1971 (83).
Vernon, Nell, actress; d. Oct. 19, 1959 (74).
Vernon, Wally, actor; b. May 27, 1904, New York; d. Mar. 7, 1970 (65).
Verrue, Betty, actress & singer; d. July 7, 1962.
Vertov, Dziga, director; b. Jan. 12, 1896, Bialystok, Poland;
    d. Feb. 12, 1954 (58).
Ve Sota, Bruno, actor; b. Mar. 25, 1922, Illinois; d. Sept. 24, 1976
    (54).
Vespermann, Kurt, actor; b. May 1, 1887, Kulmsee; d. July 13, 1957
    (70).
Vestry, Art, actor; d. Nov. 7, 1976 (36).
Vibart, Henry, actor; b. Dec. 25, 1863, Musselburgh, Scotland;
    d. 1939 (76).
Vickers, Martha (Martha MacVicar), actress; b. May 28, 1925, Ann
    Arbor, Mich.; d. Nov. 2, 1971 (46).
Victor, Charles, actor; b. Feb. 10, 1896, England; d. Dec. 23, 1965
    (69).
Victor, Henry, actor; b. Oct. 2, 1892, London, England; d. May 15,
    1945 (52).
Vidacovich, Irvine "Pinky" (Cajun Pete), actor & jazz personality;
    b. Sept. 14, 1904, New Orleans, La.; d. July 5, 1966 (61).
Vidal, Henri, actor; d. Dec. 10, 1959 (40).

Vidor, Charles, director; b. July 27, 1900, Budapest, Hungary;
    d. June 4, 1959 (58).
Vidor, Florence, actress; b. July 23, 1895, Houston, Tex.; d. Nov. 3,
    1977 (82).
Viertel, Berthold, director; b. June 28, 1885, Vienna, Austria;
    d. Sept. 24, 1953 (68).
Viertel, Salka, writer; b. Poland; d. Oct. 20, 1978 (89).
Vignola, Robert G., director & actor; b. Aug. 5, 1882, Italy;
    d. Oct. 25, 1953 (71).
Vigo, Jean, director; b. Apr. 26, 1905, Paris, France; d. Oct. 5,
    1934 (29).
Viking, Vonceil, actress; d. Dec. 2, 1929.
Vilar, Jean, actor; d. May 28, 1971 (59).
Vilches, Ernesto, actor; b. Feb. 6, 1879, Tarragona, Spain;
    d. Dec. 7, 1954 (75).
Villard, Juliette, actress; d. Mar., 1971 (26).
Villaret, Joao, actor; d. Jan. 23, 1961 (47).
Villarreal, Julio, actor; d. Aug. 4, 1958 (73).
Villatoro, Carlos, actor; d. Mar. 14, 1963.
Villegas, Lucio, actor; b. Feb. 25, 1883, Lota, Chile; d. July 20,
    1968 (85).
Villiers, Mavis, actress; b. Sydney, Australia; d. Mar., 1976.
Vincenot, Louis (r.n. Louis P. Vincenot de Malzeville), actor;
    b. Sept. 1, 1883, Hong Kong; d. Feb. 25, 1967 (83).
Vincent, Allen, actor & author; d. Nov. 30, 1979 (76).
Vincent, Gene, recording artist & entertainer; d. Oct. 12, 1971 (36).
Vincent, Larry, actor; d. Mar. 8, 1975 (50).
Vincent, Sailor, actor & stuntman; b. Oct. 24, 1901, Massachusetts;
    d. July 12, 1966 (64).
Vine, Billy, actor; d. Feb. 10, 1958 (43).
Vinton, Arthur, actor; b. Brooklyn, N.Y.; d. Feb. 26, 1963 (65).
Vinton, Horace, actor; d. Nov. 26, 1930 (76).
Viotti, Gino, actor; b. 1875, Torino, Italy; d. Dec., 1951 (76).
Visaroff, Michael, actor; b. Nov. 18, 1892, Russia; d. Feb. 27, 1951
    (58).
Visaroff, Nina, actress; d. Dec. 14, 1938 (50).
Visconti, Luchino, director; b. Nov. 2, 1906, Milan, Italy;
    d. Mar. 17, 1976 (69).
Viterbo, Patricia, actress; d. Nov. 10, 1966 (23).
Vitray, Georges, actor; b. Feb. 29, 1888, Paris, France; d. Sept.,
    1960 (72).
Vivian, Percival, actor; b. Mar. 13, 1890, England; d. Jan. 15, 1961
    (70).
Vivian, Robert, actor; b. London, England; d. Jan. 31, 1944 (85).
Vivian, Ruth, actress; b. England; d. Oct. 24, 1949 (66).
Vodney, Max, actor; d. May 27, 1939 (46).
Vogan, Emmett, actor; b. Sept. 27, 1893, Ohio; d. Nov. 13, 1969 (76).
Vogeding, Fredrik, actor; b. Mar. 28, 1887, Holland; d. Apr. 18,
    1942 (55).
Vogel, Eleanore, actress; d. June 26, 1973 (70).
Vogel, Henry, actor; d. June 18, 1925 (60).
Vogel, Patricia, actress; d. June 25, 1941 (32).
Vogel, Peter, actor; b. Mar. 22, 1937; d. Sept. 21, 1979 (42).
Vogel, Rudolf, actor; b. Nov. 10, 1900, Munich, Germany; d. Aug. 9,
    1967 (66).

Vogler, Walter A., actor; d. Aug. 26, 1955 (58).
Vogt, Carl-Willi, actor; b. May 28, 1890, Berlin, Germany; d. Aug., 1968 (78).
Voinoff, Anatole, actor; d. Feb. 9, 1965 (69).
Vokes, Harry, actor; d. Apr. 15, 1922 (56).
Vokes, May, actress; d. Sept. 13, 1957 (75).
Voloshin, Alex, actor; b. Apr. 20, 1886, Russia; d. Nov. 23, 1960 (74).
Volotskoy, Vladimir, actor; d. Nov. 7, 1927 (74).
Volpe, Frederick, actor; b. July 31, 1865, Liverpool, England; d. Mar. 6, 1932 (66).
Von Alten, Ferdinand, actor; d. Mar. 17, 1933 (48).
von Block, Bela, director, producer, & actor; d. Mar. 23, 1962 (73).
von Bolvary, Geza, director, actor, & author; d. Aug. 11, 1961 (63).
Von Brincken, William (William Vaughn), actor; b. May 27, 1881, Flensburg, Germany; d. Jan. 18, 1946 (64).
von Collande, Gisela, actress; b. Feb. 5, 1915, Dresden, Germany; d. Oct. 23, 1960 (45).
von Diossy, Arthur, actor; b. 1889, Austria; d. Sept. 29, 1940 (51).
von Eltz, Theodore, actor; b. Nov. 5, 1893, New Haven, Conn.; d. Oct. 6, 1964 (70).
von Gerlach, Arthur, director; b. 1876; d. Aug. 4, 1925 (49).
von Gersdorf, Frederich Johann, Jr., actor; d. May 5, 1951 (46).
Von Harbou, Thea, writer; b. Dec. 12, 1888, Berlin, Germany; d. July 1, 1954 (65).
von Ledebur, Leopold, actor; b. May 18, 1876, Germany; d. Sept. 17, 1955 (79).
von Meyerinck, Hubert, actor; b. Aug. 23, 1896, Potsdam, Germany; d. Apr. 14, 1971 (74).
von Palen, Anna, actress; b. May 26, 1875, Perleberg, Germany; d. Jan. 27, 1939 (63).
Von Rempert, Albert, actor; d. Oct., 1958.
von Ritzau, Erik, actor; b. July 6, 1877, Copenhagen, Denmark; d. Feb. 28, 1936 (58).
von Schlettow, Hans Adalbert, actor; b. June 11, 1888, Frankfurt, Germany; d. Apr., 1945 (56).
von Seyffertitz, Gustav, actor; b. Aug. 4, 1863, Tyrol, Austria; d. Dec. 25, 1943 (80).
Von Sternberg, Josef, director; b. May 29, 1894, Vienna, Austria; d. Dec. 22, 1969 (75).
Von Stroheim, Erich, actor & director; b. Sept. 22, 1885, Vienna, Austria; d. May 12, 1957 (71).
Von Stroheim, Erich, Jr., actor & assistant director; b. Aug. 25, 1916, California; d. Oct. 26, 1968 (52).
Von Twardowski, Hans, actor; b. Germany; d. Nov. 19, 1958 (60).
von Ungern Sternberg, Yury, actress; d. July 3, 1941 (40).
von Wangenheim, Gustav, actor, director, & author; b. Feb. 18, 1895, Wiesbaden, Germany; d. Aug. 5, 1975 (80).
von Winterstein, Eduard, actor; b. Aug. 1, 1871, Vienna, Austria; d. July 22, 1961 (89).
Vosburgh, Alfred (see Whitman, Gayne)
Vosburgh, Harold, actor; d. Nov. 17, 1926 (56).
Vosper, Frank, actor; b. Dec. 15, 1899, London, England; d. Mar. 6, 1937 (37).
Vosper, John, actor; d. Apr. 6, 1954 (52).

Voss, Frank (Fatty), actor; d. Apr. 22, 1917.
Vroom, Frederic, actor; b. Nov. 11, 1857, Clement, Nova Scotia;
    d. June 24, 1942 (84).
Vuolo, Tito, actor; b. Mar. 22, 1893, Italy; d. Sept. 14, 1962 (69).
Vye, Murvyn, actor; b. July 15, 1913, Quincy, Mass.; d. Aug. 17,
    1976 (63).


Wack, Edward W. (see Wallock, Edwin N.)
Waddy, Edward, actor; d. June 20, 1968 (74).
Wade, Bessie, actress; d. Oct. 19, 1966 (81).
Wade, John P. (r.n. John Patrick Wade), actor; b. June 30, 1876,
    Indiana; d. July 13, 1949 (73).
Wade, Warren, actor; d. Jan. 14, 1973 (76).
Wadhams, Golden, actor; d. June 26, 1929 (60).
Wadkar, Hansa, actress; d. Aug. 23, 1971 (47).
Wadsworth, Henry, actor; b. June 18, 1902, Maysville, Ky.; d. Dec. 5,
    1974 (72).
Wadsworth, William, actor; d. June 6, 1950 (77).
Wagenheim, Charles, actor; d. Mar. 6, 1979 (84).
Wagenseller, William H., actor; d. Apr. 25, 1951 (71).
Wagner, Elsa, actress; b. 1881, Reval, Estonia; d. Sept., 1975 (94).
Wagner, Fritz Arno, cinematographer; b. Dec. 5, 1894, Germany;
    d. Aug. 18, 1958 (63).
Wagner, Jack, actor; b. Jan. 5, 1897, Ohio; d. Feb. 6, 1965 (68).
Wagner, Max, actor; b. Nov. 28, 1901, Mexico; d. Nov. 16, 1975 (73).
Wagner, Paul, actor; b. Aug. 24, 1899, Koln, Germany; d. Jan. 11,
    1970 (70).
Wagner, William, actor; b. Nov. 7, 1883, New York; d. Mar. 11, 1964
    (80).
Wainwright, Godfrey, actor; d. May 19, 1956 (77).
Wainwright, Hope, actress; d. Apr. 6, 1972 (30).
Wainwright, Marie, actress; b. May 8, 1853, Philadelphia, Pa.;
    d. Aug. 17, 1923 (70).
Waite, Charles, actor; d. Sept. 6, 1951.
Waite, Malcolm, actor; b. May 7, 1892, Menominee, Mich.; d. Apr. 25,
    1949 (56).
Wakefield, Duggie, actor; b. Aug. 28, 1899, Sheffield, England;
    d. Apr. 14, 1951 (51).
Wakefield, Florence, actress; d. Mar. 26, 1943 (52).
Wakefield, Gilbert, writer; b. Apr. 23, 1892, Sandgate, Kent, England;
    d. July 4, 1963 (71).
Wakefield, Hugh, actor; b. Nov. 10, 1888, Wanstead, Essex, England;
    d. Dec. 5, 1971 (83).
Wakefield, Oliver, actor; d. June 30, 1956 (47).
Walbrook, Anton (r.n. Adolph Wohlbruck), actor; b. Nov. 19, 1900,
    Vienna, Austria; d. Aug. 9, 1967 (66).
Walburn, Raymond, actor; b. Sept. 9, 1887, Plymouth, Ind.;
    d. July 26, 1969 (81).
Walcamp, Marie, actress; b. July 27, 1894, Denison, Ohio; d. Nov. 17,
    1936 (43).
Wald, Jerry, producer & author; b. Sept. 16, 1912, Brooklyn, N.Y.;
    d. July 13, 1962 (49).
Waldau, Gustav, actor; b. Feb. 27, 1871, Piflas/Bayern; d. May 25,
    1958 (87).

Waldbrunn, Ernst, actor; b. Aug. 14, 1907, Krumau, Bohemia; d. Dec. 22, 1977 (70).

Waldis, Otto, actor; b. May 20, 1901, Austria; d. Mar. 25, 1974 (72).

Waldmuller, Lizzi, actress; b. May 25, 1904, Knitterfeld, Austria; d. Apr. 8, 1945 (40).

Waldow, Ernst, actor; b. Aug. 22, 1894, Berlin, Germany; d. June 5, 1964 (69).

Waldridge, Harold, actor; b. New Orleans, La.; d. June 26, 1957 (50).

Waldron, Andy (r.n. Andrew V. Waldron), actor; b. Sept. 20, 1847, England; d. Mar. 1, 1932 (84).

Waldron, Charles, actor; b. Dec. 23, 1877, Waterford, N.Y.; d. Mar. 4, 1946 (68).

Waldron, Charles King, actor; d. Apr. 18, 1952 (37).

Waldron, Edna, actress; d. Aug. 24, 1940 (27).

Waldron, May (Mrs. Stuart Robson), actress; d. Dec. 22, 1924 (63).

Wales, Ethel, actress; b. Apr. 4, 1878, New Jersey; d. Feb. 15, 1952 (73).

Wales, Wally (see Taliaferro, Hal)

Walker, Aurora, actress; d. Jan. 1, 1964 (58).

Walker, Bruce, actor; d. Mar. 7, 1973 (66).

Walker, Charles H. (Tex), actor; b. Oct. 17, 1866, Altoona, Pa.; d. Aug. 21, 1947 (80).

Walker, Charlotte, actress; b. Dec. 29, 1878, Galveston, Tex.; d. Mar. 23, 1958 (79).

Walker, Cheryl, actress; b. Aug. 1, 1918, S. Pasadena, Calif.; d. Oct. 24, 1971 (53).

Walker, Christy, actress; d. Oct. 29, 1918 (20).

Walker, Hal (r.n. Harold Linden Walker), director; b. Mar. 20, 1896, Ottumwa, Iowa; d. July 3, 1972 (76).

Walker, Helen, actress; b. July 17, 1920, Worcester, Mass.; d. Mar. 10, 1968 (47).

Walker, Johnnie, actor; d. Dec. 5, 1949 (55).

Walker, June, actress; b. June 14, 1900, Illinois; d. Feb. 3, 1966 (65).

Walker, Lillian, actress; b. Apr. 21, 1887, Brooklyn, N.Y.; d. Oct. 10, 1975 (88).

Walker, Martin, actor; b. July 27, 1901, Harrow, Middlesex, England; d. Sept. 18, 1955 (54).

Walker, Nella, actress; b. Mar. 6, 1886, Chicago, Ill.; d. Mar. 22, 1971 (85).

Walker, Robert, actor; b. Oct. 13, 1918, Salt Lake City, Utah; d. Aug. 28, 1951 (32).

Walker, Robert D., actor; b. June 18, 1888, Bethlehem, Pa.; d. Mar 4, 1954 (65).

Walker, Stuart, actor, director, & author; b. Mar. 4, 1888, Augusta, Ky.; d. Mar. 13, 1941 (53).

Walker, Syd, actor; b. Mar. 22, 1886, Salford, England; d. Jan. 13, 1945 (58).

Walker, Virginia, actress; d. Dec. 22, 1946 (30).

Walker, Wally, actor; d. Aug. 7, 1975 (74).

Walker, Walter, actor; d. Dec. 4, 1947 (83).

Wall, David V., actor; d. June 1, 1938 (68).

Wall, Geraldine, actress; b. Sept. 24, 1912, Illinois; d. June 22, 1970 (57).

Wallace, Beryl, actress; d. June 17, 1948 (38).

Wallace, Edgar, writer & actor; b. Apr. 1, 1875, Ashburnham Grove, England; d. Feb. 10, 1932 (56).
Wallace, Ethel Lee, actress; d. Sept. 7, 1956 (68).
Wallace, George, actor; b. Aberdeen, New South Wales, Australia; d. Nov., 1960 (66).
Wallace, Inez, author & actress; d. June 28, 1966.
Wallace, John, actor; b. Aug. 24, 1869, England; d. July 16, 1946 (76).
Wallace, Laura V. (Laura V. Brocklehurst), actress; b. June 20, 1865, Indiana; d. Aug. 20, 1943 (78).
Wallace, Maude Powers, actress; d. Apr. 23, 1952 (58).
Wallace, May, actress; d. Dec. 11, 1938 (61).
Wallace, Milton, actor; b. Sept. 24, 1887, Austria; d. Feb. 16, 1956 (68).
Wallace, Morgan, actor; b. July 26, 1881, California; d. Dec. 12, 1953 (72).
Wallace, Regina, actress; b. Trenton, N.J.; d. Feb. 13, 1978 (86).
Wallace, Richard (r.n. Clarence Richard Wallace), director; b. Aug. 26, 1894, Sacramento, Calif.; d. Nov. 3, 1951 (57).
Wallace, Thomas Henry, actor; d. Mar. 18, 1932 (60).
Wallen, Sigurd, actor; b. Sept. 1, 1884, Tierp; d. Mar. 20, 1947 (62).
Waller, Eddy C., actor; b. June 14, 1889, Wisconsin; d. Aug. 19, 1977 (88).
Waller, Fats (r.n. Thomas W. Waller), actor & jazz musician; b. May 21, 1904, New York City; d. Dec. 15, 1943 (39).
Waller, Lewis, actor; b. Nov. 3, 1860, Bilbao, Spain; d. Nov. 1, 1915 (55).
Wallerstein, Rose, actress; d. Apr. 19, 1961 (65).
Walling, Effie B. (r.n. Effie Bond Walling), actress; b. Apr. 12, 1879, California; d. June 9, 1961 (82).
Walling, Roy, actor; d. May 7, 1964 (75).
Walling, Will R., actor; b. June 2, 1872, Sacramento City, Iowa; d. Mar. 5, 1932 (59).
Wallington, Jimmy, actor & columnist; d. Dec. 22, 1972 (65).
Wallis, Bertram, actor; b. Feb. 22, 1874, London, England; d. Apr. 11, 1952 (78).
Wallock, Edwin N. (Edward Wallock Wack), actor; b. Nov. 6, 1877, Council Bluffs, Iowa; d. Feb. 4, 1951 (73).
Walls, Tom, actor; b. Feb. 18, 1883, Kingsthorpe, Northants, England; d. Nov. 27, 1949 (66).
Walpole, Hugh, author & actor; b. Auckland, N.Z.; d. June 1, 1941 (57).
Walsh, Blanche, actress; b. Jan. 4, 1873, New York City; d. Oct. 31, 1915 (42).
Walsh, Percy, actor; b. Apr. 24, 1888, Luton, Bedfordshire, England; d. Jan. 19, 1952 (63).
Walsh, William J., actor; d. Nov. 8, 1921 (52).
Walter, Jerry, actor; d. Feb. 11, 1979 (54).
Walter, Wilfrid, actor; b. Mar. 2, 1882, Ripon, England; d. July 9, 1958 (76).
Walter, Wilmer, actor; d. Aug. 23, 1941 (57).
Walters, Dorothy, actress; d. Apr. 17, 1934 (56).
Walters, Mrs. George, actress; d. Feb. 21, 1916.
Walters, John, actor; d. Jan. 23, 1944 (59).

Walters, Laura, actress; d. Apr. 10, 1934 (40).
Walthall, Anna Mae, actress; b. Oct. 3, 1894, Alabama; d. Apr. 17, 1950 (55).
Walthall, Henry B. (r.n. Henry Brazeale Walthall), actor; b. Mar. 16, 1878, Shelby City, Ala.; d. June 17, 1936 (58).
Walton, Douglas, actor; b. Toronto, Canada; d. Nov. 15, 1961 (51).
Walton, Fred, actor; b. Aug. 29, 1866, Paisley, Scotland; d. Dec. 27, 1936 (70).
Walton, Herbert, actor; d. Jan. 16, 1954 (74).
Walton, Vera, actress; d. Sept. 1, 1965 (74).
Waltz, Patrick (Philip Shawn), actor; b. Dec. 6, 1924, Ohio; d. Aug. 13, 1972 (47).
Wangel, Hedwig, actress; b. Sept. 23, 1875, Berlin, Germany; d. Mar. 12, 1961 (85).
Wanger, Walter, producer; b. July 11, 1894, San Francisco, Calif.; d. Nov. 18, 1968 (74).
Wanzer, Arthur G., actor; b. Mar. 18, 1880, Chicago, Ill.; d. Dec. 15, 1948 (68).
Waram, Percy, actor; b. 1881, Kent, England; d. Oct. 5, 1961 (80).
Warburton, Charles, actor; b. Oct. 20, 1887, Huddersfield, England; d. July 19, 1952 (64).
Ward, Beatrice, actress; d. Dec. 11, 1964 (74).
Ward, Carrie Clarke, actress; b. Jan. 9, 1862, Nevada; d. Feb. 6, 1926 (64).
Ward, Chance, actor; b. Sept. 16, 1877, Ohio; d. Sept. 2, 1949 (71).
Ward, David, actor; d. Dec. 31, 1945 (55).
Ward, Fannie, actress; b. June 22, 1872, St. Louis, Mo.; d. Jan. 27, 1952 (79).
Ward, Fleming, actor; d. Aug. 2, 1962 (75).
Ward, Hap, actor; b. Cameron, Pa.; d. Jan. 3, 1944 (76).
Ward, Jerome B. (Blackjack), actor; b. May 3, 1891, Louisiana; d. Aug. 29, 1954 (63).
Ward, Kathrin Clare, actress; b. Mar. 31, 1871, Bradford, Mass.; d. Oct. 14, 1938 (67).
Ward, Lucille, actress; d. Aug. 8, 1952 (72).
Ward, Peggy, actress; b. Feb. 10, 1879, Pennsylvania; d. Mar. 8, 1960 (81).
Ward, Richard, actor; b. Mar. 15, 1915, Philadelphia, Pa.; d. July 1, 1979 (64).
Ward, Ronald, actor; b. Apr. 15, 1901, Eastbourne, England; d. Mar. 31, 1978 (76).
Ward, Roscoe (Tiny), actor; d. Sept. 12, 1956 (63).
Ward, Sam, actor; d. May 1, 1952 (63).
Ward, Solly, actor; d. May 17, 1942 (51).
Ward, Tiny (see Ward, Roscoe)
Ward, Warwick, actor; d. Dec. 9, 1967 (76).
Warde, Anthony, actor; b. Nov. 4, 1908, Pennsylvania; d. Jan. 8, 1975 (66).
Warde, Ernest C., director & actor; b. Liverpool, England; d. Sept. 9, 1923 (49).
Warde, Frederick, actor; b. Feb. 23, 1851, Warrington, Oxfordshire, England; d. Feb. 7, 1935 (83).
Wardell, Harry, actor & author; b. Mar. 8, 1879, New York City; d. Sept. 17, 1948 (69).
Warden, May, actress; d. Oct. 5, 1978 (86).

Wardwell, Geoffrey, actor; b. July 30, 1900, York, England;
    d. Aug. 9, 1955 (55).
Ware, Helen, actress; b. Oct. 15, 1877, San Francisco, Calif.;
    d. Jan. 25, 1939 (61).
Ware, Walter, actor; b. Boston, Mass.; d. Jan. 3, 1936 (56).
Warfield, Irene, actress; d. Apr. 10, 1961 (65).
Waring, Mary W., actress; d. Jan. 10, 1964 (72).
Warmington, Stanley J., actor; b. Dec. 16, 1884, Herts, England;
    d. May 10, 1941 (56).
Warner, Albert, executive; b. Baltimore, Md.; d. Nov. 26, 1967 (84).
Warner, Cecil, actress; d. May, 1924 (22).
Warner, Gloria, actress; d. June 8, 1934 (19).
Warner, H.B. (r.n. Harry Byron Warner), actor; b. Oct. 26, 1875,
    London, England; d. Dec. 21, 1958 (83).
Warner, Harry M., executive; b. Dec. 12, 1881, Poland; d. July 25,
    1958 (76).
Warner, J.B., actor; b. 1895, Nebraska; d. Nov. 9, 1924 (29).
Warner, Jack, actor; d. July 25, 1929 (42).
Warner, Jack L., producer; b. Aug. 2, 1892, London, Ontario, Canada;
    d. Sept. 9, 1978 (86).
Warner, Jethro, actor; d. Apr. 12, 1931 (56).
Warnow, Helen, actress; d. Dec. 25, 1970 (44).
Warren, C. Denier, actor; b. July 29, 1889, Chicago, Ill.; d. Aug. 27,
    1971 (82).
Warren, E. Alyn (Fred Warren), actor; b. June 2, 1874, Richmond,
    Va.; d. Jan. 22, 1940 (65).
Warren, Eddie L., actor & author; b. Sept. 30, 1891, Texas;
    d. Mar. 17, 1946 (54).
Warren, Edward, director & actor; d. Apr. 3, 1930 (73).
Warren, Eleanor, actress; d. Apr. 6, 1927 (34).
Warren, Eliza, actress; d. Jan. 20, 1935 (70).
Warren, Fred (see Warren, E. Alyn)
Warren, Fred H., actor; b. Sept. 16, 1880, Rock Island, Ill.;
    d. Dec. 5, 1940 (60).
Warren, Kenneth J., actor; b. Sept. 25, 1929, Parramatta, N.S.W.,
    Australia; d. Aug. 27, 1973 (43).
Warren, Leonard, opera singer; b. Apr. 21, 1911, New York City;
    d. Mar. 4, 1960 (48).
Warrender, Harold, actor; b. Nov. 15, 1903, London, England;
    d. May 6, 1953 (49).
Warrenton, Lule, actress; b. June 22, 1862, Flint, Mich.; d. May 14,
    1932 (69).
Warrington, Ann, actress; d. Nov. 14, 1934 (70).
Warrington, George (r.n. George Chalman), actor; b. May 16, 1872,
    Illinois; d. Nov. 2, 1968 (96).
Warters, William, actor; d. Aug. 29, 1953 (70).
Warwick, Ethel, actress; b. Oct. 13, 1882, London, England;
    d. Sept. 12, 1951 (68).
Warwick, John (r.n. John McIntosh Beattie), actor; b. Jan. 4, 1905,
    Bellengen River, Australia; d. Jan. 10, 1972 (67).
Warwick, Robert, actor; b. Oct. 9, 1878, Sacramento, Calif.;
    d. June 6, 1964 (85).
Warwick, Robert, Sr., actor & director; b. Apr. 3, 1868, England;
    d. Dec. 3, 1944 (76).
Wascher, Aribert, actor; b. Dec. 1, 1895, Flensburg, Germany;
    d. Dec. 14, 1961 (66).

Washburn, Alice, actress; d. Nov. 28, 1929 (68).
Washburn, Bryant, actor; b. Apr. 28, 1889, Chicago, Ill.; d. Apr. 30, 1963 (74).
Washburn, John H., actor; d. Dec. 11, 1917.
Washington, Blue (see Washington, Edgar "Blue")
Washington, Edgar "Blue," actor; b. Feb. 12, 1898, Los Angeles, Calif.; d. Sept. 15, 1970 (72).
Washington, Ford L. (Buck), actor & dancer; d. Jan. 31, 1955 (47).
Washington, Jess, actor; d. Sept. 4, 1919.
Washington, Kenny, actor; d. June 24, 1971 (52).
Waterman, Ida, actress; d. May 22, 1941 (89).
Waters, Ethel, actress & singer; b. Oct. 31, 1896, Chester, Pa.; d. Sept. 1, 1977 (80).
Waters, John, director; b. Oct. 31, 1893, New York City; d. May 5, 1965 (71).
Watkin, Pierre, actor; b. Dec. 29, 1887, Iowa; d. Feb. 3, 1960 (72).
Watkins, Linda, actress; b. Boston, Mass.; d. Oct. 31, 1976 (68).
Watson, Adele, actress; d. Mar. 27, 1933 (43).
Watson, Billy "Beef Trust," actor; b. New York City; d. Jan. 14, 1945 (78).
Watson, Bobby, actor; b. Nov. 28, 1887, Springfield, Ill.; d. May 22, 1965 (77).
Watson, Caven, actor; d. July, 1953 (49).
Watson, Fanny, actress; d. May 17, 1970 (84).
Watson, Frank M., actor; d. July 24, 1946 (76).
Watson, George A., actor; d. Dec. 5, 1937 (26).
Watson, Harry B., actor; b. June, 1876, Philadelphia, Pa.; d. Sept. 23, 1930 (54).
Watson, Henrietta, actress; d. Sept. 29, 1964 (91).
Watson, Ivory (Deek), recording artist (Ink Spots); d. Nov. 4, 1969 (60).
Watson, Joseph K., author & actor; b. Feb. 12, 1887, Philadelphia, Pa.; d. May 16, 1942 (55).
Watson, Justice, actor; b. Mar. 7, 1908, Pennsylvania; d. July 6, 1962 (54).
Watson, Kitty, actress; d. Mar. 3, 1967 (80).
Watson, Lucile, actress; b. May 27, 1879, Quebec, Canada; d. June 24, 1962 (83).
Watson, Minor, actor; b. Dec. 22, 1889, Marianna, Ark.; d. July 28, 1965 (75).
Watson, Roy, actor; d. June 7, 1937 (61).
Watson, William Henry, director; d. Jan. 20, 1967 (71).
Watson, Wylie, actor; d. May 3, 1966 (77).
Watt, Nate, director; b. Denver, Colo.; d. May 26, 1968 (79).
Wattis, Richard, actor; b. Feb. 25, 1912, Wednesbury, Staffs, England; d. Feb. 1, 1975 (62).
Watts, Charles, actor; d. Dec. 13, 1966.
Watts, Charles H. (Cotton), actor; d. Mar. 5, 1968 (66).
Watts, George, actor; b. Feb. 17, 1879, Newark, N.J.; d. July 1, 1942 (63).
Watts, Peggy, actress; d. Apr. 27, 1966 (60).
Watts, Queenie, actress; d. Jan. 25, 1980 (53).
Waxman, Franz, composer & music director; b. Dec. 24, 1906, Germany; d. Feb. 24, 1967 (60).
Wayne, John (r.n. Marion Michael Morrison), actor; b. May 26, 1907, Winterset, Iowa; d. June 11, 1979 (72).

312 *International Film Necrology*

Wayne, Justina, actress; d. Dec. 2, 1951.
Wayne, Naunton, actor; b. June 22, 1901, Llanwonno, Glamorganshire,
    S. Wales; d. Nov. 17, 1970 (69).
Wayne, Patricia (see Cutts, Patricia)
Wayne, Richard, actor; d. Mar. 15, 1958.
Wayne, Robert, actor; b. Oct. 28, 1864, Pittsburgh, Pa.; d. Sept. 26,
    1946 (81).
Wead, Frank "Spig," writer; d. Nov. 15, 1947 (53).
Weatherwax, Walter S., actor; b. May 31, 1867, Fort Scott, Kans.;
    d. Jan. 19, 1943 (75).
Weaver, Frank "Cicero," actor; b. Feb. 2, 1891, Ozark, Mo.; d. Oct.
    29, 1967 (76).
Weaver, June "Elviry," actress; b. June 23, 1891, Chicago, Ill.;
    d. Nov. 27, 1977 (86).
Weaver, Leon (Abner), actor; b. Aug. 12, 1882, Ozark, Mo.; d. May 27,
    1950 (67).
Webb, Clifton, actor; b. Nov. 19, 1889, Indianapolis, Ind.;
    d. Oct. 13, 1966 (76).
Webb, Fay, actress; d. Nov. 18, 1936 (30).
Webb, Frank, actor; d. Dec. 20, 1974 (26).
Webb, George, actor; b. Oct. 3, 1887, Indianapolis, Ind.; d. May 24,
    1943 (55).
Webb, James R., writer; d. Sept. 27, 1974 (64).
Webb, Millard, director & writer; b. Dec. 6, 1893, Clay City, Ky.;
    d. Apr. 21, 1935 (41).
Webber, John F., actor; d. Nov. 25, 1943 (74).
Weber, Christine, actress; d. Oct. 8, 1936.
Weber, Joe, actor; b. Aug. 11, 1867, New York City; d. May 10, 1942
    (74).
Weber, Joseph W., actor; d. Apr. 4, 1943 (82).
Weber, Lois, director & actress; b. June 13, 1881, Pittsburgh, Pa.;
    d. Nov. 13, 1939 (58).
Webster, Ben, actor; b. June 2, 1864, London, England; d. Feb. 26,
    1947 (82).
Webster, Lillian, actress; d. July, 1920.
Webster, Lucile (see Gleason, Lucile Webster)
Wedin, Bernard, actor; d. Aug. 5, 1948 (41).
Weeks, Barbara, actress; d. July 4, 1954 (47).
Weeks, George W., producer; b. Mar. 21, 1885, Ann Arbor, Mich.;
    d. Nov. 16, 1953 (68).
Weeks, Marion, actress; d. Apr. 20, 1968 (81).
Weeks, Ranny, band leader; d. Apr. 26, 1979 (72).
Weeks, Walter, actor; d. May 4, 1961 (79).
Weems, Ted, band leader; b. Pitcairn, Pa.; d. May 6, 1963 (62).
Wegener, Paul, actor; b. Dec. 11, 1874, Bischdorf, Germany;
    d. Sept. 13, 1948 (73).
Weidler, Virginia, actress; b. Mar. 21, 1926, Hollywood, Calif.;
    d. July 1, 1968 (42).
Weigel, Helene, actress; b. May 12, 1900, Vienna, Austria; d. May 6,
    1971 (70).
Weigel, Paul, actor; b. Feb. 18, 1867, Halle, Saxony, Germany;
    d. May 25, 1951 (84).
Weight, F. Harmon, director; b. July 1, 1887, Salt Lake City, Utah;
    d. Aug., 1978 (91).
Weih, Rolf, actor; d. Aug., 1969 (63).

Weil, Harry, actor; d. Jan. 23, 1943 (65).
Weiler, Constance, actress; b. Sept. 17, 1918, Canada; d. Dec. 10,
    1965 (47).
Weinberg, Gus, actor; b. Milwaukee, Wisc.; d. Aug. 11, 1952 (86).
Weir, Jane, actress; d. Aug. 21, 1937 (21).
Weiser, Grethe, actress; b. Feb. 27, 1903, Hanover, Germany;
    d. Oct. 2, 1970 (67).
Weiss, Ethel, actress; d. Sept. 12, 1979 (82).
Weissburg, Edward, actor; d. Aug. 30, 1950 (74).
Weisse, Hanni, actress; b. Oct. 16, 1892, Chemnitz, Germany; d. Dec.
    13, 1967 (75).
Weissman, Dora, actress; d. May 21, 1974.
Weissmuller, Peter, actor; b. Sept. 3, 1903, Pennsylvania; d. Sept. 4,
    1969 (66).
Weitz, Emile, actor; d. May 12, 1951 (68).
Welch, Eddie, stuntman; d. Jan. 15, 1963 (63).
Welch, Harry Foster, actor; b. Annapolis, Md.; d. Aug. 16, 1973 (74).
Welch, James, actor; b. Nov. 6, 1865, Liverpool, England; d. Apr. 10,
    1917 (51).
Welch, James T., actor; b. Mar. 14, 1869, New York; d. Apr. 6, 1949
    (80).
Welch, Joseph N., actor & judge; b. Oct. 22, 1890, Primghar, Iowa;
    d. Oct. 6, 1960 (69).
Welch, Katherine, actress; d. Oct. 30, 1953 (66).
Welch, Lew, actor; d. June 22, 1952 (67).
Welch, Mary, actress; b. Charleston, S.C.; d. May 31, 1958 (35).
Welch, Niles, actor; b. July 29, 1888, Hartford, Conn.; d. Nov. 21,
    1976 (88).
Welchman, Harry, actor & singer; b. Feb. 24, 1886, England; d. Jan. 3,
    1966 (79).
Weldon, Jasper (White Wash Jasper Weldon), actor; b. July 4, 1895,
    Georgia; d. Feb. 4, 1968 (72).
Welford, Dallas, actor; b. May 23, 1872, Liverpool, England;
    d. Sept. 28, 1946 (74).
Wellesley, Charles, actor; b. London, England; d. July 24, 1946 (71).
Wellesley, Marie, actress; d. Sept., 1927.
Wellington, Babe, actor; d. Dec. 28, 1954 (57).
Wellman, William A., director, author, & producer; b. Feb. 29, 1896,
    Brookline, Mass.; d. Dec. 9, 1975 (79).
Wells, Bombardier Billy, actor (gong striker for Rank Films);
    d. June 11, 1967 (79).
Wells, Charles B., actor; d. Oct. 14, 1924 (73).
Wells, Deering, actor; d. Sept. 29, 1961 (65).
Wells, L.M. (r.n. Louis M. Wells), actor; b. Feb. 5, 1862, Cincinnati,
    Ohio; d. Jan. 1, 1923 (60).
Wells, Mai, actress; d. Aug. 1, 1941 (79).
Wells, Marie, actress; d. July 2, 1949 (55).
Wells, Maurice, actor; d. June 26, 1978 (76).
Wells, Raymond (r.n. Frank Wells Martin), actor & director;
    b. Oct. 14, 1880, Anna, Ill.; d. Aug. 9, 1941 (60).
Welsh, Harry, actor; b. Apr. 23, 1891, Pennsylvania; d. Jan. 20,
    1957 (65).
Welsh, William J., actor; b. Feb. 9, 1870, Philadelphia, Pa.;
    d. July 16, 1946 (76).
Wenck, Eduard, actor; b. Jan. 1, 1894, Karlsruhe, Germany; d. May 17,
    1954 (60).

Wendell, Howard, actor; b. Johnstown, Pa.; d. Aug. 11, 1975 (67).
Wendorff, Laiola, actress; b. Feb. 25, 1894, Poland; d. Jan. 21,
    1966 (71).
Wengraf, John E., actor; b. Apr. 23, 1897, Vienna, Austria;
    d. May 4, 1974 (77).
Wenman, Henry, actor; b. Sept. 7, 1875, Leeds, England; d. Nov. 6,
    1953 (78).
Wentworth, Martha, actress; b. June 2, 1889, New York; d. Mar. 8,
    1974 (84).
Wenzel, Arthur A., actor & musician; b. May 5, 1907, Wisconsin;
    d. Feb. 10, 1961 (53).
Werbisek, Gisela, actress; d. Apr. 15, 1956 (81).
Werker, Alfred, director; b. Dec. 2, 1896, South Dakota; d. July 28,
    1975 (78).
Werkmeister, Lotte, actress; d. July, 1970 (84).
Werner, Walter, actor; d. Jan. 8, 1956 (72).
Werner-Kahle, Hugo, actor; b. Aug. 5, 1882, Aachen, Germany;
    d. May 1, 1961 (78).
Wernicke, Otto, actor; b. Sept. 30, 1893, Osterode/Harz, Germany;
    d. Nov. 7, 1965 (72).
Wertz, Clarence, actor; b. Mar. 3, 1891, Bloomfield, N.J.; d. Dec. 2,
    1935 (44).
Wery, Carl, actor; b. Aug. 7, 1897, Trostberg, Germany; d. Mar. 14,
    1975 (77).
Wescoatt, Norman (Rusty) (see Bailey, William Norton)
Wescoatt, Rusty (see Bailey, William Norton)
Weske, H. Victor, actor; d. Nov. 29, 1960.
Wessel, Dick, actor; b. Apr. 20, 1913, Wisconsin; d. Apr. 20, 1965
    (52).
Wesselhoeft, Eleanor, actress; d. Dec. 9, 1945 (62).
Wesson, Dick, actor; b. Feb. 20, 1919, Idaho; d. Jan. 27, 1979 (59).
Wesson, Gene, actor; d. Aug. 22, 1975 (54).
West, Amelia Gardner, actress; d. Jan. 11, 1947 (81).
West, Arthur Pat (see West, Pat)
West, Billie, actress; d. June 7, 1967.
West, Billy (r.n. Roy B. Weissberg), actor & assistant director;
    b. Sept. 22, 1892, Russia; d. July 21, 1975 (82).
West, Buster, actor; b. Philadelphia, Pa.; d. Mar. 18, 1966 (64).
West, Charles H., actor; b. Nov. 30, 1885, Pittsburgh, Pa.;
    d. Oct. 10, 1943 (57).
West, Claudine, writer; b. England; d. Apr. 11, 1943 (59).
West, Edna Rhys, actress; b. Greenup, Ky.; d. Feb. 7, 1963 (76).
West, Ford, actor; b. Mar. 27, 1873, Dallas, Tex.; d. Jan. 3, 1936
    (62).
West, George, actor; d. Oct. 27, 1963 (73).
West, Henry, actor; d. Jan. 29, 1936 (68).
West, Henry St. Barbe, actor; b. Feb. 7, 1880, London, England;
    d. May 10, 1935 (55).
West, Isabelle, actress; d. July 21, 1942 (84).
West, Col. J.A., actor; d. July 10, 1928 (87).
West, John S., actor; d. Feb. 8, 1944.
West, Katherine, actress; d. Sept. 26, 1936 (53).
West, Nathanael, writer; d. Dec. 22, 1940 (36).
West, Olive, actress; d. May 29, 1943 (85).
West, Pat (Arthur Pat West), actor; d. Apr. 10, 1944 (55).

West, Raymond B., director; d. Sept., 1923 (37).
West, Roland, producer; b. Feb. 20, 1885, Ohio; d. Mar. 31, 1952 (67).
West, Thomas, actor; d. July 28, 1932 (73).
West, Tony, actor; d. June 25, 1923 (56).
West, W.C., actor; d. Sept. 13, 1918.
West, Will, actor; b. Sept. 22, 1867; d. Feb. 5, 1922 (52).
West, William H., actor; d. Aug. 20, 1915.
Westcott, Gordon, actor; b. Nov. 6, 1903, St. George, Utah;
    d. Oct. 30, 1935 (31).
Westcott, Netta, actress; b. London, England; d. Aug. 9, 1953 (60).
Westerfield, James, actor; b. Mar. 22, 1913, Nashville, Tenn.;
    d. Sept. 20, 1971 (58).
Westermeier, Paul, actor; b. July 9, 1892, Berlin, Germany;
    d. Oct., 1972 (80).
Western, T.S., director & actor; d. June 8, 1931 (47).
Westley, Helen, actress; b. Mar. 28, 1875, Brooklyn, N.Y.; d. Dec. 12,
    1942 (67).
Westley, John, actor; b. Nov. 17, 1878, New York City; d. Dec. 26,
    1948 (70).
Westman, Nydia, actress; b. Feb. 19, 1902, New York City; d. May 23,
    1970 (68).
Westmore, George "Bud," make-up artist; d. June 23, 1973 (55).
Westmore, Monty (r.n. Montague George Westmore), make-up artist;
    b. June 12, 1902, Canterbury, Kent, England; d. Mar. 30, 1940
    (37).
Westmore, Perc, make-up artist; d. Sept. 30, 1970 (65).
Westmore, Walter J. (Wally), make-up artist; d. July 3, 1973 (67).
Westmoreland, Pauline, actress; d. Jan. 28, 1947 (37).
Weston, Cecil, actor; d. Nov. 17, 1945 (53).
Weston, Cecil, actress; b. Sept. 3, 1889, South Africa; d. Aug. 7,
    1976 (86).
Weston, Doris, actress; b. Sept. 9, 1917, Chicago, Ill.; d. July 27,
    1960 (42).
Weston, Joseph J., actor; b. Feb. 22, 1888, New York; d. Apr. 27,
    1972 (84).
Weston, Ruth, actress; b. Aug. 31, 1908, Boston, Mass.; d. Nov. 5,
    1955 (47).
Weston, Sammy, actor; d. Feb. 1, 1951 (62).
Westover, Winifred, actress; d. Mar. 19, 1978 (78).
Westwood, Martin F., actor; d. Dec. 19, 1928 (45).
Wetherell, M.A., actor & director; d. Feb. 25, 1939 (52).
Wexler, Paul, actor; b. May 23, 1929, Oregon; d. Nov. 21, 1979 (50).
Whale, James, director; b. July 22, 1896, Dudley, Staffordshire,
    England; d. May 29, 1957 (60).
Whalen, Harold, actor; d. Jan. 17, 1940 (45).
Whalen, Michael (r.n. Joseph Shovlin), actor; b. June 30, 1902,
    Wilkes-Barre, Pa.; d. Apr. 14, 1974 (71).
Whaley, Bert D., actor; b. May 9, 1909, Illinois; d. Jan. 17, 1973
    (63).
Whatmore, A.R., actor; b. May 30, 1889, Much Marcle, England;
    d. Oct. 15, 1960 (71).
Wheat, Lawrence, actor; b. Oct. 20, 1876, West Virginia; d. Aug. 7,
    1963 (86).
Wheatcroft, Stanhope, actor; b. May 11, 1888, New York; d. Feb. 13,
    1966 (77).

Wheeler, Bert, actor; b. Apr. 7, 1895, Paterson, N.J.; d. Jan. 18, 1968 (72).
Wheeler, Cyril, actor; d. Oct. 8, 1971 (59).
Wheeler, Jimmy, actor; b. Sept. 16, 1910, Battersea, London, England; d. Oct. 8, 1973 (63).
Wheelock, Charles C., actor; d. May 25, 1948 (73).
Whelan, Albert, actor; d. Feb. 19, 1961 (85).
Whelan, Ron, actor; b. Nov. 2, 1905, England; d. Dec. 8, 1965 (60).
Whelan, Tim, director, author, & actor; b. Nov. 2, 1893, Cannelton, Ind.; d. Aug. 12, 1957 (63).
Whelar, Lanois Mardi, player; d. Oct. 17, 1918 (20).
Wherry, Daniel, actor; d. Apr. 4, 1955.
Whiffen, Mrs. Thomas, actress; b. Mar. 12, 1845, London, England; d. Nov. 25, 1936 (91).
Whipper, Leigh, actor; d. July 26, 1975 (98).
Whistler, Edna, actress; b. 1886; d. July 11, 1934 (48).
Whistler, Margaret, actress; d. Aug. 23, 1939 (47).
Whitaker, Charles "Slim" (r.n. Charles Orbie Whitaker), actor; b. July 29, 1893, Kansas City, Mo.; d. June 27, 1960 (66).
Whitaker, Slim (see Whitaker, Charles "Slim")
Whitcomb, Barry, actor; d. Oct. 25, 1928 (56).
White, Billy (r.n. William A. Rattenberry), actor; b. Apr. 26, 1856, Sacramento, Calif.; d. Apr. 21, 1933 (76).
White, Carolina, actress & opera singer; d. Oct. 5, 1961 (75).
White, Cordon, actor; d. 1943.
White, Edgar B., actor; d. Sept. 15, 1978 (59).
White, Frances, actress; d. Feb. 24, 1969 (71).
White, Hugh, actor; d. June 23, 1938 (42).
White, J. Fisher, actor; b. May 1, 1865, Clifton, Bristol, England; d. Jan. 14, 1945 (79).
White, J. Irving, actor; d. Apr. 17, 1944 (79).
White, Jack, actor; d. July 13, 1942 (49).
White, Johnstone, actor; b. Aug. 4, 1892, Oregon; d. Apr. 7, 1969 (76).
White, Josh, actor & recording artist; d. Sept. 5, 1969 (61).
White, Lee "Lasses," actor; b. Aug. 28, 1888, Texas; d. Dec. 16, 1949 (61).
White, Leo, actor; b. Nov. 10, 1882, Graudenz, Germany; d. Sept. 20, 1948 (65).
White, Lester, cinematographer; d. Dec. 3, 1958 (51).
White, Marjorie, actress; b. July 22, 1908, Winnipeg, Canada; d. Aug. 21, 1935 (27).
White, Meadows, actor; d. Nov. 20, 1973 (72).
White, Pearl, actress; b. Mar. 4, 1889, Greenridge, Mo.; d. Aug. 4, 1938 (49).
White, Raymond, actor; d. Jan., 1934.
White, Ruth, actress; b. Apr. 24, 1914, Perth Amboy, N.J.; d. Dec. 3, 1969 (55).
White, Sammy, actor & dancer; b. May 28, 1894, Rhode Island; d. Mar. 3, 1960 (65).
White, Valerie, actress; b. Dec. 26, 1915, Simon's Town, South Africa; d. Dec. 3, 1975 (59).
White Eagle, Chief, actor; d. Jan. 18, 1946 (73).
Whitefield, Axel O., actor; b. Mar. 28, 1880, Sweden; d. Dec. 13, 1944 (64).
Whiteford, John P. "Blackie," actor; b. Apr. 27, 1889, New York; d. Mar. 21, 1962 (72).

Whitehill, Clarence, opera singer & producer; d. Dec. 19, 1932 (61).
Whitelaw, Barrett, actor; b. May 25, 1890, Cape Girardeau, Mo.;
    d. Oct. 2, 1947 (57).
Whiteman, Paul, orchestra leader; b. Mar. 28, 1890, Denver, Colo.;
    d. Dec. 29, 1967 (77).
Whiteside, Walker, actor; b. Mar. 16, 1869, Logansport, Ind.;
    d. Aug. 17, 1942 (73).
Whitespear, Greg, actor; b. Apr. 18, 1897, Oklahoma; d. Feb. 20,
    1956 (58).
Whitfield, Smoki (r.n. Jordan Whitfield), actor; b. Aug. 3, 1917,
    Pennsylvania; d. Nov. 11, 1967 (50).
Whitfield, Walter W., singer; d. Jan. 13, 1966 (78).
Whitford, Annabelle, actress; d. Nov. 30, 1961 (83).
Whiting, Charlotte, actress; d. Jan. 28, 1974 (73).
Whiting, Jack, actor; b. June 22, 1901, Philadelphia, Pa.; d. Feb. 15,
    1961 (59).
Whiting, Phil S., actor & assistant director; d. Oct. 3, 1956 (60).
Whitley, Crane, actor; b. Oct. 28, 1899, New York; d. Feb. 28, 1957
    (57).
Whitley, Ray, actor, singer, & composer; b. Dec. 5, 1901, Atlanta,
    Ga.; d. Feb. 21, 1979 (77).
Whitling, Townsend, actor; b. Oct. 21, 1869, Oxford, England;
    d. June 24, 1952 (82).
Whitlock, Lloyd, actor; b. Jan. 2, 1891, Missouri; d. Jan. 8, 1966
    (75).
Whitman, Alfred (see Whitman, Gayne)
Whitman, Ernest, actor; b. Feb. 21, 1893, Ft. Smith, Ark.; d. Aug. 6,
    1954 (61).
Whitman, Estelle, actress; d. July 14, 1970.
Whitman, Gayne (Alfred Vosburgh; Alfred Whitman), actor; b. Mar. 19,
    1890, Chicago, Ill.; d. Aug. 31, 1958 (68).
Whitman, Walt, actor; d. Mar. 27, 1928 (69).
Whitney, Claire, actress; b. May 6, 1890, New York; d. Aug. 27, 1969
    (79).
Whitney, Peter (r.n. Peter King Engle), actor; b. May 24, 1916,
    Long Branch, N.J.; d. Mar. 30, 1972 (55).
Whitney, Ralph, stuntman; d. June 14, 1928 (54).
Whitney, Robert, II, actor; d. Jan. 6, 1969 (24).
Whitney, Wendy, actress; d. Dec. 27, 1978 (55).
Whitson, Frank, actor; b. Mar. 22, 1877, New York City; d. Mar. 19,
    1946 (68).
Whitsun-Jones, Paul, actor; b. Newport, Monmouthshire, England;
    d. Jan., 1974 (44).
Whittaker, Charles E., writer; b. May 31, 1877, Ireland; d. Jan. 4,
    1953 (75).
Whittell, Josephine, actress; b. Nov. 30, 1883, Arizona; d. June 1,
    1961 (77).
Whittington, Marjorie, actress; d. Oct. 23, 1957 (53).
Whitty, Dame May, actress; b. June 19, 1865, Liverpool, England;
    d. May 29, 1948 (82).
Whorf, Richard, actor & director; b. June 4, 1906, Winthrop, Mass.;
    d. Dec. 14, 1966 (60).
Whytal, Adelaide (r.n. Mary Adelaide Whytal), actress; b. Nov. 8,
    1863, New York City; d. July 13, 1946 (82).
Wickland, Larry, director; b. June 28, 1898, Kansas City, Mo.;
    d. Apr. 18, 1938 (39).

Widom, Leonard (Bud), actor (Our Gang); d. Apr. 18, 1976 (58).
Wieman, Mathias, actor; b. June 23, 1902, Osnabruck, Germany;
     d. Dec. 3, 1969 (67).
Wiene, Robert, director; b. 1881, Sachsen, Germany; d. July 17, 1938
     (57).
Wiere, Sylvester, actor; b. Prague, Germany; d. July 7, 1970 (60).
Wieth, Mogens, actor; b. Sept. 16, 1919, Copenhagen, Denmark;
     d. Sept. 10, 1962 (42).
Wiggins, Mary L., actress & stuntwoman; d. Dec. 20, 1945 (35).
Wilbur, Crane, actor, director, & scenarist; b. Nov. 17, 1886,
     Athens, N.Y.; d. Oct. 18, 1973 (86).
Wilby, Mrs. Maurice, actress; d. Mar. 6, 1939 (32).
Wilcox, Frank, actor; b. Mar. 13, 1907, DeSoto, Mo.; d. Mar. 3, 1974
     (66).
Wilcox, Fred, director; b. Tazwell, Va.; d. Sept. 24, 1964 (56).
Wilcox, Harlow, actor & announcer; b. Mar. 12, 1900, Nebraska;
     d. Sept. 24, 1960 (60).
Wilcox, Herbert, director; b. Apr. 19, 1891, Cork, Ireland;
     d. May 15, 1977 (86).
Wilcox, Robert, actor; b. May 19, 1910, Rochester, N.Y.; d. June 11,
     1955 (45).
Wilcox, Silas, actor; b. Feb. 8, 1863, Ohio; d. Feb. 11, 1945 (82).
Wilcox, Vivian, actress; d. Jan. 5, 1945 (33).
Wilde, Ted, writer; d. Dec. 17, 1929 (36).
Wilder, Marshall P., actor; d. Jan. 10, 1915 (55).
Wilder, Robert, writer; d. Aug. 22, 1974 (73).
Wildhack, Robert, actor; d. June 19, 1940 (58).
Wilding, Michael, actor; b. July 23, 1912, Westcliff-on-Sea, England;
     d. July 8, 1979 (66).
Wilenchick, Clem (see Whitley, Crane)
Wiles, Gordon, director; b. St. Louis, Mo.; d. Oct. 17, 1950 (46).
Wiley, John A., actor; d. Sept. 30, 1962 (78).
Wilhelm, Theodore, actor; d. Nov. 30, 1971 (62).
Wilke, Hubert, actor; b. Stettin, Germany; d. Oct. 22, 1940 (85).
Wilkerson, Bill, actor; b. Sept. 18, 1902, Oklahoma; d. Mar. 3,
     1966 (63).
Wilkerson, Guy, actor; b. Dec. 21, 1899, Texas; d. July 8, 1971 (71).
Wilkerson, Herbert, actor; b. Sept. 2, 1880, New York; d. Aug. 19,
     1943 (62).
Wilkins, June, actress; d. Mar. 16, 1972 (50).
Wilkinson, Geoffrey, actor; d. Dec. 5, 1955 (66).
Willa, Suzanne, actress; d. Mar. 24, 1951 (58).
Willard, Edmund, actor; b. Dec. 19, 1884, Brighton, England;
     d. Oct. 6, 1956 (71).
Willard, Jess, actor & boxer; b. Dec. 29, 1883, Pottawotamie, Kans.;
     d. Dec. 15, 1968 (84).
Willard, John, author & actor; b. Nov. 28, 1885, San Francisco,
     Calif.; d. Aug. 30, 1942 (56).
Willat, Irvin V., director; b. Nov. 18, 1890; d. Apr. 17, 1976 (85).
Willenz, Max, actor; b. Sept. 22, 1888, Austria; d. Nov. 8, 1954
     (66).
Willets, Gilson, writer; d. May 26, 1922 (53).
Willey, Leonard, actor; b. Dec. 15, 1882, England; d. June 30, 1964
     (81).
William, Warren (Warren Krech), actor; b. Dec. 2, 1894, Aitkin,
     Minn.; d. Sept. 24, 1948 (53).

Williams, Arnold, actor; d. 1927.
Williams, Barney, actor; d. Sept. 22, 1948 (68).
Williams, Beresford, actor; d. Apr. 22, 1966 (62).
Williams, Bert, actor; b. New Providence, Nassau, British West
    Indies; d. Mar. 4, 1922 (49).
Williams, Bill, stuntman; d. Nov. 13, 1964 (43).
Williams, Bransby, actor; b. Aug. 14, 1870, Hackney, England;
    d. Dec. 3, 1961 (91).
Williams, C. Jay, actor; d. Jan. 26, 1945 (86).
Williams, Charles B., actor; b. Sept. 27, 1898, Albany, N.Y.;
    d. Jan. 4, 1958 (59).
Williams, Clara, actress; b. May 3, 1888, Seattle, Wash.; d. May 8,
    1928 (40).
Williams, Cora, actress; b. Dec. 6, 1870, Chelsea, Mass.; d. Dec. 1,
    1927 (56).
Williams, Craig, actor; d. July 5, 1941 (63).
Williams, Douglas, actor; b. Sept. 19, 1906, New York; d. Dec. 24,
    1968 (62).
Williams, Earle, actor; b. Feb. 28, 1880, Sacramento, Calif.;
    d. Apr. 25, 1927 (47).
Williams, Elaine, actress; d. May 9, 1947.
Williams, Frances, actress; b. St Paul, Minn.; d. Jan. 27, 1959 (57).
Williams, Fred, actor; d. Aug. 4, 1924 (75).
Williams, Fred J., actor; b. July 2, 1874, Chicago, Ill.; d. May 29,
    1942 (67).
Williams, George Albert, actor; d. Feb. 21, 1936 (82).
Williams, George B., actor; d. Nov. 17, 1931 (65).
Williams, Guinn (Big Boy), actor; b. Apr. 26, 1900, Decatur, Tex.;
    d. June 6, 1962 (62).
Williams, Harcourt, actor; b. Mar. 30, 1880, Croydon, England;
    d. Dec. 13, 1957 (77).
Williams, Hattie, actress; b. Boston, Mass.; d. Aug. 17, 1942 (72).
Williams, Herb, actor; b. Philadelphia, Pa.; d. Oct. 1, 1936 (52).
Williams, Hugh, actor; b. Mar. 6, 1904, Bexhill-on-Sea, England;
    d. Dec. 7, 1969 (65).
Williams, Jay, actor & author; d. July 12, 1978 (64).
Williams, Jeffrey, actor; d. Dec. 27, 1938 (78).
Williams, Josephine, actress; d. June 14, 1937 (82).
Williams, Julia, actress; d. Feb. 7, 1936 (57).
Williams, Kathlyn, actress; b. Butte, Mont.; d. Sept. 23, 1960 (72).
Williams, Lawrence, actor; b. May 24, 1889, Pennsylvania; d. Mar. 30,
    1956 (66).
Williams, Lester (see Berke, William)
Williams, Lottie, actress; b. Jan. 20, 1874, Indiana; d. Nov. 16,
    1962 (88).
Williams, Mack, actor; d. July 29, 1965 (58).
Williams, Malcolm, actor; b. Spring Valley, Minn.; d. June 10, 1937
    (67).
Williams, Marjorie Rose, actress; d. July 18, 1933 (20).
Williams, Molly, actress; d. Nov. 1, 1967.
Williams, Oscar (Chalky), actor; b. July 5, 1907, Texas; d. Mar. 13,
    1976 (68).
Williams, Rhys, actor; b. Dec. 31, 1897, Wales; d. May 28, 1969 (71).
Williams, Robert, actor; b. Sept. 15, 1899, Morganton, N.C.;
    d. Nov. 3, 1931 (32).

Williams, Robert B., actor; b. Sept. 23, 1904, Illinois; d. June 17, 1978 (73).
Williams, Spencer, actor; b. July 14, 1893, Louisiana; d. Dec. 13, 1969 (76).
Williams, William A., actor; d. May 4, 1942 (72).
Williams, Zack, actor; b. Oct. 6, 1884, Louisiana; d. May 25, 1958 (73).
Williamson, Robert, actor; d. Mar. 13, 1949 (64).
Willing, Foy, singer (Riders of the Purple Sage); d. July 24, 1978 (63).
Willingham, Harry, actor; d. Nov. 17, 1943 (62).
Willis, Leo, actor; b. Jan. 5, 1890, Oklahoma; d. Apr. 10, 1952 (62).
Willis, Richard, actor; b. Oct. 15, 1876, London, England; d. Apr. 8, 1945 (68).
Willoughby, Louis, actor; d. Sept. 12, 1968.
Wills, Beverly, actress; d. Oct. 24, 1963 (29).
Wills, Bob, singer; b. Mar. 6, 1906, Limestone Co., Tex.; d. May 13, 1975 (69).
Wills, Brember, actor; b. Reading, England; d. Dec. 1, 1948 (65).
Wills, Chill, actor; b. July 18, 1902, Seagoville, Tex.; d. Dec. 15, 1978 (76).
Wills, Drusilla, actress; b. Nov. 14, 1884, London, England; d. Aug. 6, 1951 (66).
Wills, Nat M., actor; b. July 11, 1873, Fredericksburg, Va.; d. Dec. 9, 1917 (44).
Wills, Walter, actor; b. Aug. 22, 1881, New York; d. Jan. 18, 1967 (85).
Wilmer-Brown, Maisie, actress; d. Feb. 13, 1973 (80).
Wilmot, Lee, actor; d. Mar. 9, 1938 (39).
Wilsey, Jay (Buffalo Bill, Jr.), actor; b. Feb. 6, 1896, Missouri; d. Oct. 25, 1961 (65).
Wilson, Al, actor; d. Mar. 6, 1936.
Wilson, Ben, actor; b. July 7, 1876, Corning, Iowa; d. Aug. 25, 1930 (54).
Wilson, Bobby, actor; d. July 1, 1933 (56).
Wilson, Burton S., actor; d. Oct. 14, 1956 (85).
Wilson, Carey, writer & producer; b. May 19, 1889, Philadelphia, Pa.; d. Feb. 1, 1962 (72).
Wilson, Charles C. (r.n. Charles Cahill Wilson), actor; b. July 29, 1894, New York City; d. Jan. 7, 1948 (53).
Wilson, Clarence Hummell, actor; b. Nov. 17, 1876, Cincinnati, Ohio; d. Oct. 5, 1941 (64).
Wilson, Dooley, actor & singer; b. Apr. 3, 1886, Tyler, Tex.; d. May 30, 1953 (67).
Wilson, Elsie Jane, actress & director; b. Nov. 7, 1890, Australia; d. Jan. 16, 1965 (74).
Wilson, Francis, actor; b. Feb. 7, 1854, Philadelphia, Pa.; d. Oct. 7, 1935 (81).
Wilson, Frank H., actor; b. New York City; d. Feb. 16, 1956 (70).
Wilson, George, actor; d. July 30, 1954 (100).
Wilson, Hal (r.n. Harold Wilson), actor; b. Oct. 2, 1861, New York City; d. May 22, 1933 (71).
Wilson, Harry, actor; b. Nov. 22, 1897, England; d. Sept. 6, 1978 (80).
Wilson, M.K. (r.n. Millard Kenneth Wilson), actor; b. Louisville, Ky.; d. Oct. 5, 1933 (43).

Wilson, Marie, actress; b. Dec. 30, 1916, Anaheim, Calif.;
    d. Nov. 23, 1972 (55).
Wilson, Michael, writer; d. Apr. 9, 1978 (63).
Wilson, Millard K. (see Wilson, M.K.)
Wilson, Olivia Hodge, actress; d. Aug. 27, 1976 (80).
Wilson, Roberta, actress; b. June 11, 1905, Texas; d. Feb. 2, 1972
    (66).
Wilson, Tom (r.n. Thomas H. Wilson), actor; b. Aug. 27, 1880,
    Helena, Mont.; d. Feb. 19, 1965 (84).
Wilson, Wayne, actor; d. Jan. 4, 1970 (71).
Wilson, Whip, actor; b. June 16, 1915, Pecos, Tex.; d. Oct. 23, 1964
    (49).
Wilson, William F., actor; d. May 10, 1956 (62).
Wilson, Alf T., actor, director, & agent; d. Feb. 18, 1946 (77).
Wilton, Eric, actor; b. Nov. 6, 1882, England; d. Feb. 23, 1957 (74).
Wilton, Robb, actor; b. Liverpool, England; d. May 1, 1957 (75).
Wimperis, Arthur H., author & actor; b. Dec. 3, 1874, London,
    England; d. Oct. 14, 1953 (78).
Winant, Forrest, actor; b. Feb. 21, 1888, New York City; d. Jan. 30,
    1928 (36).
Winchell, Roderick, actor; b. Oct. 19, 1911, New York; d. Nov. 22,
    1968 (57).
Winchell, Walter, news columnist & actor; b. Apr. 7, 1897, New York
    City; d. Feb. 20, 1972 (74).
Winchester, Barbara, actress; d. Apr. 20, 1968 (70).
Wincott, Rosalie Avolo, actress; d. Nov., 1951 (78).
Windheim, Marek, actor & opera singer; d. Dec. 1, 1960 (65).
Windsor, Claire, actress; b. Apr. 14, 1898, Coffee City, Kans.;
    d. Oct. 23, 1972 (74).
Winfield, Joan, actress; d. June 16, 1978 (59).
Wing, Dan (r.n. Harvey Dan Wing), actor; b. May 8, 1927, Nebraska;
    d. June 14, 1969 (42).
Wing, Red (r.n. Lillian Red Wing St. Cyr), actress; b. Feb. 13,
    1884, Winnebago Reservation, Nebraska; d. Mar. 12, 1974 (90).
Wing, Ward, actor, author, & director; b. Feb. 18, 1893, Springfield,
    Miss.; d. June 4, 1945 (52).
Wingfield, Conway, actor; d. Feb. 9, 1948 (81).
Winn, Godfrey, actor & author; b. England; d. June 19, 1971 (62).
Winnerstrand, Olof, actor; b. Aug. 26, 1875, Stockholm, Sweden;
    d. July 16, 1956 (80).
Winninger, Charles, actor; b. May 26, 1884, Athens, Wisc.; d. Jan. 27,
    1969 (84).
Winston, Bruce, actor; b. Mar. 4, 1879, Liverpool, England;
    d. Sept. 27, 1946 (67).
Winston, Helen, actress & producer; d. Aug. 24, 1972 (40).
Winston, Irene, actress & author; d. Sept. 1, 1964 (44).
Winston, Jackie, actor; d. Nov. 9, 1971 (56).
Winter, Jessie, actress; d. Aug., 1971 (84).
Winter, Winona, actress; b. Huntsville, Ala.; d. Apr. 27, 1940 (49).
Winters, Linda (see Comingore, Dorothy)
Winthrop, Joy, actress; d. Apr. 1, 1950 (86).
Winton, Jane, actress; b. Oct. 10, 1905, Philadelphia, Pa.;
    d. Sept. 22, 1959 (53).
Wisbar, Frank, director & author; b. Dec. 9, 1899, Tilsit, Russia;
    d. Mar. 17, 1967 (67).

Wise, Harry, actor; d. Dec. 26, 1947 (76).
Wise, Jack, actor; b. Jan. 2, 1888, Pennsylvania; d. Mar. 7, 1954
    (66).
Wise, Joseph, actor; d. Oct. 14, 1975.
Wise, Tom, actor; b. Mar. 23, 1865, Faversham, Kent, England;
    d. Mar. 21, 1928 (63).
Withers, Charles, actor; b. Louisville, Ky.; d. July 10, 1947 (58).
Withers, Grant, actor; b. Jan. 17, 1905, Pueblo, Colo.; d. Mar. 27,
    1959 (54).
Withers, Isabel (r.n. Isabella Irene Withers), actress; b. Jan. 20,
    1896, Frankton, Ind.; d. Sept. 3, 1968 (72).
Witherspoon, Cora, actress; b. Jan. 5, 1890, New Orleans, La.;
    d. Nov. 17, 1957 (67).
Withey, Chet, director, author, & actor; b. Nov. 8, 1887, Park
    City, Utah; d. Oct. 6, 1939 (51).
Witt, Wastl, actor; d. Dec. 21, 1955 (65).
Witting, A.E. (r.n. Arthur Eugene Witting), actor; b. Oct. 21, 1868,
    Michigan; d. Feb. 1, 1941 (72).
Witting, Arthur (see Witting, A.E.)
Witting, Mattie, actress; b. Mar. 9, 1863, Palla, Iowa; d. Jan. 30,
    1945 (81).
Wix, Florence, actress; b. England; d. Nov. 23, 1956 (73).
Wix, John, actor; d. June 24, 1935 (48).
Woegerer, Otto, actor; b. Feb. 4, 1908, Vienna, Austria; d. July,
    1966 (58).
Wolbert, Dorothea, actress; b. Apr. 12, 1874, Pennsylvania; d. Sept.
    15, 1958 (84).
Wold, David, actor; b. Feb. 28, 1898, Poland; d. June 3, 1953 (55).
Wolf, Alma, actress; d. June 23, 1968 (76).
Wolf, Bill, actor; b. Aug. 14, 1894, New York; d. Feb. 16, 1975 (80).
Wolfe, Bud (r.n. Marion Wolfe), actor & stuntman; b. June 10, 1910,
    New York; d. Apr. 13, 1960 (49).
Wolfe, Jane, actress; b. Mar. 21, 1875, St. Petersburg, Pa.;
    d. Mar. 29, 1958 (83).
Wolff, Frank, actor; b. San Francisco, Calif.; d. Dec. 12, 1971 (43).
Wolfit, Donald, actor; b. Apr. 20, 1902, Newark-on-Trent, England;
    d. Feb. 17, 1968 (65).
Wolfson, Martin, actor; b. Apr. 4, 1904, New York City; d. Sept. 12,
    1973 (69).
Wolfson, P.J., writer, director, & producer; d. Apr. 16, 1979 (75).
Wolheim, Louis, actor; b. Mar. 23, 1880, New York City; d. Feb. 18,
    1931 (50).
Wolle, Gertrud, actress; d. July, 1952 (61).
Womack, Clay, actor; b. Dec. 20, 1892, Edwardsville, Ill.; d. Oct. 30,
    1948 (55).
Wonder, Betty, actress; d. July 24, 1979.
Wong, Anna May, actress; b. Jan. 3, 1905, Los Angeles, Calif.;
    d. Feb. 3, 1961 (56).
Wong, Beal, actor; b. May 11, 1906, California; d. Feb. 6, 1962 (55).
Wong, Bruce, actor; b. Mar. 11, 1909, California; d. Nov. 1, 1953
    (44).
Wong, Joe, actor; d. Nov. 9, 1978 (75).
Wong, Victor, actor; b. Sept. 24, 1906, Los Angeles, Calif.;
    d. Apr. 7, 1972 (65).
Wontner, Arthur, actor; b. Jan. 21, 1875, London, England; d. July 10,
    1960 (85).

Wood, Allen, actor; d. Mar. 26, 1947 (55).
Wood, Britt, actor; b. Sept. 27, 1893, Tennessee; d. Apr. 14, 1965 (71).
Wood, Carl "Buddy," actor; d. Apr. 17, 1948 (43).
Wood, Donna, singer; d. Apr. 9, 1947 (29).
Wood, Douglas, actor; b. Oct. 31, 1880, New York City; d. Jan. 13, 1966 (85).
Wood, Ernest, actor; b. Apr. 17, 1887, Atchison, Kans.; d. July 13, 1942 (55).
Wood, Eugene R., actor; b. Oct. 27, 1903, Bowling Green, Mo.; d. Jan. 22, 1971 (67).
Wood, Franker, actor; b. Stromsburg, Neb.; d. Nov. 9, 1931 (48).
Wood, Freeman, actor; b. July 1, 1896, Denver, Colo.; d. Feb. 19, 1956 (59).
Wood, G.D. (see DeMain, Gordon)
Wood, Gordon D. (see DeMain, Gordon)
Wood, Grace, actress; d. May 30, 1952 (68).
Wood, Marjorie, actress; b. Sept. 5, 1882, England; d. Nov. 9, 1955 (73).
Wood, Mickey, stuntman; d. Nov. 20, 1963 (65).
Wood, Peggy, actress; b. Feb. 9, 1892, Brooklyn, N.Y.; d. Mar. 18, 1978 (86).
Wood, Philip, actor & author; d. Mar. 3, 1940 (44).
Wood, Roland, actor; d. Feb. 4, 1967 (70).
Wood, Sam, director & producer; b. July 10, 1883, Philadelphia, Pa.; d. Sept. 22, 1949 (66).
Wood, Suzanne, actress; d. Sept. 12, 1934.
Wood, Victor (David Hydes), actor; d. July 15, 1958 (43).
Woodard, Stacy, director & cinematographer; d. Jan. 27, 1942 (39).
Woodbridge, George, actor; b. Feb. 16, 1907, Exeter, Devon, England; d. Mar. 30, 1973 (66).
Woodbury, Doreen, actress; d. Feb. 6, 1957 (27).
Woodford, John, actor; d. Apr. 17, 1927 (65).
Woodruff, Bert (r.n. William Herbert Woodruff), actor; b. Apr. 29, 1856, Peoria, Ill.; d. June 14, 1934 (78).
Woodruff, Henry, actor; b. June 1, 1869, Hartford, Conn.; d. Oct. 6, 1916 (47).
Woods, Adelaide, actress; d. Mar., 1917.
Woods, Al, actor; d. June 3, 1946 (51).
Woods, Ercell, actress; d. Apr. 23, 1948 (32).
Woods, Grant, actor; d. Oct. 31, 1968.
Woods, Harry (r.n. Harry Lewis Woods), actor; b. May 5, 1889, Cleveland, Ohio; d. Dec. 28, 1968 (79).
Woods, Joseph A., actor; d. Feb. 13, 1926 (66).
Woods, Nick, actor; d. Mar. 21, 1936 (78).
Woods, Thomas (Fatty), actor; d. Dec. 27, 1932 (38).
Woods, Walter, writer; d. Dec. 7, 1942 (61).
Woodthorpe, Georgia, actress; b. Oct. 11, 1859, California; d. Aug. 24, 1927 (67).
Woodward, Bob, actor; b. Mar. 5, 1909, Oklahoma; d. Feb. 7, 1972 (62).
Woodward, Mrs. Eugene, actress; d. Mar. 29, 1947 (88).
Woodward, H. Guy, actor; d. Aug. 20, 1919 (51).
Woody, Jack (r.n. Frank John Woody), actor; b. Oct. 2, 1896, Kansas; d. Feb. 27, 1969 (72).
Woolery, Clarence (Pete), singer; d. June 4, 1978.

Woolf, Barney, extra; d. Feb. 10, 1972 (95).
Woolf, Edgar Allan, writer; b. Apr. 25, 1881, New York City;
    d. Dec. 9, 1943 (62).
Woolgar, Jack, actor; b. Tolworth, Surrey, England; d. July 17, 1978
    (64).
Woollcott, Alexander, actor, author, & critic; b. Jan. 19, 1887,
    Phalanx, N.J.; d. Jan. 23, 1943 (56).
Woolley, Monty, actor; b. Aug. 17, 1888, New York City; d. May 6,
    1963 (74).
Woolridge, Doris, actress; b. Apr. 2, 1892, California; d. July 17,
    1921 (29).
Woolsey, Robert, actor; b. Aug. 14, 1889, Oakland, Calif.; d. Oct. 31,
    1938 (49).
Worden, Louise, actress; b. Aug. 18, 1914, California; d. Jan. 6,
    1977 (62).
Worlock, Frederic, actor; b. Dec. 14, 1886, London, England;
    d. Aug. 1, 1973 (86).
Worne, Howard B. (Duke), director & actor; b. Dec. 14, 1888,
    Philadelphia, Pa.; d. Oct. 13, 1933 (44).
Worsley, Wallace, director; b. Dec. 8, 1878, Wappingers Falls, N.Y.;
    d. Mar. 26, 1944 (65).
Worth, Bill, actor; d. May 2, 1951 (67).
Worth, Constance, actress; b. Aug. 19, 1913, Sydney, Australia;
    d. Oct. 18, 1963 (50).
Worth, Peggy, actress; d. Mar. 23, 1956 (65).
Worthing, Helen Lee, actress; b. Jan. 31, 1905, Louisville, Ky.;
    d. Aug. 25, 1948 (43).
Worthington, William, actor & director; b. Apr. 8, 1872, Troy, N.Y.;
    d. Apr. 9, 1941 (69).
Worthington, William, actor; d. Mar. 9, 1966 (68).
Wray, Aloha, dancer; d. Apr. 28, 1968 (40).
Wray, John, actor; b. Feb. 13, 1887, Philadelphia, Pa.; d. Apr. 5,
    1940 (53).
Wray, John Griffith, director; d. July 12, 1929 (33).
Wray, Ted, actor; d. Jan. 26, 1950 (41).
Wren, Sam, actor; b. Mar. 20, 1896, New York; d. Mar. 15, 1962 (65).
Wright, Armand Vincent, actor; b. June 6, 1896, New York; d. Mar. 28,
    1965 (68).
Wright, Cobina, Sr., actress & columnist; b. Sept. 20, 1887, Oregon;
    d. Apr. 9, 1970 (82).
Wright, "Curly" (see Wright, Armand Vincent)
Wright, Fanny, actress; d. Dec. 29, 1954 (82).
Wright, Fred, Jr., actor; d. Dec. 12, 1928 (57).
Wright, Haidee, actress; b. Jan. 13, 1868, London, England;
    d. Jan. 29, 1943 (75).
Wright, Hugh E., actor; b. Apr. 13, 1879, Cannes, France; d. Feb. 12,
    1940 (60).
Wright, Huntley, actor; b. Aug. 7, 1868, London, England; d. July 10,
    1941 (72).
Wright, Mack V., actor & director; b. 1895, Princeton, Ind.;
    d. Aug. 14, 1965 (69).
Wright, Marie, actress; d. May 1, 1949 (87).
Wright, Otho (see Otho, Henry)
Wright, Tennant C. (Tenny), director; b. Nov. 18, 1885, Brooklyn,
    N.Y.; d. Sept. 13, 1971 (85).

Wright, Wen (r.n. Harry Wendell Wright), actor & stuntman; d. June 17, 1954 (38).
Wright, Will, actor; b. Mar. 26, 1894, San Francisco, Calif.; d. June 19, 1962 (68).
Wright, William, actor; b. Ogden, Utah; d. Jan. 19, 1949 (37).
Wu, Butterfly, actress; d. 1942.
Wu, Honorable, actor; d. Feb. 27, 1945 (42).
Wuest, Ida, actress; b. Wiesbaden, Germany; d. Nov. 2, 1958 (74).
Wunder, Harry F., actor; d. July 2, 1957 (71).
Wunderlee, Frank, actor; b. St. Louis, Mo.; d. Dec. 11, 1925 (49).
Wurman, Claude (see Justin, Morgan)
Wurtzel, Sol M., producer; b. Sept. 12, 1890, New York City; d. Apr. 9, 1958 (67).
Wyatt, Eustace, actor; b. Mar. 5, 1882, Bath, England; d. Oct. 25, 1944 (62).
Wycherly, Margaret, actress; b. Oct. 26, 1881, London, England; d. June 6, 1956 (74).
Wyler, Robert, author, director, & producer; b. Sept. 25, 1900, Mulhouse, France; d. Jan. 16, 1971 (70).
Wylie, Edith, actress; b. July 19, 1886, Wisconsin; d. Jan. 17, 1971 (84).
Wyman, Eleanore, actress; d. Sept. 1, 1940 (26).
Wymark, Patrick, actor; b. July 11, 1926, Cleethorpes, Lincs., England; d. Oct. 20, 1970 (44).
Wynant, Patrecia, actress; d. Mar. 31, 1977 (37).
Wyndham, Charles, actor; b. Mar. 23, 1837, Liverpool, England; d. Jan. 12, 1919 (81).
Wyndham, Poppy, actress; d. Mar. 14, 1928 (34).
Wynn, Dolores Casey, actress; d. May 11, 1945 (28).
Wynn, Doris, actress; d. July 14, 1925 (15).
Wynn, Ed, actor; b. Nov. 9, 1886, Philadelphia, Pa.; d. June 19, 1966 (79).
Wynn, Nan, actress; d. Mar. 21, 1971 (55).
Wynyard, Diana, actress; b. Jan. 16, 1906, London, England; d. May 13, 1964 (58).


Xirgu, Margarita, actress; b. June 18, 1888, Barcelona, Spain; d. Apr. 25, 1969 (80).


Yaconelli, Frank, actor; b. Oct. 2, 1898, Italy; d. Nov. 19, 1965 (67).
Yakovlev, Yasha, dancer; d. May 17, 1970 (58).
Yanagiya, Kingoro, actor; d. Oct. 22, 1972 (71).
Yanner, Joseph, actor; d. Dec. 12, 1949 (70).
Yanshin, Mikhail, actor; d. July, 1976 (73).
Yantis, Fanny, actress; d. July 19, 1929.
Yarborough, Barton, actor; b. Oct. 2, 1900, Texas; d. Dec. 19, 1951 (51).
Yarbrough, Jean, director; b. Aug. 22, 1900, Marianna, Ark.; d. Aug. 2, 1975 (74).
Yarde, Margaret, actress; b. Apr. 2, 1878, England; d. Mar. 11, 1944 (65).

Yarnell, Bruce, actor; d. Nov. 30, 1973 (37).
Yassin, Ismail, actor; d. June, 1972 (60).
Yates, George Worthing, writer; b. Oct. 14, 1900, New York City;
    d. June 6, 1975 (74).
Yates, Herbert J., executive; b. Aug. 24, 1880, Brooklyn, N.Y.;
    d. Feb. 3, 1966 (85).
Ybarra, Rocky, actor; b. Sept. 30, 1900; d. Dec. 12, 1965 (65).
Ybarra, Roque (see Ybarra, Rocky)
Yearsley, Ralph, actor; b. Oct. 6, 1896, London, England; d. Dec. 4,
    1928 (32).
Yeats, Murray, actor; d. Jan. 27, 1975 (65).
Yegros, Lina, actress; d. May, 1978 (63).
Yensen, Ula, actress; d. Aug. 26, 1959 (19).
Yip, William S. (r.n. William Sheung Yip), actor; b. Oct. 25, 1895,
    California; d. Oct. 18, 1968 (72).
Yonnel, Jean, actor; b. July 21, 1891, Bucharest, Roumania;
    d. Aug. 19, 1968 (77).
York, B.M. "Chick," actor; d. Dec. 22, 1969 (83).
York, Duke, actor; b. Oct. 17, 1908, New York; d. Jan. 24, 1952 (43).
York, Oswald, actor; d. Jan. 25, 1943 (76).
Yorke, Carol, actress; d. July 5, 1967 (38).
Yorke, Edith, actress; b. Dec. 23, 1867, Derby, England; d. July 28,
    1934 (66).
Yorkney, John C., actor; d. Aug. 20, 1941 (70).
Yoshiwara, Tamaki (Kyonosuke Yoshiwara), actor; d. Nov. 30, 1979 (79).
Yost, Herbert A. (Barry O'Moore), actor; b. Harrison, Ohio;
    d. Oct. 23, 1945 (65).
Yost, Robert, writer; b. St. Louis, Mo.; d. Apr. 10, 1967 (81).
Young, Arthur, actor; b. Sept. 2, 1898, Bristol, Gloucestershire,
    England; d. Feb. 24, 1959 (60).
Young, "Bull," actor; d. Aug., 1913.
Young, Carleton G. (r.n. Carleton Garretson Young), actor; b. May 26,
    1907, New York; d. July 11, 1971 (64).
Young, Clara Kimball, actress; b. Sept. 6, 1890, Illinois; d. Oct. 15,
    1960 (70).
Young, Clifton, actor; d. Sept. 10, 1951 (34).
Young, Desmond, actor & author; d. June 27, 1966 (74).
Young, Gig (r.n. Byron Barr), actor; b. Nov. 4, 1913, St. Cloud,
    Minn.; d. Oct. 19, 1978 (64).
Young, Gladys, actress; d. Aug. 18, 1975 (70).
Young, Harold, actor; d. Feb. 2, 1959 (59).
Young, Howard Irving, writer; b. Apr. 24, 1893, Jersey City, N.J.;
    d. Feb. 24, 1952 (58).
Young, J. Arthur, actor; b. Chicago, Ill.; d. Sept. 14, 1943 (63).
Young, Capt. Jack, actor; b. Oct. 7, 1894, Toronto, Canada;
    d. Oct. 28, 1966 (72).
Young, Janet, actress; d. Aug. 14, 1940 (51).
Young, Lillian Selznick, actress; b. Apr. 12, 1886, Russia;
    d. May 10, 1952 (66).
Young, Lucile, actress; d. Aug. 2, 1934 (42).
Young, Mary (r.n. Mary Marsden Young), actress; b. June 21, 1880,
    New York; d. June 23, 1971 (91).
Young, Mary E., actress; d. July 14, 1947 (45).
Young, Mary L., actress; d. Aug. 6, 1934.
Young, Ned (see Young, Nedrick)

Young, Nedrick (Ned Young; Nathan E. Douglas), actor & author;
    b. Mar. 23, 1914, Philadelphia, Pa.; d. Sept. 16, 1968 (54).
Young, Noah, actor; b. Feb. 2, 1887, Nevada, Colo.; d. Apr. 18,
    1958 (71).
Young, Olive, actress; d. Oct. 4, 1940 (37).
Young, Roland, actor; b. Nov. 11, 1887, London, England; d. June 5,
    1953 (65).
Young, Tammany, actor; d. Apr. 26, 1936 (49).
Young, Victor, composer & musical director; b. Aug. 8, 1900, Chicago,
    Ill.; d. Nov. 10, 1956 (56).
Young, Waldemar, writer; b. July 1, 1878, Salt Lake City, Utah;
    d. Aug. 30, 1938 (60).
Young, Walter, actor; d. Apr. 18, 1957 (79).
Younger, Scout, actor; d. Nov. 21, 1937 (64).
Youngson, Robert, producer; d. Apr. 8, 1974 (56).
Yowlachie, Chief (r.n. Daniel Yowlachie/Daniel Simmons), actor;
    b. Aug. 15, 1891, Washington; d. Mar. 7, 1966 (74).
Yuan-Lung, Wang, actor; d. 1959.
Yule, Joe, actor; b. Apr. 30, 1894, Scotland; d. Mar. 30, 1950 (55).
Yurka, Blanche, actress; b. June 18, 1887, St. Paul, Minn.;
    d. June 6, 1974 (86).


Zabelle, Flora, actress; d. Oct. 7, 1968 (88).
Zacconi, Ermete, actor; b. Sept. 14, 1857, Italy; d. Oct. 14, 1948
    (91).
Zahler, Lee, composer; b. Aug. 14, 1893, New York City; d. Feb. 21,
    1947 (53).
Zampi, Mario, producer & actor; b. Nov. 1, 1903, Rome, Italy;
    d. Dec. 2, 1963 (60).
Zanette, Guy, actor & dancer; b. Apr. 30, 1905, Italy; d. July 11,
    1962 (57).
Zanuck, Darryl F., producer; b. Sept. 5, 1902, Wahoo, Neb.; d. Dec. 22,
    1979 (77).
Zany, King (r.n. Charles W. Dill), actor; b. June 11, 1889, Ohio;
    d. Feb. 19, 1939 (49).
Zarova, Rini, actress; d. Dec. 6, 1966 (54).
Zayas, Alfonso, actor; d. Mar., 1961 (51).
Zbyszko, Stanislaus, wrestler & actor; d. Sept. 22, 1967 (88).
Zears, Marjorie, actress; d. Mar. 9, 1952 (41).
Zecca, Ferdinand, director; b. 1864; d. Mar. 26, 1947 (83).
Zegel, Ferdinand, actor; b. Jan. 1, 1895, New Jersey; d. June 16,
    1973 (78).
Zelaya, Don Alfonso, actor; b. Mar. 6, 1893, Nicaragua; d. Dec. 14,
    1951 (58).
Zelenka, Maria, actress; d. Aug. 30, 1975 (81).
Zeliff, Seymour "Skipper," actor; b. May 16, 1886, New Jersey;
    d. Jan. 17, 1953 (66).
Zellman, Tollie, actress; b. Aug. 31, 1887, Stockholm, Sweden;
    d. Oct. 9, 1964 (77).
Zesch-Ballot, Hans, actor; b. May 20, 1896; d. Sept., 1972 (76).
Zetina, Guillermo Gutierrez, actor; b. Feb. 10, 1918, Mexico;
    d. Mar. 5, 1970 (52).
Zimbalist, Sam, producer; b. Mar. 31, 1901, New York City; d. Nov. 4,
    1958 (57).

Zimina, Valentina, actress; d. Dec. 3, 1928 (29).
Zimmermann, Ed, actor; d. July 6, 1972 (39).
Zuber, Byrdine, actress; b. Nov. 18, 1886, Illinois; d. Sept. 5,
   1968 (81).
Zucco, Frances, actress; d. Mar. 15, 1962 (29).
Zucco, George, actor; b. Jan. 11, 1886, England; d. May 27, 1960
   (74).
Zukor, Adolph, producer; b. Jan. 7, 1873, Riese, Hungary; d. June 10,
   1976 (103).